Architectures for Distributed and Complex M-Learning Systems:
Applying Intelligent Technologies

Santi Caballé
Open University of Catalonia, Spain

Fatos Xhafa
Technical University of Catalonia, Spain

Thanasis Daradoumis
Open University of Catalonia, Spain

Angel A. Juan
Open University of Catalonia, Spain

Information Science REFERENCE

INFORMATION SCIENCE REFERENCE

Hershey · New York

Director of Editorial Content: Kristin Klinger
Senior Managing Editor: Jamie Snavely
Assistant Managing Editor: Michael Brehm
Publishing Assistant: Sean Woznicki
Typesetter: Sean Woznicki, Kurt Smith
Cover Design: Lisa Tosheff
Printed at: Yurchak Printing Inc.

Published in the United States of America by
Information Science Reference (an imprint of IGI Global)
701 E. Chocolate Avenue
Hershey PA 17033
Tel: 717-533-8845
Fax: 717-533-8661
E-mail: cust@igi-global.com
Web site: http://www.igi-global.com/reference

Library of Congress Cataloging-in-Publication Data

Architectures for distributed and complex M-learning systems : applying intelligent technologies / Santi Caballé ... [et al.], editors.
p. cm.

Includes bibliographical references and index.
Summary: "This book explores state-of-the-art software architectures and platforms used to support distributed and mobile e-learning systems"--Provided by publisher.

ISBN 978-1-60566-882-6 (hardcover) -- ISBN 978-1-60566-883-3 (ebook) 1. Educational technology. 2. Instructional systems--Design. 3. Computer-assisted instruction. I. Caballe, Santi, 1967-
LB1028.3.A735 2010
371.33'453--dc22

2009034980

British Cataloguing in Publication Data
A Cataloguing in Publication record for this book is available from the British Library.

Table of Contents

Detailed Table of Contents

This chapter presents the COLLAGE (collaborative learning platform using game-like enhancements) project as a good practice example of mobile and game-based learning that aims to integrate formal and informal learning settings through an innovative pedagogical approach. In this learning environment, students learn in context while participating in ready-made game activities or creating their own games: they gather data from their environments (at school, during visits to museums and science centres, on field trips, at home) and interpret it as information useful for learning, either on their own or through platform-mediated peer collaboration. This chapter describes the pedagogical background and technical details of the COLLAGE system, which was developed in the framework of an EU-supported e-learning project in 2005-2007. The aim of the project was to investigate the impact of the COLLAGE system focusing on results and changes the introduction of mobile game-based learning may produce in the learning process.

Nowadays, mobility offers potential opportunities for student's learning. The well-known paradigm "learning anywhere anytime" is possible thanks to mobile terminals and wireless technologies that solve the limited access of wired technologies for usage due to lack of mobility. In this scenario, many projects are dealing with the use of mobility to solve specific learning activities in different environments. This chapter presents a project called Campus Ubicuo and its architecture. The novelty of this system is the integration of several wireless technologies in an only mobility learning environment. The development of the project has been divided in four parts, isolating the user interface from the communication model and from the data management. This means that the system is available in different contexts and could be easily adaptable to several organizations such as hospitals, schools, or city councils. We explain how this architecture has been designed and developed to become a solid base of mobility learning systems.

This chapter discusses the principles underpinning the design and the development of a framework, MobiGlam, which supports ubiquitous and scalable access to learning activities. The framework allows full end to end interconnectivity among open source virtual learning environments (VLEs) and Java-enabled mobile devices. Through this framework, interoperability and adaptivity techniques are combined to address the technical, pedagogical, and institutional challenges of mobile learning. The discussed framework achieved a level of flexibility and simplicity that resulted in a wide acceptance of the framework institutionally, allowing its use in various real world settings.

Mobile learning increases both flexibility and self-determined learning, often combined with a high degree of context awareness. Flexibility and context awareness includes time and location, as well as the actual individual situation. To achieve such goals, mobile learning is not just a stand-alone and independent learning environment, but is instead embedded in a broader e-learning environment. This is true for the didactic and the pedagogic concepts and the learning (content) management system, as well as the overall software architecture. XML has been proven to be adequate and a powerful technology to store content in a presentation independent manner. By defining an additional attribute inside the XML tags, it is possible to classify the content. At the same time, this will help the author generate learning material for different devices in an efficient and structured way. Also, the content can be used in different formats (XHTML, PDF, etc.) as well as with different technologies (browser, applet, MIDlet, Ajax, etc.). In order to optimise the content presentation on different mobile devices, the content has to be adapted. A necessary precondition for the adaptation process is the identification of the connected device. The classification of the identified mobile device simplifies the mapping between device capabilities and content. The ICAT (Identification, Classification, Adaptation and Tagged XML) framework addresses these issues. The proposed design patterns will help authors to generated content for such a system.

This chapter reports on a learning architecture adopting ubiquity and pervasiveness to support communities of learning practice. The research focused on mobile devices that are capable of voice, text, video/photo interactions, and Web access, and how this can cater for the preferred learning styles of the learners while supporting the workplace learning and the educational environment. The research utilised mobile technology for planned and unplanned learning situations via its capability to send and receive multimedia files, Web objects, and live broadcasting. The information and objects created and gathered using mobile technology are in a digital format. This approach allows for customisation and flexible transferability to future intended audiences, planned learning and assessment activities, and workplace learning activities providing an engaging, learner created platform for the mobile generation.

Distant e-learning emerges as one of promising means for people to learn online. Although there is a substantial increase in computer and network performance in recent years, mainly as a result of faster hardware and more sophisticated software, there are still problems in the fields of integrating various resources towards enabling distant e-learning. Further, with the advances of technologies in RFID, sensors, GPS, GPRS, IP networks, and wireless networks, mobile learning is becoming a viable means for teaching and learning. In this book chapter, we develop a service platform for mobile learning with trustworthy service provisioning based on an organic integration of our prior research results in service grid, on demand e-learning, and trusted mobile asset tracking. In this platform, the virtual learning services for students, instructors and course providers are provided leveraging on service grid resource management capabilities on group collaboration, ubiquitous data access, and computing power. Challenges and requirements for mobile learning service platform are discussed. An RFID based e-learning data integration is proposed with integrated service networks for intelligent e-learning information access and delivery.

There have been significant developments in higher education resulting in interest in personalised educational provision. Concomitant with these changes is the evolving capability and ubiquity of mobile technologies. To facilitate personalisation and leverage the power of mobile technologies in mobile learning systems identification of individuals is a prerequisite; this can be achieved using an individual's profile (termed context). This chapter considers the background to context with related research. Context modelling, context matching, ontology, and the Semantic Web technologies are introduced. Context reasoning and inference in rule-based systems is considered and a context reasoning ontology is presented with scenario-based evaluation. The chapter concludes with a discussion, consideration of future research, and open research questions.

This chapter looks at the implementation and evaluation of mobile learning scenarios with location-based features, done under the project COLLAGE (Collaborative Learning Platform Using Game-like Enhancements). Five scenarios are examined. Evaluating different implementations within the same project gives an appraisal of the technical and pedagogical value of the mobile learning scenarios, but also informs the research community of appropriate evaluation models and evaluation parameters, which are lacking in the game-based mobile learning with location-based components. The project responds to questions about designing mobile learning scenarios that are pedagogically sound and attractive to secondary school students, and presents the pedagogical evaluation of the effectiveness of mobile game-based learning scenarios in the COLLAGE platform. The project makes a case for a close collaboration with teachers and students in elaborating and validating complex mobile learning scenarios.

Foreword

The recent spate of Horizons reports (e.g. Johnson, Levine, and Smith, 2008 & 2009) provide us with a hint of what is coming at us in education and work-based learning over the next 5 years in terms of new digital technology and media. Specifically, over the next year or two we will see the deployment in educational institutions and the work place, such innovations as the next generation mobile devices, mobile broadband, cloud computing, collaborative Webs, geo-everything, and context aware learning. Developing converged media architectures that creatively build on what we know about e-learning, but that further explore what is new will require us to make creative use of existing and emerging infrastructures and technologies. Given these trends, this book makes a timely contribution to mobile learning research. The challenge, as the editors make clear, is to overcome important non-functional requirements such as scalability, ubiquity, and interoperability. All of this needs to be done in the context of legacy systems that sometimes do not want to interoperate with each other, let alone interoperate and scale up with the systems are appearing on the horizon.

Mobile learning is an emerging and rapidly expanding field of research that cuts across schools, colleges, universities, and workplace learning. It is also gaining increasing importance in informal learning (see e.g. Cook, Pachler, and Bradley, 2008). Furthermore, mobile learning is increasingly able to make use of converged functionality such as the GPS feature of devices to enable location-based and context-sensitive learning. Definitions of 'mobile learning' tend to revolve around the mobility of the technology or the mobility of the learner; of late there has been a clear change in emphasis to the latter. Indeed, I agree with Sharples, et al., quoted below, that instead of focusing on learners' interactions with peers and technology there needs to be a greater focus on learning context, practises and the mobility of learning:

There is a need to reconceptualise learning for the mobile age, to recognise the essential role of mobility and communication in the process of learning, and also to indicate the importance of context in establishing meaning. (Sharples, Taylor, and Vavoula 2005, p. 1).

What is crucial is that context is seen as an emergent property of the activities and interactions that take place in a specific context. According to Dourish (2004), the determination of contextuality cannot be made a priori. It is an emergent feature of the interaction, determined in the moment and in the doing. In other words, context and content cannot be separated. Context cannot be a stable, external description of the setting in which activity arises. Instead, it arises from and is sustained by the activity itself (Dourish, 2004). In this sense, learning can be seen as meaning-making, that is, the 'making sense' of everyday life in contexts which are under the control of the learner. Thus, learner agency becomes a key issue in that learners may be using their own mobile phones within social structures that exist outside formal educational institutions.

This book provides a useful addition to current mobile learning research from a software architecture and computer science perspective and is structured into three sections. Section 1 examines architectural types, frameworks, and platforms for mobile learning systems. Section 2 looks at technological advances in support for mobile learning. Application and case studies on mobile learning practices is the focus of Section 3. The notion of context pervades parts one and two in particular but takes many perspectives that range from the ICAT (Identification, Classification, Adaptation, and Tagged XML) framework for mapping between devices and content (Chapter 4) through to contextual widgets, which are components which gather, process, and store contextual data in a distributed, blended learning environment (Chapter 11). Indeed, in Chapter 12 the authors draw on Dourish's notions of context mentioned above to present a context reasoning ontology which defines the entity concepts (Classes) and the semantic relationship between them. Furthermore, the notion of mobility is usefully dealt with through mobile grids (Chapter 8) and in Chapter 9 through an examination of mobility as freedom of movement across myriad contexts. Section 3 provides case studies taken from practice in a variety of sectors ranging from school to higher education. For example, Chapter 15 looks at a generic framework for interoperability with existing virtual learning environments. In Chapter 17, the authors usefully explore the key notion of learner identity as a way to support learner engagement and participation.

The above overview of this book is meant to give an indication of how the authors of the chapters tackle the issues that I have identified above; specifically those of interoperability, scalability, ubiquity, plus mobility and identity in the process of meaning making across contexts. What is striking about this book is that the editors have drawn on contributors from around the world so that we are provided with a truly international perspective. The scope of the chapters in this book is very broad indeed and I commend it to you for the simple reason that it makes a serious contribution to the issues delineated above.

Professor John Cook
Learning Technology Research Institute, London Metropolitan University, UK

***John Cook** is Professor of Technology Enhanced Learning at the Learning Technology Research Institute, London Metropolitan University. He has a cross-university role of E-Learning Project Leader. John has over 14 years previous experience as a full-time lecturer at various HEIs and in 2007 was made a University Teaching Fellow. He has over 8 years project management experience, which includes AHRB, BECTA, HEFCE-CETL and EC work. Furthermore, John has been part of research and development grant proposals that have attracted £4 million in competitive external funding. In addition, he has published/presented over 200 refereed articles and invited talks in the area of Technology Enhanced Learning, having a specific interest in four related areas: informal learning, mobile learning, appropriation and ICT Leadership & Innovation. He was Chair/President of the Association for Learning Technology (2004-06), he is the Vice-Chair of ALT's Research Committee and conducts Assessor and review work for the ESRC, EPSRC, EU, DfES and the Science Foundation of Ireland.*

REFERENCES

Cook, J., Pachler, N., & Bradley, C. (2008). Bridging the gap? Mobile phones at the interface between informal and formal learning. *Journal of the Research Centre for Educational Technology, Special Issue on Learning while Mobile*. Spring. Retrieved from http://www.rcetj.org/

Dourish, P. (2004). What we talk about when we talk about context. *Personal and Ubiquitous Computing, 8*(1), 19-30. Retrieved from http://www.ics.uci.edu/~jpd/publications/2004/PUC2004-context.pdf

Sharples, M., Taylor, J., & Vavoula, G. N. (2005). A theory of learning for the mobile age. In R. Andrews & C. Haythornthwaite (Eds.), *The SAGE handbook of e-learning research* (pp. 221-247). London: Sage.

Johnson, L., Levine, A., & Smith, R. (2008). *The horizon report: 2008 Australia–New Zealand edition*. Austin, TX: The New Media Consortium.

Johnson, L., Levine, A., & Smith, R. (2009). *The 2009 horizon report.* Austin, TX: The New Media Consortium.

Preface

INTRODUCTION

Over the last decade, the needs of educational organizations have been changing in accordance with increasingly complex pedagogical models and with the technological evolution of online learning environments, with very dynamic teaching and learning requirements. In particular, these needs involve extending and moving to highly customized learning and teaching forms in a timely fashion. Each educational organization would need to incorporate its own pedagogical approach, target a specific learning goal, and utilize its specific resources. Educational organizations' demands also include a cost-effective integration of legacy and separated learning systems from different institutions, departments and courses, which, in turn, should be implemented in different languages, supported by heterogeneous platforms, and distributed worldwide.

In addition, modern online learning environments must provide advanced enablement for the distribution of learning activities and the necessary functionalities and learning resources to all participants, regardless of where these participants and resources are located, and whether this location is static or dynamic. The aim of newest learning environments is to enable the learning experience in open, dynamic, large-scale, and heterogeneous environments. As a result, ubiquity and pervasiveness have become essential requirements to support formal and informal learning and to allow all learning community members, from a variety of locations, to cooperate with each other by means of a large variety of technology-enhanced equipment. To this end, mobile learning have come to play a major role in this context by taking advantage of the extensively used mobile and wearable technology to provide anywhere, anytime learning.

Unfortunately, in literature regarding this topic, there is an important gap of appropriate software infrastructure to build the emergent and complex e-learning systems that meet the current mobile learning needs and pedagogical models. In order to fill this gap, the latest findings in this field are presented in this book.

MAIN CONTRIBUTIONS OF THIS BOOK

This book presents solid architectural solutions for the development and adoption of the next generation of mobile learning systems in terms of non-functional requirements, such as scalability, flexibility, availability, security, interoperability, and the integration of different, heterogeneous, and legacy learning systems. To address these complex issues, several chapters propose powerful and pervasive technologies, such as Grid, distributed and wireless infrastructure. Ubiquity and pervasiveness are especially relevant in this context in order to provide not only anywhere anytime learning but also unconscious learning. The book provides an extensive background and novel solutions to meet these demanding requirements as key aspects to support the current and next mobile communities of learning practice and pedagogical models.

Some authors also point out the importance of adaptivity, personalization, and usability as well as knowledge management in mobile learning so as to greatly stimulate and improve the m-learning experience. There are key evidences of the benefits from leveraging these features by adapting the formal and informal learning process to both current pedagogical models and mobile participants' needs and preferences. To this end, a complete management of contextual information and application of advanced context-awareness techniques are suggested. The so-called "social software" referring the use of Web 2.0 and related technologies, such as Web-semantic and ontologies, are also considered in this context for the provision of customized and dynamic learning (e.g., adapting the learning content in different formats and with different technologies).

The last section of the book provides a set of relevant case studies for implementation and evaluation purposes of the previous mobile learning architectures proposed. The aim is both to show the architecture's impact on the m-learning process and to provide useful guidelines to targeted designers of mobile learning systems. Furthermore, last two chapters present interesting study cases that explore aspects of the quality learning by using mobile technologies and the potential of m-learning to engagement in learning and develop strong learner identities.

Overall, the book contributes with the following:

- State of the art and latest research findings in software architectures, computer science, and mobile technology used to support complex, distributed, mobile online learning systems.
- Worldwide best practices and case studies as for the development and use of architectural solutions for emergent m-learning systems.
- Theoretical frameworks, platforms, and architectures adopting ubiquity and pervasiveness to support the latest pedagogical models found in formal and informal mobile communities of learning practice.
- Experimental results from real m-learning practices by using complex systems and applications built upon solid software architectures.
- Provision to business, academic, and research communities with a base text that could serve as a reference for software architects and developers, as well as computer sciences undergraduate/graduate courses.

ORGANIZATION OF THE BOOK

The 17 chapters of this book are organized as follows:

- Section 1: *Architectures, Frameworks, and Platforms for Mobile Learning Systems* provides a detailed overview of research projects emerged involving solid software and hardware infrastructure for developing mobile learning systems.

- Section 2: *Technological Advances in Support for Mobile Learning* shows the latest technologies to support and enhance mobile learning, such as grid computing, Web 2.0, and ontology-based and context-aware systems.
- Section 3: *Architecture Applications and Case Studies on Mobile Learning Practices* describes a set of specific experiences in mobile learning settings mostly by using software systems built upon the aforementioned architectures, platforms and frameworks.

Section 1: Architectures, Frameworks, and Platforms for Mobile Learning Systems

Chapter 1 (Developing Tools that Support Effective Mobile and Game Based Learning: The COLLAGE Platform by Chryssafidou, et al.) presents an EU-supported e-learning project aiming at investigating the impact of mobile and game-based learning on formal and informal learning. In this context, two main aspects of the project are addressed: adaptation to the user and content authoring.

Chapter 2 (Designing an Architecture to Provide Ubiquity in Mobile Learning by Carmona-Murillo, et al.) describes a flexible context-aware architecture based on mobile technologies that seamlessly integrates various wireless technologies into a platform to develop mobility services for learning environments as well for other environments.

Chapter 3 (MobiGlam: A Framework of Interoperability and Adaptivity for Mobile Learning by Fatma Meawad and Geneen Stubbs) discusses the principles of the design and development of a framework that provides interoperability and adaptivity techniques by supporting ubiquitous and customized access to learning activities while keeping the institution's pedagogical goals and regulations.

Chapter 4 (SW-Architecture for Device Independent Mobile Learning by Christ and Feißt) also proposes to increase the flexibility of mobile learning in terms of adaptation of the learning material to the specific device. An XML-based solution is proposed, which can offer the learning content in different formats as well as with different technologies.

Chapter 5 (A Ubiquitous and Pervasive Learning Framework: Linking the Learner, the Workplace, and the Education Institute by Carroll) reports on a mobile learning architecture adopting ubiquity and pervasiveness to support communities of learning practice. This approach provides customization and an engaging, learner created platform for the mobile generation.

Chapter 6 (A Mobile Service Platform for Trustworthy E-Learning Service Provisioning by Luo and Zhang) proposes a service grid-based platform to provide on-demand m-learning with trustworthy service provisioning and location information for tracking participants and managing on-line learning assets.

Section 2: Technological Advances in Support for Mobile Learning

Chapter 7 (Mobile Web 2.0: Bridging Learning Contexts by Cochrane) discusses the potential of wireless mobile devices and Web 2.0 to create social learning environments that bridge multiple learning contexts. To this end, several experiences of mobile Web 2.0 are presented and interpreted.

Chapter 8 (Mobile Grids: An Enabling Technology for Next Generation M-Learning Applications by Andronikou, et al.) explores mobile grid as an enabling technology for next generation m-learning applications aiming at making affordable to meet demanding non-functional requirements appearing in this context, such accessibility, availability, security, and performance.

Chapter 9 (Intelligent M-Learning Frameworks: Information and Communication Technology Applied in a Laptop Environment by Owen) discusses on the effectiveness of the use of ICT and mobility for learning and teaching blended m-learning. This study is supported by reporting on a specific m-learning course and by using laptop computers.

Chapter 10 (Integrating Ontology-Based Content Management into a Mobilized Learning Environment by Kismihók, et al.) presents an educational ontology-based solution for curricula, content, and a knowledge evaluation development, whose research is piloted into a mobilized learning management system.

Chapter 11 (Context-Awareness and Distributed Events in Mobile Learning by Boticki, et al.) incorporates contextual information and the use of distributed events to better adapt and disseminate mobile learning services to teachers and learners. An information system based on these technological advances and its application are presented.

Chapter 12 ('Intelligent Context' for Personalised Mobile Learning by Moore, et al.) also uses contextual information to personalize mobile learning systems. To this end, an extensive research study is presented focusing on related contextual technologies, such as ontologies and Semantic Web. As a result, a complete context reasoning ontology is presented and evaluated in a m-learning scenario.

Section 3: Architecture Applications and Case Studies on Mobile Learning Practices

Chapter 13 (Schools in Action: Pedagogical Evaluation of COLLAGE, a Case Study on Mobile and Location Game Game-Based Learning by Barajas, et al.) implements and evaluates the COLLAGE project presented in Chapter 1. To this end, several practical m-learning scenarios are examined. This provides useful guidelines to designers in developing COLLAGE sound m-learning systems.

Chapter 14 (Technical Evaluation of Wireless Communications in a Mobile Learning Architecture by Carmona-Murillo, et al.) shows a technical evaluation of the behavior of wireless communication in the mobile learning architecture of Campus Ubicuo described in Chapter 2. The results from a testbed involving several scenarios that offer mobile services through different networks are presented.

Chapter 15 (Supporting Mobile Access to VLE Resources through MobiGlam by Meawad and Stubbs) reports on the deployment and evaluation of a case study conducted in a virtual learning environment by using the MobiGlam framework introduced in detail in Chapter 3. The results are analyzed in terms of impact on the mobile access to the VLE and the framework's usability.

Chapter 16 (Using Technology to Support Quality Learning for School Activities Involving Field Studies by Stewart, et al.) presents detailed samples of case studies of a funded project's educational approach focused on supporting a range of school teachers in their use of mobile technologies to enhance learning. The evaluation results are shown in terms of quality student learning and considering the affordances of mobile technologies.

Chapter 17 (Exploring Learning Identities through M-Learning: Learning across Regional and Knowledge Boundaries by Wallace) analyzes a range of learning programs that have utilized m-learning to understand how people learn and develop strong identities. Also, it discusses on the potential to engagement in learning and learner identities in regional areas.

TARGETED AUDIENCE AND LAST WORDS

We expect the experimented and solid architectures and frameworks proposed in this book can fully support advanced learning practices and pedagogical goals from the era of distributed and mobile learning. Thus, the book's targeted audience includes industry and software development companies involved in the generation of the latest online learning systems and applications, as well as educational institutions, which incorporate mobile learning into the very rationale of their pedagogical models.

Furthermore, we would suggest the theoretical models of these architectures to form part of the curricula of undergrad/graduate courses in the computer science degree, in particular those courses related to software architectures and software development techniques, as well as e-learning from a pedagogical perspective. Indeed, we truly believe the comprehensive view and illustrative examples and practices provided will make the book interesting for university teaching purposes.

We hope the readers find this book fruitful and help accomplish their goals. Enjoy the reading!

Santi Caballé, Open University of Catalonia, Spain
Fatos Xhafa, Technical University of Catalonia, Spain
Thanasis Daradoumis, Open University of Catalonia, Spain
Angel A. Juan, Open University of Catalonia, Spain
Editors
Barcelona, Spain
April, 2009

Acknowledgment

The editors would like to thank all who have been involved in the preparation and development process of the book. Without their support, this book could not have been completed.

Special thanks to the authors of chapters for their outstanding contributions to this project. Also, we deeply appreciate most of the authors who participated in the review process as referees and provided constructive and comprehensive reviews of the book chapters, which were essential to improve the quality of the book.

Great appreciation to Dr. John Cook for accepting our invitation to contribute with his knowledge to the foreword of this book.

We are also very grateful to the Computer Science Department of the Open University of Catalonia for their continuous support and provision of resources to our research activities.

We do not want to close without acknowledging the help of the staff at IGI Global, whose assistance during the whole edition process has been invaluable. Special thanks to Tyler Heath, Rebecca Beistline, and Jan Travers for their vigilance on keeping the book edition on schedule. We finally would like to thank Kristin Klinger and Lindsay Johnston for their invitation and motivation to start and perform the first steps of this project.

This work has been partially supported by the Spanish MCYT project TIN2008-01288/TSI. Fatos Xhafa's work is partially done at Birkbeck, University of London, on Leave from Technical University of Catalonia (Barcelona, Spain). His research is supported by a grant from the General Secretariat of Universities of the Ministry of Education, Spain.

The Editors
Barcelona, Spain
April 2009

Section 1
Architectures, Frameworks, and Platforms for Mobile Learning Systems

Chapter 1
Developing Tools that Support Effective Mobile and Game Based Learning:
The COLLAGE Platform

Evi Chryssafidou
Ellinogermaniki Agogi, Greece

Sofoklis Sotiriou
Ellinogermaniki Agogi, Greece

Pavlos Koulouris
Ellinogermaniki Agogi, Greece

Manolis Stratakis
Forthnet, Greece

Antonis Miliarakis
Forthnet, Greece

Mario Barajas
Universitat de Barcelona, Spain

Marcelo Milrad
Växjö University, Sweden

Daniel Spikol
Växjö University, Sweden

ABSTRACT

This chapter presents the COLLAGE (collaborative learning platform using game-like enhancements) project as a good practice example of mobile and game-based learning that aims to integrate formal and informal learning settings through an innovative pedagogical approach. In this learning environment, students learn in context while participating in ready-made game activities or creating their own

DOI: 10.4018/978-1-60566-882-6.ch001

games: they gather data from their environments (at school, during visits to museums and science centres, on field trips, at home) and interpret it as information useful for learning, either on their own or through platform-mediated peer collaboration. This chapter describes the pedagogical background and technical details of the COLLAGE system, which was developed in the framework of an EU-supported e-learning project in 2005-2007. The aim of the project was to investigate the impact of the COLLAGE system focusing on results and changes the introduction of mobile game-based learning may produce in the learning process.

INTRODUCTION

The future of education is outside of education. It is in the everyday life. In business, in the world. In life long learning. But the principles can be applied inside of formal education as well. They require a change in thinking, to move toward problem-centered, meaningful activities in the classroom. To exploit people's interests and subvert them to lead to natural, inspired learning activities.

(Norman, 2001)

Learning happens in various ways. Students typically learn in classrooms, but learning may also occur when they explore parks and streams playing with friends, trying and maybe failing to perform tasks. People learn by experience and involvement, by talking with peers and experts, by delving into a practical problem. Virtually any experience can be a learning opportunity, although the resources to make it one are often lacking. The conception of knowledge as something "held", "stored" in a "body of knowledge" lends itself easily to viewing learning as "knowledge acquired", collected from books, lectures, and other media. A different approach is followed here: knowledge is embedded in situations, and learning is contextual in its very nature. Knowledge happens rather than being stored and applied only when appropriate.

Contextual learning may be supported and enhanced by mobile learning applications. Mobile learning provides flexibility in accessing learning materials, students, and teachers anytime, anywhere. The use of mobile devices with Internet access can offer an appropriate educational environment for learning activities both inside and outside the classroom, motivating students through their exposure to authentic stimuli as well as their involvement in game-like activities.

The proliferation of mobile phones and other handheld devices has transformed mobile learning from a researcher-led endeavour to an everyday activity, whereby mobile personal tools help people learn everywhere through either formal training or informal support and conversation (Kukulska-Hulme, Traxker & Pettit, 2007). Even so, the effective design and development of mobile learning applications and activities, and their evaluation remain core activities where specialist expertise and insights by teachers and learners have important roles to play.

Teachers constitute a major factor for the success of such innovative interventions. Schools and classrooms, both real and virtual, ought to have teachers equipped with resources and skills enabling them to teach the subject matter exploiting technology potential. Interactive computer simulations, open educational resources, and sophisticated data-gathering and analysis tools are only a few of the resources that allow teachers to provide previously unimaginable opportunities for conceptual understanding. Traditional approaches may no longer provide prospective teachers with the necessary skills for teaching students to survive economically in today's workplace.

In this context, the aim of the COLLAGE (Collaborative Learning Platform Using Game-like Enhancements) project (Sotiriou et al., 2007) was to contribute towards an innovative, more flexible approach to learning, which would afford rich patterns of integration of formal and informal learning settings (e.g. museums, science parks, archaeological areas) through an orchestration of technologies (laptops, PDAs, mobile phones, the Internet) into a single learning-supporting and learning-enhancing environment. This project particularly aspired to support the development of a new "everywhere-learning" and "lifelong-learning" culture among secondary school students, who were facilitated to realise that classroom walls are not a barrier between school activities and everyday life, as learning is related to the world rather only to schooling.

In the COLLAGE mobile learning paradigm, school students, while participating in ready-made or their own game activities, learn to gather and interpret data from their environments, and thus build their learning either on their own, or, most importantly, through face-to-face and virtual collaboration with their peers. Together with, and supported by, their teachers, they learn how to acquire, create, use and re-use high quality e-learning content in a cross-cultural and cross-linguistic European context transcending national borders. Importantly, beside professionally produced content offered by third parties (e.g. libraries, museums, other sources of knowledge) this learning environment is filled with content generated by students within learning activities planned by their teachers. Students and teachers can select, re-purpose, use, share, and manage content created either by themselves or by other peers.

The COLLAGE system offers the integrated, coherent, and practical mobile learning service enabling students and teachers to perform these innovative learning activities efficiently. Although technological development was not the main aim of the COLLAGE project, the research team managed to demonstrate unique ways of innovatively combining existing technologies to support everyday contextualised learning. It is important to note that the development of the technological environment took place in repeated cycles integrated with extended validation in real environments, the results and outcomes of each phase providing input to the next. The repeated development cycles gave students and teachers the opportunity to actively participate in the design and redesign of the final system.

This chapter sets out to discuss the state of the art in designing technology-enhanced educational activities in informal learning environments, demonstrating current challenges in the field through the examples of various mobile and game-based learning projects. Further, the pedagogical approach is presented which guided us while supporting teachers to design, create and evaluate mobile-based educational games. This approach also informed the development for the technology, a description of which is provided next in this chapter. Finally, future plans of the COLLAGE project consortium are presented.

This chapter is complemented by the following one in this volume, which presents a series of indicative scenarios of use of the COLLAGE system, along with the systematic evaluation that was realised in the framework of the project.

BACKGROUND

The real key to future development is likely to be personalisation: of interpretation to significantly enhance social and intellectual inclusion; [...] of learning to finally facilitate an escape from the deficit models so prevalent in educational institutions and release untold potential, as the individual learner is able to use technologies to exercise choice and to take responsibility for his/ her own learning.

(Hawkey, 2004)

Linking Formal and Informal Learning

The proposition of informal learning as a response to the strict formality of processes in the education systems dates back to the 1970s (cf. McKenzie & Kernig, 1975). More recently, the characteristics of learning outside the classroom and the tensions or links between this and formal learning practices have increasingly preoccupied pedagogical thought in the last fifteen years. Current pedagogical discourse and research often emphasise the differences between these two ways to knowledge – maybe understandably, as informal learning is usually defined through its distinction to the learning taking place in structured teaching contexts applying specific curricula. However, formal and informal learning do not necessarily stand in the mutually exclusive relation to each other that traditional boundaries may misleadingly imply. As Cook, Pachler and Bradley (2008) remark, formal and informal learning can be viewed as being 'part of a continuum of a multi-dimensional clustering of informal and formal learning activities rather than positioned in an either-or relationship' (p. 4). In the field of educational technology, in particular, there has been a strong interest in utilising technological features to facilitate the development of links between the two 'loci' of learning.

The potential for technology-supported synergies between formal and informal learning settings are particularly evident in sites such as museums, science centres, or areas of historical interest. Visiting such places can be an inspirational learning experience for students. A variety of digital tools are used within such informal learning spaces aiming to enhance the learning experience, widen the scope of learning and make resources as widely available as possible. Technology enhanced on-site learning may involve visualisation, interactivity with the exhibit, learner participation, personalisation and adaptation to visitors' needs and preferences. Online learning is also promoted by science centres and museums in advanced websites, where the user can have online tours and access rich learning resources (e.g. multimedia, simulations, games).

The transcending of spatial barriers naturally offered by mobile technologies readily offers itself to aspirations of supporting learning outside the classroom, leading to an increasing interest in the ways in which mobile devices may bridge the gap between formal and informal learning (Cook et al., 2008).

The Mobile Learning Paradigm

Laurillard (2007) defines mobile learning, or m-learning, as "the digital support of adaptive, investigative, communicative, collaborative, and productive learning activities in remote locations" (p. 173). She further summarises the new opportunities offered by mobile learning as "[placing] learners in challenging active learning environments, making their own contributions, sharing ideas, exploring, investigating, experimenting, discussing" (p. 174). Patten, Arnedillo-Sánchez and Tagney (2006) define the following roles for handheld devices in learning (p. 296): administrative; referential; interactive; "microworld"; data collection; location awareness; collaborative. Similarly, Song & Fox (2008) identify a number of relevant affordances of PDAs, organising them into seven categories: multimedia collection, multimedia access, communication, scheduling, data processing, connectivity, and representation. Most of these functionalities, of course, already exist in other computer technologies used forlearning, too. However, what is unique and therefore of potential in mobile learning, is its place-independent nature.

In mobile learning activities, place should be seen not only as context, but importantly also as subject and resource for learning: mobile learners can now gain deeper consciousness of place and, through interaction with the others, multiple perspectives on it. Tatar, Harisson, Crandell and

Schaefer (2008) have provided an example of how mobile devices and software can help learners reflect on their relationship to particular places, and the relationship between their own experience and other people's experiences of those spaces. Learner's new interactions with place are multiplied and diversified through the combination of mobile technologies with digital augmentation, integrated into learning experiences in various contexts (Price, 2007).

Mobile learning is often approached as a different way of learning, deserving its own methodologies for designing learning activities so that the potential of innovation is fully exploited. Cook, Bradley, Lance, Smith and Haynes (2007), for instance, focus on the affordance of mobile devices for learner-generated context, and propose this as the core concept for pedagogically effective design of mobile learning activities. Oloruntoba (2006) discusses strategies that would encourage adoption of m-learning and reduce the cognitive overload that may be induced from the technological novelty.

As Bruce and Hogan (1998) point out, technologies are ideological tools embodying social values. The advent of mobile devices in the world of learning can thus only be fully interpreted and appreciated if visited from a social-cultural perspective, too. From such an angle, Kress and Pachler (2007) show that the change that mobile learning brings, or indeed is part of, is of a social, political and economic nature, in a globalised world where learning is central and digital technologies "hold out the promise of unlimited access to educational commodities and of the consumer-learner's sovereignty of choice" (p. 9). They argue that mobility is a feature not only of the technological world, but also of the contemporary social, political, and economic environment. Mobile learners have a new "habitus" of learning, in which they are accustomed to immediate, ubiquitous access to the world. The world, they argue, has become the curriculum, and the individual someone "always expecting and ready to be a learner" (Kress & Pachler, 2007).

Irrespectively of how one may theorise mobile learning as a cognitive, social or cultural process, it remains a fact that the use of mobile devices in formal and informal settings by both formal and informal learners, in any of the possible combinations among these, raises expectations for more and better access to learning. In this emerging landscape, the idea of mobility is often linked to experiential learning in-situ: on the field, in the museum, at the cultural site. Further, readily available connotations of mobile devices have almost naturally lead many pedagogues to experimentations in the cross-section of mobile learning with game-based learning.

Technology-Enhanced Learning Experiences through Games

Play is an element of human nature, and as such, it has naturally been considered as important for learning. In the contemporary era, a great potential is anticipated of digital games and simulation in education, and positive effects on learning outcomes are reported (Amory, 2007; Kiili, 2005; Quinn, 2005).

Games seem to match contemporary views on learning and pedagogical concepts such as experiential learning, authentic learning contexts, or competence learning, which all tend to require the immersion of learners in complex learning contexts (Gee, 2003). Games may provoke active learner involvement through exploration, experimentation, competition and co-operation. They support learning through increased visualisation and challenged creativity. They also address the changing competences needed in the information age: self-regulation, information skills, networked co-operation, problem solving strategies and critical thinking.

The potential of learning based on digital games is multiple, including also aspects such as motivation. Motivation sustained through feedback, reflection and active involvement is a key to effective learning. Game-based learning is particularly helpful in this direction, and many learning games have been developed for groups with difficulties of sustaining motivation. One other important observation on game-based learning is that it allows for the spontaneous formation of communities of practice offering a context for access to expertise and support. What is more, integrating a range of tools with potential uses for education has been a key challenge for e-learning. Game-based learning offers enhanced potential to integrate different tools such as discussion forums, bulletin boards and concept mapping software. In some cases, games are used as an interface to e-learning materials, resources and courses.

The use of games for learning may need to be differentiated according to learners' specific characteristics and requirements. It may be most effective with particular learners who enjoy this learning approach (de Freitas, 2006). It is of importance, also, that games have become particularly adopted by new generations of learners, the so-called digital natives immersed in new communication technologies (Prensky, 2006).

In this context, game-based learning ought to have a particular place in the school. While discussions on the usefulness of game-based learning are widely reported, the actual effectiveness is subjected to embedding games into the school practice, providing guidelines to practitioners, allowing for opportunities to practitioners in terms of time and effort allocated. According to the JISC review on game-based learning (de Freitas, 2006), there is great potential for tutors and practitioners to become involved with games development for learning. The main difficulties related to tutor engagement refer to:

- Fixed lesson duration and time constraints both for planning and implementing game-based learning (Sandford, Ulicsak, Facer & Rudd, 2006)
- The particular context and manner a teacher is used to work, i.e. their experience, their teaching style, and the wider context of the institution (Sandford et al., 2006)
- The ability to link the game objective and possible learning outcome with the curriculum; in particular Sandford et al. (2006) noticed that while teachers needed a certain level of familiarity with a game to be able to use it in their teaching, achieving particular educational objectives through the use of the game was more dependent upon a teacher's knowledge of the curriculum with which they were working than it was on their ability with the game.
- Lack of dedicated guidelines, toolkits and frameworks for supporting innovative practice, which may be produced by the research community of game-based learning (Sandford & Williamson, 2005).

Two Further Conceptual Pillars of COLLAGE

In addition to the above discussed concepts, the COLLAGE project aimed to address two further aspects of the contemporary e-learning discourse: adaptation to the user, and content authoring. These two aspects are discussed below.

Adaptive and Adaptable Learning Environments

Adaptive learning systems or intelligent tutoring systems have attempted to address problems such as the insufficient understanding of human language semantics by the machine. However, they remain unable to reliably capture user's mood, behaviour, or interest, so as to satisfyingly adapt to user's needs. Thus, they tend to be specialized in certain domains or situations (Lin & Liu, 2006; LISTEN, 2005). Adaptable systems, on the other hand, follow the opposite approach: instead of trying to adapt to the user, they provide functionality for the user to actively adapt the system to his/her needs (e.g. Squeak, 2007). Hereby, users are required to become active and effort is required by the user. In contrast, the COLLAGE project aimed to take load away from the user. Looking at advantages and disadvantages of both adaptive and adaptable systems, we have introduced an innovative concept that utilizes simple methods to achieve user-driven adaptation, and which we call auto-adaptability. This is based on the idea that users, when interacting in mixed realities, leave context and content traces. These traces are tracked for each learner or group of learners in real world space, leading to an information space which will then be mapped into the real world environment. Further interaction refines this space and allows for prediction functions distributed over time and users.

Content Origin and Authoring

In projects demonstrating the use of mobile devices as ways to enhance user experience during visits in places of educational interest, the relevant digital content is provided either by the place of interest (e.g. materials developed by museum staff), or it comes with the mobile learning platform as a demonstrator (Facer et al., 2004). In some cases, people other than teachers, such as researchers or experts, are involved during the design of the activity and content (Facer et al., 2004; Luyten et al, 2006). However, the production of educationally authentic and valid content is crucial, and the role teachers and even students should be given for participatory co-design in this direction is evident. The COLLAGE project recognised the need for providing easy-to-use content authoring tool to the school community, and particularly teachers.

Authoring and content creation tools cover a wide range of content types and required user skills. Somewhat informally, they can be divided into creation of static documents (text editing, desktop publishing) or graphics (images, drawings) and dynamic – sometimes even interactive – content, such as movies or animations. While most of the relevant tools truly excel in their specific domain, especially the tools for dynamic media require a high level of user skills to master. Tools for mixed mode content like PowerPoint presentations are static, slide-oriented in nature. Systems like Squeak and e-toys transcend this limitation and open up the "application" itself, allowing for a much profounder and deeper level of user involvement and creativity. Unfortunately both are considered research prototypes and although they are in widespread use in schools mainly in the US and Japan, content creation is rather tedious. Sophie (sophieproject.org) tries to bring these two worlds together, bringing ease of use to editing and media assembly but still lacks the interactivity Squeak and e-toys offer. The COLLAGE project has integrated established tools for content creation, such as e-toys, but also design new ones, tailored to the requirements of the proposed pedagogical approach. Combining the best of these worlds promises to deliver low-threshold, high ceiling content creation tools, and allows for users to create content in context.

Other Related Projects

There is a long history of digital games in education, from early simulations to immersive worlds for learning supporting social constructivist theories (de Freitas, 2006). The recent proliferation of mobile games has made them into a fertile ground for the development of new resources for learning (Facer et al., 2004). The following selection of eight projects presents a brief overview of mobile games that have successfully explored playing and learning across locations.

Environmental Detectives was an early mobile game that used personal digital assistants (PDAs). The game engaged high-school and university students in a real-world environmental consulting scenario constructed to immerse players in the practices of environmental engineers. The main focus of the game was on planning an effective investigation that balanced quantitative and qualitative data (Klopfer, Squire & Jenkins, 2002).

The Ambient Wood project was designed to enable children to switch between the experiences of the physical world (for example, observing a butterfly drinking nectar from a thistle) and to reflect upon the ecological processes behind this interdependency (for example, pollination). Mobile devices and visualization tools were provided for the children to access and share contextually relevant digital information (for example, the animation of seasonal changes) when indoors and outdoors (Price, Rogers, Stanton & Smith, 2003).

Learning games in mixed realities also emerged, where experiences may include, for instance audio overlays on physical space (Owen, 2006). Savannah was a mobile game that re-created the African savannah outside on local school grounds. Children were given global positioning systems (GPSs) devices linked to personal digital assistants (PDAs) through which they "saw", "heard" and "smelled" the world of the savannah as they navigated the real space outdoors. In addition, in an indoors space children reflected on how well they had succeeded in the game, accessed other resources to support their understanding and developed strategies for surviving as lions in the virtual savannah (Facer et al., 2004).

Frequency 1550 was a historically based game in which groups of students were competing acting as pilgrims in old Amsterdam while trying to find a missing holy relic. They communicated via videophones and use a GPS-equipped mobile phone for the game and for position-tracking while at headquarters they had a laptop connected to the Internet. The teams at headquarters tracked all the teams and directed their own team in the street to solve the mystery (Raessens, 2006).

In the Hewlett-Packard Mediascape, experiences are context-aware rich multimedia delivered to mobile devices that specify the relevance they have to the physical situation (Stenton, 2007). Many Mediascapes have been developed for education and for general purposes such as art exhibits and location-based experiences. Several projects have been launched from this initiative, including CreateAscape, designed for educational use, and the general Mediascape, an open toolkit for everyone.

AMULETS (Advanced Mobile and Ubiquitous Learning Environments for Teachers and Students) project at Växjö University explores how to design, implement and evaluate innovative educational scenarios combining outdoors and indoors activities supported by mobile and ubiquitous computing. AMULETS is based on the premise that the design of innovative mobile learning activities should be guided by collaborative learning scenarios in context in authentic settings. Educational scenarios were designed together with teachers to support the regular curriculum in a wide range of topics including geography, history and biology (Spikol & Milrad, 2008).

The UNITE project (Zoakou, Tzanavari, Papadopoulos & Sotiriou, 2007), set out from a state-of-the-art analysis of the existing educational platforms, mobile learning and eLearning pedagogical frameworks with the view to structuring an eLearning environment capable to meet the learning needs of the schools it addressed. The main output of the project was the UNITE eLearning environment, as well as a series of eLearning scenarios covering a great range of thematic axes, which could be customized to the needs of each learning audience.

The recently launched (2008) EXPLOAR project (www.ea.gr/ep/exploar) demonstrates an innovative approach that involves visitors of science museums and science centres in extended episodes of playful learning. The EXPLOAR approach considers informal education as opportunity to transcend from traditional museum visits to a "feel and interact" user experience, allowing for learning "anytime, anywhere", open to societal changes and at the same time feeling culturally conscious. A set of demonstrator learning scenarios are being implemented employing advanced and

Figure 1. The EXPLOAR project introduces the idea of the "Science Centre to Go" through the augmentation of physical phenomena on miniature models of common science centres exhibits (Buchholz & Wetzel, 2009). Students can create their own exhibition and explore the physical phenomena (Image Source: Fraunhofer Gesellschaft).

highly interactive visualization technologies in personalised ubiquitous learning paradigms. The service demonstrates the potential of mobile Augmented Reality (AR) technology to cover the emerging need for continuous update, innovation and development of new exhibits, new exhibitions, new educational materials, new programmes and methods to approach visitors.

The examples described above are indicative of real results of the use of mobile games in educational contexts. Like the COLLAGE project, Mediascape and AMULETS projects additionally offer tools and scenarios for teachers and students to design location-based learning activities. The COLLAGE approach, combining mobile learning technology and game-based learning, provides multiple challenges for the design of learning activities that go beyond individual learning in front of computers and take students outside the classroom to collaborate with their peers and to explore the world through their own eyes and questions. Moreover, it provides a library for new teachers to work from, as well as useful evaluation results of past trials.

THE COLLAGE PROJECT

The COLLAGE project has managed to go beyond the state of art by offering innovative tools and supporting active learning without the constrains of time and space, thus paving the way for the realisation of a feature that literature regards as a future step: personalisation. This becomes true using the COLLAGE platform, by providing a chance for the user to participate in learning experiences adapted to his/her own needs and preferences. Furthermore the, project has demonstrated that spatial limitations of informal learning spaces can be counterbalanced with the proper pedagogical approach and the right tools. The student is not limited to pre-generated expert content, but is able to provide other students with his/her unique knowledge and experience, thus belonging to a community of learners. As mobile learning continues to challenge the boundaries imposed by traditional classroom learning, it raises questions about its significance in relation to wider ambitions to improve education and exploit technology in furthering that aim. What shifts in pedagogical and theoretical perspectives have been observed? To what extent are e-learning policy and initiatives taking account of research project results and the potential of mobile learning?

The COLLAGE project emphasises the perspective of game-based learning. Modern academic research strongly backs up the idea that when students are engaged in the learning process, they learn and retain more. Engagement may come through emotion, relaxation and especially through fun. It is obvious that games are a strong motivating and engaging factor. Students in the COLLAGE project were involved in entertaining and fun activitiesin the form of web-based games. By placing a game at the core of an interactive learning environment, the use of the COLLAGE platform provided students with the opportunity to participate in an active learning process, enabling them to gain knowledge and skills beyond "traditional" classroom results. Further, a communicative approach was adopted, so that students' communicative activities with experiential value were used for the acquisition of knowledge and the development of communicative competence.

Added Value

In the educational scenarios implemented, the content was experience-based rather than theoretically transmitted. As research in pedagogy demonstrates, successful learning can be achieved in authentic situations. Furthermore, according to constructivist learning theories the learner should be encouraged to actively explore "the world" on his/her own rather than being subjected to "knowledge transmission" by the teacher. Without denying the potentials of traditional classromm education, it is attempted here to create a link between traditional methods and the potential of mobile technologies, which still needs to be further explored. Furthermore, our approach takes into account the need for more interdisciplinary and collaborative school education, which is crucial for enhancing the effectiveness of education. This can provide a unique way of strengthening learning processes, such as discovering analogies, similarities etc., while providing topics which are inherently closer to real world problems. The goal is to induce the learner into a "culture of practice" which makes knowledge meaningful. Another implication is that the feedback ideally should be intrinsically embedded into the context in which the activity is performed. A further implication is to have the learning challenge carefully balanced to keep it within a "zone" that matches the learner's ability. What we see is that elements that contribute to effective learning environments include a thematically meaningful story ("situating" the application of the knowledge), relevant and rapid feedback, and a carefully managed level of challenge.

Contextual Learning

Our approach has assigned importance to learning in context and demonstrated innovative ways to integrate game-based learning within specific contexts. Contextual learning occurs in close relationship with actual experience, allowing students to test academic theories through real world applications. Contextual teaching and learning strategies emphasize problem-solving; recognize the need for teaching and learning to occur in a variety of contexts such as home, community, and work sites; teach students to monitor and direct their own learning so they become self-regulated learners; anchor teaching in students diverse life-contexts; encourage students to learn from each other and together; and employ authentic assessment. The Contextual Model of Learning (CML), developed by Drs. John H. Falk and Lynn D. Dierking, was selected as such a framework (Falk & Dierking 2000) for the project. This model posits that there are three contexts that influence the nature of learning (Personal, Physical, and Sociocultural), and that in order to design effective learning environments and tasks one needs to consider suites of factors within each of these contexts.

Personal Context factors relate to what each learner brings to the learning task: their interest and motivations, their preferences for how to learn and their prior knowledge and experience. At the heart of this context is the knowledge that learning is facilitated when: 1) the learner is motivated and affected emotionally; 2) when personal interests are tapped into; and 3) when "new" knowledge is constructed on a foundation of prior experience and knowledge. Thus, three aspects of the Personal Context were emphasized within the pedagogical design of COLLAGE emotional context by connecting to and facilitating: 1) the prior knowledge and experience of students including efforts to create meaningful pre-visit activities; 2) student interest in, and motivation for, the topic and tasks they are engaged in; and 3) opportunities for choice and control enabling students to be in charge of their own learning.

Physical Context factors encompass the notion that learning is best facilitated and expressed within appropriate and authentic contexts with objects and experiences from the real world (see Figure 2). In the framework of the project learners had opportunities to engage actively in learning tasks, in some cases physically interacting with

Figure 2. Learning History in situ: In the framework of the COLLAGE project a series of educational activities were developed around the Knossos Palace in Crete. Students had to accomplish specific missions in order to locate the area of the Labyrinth. Following different paths and answering different sets of questions, students were exploring the area and at the same time learning about the Minoan Civilization.

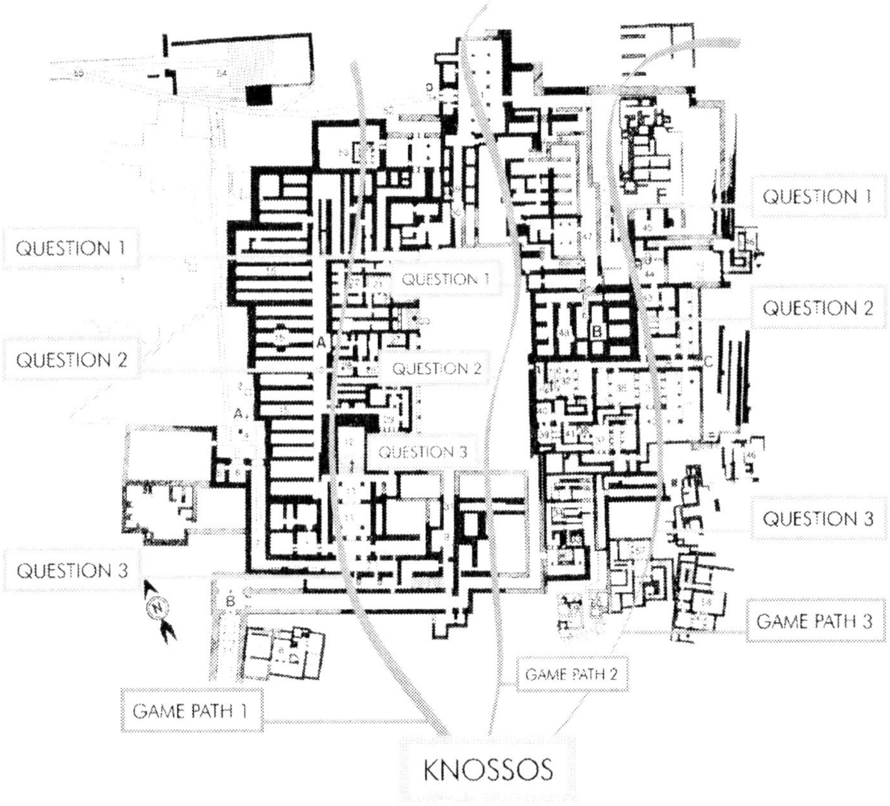

an archaeological monument, science centre or museum exhibit, water biotope and small animals. The COLLAGE approach can facilitate 1) physical orientation to the space and the experience of investigating a problem in situ by introducing mobile and context awareness technology 2) conceptual organisation of objects and concepts involved in the problems (e.g. with the help of a related ontology) 3) subsequent reinforcement of recording and reporting experiences back at school and at home.

Sociocultural Context factors encompass the notion that learning occurs within a sociocultural milieu; learning is both an individual and a group process. What someone learns, let alone why and how someone learns, is inextricably bound to the cultural and historical context in which that learning occurs and to the people collaborating in the learning process. In fact, for many learners learning is best accomplished through collaboration and group problem solving. The COLLAGE educational games provided ample opportunities for collective work on problems and challenges. There were also opportunities for students to interact with staff and volunteers at the archaeological sites, science centres and museums, or local people affected by the problem researched. Problem-solving with the educational games has demonstrated that it can support the identification of crucial actors (e.g. local people, scientists) in problem identification and decomposition, and expose already applied solutions to similar problems.

The model also includes a fourth and very important dimension, Time. Learners build experiences and concepts layer upon layer; the best learning occurs when experiences are reinforced and connected across the settings in which learners participate.

The Educational Activities

The COLLAGE educational activities included four main phases of implementation (see Figure 4):

1. **Preparatory phase:** After defining a problem-based activity, the teacher works with the platform to fine-tune the domain model, the necessary skills and skills that

Figure 3. Following the steps of Theseus. During their missions students worked in groups to accomplish the tasks assigned to them. In the case of the Knossos educational game, students had to search for additional information on the web, to interact with experts or even to use information from cartoons and TV series referring to the Greek Mythology. The COLLAGE educational games provided ample opportunities for collective work on problems and challenges.

can be acquired, planning the didactical and practical aspects of the activity. This is when the time dimension is initiated.

2. **Problem identification phase:** This phase may coincide with the pre-visit phase if learners are involved in a field trip or visit, or a pre-investigation phase in any other case. This phase may take place in the classroom. Students get informed about the domain, the possible research areas and develop a research plan. Besides this, students are supported by the platform to develop a relation to the problem and its domains. A research plan includes: i) a description of the phenomenon or the problem the students want to do research on, and ii) a predictive explanation about the phenomenon or a set of possible solutions to a problem.
3. **Solution phase:** During the solution phase, time counts to the benefit of learners. While defining their solution plan and executing it, the learners may work individually or as group. Data, information and circumstances are weighted with a certain rationale.
4. **Post-solution phase:** The final phase may include reporting back to classroom, or taking a decision regarding a construction or purchase, to review the pathway to possible problem solutions and to solution execution. Knowing why a certain solution is given to a problem and not just what is the solution to the problem will contribute greatly to self-organised and self-regulated learning as well as to the development of meta-cognitive learning competences such as elaboration and solution strategies.

Figure 4. An overview of the four phases of organising the educational activities according to the COLLAGE approach explaining their relationships

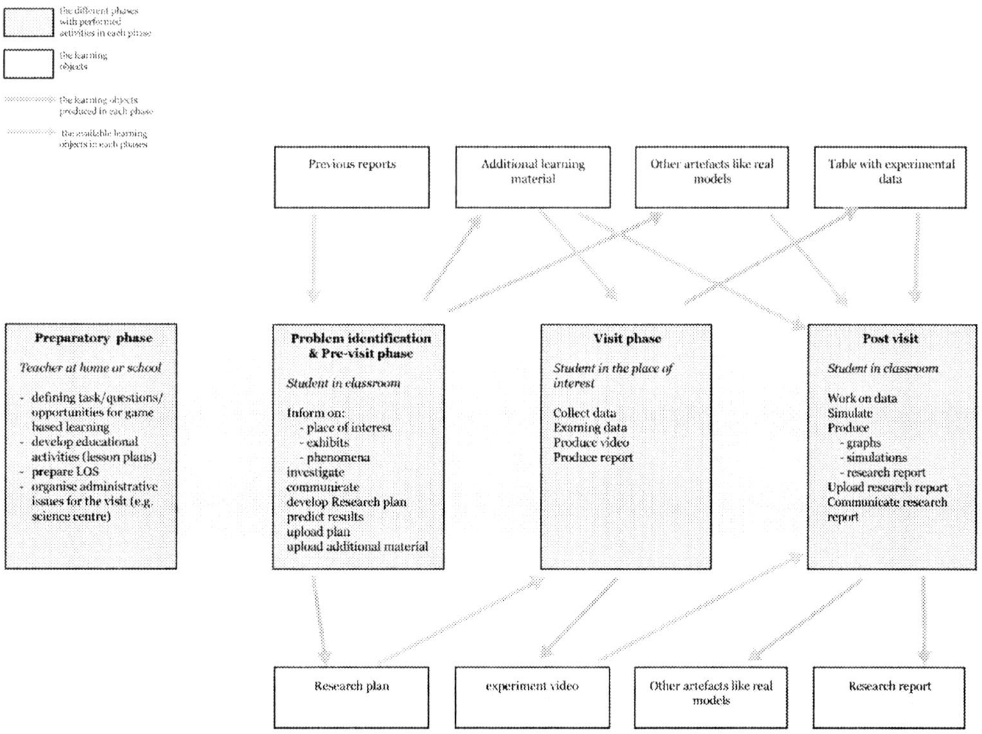

THE COLLAGE SYSTEM

The COLLAGE system was developed to facilitate the implementation of the approach described in the previous section. The integrated system is presented in Figure 5. The system was developed in a multi-tier architecture, having three levels:

1. The educational content level, containing the educational modules and courses, together with metadata about their possible use. This level is in fact distributed in various Internet-enabled sites, which are accessed in ways transparent to the user.
2. The educational services level, which contains the software modules and agents that implement the system services, together with the ontologies that support their personalisation. Ontologies constitute the core of content representation and the means that the COLLAGE system uses in order to re-use existing content, to personalize services and to maximize efficiency of education. This task is closely interrelated with user profiling, content and scenario description and platform design.
3. The user level, which contains the Personal Learner's Apprentice, responsible for establishing and maintaining an educational session that meets user requirements

The COLLAGE Platform

The COLLAGE platform is designed as a three-tier web platform to serve a wide variety of user needs beyond static document access and browsing of static content. The technology is platform independent, as it is directly interpreted within a browser that is capable of accessing HTML and dynamic ASP web pages with java and VB script support. Sound collaboration among different server side modules and applets has been achieved using Scripts, server side Java applets and asynchronous JavaScript and XML (AJAX) techniques. The result is the provision of a unified, dynamic, interactive Web platform. A number of plug-ins

Figure 5. The architecture of the COLLAGE system

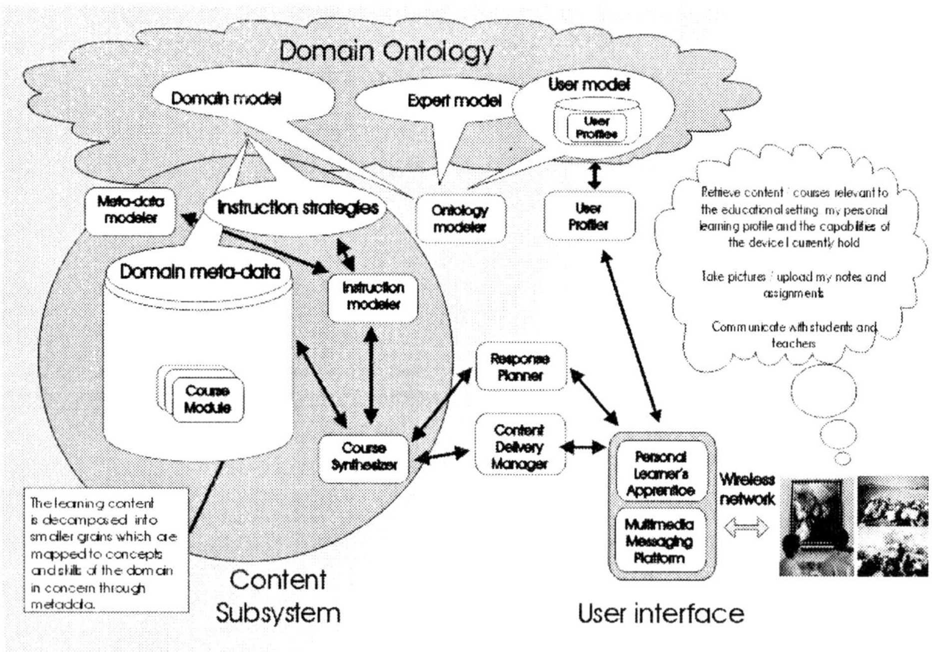

has been used in order to support the process of video and audio files on the client's device.

The philosophy of the COLLAGE platform is to provide services that promote data sharing and collaboration among different web users, while role-based access restrict platform access to different levels of authorized users. A number of mechanisms enable users to search for classified educational material according to specific search criteria and meta-information. These services allow users not only to share but mainly to reuse, evaluate and comment revised educational material and finally reformat information in order to produce new educational content. The platform is mainly designed to support mobile users and therefore the web service interface is specially designed to fit the platform on low and medium sized devices' screen with optimized navigation structure. The system manipulates data (using buffer, cache and content resize techniques) in order to achieve minimum data transfer and high interaction experience over any available wireless

Figure 6. The different sessions of the COLLAGE platform. Teachers are able to create a series of game-like educational activities (design the game, allocate roles, create teams) and then, during the visit to a specific place, to give to their students the opportunity to get involved in the educational activities by playing the game. All the materials are stored in the library for future use.

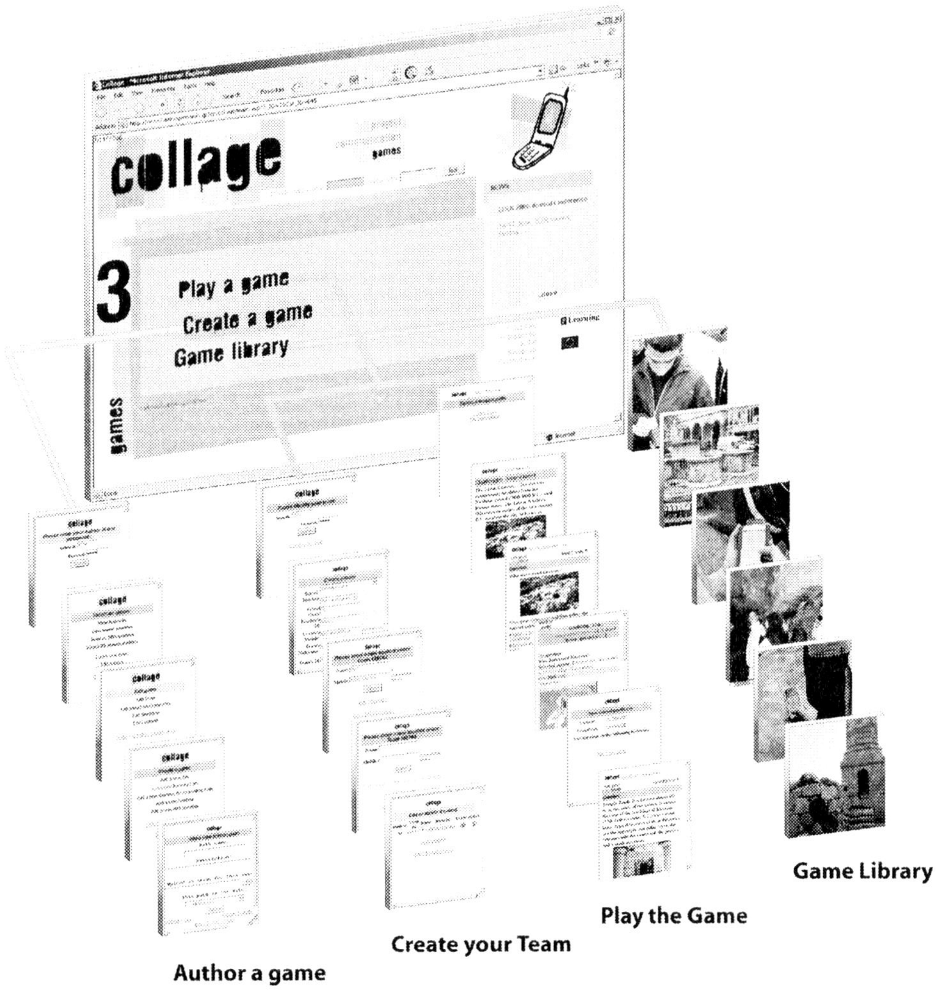

Figure 7. The platform services are delivered to the user via an advanced user interface. The main components of the user interface are the Personal Learner's apprentice and the Multimedia Messaging Platform.

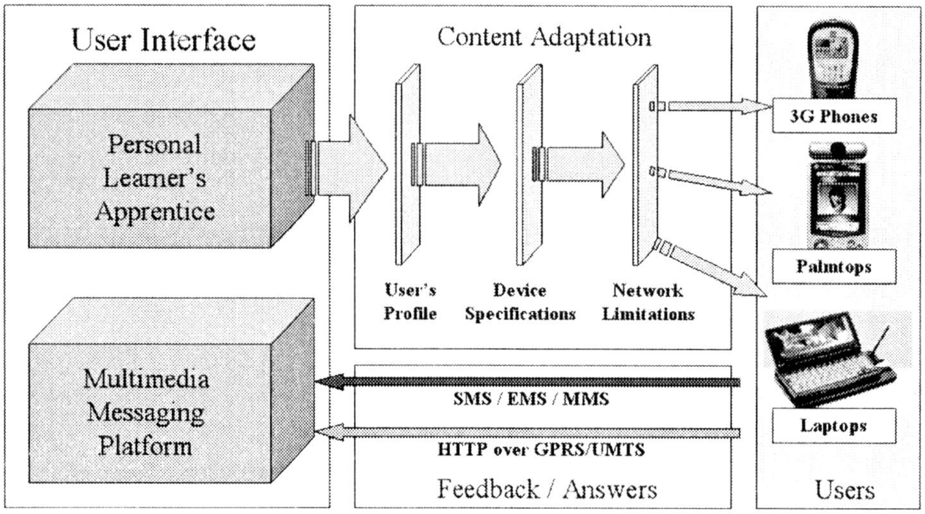

network that is able to establish an internet connection between the platform and the end user's terminal device. A number of data and communication technologies have been used to enrich the platform with 2-way SMS, tele-voting, location based content and GIS functionalities.

Based on user's model and profile, the COLLAGE platform synthesizes the user interface for the particular educational activity "on the fly", using frames that combine interaction templates with aspects of context. By decomposing the user interface into dialogue description, content, layout and device capabilities, the system supports flexibility, adaptability of interaction, while taking into account linguistic and cultural preferences of the users.

The Two-Way SMS System

Anytime-anywhere communication services are also supported by a 2-way messaging mechanism that provides users with the capability to send targeted SMS messages to selected groups of recipients (e.g. a group of students). The equipment needed for the Two-Way SMS System is a GSM/GPRS modem with a GSM card and a PC with an Internet connection. The modem is connected to the computer via an RS232 cable. The communication process is made using AT commands and the programming language used is Java. The SMS messages containing the questions are sent to students' personal mobile phones. The students' mobile numbers are collected during the team's registration process. The SMS messages are sent using the B2B Server mechanism of GroupSMS service provided by Forthnet S.A. (www.forthnet.gr), a programmatic access to the "groupSMS" SMS gateway centre from a custom application via TCP/IP and the Internet via HTTP.

Sending the Replies

Answers to the SMS system were sent through the students' mobile phones. The reply should have had a specific format in order to be recognised by the system as the answer to a specific question. The format of the SMS message with the student answer had to be:

Figure 8. The 2Way SMS mechanism that was implemented in the COLLAGE system

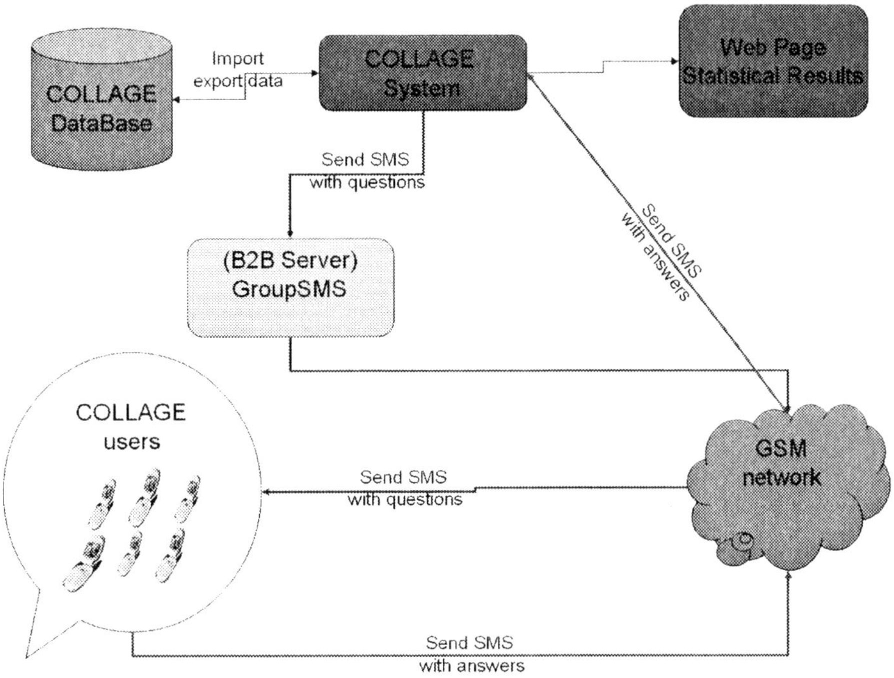

"Question code" (4 letters/ numbers - no spaces - provided in the question SMS)
followed by: 1 space character
followed by: "answer_code" (eg "1" for the first choice or "2" for second choice etc)

Receiving the SMS Messages

The SMS replies sent by the students were received through the GSM/GPRS modem. A mechanism was always running and waiting for the SMS messages. When a new SMS message had been received, the listener received the components needed. These components were the SMS text and the SMS originator (mobile number). When the SMS text was extracted, it was sent to the Message Parser. The Message Parser extracted the question code and the answer code from the answer SMS and checked whether the student had recognized correctly which answer was the correct one.

Statistical Results

All the question codes for each teacher can be seen in the 2WaySMS web page. Through this page the teacher can see the statistical results for every question as a pie chart. In the pie chart the teacher can see how many answers were wrong, how many were right and how many students have not answered the question at the specific moment. He/she is also capable of seeing the students' names of each category (right answer, wrong answer, not answered). The statistical results page is further described below, in the section titled "Using the COLLAGE Platform".

Server Side Implementation

A server side Java application is responsible to route messages to mobile phones through a group SMS gateway and receives answers that are automatically processed and stored in the local database. The 2WaySMS Platform connects to the COLLAGE database through a JDBC-ODBC Bridge. GPS technology, Google and Yahoo maps have been used to locate mobile users during their educational activities. Ajax, CGIs and server side VB and java scripts monitor users' position on Yahoo Maps 3.0 and provide location based information as text messages, describing nearby places of interest for different learning paths. Although final users may use almost any browser enabled mobile device to access the COLLAGE platform, a Java-enabled device is required for using the location based functions. On the other hand, the use of a GPS is optional and therefore the platform is functional even in cases that the user has a non-GPS enabled mobile device.

Locating Mobile Users through "GpsData" Application

For the COLLAGE system requirements, the Global Positioning System was selected as positioning method due to its accuracy. Furthermore, GPS works anywhere in the world, under any weather conditions, 24 hours a day without paying any fee or subscription, or without the need to develop any infrastructure or network. The only equipment that is needed is a GPS receiver that follows the NMEA 183 protocol and is able to export data for the PDA.

In order to read the NMEA sentences, a special application was developed using JAVA. GpsData is a software application developed in order to read and send location data from a GPS-enabled PDA to a central server through a network connection (usually GPRS Internet). It has been designed to work on every PDA with a connected/embedded GPS device running Windows Mobile 2004/2005. The most interesting of the NMEA commands is the GLL and the GGA, as these sentences contain information about the current position of the GPS receiver. It has been found that the GLL sentence is not supported by some PCMCIA card GPS re-

Figure 9. Teachers were able to interfere with and alternate the normal flux of the game through the 2-way messaging mechanism, by assigning new tasks or in some cases providing support to the teams that were not able to proceed in the next tasks

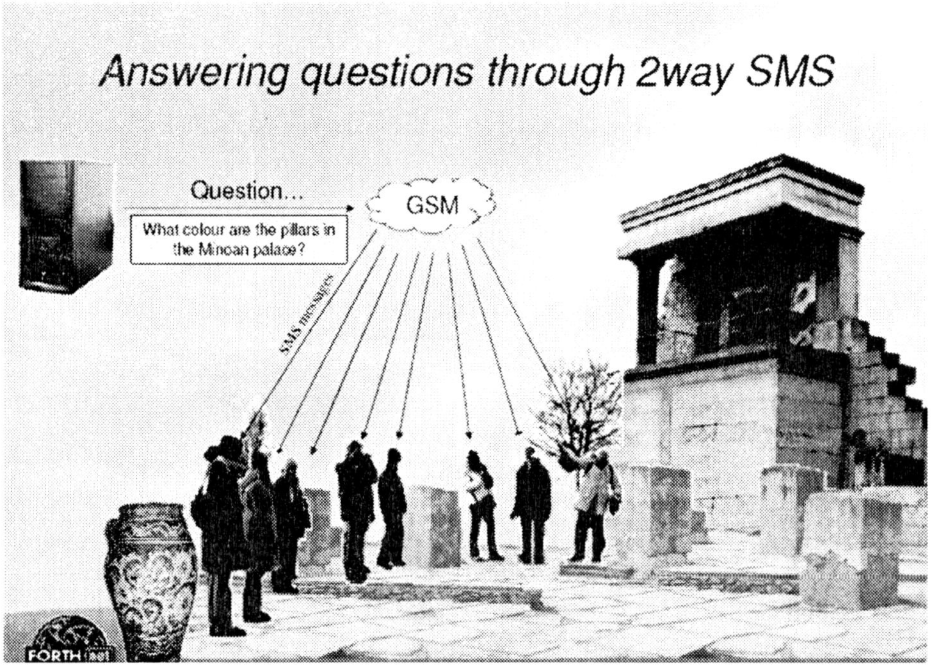

ceivers; therefore, the COLAGE GpsData mobile application uses the GGA sentence in order to extract the desired data.

The Global Positioning System Fix Data GGA sentence is analyzed below:

```
$GPGGA,094655.404,4318.7911,N,01120.3136,
E,1,07,1.1,355.8,M,,,,0000*0D
```

where:

094655.404	Fix taken at time of measurement
4318.7911,N	Latitude 43 deg 18.7911' N
01120.3136,E	Longitude 11 deg 20.3136' E
1 Fix quality:	0 = invalid
	1 = GPS fix
	2 = DGPS fix
07	Number of satellites being tracked
1.1	Horizontal dilution of position
355.8,M	Altitude, Metres, above mean sea level
(empty field)	Height of geoid (mean sea level)
(empty field)	time in seconds since last DGPS update
(empty field)	DGPS station ID number

The mobile application reads the incoming NMEA data and seeks for the GGA sentence which contains all necessary information in comma delimited format. The GpsData mobile application parses the sentence and isolates the latitude and longitude elements (at the "GPS settings" sector, "Lat" and "Lot" text fields), which then transmitted to the main server. Having in mind to integrate this application as part of an enterprise level environment, each PDA has its own Unit ID, which uniquely identifies the PDA Unit to the server. Each request to transmit location data includes Unit's ID, enabling the central Server to recognize who is actually sending the data. GpsData has been designed to be simple in its use and completely transparent to the user.

Mapping Technology

An integral part of "everywhere learning" is representing the learning activities in the physical world. Parts of the overall architecture of COLLAGE are a suite of web applications to visualize the learning activities and to provide reflections of the scenarios.

COLLAGE utilized the GPS data from the mobile phones in the general architecture together with Application Programming Interfaces (APIs) of available Internet mapping services from Google and Yahoo Maps to create these applications. These APIs enabled live team tracking and activity summaries of the different learning summaries taking place in real time. The activity summary feature displayed user generated photographs and comments from each of the teams in the learning scenarios. This provided a space for reflection that also combined the actual path that they followed, rendered via the mapping technologies. Additionally the technology supplied a live map with a GPS position on the mobile device helping the learners navigate through the environment (see Figure 10).

Using the COLLAGE Platform

The COLLAGE platform is available with Internet Explorer version 4 or later, Mobile Internet Explorer or Opera 8.6 for Pocket PC. Active Server Pages (ASP®) is the main language used for the server side development of the COLLAGE platform. Each time the user browses to COLLAGE ASP® web pages, the web server generates the HTML code which is then passed to user's browser and creates a page on the user's screen. There are 4 main areas for the user to choose:

- Administrator (for the administrator only)
- Play a game
- Author's area
- Library

The Administrator Panel

The administrator panel is available only for the COLLAGE administrator, who is provided with a username and a password by the COLLAGE system. The main tasks of the COLLAGE administrator are described below.

Figure 10. Through the COLLAGE platform the teacher is able to monitor students' teams. The mapping technology offers detailed information about the activities taking place in the different locations of interest.

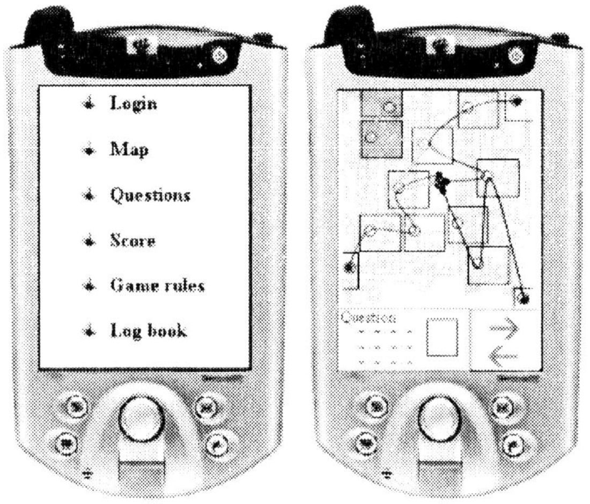

Add a School

The administrator is able to create a list of the schools that are going to participate in the game and use the COLLAGE platform. A number of details are needed in order to add a school at the list: school's name, level, country, while a unique id is needed for each school. By clicking on the "submit" button, an ASP form reads, verifies and stores the submitted data through intermediate ASP page.

Add a New Author (Teacher Account)

The administrator is able to add a teacher (game author) for an existing school providing his/her details such as name, a unique id number and a password. The administrator can also edit the information for active authors' accounts using the "edit" procedure from the "Edit teacher" page (see Figure 11).

Figure 11. Create a teacher account

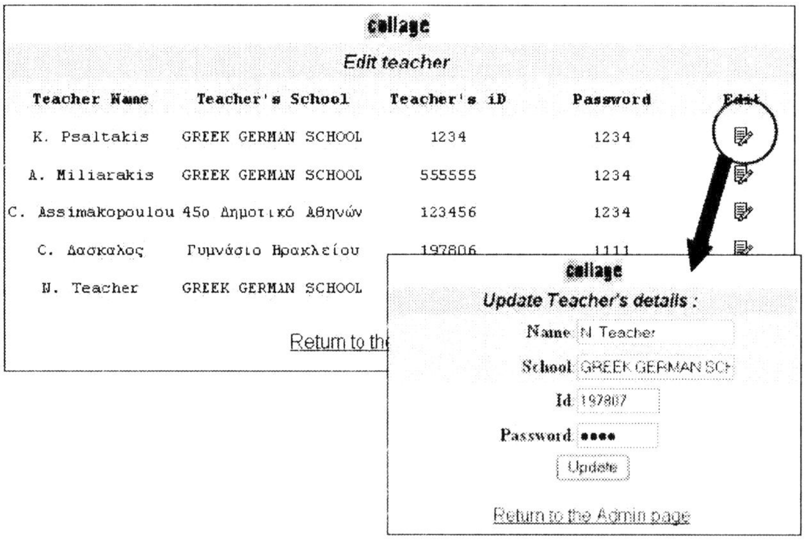

Author's Area

Only authors (teachers) registered to the COLLAGE system through the administrator panel are able to create games. In order to be a game author, the user should fill in and submit a form with personal details such as his/her name, his/her school name and level, his/her country and his/her email address. By submitting the form, an automatically generated mail is sent to the COLLAGE administrator in order to complete the registration process. Game authors are able to access a number of functionalities, like creating a new game or editing an existing game through a static html page.

Create a Team

The students' teams must be registered to the COLLAGE system before taking part in a game. During the registration process, the author has to select the school's and teacher's name, to declare the desired team's nickname, and enter a desired unique id and password, the "submit" procedure reads, verifies and stores the submitted data through intermediate ASP page. Each team consists of one ore more students. After the team registration, the author is able to add one or more students to the team by submitting the above form.

Add a New Site

Each game is linked with a site (an archaeological site, a museum etc). The author can add a new site providing a name, the school that is linked with this game, author's name, preferred language and a small description about the new site submitted. The "School Name", "Teacher Name" and "Language" are automatically exported from the "School", "Teacher" and "Country" tables respectively.

Add a New Learning Path

Each site consists of one or more learning paths. The author can create new paths for the specific site providing a small description about the path, the path's name, a few relevant keywords, the subject that is strongly related to the path, the language used, and the age levels related with the educational

Figure 12. Add a new learning path

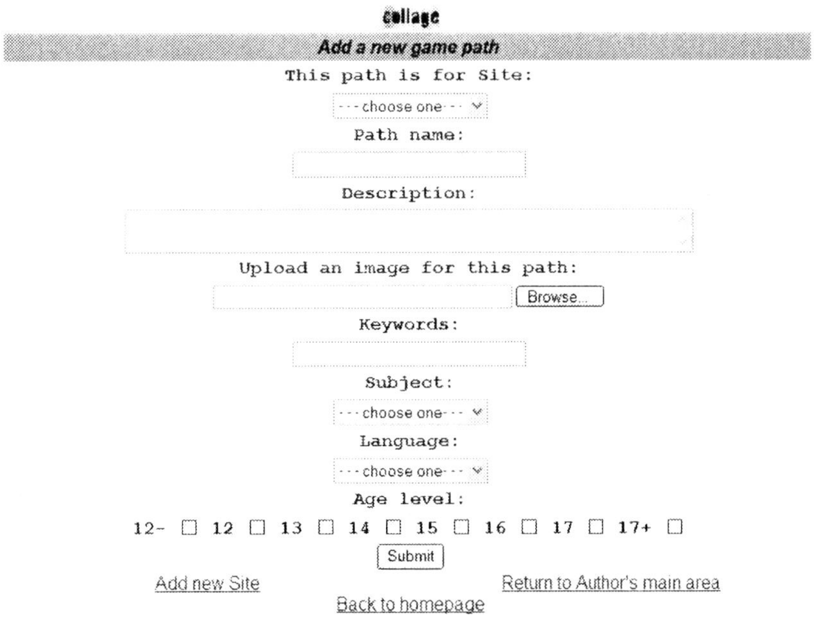

material of this path. He/she is also able to upload additional information (e.g. a picture) concerning the specific path. (Figure 12)

Add a New Question for an Existing Path

The author has the ability to create multiple choice questions for under a path. The data provided will be the question text and two or three possible answers for every question.

If no possible answer is provided, the question is considered as a task which prompts the team to take some action relevant to the educational material of the path. The author is able to upload multimedia content (video or sound file) instead of a photograph or image. Acceptable video and sound formats are "wmv", "wma" and "mp3". (Figure 13)

Add Questions from an Existing Path

The author is able to select questions from existing paths, owned by other authors, to be added in his/her own one. First he/she has to choose the desired existing site and path. By submitting the form, the author is able to view all the questions belonging to the relevant site and path, and then to select one or more of them to be added to a specific destination. The selected destination can be any of the sites and paths that the author has previously created. (Figure 14)

Add a New Territory

The author of the game should be able to declare in the game some geographic territories with special interest, using the Geographic coordination of the desired territory. The interface for this functionality is shown in Figure 15.

Add a New SMS Question

For each path, the author is also able to create one or more SMS questions. These questions can be sent to students' mobile phones. Each SMS question consists of a unique question code (4 digit alphanumeric value), the question text and two possible answers. The author should finally choose the right answer. (Figure 16)

Edit Games and Teams

Through the "edit" procedures, the game author is able to access a number of functionalities relative with the editing of a COLLAGE game

Figure 13. Add a new question/task

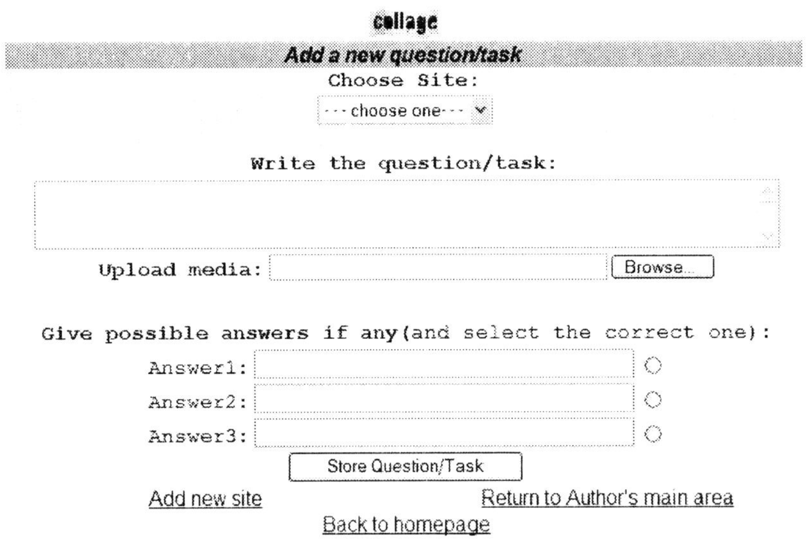

parameters such as sites, paths and territories. As for the teams, author is able to edit his/her existing teams details (the team's nickname and password, the team's points and the leader's mobile). The game author can also initiate or clear the team's GPS positions from the database by selecting the relevant option.

Figure 14. Select destination and the relevant questions

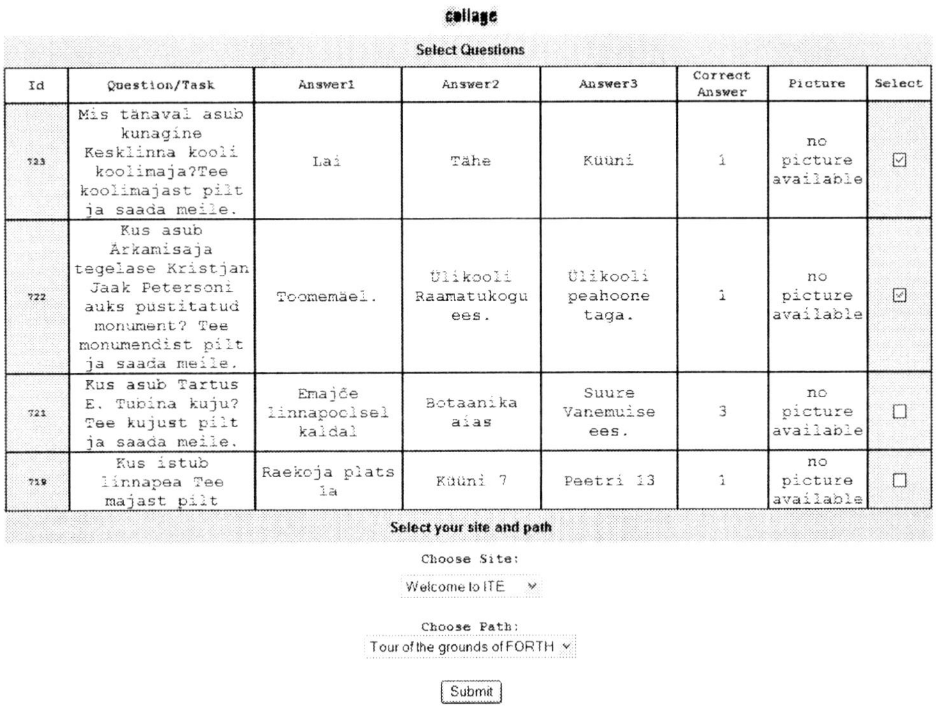

Id	Question/Task	Answer1	Answer2	Answer3	Correct Answer	Picture	Select
723	Mis tänaval asub kunagine Kesklinna kooli koolimaja?Tee koolimajast pilt ja saada meile.	Lai	Tähe	Küüni	1	no picture available	☑
722	Kus asub Ärkamisaja tegelase Kristjan Jaak Petersoni auks püstitatud monument? Tee monumendist pilt ja saada meile.	Toomemäel.	Ülikooli Raamatukogu ees.	Ülikooli peahoone taga.	1	no picture available	☑
721	Kus asub Tartus E. Tubina kuju? Tee kujust pilt ja saada meile.	Emajõe linnapoolsel kaldal	Botaanika aias	Suure Vanemuise ees.	3	no picture available	☐
719	Kus istub linnapea Tee majast pilt	Raekoja plats 1a	Küüni 7	Peetri 13	1	no picture available	☐

Figure 15. Add a new territory of interest

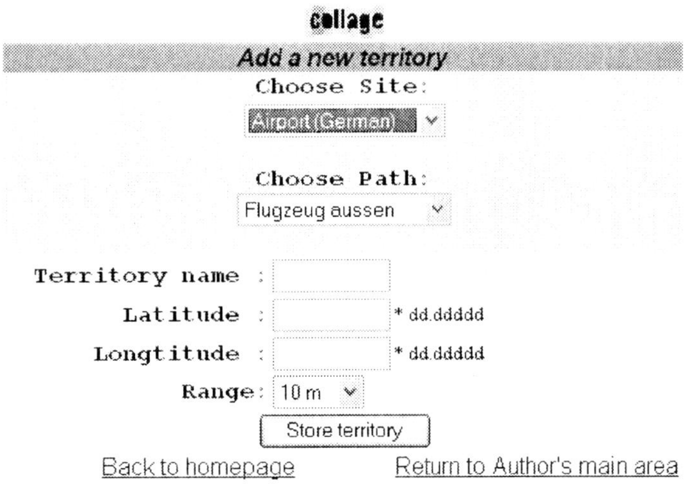

Figure 16. Add a new SMS question

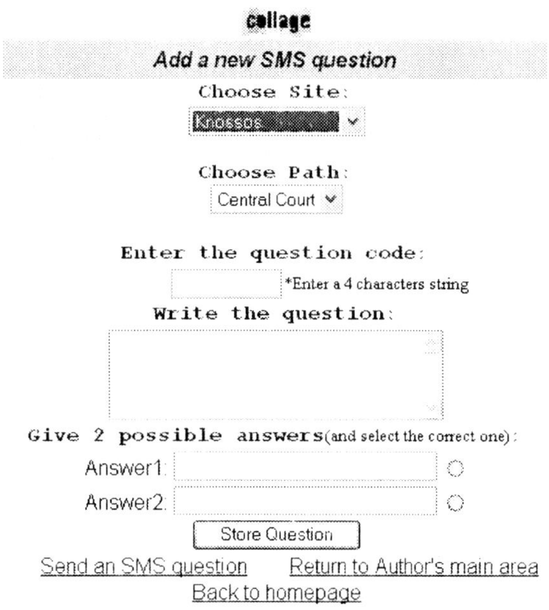

Edit Questions/Tasks

The author of a game through this section is able to edit or delete the relevant questions/tasks and relevant questions of a selected learning scenario. The author through this section has also the ability to change the questions/tasks order.

Edit Logbook

During a game, students are able to upload pictures and comments to the platform. These pictures and comments are accessible from other teams or students, in order to encourage collaboration among students. The author of the learning scenario is able to delete or edit some or all of these comments after the end of the game.

Send an SMS Question

When the teacher plans to send an SMS question to a group of students he/she has to choose the desired site and path. By clicking on the "Submit" button, the questions that are available for the specific site/ path are shown in an ASP page. Using this page the teacher is able to select which question should be sent to students / recipients.

Answer Statistics

SMS statistics is an ASP page where the teacher is able to see how many students have answered to the previously sent SMS question. In order to see the COLLAGE Statistics page, the PDA browser should be Java enabled. There are details about students that have answered wrong or right and how many questions have not been answered yet. The students' names can also be seen. (Figure 17)

View Logbooks

Through this area, the game author is capable to watch the activity of his/her teams during a game. He/she is able to see all the answers and comments made by his teams' members and their total points. He/she can also submit his own comments when needed.

View Teams Positions

Through this section, the author of the game is able to see in which geographic territory is located each one of the teams that participate to the game. (Note: the territories should have been declared by the author in advance using the "Add a new territory" in "authors' area").

Play a Game

Students can play the games that have been created and stored in the COLLAGE database. A game consists of one or more learning paths, while each learning path has one or more multiple answer question, tasks and a logbook. The logbook is the area where students are able to collaborate, by uploading comments and pictures related to the learning path.

Selecting a Site/Course

In order to play a game, the student has to select the desired site. A site/course is a thematic unit referring to a specific place (e.g. an archaeological site) or course (e.g.: history).

Figure 17. Analysis of the results

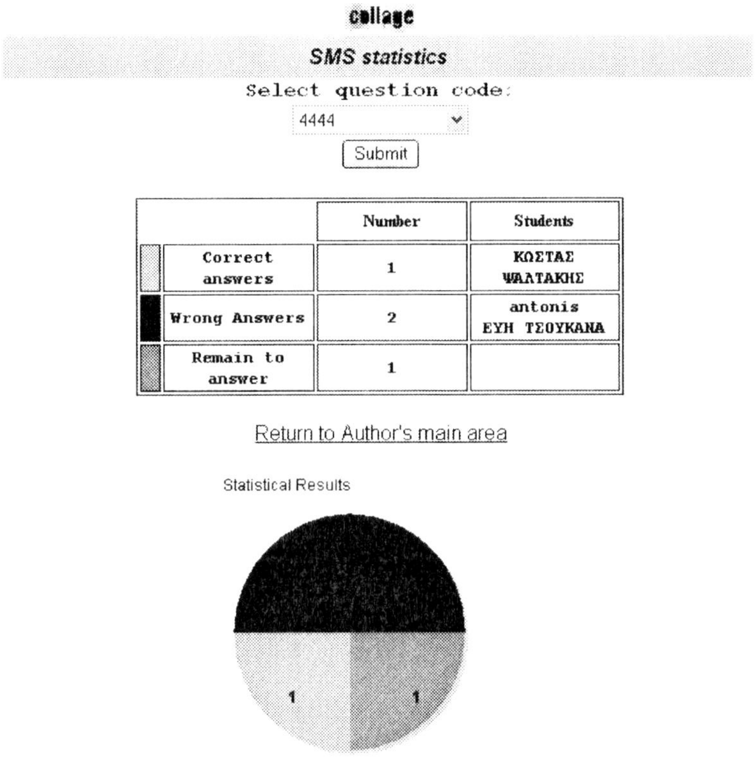

The students have two options:

1. They are able to select only sites which have been created by their own teacher. If a team wants to play another site, that has to be selected through the library section.
2. They have the ability to continue an unfinished game without losing their points.

Site names are automatically gathered from the "Scenarios" table. The second step for the team is to select one of the available learning paths for the selected site. During this second step, the user is able to see and select only the learning paths that are connected with the selected site. The relationship between "sites" and "paths" is one to many, which means that each "site" may consist of many "paths", while each "path" belongs to only one "site". When the path has been selected the game starts with a short description of the purpose of the selected path. After reading the introduction, the student is able to proceed to the first available question/task. (Figure 18)

On the top right corner, the team can check its total points (points which have been achieved totally from all the COLLAGE paths that have been played by a specific team) and is also able to watch the points collected for an individual path. The team is also able to see other teams' points (only if these teams are taking part in the same game and are owned by the same teacher). When an answer is provided about a question, the question's points will be collected for the specific team and the student is automatically transferred to the logbook area where he can upload a comment. There is also the option of skipping the specific question and continuing the game with the next available question/task without earning any points.

Figure 18. The interface of the COLLAGE platform that supports the educational activities. The platform provides information about the score of the team, the team location in relation with the other teams. The students can also add information to their logbook for future reference.

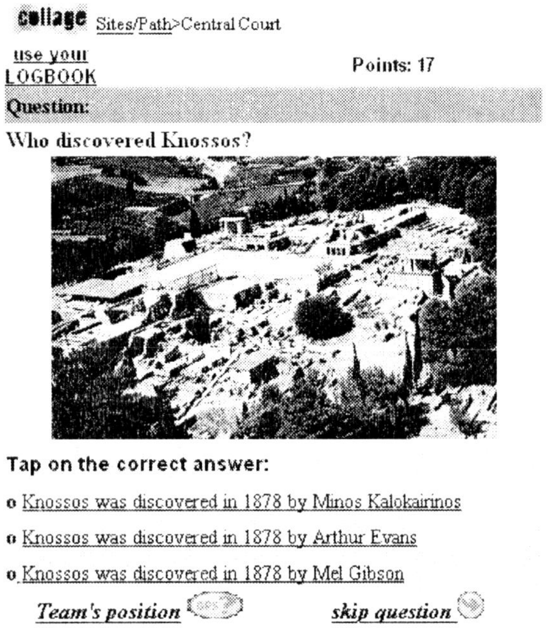

The Logbook - The Learning Scenario

The main activity area of the platform is the logbook as it is a point of collaboration and discussion among students. In the LogBook area students can see their classmates' photos/comments and add their own material in order to discuss and collaborate on-line. A different logbook is created for each learning path. The logbook is a record of how the team dealt with the questions of each Game Path. The Players have to add a comment in order to support their answer, whether that is right or wrong. However, on entering the Logbook the player can infer from the Points collected whether they have chosen the correct answer. The pedagogical objective of the Logbook is to allow the players and the teams to review their playing strategy and their performance. On entering the logbook the team has an overview of their situation, how many points they have, how many questions they have answered and how. Every entry in the Logbook corresponds to a Game Path question. The player is usually required to back up his or her chosen answer with a written comment, a photo taken on site or other information from the web, e.g. a hyperlink. Other players of the same team can add their own comments to back up the chosen answer or the comment initially add to support the chosen answer. Furthermore, a player that disagrees with the team's chosen answer can declare his or her disagreement with a comment. After answering all available questions under a path, students are able to select another learning path or even a completely different site/course. They are also able to review their logbook or their total points.

Geographic Territories and Users' Localization

During a game each team is able to watch its actual position through this section. Specific game territories can be declared to the platform as key points. When a key point is reached by a team an automatically generated SMS is sent to all the members of this team with information about the area. This functionality is fully operating if the GPS Data application is activated on the students' PDAs and the author has marked the key points with actual geographical coordinates. A Yahoo map facility has been added to this page, where a team can watch its actual position on a yahoo map. When team is not within a pre-defined territory or there are no GPS coordinates available for the specific team, an information message appears on the screen.

Library Section

Registered users of the COLLAGE platform are able to search for specific games that match their educational standards. Choosing the subject, language, the age levels, and submitting up to three keywords, the users are able to search for a desirable COLLAGE path (if there exists one) which then can play or use for the creation of their own games.

Testing the COLLAGE Platform with Different Terminal Devices

To access the COLLAGE platform, a laptop, PDA or mobile phone with internet access and web browser is required. The web browser should be capable of accessing HTML and Active Server Pages (ASP). The latest versions of the most popular web browsers for desktop and mobile devices (such as Internet Explorer, Mobile IE, FireFox and Opera) support ASP and therefore can access the COLLAGE platform.

The terminal device should provide internet access, through any wired (DSL, Cable, LAN etc) or wireless network such as GPRS, 3G or WiFi. Although the platform is accessible even on low bandwidth networks (such as 9.6kbps GSM, or 14,4 HSCSD), it is recommended to access the Internet through faster and more cost-effective networks, such as GPRS, 3G or WiFi where available. For maximum usability, it is recommended that the teachers and users who wish to upload questions or extended text should use devices equipped with a full QWERTY keyboard and minimum screen resolution of 480x640 or, even better, to use a desktop, laptop, or ultra portable PC.

On the other hand, students and final users who answer questions and upload short comments in the framework of a logbook may use any mobile device that meets the web browser and internet access criteria mentioned above. It is also recommended to use a device with colour touch screen, as well as screen resolution adjusted to 240x 240 pixels or higher. Furthermore, the user may need a device with embedded (or in combination with) camera or GPS receiver in case they want to use COLLAGE "advanced" features, like uploading photos in questions and comments or location based gaming.

Ideal Device

The ideal terminal device for the COLLAGE user should meet the following functional requirements:

- Java / VB script enabled browser
- Wireless Access to the internet
- Full QWERTY keyboard
- Embedded GPS receiver
- Embedded 1.3 mega-pixel camera or better
- Touch screen displaying a resolution of at least 320 x 240 pixels
- SD or MiniSD I/O slot
- Long battery life (more than 2 hours of continuous operation)
- Good Portability (weight less that 250gr)

Accessing COLLAGE Platform with Different Devices

In order to test the functionality of the COLLAGE web pages, a number of different devices and platforms (Windows, Widows Mobile, Symbian) in combination with various web browsers (Internet Explorer, Mobile IE, Opera, Netfront and Symbian 60 web browser) were tried.

NOKIA 6630 (Symbian 60) Smartphone

NOKIA 6630 is a GSM/GPRS/3G enabled mobile phone based on the Symbian 60 platform and thus its functionality is not different from other Nokia S60 smart phones. It is equipped with an HTML web browser, good quality digital camera and mini SD memory card slot. The Symbian 60 smart phone operated successfully with the COLLAGE platform over GPRS network, with the main disadvantage being the small non-touch screen. It is recommended to install a third party web browser for Symbian60 like Opera or Netfront Web Browser (full screen images, different view modes, better interaction with forms etc). (Figure 19)

Although, NOKIA Symbian60 platform is compatible with the main functionalities provided with the COLLAGE platform (answers questions, upload a picture, add comment etc), it is not recommended due to its small, non-touch screen. On the other hand, the device can be used by users who already own it as long as data services (GPRS / 3G) are activated.

qTek 9000 (Windows Mobile 5.0)

qTeK 9000 is produced by HTC while its functionally is identical to i-mate JASJAR, O2 XDA Exec and T-Mobile MDA IV. (Figure 20)

Qtek 9000 is a GSM / GPRS/ 3G device based on Windows Mobile 5.0. It is equipped with a full QWERTY keyboard, WiFi and digital camera. The display measures a resolution of 480 x 640 pixel

Figure 19. Using COLLAGE platform through a Symbian 60 smartphone

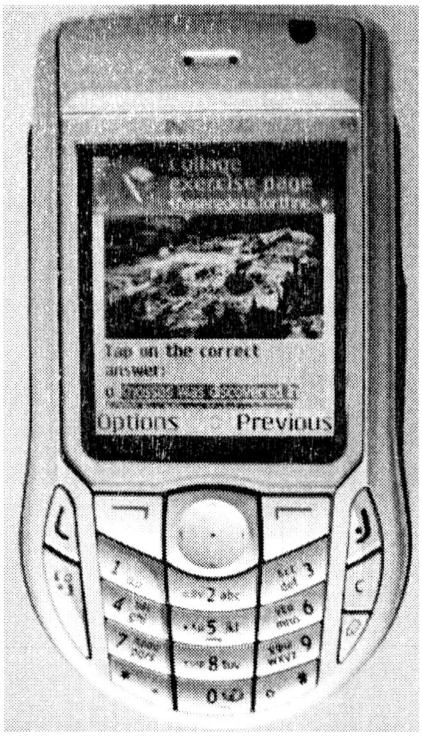

(VGA) and it is able to swivel and close back up on itself, in order to allow either two handed typing or PDA touch screen use. The qTek 9000 is a recommended device for COLLAGE platform, due to high resolution display and full QWERTY keyboard, while the only restriction is the lack of embedded GPS receiver. The user has to use an extra GPS receiver to use the location based functions provided by the platform.

iPAQ hw6515 (Windows Mobile 2003)

The hw6515 runs Windows Mobile for Pocket PC 2003 Second Edition while it is equipped with a 240x240 pixels display, which is rather small for a PDA (this may also cause problems with applications that are usually optimized for larger 240x320 screens). It has an embedded GPS receiver, GSM/GPRS modem and a full QWERTY keyboard. Although hw6515 has a bult-in GPS receiver, it is not recommended for the COLLAGE platform because of its small screen, the lack of embedded WiFi and the "old" Windows mobile 2003 version, due to the restrictions of the Mobile IE 2003, that does not support the uploading of files (an Opera browser may be used to overcome this problem). (Figure 21)

Compatibility with Other Devices

Apart from the devices mentioned above, many other mobile smart phones, tablet or PDAs could also be used for accessing the COLLAGE platform as far as they meet the criteria described under the "general characteristics" section above. Although final users may use almost any Symbian60 or similar mobile phone for the basic COLLAGE functionalities, a java enabled PDA is required for using the GPS functionalities of the platform.

FUTURE DIRECTIONS

The COLLAGE project achieved most of its goals, integrating new learning strategies with the use of mobile technologies. The level of en-

Figure 20. Using COLLAGE platform through a Qtek 9000 (landscape)

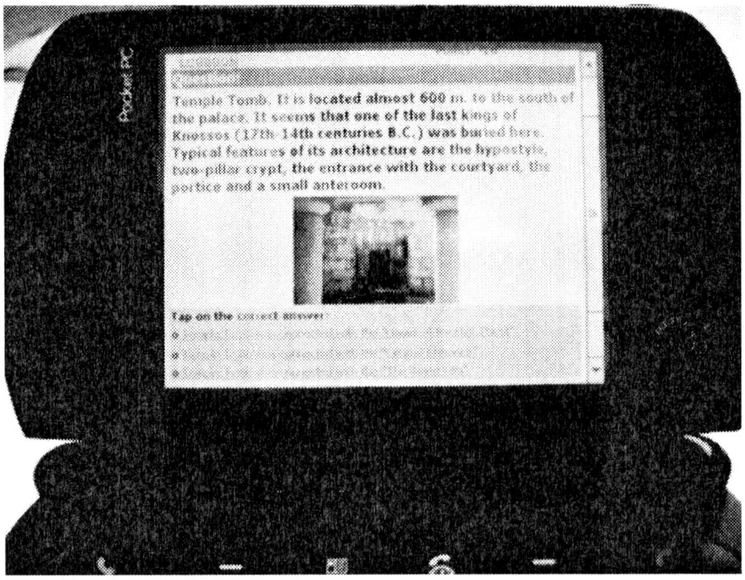

Figure 21. Using COLLAGE platform through a hw6515

gagement of all actors was very high, especially in the scenarios that evolved in time. Teachers were enthusiastic using the platform in learning situations outside the classroom. The same can be said about students, who were always very keen on using mobile technologies in the different scenarios. Consequently, the COLLAGE consortium is planning to exploit this work further through the following activities:

1. The COLLAGE approach has been already introduced in schools in Greece and Austria through the integration of the developed scenarios in a series of national initiatives. For example in Greece schools participating in the "Environmental Activities" national programme are using the COLLAGE platform to create new game-based scenarios for field trips and other relevant educational

activities. In Austria COLLAGE materials are available through the "Virtual School" portal of the Austrian Ministry of Education (see http://www.virtuelleschule.at/collage/index.html).

2. The COLLAGE consortium is closely cooperating with the FP6 research project UNITE (http://www.unite-ist.org/) which is developing an eLearning platform aiming to bridge the gap between formal and informal learning settings. The COLLAGE platform is already used in the framework of the UNITE project, as it was easily integrated with the UNITE pool of tools.
3. Växjö University and Forthnet are designing future directions for the COLLAGE platform, aiming at advanced robustness and scalability, as well as introducing the COLLAGE concepts into an existing Course Management System (CMS) like Moodle (http://www.moodle.org), which may hold the largest share of CMS deployed in the world. At FH Joanneum University, the COLLAGE group has already worked on a prototype module for Moodle called the Mobile Classroom; together with Växjö University mapping technology this could provide a framework for a future system enabling wide-spread use within Moodle communities. The adaptation of an open source software framework would quickly enable a global market for COLLAGE allowing for wide dissemination and adoption.

Business opportunities may also arise from a consulting point of view, providing services in the design of mobile learning scenarios for site-specific locations and course material.

CONCLUSION

The emergence of mobile game-based learning is offering the learning and teaching communities new opportunities to reach and motivate hard-to-engage learner groups and support differentiated and personalised learning. Policy perspectives over the last few years have increasingly become more supportive of learning with games, and a series of high-profile studies (e.g. de Freitas, 2006; Sandford et al., 2006) have demonstrated a wide range of case studies of effective game-based learning practice.

While the benefits of learning with games have been demonstrated, also by the COLLAGE project (see next chapter), the challenges for providing a sufficient level of institutional support, both technical and pedagogic, are not insignificant, and the emphasis upon "early adopters" leading the way reflects that of other areas of e-learning. However, as research within the COLLAGE project is demonstrating, game-based and contextualised learning approaches can bring learning alive, can inspire and motivate interest for the subject beyond the end of formal learning, and therefore offer new opportunities for tutors and learners alike. The COLLAGE approach has demonstrated innovative ways to integrate game-based learning within specific contexts. It demonstrated ways to eliminate the distinctions between the different educational environments (school, home, libraries, cultural places etc.), and to bridge every day personal activities.

Although the COLLAGE system used front-end technology, the aim was not to test this technology, but to investigate its impact on education, and focus on the results and changes that it can produce in the learning process. Game-based learning has been effective in these situations, offering a wide diversity of approaches and tools for tutors to make use of in their practice. Game-based learning also offers the student a chance to become more central in their own learning through generating their own content, learning collaboratively in teams and becoming more engaged in the processes of learning.

Mobile learning is the other major field of pedagogical inquiry the COLLAGE project has entered. There are many issues that deserve further in-depth investigation in this relatively new, still exploratory field. Initiatives have demonstrated how mobile technologies can work in learning contexts, but the need for a better defined research agenda for m-learning becomes now evident (Pachler, 2007). More specific research is necessary on the cognitive as well as social and cultural aspects of the introduction of mobile learning in formal and informal learning practices. As recent relevant literature demonstrates, research stemming out of the COLLAGE project could look closer into aspects such as affective issues and the options for learner sensitive scaffolding from the tutor (Cook et al., 2008), optimal design of mobile learning activities so that they support innovative educational practice and user involvement (Cook et al., 2007), even the impact of the fact that pupils readily have mobile phones and other handheld devices at their personal disposal (Bachmair, 2007).

Investigations of mobile learning often naturally tend to start from exploring designed research or experiments, in which students use the technology in prescribed learning tasks (Song & Fox 2008). Users' initiative, content generation and imaginative exploitation of the functions offered by mobile devices in the context of everyday learning, outside predefined activities, should constitute the next subject of close study in this process.

The more one experiments with mobile learning, the more existing and potential interfaces between formal and informal learning are revealed. As Cook et al. (2008) have pointed out, it is necessary to continue with further conceptual work aiming to define the gaps and possible links between informal and formal settings of learning with mobile devices, taking into account cultural variants that characterise both fields. as a precursor to trying to create synergies between them.

ACKNOWLEDGMENT

The COLLAGE project was partially financed by the European Commission under the e-Learning Programme (Contract Number: 2005-3873). The authors would like to thank the colleagues of the COLLAGE consortium for their contributions and support during the life cycle of the project. They are also grateful to the teachers and students that participated in the numerous validation activities that were realized in Greece, Estonia, Denmark, Spain and Austria.

REFERENCES

Amory, A. (2007). Game object model version II: A theoretical framework for educational game development. *Educational Technology Research and Development*, *55*(1), 51–77. doi:10.1007/s11423-006-9001-x

Bachmair, B. (2007). M-learning and media use in everyday life: Towards a theoretical framework. In N. Pachler (Ed.), Mobile learning: Towards a research agenda. WLE Centre Occasional Papers in Work-based Learning 1. London: The WLE Centre, Institute of Education.

Bruce, B., & Hogan, M. (1998). The disappearance of technology: Toward an ecological model of literacy. In D. Reinking, M. McKenna, L. Labbo & R. Kieffer (Eds.), Handbook of literacy and technology: Transformations in a post-typographic world. Mahwah, NJ: Lawrence Erlbaum Associates.

Cook, J., Bradley, C., Lance, J., Smith, C., & Haynes, R. (2007). Generating learning contexts with mobile devices. In N. Pachler (Ed.), Mobile learning: Towards a research agenda. WLE Centre Occasional Papers in Work-based Learning 1. London: The WLE Centre, Institute of Education.

Cook, J., Pachler, N., & Bradley, C. (2008). Bridging the gap? Mobile phones at the interface between informal and formal learning. *Journal of the Research Center for Educational Technology, 4*(1), 3–18.

de Freitas, S. (2006). Learning in immersive worlds: A review of game based learning. Joint Information Systems Committee (JISC). Retrieved on October 10, 2008, from http://www.jisc.ac.uk/media/documents/programmes/elearninginnovation/gamingreport_v3.pdf

EXPLOAR Project. (2008). About the EXPLOAR project. Retrieved on February 16, 2009, from http://www.ea.gr/ep/exploar/

Facer, K., Joiner, R., Stanton, D., Reid, J., Hull, R., & Kirk, D. (2004). Savannah: Mobile gaming and learning? *Journal of Computer Assisted Learning, 20*(6), 399–409. doi:10.1111/j.1365-2729.2004.00105.x

Falk, J. H., & Dierking, L. D. (2000). Learning from museums. Walnut Creek, CA: AltaMira Press.

Gee, J. P. (2003). What video games have to teach us about learning and literacy? New York: Palgrave MacMillan.

Hawkey, R. (2004). Learning with digital technologies in museums, science centres, and galleries. Report No. 9, NESTA FutureLab. Retrieved on February 16, 2009, from http://www.futurelab.org.uk/resources/documents/lit_reviews/Museums_Galleries_Review.pdf

Kiili, K. (2005). Digital game-based learning: Towards an experiential gaming model. *The Internet and Higher Education, 8*, 13–24. doi:10.1016/j.iheduc.2004.12.001

Klopfer, E., Squire, K., & Jenkins, H. (2002). Environmental detectives: PDAs as a window into a virtual simulated world. IEEE International Workshop, Wireless, and Mobile Technologies in Education, 95-98.

Kress, G., & Pachler, N. (2007). Thinking about the 'm' in m-learning. In N. Pachler (Ed.), Mobile learning: Towards a research agenda. WLE Centre Occasional Papers in Work-based Learning 1. London: The WLE Centre, Institute of Education.

Kukulska-Hulme, A., Traxler, J., & Pettit, J. (2007). Designed and user-generated activity in the mobile age. *Journal of Learning Design, 2*(1), 52–65.

Laurillard, D. (2007). Pedagogical forms for mobile learning: Framing research questions. In N. Pachler (Ed.), Mobile learning: Towards a research agenda. WLE Centre Occasional Papers in Work-based Learning 1. London: The WLE Centre, Institute of Education.

Lin, C., & Liu, D. (2006). An intelligent virtual piano tutor. ACM International Conference Proceedings: Virtual Reality Continuum and Its Applications, Hong Kong, China (pp. 353–356).

LISTEN. (2005). Project LISTEN–a reading tutor that listens. Retrieved on February 16, 2009, from http://www.cs.cmu.edu/~listen/

Luyten, K., Van Loon, H., Gabriels, K., Teunkens, D., Robert, K., Conix, K., & Manshoven, E. (2006). Designing for interaction: Socially-aware museum handheld guides. Document Server@UHasselt, Research Groups, Dept. Mathematics, Physics, Informatics (WNI), Expertise Centre for Digital Media (EDM). Retrieved on October 25, 2008, from http://hdl.handle.net/1942/1740

McKenzie, M., & Kernig, W. (1975). The challenge of informal education: Extending young children's learning in the open classroom. London: Darton, Longman, and Todd.

Norman, D. A. (2001). The future of education: Lessons learned from video games and museum exhibits. Commencement address, Northwestern University, School of Education and Social Policy.

Oloruntoba, R. (2006). Mobile learning environments: A conceptual overview. Retrieved on October 1, 2008, from https://olt.qut.edu.au/udf/OLT2006/gen/static/papers/Oloruntoba_OLT2006_paper.pdf

Owen, M. (2006). Social software and learning. Bristol: Futurelab.

Pachler, N. (2007). Mobile learning: Towards a research agenda. WLE Centre Occasional Papers in Work-based Learning 1. London: The WLE Centre, Institute of Education. Retrieved on February 16, 2009, from http://www.wlecentre.ac.uk/cms/files/occasionalpapers/mobilelearning_pachler2007.pdf

Patten, B., Arnedillo-Sánchez, I., & Tangney, B. (2006). Designing collaborative, constructionist, and contextual applications for handheld devices: Virtual learning? *Computers & Education*, *46*(3), 294–308. doi:10.1016/j.compedu.2005.11.011

Prensky, M. (2006). Don't bother me, Mom, I'm learning!: How computer and video games are preparing your kids for 21st century success and how you can help! St. Paul, MN: Paragon House.

Price, S. (2007). Ubiquitous computing: Digital augmentation and learning. In N. Pachler (Ed.), Mobile learning: Towards a research agenda. WLE Centre Occasional Papers in Work-based Learning 1. London: The WLE Centre, Institute of Education.

Price, S., Rogers, Y., Stanton, D., & Smith, H. (2003). A new conceptual framework for CSCL: Supporting diverse forms of reflection through multiple interactions. In B. Wasson, S. Ludvigsen & U. Hoppe (Eds.), Designing for change in networked learning environments. Proceedings of the International Conference on Computer Supported Collaborative Learning 2003.

Quinn, C. N. (2005). Engaging learning: Designing e-learning simulation games. San Francisco: Pfeiffer.

Raessens, J. (2006). Playing history. Reflections on mobile and location-based learning. In T. Hug (Ed.), Didactics of microlearning. Concepts, discourses, and examples. Waxmann Verlag.

Sandford, R., Ulicsak, M., Facer, K., & Rudd, T. (2006). Teaching with games: Using commercial off-the-shelf computer games in formal education. Bristol: Futurelab.

Sandford, R., & Williamson, B. (2005). Games and learning. NESTA Futurelab. Retrieved on October 1, 2008, from http://www.nestafuturelab.org/download/pdfs/research/handbooks/games_and_learning.pdf on 02/03/2006

Song, Y., & Fox, R. (2008). Affordances of PDAs: Undergraduate student perceptions. *Journal of the Research Center for Educational Technology*, *4*(1), 19–38.

Sotiriou, S., Chryssafidou, E., Owen, M., Barajas Frutos, M., Zistler, E., Lohr, M., et al. (2008). The COLLAGE project: Guide of good practice on mobile and game based learning. Athens, Greece: EPINOIA Ed.

Spikol, D., & Milrad, M. (2008). Combining physical activities and mobile games to promote novel learning practices. Fifth IEEE International Conference on Wireless, Mobile, and Ubiquitous Technology in Education (pp. 31-38).

Squeak. (2007). About squeak. Retrieved on October 10, 2008, from http://www.squeak.org

Stenton, S. P. (2007). Mediascapes: Context-aware multimedia experiences. *IEEE MultiMedia, 14*(3), 98–105. doi:10.1109/MMUL.2007.52

Tatar, D., Harrison, S., Crandell, A., & Schaefer, M. (2008). Using place as provocation: In Situ collaborative narrative construction. *Journal of the Research Center for Educational Technology, 4*(1), 49–60.

Zoakou, A., Tzanavari, A., Papadopoulos, G. A., & Sotiriou, S. (2007). A methodology for e-learning scenario development: The UNITE approach. In D. Remenyi (Ed.), The 6th European Conference on e-Learning, Copenhagen Business School, Trinity College Dublin, Ireland (pp. 683-692).

Chapter 2
Designing an Architecture to Provide Ubiquity in Mobile Learning

Javier Carmona-Murillo
University of Extremadura, Spain

David Cortés-Polo
University of Extremadura, Spain

José Luis González-Sánchez
University of Extremadura, Spain

ABSTRACT

Nowadays, mobility offers potential opportunities for student's learning. The well-known paradigm "learning anywhere anytime" is possible thanks to mobile terminals and wireless technologies that solve the limited access of wired technologies for usage due to lack of mobility. In this scenario, many projects are dealing with the use of mobility to solve specific learning activities in different environments. This chapter presents a project called Campus Ubicuo and its architecture. The novelty of this system is the integration of several wireless technologies in an only mobility learning environment. The development of the project has been divided in four parts, isolating the user interface from the communication model and from the data management. This means that the system is available in different contexts and could be easily adaptable to several organizations such as hospitals, schools, or city councils. We explain how this architecture has been designed and developed to become a solid base of mobility learning systems.

INTRODUCTION

Although the basic applications and guidelines that make the Internet possible had existed for almost a decade, it wasn't until the late 1980s and early 1990s that the network began to grow at a dramatic rate, modifying little by little our lives. As the Internet continues with its evolution, there is a parallel phenomenon taking place in wireless communications which is equally influential. Nowadays everyone owns, at least, a mobile device so the current demand of ubiquitous connectivity has turned into a reality that is necessary to satisfy, so those services traditionally offered in wired networks must also

DOI: 10.4018/978-1-60566-882-6.ch002

be offered in mobile network (Koodli & Perkins, 2007).

When we think of why mobility is so important, we can show some data. For example, at present, the number of subscriber connections in mobile telephony is over 3.500.000.000 (GSM World, 2008). This means that if there was one active subscription per person, more than half the world's population would use a mobile device.

In the field of education, the evolution process has been the same. First of all, education based in computer technology, where no in-person interaction takes place was called e-learning. Then, when mobility devices are essential in our lives, a new paradigm in educational science has arisen to take advantage of learning opportunities offered by portable technologies (Hadzilacos & Tryfona, 2005).

This new **learning system** has different definitions, depending on who is going to use it because each one of them has its own idiosyncrasy and its scope of application. From the point of view of its conception and development as an educational tool, this kind of learning systems has a pedagogical and technological duality (Georgiev, Georgieva & Trajkovski, 2006).

The aforementioned evolution must be accompanied by the development of new applications, architectures and systems to offer mobility services that can complement the learning process.

In last years the research community has started to focus some attention on this topic and some proposals and contributions have been made. In this sense, GITACA Research Group (Gitaca, 2008) contributes in this subject with a mobility project that takes in account three main features that are the basis of the whole design: User mobility in wireless networks; the Quality of Service (QoS) in the mobile communications; and finally, security issues of the information transmitted across mobile networks. Ubiquitous Campus (hereafter **Campus Ubicuo**) project proposes to interrelate them by means of **free software**, which contributes with new some advantages.

This project is the outcome of the experience obtained after some years of research into communications, mobility, educational improvement, free software and applied telematic systems, and comes up to take advantage of the mobile and portability possibilities of PDA (Personal Digital Assistant) devices, mobile phones and laptops. Thanks to these elements as well as technologies like GSM (Global System for Mobile Communications), GPRS (General Packet Radio Service), UMTS (Universal Mobile Telecommunications System), Bluetooth or WiFi (Wireless Fidelity).

The rest of the chapter is organized as follows. First, a brief background about technologies used in the design, as well as, an overview of other mobile learning architectures is presented. Then, in the main section of the chapter, the development is described in detail. Finally, conclusions and future work are discussed.

BACKGROUND

Mobile Computing in the Learning Process

Learning centers (universities, high schools, training centers,...) and, in general, all kind of organizations (city councils, museums, hospitals, ...) are very interested in the emergence of wireless communications. Workers, professionals and learners use their portable devices to be connected to the Internet in their daily activity, using them to address many of the needs of today's learners.

Mobile communications are the basis that makes possible this new learning method. The scene of an organization is composed by several wireless technologies. Some of them are shown in Figure 1. In this image a hospital (a) and a high school (b) are presented with a network infrastructure that allows user mobility. WLAN (Wireless Local Area Network) or Wi-Fi networks are the most common wireless technologies in a local institution; GPRS and UMTS allows mobility in

Figure 1. A well-designed wireless infrastructure can offer mobility services in an organization

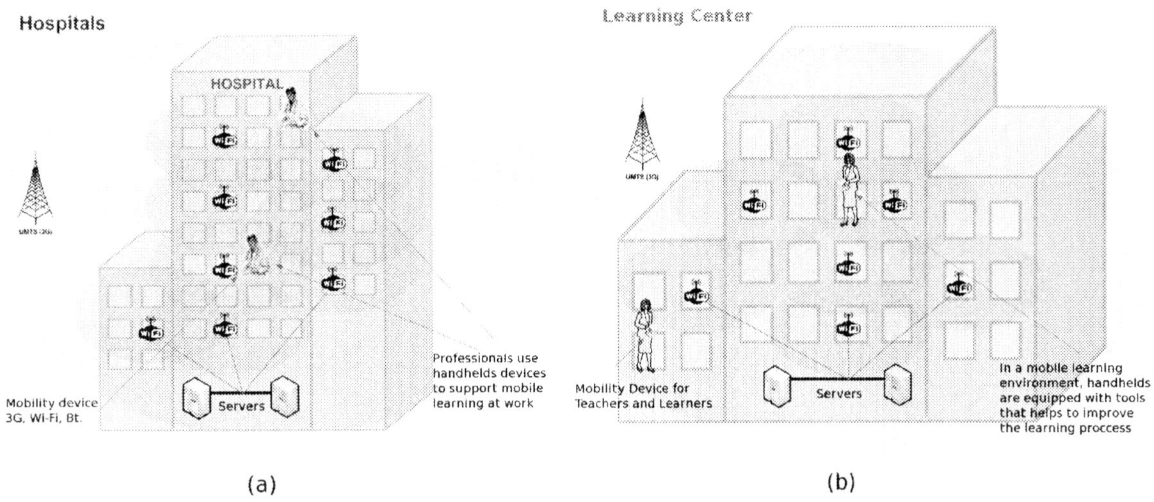

wide areas and are used to be always connected when local Wi-Fi networks are not available. In these days, it is common to find all the aforementioned technologies available in learning centres, so it is necessary to manage these technologies to obtain the greatest benefits that can help in the learning process.

Platform for Advanced Learning Systems

When a learning system platform is going to be designed, there are several key elements that are necessary taken in account. Usually, it is common to distinguish three stages (Andronico, Carmonaro, Colazzo, Molinari, Ronchetti & Trifonova, 2003):

- Firstly, the model that is going to be designed is analyzed and seen as a whole. This model will bear the communications between the users and the elements that compose it.
- The second issue is dedicated to the evaluation of the model as a function of the induced quality in the learning process. This task is not easy to solve because there are different opinions about what means a quality in a formative intervention. Once the model is operation, a key element is to monitoring the model to evaluate it and check that is carrying out the planned objectives.
- Finally, the third task is focused on complete the information necessary to the operation of the systems (databases, user information, authorization, etc.).

Our experience is presented in the next section. Campus Ubicuo is a platform designed to provide mobility and ubiquity in a university campus environment, easily adaptable to several organizations.

Related Projects

In last years, several projects are dealing with mobile learning. From the technical point of view, these projects utilize different mobile devices ranging from mobile phones (Markett, Arnedillo Sanchez, Weber & Tangney, 2006), (Levy & Kennedy, 2005) to **PDAs** (Waycott & Kukulska-Hulme, 2003), (Benford, Rowlanda, Flintham, Hull, Reid, Morrison, Facer & Clayton, 2004),

(Kneebone & Brenton, 2005) or tablets (MILE, 2009) and diverse wireless technologies such as GPRS (McGreen & Arnedillo Sánchez, 2005), 3G (Cityware, 2009) (Cheng, Tsai & Chen, 2008), Wi-Fi (Pastore, 2005), Bluetooth (Zhang, Li & Fu, 2007), GPS (Collage, 2009) or RFID (Contsens, 2009) The final goal of all these systems is to support "learning anywhere anytime" paradigm (Sharples, 2002) and solve a specific learning activity in different environments such as museum tours, fieldwork, medicine, secondary schools or university campus.

In this scenario, Campus Ubicuo has been developed to provide mobile learners the technological environment where they can overcome the limitation of educational flexibility with wired technology. To achieve these goals, students and educators are equipped with mobile devices (laptops, PDAs and mobile phones) which have hardware that makes possible the connection through different wireless technologies (GSM, GPRS, 3G, WiFi or Bluetooth). The integration of all this technologies in a platform is one of the main strengths of this project.

In addition to the technological aspects, mobile learning systems are developed to offer new possibilities for interaction and communication in education so, they are also evaluated by the pedagogical principles they use.

The pedagogical challenge related to Campus Ubicuo is to find ways on how mobile devices can be integrated into classroom activities as well as successfully address all the parameters related to and influence mobile devices integration in education. A pedagogical opportunity is that the m-learning widens the educational horizons of students as well as enhances the educational options for educators (Ktoridou, 2005).

Campus Ubicuo is a context-aware system. This means that the system is available in different contexts. Besides, the systems should not be perceived as the object of learning but as a means to support student's learning activities. Taking this view allows us to develop more useful learning environments and interpretations of student's experience (Uden, 2007).

In next section the Campus Ubicuo platform is presented.

CAMPUS UBICUO: A PLATFORM BASED ON MOBILE TECHNOLOGIES

Campus Ubicuo Architecture

As was exposed in the previous section, the first step in the design of a learning platform is to develop a model and to deploy it. In this section we present Campus Ubicuo, which architecture is shown in Figure 2. This is an infrastructure over which ubiquity services can be offered through mobile communications technologies.

The project has been divided in four stages: Movicuo, GNU/LinEx in PDA, SARI and MeUbicuo. Now, we present each sub-project briefly and in next sections, each one is explained in detail.

In Campus Ubicuo, we devote a great amount of our efforts to develop software that contributes mobility to user of free operating systems like GNU/Linux. **Movicuo** is the project subsystem where we carry out these tasks. The technologies used in Movicuo are GSM, GPRS and UMTS. As result of this subproject, a tool called Gnome-GPRS has been developed. It simplifies that process by offering Campus Ubicuo users the possibility of establish a connection using portable devices and mobile technologies from GNU/Linux.

The second stage is focused on building a GNU/LinEx distribution for PDA devices. Once developed, this platform will allow us to design advanced learning tools for mobile devices. To achieve this goal, we have used two portable devices: Nokia 770 Internet Tablet and HP iPAQ H6340.

Next, a remote administration system has been developed. This tool is called **SARI** (Wireless Remote Administration System) and it is available

Figure 2. Campus Ubicuo architecture

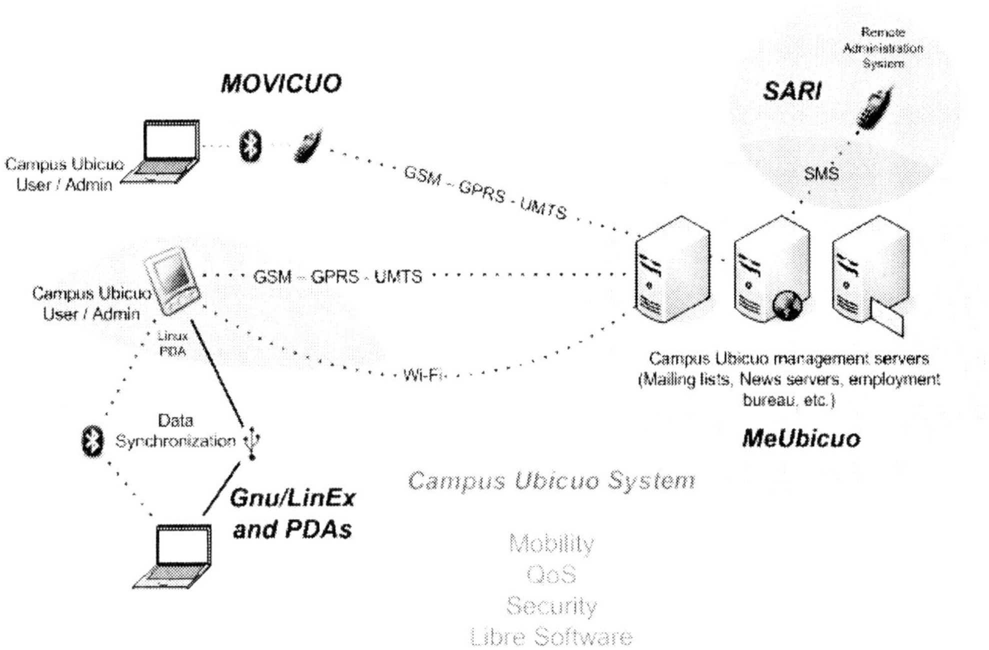

for the admin, learners and teachers. We offer a new medium of communication easily adaptable to the specific needs of the organization. This communication is based on SMS (Short Message Service) messages.

Finally, Campus Ubicuo project has a set of servers where the information that must be managed is stored. This management tasks have been isolated from the rest of the system, because all the services offered are controlled from these servers. This is why an independent subproject called **MeUbicuo** has been developed. If some changes were necessary due to modifications of initial conditions or to adapt the system to other environments, only MeUbicuo has to be modified. In order to allow the users to access the information, a web portal has been developed. This PHP+MySQL application is used by the users to register in the system and to modify or configure their preferences, e.g. subscribed services or access technology. This method complements the SMS subscription and management service.

This way, MeUbicuo can be viewed as the third key stage defined in the design of a platform mentioned in the previous section.

Besides, the structural design shown in Figure 2 has been developed keeping in mind several challenges that are the main contribution of this architecture to the mobile learning field:

- **Mobility:** This model tries to take advantage of mobility and portable features of modern devices. It is also based on those technologies that allow users ubiquity capabilities.
- **Quality of Service:** Next generation wireless networks can provide quality of service in communications. This feature has been taken into account in the development of the tools and applications carried out.
- **Security:** The wireless environment is exposed to security problems due to its own nature. For this reason, security must be considered as a main challenge when an architecture is proposed. In all Campus

Ubicuo implementations, this topic has been in mind.

- **Free Software:** Campus Ubicuo is a R&D project where all software development is released under a free software license. Free Software allows the technological innovation and makes easy the technological transfer to the m-learning market (Carmona-Murillo, González-Sánchez, Castro-Ruiz, 2007)

Involved Technologies and Hardware Devices

Just like the relationship between e-learning and classroom instruction, the development of mobile learning is not intended to replace the classroom learning, but to enhance the value of wireless communication network.

In Campus Ubicuo project, several wireless technologies are involved in the architecture design as it was shown in Figure 2. Mobile communications technologies such as GSM, GPRS or UMTS are used to offer global mobility and others like Wi-Fi or Bluetooth have a local range. In this section we present briefly each of these technologies.

Since the first public GSM call was made in 1991, the evolution in mobile telephony has been an overwhelming success, which was difficult to predict at early stage. From the user perspective, there is now a growing demand for value-added non-voice services, which the existing GSM infrastructure is not well suited to deliver effectively due to its circuit switched nature.

Because of this, GSM was adapted to a packet switched core network where data traffic could be delivered in a better way than the 9.6 kbps circuit switched voice network used in GSM. In many cases, GPRS is seen as an evolutionary step towards 3G, and hence is often referred as 2.5G.

The goal of 3G is to provide a network infrastructure that can support a much broader range of services than existing systems. Since GPRS design, new infrastructures provide facilities, adequate bandwidth and quality for end-users and their applications. This facility provision, bandwidth allocation and connection quality together is commonly called quality of service. In an educational environment, these technologies are well suited to provide global mobility to m-learning users with requirements of multimedia and QoS features.

Apart from those global technologies, in Campus Ubicuo other localized wireless technologies such as Bluetooth and Wi-Fi are involved.

Bluetooth is a wireless data transmission technology that offers a connection with two or more devices over a short distance. It is now been included in many devices, including cell phones and PDAs. This makes possible to use them as peer-to-peer devices over a short distance. As bluetooth uses the unlicensed ISM (Industrial, Scientific, Medical) frequency band, there's no charge for data communications using bluetooth.

On the other hand, Wi-Fi is a Wireless Local Area Network (WLAN) technology widely used in localized organizations to offer mobility within the range of hundreds of meters. Actually PDA and some cell phones are equipped with Wi-Fi cards.

On the other hand, the learning materials need to be developed in a small, consumable bytes of format, which can be delivered through the wireless networks mentioned in the previous section. Campus Ubicuo project enables mobile learning from anywhere using a variety of devices, including cell phones, **PDAs** (Personal Data Assistant) and laptops (Zhang, Zhang, Vuong & Malik, 2006). These portable devices and mobile technologies make learning possible from anywhere at any time in the proposed architecture. In this section, the specific hardware devices are explained. Figure 3 shows the hardware devices used in the project.

As we can see in the previous image, two PDAs have been used: HP iPAQ h6340 and Nokia 770. These pocket-sized computers are in compliance with the required features because they have Wi-Fi

Figure 3. Portable devices and spectrum analyzer

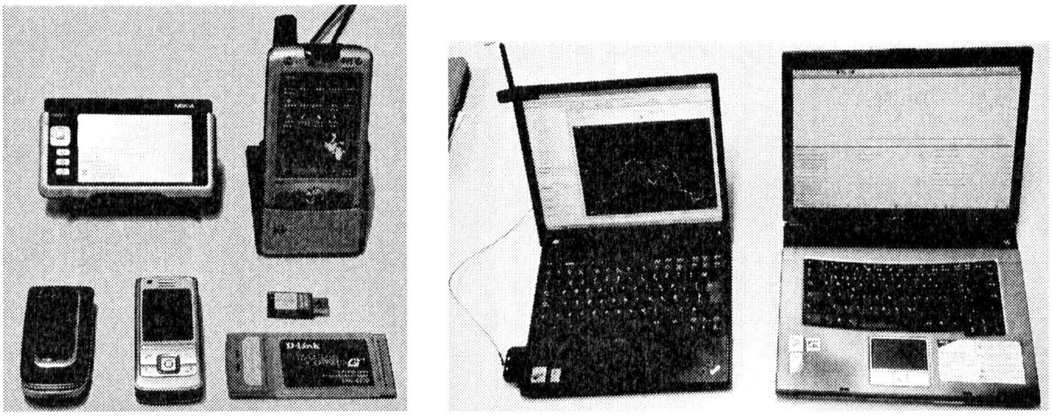

(a) *(b)*

and Bluetooth capabilities. One of the main challenges of the project related to these terminals is to build a free software Linux distribution to be installed on PDA devices. This Linux distribution is called **LinEx Mobile**, a lightweight version of GNU/LinEx (GNU/LinEx, 2008), a Debian based operative system developed by the regional government of Extremadura (Spain) to be used in all primary and secondary schools in Extremadura, as well as in official institutions. This way, LinEx Mobile is intended to be used by these institutions as a base where offer mobile learning services. The details about this development are explained in "Campus Ubicuo development" section.

In Figure 3 (a), some mobile phones are shown. Cell phones use the wireless technologies aforementioned in the previous section to exchange voice and text messages, email, and small web pages, anywhere and anytime.

Besides PDAs and cell phones, laptops are used in Campus Ubicuo project. Although its size is bigger that PDAs, some applications require a bigger display or high computing capabilities. Some applications have been developed to be executed in laptops, for example PDACC (used for PDA – Laptop synchronization) or GNOME-GPRS (it makes possible a 2.5/3G Internet connection using the cell phone as a modem). This software is explained in following sections.

Finally, it has been necessary the use of a spectrum analyzer to measure the wireless network performance. Figure 3 (b) shows this analyzer.

Campus Ubicuo Development

The project architecture shown Figure 2 is based on the four main features: mobility, QoS, security and free software. In following sections, we describe each task in which the project development has been split: GNU/LinEx Mobile, Movicuo, SARI and MeUbicuo.

GNU/LinEx Mobile

One of the main challenges of the project, apart from the mobile architecture design, is to develop free software applications available for users in a M-Learning platform. Those applications will run in a Linux operative system installed in portable devices. There are several Linux-based distributions for laptops, however it is not common to find a PDA with a Linux-based system. Furthermore, taking into account that the project is funded by Extremadura Government, where GNU/LinEx has been developed, it has been necessary to build a Linux-based distribution that will be installed in

Figure 4 Cross-compiling process

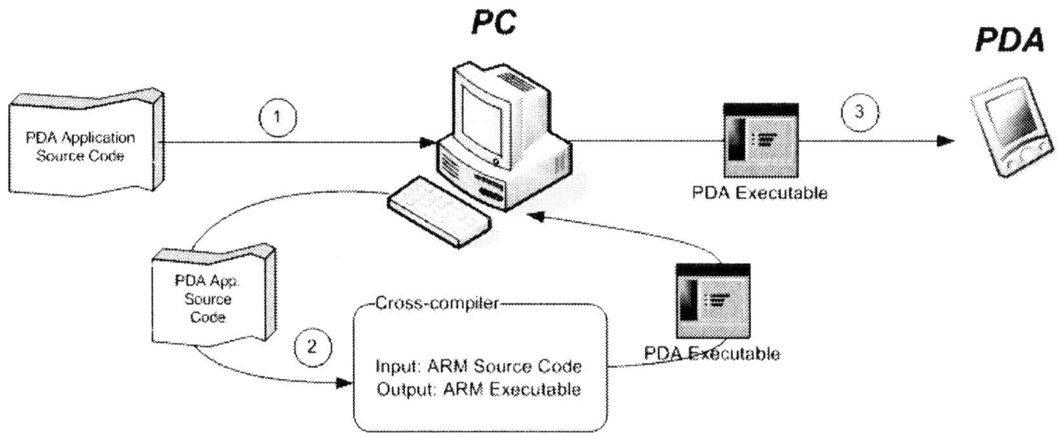

PDAs. This distribution has been called LinEx Mobile. Next, some details about its building are given.

Building a Linux embedded system in a PDA is a complex task. PDA devices have a different hardware architecture with respect to a conventional computer. Embedded devices like PDAs are equipped with a 32-bits RISC processor called ARM, because of their power saving features. For that reason, building an embedded Linux distribution requires a wide knowledge in operative systems, Linux systems and device specific architecture.

This means that the software developed for a PC is not compatible for a PDA, so the whole software executed in this device must be specifically compiled for it. However, due to limited resources in embedded devices, is not possible to run a complex compilation. Since debugging and testing may also require more resources than is available on an embedded system, a process has been created to avoid native compilation. This process is called cross-compiling. In fact, cross-compiling process consists in creating executables binaries for a platform other than the one on which the compiler is running. This process is shown in Figure 4.

At present, many projects are focused on Linux system development for embedded devices, among which we can mention EmDebian (Embedded Debian, 2008) or Familiar (Familiar Project, 2008), as well as tools to make easy the cross-compiling process like Scratchbox (Scratchbox, 2008) and OpenEmbedded (Openembedded, 2008). The first one offers several tools designed to facilitate the process, whereas OpenEmbedded is an environment that simplifies the task of building complete Linux distributions for embedded devices.

In Campus Ubicuo project we use the PDAs shown in Figure 3 (a), one of them is HP iPAQ h6340, which incorporates an ARM TI OMAP 1510 microprocessor. Building a GNU/LinEx distribution for iPAQ means to get each part in which the system is composed: kernel, filesystem and bootloader.

Kernel sources for this microprocessor are omap-linux (are also necessary some patches for this specific device). Cross-compiler used for kernel sources is GCC for ARM (arm-linux). This compilation results in an image which will be loaded in boot process. Besides the kernel, the operating system requires user interactivity tools and the hierarchical Linux filesystem (we call this structure rootfs). Compiling each library and application one on one is not acceptable in time and effort terms, so we use Openembedded to make easy this task. Regarding the bootloader, we use Uboot, because it is supported in the device architecture.

Once we have these three elements (kernel image, rootfs and bootloader) GNU/LinEx system can be booted. The PDA platform built, which can be extended to other Linux distribution, is the base of other developments and activities in the project. Additional details about how to build this distribution can be found in (Carmona-Murillo, González-Sánchez, Castro-Ruiz, 2007).

As a result of this development, LinEx Mobile has been built for HP IPAQ h6340 and Nokia 770. With this operative system, other applications such as GPRS connections or PC synchronization have been developed to use this portable device in the learning process.

Movicuo

Movicuo is the subsystem where develop mobility software for operative systems like GNU/Linux. Mobile phone networks offer this capability. As we explained in previous sections, GPRS (2.5G) complements the design of GSM (2G) by adding a packet switched network to carry data traffic; moreover, it allows **QoS** parameters negotiation. However, traffic rates achieved by GPRS (171.2 Kbps in ideal situation) are not adequate to support some particular services as, for example, multimedia traffic. UMTS (3G) uses a new media access method that adds complexity but allows achieving higher traffics rates (Perez-Romero, Sallent, Agustí & Díaz-Guerra, 2005).

In this section we give details about how GNU/Linux systems support GPRS and UMTS connections, following standard recommendations published by 3GPP organization (3GPP, 2008). Once the operative system support this connections, will be possible to develop advanced mobile applications with quality of service support. According to Figure 2, Movicuo is focused on the development of advanced tools that allow users of the m-learning platform to access to the resources through mobile communications technologies. With these tools, we are able to offer advanced capabilities such as quality of service negotiations. This way, network access is possible by means of portable devices with at least a GPRS or UMTS interface. However, laptops are not equipped with GPRS or UMTS interfaces, so it is necessary a mobile phone working as a modem. Figure 2 show this scene.

In order to establish a 2.5G or 3G connection from GNU/Linux, the first step is to connect the devices. If we are using a laptop and a mobile phone, that connection will be done by means of USB, serial line or Bluetooth technology. If we are using a PDA, the physical link will be established without user intervention.

One of the most interesting features in the connection process is the access to the physical hardware. GPRS/UMTS defines a set of AT+ commands to allow the developers to access to the terminal hardware and the GPRS/UMTS network properties. These AT+ commands extend the usual AT commands assigned to control the modem (ETSI TS 07.07, 2003). The application developed in Movicuo, simplifies the connection process.

From the research point of view, thanks to this tool, we have analysed 2.5G and 3G connections, studying parameters like throughput, delay and jitter. We have also evaluated the network behaviour depending on the kind of traffic sent and the negotiated QoS level. This is a key element in a mobile learning environment, because it is fundamental to know how the network responds to the different services offered.

The applications developed in Campus Ubicuo have been carried out for laptops with Linux and PDAs with LinEx Mobile. This way, both laptops and PDAs are going to be connected anywhere through GPRS or UMTS, global communications technologies adequate for multimedia traffic or high data rates connections.

This graphical tool has been developed to simplify as much as possible the connection process. Most m-learning users don't know anything about

GPRS, UMTS or quality of service, so the connection must be transparent to the user. However, it is possible that some users are experts in this kind of mobile technologies. One of the challenges in the development of Gnome-GPRS is that this tool should be useful to all kind of users, from inexperienced to experts. To achieve this goal, the application windows have been designed for both novice and advanced users.

When the application is first launched, it is necessary to configure it, so a window is shown to inform the user about this situation. At the beginning, some buttons in the main window are not active, so the first step is to configure Gnome-GPRS with the correct values. When the configure button is clicked, appears the Configure window (Figure 5).

Although there are four tabs in this window, the first tab is the only one that you have to fill in. So, a novel user will connect its mobile to the laptop through bluetooth just clicking the "Automatic Detection" button and selecting the mobile phone from the list of Bluetooth devices found. Gnome-GPRS has been developed to offer advanced features. Next tabs allow configuring DNS servers, the program appearance, graph support, QoS activation or other configure options. If QoS checkbox is active, last two tabs are used to define QoS class. In GPRS connections, each flow of data has a QoS associated with it, which defines the following clases:

- **Precedence:** Under normal operating conditions the network will attempt to meet the requirements of all service commitments. However, under abnormal conditions it may be necessary to discard packets etc. The precedence class priority level determines which flows will be maintained and which flows will be affected first. There are three precedence classes.
- **Delay:** This is the round-trip-time for a packet in the network. There are four delay classes defined that can be selected.
- **Reliability:** This class is defined in terms of residual error rates, which include probability of loss of data, probability of data delivery out of sequence, probability of duplicate data and probability of corrupted data. Each different flow of data will require specific reliability classification according to its particular requirements.
- **Peak throughput:** Throughput of used data is characterized in terms of bandwidth, split into a peak and mean throughput class. The peak throughput class defines the maximum rate at which the data is expected to be transferred. The class provides no guarantee that the defined rate will be reached, as this depends on both the resources available in the network, and the capabilities of the mobile device.
- **Mean throughput:** Defines the average data rate in bits per second. The actual definition is in terms of bytes per hour, as the bursty nature of most data applications means that although there may be high instantaneous demand for resources, on average the throughput can be quite low.

These QoS parameters are requested during the activation but this may be modified by various elements within the network in accordance with resources available. In any case, the application will inform if the network is able to offer the requested parameters.

SARI

Coming back to the architecture shown in Figure 2, Campus Ubicuo has a remote administration system called SARI (Wireless Remote Administration System).

Any system must be controlled by computers that should be managed and maintained by an administrator; moreover, it should be always available for management tasks. Of course, Campus Ubicuo servers and applications also

Figure 5. Gnome-GPRS configure window

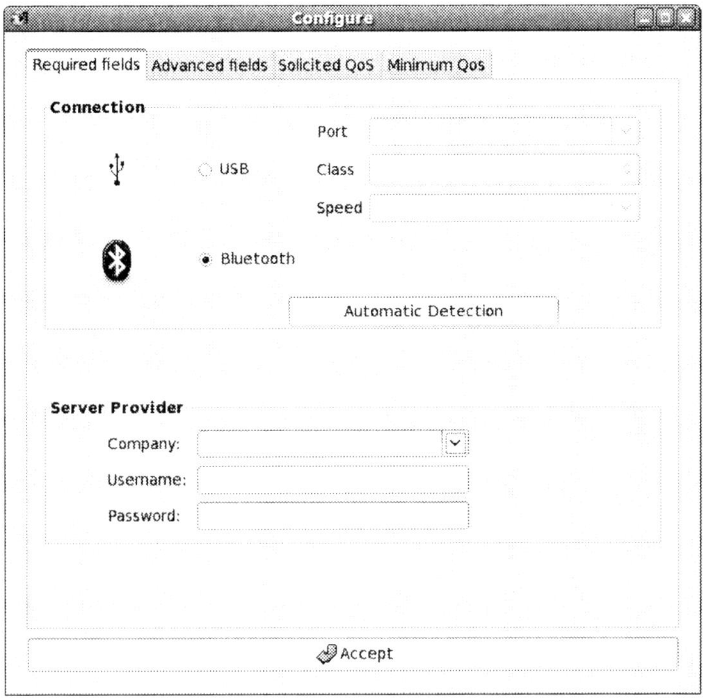

have this requirement. Some tasks like software update, access control, security system management, connectivity, etc. keep the system alive and working correctly and must be carried out by an administrator. However, sometimes the person who is responsible for the system is not near of the place where servers are located, and a critical process must be carried out immediately. In this sense, capabilities of instant messaging technology make it especially interesting to handle some critical systems that require to be controlled everywhere and at any time. SARI allows administrators to manage a system wherever they are, through global mobile technologies such as GSM. In this section, we describe SARI system.

SARI is a robust and extensible application developed to administrate a system via SMS, it is able to cover the administration needs of modern computing systems. But SARI also has been developed to interact with the own Campus Ubicuo system. M-Learning users (teachers, pupils, administrators) can find in SARI another option to be connected to the platform.

Therefore, SARI allows remote GNU/Linux commands execution as well as managing subscriptions to the information broadcast system in Campus Ubicuo. These features offer the system administrator the necessary ubiquity in order to carry out administration task and allow Campus Ubicuo users to send and receive information to the system via SMS and e-mail. In Figure 6 we can see the interaction between users and SARI.

One of the main goals in SARI development has been to make easy to modify and add new features. This makes possible to adapt the tool to the specific needs of the learning model. So the main application, or base system, is executed as a daemon that will not be modified. The way of adding new features or new methods to communicate between users and the core daemon is adding different plugins for each kind of technology.

At present, we have implemented two plugins; one of them in charge of Bluetooth - terminal com-

Figure 6. Interaction between users and SARI system

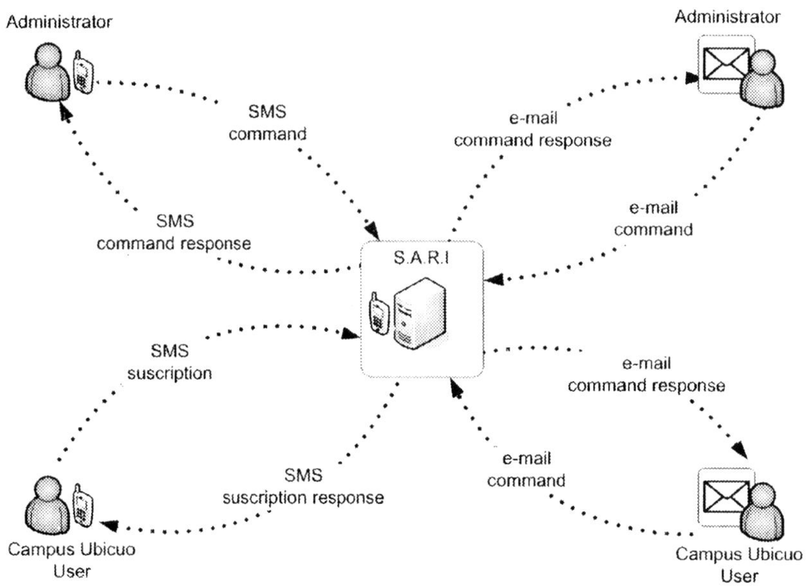

munication to manage SMS functionality (send/receive), and the other intended to manage the communication via email messages. This way, the daemon executes the corresponding procedures depending on the type of technology supported by the installed plugins. Simultaneously, each plugin follows a set of stages and maintain these stages in a queue. Although the execution of a stage is not parallel with respect to the other ones in the rest of the plugins, the global process is concurrent, so that, different type of technologies can be used at the same time.

Each plugin manages the communication to make it non-blocking. Their implementations have to avoid software blockages if the device or the server does not send a response for a request. Each plugin follows the classic connection stages: establishment, maintenance and closing. The operation of SARI daemon is similar to the rest of the GNU/Linux services. Its configuration file is located at /etc/sari/sari.conf, and can be launched from /etc/init.d/sari. When SARI is running, it allows administrative operations as well as task related to Campus Ubicuo users' subscriptions. To do that, there are several configuration files in /etc/sari to set up the SARI settings.

MeUbicuo

Campus Ubicuo project has a set of servers where the information that must be managed is stored. This management tasks have been isolated from the rest of the system, because all services offered are controlled from these servers. This is why an independent subproject has been developed. MeUbicuo is the public information system in Campus Ubicuo platform. Data structuctures, user information, news, messages, etc. are stored and managed in MeUbicuo servers. If some changes were necessary due to requisites modifications or to adapt the system to other environments, one only has to modify MeUbicuo.

SARI is executed in these servers, allowing users to send and receive information related to the learning process, as well as some administrative tasks. The databases and the data structures necessary to manage the system and the information broadcast system are placed there.

Figure 7. Campus Ubicuo information system (MeUbicuo) web application

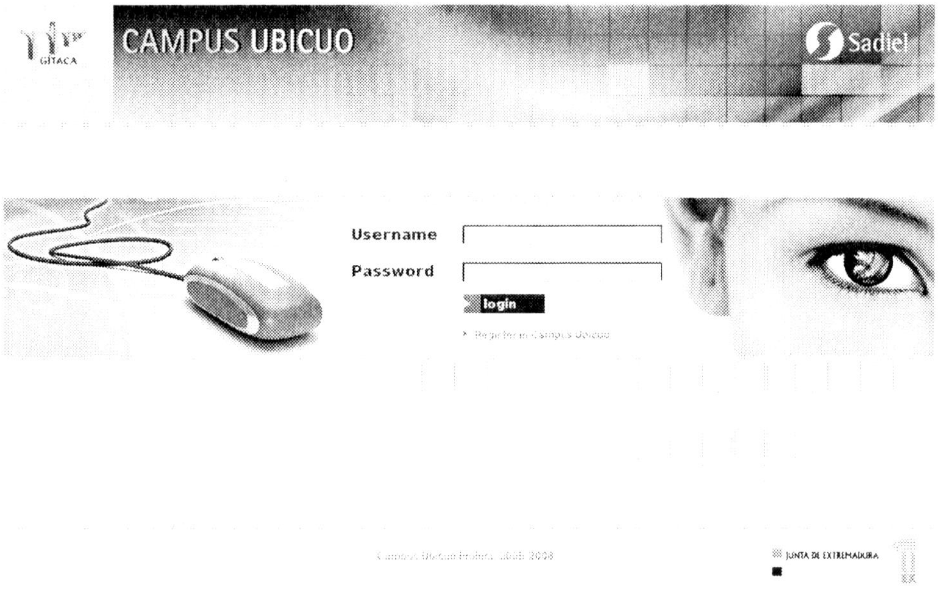

With this framework, teachers (wherever they are) can user the system to inform to their pupils about a new or about a learning task, just sending an SMS message, which will be spread to the rest of the users subscribed to the specific category.

In order to allow the users to access the information, a web portal has been developed. This PHP+MySQL application is shown in Figure 7, and is used by the users to register in the system and to modify or configure their preferences, e.g. subscribed services or access technology. This method complements the SMS subscription and management service.

Initially, in a university environment there are different profiles: Admin, teachers and students. Due to the fact that each agent needs its own services in the learning process, the web application detects the user's profile and shows a personal interface for each of them. Figure 8 shows the interface for the admin user.

FUTURE WORK

The mobility project presented in this chapter has been developed initially to be deployed in a Universitary Campus but, as we have explained through the previous sections of the chapter, this architecture has been designed to be easily adaptable to other mobile learning environments. In fact, the good results obtained in Campus Ubicuo have made possible this model to be adapted to other organizations.

In one hand, in last months we have developed Meseas, a project funded by Spanish Government and now is being implemented in different hospitals in Extremadura, a region in the south west of Spain. This project is focused on the improvement of healthcare services through mobile communications.

In the other hand, Libre Movicuidad is a project recently granted by the Regional Government of Extremadura that will be developed in next years. Its goals are the tourism promotion in a city by means of mobility technologies and an architecture very similar to Campus Ubicuo.

Figure 8. Admin user interface

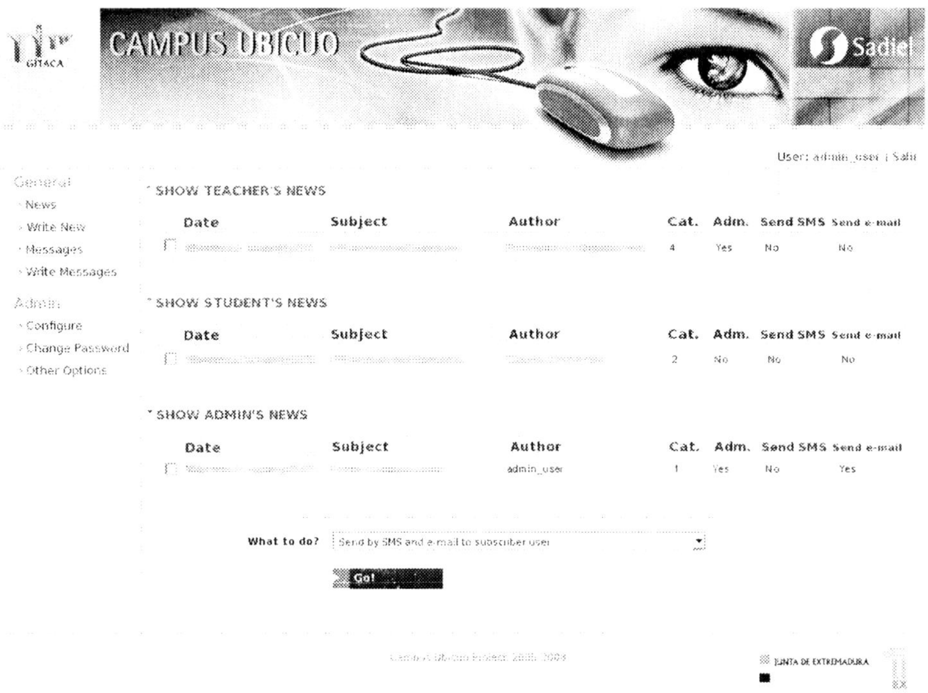

In this case, tourists get a portable device (PDA) and thanks to services provided by the system architecture are going to visit the city with the information related to the places they are visiting. The system will propose different itinerary that can be updated while the person visits the city and moves through different places. They will have the possibility of interact with the system to carry out tasks like getting in contact with tourist office, booking restaurants near they are, etc.

As we can see, Campus Ubicuo is well suited to other organizations different to a Universitary Campus. These two projects are being developed to adapt this architecture to a hospital and a city environment, but there are several areas in which this mobility model could be implemented to solve a learning need.

CONCLUSION

Before concluding this chapter, the main conclusions are presented. With the evolution of computer network and wireless network, mobility services are more and more required. The field of learning is not apart from this change and has evolved from face-to-face learning, to mobile learning Some authors expose that one of the factor fostering the evolution is not the learning itself; insead, it is the service needed for utilizing the mature information technologies and wireless networks (Yu-Liang, 2005). Under this scenario we have proposed an architecture for mobile learning based on next generation wireless networks that can be easily implemented in other environments. In fact, that is one of the main goals of the project, and supposes that Campus Ubicuo will be unfinished until it has been deployed in different organizations different from the university.

The implementation of Campus Ubicuo in other different environments, where could be directly applied, is now being carried out: hospitals, secondary education centres and tourist services in a local council. In secondary education centres and hospitals, this project can be used to make easier and faster every administrative process for students and patients. In relation to tourist services, Campus Ubicuo can be a support to provide advanced mobile communications services to tourists; e.g. using a PDA or a mobile phone. In both cases, the interaction between the system and the users could be done anywhere the user is located thanks to the tools developed in the project. Furthermore, in some cases, the communication between them is done with quality of service, an added value very important when we want to offer some services over 3G networks such as video or audio streaming (virtual classes).

ACKNOWLEDGMENT

This work is sponsored in part by the regional Economy, Commerce and Innovation Ministry belonging to the Extremadura (Spain) Regional Government, through the following projects: Campus Ubicuo (numbered as PDT05A041) and LibreMovicuidad (numbered as PRI08A079).

REFERENCES

Andronico, A., Carmonaro, A., Colazzo, L., Molinari, A., Ronchetti, M., & Trifonova, A. (2003). *Designing models and services for learning management systems in mobile settings.* Udine, Italy: Mobile and Ubiquitous Information Access.

Benford, S., Rowlanda, D., Flintham, M., Hull, R., Reid, J., Morrison, J., et al. (2004). Savannah: Designing a location-based game simulating lion behaviour. *International Conference on Advances in Computer Entertainment Technology.*

Carmona-Murillo, J., González-Sánchez, J. L., & Castro-Ruiz, M. (2007). Technological innovation in mobile communications developed with free software: Campus Ubicuo. *UPGRADE. The European Journal for the Informatics Professional, 8*(6), 27–33.

Cheng, S., Tsai, W., & Chen, Y. (2008). Rescue knowledge m-learning system by 3G mobile phones. *Fifth IEEE International Conference on Wireless, Mobile, and Ubiquitous Technology in Education (WMUTE08)*, Beijing, China. Cityware Project Home Page. Retrieved on January 26, 2009, from http://www.cityware.org.uk/

Collage Project Home Page. Retrieved on January 26, 2009, from http://www.ea.gr/ep/collage/main.asp

CONTSENS (Using Wireless Technologies for Context Sensitive Education and Training) Project Home Page. Retrieved on January 26, 2009, from http://www.ericsson.com/ericsson/corpinfo/programs/using_wireless_technologies_for_context_sensitive_education_and_training/

Embedded Debian Home Page. *The universal embedded operative system*. Retrieved on October 15, 2008, from http://www.emdebian.org

ETSI TS 07.07. (2003). *Digital cellular telecommunications system (phase 2+); AT command set for GSM mobile equipment (ME)*. Familiar Project Home Page. Retrieved on October 15, 2008, from http://familiar.handhelds.org/

Georgiev, T., Georgieva, E., & Trajkovski, G. (2006). Transitioning from e-learning to m-learning: Present issues and future challenges. *Proceedings of the Seventh ACIS International Conference on Software Engineering, Artificial Intelligence, Networking, and Parallel/Distributed Computing (SNPD '06)*, Las Vegas, NV. GITACA Research Group Home Page. Retrieved on October 15, 2008, from http://www.gitaca.com

GNU/LinEx Operative System Home Page. Retrieved on October 15, 2008, from http://www.linex.org

Hadzilacos, T., & Tryfona, N. (2005). *Mobile learning: Current trend and future challenges*. Paper presented at Fifth International Conference on Advanced Learning Technologies (ICALT '05), Kaohsiung, Taiwan.

3Home Page, G. P. P. Retrieved on October 15, 2008, from http://www.3gpp.org/

Kneebone, R., & Brenton, H. (2005). Using PDAs to support a new professional healthcare role: A case study. In A. Kukulska-Hulme & J. Traxler (Eds.), *Mobile learning: A handbook for educators and trainers*. London: RoutledgeFalmer.

Koodli, R. S., & Perkins, C. (2007). *Mobile internetworking with IPv6: Concepts, principles, and practices*. Hoboken, NJ: John Wiley & Sons, Inc.

Ktoridou, D., & Eteokleous, N. (2005). Adaptive m-learning: Technological and pedagogical aspects to be considered in Cyprus tertiary education. In *Recent research developments in learning technologies* (pp. 676-683). Spain: Badajoz.

Levy, M., & Kennedy, C. (2005). Learning Italian via mobile SMS. In A. Kukulska-Hulme & J. Traxler (Eds.), *Mobile learning: A handbook for educators and trainers*. London: RoutledgeFalmer.

Maginnis, F., White, R., & Mckenna, C. (2000). Customers on the move: M-commerce demands a business object broker approach to EAI. *eAI Journal*, 58-62.

Markett, C., Arnedillo Sánchez, I., Weber, S., & Tangney, B. (2006). Using short message service (SMS) to encourage interactivity. *Computers & Education*, *46*(3), 280–293. doi:10.1016/j.compedu.2005.11.014

McGreen, N., & Arnedillo Sánchez, I. (2005). Mapping challenge: A case study in the use of mobile phones in collaborative, contextual learning. *International Association for Development of the Information Society Press*, 213-217. MILE (Mobile and Interactive Learning Environment) Project Home Page. Retrieved on January 26, 2009, from http://www.mile-project.net/

Openembedded Home Page. *The cross-compile environment*. Retrieved on October 15, 2008, from http://www.openembedded.org/

Parsons, D., Ryu, H., & Cranshaw, M. (2006). A study of design requirements for mobile learning environments. *Sixth International Conference on Advanced Learning Technologies (ICALT '06)*, Kerkrade, The Netherlands.

Pastore, S. (2005). Experiences of mobile learning in science: Technological solutions for wireless network and content delivery. *7th Internet Users Conference*, Dubrovnik, Croatia.

Perez-Romero, J., Sallent, O., Agustí, R., & Díaz-Guerra, M. A. (2005). *Radio resource management strategies in UMTS*. West Sussex, England: John Wiley & Sons.

Scratchbox Home Page. *The cross-compilation toolkit project*. Retrieved on October 15, 2008, from http://www.scratchbox.org/

Sharples, M. (2002). Disruptive devices: Mobile technology for conversational learning. *International Journal of Continuing Engineering Education and Lifelong Learning*, *12*(5/6), 504–520. doi:10.1504/IJCEELL.2002.002148

Uden, L. (2007). Activity theory for designing mobile learning. *International Journal of Mobile Learning and Organisation*, *1*(1), 81–102. doi:10.1504/IJMLO.2007.011190

Waycott, J., & Kukulska-Hulme, A. (2003). Student experiences with PDAs for reading course materials. *Personal and Ubiquitous Computing*, *7*(1), 30–43. doi:10.1007/s00779-002-0211-x

World, G. S. M. (2008). *Subscriber connections-Q2 2008*. Retrieved from http://www.gsmworld.com/news/statistics/pdf/gsma_stats_q2_08.pdf

Yu-Liang, R. (2005). *Mobile learning: Current trend and future challenges*. Paper presented at Fifth IEEE International Conference on Advanced Learning Technologies (ICALT'05), Kaohsiung, Taiwan.

Zhang, Y., Li, W., & Fu, Y. (2007). A mobile learning system based on bluetooth. *Third International Conference on Natural Computation, 2007 (ICNC 2007)* (Vol. 5, pp.768-771).

Zhang, Y., Zhang, S., Vuong, S., & Malik, K. (2006). Mobile learning with bluetooth-based e-learning system. *Wireless Ad Hoc and Sensor Networks Symposium*, Vancouver, Canada.

Chapter 3
MobiGlam:
A Framework of Interoperability and Adaptivity for Mobile Learning

Fatma Meawad
German University in Cairo, Egypt

Geneen Stubbs
University of Glamorgan, UK

ABSTRACT

This chapter discusses the principles underpinning the design and the development of a framework, MobiGlam, which supports ubiquitous and scalable access to learning activities. The framework allows full end to end interconnectivity among open source virtual learning environments (VLEs) and Java-enabled mobile devices. Through this framework, interoperability and adaptivity techniques are combined to address the technical, pedagogical, and institutional challenges of mobile learning. The discussed framework achieved a level of flexibility and simplicity that resulted in a wide acceptance of the framework institutionally, allowing its use in various real world settings.

INTRODUCTION

Mobile learning brings together various evolving research areas with on-going challenges; ranging from the limitations and poor usability issues facing mobile technologies to the social and the pedagogical aspects of introducing a new technology for learning. Such challenges are viewed as major concerns for mainstreaming mobile learning (Doering, 2007; Keegan, 2005; Stead, 2005); yet, collectively, they are not well investigated by current research (Seong, 2006). Consequently and despite the significant amount of literature in mobile learning, it is not yet being used as a truly ubiquitous technology. Meanwhile, the success of mobile learning is closely related to the degree of its ubiquity. A similar statement was made in the conclusion of a comprehensive literature review in mobile learning:

In the future, the success of learning and teaching with mobile technologies will be measured by how seamlessly it weaves itself into our daily lives, with the greatest success paradoxically occurring at the point where we don't recognise it as learning at all. (Naismith et al., 2004)

DOI: 10.4018/978-1-60566-882-6.ch003

Based on this, there is a need for a solution that will support flexible and large scale use of mobile learning. Mobile learning has shown several empirical successes in different settings and modes: work based, distance based, independent, classroom based learning, or field work (Chen et al., 2005; Goh & Hooper, 2007; Kramer, 2005; Naismith et al., 2005; Rogers et al., 2004; Wentzel et al., 2005). However, as yet, incorporating mobile access in an institutional infrastructure is not a practical or a seamless process. As such, the importance of providing a flexible architectural solution for accessing learning material through mobile technologies is identified. The term flexibility in this context implies (a) applicability in different learning settings without influencing the pedagogical soundness or being influenced by institutional issues (e.g. security policies, extra staff time and extra costs) and (b) readiness to accommodate different adaptivity techniques for enhancing the overall user experience. Interoperability will create opportunities for making use of existing expertise in e-learning and the opportunity to merge with established infrastructures. Furthermore, adaptivity techniques can support the implementation of automated intelligent behaviours according to the changing elements of a user's context. In this chapter, the MobiGlam framework through which these two concepts are pulled together is described.

In order to highlight the significance of the discussed solution in the area of mobile learning, the chapter starts by a discussion in which the challenge for mobile learning is formalised as the problem of enhancing mobile usability in light of the requirements for pedagogical usability and institutional deployment. Then, several guidelines for designing a mobile learning solution are discussed.

USABILITY REQUIREMENTS FOR MOBILE LEARNING

The success of a mobile learning application significantly relies on the human and the organisational factors in adopting the continuously evolving wireless technologies (Kukulska-Hulme, 2007; Wagner, 2005). Such statement suggests the need to focus on best practices in usability. It is a challenging task to define the usability requirements for mobile learning due to its multidisciplinary nature. Besides the issues associated with using wireless technologies, the early attempts in the field uncovered pedagogical, institutional, social and economical challenges (Economides, 2007). The following discussion starts with the elements of a positive mobile user experience, and then involves the elements from the user's educational context.

In the Mobile Context

A recent review of literature in mobile usability proposes that the essence of a positive mobile user experience lies in the simplicity by which a user can complete a particular goal (Coursaris & Kim, 2006). Mobile usability is obviously heavily context dependent. Whether the context relates to the handset, the connection, the application or the user, different related elements could interfere with the simplicity by which a user can accomplish a certain goal. It is strongly believed that whether it is for leisure or work, mobile users usually have immediate goals when using mobile devices (Weiss, 2002). Therefore, it is important to give mobile users exactly what they need and allow them to finish their goals in a timely manner, with the least attention and according to their context. User-centered design, adaptive interfaces, personalisation and context-awareness are promoted for enhancing usability in mobile learning. Finally, it is important to note that the usability requirements involve more than enhancing the presentation or the interaction with the mobile application. Users must want to use a system (Dix et al., 2004). Therefore, enhancing the added-value of the content and engaging users with an application are key design requirements.

In the Educational Context

Pedagogical soundness and adherence to best practices in learning and teaching should be maintained. Existing work suggests several criteria for pedagogically sound mobile learning content: just-in-time, just-enough, engaging and goal oriented. Additionally, some practices are highlighted when introducing the use of mobile technologies to a group of users. Firstly, mobile devices are personal devices; therefore, it is important to preserve users' sense of ownership (Kukulska-Hulme, 2005). Secondly, users should be given the control over how and when they can access or be accessed through their mobile devices. It is not surprising to see a clear relation between the criteria recommended for pedagogical usability and mobile usability, as discussed in the previous section, for example, timely and just-in-time or relevant and goal-oriented.

It is important to note that any chosen approach for mobile learning should seek institutional acceptability. Educational institutions are responsible for the proper introduction and maintenance of any new technology for learning and teaching through various practices, for example, staff training and development, technical support, administration, quality assurance or cost management. Moreover, institutions are responsible to motivate learners and teachers to adopt new technologies in a pedagogically-sound way especially with non-traditional learners such as distance or work based learners. The practical considerations for these factors are not well researched among existing case studies and projects in mobile learning. However, the need to pay attention to such factors is highlighted by several researchers (Luckin et al., 2005; Traxler & Kukulska-Hulme, 2005).

HOW TO DESIGN FOR MOBILE LEARNING?

Design for a user on the move. (Weiss, 2002)

The usability requirements of mobile learning will keep changing which will make it difficult to strictly follow specific guidelines. However, considering a user on the move in our design process brings up the same criteria that support better mobile, pedagogical and institutional usability, for example timely, unobtrusive, just-in-time, just-enough, on-demand, engaging, affordable and controllable. Another useful technique that can assist in a good design is to consider possible extensions that would enhance the way people interact and communicate as proposed by Preece et al. (2002).

It is noticeable that the criteria for enhancing mobile learning and supporting its large scale use are evolving to the notion of pervasive learning. There are fewer boundaries on what constitutes a pervasive learning context. In discussing the philosophy of pervasive learning, Nyiri (2002) stated:

Learning will occur not only with less effort, but also without us being conscious that we are learning (as indeed is the case for most of the knowledge we acquire in life!).

According to this, learning will take place in the background of our daily lives. Moreover, in order for mobile learning to support this concept, a presentation layer should be designed that will work efficiently on different platforms (Wagner, 2005). With this vision in mind, the authors have developed the following values for designing a solution for mobile learning:

- **Use structured and dynamic content**: It is important to make use of the already existing expertise adopted in e-learning and adapt it to suit mobile learning (Jawad et al., 2006). If the richness of content serves a need in the application context, then extending dynamic and structured content that follows e-learning specifications, standards or authoring tools will improve its quality. Naturally, the type of content used and level of interaction will define the difficulty level of designing a mobile application. For example, an application that aims to provide unlimited on-line browsing and a high level of interaction with content will have more concerns than an online application that provides display and interaction with static content. The on-line mobile application might come across large amount of text that was designed for desktop computers causing a high percentage of invisibility on mobile device screens.

- **Use simple in hand and cost effective technologies**: Technological sophistication is not necessarily a measure of usefulness. The value should be measured by how well the developed solution fits into the user's and the application's context. This understanding was reflected in the success of mobile solutions based solely on messaging. In the mobile world, the success of SMS and its widespread uptake as opposed to WAP was much unexpected. If we contemplate the reasons that led to such results, we can see that simplicity and cost-effectiveness enabled SMS to be a pervasive technology.
- **Combine the advantages of Hybrid solutions:** Hybrid solutions bring together the benefits of an enhanced display on mobile devices with less dependence on their limited resources. Relying on server side processing or on distributed networked servers can provide optimised performance to the mobile client.
- **Employ adaptivity and context-awareness techniques:** Sensitivity to the user and the application context is believed to be an important component of any mobile learning application (Cobcroft, 2006; Ghim et al., 2004; Parsons et al., 2006). It is not possible to build one static application that would handle all scenarios. Thus, the need emerged for a flexible middleware that can provide various components for context-sensitivity, personalisation and content-adaptation to realise ubiquitous access. However, best practices for context-aware mobile learning will take considerable time to develop as suggested by Wang (2004).

A Mobile Learning Scenario

Imagine the scenario of a learner who was on the move when he got a notification that a new quiz was added by the tutor for one of his courses. The learner read the message and continued towards his original destination. The learner ended with a few minutes to spare (sitting in a cafeteria or waiting for a bus) when he felt the urge to check out the new quiz in this unused time. The learner was able to access the quiz in a couple of clicks and the questions were clearly displayed which encouraged him to attempt answering some questions. After answering a few questions, some friends came over, so the learner closed his phone and joined his friends. On the way home, while sitting in the train, the learner started working on the quiz again from where he stopped before. He finished many of the questions till the train arrived at his station and he had to leave. The learner went back home where he accessed the quiz form his desktop connection and finished of the quiz.

This scenario is one of endless possible scenarios that could be encountered by a learner on the move. The value that needs to be stressed in this scenario is that the learner was able to use the technology available, not necessarily mobile, to finish a task in his own chosen time as envisaged by Thomas (2005) for pervasive learning. It is interesting to analyse how the use of mobile technologies contributed to the success of this experience. There are many assumptions that were collectively important to support the above scenario.

- **Automated contextual notifications**: When a tutor added a quiz, notifications were automatically triggered to students (only the ones who were supposed to take the quiz). Tutors cannot be expected to manually maintain such functionality.
- **Clear Display and Easy Navigation:** The learner was able to easily access the quiz and view the content clearly which encouraged him to further interact with the content and attempt to answer questions after just intending to take a quick look.
- **Consistency with an existing resource:** The learner was able to instantly access the latest version of content without the need to synchronise. Also, he was able to resume from where he left off, from a different connection and a different device.
- **Supported by Institutions:** The process of quiz submission from the phone or from a desktop does not affect the learner's assessment and it is seamless to the tutor. This also implies that such activity is supported by the institution.
- **Affordable:** The learner was not worried about the involved cost as he accessed content. This could be due to further institutional support or awareness that the costs incurred are affordable.

The use of mobile technologies certainly supported the learner's experience in the above scenario as a "companion of E-learning" to optimise time, as well put by Kember (2001). The authors envisage that supporting this scenario and similar experiences for learners and teachers can be reached with large scale and pervasive access. Additionally, the assumptions made as simple design guidelines should be achieved by the final outcome of this work.

AN OUTLINE OF A SOLUTION

Based on the previous discussion, the need for a framework that would embrace practices of interoperability and adaptivity to improve access for mobile learning is established. Accordingly, the authors clearly identified the direction to be followed, more specifically, using a hybrid solution based on a Java-ME MobiGlam client that interacts through web services with server-side e-learning content authoring tools, VLEs in particular. Additionally, full automation in responding to users according to their context with the least intervention is envisaged. Clearly, this vision requires using techniques for context-awareness and adaptation. In this section, the design and development of such framework which are key challenges for this research are discussed.

Content Modelling

Content modelling is key for a mobile solution. It is particularly emphasised in the educational context since the concept of what is pedagogically usable for mobile learning is not well defined yet. The aim is to bring together the advantages of reusing existing content and allowing educators to create novel opportunities for learning on mobile devices. Thus, the idea of inter-operating with available virtual learning environments (VLEs) was adopted. VLEs, such as Moodle, Sakai and ATutor are web-based applications that organise authoring and accessing content for learners, educators and support staff. Due to their popularity and wide-spread, it is believed that there is much hope for pervasive e-education through extending VLEs to every end device (Holzinger et al., 2006). However, practically speaking, there are very few working mobile access implementations for VLEs to date (Zanev & Clark, 2005). Several advantages from inter-operating with VLEs rather than developing a new authoring tool are envisaged:

- Giving instant access to a substantial amount of existing learning content with no need for replication.
- Allowing enthusiastic educators to use their regular VLEs to create novel opportunities for learning on mobile devices such as using forums or blogs on a mobile device for reflection during field trips or using polls or quizzes to emulate a response system.
- Enhancing the ubiquity of the content through accommodating for both web access and mobile access without inconsistencies or synchronization problems.
- Promoting the use of mobile learning among educators who might be concerned about extra time in using or learning additional tools. This advantage will benefit institutions as well by avoiding costs of extra staff time and extra maintenance costs, hence more enthusiasm for adopting mobile learning.

Regardless of the underlying pedagogical principles or the infrastructure of open source VLEs, they essentially provide a set of activities that are well designed to promote communication, interaction, time management and collaboration, for example, forums, news, time schedules, chats or quizzes. These types of activities are simple, yet valuable in supporting learning. The immediacy and the simplicity of these activities fit perfectly into the context of a mobile learner rather than the actual act of learning. For example, imagine the scenario of a student travelling by train and checking his time schedule, grades, deadlines, notes or communicating with other students or tutors in his course. Many surveys revealed that learners are most interested in mobile access for such supportive learning activities (Trifonova, 2006). It is noticeable that these findings comply with the emerging thinking among researchers that the use of task-oriented, goal-driven or activity-oriented content underpins effective mobile learning (Uden, 2007; Uther, 2002; Weiss, 2002). Therefore, in this work, the main interest lies in these forms of activities when modelling content authored by VLEs.

A Conceptual Model for Mobile Activities

The need to devise a form of abstraction that can realise different designs and structures of learning activities has led us to develop a conceptual model through which high level representations of activities can be systematically generated. The model is based on the assumption that an activity can be represented through a combination of predefined templates. Each template is programmed to provide a well defined task that can be completed on the move whenever and wherever it suits the user. Moreover, some specific templates can be used to reconceptualise activities to fit into mobile scenarios. Figure 1 shows a structured view of the main components that guide our content modelling. Additionally, the authors make the assumption that learning activities in a VLE can be modeled in association with a user or in association with courses.

The framework currently supports three categories of templates that can be used by developers to construct mobile-friendly representations of activities: basic, mobile-specific and user-oriented. The basic templates provide a simplified representation of an activity to minimally match the way it is used through a desktop PC; for example, browsing information through listing, viewing detail or searching. Additionally, interaction is allowed through different forms of input templates, such as single choice, multiple choice or free text forms. The mobile specific templates can be used to optionally add some interesting features that are more useful and applicable on mobile devices; for example, using the device's camera to upload pictures or scheduling events to the device's calendar. The user oriented templates are usually needed for checking access permissions for protected items, explicitly collecting user preferences or saving items for off-line access.

In order to illustrate the modelling process, we will work through an example to reconceptualise the forum activity. First, three View List templates are used to correspond to browsing forums in a certain course, discussions in a selected forum and posts in a selected discussion. Reading a certain post requires one View Detail template. Another two TextArea Input templates are used for posting replies or adding new discussions. Optionally, a Search template can be included to search posts or discussions. So far, this selection of templates minimally represents a forum activity. Note that there are other optional features to be added according to a developer's vision of how a forum activity could be used on a mobile device. For example, mobile specific templates can be added to access the device's calendar to schedule events and upload pictures to posts or to schedule general SMS notifications for new posts to forums. With such combination of templates, the first step in content modelling is completed resulting in an abstract representation of what can be required in a forum activity (see figure 2). Any additional functionality that requires an unsupported template will be excluded.

The next step in modelling is expanding the constructed template representation into detailed pages that are specific to a selected activity. Step two in figure 2 shows how the templates, chosen for the forum activity, were expanded into several specific pages. These pages need to be created and stored in the local database of the framework only once for the forum activity, regardless of the number of different target VLEs. The currently supported templates are enough to minimally design a wide range of activities that

Figure 1. A high level conceptual model for mobile activities based on the use of task-based templates

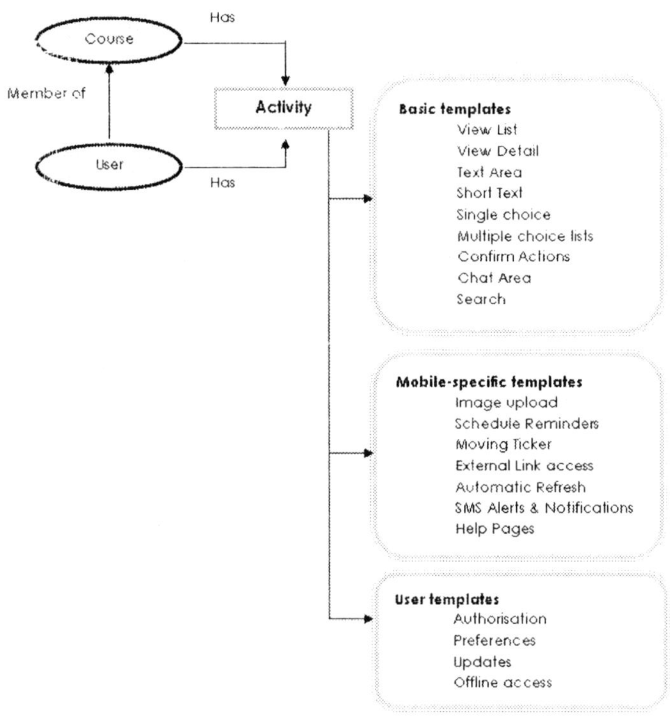

could support learners and educators. The range of activities and how they were reconceptualised evolved throughout the course of this study from the continuous feedback of users in supervised evaluations (Meawad and Stubbs, 2008). At the time of writing, the framework supports the following services based on the discussed conceptual model: participants (users), news, events, messages, forums, lessons, assignments, workshops, personal profile, grades, wikis, contacts, groups, exercises and chat.

Behaviour Modelling

The process of content modelling, discussed in the previous section, takes place only once for each activity. In the mean time, the output of this process is configured to generate three types of interfaces that model the overall behaviour of the framework: database interfaces, navigational interfaces and service call interfaces. Interfaces are protocols through which heterogeneous entities can interact. They are standards that can be very useful in hiding the underlying system complexity and extending systems without changing implementation code. Based on the one instance of pages per activity stored in the local database of the framework, many interfaces can be generated as needed to extend that same activity for different VLEs. In this section, we focus on how these interfaces are created and how they support the automated behaviour of the framework.

Database Interfaces

The discussed framework targets seamless interoperation with open source VLEs that could have different infrastructures without interfering with how a VLE normally works. One way of doing this, while avoiding replication or inconsistencies, is to establish a direct connection with the database of a VLE through an SQL-based interface. This way, many levels of differences among the target VLEs can be bypassed and narrowed down to database-related differences. For example, the fact that a VLE is Java based or PHP-based is irrelevant to how the framework works.

In the previous section, the modeling process reached to a point where the proposed conceptual model was used to construct detailed representations of pages for a specific activity. From this point, the only configuration needed to create the database interface is to provide the corresponding SQL statement for each specific page in relation to a target VLE. For example, based on the cre-

Figure 2. The two steps of content modeling–selecting templates and expanding them into specific pages

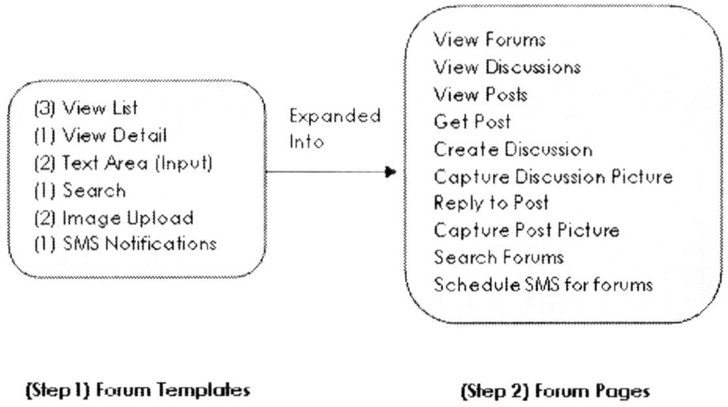

ated set of pages shown in figure 2, providing the SQL statements to list forums, discussions or posts for different types of VLEs, such as Moodle, Sakai or ATutor, is the only step needed to achieve interoperability with that database of each VLE type. It does not matter at this stage the significant differences among these databases in terms of size and schema because the framework interacts with them through the same pages. This process is completely separate from the framework programming logic; therefore, it does not require any implementation steps. Figure 3 shows an overview of the generic interoperability with specific versions of different VLEs based on the author's experimentation of the use of the SQL interface with them.

Navigational Interfaces

With some additional configuration to the constructed pages of an activity, a navigational interface that defines the display on the mobile device is created. More specifically, the following configurations are stored for each page: the order, the hierarchical structure, the title and the permissions. Figure 4 shows one way of navigating the forum activity on a mobile device.

There are several advantages to the proposed database driven approach for configuring navigation. First, the whole interface can be managed from the database which provides great flexibility and control over the user interface. Accordingly, the framework provides a web interface to manage the navigational structure as envisaged by developers (see figure 5). Second, different naming patterns can be used for each page corresponding to how different VLEs refer to the same pages. For example, Moodle uses the term "Discussions", while Sakai and ATutor use the term "Categories" and "Threads" respectively to refer to the same page in the forum activity. This difference can be easily reflected through configuring pages to change their titles without affecting the use of the same templates or the database interface. Additionally, the titles can be changed on the web to translate the mobile interface to different languages. Another advantage of this database-driven definition of the user interface is allowing the use

Figure 3. A figure showing generic interoperability with different VLEs–the templates used are the same but the SQL statements differ for different databases

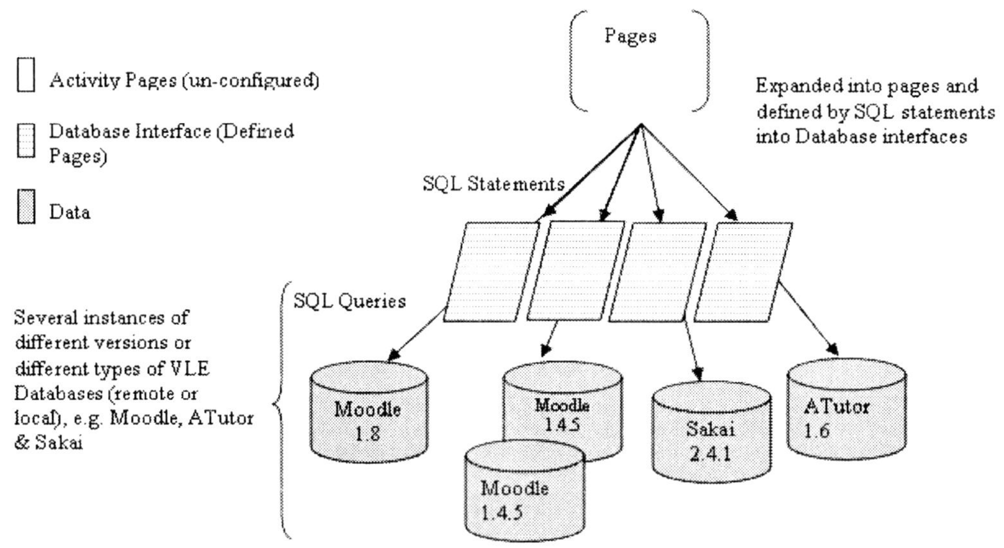

Figure 4. The flexibility of managing the navigational structures for the forum activity for the Sakai VLE

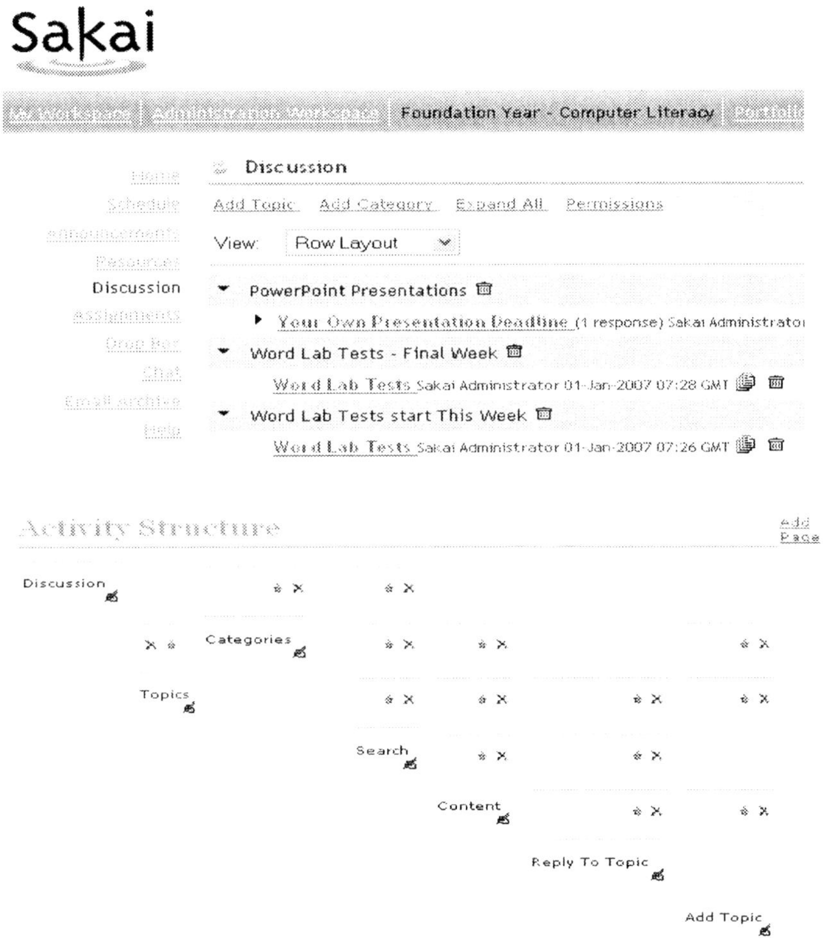

of context related data to adapt or personalise the navigation for different users.

Service Call Interface

As discussed earlier, the process of content modelling relies on task-based templates that are supported by the framework logic. This task oriented view of templates is useful on an abstract level; however, at runtime, in order to complete a certain task, a series of lower level functions has to be loaded. These functions are essential to the operation of the framework, for example, setting up all the parameters needed for the selected VLE, or setting up the permission and preference levels required. This series of local functions combined with loading the database interface, the navigational interface and the task-based template constitute a *Service*. The following is an example of a series of functions loaded by the framework to execute a request for listing the courses of a student:

1. Set VLE database parameters (e.g. url of the database or login information)
2. Authorise Remote User
3. Load User preferences

Figure 5. A block diagram to show the navigational structure for the forum activity

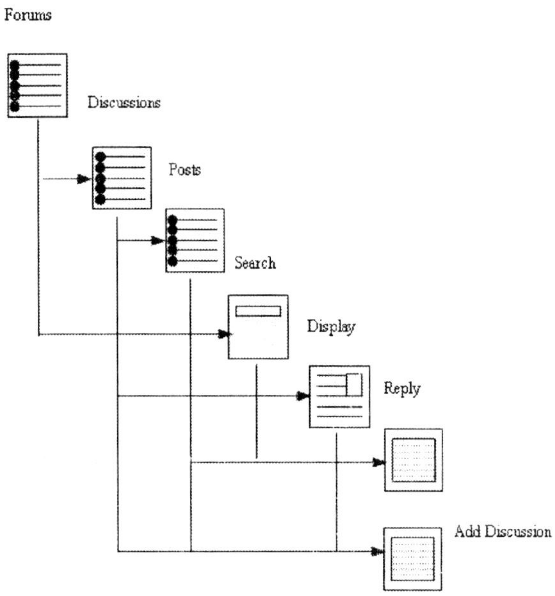

4. Load mobile context-related Data (e.g. Display and download parameters)
5. Load SQL Interface Data (Page: getStudentCourses)
6. Execute (Template: View List)
7. Load Navigational Interface Data (Page: getStudentCourses)
8. Set Log information

A service is a modular component that can be invoked from heterogeneous client environments through the web services technologies. Web services provide a layer of interoperability that allows services to be published and invoked irrespective of underlying architectures. The use of web services ensures the system's scalability and reusability by providing a standardised means of communication that could be extended by other clients in the future. Moreover, web services give the user the freedom to invoke services through any of the mobile Internet technologies, for example, WiFi, GPRS or Internet over Bluetooth. These criteria are essential for pervasive access.

The Remote Procedure Call (RPC) technique of deploying web services is used to invoke the framework's services through a call interface as methods. These interfaces are meant to act as gateways that expose all the available services and the parameters required to invoke them. We have chosen to use XML-RPC to develop our services call interface due to its simplicity and minimalism. These criteria have observable benefits over the speed of communication (Lafon, 2008). XML-RPC uses XML over HTTP to invoke remote procedures. Thus, the framework services are XML-based. Each service has to be constructed once for any activity, and then it can be invoked with different parameters for different instances of VLEs.

Putting it all Together

This section discusses how the outlined models and theories fit together through a set of open source tools and technologies forming the architecture of the framework. The use of open source tools and standards enhances the potential for large-scale use and scalability of this framework.

These criteria have positive implications on institutional enthusiasm which is essential for achieving pervasive access. Figure 6 shows the detailed architecture of the framework. The figure shows where the models and the interfaces, discussed in the previous sections, fit in the architecture. The architecture consists of three main distributed layers: a mini browser on the mobile device, a server side middleware and VLE databases. These layers are distributed in the sense that they run on remote machines; yet, communicate through the interfaces and various technologies used by the middle-ware of the framework.

The Middleware

The server side middle-ware is a central point of control of the whole framework. On one side, it communicates with mobile devices through the

Figure 6. An overview of the architecture and the technologies used by the framework

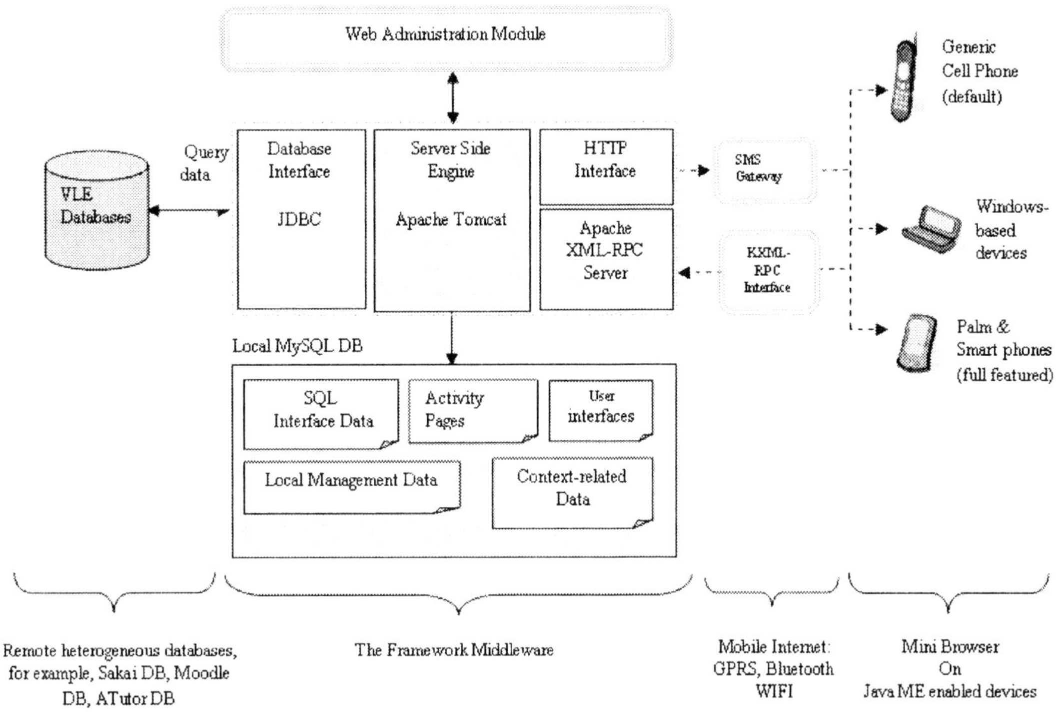

service interface implemented over the Apache XML-RPC Server or through a third-party HTTP Interface for messaging. On the other side, it communicates with heterogeneous VLE databases through the database interfaces using JDBC driver technology. Thus the middle-ware sits in the middle of an end-to end communication between mobile devices and VLEs. This centralized setting of the middle-ware allows several practices for adaptivity, management and monitoring of the whole framework operation.

A web based administration module was built to facilitate the management and monitoring process for administrators, tutors or any permitted roles. Through this web module, administrators can register their VLEs with the framework in one step. Once registered, the framework automatically extends the content of the VLE and provides several management features. For each course, an administrator can manage supported activities, monitor users or view statistics about the framework's activity level. Moreover, as discussed earlier, the web module can be used to manage the navigational interface on the mobile device (see figure 5).

The middle-ware keeps a local MySQL database to store the modeled activity pages and the configuration data for both the SQL and the navigational interfaces. This data is locally stored for any supported VLE. At the time of writing, the different versions of Moodle starting from version 1.5.2 to version 1.8 are fully supported by the framework; while Sakai version 2.4.1 and ATutor version 1.6 are minimally supported for illustrating the concept of generic interoperability. The local storage is also used to store context re-

Figure 7. The browser's views–login, courses and activities are the only required views and the rest of the view are dynamic and depend on the server side design

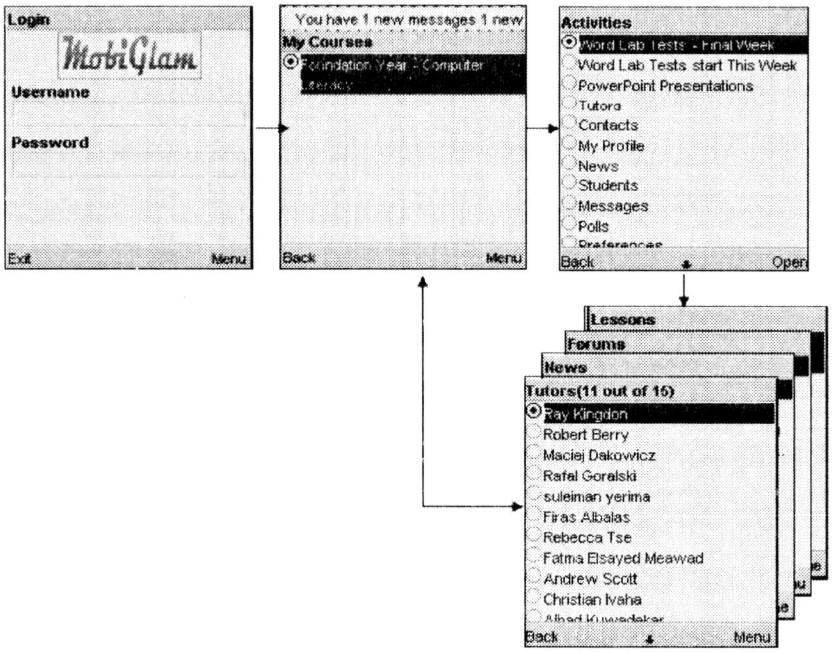

lated data to serve different adaptivity techniques used by the framework.

A Light-Weight Browser

In order to promote wide participation among potential users and support using in-hand technologies, Java-ME was used to develop a light-weight platform independent mini browser (figure 6). Based on this, users who own data enabled phones with minimal features should be able to participate. Using Java-ME provides a pleasant interface while making use of the full display of the mobile device without losing any space for unnecessary display items, such as tool bars or extra frames. Additionally, relying on the fact that Java-ME is platform-independent and available for devices manufactured all over the world, we can support devices that have never been seen or used locally. This increases the reliability of using the framework internationally.

The Java-ME application follows a simple design in order to combine the advantages of unlimited browsing and light weight processing. All the views used by the browser are dynamic and optional except for three required views: login, courses and activities. The identity and the role of a user has to be determined from the start; therefore, users have to login before they can use the activities from the mobile device. As discussed earlier, the conceptual model assumes that activities are user oriented or course oriented. Therefore, the first page seen by users after logging is a list of courses that they are enrolled in or sites that they belong to. From this page, users can navigate to different possible activities as designed for a certain VLE or they can view a list of all activities, as shown in figure 7.

The Java-ME mini browser is light weight in the sense that the entire heavy processing takes place on the server and it only processes specific commands sent by the server. This design results in a very thin mobile browser application with a maximum of 60 kilobytes, even though the application provides unlimited browsing of activities. As shown in figure 6, the mini browser communicates with the server side through KXML-RPC. KXML-RPC is a light weight open source tool for making remote procedure calls that is compliant with Java-ME. Despite of the wide success of Java-ME, it is still an evolving technology which suffers from some challenges. Java-ME's biggest challenge is fragmentation. Fragmentation is the possible incompatibilities in how different virtual machines operate on different devices or if a device refuses to run an application even though it fully supports its Java implementation. Fragmentation is a serious challenge because it is a threat to the platform independence notion "Write Once, Run Anywhere".

Messaging and Notifications

The use of SMS messaging in a mobile learning application is very valuable as a tool for engaging learners (Goh & Cooper, 2007). This is especially true for the learners who are not well involved with the online VLE which makes them unaware of the events that could be interesting for them. This problem increases with distance learners or work-based learners whose main source of information is the on-line learning system. Additionally, many educators find some students unreachable even through their emails. In some cases, these learners could be missing out on some urgent information about their grades or courses.

The use of SMS notifications should be embedded in a VLE the same way, email notifications are. It should be part of the VLE's overall behaviour while providing proper management tools to control this feature. The MobiGlam framework is designed to seamlessly enable SMS messaging for supported activities either through instant or scheduled notifications. Currently, the instant type of notification is programmed into templates that allow communications through sending messages, replying to posts or any similar tasks. On the other hand, the scheduled notifications are triggered by a general scheduler controlled by the framework. The scheduler checks for updates related to registered users every five minutes and triggers notifications accordingly. For example, figure 2 shows a page created for scheduling notifications for the forums activity. Through the corresponding SQL provided for this page, the scheduler checks for new posts to forums or new replies to users' posts and sends notifications accordingly. Users are given the option to personalise receiving notifications or arrange for notifications to be triggered based on certain actions. This is an important feature to maintain the personal use and the privacy of these mobile devices for users.

ADAPTIVITY TECHNIQUES

Considering the diversity of devices that can be potential clients of the framework and in order to maintain the notion of pervasive access, it is essential to be prepared to adapt content delivery for any accessing device. This section discusses how several technologies are embedded on the server side to automatically extract knowledge from accessing devices. Furthermore, it discusses how this knowledge is interpreted and used to adapt content delivery while giving the necessary control to the user.

Device Recognition

The device of a new user is completely anonymous to the framework. Therefore, a technique for device recognition should be provided to enable efficient communication with accessing devices. It is not possible to rely on users' knowledge to enter detailed information about their devices. Most users are not familiar with the technical specifications of their mobile devices. Additionally, explicitly requiring users to enter such information is not a reliable or a user-friendly approach. It is important to note that as new devices enter the market everyday from manufacturers all over the world, a comprehensive up-to-date list of the existing varieties of mobile devices world-wide does not exist. As such, it is believed that device recognition should take place at run-time without relying on static data or user interference.

In the context of this work, using a combination of technologies is proposed to guarantee the creation of a device profile that is as accurate as possible by the end of the recognition process and before processing any data requests for a device. The following three technologies were specifically used by the authors:

1. The HTTP header is probably the simplest technology for device recognition. It has always been used to recognise browser types and resolve browser differences for the Web. Similarly for mobile browsers, mobile operators and manufacturers attach several attributes to the HTTP header to recognize the accessing device.
2. The User Agent Profile (UAProf) which is introduced by the Open Mobile Alliance (OMA) is a thorough definition of the capabilities of mobile devices based on Resource Description Framework (RDF) (Kiss, 2007). One of the attributes defined in the HTTP header is a link to the device's UAProf. The UAProf represents device capabilities as a two level hierarchy consisting of components and properties (Dixit & Wu, 2004). These profiles can be optionally defined by the device manufacturer or the mobile operator.
3. The Wireless Universal Resource File (WURFL) (Passani, 2008b) is an open source package that can be used to access a comprehensive list of device capabilities. The package stores device specification data in an XML file that can be maintained off-line. The information in this file is the result of the collaboration of developers around the world.

The use of the HTTP header and the UAProf takes place on-line as the user makes a request to the server side. On the other hand, the WURFL file can be stored for offline use. As mentioned before, none of these technologies promises availability or accuracy. However, they are becoming widely accepted among manufacturers and mobile operators which increase their value for future use. The device recognition process is required only once for any new accessing devices that do not have matching profiles in the local database kept by the framework. The process starts when the user attempts to download the Java-ME browser and continues when the user first makes a request for data.

The aim in extracting device capabilities is to collect any properties that are essential for the framework's intelligent behaviour when responding to various devices. In other words, a device adaptivity profile should be created containing the following variables: the maximum granule size, the page size, the number of menu items, the number of list items, the recommended image size, screen resolution and colours. These are control variables that help the server make some intelligent decisions about adapting and encapsulating content into granules.

Content Adaptation

Content adaptation is a widely acknowledged need for any mobile application especially if it targets a wide variety of devices and allows unrestricted access to content. The MobiGlam framework generates content in real time as demanded by users without relying on stored multiple versions of the same content, style sheets or caching mechanisms. Thus, in order to adapt content delivery inline with the recommended criteria for mobile and pedagogical usability, the framework processes any content in download units that is referred to as granules. In the context of this work, a granule is defined as a dynamic structure of content that is deliverable and displayable on mobile devices. Each granule contains one or more associated pages, where each page is a list of ordered display units, for example, regular text, image, link or title text. A granule is also packed with presentation metadata, the navigational menu items and any contextual data required by the application. The presentation metadata determines the layout of the pages, how and where to display each item on the mobile device (see figure 8). These presentation metadata are completely device independent since they display content regardless of its capabilities. Thus, the advantage is reduced processing on the mobile device itself as all the adaptation load is completed on the server prior to delivery.

Obviously, automatically generating the granular structures to suit different device capabilities requires some real time decisions on the variables that control the content generation process for each device. Some of these variables rely on user or administrator preferences; while the rest come from the device adaptivity profile as described in the previous section.

Parsing Content

Content retrieved from the database has to be stripped of any formatting such as XML or HTML tags. Then, only the predefined formats by the framework are extracted while everything else is retrieved as plain text. Figure 9 shows the steps taken to parse content upon request from a user. The process is dependent on the device adaptivity profile and user preferences. Thus, the first step taken is loading the device profile corresponding to the identifier in the user's request and loading the user's preferences. After extracting all nodes, a loop starts that goes through all the extracted nodes until they are finished or till the maximum granule size is reached. Inside the loop, the type of each node is checked and accordingly, it is wrapped with presentation metadata and added to the current page. After checking every node, counters for the granule size and for the page size are incremented. When the current page size is reached, a new page is created and linked to the previous page through the menu. The result of this process is a granule with one or more connected pages that are compliant with the device characteristics and the user preferences. The result of the content adaptation process is shown for the Qtek

Figure 8. The structure of a granule with a list of pages and list of display items per page. The pages are associated through the navigational items.

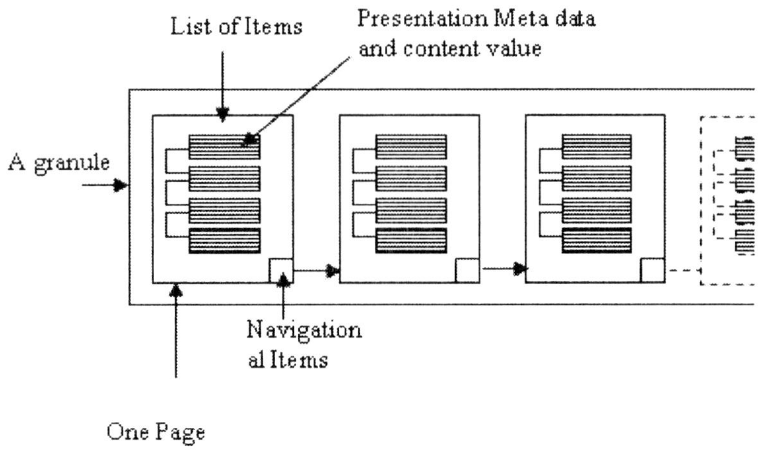

Figure 9. The algorithm of generating granules according to device adaptivity

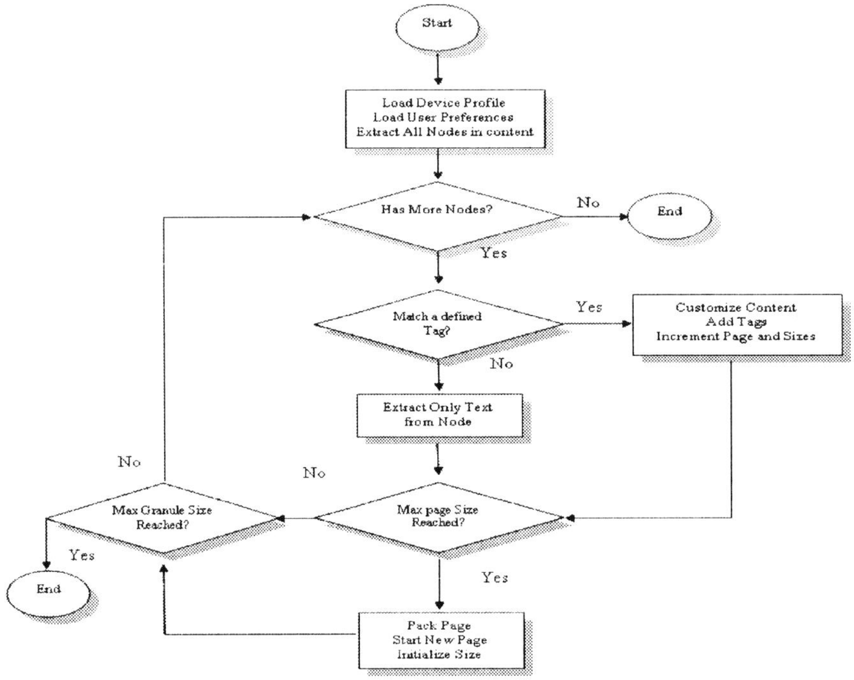

9100 (figure 10) and the Nokia 6230i (figure 11) according to their device adaptivity profile.

EXPERIENCES

This chapter discussed MobiGlam, a framework that enables seamless integration and use for mobile learning with the goal of supporting its large scale use. Since this goal assumes flexibility with respect to the type of users, devices, activities involved, MobiGlam was put through three real world evaluations with different settings: campus based, work based and distance based. The three settings differed in their learning mode, user roles, use of learning activities, host institution, geographic location and more. The work based and distance based evaluation settings involved only remote communication between tutors and students with no face to face interaction. The distance based evaluation settings was the only one that used mock content just for testing, while the others used the framework in the real course delivery. Involving such diversity was crucial to provide more insight to the value of the framework as a tool to support mobile learning. Within these settings, the aim was to observe the degree by which the framework can integrate into the participants' lives while supporting the activities taking place in their specific context.

The user analysis conducted in those evaluations showed various backgrounds for the participants, for example they belonged to different age groups, had different attitudes towards mobile learning, and different knowledge of mobile technology. Some tutors were enthusiastic about trying out the new technology, while others were overloaded with extra teaching work and they were only looking for a way to optimise their use of the VLE without any extra effort. Some students were reluctant to use the technology while others recognised their need for it from the start. The different mode of learning in each setting was very informative since it emphasised the value

Figure 10. Adapted assignment detail on the Qtek 9100

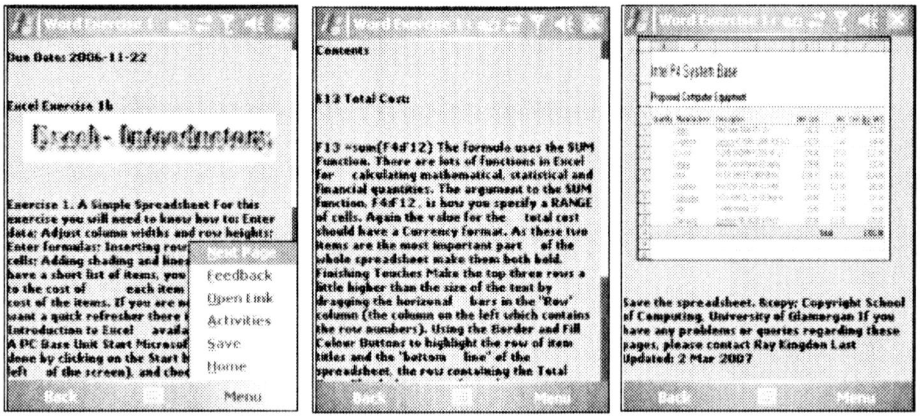

Figure 11. Adapted assignment detail on the Nokia 6230i

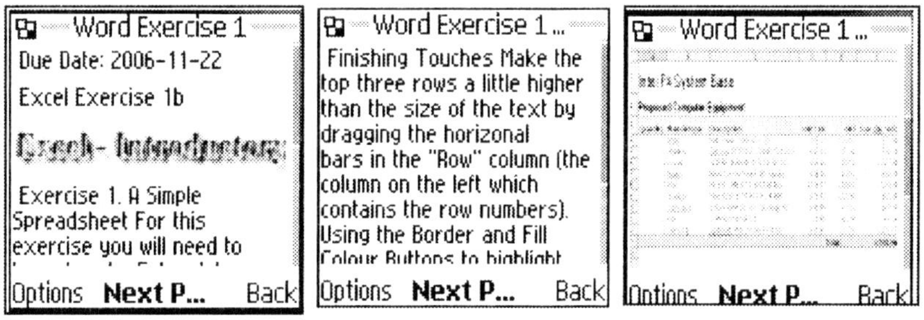

of the different roles involved in the educational process and their specific needs that were not fully accounted for before, for example, course creators and customer support. Finally, the evaluations took place in different country locations (Canada and the UK) and that had a surprising impact on the participants' experience in using MobiGlam. This highlighted the different patterns of use of mobile devices in different countries and the restrictions imposed by mobile operators.

The analysis of the participants' feedback showed a mixture of feelings of satisfaction and dissatisfaction to the same services but within different contexts. The majority of the participants from the campus based and work based evaluation settings enjoyed using the technology and expressed positive reactions to other potential users or institutions. In the meantime, many of the distance based mature participants expressed disappointment and overall unhappiness with their experience of using MobiGlam. Even though such reaction rooted from their dissatisfaction with the capabilities of their mobile devices, the main contributing factor in such disappointment is believed to be that they were using MobiGlam with mock content that did not have a value towards their learning.

The framework is still being used and is starting new phases of use in September 2008 within 4 different institutions: Bridgend College, Swansea College, Coleg Glan-Hafren and Merthyr College. Even though the four institutions are campus based, there is an expected diversity among the users of MobiGlam within these four contexts. For example, the Bridgend College participants are Masters level mature students while the Merthyr participants are foundation level students. Additionally, the number of participants will vary from 20 till 60 participants in each context. The four projects are deployed with only one instance of MobiGlam. This is evidence of the ease of integrating MobiGlam for large scale use.

REFERENCES

Chen, Y. S., Kao, T. C., & Sheu, J. P. (2005). Realizing outdoor independent learning with a buttery-watching mobile learning system. *Journal of Educational Computing Research, 33*, 395–417. doi:10.2190/0PAB-HRN9-PJ9K-DY0C

Cobcroft, R. (2006). *Literature review into mobile learning in the university context.* Queensland University of Technology Creative Industries Faculty.

Coursaris, C. K., & Kim, D. J. (2006). A qualitative review of empirical mobile usability studies. *In Proceedings of the Twelfth Americas Conference on Information Systems*, Acapulco, Mexico.

Dix, A., Finlay, J., Abowd, G., & Beale, R. (2004). *Human computer interaction* (3rd ed.). Harlow, UK: Prentice Hall.

Doering, N. M. (2007). The mainstreaming of mobile learning at a German university. In *Pervasive Computing and Communications Workshops (2007). PerCom Work Fifth Annual IEEE International Conference* (pp. 159-164).

Economides, A. A. (2007). Requirements of mobile learning applications. *International Journal of Innovation and Learning.*

Ghim, S. J., Yoon, Y. I., & Ra, I. (2004). *A context-adaptive model for mobile learning applications.* (LNCS 3307/2004, pp.102-113). Springer Berlin / Heidelberg.

Goh, T. T., & Hooper, V. (2007). To txt or not to txt: That's the puzzle. *Journal of Information Technology Education, 6*, 441–453. doi:10.3923/itj.2007.441.447

Jawad, B., Rachid, B., & Yacine, A. (2006). Ontology-based framework for context-aware mobile learning. In *IWCMC 2006, Proceedings of the 2006 International Wireless Communications and Mobile Computing Conference* (Vol. 2006, pp. 1307-1310).

Keegan, D. (2005). Mobile learning: The next generation of learning. *Distance Education International.*

Kember, L. (2001). *Introducing mobile learning.* IT Solutions, SYS-CON Media.

Kramer, B. J. (2005). *Mobile learning: The next generation of learning, fernuniversitts contributions to the 2nd year of the leonardo project mlearn2.* (Tech. Rep.) ISSN 0945-0130, 5/2005, FernUniversitt in Hagen, 58084 Hagen, Germany.

Kukulska-Hulme, A. (2007). Mobile usability in educational contexts: What have we learnt? *The International Review of Research in Open and Distance Learning, IRRODL*, 8. ISSN: 1492-3831. Holzinger, A., Nischelwitzer, A. K., & Kickmeier-Rust, M. D. (2006). Pervasive e-education supports lifelong learning: Some examples of x-media learning objects (xlos). In *10th IACEE World Conference on Continuing Engineering Education (WCCEE)*, Vienna University of Technology, Vienna.

Luckin, R., Brewster, D., Pearce, D., Siddons-Corby, R., & du Boulay, B. (2005). *Mobile learning: A handbook for educators and trainers* (pp. 116-124). London: Routledge.

Naismith, L., Lonsdale, P., Vavoula, G., & Sharples, M. (2004). *Literature review in mobile technologies and learning.* (Tech. Rep. 11). FutureLab Series.

Naismith, L., Sharples, M., & Ting, J. (2005). *Evaluation of caerus: A context aware mobile guide.*

Nyiri, K. (2002). Towards a philosophy of m-learning. In *Wireless and Mobile Technologies in Education 2002. Proceedings. IEEE International Workshop* (pp. 121-124).

Parsons, D., Ryu, H., & Cranshaw, M. (2006). A study of design requirements for mobile learning environments. In *Advanced Learning Technologies 2006. Sixth International Conference* (pp. 96-100).

Preece, J., Rogers, Y., & Sharp, H. (2002). *Interaction design: Beyond human-computer interaction.* New York: John Wiley

Rogers, Y., Price, S., Fitzpatrick, G., Fleck, R., Harris, E., Smith, H., et al. (2004). *Ambient wood: Designing new forms of digital augmentation for learning outdoors* (pp. 3-10).

Seong, D. S. K. (2006). Usability guidelines for designing mobile learning portals. In *Mobility '06: Proceedings of the 3rd International Conference on Mobile Technology, Applications, & Systems*, 25. New York: ACM.

Stead, G. (2005). Moving mobile into the mainstream. In *4th World conference on m-Learning.*

Thomas, S. (2005). Pervasive, persuasive e-learning: Modeling the pervasive learning space. In *Pervasive Computing and Communications Workshops, 2005. PerCom 2005 Workshops. Third IEEE International Conference* (pp. 332-336).

Traxler, J., & Kukulska-Hulme, A. (2005). Evaluating mobile learning: Reactions on current practice. In *Proceedings of MLEARN*, Cape Town, South Africa.

Trifonova, A. (2006). *Towards hoarding content. In m-learning context.* Unpublished doctoral dissertation, DIT-University of Trento.

Uden, L. (2007). Activity theory for designing mobile learning. *Int. J. Mobile Learning and Organisation, 1*, 81–102. doi:10.1504/IJMLO.2007.011190

Uther, M. (2002). Mobile Internet usability: What can 'mobile learning' learn from the past? In *Wireless and Mobile Technologies in Education 2002. Proceedings. IEEE International Workshop* (pp. 174-176).

Wagner, E. D. (2005). Enabling mobile learning. *EDUCAUSE Review, 40*, 4053.

Wang, Y. K. (2004). Context awareness and adaptation in mobile learning. In *the 2nd IEEE International Workshop on Wireless and Mobile Technologies in Education* (pp. 154-158).

Weiss, S. (2002). *Handheld usability.* Chichester: John Wiley & Sons.

Wentzel, P., Lammeren, R. v., & Molendijk, S. M. Bruin, & Wagtendonk, A. (2005). Using mobile technology to enhance students' educational experiences. *Educause, (ECAR Case Study 2)*, 18. Boulder.

Zanev, V., & Clark, R. (2005). Wireless course management system. *In ACMSE 43: Proceedings of the 43rd Annual Southeast Regional Conference* (pp. 118-123). New York: ACM Press.

Chapter 4
SW-Architecture for Device Independent Mobile Learning

Andreas Christ
University of Applied Sciences Offenburg, Germany

Markus Feißt
University of Applied Sciences Offenburg, Germany

ABSTRACT

Mobile learning increases both flexibility and self-determined learning, often combined with a high degree of context awareness. Flexibility and context awareness includes time and location, as well as the actual individual situation. To achieve such goals, mobile learning is not just a stand-alone and independent learning environment, but is instead embedded in a broader e-learning environment. This is true for the didactic and the pedagogic concepts and the learning (content) management system, as well as the overall software architecture. XML has been proven to be adequate and a powerful technology to store content in a presentation independent manner. By defining an additional attribute inside the XML tags, it is possible to classify the content. At the same time, this will help the author generate learning material for different devices in an efficient and structured way. Also, the content can be used in different formats (XHTML, PDF, etc.) as well as with different technologies (browser, applet, MIDlet, Ajax, etc.). In order to optimise the content presentation on different mobile devices, the content has to be adapted. A necessary precondition for the adaptation process is the identification of the connected device. The classification of the identified mobile device simplifies the mapping between device capabilities and content. The ICAT (Identification, Classification, Adaptation and Tagged XML) framework addresses these issues. The proposed design patterns will help authors to generated content for such a system.

INTRODUCTION

While at home it is often more convenient to use a PC, but while on the move and using mobile learning, a learner would like to access comparable learning content with the same look and feel. So a system is necessary which is device sensitive from the point of communication functionality, interactivity, information presentation and information depth. But at the same time it must be a system which is

DOI: 10.4018/978-1-60566-882-6.ch004

device independent from the point of information access, and (a-) synchronous communication possibilities.

Typically, learning content management systems are unable to handle these two opposing facts with one common data base for the content. In order to surround this problem many content providers offers multiple versions of the same information. In this way, maintaining content will be labour-intensive and therefore costly. Another disadvantage is that the authors and content developers need to have knowledge on different devices and their behaviour in order to be able to generate content using the abilities of these devices. But most authors and content developers do not have this precise technical knowledge. They want and should concentrate on the content and, in the case of e-learning and mobile learning systems, on the didactic. However, this is not on a device optimised presentation. On the other hand, people with the technical knowledge do not have necessarily the knowledge to convert the content in a proper way.

All the content pieces motivated by the didactical purpose without considering the technical or graphical constrains composes the so called generalised content.

Systems that can transfer generalised content into a device adapted version of the content are a solution for this problem. Such systems are especially important for mobile learning because of the large amount of varying devices with significantly different features and functionalities. This is true not only to support different learners, e.g. all learners within one learning community, but also to support the same learner using different equipment parallel and/or at different times. For mobile learning purposes, it is impossible to develop and adapt content for all mobile devices individually due to cost issues and author's requirements. But new concepts and technologies enable the automation of the content adaptation process.

The following example illustrates the need for the adaptation requirement. Figure 1 shows a small XHTML page containing a SVG images (vector based, 31KB) on three different mobile devices without adaptation. The image is perfectly scaled and displayed on the first two devices (labelled a and b). Unfortunately, the third device does not support SVG, therefore the image is not visible on this device without adaptation (media format conversion). A second example is shown in Figure 2, where the XHTML page contains a JPEG image (640x480 pixels, 68KB) shown on the left. The figure on the right (labelled b) shows an adapted device version of the same image (128x96 pixels, 10KB). The advantage is that this media format is widely supported. Transmitting an image that is not adapted has the disadvantages that the scaling process is performed at the mobile device. This scaling process can cause a blur or raster effect that can make image text difficult to read. But the combination of figures and text is an important and common mobile learning means. Adaptation on the server side with specialised image processing software can reduce this bur or raster effect as well as the data amount which is an additional advantage because it can save cost/time (transmission cost/bandwidth).

XML (eXtensible Markup Language) (XHTML 1.0 Recommendation, 2000) is a key technology today with huge potential to reach the goals mentioned. XML can be and is used with quite different concepts for interactive distributed applications for both PC-based and mobile networks using internet technologies. It offers the perfect solution for handling data for device dependent presentation because it structures the data without specifying the visual presentation contrast to HTML (HyperText Markup Language) (HTML 4.01 Specification, 1999). Thus it allows reusing data to generate different device specific presentations with the help of templates.

In order to realise such an approach it is very important to be familiar with the specific device actually used. The accelerating evolution in the mobile device market has shown that a simple division into desktop and mobile presentation

Figure 1. SVG on three mobile devices--a) Nokia, b) SE P1, and c) HTC Touch. The Touch does not support SVG.

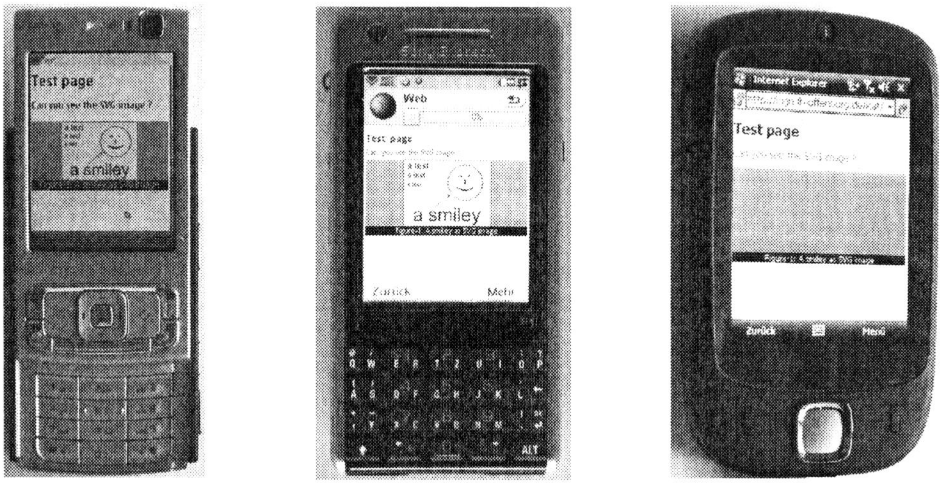

a. b. c.

is not applicable (M. Gaedke, M. Beigl, H-W Gellersen, C. Segor, 1998). Also, it is more and more difficult to distinguish mobile devices on a rough and general classification such as PDA, smart phone or mobile phone (M. Feisst, D. Santos, J. Mitic, A. Christ, 2005). On the other hand, it is much too cumbersome to deliver content and its visual presentation with respect to all specific models available (M. Ally, F. Lin, R. McGreal, B. Woo, 2005), (R. Omari, 2006). One solution is a combination of important capabilities of mobile devices used to define a classification of the device. However, as few as possible relevant classification parameters should be taken into account in order to simplify the classification process.

A device independent system is able to deliver content to any device in such a way that the received content can be presented. This task can be approached in the two following ways: either content for every device exists or the system is able to adapt content for each device. In case the system is capable of adapting content to a device

Figure 2. a) Original JPEG image, b) scaled JPEG image

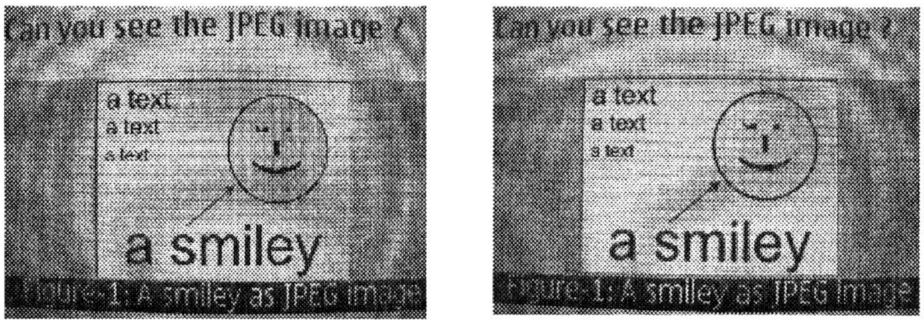

a. b.

dependent presentation, the content has to be available in a generalised form. Additionally, such a system should support a device independent authoring process where the author can focus on the content generation and not on device dependent content adaptation.

In order to realise such an e-learning system for mobile learning purposes, two major requirements have to be fulfilled:

- Generation, structuring and storage of generalised content
- Transformation process from general content to optimised and device dependent content

The next sub-chapters will explain what methods and systems can provide these functionalities. As a starting point, a short technical introduction will be given, followed by definitions and short explanations of the most important technical terms. Following will focus on the process of device dependent content presentation and how to perform such a process. The last two sub-chapters describe implementation details of an experiment and the comparison of different approaches.

TECHNOLOGICAL BACKGROUND

N-tier Software Architectures

From a system architectural point of view, mobile learning is a typical client-server application with mobile devices as clients. Well known concepts can be used and adapted to structure the software into modules responsible for the different kind of tasks that have to be executed. Basically, one distinguishes presentation tasks, (application) logic tasks and data storage tasks. Different

Figure 3. N-tier architecture

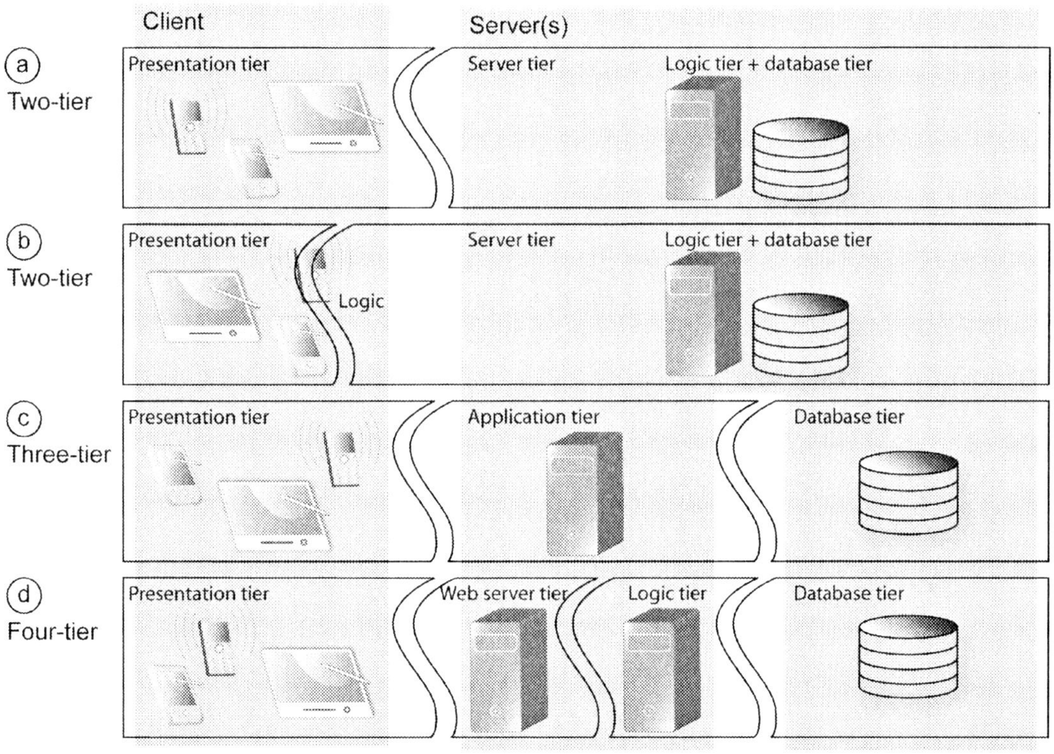

architecture models distribute these tasks differently on components running on client and server machine(s).

There are different definitions for a tier. In this chapter a tier is referred to as a logical software unit, often but not necessarily corresponding with **one** underlying physical device (server/client). The classic two-tier structure consists of a client, performing the presentation tasks (presentation tier) and a server executing the logic tasks and storing the data, all within one tier (sometimes called as server tier). This is often referred to as a client-server architecture (Figure 3, labelled a). Part b of Figure 3 shows a slightly modified two-tier architecture where the server is responsible for persistent data storage with the help of a database and/or directly on a file system but the logic tasks are split somehow between client and server. Three-tier architecture concentrates all logic tasks within an additional application tier, or middle tier, running on a server machine (part c). What is important is that in a three-tier architecture, the client never connects to the data tier directly. This is the most used architecture on the Internet.

Professional and large scale applications further divide the middle tier into a web server tier responsible for the receipt of requests and for pre-processing of the answer and into a logic tier performing the application logic in a stricter sense. This is commonly known as a four-tier architecture (Figure 3, part d). Web server tier and application tier can run on different server machines or on a server cluster. For IT-security purposes, an additional DMZ (DeMilitarized Zone) is often realized by adding another server machine between internet and web server tier with firewalls on both sides (Figure 4).

In comparison with the server, a mobile device has restricted computing power. Therefore, only the presentation tier is typically performed on the client side. This is called a thin client. For mobile learning a wide spread of different devices are used by the learner and therefore have to be taken into account. This sometimes includes also laptops and desktops. It is necessary that the application tier and web server tier, respectively, are able to deliver content to a presentation tier with quite different functionalities and abilities.

XML, HTML, XHTML MP, CHTML and PDF

Mark-up languages are used to structure, classify, store and transfer data objects. XML (XHTML 1.0 Recommendation, 2000) is a specification of the W3C to define such languages in a structured manner mainly for web applications. It allows storing data in a strong hierarchical manner using a tree structure by defining a general syntax. Any derived mark-up language must conform to the recommendation to be called a well-formed XML document.

In regards to mobile devices, the XHTML MP (eXtended HTML Mobile Profile) (XHTML

Figure 4. Four-tier with firewall

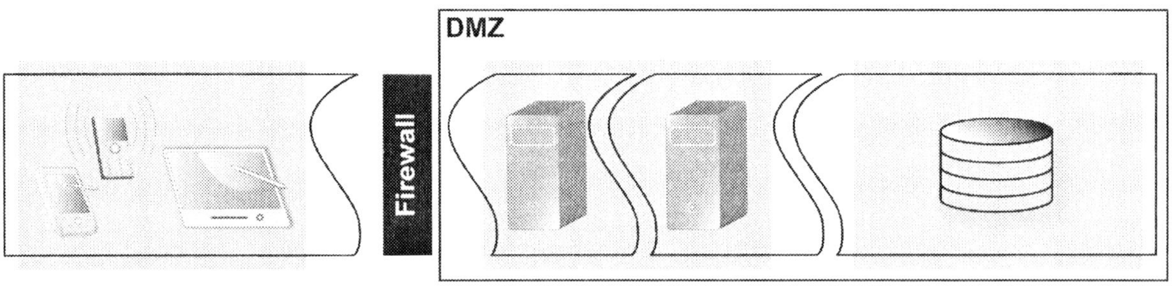

1.0 Recommendation, 2000) is a very important mark-up language to exchange web pages.

Any document that conforms with XML consists of elements which themselves may include character data as data object, attributes to additionally specify the data object and further nested elements to build up a tree structure. The whole document is built by a prolog and the so called root element. All elements are delimited by start- and end-tags. Data objects as well as tags are represented by readable text. Therefore XML documents are human readable but at the same time much longer than binary code.

XML allows specifying different element types with a specific meaning of its data object and with different attributes. They are distinguished within the XML document by different tag names. The element structure is described by either a DTD (Document Type Declaration) or a XML-scheme (XML Schema, 2004). It defines for each element type its tag name, the valid attributes, eventually allowed nested elements and whether a data object is permitted. A valid XML document must fulfil the structure given by the DTD or XML-scheme.

By using XML to describe documents like web pages, it separates the content, i.e. the data object, and the meaning of the content, given by the tag name. To present the content on a screen in a graphical representation, the client needs an application such as a web browser for PCs or a micro-browser for mobiles. The browser itself and possibly an additional CSS (Cascading Style Sheet) are responsible for interpreting the content and formatting its actual representation based on the type of the individual elements and its attributes. By delivering both the XML document and a device specific CSS by the web server, quite different mobile devices can be served. This functionality should be performed by the web server tier (Fig 1d).

To manipulate XML documents at the client side, the document is internally represented as DOM (Document Object Model) structure. A parser transfers the text based XML document by reading it and building up the DOM. Like the XML document the internal representation is a hierarchical tree structure with nodes. Elements, attributes and data objects are regarded as nodes. Because elements may be nested so do nodes.

An API (Application Programming Interface) – e.g. for JavaScript – allows to process nodes by adding, removing and replacing nodes, getting the type of the node, reading and writing data objects and attribute values etc. Doing this the presentation of a web page on a screen can be manipulated directly by processing its DOM using JavaScript statements. Since DOM includes the CSS information, the layout can also be manipulated. DOM and its manipulation are used by Ajax (Asynchronous JavaScript and XML).

The most important mark-up languages for web pages are HTML (HTML 4.01 Specification, 1999) and XHTML (XHTML 1.0 Recommendation, 2000). HTML was the first mark-up language to describe web pages. XHTML 1.0 was created as a redefinition of HTML 4.01. However, unlike HTML, XHTML documents meet the structural requirements of the XML paradigm. They are therefore well-formed and are valid XML. Since this simplifies parsing and manipulating of web pages at the client side, almost all internet compatible mobile devices are able to process XHTML MP (XHTML Mobile Profile, 2001), an adjusted subset of XHTML for mobile devices.

Initially, CHTML (Compact HTML) was created as mark-up language for mobile devices. Originally based on HTML 2.0, it is not well-formed XML but is also adapted to the properties of mobile devices.

The PDF (Portable Document Format) (Document management, 2008), another commonly accepted standard, is a widely used file format for ready designed documents including text, fonts and images. In contrast to XML documents, all layout requirements are included. Therefore, PDF fits best for file exchange for printing purpose, for electronic books (e-books) and for long-term archiving of documents.

Originally created by Adobe Systems Inc. it is now an open ISO (International Organization for Standardization) standard. For free of charge, readers are available for all common platforms especially for mobiles. Increasing size and resolution of the display of mobile devices make it more and more comfortable to read, at least for short documents.

Appropriate software can transform XML documents into PDF documents. This is done by transforming the XML document into an XSL-FO (Extensible Stylesheet Language – Formatting Objects) (Extensible Stylesheet Language, 2006) document with the help of XSLT (Extensible Style sheet Language Transformations) style-sheets in a first step and into the final PDF document in a second step.

Java and JavaScript

Java is a programming language developed and maintained by Sun Microsystems. The Java source code is a human readable ASCII based text file with ".java" as file extension. The source code is compiled with the help of a Java compiler into so called "byte code" with ".class" as file extension. The resulting byte code is operating system independent and can therefore be executed on any platform that supports the installation of a Java Interpreter. Since the byte code is not native machine code, a Java Interpreter that translates the byte code into native machine commands is needed in order to execute any Java program.

For distribution purposes, all class files can be packed together into JAR (Java ARchive) file. A JAR file is a GNU zipped file containing all class files together with an additional manifest file that describes the application.

Java Applets are a special type of Java applications that are designed to work within a browser. In order to execute an Applet, a plug-in has to be installed into the browser.

Java MIDlets are a special type of Java application, designed to run on mobile phones, smart phones and PDAs.

JSP (Java Server Pages) and JavaBeans are used for server side programming. JSP is a mix out of Java code and (x)HTML, which is interpreted by a Servlet Engine (ex. Tomcat, JBoss). JavaBeans are Java classes fulfilling special requirements (ex. class attributes are changed via get/set methods) used to process logical functions.

ECMAScript (ISO/IEC 16262:1998) is the standardised version of the browser scripting language and both JavaScript (Netscape/Mozilla) and JScript (Microsoft) are compatible with ECMAScript. These scripting languages are executed at the client side and can be used to manipulate the DOM structure.

Micro-Browser, Web Service & Ajax

For all relevant mobile platforms, browsers for internet access are available that are adapted to the restrictions of mobile devices. The main task of these agents is to display content and to navigate. To distinguish them from PC based browsers they are often called micro-browser. Nowadays almost all micro-browser can process and display XHTML MP documents, some of them HTML as well.

PDF files can also be displayed on a handheld with the help of a PDF reader started as application by the micro-browser.

Due to growing importance of mobile internet access, original PC based internet technologies like web services/SOAP (Simple Object Access Protocol) and Ajax will get a similar importance for mobile devices. Web services allow machine-to-machine interconnection within distributed systems. Requests and responses are transferred via HTTP and HTTPS protocol by using the XML based SOAP protocol. Thus data exchange is performed in a standardized and platform independent way.

The mark-up language UDDI (Universal Description, Discovery and Integration) (OASIS UDDI Specifications, 2002), being in conformity with XML, was created by OASIS (Organization for the Advancement of Structured Information Standards) for publication of web services offered by a server and for its retrieval. Furthermore for defining the interfaces to the web service WSDL (Web Services Description Language) (WSDL 2.0, 2007).

Ajax is a set of different internet technologies to create dynamic web pages. A JavaScript code, usually packed into a library, manages the access to web services via XML. Additionally, it delivers an API to perform dynamic changes of the presentation of a web page on the screen by manipulating its internal DOM structure. The manipulation of the DOM structure is performed at the client side, after exchanging partial data with the server. This allows Ajax to reduce the network load by an incremental web page update. Together with XHTMLMP which has a well-formed and valid XML syntax these technologies also fit to the requirements of mobile internet access with clients having restricted properties.

DEVICE DEPENDENT CONTENT PRESENTATION

General Software Architecture for Device Independent Systems

The four-tier software architecture (Figure 3, part d) fulfils the requirements for device adapted content presentation. The presentation tier is the graphical front end of the used device. The transmitted information generated and adapted by the web server tier consists of the data and additional layout information (e.g. XHTML + CSS). The web server tier receives the client request, while the logic tier evaluates the request, collects the data and sends the answer back to the web server tier.

The database tier stores the data of the application. In order to realise a device dependent content presentation where the information is adapted to the device, no layout information is stored in this tier. Old fashion systems realise a pseudo content adaptation by storing multiple versions of information (data and different layout) at the database tier.

Steps for Device Dependent Content Presentation

The task of device dependent content presentation consists of three different steps which have to be performed:

1. Device identification
2. Device classification
3. Content adaptation

The first step is to identify the device. After the device is identified, its capabilities are known and it is therefore possible to adapt the content to the connected device and to realise an optimal presentation. In the following sub-chapters different possibilities and methods to solve the problem of devices identification is explained.

The second step is the process of device classification which results in the assignment of a mobile device to a device class. In some frameworks this step is included in the content adaptation process and thus it is not an independent process. In any case, a classification process has to be performed because the decision has to be made on what kind of content will be displayed on what device. Systems with an independent device classification process tend to be more flexible, because the classification process can be changed without changing the process of content adaptation.

The last step of the device dependent content presentation process is the adaptation of the content. In order to resolve this process, the device class is taken into account to adapt the requested content to the connected mobile device. In case the framework does not perform an independent device classification process, the capabilities of the connected device, identified by the first step, are taken into account directly. A precise description of different possibilities and methods to resolve the content adaptation process are explained in the following sub-chapters.

Device Identification

Device Identification by WURFL

The WURFL (Wireless Universal Resource File) was introduced and is maintained by Luca Passani. The main reason for the introduction of WURFL was the need to get the capabilities of mobile devices.

The WURFL database is available at no cost for downloading. It contains currently about 7,000 different mobile devices including subversions of installed micro-browser or operating systems. Additionally, the downloaded database can be changed by so called patch files.

The mobile devices are described by their capabilities denoted in XML format. A mobile device inherits the capabilities of the group it belongs to. This way only information that is different between the mobile device and the group has to be overwritten. Therefore, the WURFL database stores only incremental device data and reduces the needed resources (by WURFL called "fall-back function").

An example of the most known commercial service that uses the WURFL is the DeviceAtlas (http://deviceatlas.com). This service uses, in addition, the UAProf (User Agent Profile) information. Other information is used as well but the sources are not specified.

Device Identification by W3C with UAProf

The RDF (Resource Description Framework) (W3C Semantic Web Activity, 2004) is developed and maintained by the W3C and is used to process metadata (information about information). RDF is a description framework for defining vocabularies used to describe new XML tags. The CC/PP framework (Composite Capabilities/Preference Profiles) (Composite Capabilities, 2007) is also developed by the W3C and uses the RDF to define the available vocabulary for UAProf. The CC/PP schema is a semantic description of the used vocabulary. It is well-formed XML. The idea behind this approach is to obtain the ability to add new vocabularies in the future. Thus it is possible to add new tags to describe device capabilities which are currently not known. This way the UAProf is future-proof. An instance of a schema is usually called a profile. An implemented profile of the CC/PP framework is the UAProf. Hence the UAProf is a description of the capabilities of a mobile device with the vocabulary specified in the CC/PP. Figure 5 shows an example of UAProf.

The current profiles consist of components of the following six different groups of characteristics:

- Hardware platform
- Software platform
- Network characteristics
- Browser UA
- WAP characteristics
- PUSH characteristics

In a query to a server, the newer mobile devices send the URL at which point the UAProf can be found as value in the HTTP-header parameter. There are two reasons why the UAProf itself is not transmitted directly to the server/application. First, the HTTP communication does not directly define such a header parameter and second the end user has to pay additional costs for the transmission of this information. If the server side application needs the UAProf, it can be downloaded from the specified URL and can be parsed to receive the mobile device information.

A tool that performs this task is the DELI framework (a Delivery context Library for CC/PP and UAProf). DELI is an open source library developed by the open mobile alliance and is written in Java.

Figure 5. UAProf structure

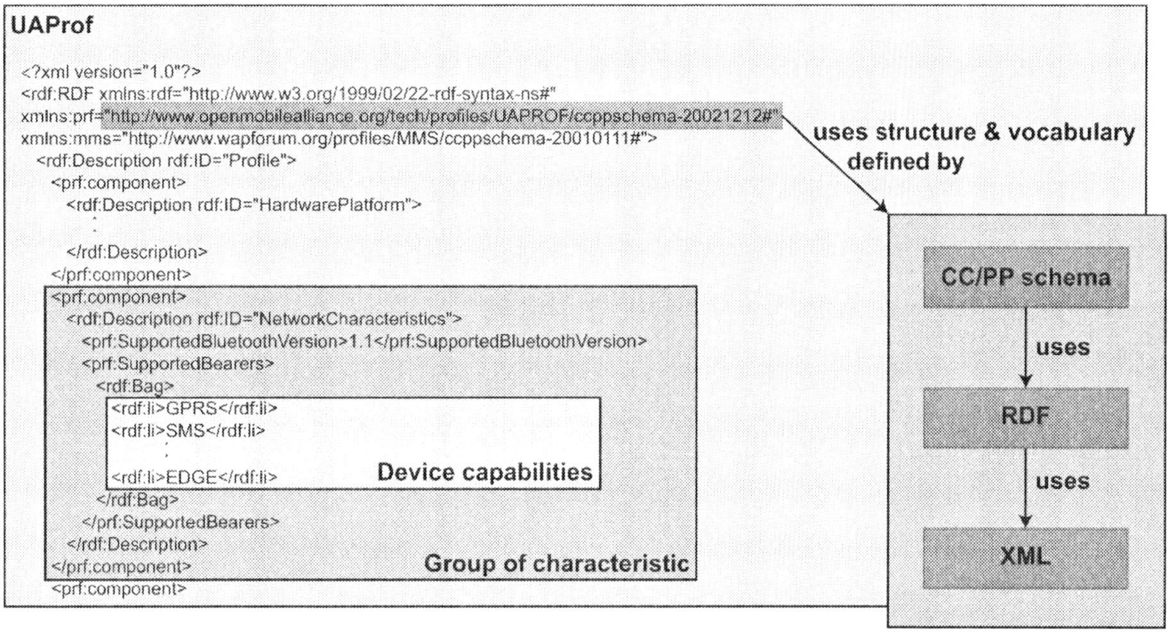

Device Identification by ICAT with UAProf

The system design ICAT (Identification, Classification And Tagging) developed by the University of Applied Sciences Offenburg uses a combination of the UAprof and local database. The flowchart in Figure 6 explains the whole process.

First, it is detected whether the user is connecting to the system via mobile device or by desktop device by analysing the user-agent parameter of the HTTP-header. In case of mobile devices, the local database is checked whether the device is listed and the available information is up-to-date. Outdated device information is determined using the UAProf, which is accessed on the manufacturer's server.

Device Classification

Device Classification by WURFL

WURFL uses the concept of inherited group capabilities to classify a device. The mobile device capabilities are the sum of all capabilities described by groups the device belongs to. Also it is possible for a group to inherit these capabilities from another group. Thus, the concept of WURFL can be considered as a kind of "reverse device classification": The mobile device is classified by the conjunction of the groups the device is a member of.

Device Classification by W3C

In the "Mobile Web Application Best Practices" document (Mobile Web, 2008) the W3C emphasises the importance of a device classification in order to simplify the content adaptation process. Nevertheless there are currently no drafts for an elaborated device classification concept available.

Device Classification by ICAT

The concept of device classification is based on isolating the important capabilities, described by classification parameters. The reason behind this is

Figure 6. Flowchart device identification ICAT

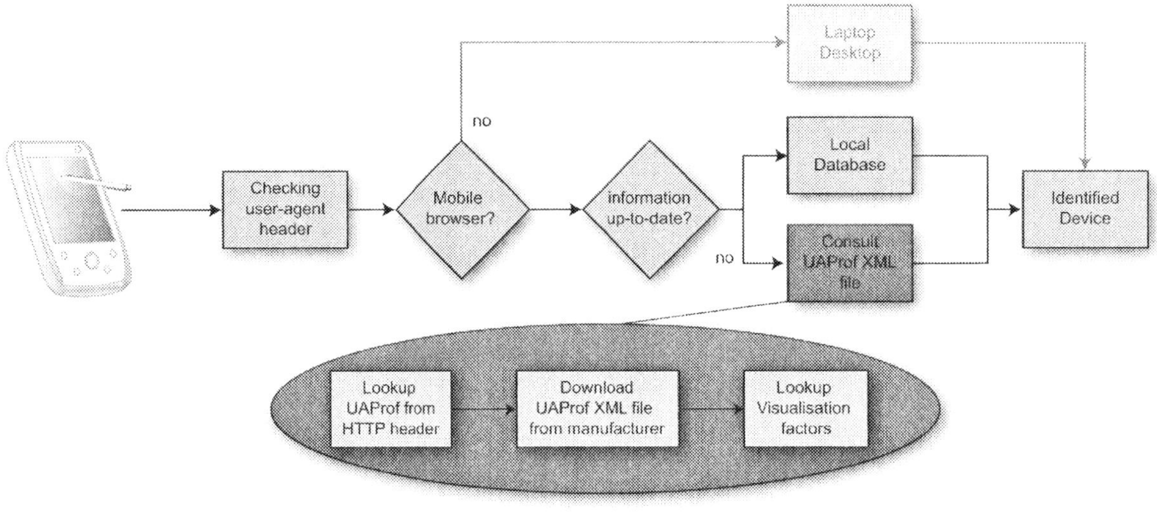

that in most applications not all device capabilities are important to generate an adequate presentation. Often it is sufficient to take two or three capabilities into account like the screen size, the bandwidth and the supported media.

In order to obtain the device class, all classification parameters can be combined to a vector which spreads out a parameter space. Finally, the parameter space is transformed into a low-dimensional space which is then divided into the targeted number of classes. Figure 7 models an example space for an application which is designed to offer 7 different presentations depending on the visual and connection capabilities of the devices. Note that device class 1 is intended for desktop devices (PCs and laptops).

This concept has the advantage of flexibility in the selection of the classification parameters, and the number of device classes. However, the more parameters are taken into consideration, the more complicated the system gets.

Another advantage is that the classification parameters are not restricted to device capabilities. Thus, user and environment settings can be seen as classification parameters too.

To simplify the generation of the device class, it is possible to use multiple nested classification processes, e.g. the first classification process takes bandwidth and QoS (Quality of Service) into account and generates a connectivity class. This class is used as classification parameter for the next classification (chained classification).

In order to obtain meaningful results, classification parameters that are related to each other are grouped into a category of capabilities. The following categories of capabilities were detected as most important:

Visual category: There is a huge spread in the visual capabilities of available mobile devices in the world wide market. Content presented on devices with a small screen size and limited number of colours will face a lot of visual limitations, while other more visual oriented mobile devices do not. Hence, it is important to take into account the whole range of visual capabilities in order to generate an optimal user experience on each device. The most important classification parameters found to vary from one device to another are:

- the display size
- the screen resolution
- the screen size in characters
- the number of colours
- the orientation of the device

Figure 7. Device classification with two classification parameters

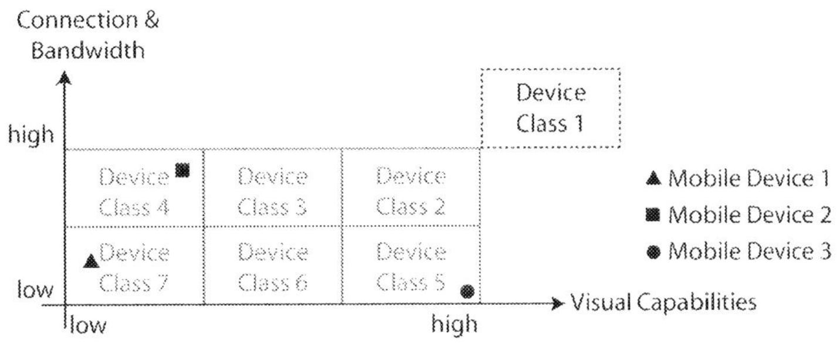

Media category: Mobile devices differ also in a wide range of media presentation capabilities (i.e. acceptable MIME media types). Additionally, it has to be distinguished between supported media types and supported file formats of the media type, e.g. in case a mobile device supports the media type "image" it does not necessarily support the "gif " file format. The most important media types are:

- text
- image
- audio
- video

Connectivity category: Applications have to pay attention on the connection speed and the Internet access method, which specifies whether the device is connected to the Internet via a mobile network service provider or a Wireless LAN, Bluetooth, etc. The most important connectivity classification parameters are:

- Available bandwidth
- QoS
- Tariff model (flat rate, pay per minute or kB)

Content Adaptation

Content Adaptation of WURFL – WALL

Additional to the WURFL database, there exists the WALL (Wireless Abstraction Library from WURFL) library to realise content adaptation according to the mobile device. The WALL is a Java tag-lib that is used to generate the content to be presented at the device according to its capabilities. In such a way, an author can mark-up his content with WALL tags that are automatically transformed to the correct tags supported by the connected device afterwards, e.g., the tag *<wall:br>* is transformed into *
* for devices which uses CHTML and to *
* for WML or XHTML MP enabled devices. Figure 8 shows a more complex example of a WALL document.

Additionally, WALL is able to assign specific content on the basis of the individual device capability provided by the WURFL database. The following fragment of a WALL document shows the principle on the example of the supported image format. In case the connected mobile device supports GIF images, the "test_image.gif" is used, otherwise the WBMP image "test_image.wbmp" is used.

```
<c:choose>
 <c:when test="${capabilities.gif}">
   <img src="test_image.gif" alt="An test
image" />
 </c:when>
```

Figure 8. Use of WALL library

WALL
```
<wall:menu colorize="true" autonumber="true">
  <wall:a href="http://url1" title="URL 1">Url 1</wall:a>
  <wall:a href="http://url2" title="URL 2">Url 2</wall:a>
  <wall:a href="http://url3" title="URL 3">Url 3</wall:a>
</wall:menu>
```

WML 1.x
```
<p>
  <a href="http://url1" title="URL 1">Url 1</a><br/>
  <a href="http://url2" title="URL 2">Url 2</a><br/>
  <a href="http://url3" title="URL 3">Url 3</a><br/>
</p>
```

CHTML
```
<br clear="all">
  &#59106; <a acceskey="1" href="http://url1">Url 2</a><br>
  &#59107; <a acceskey="2" href="http://url2">Url 2</a><br>
  &#59108; <a acceskey="3" href="http://url2">Url 3</a><br>
```

XHTML MP
```
<p>
<ol>
  <li><a acceskey="1" href="http://url1" title="URL 1">Url 1</a></li>
  <li><a acceskey="2" href="http://url2" title="URL 2">Url 2</a></li>
  <li><a acceskey="3" href="http://url3" title="URL 3">Url 3</a></li>
 </ol>
</p>
```

```
 <c:otherwise>
   <img src="test_image.wbmp" alt="An
test image" />
 </c:otherwise>
</c:choose>
```

Content Adaptation by W3C – DIAL

DIAL (Device Independent Authoring Language) provides a mark-up language to adapt content. DIAL filters and presents web pages facilitating an optimal user experience available across different delivery contexts. The filtering mechanism adapts the DIAL instance document in such a way that the presentation fits best. The technology behind DIAL is based on W3C XML vocabulary and CSS modules. In this way web page structure, presentation and form interaction are realised with standard mechanisms. Additionally, the DIAL uses the DISelect metadata vocabulary for the adaptation process for multiple delivery contexts. In other words, with the help of DISelect the client device displays only tags fulfilling the DISelect condition (Mobile Web Authoring Language, 2007). The content adaptation process of DIAL takes place at the client side. Therefore, no device identification like UAProf is needed because build-in processing application knows the mobile device capabilities.

Content Adaptation by ICAT

The analysis of current mobile device market studies has shown that all micro-browsers of the mobile devices currently delivered by the worldwide market leaders fully support the WAP 2.0 standard (8). That implies complete support of XHTML MP. Of course this is not true for older devices, except they support full XHTML. Therefore, this approach supports only newer devices. Another requirement is the availability of the generalised content as well-formed XML data.

Using the ICAT approach the actual demanded content can be selected individually depending on the request details and the result set is formed according to the user's needs. This predefined subset of the generalised content is referred to as a content class.

For technical realisation, the generalised content is divided in a large number of small pieces. Each of them is represented as a XML element. This gives the possibility to add a new XML attribute to each element. This new XML attribute is called level and defines the importance of the content for learning purpose. With help of the level attribute, all content that belongs to one content class is selected. This can be a one-to-one selection. However, a content class can also contain content pieces of different levels, e.g. a content class 'Relevant' contains content pieces the XML level attributes of which are equal to 'Essential', 'Important' and 'Relevant'. Therefore, those content pieces of the same level that belong to several classes have to be stored only once.

Finally, in order to obtain the content that has to be delivered to the user's mobile device, a mapping between a content class and the device class has to be carried out. In the easiest case, one content class is mapped onto one device class.

In regards to multimedia assets, this mapping has to take care of the possible media formats supported by the mobile device, e.g. for image vector-based media formats are the best solution because they can be scaled without loss of quality, SVG (Scalable Vector Graphics). Unfortunately in most cases such media formats are not supported by low end devices. In order to display such a media format on a low end device, a media format conversion has to be performed at server side. The output of such a conversion has to be a media format that is supported by the corresponding device, e.g. JPEG. Although a conversion has to be performed to present vector based media formats on most of the devices, these formats are preferable. The reason is that such a format can be scaled without quality loss and afterwards the conversion to a pixel based format (GIF, JPEG, etc.) can be performed. This way the resulting quality will be higher compared to a scaling process of pixel based formats. It must be pointed out that scaling often happens additionally on mobile devices in order to adjust the media to the screen. But scaling such material may have dangerous side effects. For example, thin lines can disappear in a scaled down image. To avoid an unpredictable scaling on a mobile device, pixel based format has to be adequately "pre-scaled" by ICAT according to the device class.

As a consequence, the discussed approach is not an adaptation process where only layout information is transformed into a device supported form. The adaptation process can additionally change the amount and form of the content. The process of content reduction always includes a certain kind of threat. However, in contrast to other automated processes, the reduction of content is defined by the author and content developer. An interesting aspect at this point is the possibility to extent the content adaptation process by including user preferences and user settings. It is therefore an adaptation process that optimises according to a combination of device capabilities and user preferences (Figure 9).

As an example: The processing of the generalised content and the transformation into different result set formats (e.g. XHTML MP and PDF) can be realised by the web server tier (Figure 10). Different XSLT style-sheets are used for dynamic generation of XHTML MP and PDF, respectively.

The benefits of the authoring process are as follows:

- Flexibility and portability of information is guaranteed by using XML format.
- Only one additional attribute within XML tags - the level attribute – is necessary.
- The author is able to arrange the content in a hierarchical manner. However the author does not need to know anything about device capabilities.

Figure 9. Device classification process

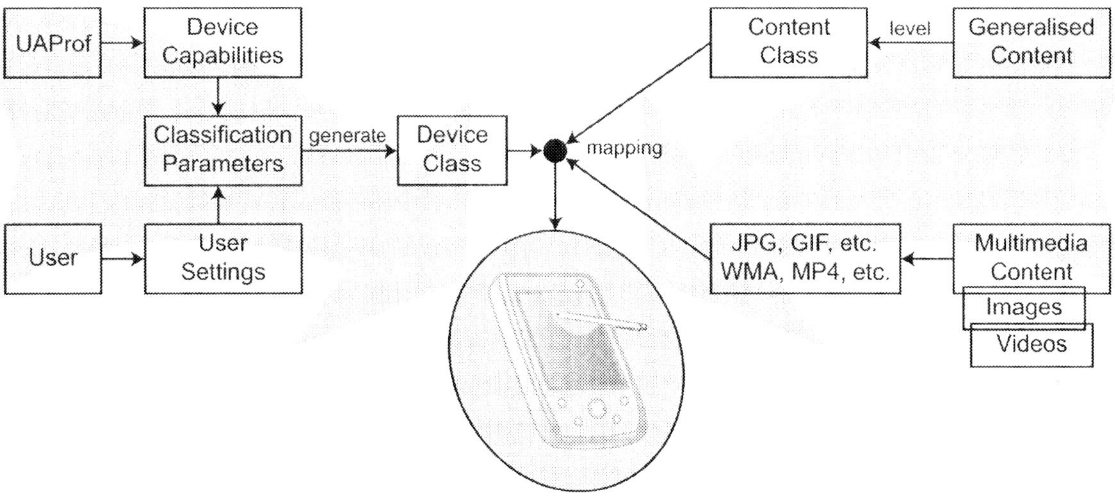

Figure 10. Generation of different output formats

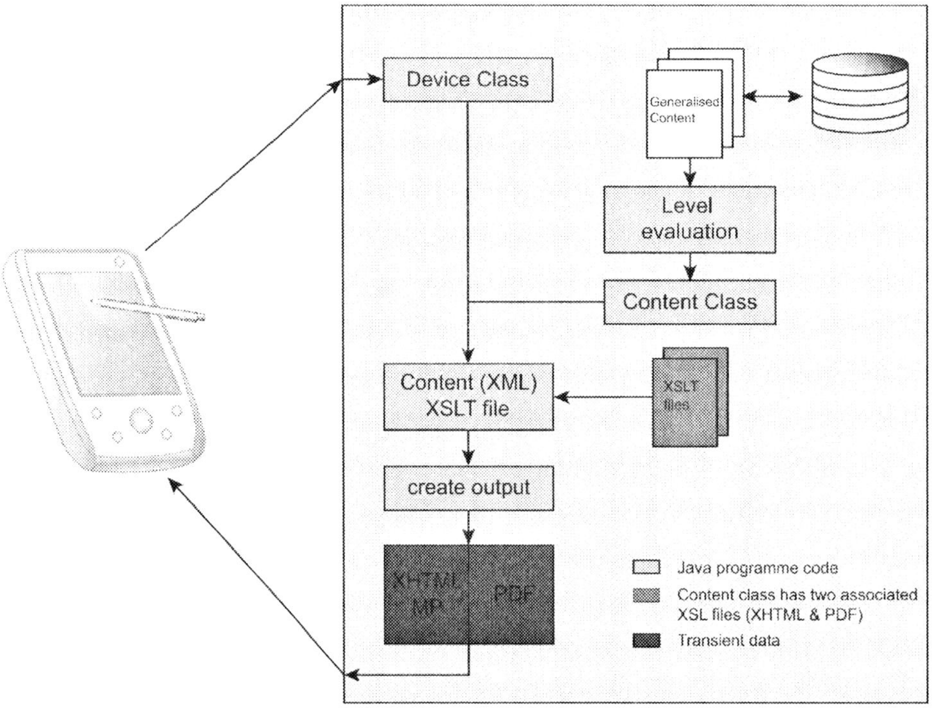

Essential information is included in all the result sets, i.e. tagged with a level that is always included in the result set. All supplementary information is added to this content incrementally. The next sub-chapter explains this authoring process.

Design Patterns

The XML based data storage allows the author to classify their content according to the importance of the content and not according to different devices. Usually authors tend to generate their learning material for PC and laptop usage and later on strip it down to adjust the content to lower end devices. As a result, content may become incomprehensible and nearly unreadable. Furthermore, cutting down content important relationships may be lost.

In ICAT content, which is less important, can be omitted on lower end devices without losing the relations of the learning content because the author has to start with the essential learning content (Figure 11). This information has to be presented on all devices, either on mobile phones or on high end personal computer.

In the next steps, the author can add further learning content. That additional information has to be tagged (e.g. level: important, relevant or optional, Figure 11). Thus, the author ensures that the learning content stays comprehensive on low end devices because the essential content is transmitted. In order to omit that, the same content is stored multiple times, a less important content class also contains the information of all the more important content classes (e.g. content class 'Relevant' includes content of content class 'Important' and 'Essential').

Indeed, the system evaluates which content class fits best to a device class, though the system does not automatically decide on the importance of the content. Specifying the level attribute remains the author's task (and has to remain).

Categorising text into different content classes is not problematic but is time consuming. A problem can occur with other media formats like images, sounds and videos. It cannot be guaranteed that all mobile devices are able to present all media formats. Consequently, media formats have to be used with care especially if the learning content is highly important (e.g. content of level 'Essential').

TECHNICAL IMPLEMENTATION OF THE ICAT SYSTEM

The current ICAT system is a four-tier software architecture, actualised with a MySQL database and the Tomcat Servlet Engine. The Web-server tier functions with JSP (Java Server Pages) and the logic-tier with JavaBeans. The web-server tier handles the request from the client and the

Figure 11. Content classification

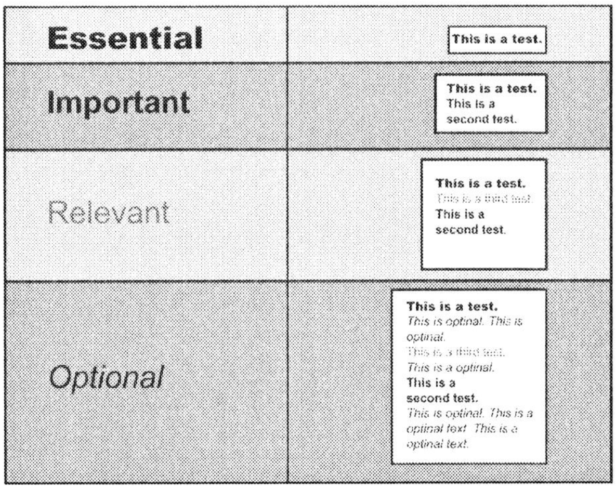

response to the client. The logic tier implements the MVC (Model View Controller) concept. The Controller implements the device identification and classification, collects data and updates the data in the model. The view assembles the output for the connected client according to the device classification and the data available in the model.

The output for Web browsers (PC based systems) is HTML or PDF and for micro browsers (mobile devices) it is XHTML-MP. For PC based systems, additional information can be exchanged via Applets and content is dynamically modified via Ajax. The Applets and Ajax functions are accessing the data via (simple) SOAP. For mobile devices, it is possible to download additional MIDlets in order to access more information. In contrast to Applets and Ajax, the MIDets can not be seamlessly integrated into the XHTML-MP output. Therefore, it is important that MIDlets only access optional information.

Device Identification

The ICAT system identifies the connected device via the UAProf (see Figure 5 and Figure 6). The current version of the ICAT system can only extract little information, as follow:

- Phone name (Vendor and model)
- Image type (gif, jpeg, wbmp, etc.)
- Screen resolution and type (colour or monochrome)
- Supported network bearers (GSM, GPRS, HSCSD, UMTS)

The current version extracts this information via a simple Java parser class. The future version will use the DELI framework to parse all information existing in the UAProf. In case the user visits the web page for the first time, detected via Cookie and/or after login, the user is ask about his/her tariff model (flat rate, volume flat rate, time rate). This information is stored in the Java device class. In the case the phone is already known (Vendor/model), the information of the device is retrieved from the database, otherwise the UAProf has to be downloaded and needs to be parsed.

Device Classification

The device classification is performed with the help of the information stored in the Java device class. This information of the Java device class is a subset of the device capabilities of the real device. The current ICAT system uses seven different classes (Figure 7). The device class one defaults to PC based browsers, where as device class two to class seven are for mobile devices. The classification of the device depends currently only on the visual capability (screen resolution/colour) and on the network capability (tariff model/bearer technology). While the visual capability is easy to evaluate, the network capability is problematic. Although it is possible to detect the bearer technology the device can handle, we can not reliably detect which bearer technology is used. For example, a device which has the capability to connect over a UMTS network may be connected via a slower GPRS connection because UMTS is currently unavailable or the users' contract does not allow UMTS connection. On the other hand, a user can be connected via UMTS but due to network overload, the current bandwidth is much lower. Therefore, we decided the more important factor in the ICAT system is tariff model.

In a simplified way, the classification can be performed by first evaluating the network capability. In the case the user uses a flat rate; his/her device is in class two, three or four. In the case he/she has a volume or time rate, his/her device is in class five, six or seven. Devices with a screen resolution equal or higher to 300 pixels are in class two or four, between 120 and 300 pixels in class three or six. Devices with a screen resolution lower than 120 pixels are in class four or seven. Merging visual and network capabilities results in the following device classes (Table 1).

Table 1. Definition of the device classes for the implemented ICAT system

Device class	2	3	4	5	6	7
network	flat	flat	flat	volume/time	volume/time	volume/time
screen	>= 300 px	< 300 px >=120 px	< 120 px	>= 300 px	< 300 px >=120 px	< 120 px

The first results show that this approach is working well and fits into mobile learning needs. It is easy for an author of mobile learning content to distinguish this low number of different content importance. It takes into account that mobile learning material is typically based on text with short sentences and small figures. It uses technologies that are available on typical mobile devices used in learning and business environments.

Nevertheless, the relatively hard decision and the low number of capabilities taken into account results in same case in an insufficient adapted content generation. Therefore, the future version of the ICAT system will take more capabilities into account and make softer decisions. As a consequence, there will be more device classes.

Content Adaptation

The adaptation of the content is done with the help of the device class. The generalised XML content is stored in a tree structure, where a tree can have one or more XML content items or another XML tree element. A XML item element contains additional information like level, media type and media format, besides the content. Together with device class, the content elements can be selected from the XML items. For example, if a device has the level three, all XML items are selected with a level higher or equal to three. This is done because often mobile learning material can be structured in a hierarchical manner. The most important content must be known; some content is just for repetition or for further interest. The inclusion of appropriate levels starting with the most important essentials (see sub-chapter "Design Pattern") reflects this. The resulting items are transformed into XHTML. The Java device presentation class is collecting the data and coordinating the needed operation. As well, this class performs with the help of a media transformer class (*MediaTransform*), the transformation and or adaptation of media formats. For example, a TIFF image can be transformed into a JPEG image that will be scaled down to a reasonable size. A reasonable size of the images is achieved if the resulting pixel size is smaller than the mobile device maximum pixel resolution. The importance of such an image adaptation is shown in Figure 1 and 2.

ICAT System Implementation

The following class diagram is a stripped down version of the real system (Figure 12). The class diagram shows the most important classes and relations. The central class is the *DevicePresentation* class. This class evaluates the client request and requests the device identification via the *CoreOperation* and the *MobileDevice* class. The content is handled as a XML tree structure via the *XMLTree* class. The *DevicePresentation* class generates the client output by filtering the XML tree structure according to the content level and the supported media formats. In case of unsupported media, a conversion of the media is performed by the *MediaTransform* class. This class is additionally responsible for media adaptation (ex. Scaling of images).

Figure 12. Stripped down class diagram of ICAT system

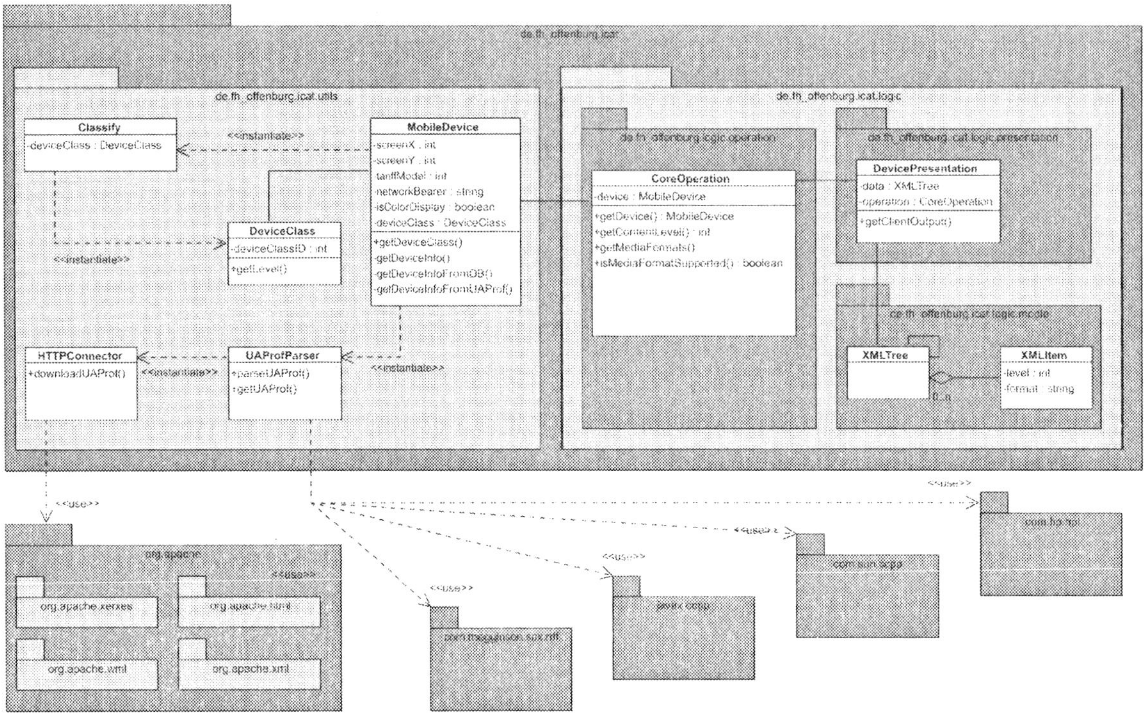

COMPARISON W3C, WURF, ICAT

The W3C has no common concept and/or system. They provide for each task only drafts or best practice guides. Each of the 3 tasks is discussed in different working groups, which makes it difficult to develop an overall concept. Nevertheless, they are aware of that problem, the importance of mobile web and an adaptation to mobile devices.

The WURFL project has a long history and therefore much knowledge on device identification and adaptation is already known. This project (claims to) has the biggest device database and therefore it is able to handle almost all devices. It has support for a lot of different languages (PHP, Java, Perl, Ruby, Python, dotNet and C++) and is relatively easy to use if the developer has at least basic knowledge in the targeted programming language. A content provider can specify according to device capabilities if a feature should be displayed or not. The possibility to automatically adapt generalised content (ex. XML) is not possible.

The ICAT system is a research project from the University of Applied Science Offenburg. The system was originally designed to access an on-line simulation tool with mobile devices. Nowadays the system is improved and extended with a focus on a mobile learning system. Due to the research project's history, the system uses the new UAProf possibility to perform the device identification. The device classification is actualised by isolating the important device capabilities. An important goal from this project is to be able to adapt generalised content on base of the system identified device information. This way an author does not need to have programming skills or to learn a new meta language to develop content. The authors can concentrate on content and the didactic; the device adaptation is done by the system. Due to

Table 2. Comparison of the W3C-, WRUFL/WALL- and ICAT- concept

	W3C	WURFL/WALL	ICAT
Overall concept for identification, classification & adaptation	No	Yes	Yes
Used programming language	Java (DELI)	PHP, Java, Perl, Ruby, Python, dotNet and C++	Java
Identification correctness	Limited to UAProf	Almost all (over 7000 devices)	Limited to UAProf
Device Classification	No, only guide (Mobile Web, 2008)	Inherited groups	Device class
Concept of generalised content adaptation	No Draft (DIAL)	Partially (adaptation according capability via WALL)	Yes Mapping of device class and content class
Difficult to setup (Basic knowledge in PHP and/or Java available)	No system available	Low/medium	Medium/high
Use only parts of the system	Yes only libraries available	Yes	No

the complexity of ICAT, it is not possible to use only parts of the system (except the internally used free available libraries like DELI).

CONCLUSION

The realisation of a mobile learning system has to take into account different devices in order to produce an optimised content presentation and therefore support the learning process on PCs and laptops as well as on mobile devices best. In the previous sub-chapters, different approaches with different ideas were discussed. All of these systems have advantages but as well disadvantages. In order to help the reader to rate these systems a short summary with advantages and disadvantages for every system will be given.

The strength of the WURFL/WALL project is the big device database. It contains, more than 7,000 different devices according maintainer (Luca Passani, 2006). This high number is explainable by the fact that any firmware or software subversion is considered as a new device. This project supports old or older mobile devices very well. As a result of the early start of the WURFL/WALL project in 2001, it supports as output format, besides XHTML and CHTML, the older WML format. Another advantage is the availability of libraries and tools in different languages. Besides the strongly supported Java and PHP tools, there are at least basic libraries and functionalities available for Perl, Ruby, Python, dotNet and C++. The device database, as well as the libraries, is available without licence fees under different open source licences. Device information can be overwritten or added by applying so called patch files. The WURFL database is maintained mainly by Luca Passiani. In the case that device information is not be up-to-date, they can be corrected by patch files.

Classification of mobile devices is possible with the WURFL framework; nonetheless there is no concept of mapping device classes and related content classes.

The lack of such classification mechanisms requires extensive technical background knowledge for authors. Even though WURFL provides very extensive device recognition functionality, it is together with WALL that it does not take into account any other parameters for the adaptation process.

WALL and WURFL are a perfect solution to transform content into a device supported format. Nevertheless, this combination is not able to perform a higher level abstraction.

The most important advantages of the UAProf are the future-proof implementation, the fact being an official accepted standard and the wide support by the device manufacturers. The UAProf that implements the CC/PP profile is maintained and stored by the device manufacturer. Thus, information of newly available mobile devices can be obtained, in best case even before they are on the market. The information stored in the UAProf can be accessed by the open source library DELI. Unfortunately there exists only a Java implementation of the library. No other framework in any other programming language is available. There is no global database available that stores the UAProf information.

The W3C has shown the awareness of the need for a device classification concept. Nevertheless, there are neither drafts nor any implementations available.

The W3C approach DIAL, realises device dependent content adaptation, is based on well known and proven standards and mechanisms. DIAL is a client side based approach with the advantage that no device identification is needed because the capabilities of device are mapped into the software on the mobile device itself. A disadvantage is that content is transmitted to the mobile device, which may not be supported by the device. Additionally, authors and content providers do not have any possibility to influence the adaptation process.

The ICAT framework uses the UAProf for the detection of the device capabilities. Thus the detection progress has the same advantages and limitations. A local database is used, which additionally caches the device information. In this way, the problem of old, and by the UAProf unknown, mobile devices could be solved too. This approach is similar to the patch file functionality of the WURF project.

The main distinguishing feature of ICAT is the device classification progress and the mapping between the content class and the device class. As classification parameters, the system can take into account user settings in addition to the mobile device capabilities too. Thus, the device classification will include a personalisation process. The tagged content pieces stored in valid and well-formatted XML will be transformed with the help of the device class into the result set. Further, the mapping process takes care of delivering only such multimedia formats to the client that is supported by the mobile device. Otherwise a conversion into a format supported by the mobile device will be performed.

With the help of content adaptation, e.g. done by ICAT, mobile learners with varying devices can be supported well. This is important for the wide spread of mobile learning and for its different scenarios of the didactical meaningful implementation and at the same time for its cost efficiency.

REFERENCES

W3C Semantic Web Activity/Resource Description Framework (RDF). (2004). Retrieved from http://www.w3.org/RDF/

Ally, M., Lin, F., McGreal, R., & Woo, B. (2005). *An intelligent agent for adapting and delivering electronic course materials to mobile learners*. Retrieved from http://www.mlearn.org.za/CD/papers/Ally-an intelligent.pdf

Compact HTML for Small Information Appliances. Retrieved on February 9, 1998, from http://www.w3.org/TR/1998/NOTE-compactHTML-19980209/

Composite Capabilities/Preference Profiles Retrieved on October 25, 2007, from http://www.w3.org/Mobile/CCPP/

Device Independent Authoring Language (DIAL). (2007). Retrieved from http://www.w3.org/TR/dial/

Document Management-Part 1: PDF 1.7: ISO 32000-1:2008. Retrieved from http://www.iso.org/iso/iso_catalogue/catalogue_tc/catalogue_detail.htm?csnumber=51502

Feisst, M., Santos, D., Mitic, J., & Christ, A. (2005). *Adaptive heterogeneous learning system, mLearn2005*. Retrieved from http://www.mlearn.org.za/CD/papers/Feist.pdf

Gaedke, M., Beigl, M., Gellersen, H.-W., & Segor, C. (1998). *Web content delivery to heterogeneous mobile platforms*. University of Karlsruhe. Retrieved from http://www.teco.edu/~gaedke/paper/1998-lncs1552.pdf

HTML 4.01 Specification. Retrieved on December 24, 1999, from http://www.w3.org/TR/html401/

Language, E. M. (XML) 1.0, 16. Retrieved in August 2006, from http://www.w3.org/TR/xml/

Language, E. S. (XSL) Version 1.1.5. Retrieved in December 2006, from http://www.w3.org/TR/xsl11/

Mobile Web Application Best Practices. Retrieved on July 29, 2008, from http://www.w3.org/TR/mwabp/#bp-devcap-classify

OASIS UDDI Specifications TC–Committee Specifications. Retrieved from http://www.oasis-open.org/committees/uddi-spec/doc/tcspecs.htm

Omari, R. (2006). *A SW module for mobile device content delivery*. Master thesis, University of Applied Sciences Offenburg. Web Services Description Language (WSDL) Version 2.0 Part 0: Primer. Retrieved on June 26, 2007, from http://www.w3.org/TR/wsdl20-primer/

Passani, L. (2006). *DDR Workshop WURFL, WALL and the Community of Mobile Developers*. Retrieved from http://www.w3.org/2005/MWI/DDWG/workshop2006/presentations/WURFL/WURFLandWALL.pdf

Schema Part, X. M. L. 0. Retrieved on October 28, 2004, from http://www.w3.org/TR/xmlschema-0/

XHTML 1.0 Recommendation. Retrieved on January 26, 2000, from http://www.w3.org/TR/xhtml1/

XHTML Mobile Profile. Retrieved on October 29, 2001, from http://www.openmobilealliance.org/tech/affiliates/wap/wap-277-xhtmlmp-20011029-a.pdf

Chapter 5
A Ubiquitous and Pervasive Learning Framework:
Linking the Learner, the Workplace, and the Education Institute

Rodger Carroll
Chisholm Institute and Victoria University, Australia

ABSTRACT

This chapter reports on a learning architecture adopting ubiquity and pervasiveness to support communities of learning practice. The research focused on mobile devices that are capable of voice, text, video/photo interactions, and Web access, and how this can cater for the preferred learning styles of the learners while supporting the workplace learning and the educational environment. The research utilised mobile technology for planned and unplanned learning situations via its capability to send and receive multimedia files, Web objects, and live broadcasting. The information and objects created and gathered using mobile technology are in a digital format. This approach allows for customisation and flexible transferability to future intended audiences, planned learning and assessment activities, and workplace learning activities providing an engaging, learner created platform for the mobile generation.

INTRODUCTION

Parents place pressures on their young in regard to individual achievement. They provide televisions and playback devices in their bedrooms, removing them from the communications and the learning that comes from within the family unit. They provide multiple personal technologies such as hand held game stations so they can amuse themselves. You may not even know what music they are listening to any more, thanks to personal music players.

The young of today may be having unsupervised, unmonitored communications with strangers via the Internet, regardless of the dangers. The need that they be contactable in case of an emergency at any time and anywhere, has unwittingly promoted a youth culture with no concern for socially acceptable times of communications.

This has created a generation where individuality is the norm. From their early years we are training young people to be independent in the ways they amuse themselves, socialise and communicate.

DOI: 10.4018/978-1-60566-882-6.ch005

The youth of today are the consumers of our generation's technological revolution backed by investors demanding higher dividends and a bigger share of the market. This has resulted in aggressive marketing tactics aimed at our youth.

Expecting this new "mobile generation" to learn as passive receptors, sitting in rows, learning by rote, and preparing for an exam that may determine career choice, as once was the case, may result in disengagement from the learning process. Traditional educational communication is facing extinction unless we are prepared to adopt the communications media utilised by our youth. If we recognise issues within this generation, then imagine how removed education will be to the next generation if we fail to change practices now.

A convergence of technology has created a society who can access unlimited forms of information, allowing for contextual and relevant content choices to be in the hands of the learner. This generation is in a transitional stage from being the digital generation to the Ubiquitous Generation, driven by the need for content regardless of time or place, with a new paradigm being driven by personalisation, self created content and self publishing. This attraction to self created content and self publishing is evident by the uptake of Web 2.0 technologies such as YouTube and the variety of personal blogs and wikis. The learning architecture presented in this chapter is considerate of available technologies and a self publishing society.

BACKGROUND

In 1984 John Goodlad wrote about the implications of education and schooling in regard to the youth culture of the time. He talks of a generation preoccupied with itself and made up of individuals less influenced by the home, religion and school. These writings bear resemblance to the youth of today and raise the same question that Goodlad (1984) asked. Is school relevant to this new generation?

Comparisons can be made between the changes affecting schooling back in 1984 and the changes affecting our society at present. We have gone through an immense technological advancement over the last 10 years and are now faced with a society that is no longer in awe of wizardry and gimmicky efforts to engage them. In education today, we can run a class with learners accessing the class from anywhere in the world utilising synchronous communications, application sharing, web tours and collaborative editing, something that was only dreamed about in 1984.

Technology Triggering a Generational Divide

Jukes (2005) sees our schools as reflecting our past, our values, our thinking and not reflecting the reality of the world as it is. He believes if we can't connect with our children and build relationships with them by understanding their learning and communication practices and applying this understanding in the classroom, we have no hope of increasing student achievement, and risk creating a disconnect between the digital native and the school.

Tracey (2004) informs us that this age of technology has limited the exposure of expectations of society in terms of social protocol. The previous social and physical barriers of connectivity have been broken down by the always reachable mindset of young users of this technology as Aakhus & Katz 2002 in Tracey (2004) comment, the taking of calls in a public domain is quite the norm for young people and that such behaviour privatises public spaces.

The Australian Psychological Society (APS) conducted a report on the psychological aspects of mobile phone use among adolescents in Australia. The paper looked at areas such as how mobile phones contribute to the development of social relationships.

The report found that 47% of adolescents who did not have a mobile phone reported feeling left out of social interactions. Not surprisingly, given that communication is the catalyst of the social engagement, 27% of adolescents say that having a mobile phone has improved their friendships. These adolescents were more at ease with this communication method than they were in a face to face environment. This indicates that adolescents feel more confident in utilising a text messaging system for communications (A.P.S, 2004).

As mobile phones have been described as intimate devices, capable of creating social networks and aiding in the development of this new generation, what effect will the delivery of course content have? Attewell (2005) informs us that offering services to someone's mobile phone may encroach on their personal space. Educators should investigate the impact of a ubiquitous intervention prior to implementation.

Jukes (2005) claims many of us are digital immigrants, struggling to deal with changing technologies in a different world than the one that we grew up in, while this generation, the digital natives, interact with information and communication in different ways than the previous generations. It is because of this interaction with information and communication technology that this new generation learn differently. This makes this generation more assertive information seekers and shapes how they approach learning in the classroom. The use of the Internet and indeed the mobile Internet has created a generation with a need for immediate, quick access to information and has built an expectation of immediate answers. This generation will not tolerate delayed feedback. This is described as twitch speed (Jukes, 2005, Barnes, Maratao, & Ferris, 2007).

Oblinger and Hagner (cited in Barnes et al., 2007) observe that digital age students are bored with traditional learning methods and have a desire for varied forms of communication. Glenn (cited in Barnes et al., 2007) notes that to create personally meaningful learning experiences, this generation prefers interactive environments and self-directed activities.

Jukes (2005) calls them digital kids living in a visual world where they are completely comfortable with the bombardment of simultaneous images, texts and sounds as they provide relevant and compelling experiences. This fits with their preference for multitasking where they can be listening to music while doing their homework, while talking on the phone while having the Internet chat line open on the computer, replacing what we did in the park or on the street, where we gained our social experiences (Jukes, 2005). It's as if they learn from peripheral vision, absorbing all that is around them, unlike the older generation, who were taught to sit straight and focus on one thing, generally the teacher or the blackboard.

A quick test of this theory was the purchase of a new smart phone. A digital immigrant makes sure to follow the printed manual that comes with the phone, familiarising himself with the basic features and being careful to do everything in order as dictated in the manual. In comparison, a 14-year-old child, who has a basic mobile phone, had no problem navigating and mastering the features of my new phone with no access to the manual or instruction from others. She can take photos and video, surf the Web, and send multimedia messages, text messages and digital audio files within ten minutes of being given the phone.

What were the clear differences? The digital immigrant studied the phone, studied the manual, analysed the information and bundled it into a sequence that I can understand. The 14-year-old child however experimented without long analysis and learnt as she went. Was this a presentation of what Barnes et al., (2007) describes in their research, that the net generation lack critical thinking skills? Or is it that we focus too greatly on the one single goal, while the new generation learn from all the interceptions on their journey to the same goal? Or is this a high level of confidence that comes with digital literacy?

It is not just technology that has created a different learner; it is also the changing pressures on families.

Jukes (2005) presents statistical representations of the differences of the family unit. They state that parents today spend 40% less time with their children than parents did 30 years ago. That 64% of kids come home from school to an empty house because their parents or the only parent are at work. That kids of today watch more than 25 hours of television each week. Also 62% of school-age kids have TV sets in their own bedroom, and 82% of kids play video games on a regular basis.

We live in an age where 28% of families are led by a single parent. In 68% of American homes, the only parent or both parents work in order to survive (Jukes, 2005).

Baby Boomers, a Retiring Workforce

There is an emphasis on lifestyle factors within the Australian workforce, whether in the adolescent years or in early retirement. Vast numbers of early retirees are craving a lost teenage and have now created the opportunity to re-live those years. While the new adolescents are not prepared to let go of these carefree times, the adolescent years now span from 13 to 30 years old. This has resulted in a reduction of adult income generating years, possibly as a result of an inheritance mindset. This generation will inherit the wealth of the past generation, leading to a relaxed lifestyle (Salt, 2007).

With a vast majority of baby boomers reaching retirement age, we are faced with a critical workforce shortage. This current school generation will benefit from a supply and demand environment, with them in the demand sector. They will be educated, opportunistic and global (Salt, 2007).

Australia is witnessing a rise in population shifting to coastal areas and the hills surrounding them, removed from the large city. This demographic shift of population, aided by technology, has provided the mobility to work from any where; this is referred to as telecommuting, an ability to successfully work from home. Although this has also removed them from the infrastructure embedded within the large city, in particular the learning infrastructure (Salt, 2007).

A diminishing workforce creates a need to provide fast solutions to training and education needs. Recognition of prior formal learning, informal learning and workplace learning will become a driver in Education and Training as a valid pathway to qualification.

Informal and Workplace Learning

The word 'informal' in learning, implies the learning is of no value. That learning needs to be formal in order to be recognized. Yet many organisations recruit on the basis of not only qualifications but substantiated experience in the field, often requiring referee verification. This experience is given some measure of credit and the employers recognize that qualification alone is not enough.

Eraut (2004) discusses informal learning in the workplace as a non-planned event that occurs as a result of formal working activities. It is important to understand that learning is not a given in participating in a social working environment. It is the individual who subscribes to participate and at what depth, therefore determining what learning or value of learning is derived from the experience (Billett, 2004).

Educational Institutes create a simulated workplace environment to carry out holistic, project based assessments of competencies. The teacher observes the interaction between the learners, how they communicate to solve problems and identify issues relative to the task, for example; safety, materials required, team organisation and task organisation. The focus is on carrying out the task to an industry standard with the learning being a combination of collaborative group work, individual task with the added inclusion of peer guidance and review, with the teacher in a guiding, facilitating mode.

Within this environment it is the learning that is structured, with the task, or work, being the vehicle to learning and assessment. The problem is the transfer and the application of this knowledge to the workplace (Jorgensen, 2004).

In a workplace environment the predominant focus is on the work. The end product of the task is for the intended client, with the employer having a contractual agreement to complete the work within the required time frame and price. This is the environment that Eraut (2004) describes as formal work activities and one that Jorgensen (2004) talks of as a production workforce with the work being the vehicle to income and further employment. This production focus produces a business only interested in education that has a direct and immediate effect on its workforce. This however, could lead to part of the workforce obtaining only limited skills at carrying out specific tasks.

The factors that link between work experiences and learning in the workplace can be described as implicit learning, reactive learning and deliberative learning. Implicit learning being experience unconsciously entering the action of work, Reactive learning is a brief conscious reflection on the past experiences, and deliberative learning is a planned, deliberative, review of past actions (Eraut, 2004). All of these factors aid in problem solving abilities and follow a similar link to Blooms taxonomy in relation to high level skills of synthesis, and evaluation. The product becomes new knowledge available for others at the lower level of Blooms taxonomy, the new entrants of the workplace.

The difficulty facing educational institutes in relation to the recognition of informal learning in the workplace lies in the assessment. In a simulated environment the teacher is present, observing, guiding, assessing and ultimately validating and recording the achievements of the individuals.

In the workplace however this does not occur, or it occurs with less frequency, to a standard set by the employer which may not be in line with national qualification standards and the observations carried out by a supervisor or employer who may lack the required assessor qualifications.

Jorgensen (2004) discusses three players in Vocational Education and Training.

- The Education Institute is to deliver theoretical knowledge and a production rationale based on the needs for useful skills in the workplace.
- The employer expects the training and education to support the business aims, the business development and business efficiency.
- And the student expects to be able to use the skills and knowledge gained in the Education Institute in their working life.

All three elements need to be synchronised in order to achieve the same goal.

Jorgensen (2004) presents a fourth proposition that training and education be personal, based on the learners individual learning and development requirements. The new generation of learners will not engage with education that is relevant to the curriculum or relevant to the businesses in which they are employed. They prefer education and training that is centred on their personal motivation and personal development.

This is relevant to an education system that has had a focus on individuality, in order to lower the dropout rate and ensure engagement in lifelong learning.

The world is in a time of Industry led training systems that focus on the skills needed in the workplace. This has resulted in industry demanding a more differentiated and flexible workplace training and assessment method. These demands for customisation are bringing about new and intensified professional, technical and educational roles for Education providers (Mitchell &Young, 2005).

The gap is widening between the many skills that the businesses expect from the employees and the skills that the employees are able to develop at work. It is because of this that Jorgensen claims learning outside of the workplace has grown even more important (Jorgensen 2004).

Where industry demand for localised training and assessment is combined with the technical and cultural differences between generations, there is need to find a way to engage the learners and provide not only the skills to carry out a task, but also the lifelong learning skills that will foster further development of the learners in the future.

Population Acceptance of Ubiquitous Technology

The issue of technology division is recurring, not at a time of the technological breakthrough, but at a time of technological saturation when that technology becomes embedded in people's working and private lives. Mobile technologies have reached saturation point with mobile penetration in many countries near 100%, and the systems requirements are relatively inexpensive thus creating a climate for knowledge distribution whether by social means or education availability that was once inaccessible.

Near the end of 2006, Australia had more than 20 million registered mobile phone accounts. (Australian Mobile Data, 2006a) This is nearly equal to Australia's total population of 20,811,855 as reported by the Australian Bureau of Statistics (2007) at 10.00am on the 27th April 2007.

With the market forecasting a further 2 million contacts to be realised within a further two years (Australian Mobile Data, 2006a), we can conclude that mobile usage within Australia is indeed at saturation point. The Australian adoption of the mobile phone reflects in the total number of text messages being sent in a twelve month period between 2005 and 2006 at greater than 8 billion (Australian Mobile Data, 2006b).

In comparison, England sent 48.1 billion text messages in 2006, with 205 million recorded on Christmas Day, an average of 8 million an hour. The USA averages over 1.6 billion SMS messages per day, leading to a worldwide total of over 2.3 trillion SMS messages sent annually (Text. it. 2007). This is an indicator of how mobile phone users have accepted SMS as a communication medium.

Mobile phone enhancements and applications have developed with photo/video ability, web access, live TV, live video calls, email, and the ability to send, receive and edit office documents such as power point, excel and word documents. Telecommunication businesses have invested heavily in the development of such networks, allowing an opportunity to explore an educational application.

The continued investment and increased customer usage of mobile applications is a strong indicator that education based around mobile communications will be sustainable.

With price becoming more affordable and increasing utility, Prensky (2004) concludes that all students will have a mobile phone, in the not too distant future.

A survey of Southern Institute (pseudonym) Building studies students in 2007 found that a ratio of 1: 220 did not own a mobile phone, with over 95% reporting their phones have cameras and web access. Attewell (2005) reinforces this by reporting more camera phones sold than digital cameras in 2003 when 84 million camera phones were purchased.

A MOBILE LEARNING ARCHITECTURE: UBIQUITOUS TECHNOLOGY PROVIDING AN EDUCATIONAL SOLUTION

Educators could utilise mobile technology to enhance the interactions of the education process and therefore have an increased expectation of catering to the varied learning styles of our students. This age cohort is already engaged with mobile phones, therefore usage of mobile devices for education will inherently have client engagement. Attewell (2005) reports on a project using mobile phones to deliver language courses to learners who had already dropped out of education or were at risk of dropping out of education. 89% of these learners had literacy or numeracy needs while 32 were homeless and 80% of the learners were unemployed.

The key finding of this project was the re-engagement with learning, with 62% of the participants expressing an interest in taking part in future learning after trying mobile learning.

Project observers reported the participants having a more positive attitude towards reading and that the participants are remarkably focused and calm spending up to two hours in a session although this focus may be due to the novelty of using mobile devices (Attewell, 2005).

Barnes et al., (2007) suggest that educators can best serve the needs of net generation learners and meet teaching goals by modifying pedagogies to accommodate their need for independence and autonomy in learning.

As Dr Elizabeth Hartnell-Young from the University of Nottingham found, the mobile phone that includes video, camera, voice recorders and other software is a perfect fit for creating e-portfolios. These e-portfolios are a repository of information about the student's learning and achievement, a tool to allow students to demonstrate understanding and skills in multiple ways, a tool for students to reflect on their learning and their learning style and a tool for planning future learning and career pathways. Mobile devices allow video, images and messages to be created at any time the need arises and can be sent directly to a blog for sharing with others or uploaded to a PC for digital archiving. (Hartnell-Young, E., 2004).

The outcomes of the projects reinforce the suggestion that mobile technologies can enhance the learning environment and result in engagement or re-engagement of the learner. This new technology will emphasise two-way communication among students themselves or between students and teachers as useful in helping students achieve higher order objectives. Learner access to information far exceeds the access afforded to learners in the past. Technology has created opportunities for the learner to experience new and varied teaching styles (Gulliver, Randall, & Pok, 1999). This technology could allow the teacher to be more creative and imaginative in providing an environment to support the cognitive development of the students.

Implementing Ubiquitous Technology in the Education Domain

The use of a Moblog, which is similar to a blog or journal but is also accessible via mobile device, was chosen to provide opportunities for continuing social interaction, advice and validation. This was trialled with a group of 15 year old learners remote from the Institute. The inclusion of mobile camera phones and the uptake of our teen students in camera phone ownership further validated the set up of a Moblog. With camera phones commonplace, the opportunity to capture special moments and events and post them on the Moblog for a select few or even a public view has grown considerably.

Exhaustive research led to the selection of a suitable platform. This had a rating of PG 13 years, suitable for education purposes. Many other platforms are not suitable as some content would be deemed undesirable. This content is what other parties would enter on their Moblog and be easily accessible via internal search engines.

The platform allowed for picture postings, video postings, digital sound files and even short text postings. The Moblog had a comment platform in which the learners or facilitator could respond or add comment and continuing comment to a posting.

The Moblog was used to create a positive social environment with the freedom to post whatever the students feel is important to them, be it a new surfboard, motorbike, music they like and so on. This then allows others with similar interests to add comment, therefore building relationships and creating a more social environment. This enhanced social environment creates an inviting educational atmosphere, resulting in greater participation and greater engagement.

The inclusion of a Moblog to enable flexible, mobile access for these students and even their families allowed acknowledgement of student achievements, and gave friends and family an insight into the students Vocational Education environment. It is hoped this exposure of the Institute to the broader community will spread a positive Institute experience and provide future learners with the confidence to enter or re-enter the education and training environment with the likelihood that they will choose an Institute in which they have some knowledge about.

The tracking facility on the Moblog site recorded an average of 1,200 hits over 14 day cycles. This translated to 86 visits per day by the student cohort and allowed family and friends.

The student access is voluntary and most feel that the ability to see what others are doing and what interests them is of importance.

Part of the remote delivery to this student group, is an online component. This online access is afforded via a link from the Moblog to the course homepage on WebCT. The completion rate was extremely high, with all students successfully completing the course with an average of 160 visits to the formal learning site on WebCT.

The inclusion of the social Moblog became a driver to log on to the learning environment to see what the others are doing, and while logged on, the learners can then can access the formal learning content as well. The success of online delivery programs is reliant on the student's willingness to log in. The inclusion of class activities posted on the Moblog creates a sense of achievement in the students, providing new learners with pictures of what they will also be taking part in and creating a sense of belonging within the student group; an important sense of community.

The confidence and skills gained in communicating and posting are designed to be transferred to the formal learning environment where pictures, comments, discussion of learning materials, celebration of achievements can take place, encouraging reflection on the learning, giving ownership and acknowledging achievement.

The use of mobile technologies also provided exposure of the technology to the learners and teachers and created an environment that builds great value and supports lifelong learning.

A second project group of the Shopfitting and Aluminium Fabrication students commenced. In order to provide quality training delivery to a small group of learners with limited physical up to date resources, the use of mobile phones to support onsite delivery and assessment became a successful strategy in addressing the concern of providing costly specialist physical resources.

The Moblog platform provided for the inclusion of third party evidence. The third party evidence gained via the employer/supervisor videoing the student carrying out a task and adding audio commentary, overcome the need for written reports. Validation is also addressed via the visual image of the actual student doing the actual work. The image can be checked via student record photographs.

One of the strategies used was to have the students post one or two pictures per week from their mobile to the Moblog; just pictures of their everyday work life. This is important in validating the onsite assessed unit via the student's constant exposure to the task. For instance, a worker assembles aluminium windows and doors as his main work duty, so formal onsite assessments that address this field are validated by evidence of constant participation in such tasks.

The ability for the teacher, assessor, employers, students and even parents and friends to be able to visit this learning environment allows for social dialogue, recognition of employer input into training and acknowledgement of student achievements. This gives friends and family an insight into the student's work environment, with a greater understanding of the stresses and rewards of a career in this field. The average number of visits to the Moblog site was 92 per day.

An auditor may also visit the moblog as a means of validating assessment and learning strategies and outcomes.

The Moblog is able to be accessed via an internet connected computer or internet enabled mobile phone, providing anytime access to view photos and video, view comments, add comments, all in a mobile context. The cost of accessing the site is quite inexpensive at approximately 12 to 16 (AU) cents to open the page. Adding comment is a further 12 to 16 cents (AU).

The ability to add comment provides feedback to the student on their work processes and is shared collaboratively via fellow student access to picture and comment, giving added context to the written comment. All participants then learn from the one experience.

The inclusion of third parties in the learning and assessment process builds a closer relationship between the parties and the Institute, providing an opportunity to review and improve course design and course outcomes in line with Industry and Community requirements. This re-enforces the validity of training programs and supports assessment to real industry standards and not to a standard experienced years before.

The use of mobile phones to support onsite delivery and assessment provided a successful strategy to address the cost of adequate physical resources for a small group of students.

Employer/supervisor participation in the education process not only creates opportunities for the employer to be more involved and more aware of Institute based learning, but also provides the employer/supervisor with recognition of their role in the training. The employer/supervisor also gains by participative inclusion in the learning via enhanced ICT skills and digital literacy that will translate into a higher skilled workplace, meeting the challenges of an economy driven by innovation.

Including all parties in the learning process encourages reflective practice, collaborative practice and comparative practice, embedding an awareness of the competition. This enables self design and implementation of strategies to ensure productive growth and development.

Responding to a Self-Publishing Generation

The picture and video evidence created by a student or a group of students for assessment purposes can be self published by the students (with teacher approval) to the wider learning community, via an Institute resource library or blog. The project will allow for currency in learning resources constantly updated via student input and teacher validation. The validation is not only used as an assessment component but can be used to determine if a student is ready for a formal assessment.

The advanced student can move forward and commence the next phase of learning and assessment at their preferred pace giving flexibility within a workshop and project based environment. Student group work within the project allows for a collaborative environment, creating a learning environment where the students help and teach other students, creating greater learner responsibility, recognizing student input and achievement and promoting mutual respect.

A learning repository will not eliminate the need for individual tuition but will offer students a peer created resource at a level that is relative to their learning while providing the at risk student with more access to the teacher. This will meet the varied needs of our students who come to us with differing needs and styles. The struggling student can reinforce teacher instruction via access to the learning repository, gaining valuable insight into the task required. This utilises the digi-stories created for assessment purposes as a re-useable learning object.

Limiting student created learning objects to assessment purposes would be short sighted when addressing the need for student engagement and the concept of student created content. An initial phase of the project was to trial the hypothesis with a control group. An advanced group of students was chosen who were familiar with the Vocational environment. The students were broken into small groups with each group given an assigned task. The individual group tasks were to research and source the relevant Industry standards for construction, to research and source the relevant competency standards for assessment and to source available physical resources and materials.

The task began with the learner finding meaning of the competency elements, constructing their view of the competency and how that fits within their existing knowledge. This allows for the identification of the desired knowledge and via collaborative environments provides for the formation of partnerships with others who possess the desired knowledge. The groups that form as a result of this process then work together to gather the information required to design a collective but personalised learning and assessment project. A shared learning agenda results from student control of the task design.

The learner was allowed to enter industry in order to source picture and video evidence of current industry trends in the topic. The students could utilise their own workplace or search for other appropriate workplaces in the process of undertaking the application of the learning topic. The students re-group to determine a learning and assessment project that meets the National competency requirements and the industry requirements within the available resources of the Institute.

The student group then designs and creates the instructional resources, including print, with diagrammatic and multi media content. The evaluation of this phase returned some very positive responses from both the students and the teacher. The teacher reported that the class were very responsive to the opportunity to create their own learning with student to student interaction being extremely heightened and a relaxed talkative but educative environment ensuing.

The process could be viewed as collective learning, learner content being created by the learners, exploiting the collective knowledge of the group to achieve the desired outcome.

The Inclusion of Ubiquity and Pervasiveness in the Learning Architecture Adopted to Support Communities of Learning Practice

Mobile technologies have allowed the negotiated learning and assessment project to be undertaken in industry, outside of the institute. Partnerships include people external to the institute but related to the desired learning. This may be the employer or supervisor, another apprentice, or even a different employer identified as having valued knowledge.

The requirement for the learner to provide evidence of the learning and assessment process via narrated video and blogs provide digital evidence that can be used for audit purposes and be re-used as a resource for other learners. The resource is industry current, and relevant to the generation who produced the resource and the generation that will use the resource.

The process becomes an engaging platform that fits this generation of learner by utilising mobile technology and providing for self publishing opportunities in a social environment.

This emergent model operates under the existing authority of the teaching profession where the teacher still uses the judgement and direction afforded in the past, combined with the selection of pedagogical principles and theories in order to support the development of the individual student (See Figure 1).

The impact of these technologies on the learner is the ability to create, capture and share objects of interest or learning objects that occur wherever

Figure 1.

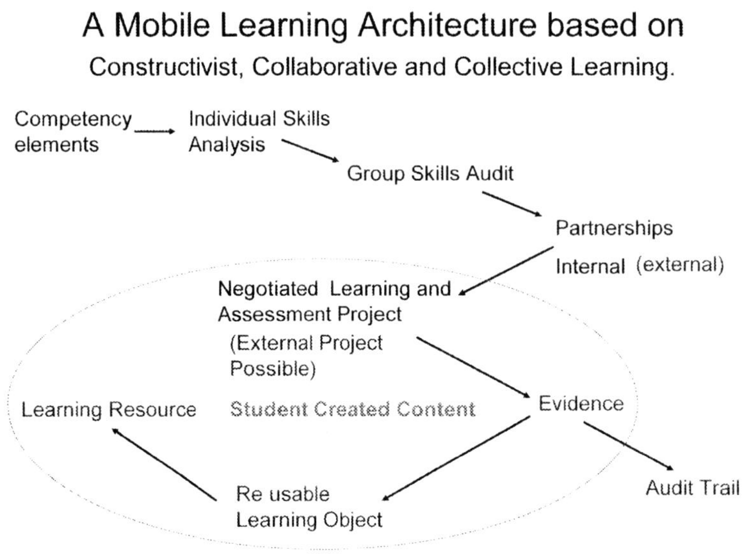

the learner is, in the classroom, the workplace or in life. The objects can be used for collaborative reflection empowering the learners to act as investigators (Naismith, Lonsdale, Vavoula, & Sharples, 2004).

Mobile technology has the capacity to support the learner and the learning in the workplace, not just the assessment, by utilising a platform to enable content delivery to mobile devices (Figure 2). The platform exploits the ability to create information, to carry out self assessment and to have secure scored formal assessment accessible via mobile devices (Figure 3), thus creating a whole of learning environment whilst the learner is in the workplace.

The platform operates on the Institute's existing server structure, creating a cost effective implementation of a new e-learning environment. It enables the distribution of learning activities with the necessary functionalities and learning resources to all participants, regardless of where they are located, and whether the location is static or dynamic.

The creation of online learning resources accessible via mobile device containing self checks to aid learning retention, reinforcement, an option to undertake a scored formal assessment and instant feedbacks via the mobile device has indeed integrated ubiquitous technologies into mainstream Vocational Education and Training.

Inclusion of Synchronous Technology Delivered Education

The integration has created the opportunity to webcast events live via mobile device allowing critical aspects of instruction to be filmed utilising Comvu (2007) software installed on a mobile phone. The system notifies a selected group, for example, the on-site or workplace students, who are then able to see the instruction real time via mobile device or computer, with an option to view the archive at a later more convenient time. Students are also able to broadcast critical events in their workplace, relevant to the learning, to the rest of the group and the Institute.

This allowed for specific contextual content to be viewed, discussed and reflected upon, either collaboratively or individually, enabling learning and knowledge construction wherever the learner is situated.

Figure 2.

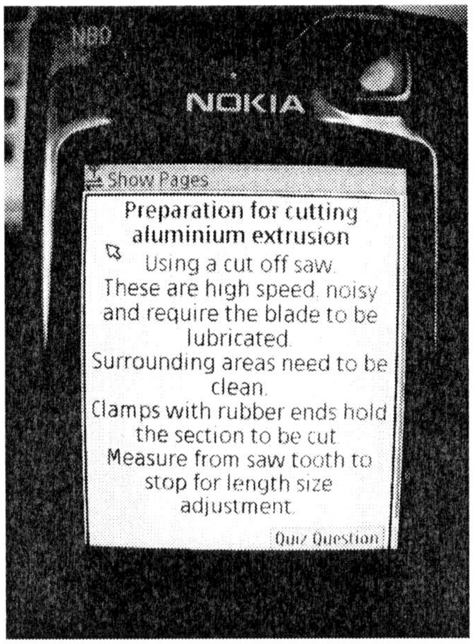

Figure 3.

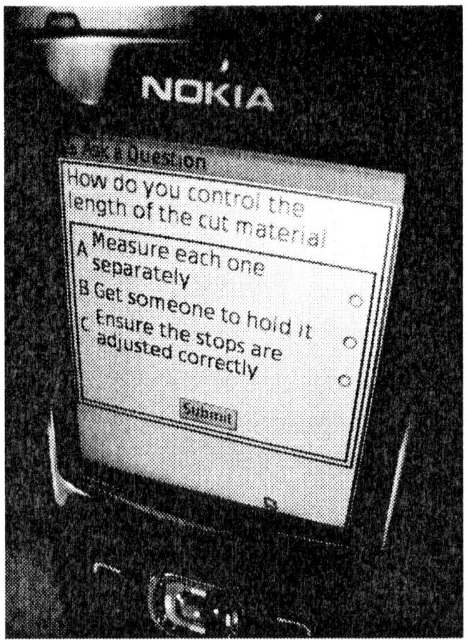

Participation in this project provided professional development for the teachers via enhanced skills in the use of technology to create learning resources in a student centred environment utilising sound pedagogical theories. The opportunity to participate in the design, implementation and evaluation of student created learning resources provides for an enhanced understanding of flexible learning strategies, student needs, engagement, cultural and generational differences. This awareness had a positive cultural impact within the Institute.

CONCLUSION

What becomes apparent from the research is that educators are generally slow in integrating new technologies within the pedagogical context, which reinforces the importance of continual research and development.

The current convergence of technology has created a generation who can access almost unlimited forms of information, allowing for contextual and relevant content choices to be in the hands of the learner. I believe that this generation is in a transitional stage to becoming what I would call "the Ubiquitous Generation", having moved on from the digital generation with the new paradigm being driven by the need for personalisation and self created content, regardless of time or place, blending perfectly into workplace and informal learning practices.

The teacher's control of the content will diminish, giving the learner the freedom and the mobility to discover, interact and create new content. The new teacher will be seen as a navigator, guiding the student's direction, choices and knowledge creation whilst reserving the authority and judgement that is embedded within the professional practice of teaching.

Mobile technology has provided a cost effective, ubiquitous, engaging platform that allows the three parties in the training contract, the learner, the employer and the Institute to work collaboratively in the delivery of training and education.

FUTURE DIRECTIONS AND OPPORTUNITIES

Technology will evolve, systems will morph with users being able to create, publish and interact on any device from anywhere (Openwave, 2007). When we look at the advancement of technology over the past ten years and what the technology is now capable of doing, can we as educators, with some degree of certainty, predict how we will use technology in ten years time? Not really. The technology that is in an introductory or a trial phase at present can be an indicator of what may be available in the next two or three years.

For example;

- A Microsoft Windows operating system available on mobile phones
- A projected keyboard
- A mini data show

The merger of these technologies into a mobile device leads us to deduce that the mobile phone may very well become the laptop computer of the future.

Whatever the future holds in regard to technological advancements, the thing not to forget in utilising technology is that the learning needs to be the focus, not the technology. If we focus on the technology we will certainly be left behind and the message of Goodlad (1984) will again become relevant.

These technology based tools enable rich learning environments built around context sensitive material, learner controlled material with the added benefits of flexibility. In education we must remember that technology provides nothing more than a delivery infrastructure to enable teachers to be innovative yet still use the theoretical foundations that underpin pedagogical processes (Gulliver et al., 1999).

REFERENCES

Attawell, J. (2005). Mobile technologies and learning: A technology update and m-learning project summary. London: Learning and Skills Development Agency.

Australian Bureau of Statistics. (2007). Retrieved on April 27, 2007, from http://www.abs.gov.au/ausstats/abs%40.nsf/

Australian Mobile Data. (2006a). Retrieved on December 1, 2006, from http://www.budde.com.au/e-Newsletters/Contents/Australia-Mobile-Communications-Data-1180.html

Australian Mobile Data. (2006b). Retrieved on December 1, 2006, from http://www.budde.com.au/publications/annual/australia/australia-mobile-data-and-content-markets-summary.html

Barnes, K., Marateo, R., & Ferris, P. (2007). Teaching and learning with the Net generation, Innovate Journal of Online Education, 3(4). Retrieved on April 1, 2007, from http://www.innovateonline.info/index.php?view=article&id=382

Beckett, D., & Hager, P. (2000). Making judgements as the basis of workplace learning: Towards an epistemology of practice. *International Journal of Lifelong Education, 19*(8), 300–311.

Billett, S. (2004). Workplace participatory practices, conceptualising workplaces as learning environments. *Journal of Workplace Learning, 16*(6), 312–324. doi:10.1108/13665620410550295

Comvu. (2007). Press release 04/24/07 Comvu Media Inc. Retrieved on April 26, 2007, from http://www.comvu.com/comvu/presscenter/News042407.htm

Eraut, M. (2004). Informal learning in the workplace. *Studies in Continuing Education, 26*(2), 247–273. doi:10.1080/158037042000225245

Goodlad, J. (1984). A place called school: Prospects for the future. New York: McGraw-Hill.

Gulliver, R., Randall, B., & Pok, Y. (1999). The orbicular model-cognitive learning in cyberspace. *Association for the Advancement of Computing in Education, 1*(12), 18–22.

Hartnell-Young, E. (2004). Mapping the e-portfolio territory. Personal hand out, International Society for Performance Improvement, Melbourne chapter, Presentation, November 2004.

Jorgensen, C. (2004). Connecting work and education: Should learning be useful, correct, or meaningful? *Journal of Workplace Learning, 16*(8), 455–465. doi:10.1108/13665620410566423

Jukes, I. (2005). Understanding digital kids. The Infosavvy Group. Retrieved on February 23, 2007, from http://ianjukes.com/infosavvy/education/handouts/ndl.pdf>

Mitchell, J., & Young, S. (2005). Innovation and the national training system: Core ideas. Elizabeth, South Australia: Reframing the Future.

Naismith, N., Lonsdale, P., Vavoula, G., & Sharples, M. (2004). Literature review in mobile technologies and learning. Futurelab. Retrieved on April 18, 2007, from http://www.futurelab.org.uk/research/lit_reviews.htm

Openwave. (2007). 5 things you need to know about personalization. Openwave Systems Inc. Retrieved on April 18, 2007, from http://www.openwave.com/docs/openwave_5things_about_personalization.pdf

Prensky, M. (2005). What can you learn from a mobile phone?–almost anything! Innovate Journal of Online Education, 1(5). Retrieved on October 30, 2006, from http://innovateonline.info/index.php?view=article&id=83

Salt, B. (2007, May 7). Will learning communities cope with our future. Presentation, Frankston Arts Centre.

Text.it. (2007). Media Centre. Retrieved on April, 19, from http://www.text.it/mediacentre/press_release_list.cfm?thePublicationID=351A37F2-C5A0-881E-03C5B18AAC2AE745

The Australian Psychological Society. (2004, November). Psychological aspects of mobile phone use among adolescents. The Australian Psychological Society, 3. Retrieved on March 2, 2007, from http://www.pshychology.org.au/news/psychology_week/10.10_2.asp

Tracey, I. (2004). Social protocol: Mobile phone and Internet. M/cyclopedia of New Media, Creative Industries Faculty, QUT. Retrieved on March 20, 2007, from http://wiki.media-culture.org.au/index.php/Youth_Culture_and_New_Technologies_-_Social_Protocol>

Chapter 6
A Mobile Service Platform for Trustworthy E-Learning Service Provisioning

Zongwei Luo
University of Hong Kong, Hong Kong, China

Tianle Zhang
Beijing University of Posts and Telecommunications, China

ABSTRACT

Distant e-learning emerges as one of promising means for people to learn online. Although there is a substantial increase in computer and network performance in recent years, mainly as a result of faster hardware and more sophisticated software, there are still problems in the fields of integrating various resources towards enabling distant e-learning. Further, with the advances of technologies in RFID, sensors, GPS, GPRS, IP networks, and wireless networks, mobile learning is becoming a viable means for teaching and learning. In this book chapter, we develop a service platform for mobile learning with trustworthy service provisioning based on an organic integration of our prior research results in service grid, on demand e-learning, and trusted mobile asset tracking. In this platform, the virtual learning services for students, instructors and course providers are provided leveraging on service grid resource management capabilities on group collaboration, ubiquitous data access, and computing power. Challenges and requirements for mobile learning service platform are discussed. An RFID based e-learning data integration is proposed with integrated service networks for intelligent e-learning information access and delivery.

INTRODUCTION

Over the past few decades, Computer Based Training (CBT) solutions evolve from standalone to web-based package (Web Based Training – WBT) with rich multimedia content. Today, most of the web-based solutions leverage on various load-balancing techniques to increase their performance, availability and reliability. Such techniques suffer from the fact that the solution must be able to handle the load of the estimated maximum number of participants and the system resources must be powered by homogeneous platform (both hardware and software). On the other hand, most of the CBT

DOI: 10.4018/978-1-60566-882-6.ch006

and WBT solutions available today advocate "self learning" (Zemke, R., & Zemke, S. 1995) and provide limited interactivity and instantaneous feedback mechanisms that are provided in traditional teaching environment. The sequencing of the courseware is pre-built and thus it may not be applicable for all types of learning. It also fails to facilitate the learning process by creating learning community.

Furthermore, multimedia rich courseware and community portal demand huge data storage that may growth with time. Flexible data storage scheme is required to tackle the on-demand storage needs.

The approach of "On-Demand e-Learning" intends to tackle the problems inherited from the inefficient use of data resources of existing database technology and traditional approach in offering e-learning package (Luo, Z., Fei, Y., & Liang, J., 2006). The primary objective is to develop virtual learning service community for all community participants including students, instructors, and courseware providers leveraging on Service Grid technologies (Luo, Z., Zhang, J., & Badia, R. 2005), for e-learning services development and access, ubiquitous data access, group collaboration, and computing resource management.

Furthermore, today's world has witnessed the trend of convergence of computing and communication, and integration of sensor and mobile technologies for enabling a new generation of e-learning applications in a mobile and pervasive manner. With mobile applications becoming more and more attractive, location awareness is becoming a fundamental requirement in mobile e-learning solutions offering functions for such as mobile e-learning asset management to enable efficient utilization of resources. A key enabling technology for such location awareness is through positioning technologies, of which GPS, global poisoning system, is becoming more and more popular in outdoor environment. Other enabling technologies include Radio Frequency Identification (RFID), which could be used to uniquely identify an object. This RFID technology is particularly helpful in pushing asset management at an even finer granularity, e.g. from case level to item level.

Location aware e-learning applications and services, e.g. track and trace for managing asset, are especially helpful in identification of the move paths of the asset and can help identify e-learning patterns, enabling more efficient e-learning information exchange and asset utilization. However, these features would incur a few problems as well. The feature, if wrongly used, e.g. by an un-authorized party, would lead to leakage of patterns (such as utilization, trend, etc.) about the e-learning asset under management as well as individual's behavior. The rapid technology advances in business intelligence tools, e.g. data mining and knowledge discovery has made this type of threats even more severe. Thus, to protect the privacy of individuals as well as companies' trade secret, it is necessary to develop a secure system for managing the e-learning asset, raising the bar for obtaining valuable information to breach the location information integrity for managing the e-learning participant and asset (Zhang, T., Luo, Z., et al., 2008).

All of these require for a holistic view on integrating related technologies, such as position technologies like GPS, sensing and identification technologies like RFID, and security technologies like authentication and authorization. Thus, we need an integrated service network approach that supports sharing, accessing and managing e-learning resources and leverages various positioning, sensing and security services that are available to the network. Through this integrated service network, information about e-learning participants and the e-learning asset shall be made available to the network participants. E-learning participants and asset tracking then could be developed and services could be offered to deliver the information securely to interesting participants.

In the book chapter, we will present a service platform for mobile learning with trustworthy service provisioning, called MiQ-SP, for tracking e-learning participants and managing e-learning asset, developed based on an integrated service network concept. In MiQ-SP location information about e-learning participants and asset could be obtained via several location positioning technologies. Status about the asset could be monitored via sensing technologies. MiQ-SP could be able to deliver the asset information to the interesting parties via integrating various communication technologies. Furthermore, MiQ-SP would ensure asset information integrity in order to provide trusted e-learning services to its service customers.

BACKGROUND

Learning process can be classified as "synchronous" and "asynchronous" (Dennis, T., & El-Gayar, O., 2005). Asynchronous Learning is a process in which interaction between instructors and students occurs intermittently with time delay. Examples are self-paced courses taken via Internet or CD-ROM, online discussion group, and email (Bourne, J.R., 1998). Synchronous Learning is instructor-led real-time event in which all participants are logged on at the same time and communicate directly with each other. Instructor maintains control of the class (may be virtual classroom) with the ability to call on participants. Students and instructors can use a whiteboard to see work in progress and share knowledge. Interaction may also occur via audio or videoconferencing (Chen N. S., et al., 2005).

Distance Education refers situation in which time, location, or both separate the instructors and students (Luo, Z., Zhang, J., & Badia, R. 2005). Education course could be delivered to remote locations via synchronous or asynchronous means of instruction. Asynchronous Distance Education plays a critical role in the adult community and the key success factors of such education model include, but not limited to, the initiative and discipline of learners. It may not be effective model for communities such as primary or secondary students. Synchronous Distance Education Model (SDEM) (Williams, K., & Paparozzi, E., 2002), which advocates interactivity, adaptive and experience sharing, may be the direction for such community. Further, moving to virtual classroom leveraging on the existing Internet infrastructure triggers the following problems like lacks of reliable, scalable and flexible computing infrastructure to handle the dynamic training needs. On the other hand, data users like Students, Instructors and various Service Providers need data storages for maintaining the valuable information. Each of the data users needs maintain its own data storage facilities that are capable to meet the requirements and service level. Such data storage architecture has the following problems:

- Data users are responsible for all maintenance activities for their own data storage.
- Each Service Provider needs to invest data storage facilities based on their projection of the maximum data consumption pattern in a certain period. Start up cost is relatively high.
- Application developers need to adopt different programming model in accessing data.

This chapter attempts to tackle these problems by developing mobile e-learning infrastructure for managing e-learning asset and providing a trustworthy service platform for accessing various e-learning resources including data, collaboration channels, computing resources, etc.

E-learning participant and asset location is one of the key information for developing mobile e-learning solutions. Location information needed for tracking e-learning participants and managing e-learning asset is usually derived from location positing information. Various positioning technologies are developed including mobile cell positioning (utilizing the cell of origin or cell ID to approximate the location of the user), mobile handset positioning (involving analysis of the angle or time features of a signal between the mobile phone and the cellular antenna.), GPS positioning, and RFID positioning. While mobile cell positioning has a large degree of uncertainty, GPRS provides a means of positioning a mobile handset, even when the handset is in idle state. RFID positioning relies on analyzing the tag position information when a reader picks up a signal from the RFID tag attached to it. The most widely recognized positioning system is the Global Positioning System (GPS). GPS uses satellites to provide accurate positioning information. This makes it a good candidate in open outdoor space.

RFID positioning provide both positioning and locations for mobile users. However, due to the limitation of RFID power range, RFID positioning could not reach as pervasive as other positioning technologies like GPS, and mobile cell and handset positioning. It is usually used in the last mile to report an asset passing by with known location information.

Mobile cell and handset positioning provides positions for mobile users when these is network coverage is available. However, current wireless networks alone can not achieve complete coverage due to network deployment restrictions. It is even worse when people may sign up different network services, such as broadband, or 3G. Interconnections among these networks would yield a better coverage. Thus, a feasible way to improve network convergence is through interconnections among Wi-Fi, 3G, GPRS, IP networks, RFID, etc.

GPS plays an important role in providing location information about asset in outdoor environment. However, GPS works in a passive mode by calculating position information using the signals from GPS satellites. This helps its popular usage base by making it possible to build very cheap GPS receiver. However, it is lack of bi-direction communication capability. That is, while GPS receiver can calculate position information, it can't send the information out to interested parties. Thus, it is necessary to develop communication modules to work with GPS in order to provide asset location information to interested parties other than the receiver holder. A GPS tracking unit has been developed that uses GPS to determine asset location at regular intervals. The recorded location data can be stored and transmitted to interested parties via various means, including GPRS, radio, or satellite modem.

Furthermore, unstable GPS signals could pose problems to its applications. Temporary unavailability or a weak GPS signal may lead to a miss read of location. This could cause problems if at that very moment a location query arrives. Asset location information can be wrong if transmitted without correction.

In the meantime, those positioning technologies have to work with other sensing technologies to provide a needed status report about the e-learning participants being tracked and e-learning asset under managed. An asset may need different sensors to keep track of various asset properties such as active usage duration, number of concurrent sharing, etc. Thus, it demands a good sensing integration to coordinate all these sensors to provide valuable tracking information about the e-learning participant and asset as well.

In summary, there are a few challenges for tracking e-learning participants and managing mobile e-learning asset:

- E-learning participants and asset information capturing. The challenge is that which method or technology shall be used for capturing different information about the e-learning participant and asset including location.
- E-learning participants and asset information reporting. The challenge is once location information is captured, how shall it be reported? Shall it reside with the capturing device or a central location?

generates the executable e-learning function image corresponding to the defined workflow.

- Using the deployment facility, the workflow executable will be downloaded to the mobile e-learning participants' execution environment, such as mobile phone, PDA, etc.
- If necessary, the software service provider could help test the executable image in the local company's environment.
- If everything is alright, the software service provider will inform the mobile e-learning service platform operator and the execution image will be ready in production with charging started.

M-LEARNING SERVICE PLATFORM

The essential goal of MiQ-SP is to share, access, and manage diverse e-learning technologies and resources, widely ranging from raw location positioning data and servers to location based e-learning applications and services. It brings together players in the location based e-learning services and applications related domain and provides mechanisms for them to interact and collaborate, for the purpose of e-learning service provisioning and resource exchange in an mobile and persuasive manner. MiQ-SP relies on an integrated service network to integrate various technologies like data capturing, information replay and delivery, information access.

RFID Based Data Capturing

In tracking the e-learning participant and asset, it is necessary to monitor different properties of the tracked assets, such as active learning duration, interactive parties, location, etc. This poses a need to integrate these data to provide useful tracking information. Here we present an RFID based multi-sensing mechanism for this purpose. Each sensor such as a GPS device is associated with an RFID, uniquely identifiable. All the RFIDs will then be put in a hierarchical structure with each sensing RFID representing a particular sensing property. And the root RFID represents the e-learning participant and asset to be tracked. In this way, it can be easily to associate the sensing data with the tracked e-learning participant and asset and identify the sensing property of the e-learning participant and asset. This is quite similar to object oriented programming. The asset to be tracked is the object. The to be sensed properties are the object properties. Further, this RFID based tracking data integration provides even convenient means to exchange data among different parties and applications as it leverages product code standardization technologies like Electronic Product Code (EPC) (EPC, 2008) in tagging e-learning participant and asset. With it, we can provide a finer sensing granularity at the same time.

Information Relay and Delivery

MiQ-SP provides information relay and delivery through intelligent and ubiquitous information access, relay, search and delivery for managing mobile e-learning asset. Relying on timely information acquisition, relay and delivery over the integrated service network, MiQ-SP provides a critical and ubiquitous infrastructure with convergence of RFID, sensor, Wi-Fi, IP network. MiQ-SP is able to provide seamless dynamically interconnections to leverage mobile nodes to "bridge the gap" by serving as relay for delivery of mobile queries with or without direct network access.

MiQ-SP will leverage available network connections and mobile nodes to provide a seamless convergence network in which mobile relay nodes (Ad hoc Wi-Fi or RFID enabled) roaming to piggyback information to relay and deliver information. This converged network can fill the gap among multiple networks such as Wi-Fi, Internet, GPRS, 3G etc.

In short, MiQ-SP relies on an integrated service network to take advantages of each technology and overcome their shortcomings. For example, MiQ-SP could provide functions to convert positioning information into useful location information and make it available for location based e-learning services and applications. One of the key value aspects of the MiQ-SP is to enable the use of various positioning and sensing technologies in conjunction with various location bases e-learning services and applications.

Information Access

MiQ-SP provides Query Information Service (MiQ-QIS) to enable mobile information access. The MiQ-QIS can retrieve information through the integrated service network. If information services providers (logistics players, hospitals, library or bank) want to join the MiQ-SP, they have to subscribe to the integrated service network so they can supply their information for MiQ-QIS query.

When a user wants to accesses the MiQ-QIS, his/her handle devices (e.g. mobile phone) can sense the availability of an integrated service network and if available, will relay the query for MiQ-QIS execution. Otherwise, if a MiQ-SP's access network is not available (e.g. s/he is not in a Wi-Fi zone), the phone can store the query and will start sense the network availability for resuming the query delivery.

The mobile relay of the integrated service network works in an energy-aware manner (Ocakoglu, O., & Ercetin, O., 2006). For example, the mobile nodes would execute sleep wakeup scheduling when sensing the network availability, considering the density of neighbors and the frequency of relaying (Grossglauser M., & Tse, D., 2002; Chaintreau, P., et al., 2006; Su, J., et al., 2004). User can access the MiQ-SP services through the provided channels of service delivery including: SMS, GPRS, 3G, Wi-Fi, IP network, broadband network, etc.

MiQ-SP designed based on the delay tolerant concept provide very reliable access to the MiQ-SP services. For example, during a typhoon period, the communication systems often become congested and disrupted. The MiQ-SP can still leverage bluetooth available in the mobile phone or other channels with limited bandwidth to help achieve reliable information delivery over the integrated service network through mobile relay even in such extreme occasions.

Trusted MiQ-SP

Besides what is already described, other features for trusted e-learning tracking in MiQ-SP are reflected in trusted data integration, trusted information delivery and access, and pervasive data integrity.

Trusted Data Integration

As said, in tracking e-learning participant and asset, it is necessary to monitor different properties of the tracked assets, such as active learning duration, interactive parties, location, etc. The RFID based data capturing provide a means to integrate these data to provide useful tracking information. With an RFID associated with each e-learning participant and asset and its properties to be monitored, we provide trustworthy data integration for information exchange based on standardization efforts in e-learning asset code like EPC and asset descriptions. Further, it provides an automatic way for exchange sensing data at any granularity. This automatic feature in data exchange in tracking the e-learning asset helps improve the reliability of information relay and delivery.

Reliable Information Delivery and Access

Trusted system for e-learning participant and managing mobile e-learning asset involves reliable information capturing, reporting, delivery, storage, and access. To provide a trusted system, a collaborative data filtering mechanism is developed to report any missing capturing and correct wrong capturing leveraging the tracking route information and application processes (Peng, P., 2008). A lightweight authentication and authorization protocol is developed based on PKI for secure access of the QIS (Zhang, T., et al., 2008). MiQ-SP leveraging collaborative data filtering and PKI based authentication and authorization, provides reliable information capturing, reporting, and delivery and access. The integrated service network in MiQ-SP works in a delay tolerant methodology for information relay and delivery in a store and forward manner. The delay tolerant routing protocol is designed for reliable connection among different relay networks (20).

Sensing Data Integrity

To ensure data integrity, reliable data storage called black box is provided for storing the location, time and sensing information. This black box is developed based on mutual trust among the tracking participants (Luo, Z., Chan, T., Li, J., 2005). It will ensure that data captured are not tampered. The lightweight mutual authentication and authorization based on PKI will help the data used in the way according to a priori or on the spot agreement made among the tracking participants. Mutual trust is established among these parties to establish a smooth, effective, and efficient operation environment.

SYSTEM IMPLEMENTATION

Platform Architecture

The MiQ-SP platform will support role-based scenarios. For example, there are three types of roles in e-learning: student, instructor, and courseware developer. Certainly there are other roles as well like administrator, platform operator, etc. Each role will be associated with some typical scenarios to be enabled by e-learning platform. The platform will provide various access means including online and mobile/wireless access. The architecture of the platform composes of 3 major application service layers and 1 cross-domain data service layer.

- Web Services layer acts as the fundamental building blocks for rendering generic functions to build mobile e-learning applications. This layer can be further classified for Mobile e-learning, Virtual Classroom Management, Multimedia Streaming / Storage. All services at this layer provide transient function access to the Service Requester that is responsible for maintaining the persistent storage. Service Providers of Virtual Classroom and Multimedia Streaming will share a mechanism in handling the authorization and authentication functions.
- Learning Application Portal application layer aggregates functions provided by On Demand Service Grid (ODSG) (ODSG, 2008) providers and is responsible for state / session management and persistent storage. It also provides the web access interfaces for Instructor / Students to participate in the interactive e-learning process.
- Client Application Layer is a client-side (Instructor / Student) application (for capturing / displaying multimedia data) for enhancing the user experience during the e-learning process.
- Cross Domain Data Access Layer is the information servicing layer through which all service providers and applications access data remotely stored in data stores provided by data storage service provider using OGSADAI (OGSA-DAI, 2008) technologies.

Collaboration Implementation

The MiQ-SP platform supports large-scale distributed meeting, messaging, collaboration, lectures, training sessions, seminars, and tutorials. It makes it possible for multiple, group-to-group interaction as well as one-to-one or one-to-many communications. To enable such large-scale collaboration on the e-learning platform, we have integrated AccessGrid technologies (AccessGrid, 2008) into our e-learning platform for the collaboration enablement.

- The collaboration enablement built upon AccessGrid (AccessGrid, 2008) takes advantage an integrated set of software and hardware resources that support large-scale group-to-group interactions across the network.
- The collaboration enablement manages an ensemble of resources and collection of multicast backbone supporting video conferencing targeted for group-to-group interactions, large-scale distributed meetings, collaborative work sessions, seminars, lectures, tutorials, and training. It serves as effective platform for group-to-group interaction and collaboration and teaching among different campuses.
- The collaboration community consists of a group of collaboration nodes that serves as access point for participants joining a collaboration session. Each node acts as Virtual Venue over which Virtual Classroom could be instantiates. Virtual Classroom is the premise in which participants in the class collaborate. In other words, Virtual Venue is the Event Server that broadcast the events / data streams to the participants of the Virtual Class.

Application Portal Implementation

This application layer aggregates functions provided by ODSG (ODSG, 2008) providers and is responsible for state / session management and persistent storage. It also provides the web access interfaces for Instructor / Students to participate in the interactive e-learning processes.

Web Services are emerging as a popular approach for business-to-business applications resulting of its interoperability. However, many problems like their availability, service level and recoverability, etc, can arise that causes headaches for a Web Service based application. Service Domain technology addresses all of the web service difficulties and provides the best service available from a pool of dynamically assembled service providers in order to meet the user's needs.

There are three major components in this framework: Service Requestor, Service Hub Operator and Service Provider. Service Hub Operator aggregates "services" offered by different Service Providers into general Service portTypes, which could be accessed by Service Requestor. Service Hub Operator is responsible for all administrative tasks like managing and matching service agreements for both Provider and Requestor, selecting, filtering, routing, managing, and dispatching service requests.

Cross Domain Data Access

The cross-domain data access resides in the information service layer. This layer provides all service providers and applications the capabilities to access data stored in virtual data stores either locally or remotely provided by data storage service provider using OGSADAI (OGSA-DAI, 2008) technologies.

The Service Grid is an infrastructure that supports the Discovery, Access and Use of distributed computational resources (Luo, Z., Zhang, J., & Badia, R. 2005). This emergency raises the question of how database management systems and technologies can be deployed or adapted for use in such environment. The information service layer built upon OGSA-DAI is the middleware technology to interface existing databases in a common way based on the Open Grid Service

Architecture (OGSA). It provides basic services and data source abstraction for accessing data sources implemented in different technologies without mandating any particular query language or data format within the OGSA framework. They take XML document as input/output and support parameterized database operations through SQL Statement or XPath / XQuery.

By taking advantages of OGSA-DAI, the information service layer provides data access and integration functions for computing Grids using standard OGSI framework. It allows Grid application to access existing data resources, either as Relational DBMS or XML-DBMS, for supporting business applications today. The querying interface adopts the existing standards like SQL, XPath and XQuery for accessing data resources.

In addition, it has a RoleMapper bridges the security standard X.509 in Grid community to the existing database security framework (role-based or user-based authorization). Database developers don't have to change its product line in adapting the Grid standard and Grid Application developer could adapt the X.509 standard in accessing legacy database systems.

Computing Resource Management

Grid Computing is an emerging approach for enabling applications to run in large-scale distributed computing environment. However, the Grid concept triggers the problem of coordinating resources sharing in the dynamic, multi-institutional Virtual Organization. Community Scheduler Framework (CSF) is a grid middleware technology that represents the heterogeneous lower-level resources with higher level for providing uniform access (CSF, 2008).

The Community Scheduler Framework is an open-source implementation of a number of Grid Services as a grid meta-scheduler providing high-level of abstraction that provides basic capabilities for scheduling and can be used as a development toolkit for implementing community scheduler. It allows end-users to interact with the underlying resource managers, including LSF, Condor, SGE, PBS, etc, in a system independent fashion.

The CSF consists of Metascheduler, Global Information Service and Resource Manager Adapter as core services (CSF, 2008). Metascheduler, consisting of Job Service, Queuing Service and Reservation Service, allow end-users to interact with the underlying resource managers in a system independent fashion by defining the protocols that interact with resources manager. Moreover, the CSF provides common interface to accept user requests to run jobs on distributed heterogeneous computing environment. It acts as the entry point for accessing computing resources of a Virtual Organization.

FUTURE RESEARCH DIRECTIONS

In this chapter we intend to develop an intelligent mobile e-learning platform, i.e. MiQ-SP, to bring various e-learning participants together in building an integrated e-learning environment. We tackle the problems inherited from the inefficient use of data resources of existing database technology. Future work includes implementation of the e-learning community infrastructure, services and tools for various participants including students, instructors, and courseware to access, develop, and maintain e-learning services. Moreover, advanced polices for orchestrating Grid resources for meeting the on demand requirements have to be designed and implemented.

MiQ-SP is developed for managing e-learning participant and asset, developed over an integrated service network. In MiQ-SP location information about e-learning participant and asset could be obtained via several location positioning technologies. MiQ-SP could be able to deliver the asset location information to the interesting parties via integrating various communication technologies. Further we developed an RFID based multi-sensing mechanism to integrate sensing data. Each sensor such as a GPS device is associated with an RFID, uniquely identifiable. This RFID based tracking data integration provides even convenient means to exchange data among different parties and applications as it leverages product code standardization technologies like EPC in tagging e-learning participants and asset. With it, we can provide an even finer sensing granularity at the same time. Our current research efforts are further on focused on a large scale deployment of such a moving asset tracking solution.

A lot of more potential information services can be added to the MiQ-SP to supply valuable information (e.g. pattern analysis, trend analysis, behavior analysis about e-learning participants and asset being tracked and managed) and provide information services for mobile e-learning. We can even extend this MiQ-SP to manage various devices like the office and classroom electronics, e.g. query the status and send turning-off control to turn the air conditioner on/off while away from office and classrooms.

CONCLUSION

E-learning through Grid technology is not a new idea. For example, ChinaGrid (ChinaGrid, 2008) has been exploring Grid technologies in enabling video sharing for e-learning. This project taking advantages of the Grid network infrastructure, intends to achieve virtual access to those video class materials online. In the world, there are many campus Grids built for the purpose to share education resources, for example EU-US Learning Grid (E-Grid, 2008). ChinaGrid, one of largest efforts in the world, eventually will connect virtually all universities in China to allow them to share computing resources. However, those projects differ from our approach. These projects focus one type of computing resources, either on video resource sharing, or on high performance computing, lacking integrated view over managing the Grid resources.

Our approach takes an integrated service approach, applying Service Grid technologies in describing the Service grid resources for all e-learning participants, for example, in Web Services Description Language (WSDL), and use orchestration to manage all of these resources for all e-learning participants. Different resource management systems and tools are integrated for managing specific resources, while presenting WSDL interfaces for easy integration. Moreover, these resources would be flexibly composed to enable dynamic and adaptive e-learning solutions, such as flexible courseware development, student's adaptive e-learning capability enabling, and instructor's flexible course offerings.

While plenty of asset tracking solutions are available today such as GPS based tracking, WiFi based tracking, and RFID based tracking (Wang, J. et al., 2007), our approach of MiQ-SP differs from these approaches by providing an integrated service network leveraging various technologies to provide a trusted system for managing mobile e-learning asset:

- It provides energy aware information relay to bridge the multiple existing networks, leveraging mobile nodes. The mobile relay of the MiQ-SP works in an energy-aware manner to extend the life time of the tagging and relaying mobile nodes. Mobile relay technology in MiQ-SP can fill the gap between isolated information islands, connecting people with different mobile devices (3G, GPRS, Wi-Fi, etc).
- It provides tunable features to adjust network node availability to meet different e-learning application needs and performance requirements. By adjusting the on/off property for mobile tagging and relaying nodes and network availability, we can get different expected delay results. With this, MiQ-

SP could leverage allowed delay tolerance to provide satisfactory tracking services while considering available resources and different tracking requirements.

- The trustworthiness features provided in MiQ-SP for the tracking system development to provide reliable information capturing, reporting, delivery, storage and access. It leverages collaborative data filtering and mutual trust establishment plus available security technologies to provide a trusted system for tracking e-learning participants and assets.
- Further, the RFID based data capturing provide a means to integrate various sensor data and associate them with corresponding e-learning parties (such as student, instructor, e-learning facility and service platform operator, etc.) to provide useful tracking information. With an RFID associated with each e-learning participant and asset and its properties to be monitored, we provide trustworthy data integration for information exchange based on standardization efforts in e-learning asset code like EPC and asset descriptions.

REFERENCES

AccessGrid. (2008). *Access grid.* Retrieved from www.accessgrid.org

Bourne, J. R. (1998). Net-learning: Strategies for on-campus and off-campus network-enabled learning. [JALN]. *Journal of Asynchronous Learning Networks, 2*(2).

Burleigh S., et. al. (2003). Delay-tolerant networking: An approach to interplanetary Internet. *IEEE Communications Magazine*, June.

Chaintreau, P., et al. (2006). Impact of human mobility on the design of opportunistic forwarding algorithms. In *Proceedings of IEEE INFOCOM*, 2006.

Chen, N. S. (2005). Synchronous learning model over the Internet. *Innovations in Education and Teaching International, 42*(2). doi:10.1080/14703290500062599

ChinaGrid. (2008). Retrieved from http://www.chinagrid.edu.cn/chinagrid/index.jsp

CSF. (2008). *Community scheduler framework, CSF*. Retrieved from www.globus.org

Dennis, T., & El-Gayar, O. (2005). Effectiveness of hybrid learning environments. *Issues in Information Systems, 6*(1).

E-Grid. (2008). *EU-US learning grid.* Retrieved from http://us-eu.ncsa.uiuc.edu/domains/elearning.htm

EPC. (2008). Retrieved on January 27, 2008, from http://www.epcglobalinc.org

Fall, F. (2003, August 25-29). A delay-tolerant network architecture for challenged Internets. *SIGCOMM 2003*, Karlsruhe, Germany.

Grossglauser, M., & Tse, D. (2002). Mobility increases the capacity of ad hoc wireless networks. *IEEE/ACM Transactions on Networking, 2002.*

Luo, Z., Chan, T., & Li, J. (2005). A lightweight mutual authentication protocol for RFID networks. *ICEBE, 2005*, 620–625.

Luo, Z., Fei, Y., & Liang, J. (2006). On demand e-learning with service grid technologies. *Edutainment, 2006*, 60–69.

Luo, Z., Zhang, J., & Badia, R. (2005). *Service grid for business computing. Grid technologies: Emerging from distributed architectures to virtual organizations*. WIT Press.

Ocakoglu, O., & Ercetin, O. (2006). Energy efficient random sleep-awake schedule design. *IEEE Communications Letters*, *10*(7), 528–530.

ODSG. (2008). *On demand service grid, ODSG*. Retrieved from www.ibm.com

OGSA-DAI. (2008). Retrieved from www.globus.org

Peng, P. (2008). A P2P based collaborative RFID data cleaning model. *The 2008 International Symposium on Advances in Grid and Pervasive Systems (AGPS 2008)* in conjunction with the *3rd International Conference on Grid and Pervasive Computing (GPC 2008)*, Kunming, China.

Su, J., et al. (2004). User mobility for opportunistic ad-hoc networking. In *Proceedings of IEEE WMCSA*.

Wang, J., et al. (2007). RFID based object tracking for automating manufacturing assembly lines. *ICEBE 2007*, Hong Kong.

Williams, K., & Paparozzi, E. (2002). Model to develop a synchronous interinstitutional course using distance technologies. *NACTA Journal*.

Zemke, R., & Zemke, S. (1995). Adult learning: What do we know for sure? *Training (New York, N.Y.)*, *32*(6), 31–40.

Zhang, T., et al. (2008, June 11-13). Mobile intelligence for delay tolerant logistics and supply chain management. *SUTC 2008*, Taichung, Taiwan.

Zhang, T., Li, Z., & Liu, M. (2006). Routing in partially connected wireless network. *Journal of System Simulation*, *18*(10), 2972–2975.

Zhang, T., & Luo, Z. (2008). Developing a trusted system for tracking asset on the move. *ICYCS, 2008*, 2008–2013.

Section 2
Technological Advances in Support for Mobile Learning

Chapter 7
Mobile Web 2.0:
Bridging Learning Contexts

Thomas Cochrane
Unitec, New Zealand

ABSTRACT

Blogs, wikis, podcasting, and a host of free, easy to use Web 2.0 social software provide opportunities for creating social constructivist learning environments focusing upon student-centred learning and end-user content creation and sharing. Building on this foundation, mobile Web 2.0 has emerged as a viable teaching and learning environment, particularly with the advent of the iPhone (nicknamed "the Jesus phone") and iPod Touch. Today's wifi enabled smartphones provide a ubiquitous connection to mobile Web 2.0 social software and the ability to view, create, edit, and upload user generated Web 2.0 content. This chapter explores the potential of wireless mobile devices and Web 2.0 (social software) to create social constructivist learning environments that bridge multiple learning contexts. The chapter provides an overview of current literature in the field, and discusses the pedagogical design of six example mobile Web 2.0 trials undertaken during 2007 and 2008 as part of research into the potential of mobile Web 2.0 to enhance tertiary education. The trials were based in three different courses and illustrate the application and integration of mobile Web 2.0 to bridge a range of learning contexts. The chapter argues that wireless mobile devices can be used to intentionally create disruptive learning environments that facilitate a social constructivist approach to teaching and learning.

INTRODUCTION

This chapter is based upon the experiences gathered from six mobile learning (mlearning) trials beginning in 2007 and continuing throughout 2008. After an introductory trial in 2007 (Cochrane, 2008c), five small (each involving between 6 and 10 students and their lecturers) mlearning projects were implemented and evaluated during 2008 (Cochrane, 2008a). Feedback from the 2008 mobile projects was very enthusiastic:

DOI: 10.4018/978-1-60566-882-6.ch007

It isn't 'easy' working in this way but it is immensely valuable and exciting. I think that it would be very hard go back to traditional teaching only methods now I have begun to use blogging and mobile blogging (Third year Bachelor Product Design lecturer).

I really, really enjoyed the process, it was great. The things I liked were being able to be completely mobile, and having access to the Internet – you know, if I was lost or if I needed to find someone, or I needed to ring a business. I could go on the Internet, Google their website, look up their opening hours, things like that... (Bachelor Product Design student)

Compilations of 2008 student and staff VODCasts (Online video recordings) are available on YouTube:

1. Bachelor Product Design Year 1: http://www.youtube.com/watch?v=8QUfw9_sFmo
2. Bachelor Product Design Year 2: http://www.youtube.com/watch?v=6jwAFXBZAz0
3. Bachelor Product Design Year 3 (and Lecturers): http://www.youtube.com/watch?v=8Eh5ktXMji8
4. Diploma Contemporary Music: http://nz.youtube.com/watch?v=0It5XUfvOjQ
5. Diploma Landscape Architecture: http://nz.youtube.com/watch?v=c8IZSVtaMmM

The focus of using mobile web 2.0 technologies (described below) is to harness easy to use, mobile friendly tools that students can use to create their own content and learning contexts, guided by their lecturers and supported by their peers, beyond the limitations of institutional systems. Recent mlearning projects based at the University of Wollongong (Herrington *et al.*, 2008) follow a similar pedagogical and staff professional development approach to that utilised in this research project, but do not explicitly link web 2.0 tools with mlearning as this project does.

Defining Mobile Learning

Definitions of mobile learning have focused initially upon the mobility of the devices and more recently the mobility of the learners. Sharples proposes a form of Laurillard's conversational framework (Laurillard, 2001), excluding the teacher, to define mobile learning by its contextual and informal learning characteristics. "The processes of coming to know through conversations across multiple contexts amongst people and personal interactive technologies" (Sharples *et al.*, 2006). However, a key element in the conversational framework is the dialogue between teacher & student. In contrast to Sharples et al (2006), Laurillard (2007) emphasizes the teacher's input in mobile environments through good pedagogic design that facilities continuity between the face to face and remote peer learning contexts. Her definition of mobile learning incorporates the critical pedagogical design input of the teacher: "Mlearning, being the digital support of adaptive, investigative, communicative, collaborative, and productive learning activities in remote locations, proposes a wide variety of environments in which the teacher can operate" (Laurillard, 2007).

Wali et al (2008) take 'context crossing' as the basis for their conceptualisation of mlearning. They use Activity Theory to define mlearning. The resultant definition is extremely broad: "learning that occurs as a result of pursuing learning activities that are directed towards achieving some objective in multiple contexts (physical and social)" (Wali *et al.*, 2008) p45. Wali et al believe "definitions of mobile learning should cover conventional devices as well as any other technology" – they want to get away from a technology focus within the definition of mlearning, to a focus upon the 'continuity of learning activities in different contexts'. However, non wireless devices cannot bridge communication across multiple contexts.

It is the potential for mobile learning to bridge pedagogically designed learning contexts, facilitate learner generated contexts, and content (both personal and collaborative), while providing personalisation and ubiquitous social connectedness, that sets it apart from more traditional learning environments. Mobile learning, as defined in this chapter, involves the use of wireless enabled mobile digital devices (Wireless Mobile Devices or WMD's) within and between pedagogically designed learning environments or contexts. From an activity theory perspective, WMD's are the tools that mediate a wide range of learning activities and facilitate collaborative learning environments (Uden, 2007).

Context Bridging

Recent research into mlearning has highlighted the context 'awareness' of mobile devices, and the ability to 'span' learning contexts. However, what is unique about WMDs for mlearning is their ability to BRIDGE contexts (Vavoula, 2007) – i.e. to provide ubiquitous connectivity independent of the context of use, thus linking multiple contexts into the learning environment, continuing learning 'conversations' via social presence and communication technologies.

Mlearning can support and enhance both the face to face and off campus teaching and learning contexts by using the wireless mobile devices as a means to leverage the potential of current and emerging collaborative and reflective e-learning tools (e.g. blogs, wikis, RSS, instant messaging, podcasting, social book marking, etc…). These are often called social software or web 2.0 tools. The WMD's wireless connectivity and data gathering abilities (e.g. photoblogging, video recording, voice recording, and text input) allow for bridging the on and off campus learning contexts – facilitating "real world learning". In particular, the context bridging and media recording capabilities of today's smartphones make them ideal tools for mobile blogging. Smartphones allow a user to send text, photos, video and audio directly from the site of recording to the users online Blog. An example of the potential of mobile blogging is the rise of citizen journalism (Cameron, 2006; Elmendorp, 2007; Fulton, 2007; Skoeps, 2007). Collaboration and communication with peers and tutors can be maintained in any context using WMDs with a variety of communication technologies (email, online LMS, Instant Messaging, audio and video conferencing, SMS, MMS, mobile phone calls etc…).

BACKGROUND

Why Mobile?

The convergence of ubiquitous broadband, portable devices, and tiny computers has changed our concept of what a phone is meant to be. A pocket-sized connection to the digital world, the mobile phone keeps us in touch with our families, friends, and colleagues by more than just voice. Our phones are address books, file storage devices, cameras, video recorders, wayfinders, and handheld portals to the Internet—and they don't stop there. The ubiquity of mobile phones, combined with their many capabilities, makes them an ideal platform for educational content and activities. We are only just beginning to take advantage of the possibilities they will offer. (New Media Consortium, 2007)

Today's mobile phones are powerful computers. The catch phrase of Nokia's current add campaign for its N-Series smartphones is: "It's what computers have become" (Nokia, 2007). Its rise to ubiquity is described as a

…stealthy but rapid shift from a telephony device towards a portable, personal media hub that enables an increasing range of personalised and customised communication, entertainment, relationship management and service functions. Its reach is pervasively global and trans-cultural, possibly more so than any other media form including the internet and world wide web (Cameron, 2006).

The largest growth area of Internet usage is mobile access. "'Mobile, mobile, mobile,' were the words of Google chief executive Eric Schmidt recently when asked what technologies are most intriguing to the computer Web search leader" (Wakabayashi & Auchard, 2007). Marc Prensky remarks: "What can you learn from a cell phone? Almost anything!" (Prensky, 2005b).

Pedagogy and Today's Learners

Pedagogical approaches to teaching and learning environments range from teacher-centred (instructivism) to student-centred collaboration (social constructivism). Traditional tertiary education has followed an instructivist pedagogy. However, increasingly school leavers are entering tertiary education with content creation skills honed from their immersion in digitally facilitated social network sites (Boyd & Ellison, 2007). They have been nick-named the 'net-generation' and 'digital natives' (Oblinger & Oblinger, 2005; Prensky, 2005a). These learners have also been named 'generation C', the content creation generation. As Bruns argues (2007), this is not necessarily age related, but "a loose but significant grouping of participants who (on average, and perhaps implicitly rather than explicitly) share a set of common aims and practices." While this portrayal of today's school leavers immersed in web 2.0 use has been challenged (Kennedy *et al.*, 2007), it is in general their willingness (and in many cases preference) to adopt new technology (JISC, 2007) that sets them apart from previous generations of learners. There is potential to engage and guide these learners in education by leveraging web 2.0 tools within collaborative, technologically rich social constructivist environments.

E-learning is not an experiment. It has moved into the mainstream of higher education and is beginning to be recognized as a strategic asset... The challenge for institutions is to adopt what is, in the short term, a disruptive technology, in such a way that it enhances core values while positioning the institution for the demand and opportunity of innovative technology (Garrison & Anderson, 2003).

The use of Wireless Mobile Devices (WMDs) as part of the teaching and learning environment requires changes in pedagogy and integration into the teaching and learning processes. Changes in pedagogical strategies, content (reformatted for small screens and lower data bandwidths), and contexts (beyond the face-to-face classroom environment) are required. Mishra et al (2007) argue that "appropriate use of technology in teaching requires the thoughtful integration of content, pedagogy, and technology".

The addition of a new technology reconstructs the dynamic equilibrium between all three elements forcing instructors to develop new representations of content and new pedagogical strategies that exploit the affordances (and overcome the constraints) of this new medium. Similarly, changing pedagogical strategies (say moving from a lecture to a discussion format) necessarily requires rethinking the manner in which content is represented, as well as the technologies used to support it (Mishra et al., 2007).

Mobile devices coupled with wireless networks have been described as 'disruptive technologies' (Sharples, 2000, 2001, 2005; Stead, 2006), and so have the web 2.0 social software tools that have developed (Blogs, Wikis, podcasting, vodcasting, online photo blogging etc…) (Alexander, 2004, 2006; Fielder, 2004; Lamb, 2004). Disruptive technologies are those technologies that challenge established systems and thinking, requiring change and are thus viewed by many as a threat to the status quo. Disruptive technologies democratise education environments challenging the established power relations between teachers and students. Their disruptive nature forces a rethink of pedagogical strategies and relationships in education.

A pedagogical framework for implementing social software tools via wireless mobile devices can be developed by drawing on concepts from: constructivism (Bruner, 1966; Piaget, 1973), social constructivism (Vygotsky, 1978), communities of practice (Wenger, 2005), a conversational model of learning (Laurillard, 2001), and the social construction of technology (Bijker, 1995). Thus a mobile (mlearning) pedagogical model will focus upon enhancing communication and collaboration within a dynamic learning environment, and will be student-centred. In a social constructivist view of learning, creating a student centred, self-directed learning environment is seen as necessary for deep learning to occur. Hence it is postulated herein that WMDs are disruptive technologies that are useful in challenging established pedagogies, providing a catalyst to move tertiary education towards social constructivism.

Web 2.0

Web 2.0 is a recently coined term (O'Reilly, 2005) referring to a new wave of Internet tools and usage. Kress and Pachler describe web 2.0 as a "fundamental shift in agency from broadcast to content generation, a decentralization of resource provision and, … an enhanced organization and categorization of content with an emphasis on 'deeplinking'" (Kress & Pachler, 2007). 'Social Software' (interactive collaborative software) is one of the key features of 'Web 2.0'. Examples of current and emerging social software tools include Blogs, Wikis, RSS, instant messaging, podcasting, social book marking, etc… (Farmer, 2004; Glogoff, 2005; Kaplan-Leiserson, 2004). The key characteristics of social software fit well with the pedagogies described above, enabling a natural and relatively simple approach to creating collaborative learning communities.

Web 2.0 is about:

1. Moving beyond CONTENT
2. Ease of use
3. Interactivity
4. Collaboration & sharing
5. Customisation
6. Personal Publishing
7. Exploiting multiple communication channels

The educational implications of web 2.0 social software are the source of recent interest (Alexander, 2006; Alexander *et al.*, 2006; Anderson, 2007; Becta, 2006, 2007; Bryant, 2006; New Media Consortium, 2007). Many educators have harnessed web 2.0 tools for creating engaging student-centred learning environments. This appropriation of web 2.0 tools within a social constructivist pedagogy facilitates what has been termed "pedagogy 2.0".

Pedagogy 2.0 integrates Web 2.0 tools that support knowledge sharing, peer-to-peer networking, and access to a global audience with socioconstructivist learning approaches to facilitate greater learner autonomy, agency, and personalization (McLoughlin & Lee, 2008).

Building on this foundation, Wireless Mobile Devices coupled with open-source Social Software tools potentially provide the basis for enhancing teaching and learning in virtually any discipline, providing an environment that stimulates reflection, critique, collaboration, and user generated content – i.e. a social constructivist environment.

Mobile Pedagogies

Approaches to mobile learning can be categorised within three broad approaches (Stead & Colley, 2008):

1. **Shallow or supplementary learning:** Typically, these may be SMS prompts, School-generated podcasts, and mobile games. They are good as a supplement to other activities.

2. **Focused Learning:** Typically these resemble a mobile-friendly version of classic "e-learning", with targeted nuggets of learning that can be engaged with while on the move - possibly context aware.
3. **Deep Learning:** Deep learners are immersed in a mix of mobile technologies, as creators or originators as well as the more common consumers of mobile media, following a constructivist model.

This chapter focuses on the third approach by using a mix of mobile web 2.0.0 tools. While web 2.0 tools are characterised by user-generated content and social networking, mobile devices add the extra dimension of user-generated contexts. "The intrinsic nature of mobile technologies is to offer digitally-facilitated site-specific learning, which is motivating because of the degree of ownership and control." ((Laurillard, 2007) p157)

The majority of today's learners can be described as:

- Technically literate
- Multitasking
- Collaborative
- Connected

To engage these learners a lot of thought must be given as to how their preferred means of communicating can be integrated into the teaching and learning environment. Mobile devices are inherently social, enabling rich social interaction, and have the potential for enhancing group work and communication within educational settings. In general today's younger tertiary learners are constantly connected to their social networks via their wireless mobile devices. A 2006 survey of Australian students born since 1980 indicated - 95% owned mobile phones, 73% owned MP3 players or iPods, 23% had their own games console and 15% had a personal digital assistant (Litchfield *et al.*, 2007). Their preferred method of communication is text messaging (65% (Cameron, 2006)), followed by instant messaging (New Zealand Herald, 2006). A recent ECAR survey of 27,846 students at 103 USA higher education institutions indicated 84.1% of students use instant messaging daily while 81% use social networks daily (Caruso & Salaway, 2007).

In comparison, many of today's lecturers may be unfamiliar or uncomfortable with the use of the tools described above (Blogs, wiki's, RSS, instant messaging etc…). Before lecturers can implement mobile learning they require understanding and experience of a range of foundational learning technologies. Most mobile learning trials involve only a small number of lecturers, who are already techno-savvy enough to be confident incorporating mlearning. To move mobile learning into the mainstream of an institution requires a strategy for up-skilling academics in integrating technology into their pedagogies (Kukulska-Hulme & Pettit, 2007; Moser, 2007).

Intentional Disruption

The disruptive nature of Web 2.0 and mobile technologies facilitates a move from instructivist pedagogies to social constructivist pedagogies. The personal, social networking, and context awareness of mobile devices democratise power relationships and are best suited to open learning environments. The disruptive nature of mobile devices requires educators to rethink learning environments and assessments in order to integrate the technology into their pedagogical approach. As Laurillard reinforces (2007), the role of the educator in designing/facilitating effective mobile learning environments is critical. This disruption is not limited to the role of the educator, but also to students' workflow and perceptions of education. For many students the facilitation of anytime anywhere learning and the use of their social devices will be met with feelings of intrusion and resistance. However, some students will find a new sense of empowerment and connectedness in this new educational environment. Both of these reactions have been experienced during the mobile trials at Unitec referenced later in this chapter.

Supporting Mobile Learning

The disruptive nature of mobile learning requires significant pedagogical support. One approach to facilitate this is the development of academic peer group support guided by a teaching and learning professional, i.e. a Community Of Practice (Cochrane, 2007b; Cochrane & Kligyte, 2007), investigating the use of Web 2.0 social software tools and then mobile learning in education guided by a 'technology steward' (Wenger et al., 2005). This Community of Practice also provides a model for academics to use in their own student classes as they later integrate social software and mobile technologies into their courses. However, it must be noted that nurturing successful intentional Communities of Practice requires significant effort (Langelier, 2005; Wenger et al., 2002). In the following research project, the author has taken on the role of the technology steward to guide academic staff and their students using an intentional Community of Practice model. This has proven to be a key strategy in the success of the mobile learning trials. Academics who have participated in COPs feel better prepared for today's technology adept learners.

MLEARNING CASE STUDIES

This section illustrates social constructivist learning environments facilitated via WMDs and social software with several qualitative action research learning trials being run to investigate the impact of WMDs on teaching and learning in higher education. The anticipated learning outcomes of these trials for students are:

- Developing critical reflective skills
- Facilitating group communication
- Developing an online eportfolio
- Developing a potentially world-wide peer support and critique network
- Learning how to maximise technology to enhance the learning environment across multiple contexts

Methodology and Participants

The research is qualitative using a participatory action research methodology to build upon lessons learnt in each successive trial, and to allow flexibility and critical reflection leading to appropriate trial redesign within each trial. The researcher is interested in bringing about positive change within the teaching and learning environment. Yoland (Wadsworth, 1998) identifies the key characteristics of 'participatory action research': the researcher is a participant, the researcher is the main research instrument, it is cyclical in nature, involves action followed by reflection followed by informed action, and is concerned with producing change. This change is ongoing throughout the process, and the research is interested in input from participants/stakeholders. Teaching staff (9) were invited to be potential participants for the research trials by the researcher, and were all previously participants in communities of practice facilitated by the researcher focusing on the potential of educational technologies to enhance teaching and learning. Each trial was created as the result of collaborative discussions between the researcher and each set of tutors, choosing appropriate mobile devices and project goals to enhance each respective course. Tutors then called for volunteer student participants from each of their courses (a total of 50 students over 8 courses), outlining the scope and participation requirements. All participants were provided with the chosen mobile device, wifi access on campus, and a variety of 3G data accounts for use during the period of each trial. Students and staff were surveyed pre-trial to gauge their previous experience of the mobile web 2.0 tools. They were also provided with outlines of the research, an acceptable use policy and ethics consent forms. An intentional community of practice was then established for each trial, consisting of the researcher (technology steward), the course tutors, and the student participants. Each community of practice aimed to meet regularly and formed the basis for scaffolding the use of the technology and the integration into each courses curriculum. Survey instruments and focus group discussions gathered feedback from all participants mid and post trial. The first trial (Diploma Landscape Design 2007) provided a basis for informing the second trials in 2008. The three 2008 trials were being conducted in parallel with one another, and issues raised by one trial were then identified and used to modify the other two trials, providing an inter-connected action research environment.

Research Questions:

1. What are the key factors in integrating Wireless Mobile Devices (WMDs) within tertiary education courses?
2. What challenges/advantages to established pedagogies do these disruptive technologies present?
3. To what extent can these WMDs be utilized to support learner interactivity, collaboration, communication, reflection and interest, and thus provide pedagogically rich learning environments that engage and motivate the learner?
4. To what extent can WMDs be used to harness the potential of current and emerging social constructivist e-learning tools?

Data gathering consists of:

1. Pre-trial surveys of lecturers and students, to establish current practice and expertise
2. Post-trial surveys and focus groups, to measure the impact of the wireless mobile computing environment, and the implementation of the guidelines.
3. Lecturer and student reflections via their own blogs during the trial.

The survey tool and focus group questions can be viewed in the appendix. Additionally each trial has used the mid semester and end of semester breaks to provide opportunities for reflection on the progress of each trial, gather formative feedback from participating students and staff, and brainstorming with the tutors on how to better integrate the technologies into each courses curriculum. Students and tutors have been encouraged to create summary VODCasts (video blogs) providing critical reflection on the trial at these points. These VODCasts, along with the wide variety of media students have uploaded to their blogs, have provided rich media for later analysis and reflection.

Communities of Practice

The tutors involved in the trials have previously been involved in the development of academic peer support groups guided by a teaching and learning professional, i.e. an intentional Community Of Practice (Cochrane, 2007b; Cochrane & Kligyte, 2007), investigating the use of Web 2.0 social software tools and then mobile learning in education. This Community of Practice also provides a model for academics to use in their own student classes as they later integrate social software and mobile technologies into their courses. The project is guided and supported by weekly "technology sessions" facilitated by a 'technology steward' (Wenger et al., 2005) who is the researcher and an Academic Advisor in elearning and learning technologies in the Centre for Teaching and Learning Innovation (CTLI) at Unitec. The projects are collaborative projects between the 'technology steward', the course tutors, and the students on the course. While still in early days, the uptake throughout the institution of COPs for educational technology is encouraging. Staff who previously struggled with integrating technology into their pedagogical approaches are now implementing mobile learning projects with students, and thus we are seeing the awareness and uptake of mobile technologies in tertiary learning increase at Unitec (A tertiary education Polytechnic institution). Key to the models success is its flexibility: recognizing that every COP formed is unique, requires negotiable content, motivational goals, and appropriate access to resources. Every COP will require a different approach for nurturing and motivation.

Scaffolding the Learning

As part of the role of the 'technology steward' for the trials the researcher has also taken on developing the technical and learning support for the trials. This has involved the investigation and purchase of appropriate smartphones and folding Bluetooth keyboards for the smartphones. The best option for providing voice and data connectivity for the trial participants (within the project budget) was investigated with Vodafone New Zealand. The smartphones were pre-configured with the wireless settings and software appropriate for the trial (e.g. Vox client, GMail client, Shozu client, Google Mobile and Moodle shortcuts etc...). Tutorial courses have been created for each trial within the Learning Management System (LMS) used by the course (either Moodle or Blackboard). Demonstration tutorials have been created using screen captures of the smartphones accessing the various web 2.0 tools utilized and embedded as interactive slideshows within the LMS. Support has been provided for the course tutors in the form of pre-trial tutorials on using the smartphone and web 2.0 tools. Finally the core support element of the trials is a weekly 'community of practice' investigating the use and integration of the smartphones and web 2.0 tools involving: the technology steward, the course tutors, and the students. Each trial 'learning community' is also supported by the 'neighbourhood' social networking feature of Vox, and the use of instant messaging for facilitating communication and a sense of social presence.

Figure 1. Mobile Web 2.0 concept map

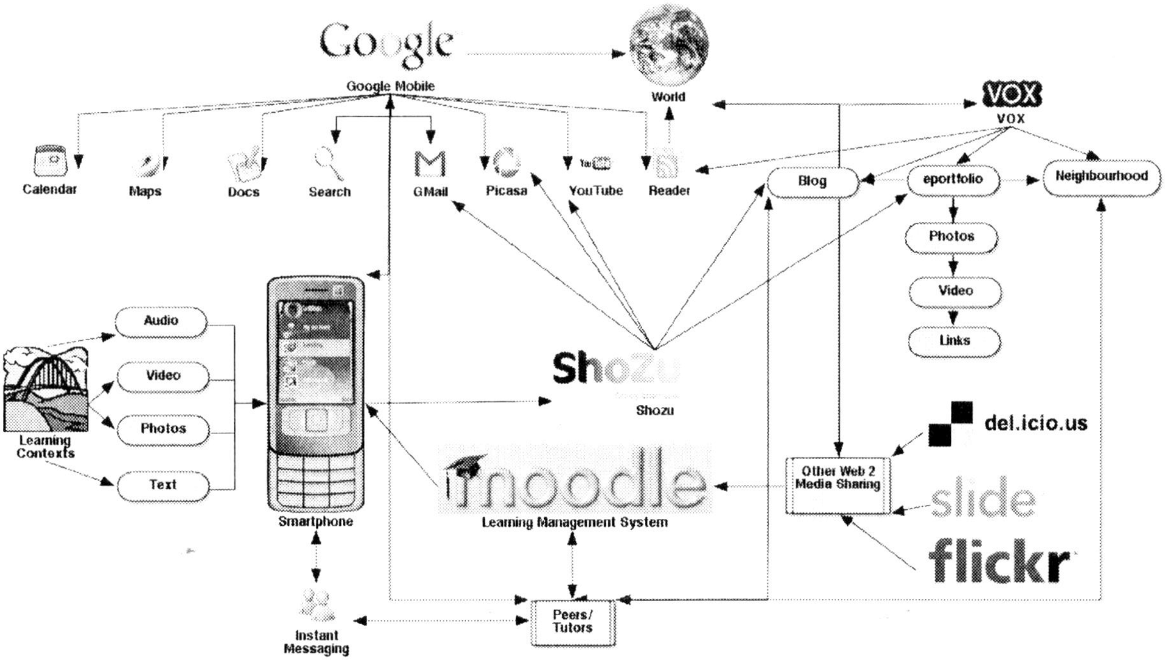

Pedagogical Design

The core activity of each trial is the creation and maintenance of a reflective Blog as part of a course group project. Additionally a variety of mobile friendly web 2.0 tools are used in conjunction with the smartphone. The trials investigate how the smartphone can be used to enhance almost any aspect of the course. The project uses the smartphone within a wide range of activities (see the following diagram, Figure 1, Table 1 and Table 2 that attempt to illustrate the alignment of these activities with the projects underlying social constructivist pedagogy. There is an interactive online version available at http://ltxserver.unitec.ac.nz/~thom/mobileweb2concept2.htm):

The trials are exploring how a mix of mobile web 2.0 tools can enhance the student's learning throughout their whole course.

Table 3 below outlines the implementation timeline model developed to facilitate the mobile web 2.0 trials. It must be emphasized that experience indicates that this process involves significant time for staff and student develop-

Table 1. Table of trial activities aligned to social constructivist pedagogical outcomes

Activity	Overview	Pedagogical outcomes
A reflective Blog	A blog post (including media) can be uploaded directly to VOX using the Vox client on Nokia smartphones, or Shozu (http://www.shozu.com), or emailed to VOX xxxxxx@moblog.vox.com	Developing critical and reflective thinking
An eportfolio	VOX (http://www.vox.com) includes media sharing (video, audio, documents, images, links…) and linking (YouTube, Flickr etc…) as well as social networking.	Collaborative sharing of media and peer critique also forms the basis for a career portfolio.
Email	GMail (http://gmail.com) provides a free email account that can be used on almost any Internet capable device. A GMail account also opens free access to all other Google web services. The Google Java application optimises GMail for phones.	Communication and collaboration
RSS	RSS enables subscribing and tracking/sharing of online activity. It provides a link between all your web 2.0 media sites. Google reader (http://reader.google.com) is a great web based RSS reader, while Newsgator (http://www.newsgator.com) also provides RSS clients for synchronisation via PC, Mac or mobile.	Collaboration
Shared Calendars	Google Calendars (http://calendar.google.com) can be shared between groups of people via invitation. Google Calendars use an open format that provides interoperability between many calendar systems – e.g. iCal on Mac OSX	Time scheduling and collaboration of activities
Image Blogging	Dedicated image sharing repositories such as Flickr and picasaweb offer more interactive features than Vox's image repository, and are linkable to Vox and other Blogging systems. Direct mobile upload to Flickr can be achieved via either the Vox client, or email. Picasaweb mobile is supported via Shozu destination uploads.	Event, data and resource capturing and collaboration. Creativity.
Video Blogging	YouTube (http://www.youtube.com) is currently the most popular video-sharing site. The mobile version supports viewing of videos online in the mobiles web browser, or via a downloadable Java client for specific phones. Uploading mobile videos to YouTube is achieved via email attachments.	Event, data and resource capturing and collaboration. Creativity.
Shozu	Shozu is a service for linking all your online mobile Blog and Media sites together via either the Shozu client application, or an email sent to go@m.shozu.com	Shozu provides links between all the pedagogies described.
Podcasting	Uploading an audio file to Vox creates a podcast episode that others can subscribe to via an automatically created RSS feed.	Interviews, critiques, reflections, shared collaboration.
Instant Messaging and Skype	Fring (http://www.fring.com) is a free Instant Messaging and Skype client for most mobile phones. It allows messaging between the most popular IM systems. It works best over a WiFi connection, or good 3G connection.	Communication and collaboration

ment. The timeframe of the trials was designed to firstly familiarise the tutors with the tools and technology before introducing it to their students. Semester one goals of mobile web 2.0 projects are mainly to get tutors and students experimenting and confident with the tools, embedding them into their course workflows, followed by more explicitly targeted pedagogically designed learning experiences in semester two.

Tables 4, 5, 6, 7, 8 and 9 provide a comparative outline of the six mobile web 2.0 trials conducted during 2007 and 2008. Each trial uses a Learning Management System (LMS) to provide scaffolding and support for both tutors and students (either Blackboard or Moodle). Each project also uses a different 'smartphone' device, appropriate to the requirements of the course, and each project has a specific timeline that has been negotiated between the course tutors and the researcher.

Disruptive Pedagogical Implications

The 2007 mobile web 2.0 trial illustrates the disruptive nature of the introduction of these technologies into a learning environment. The project began by using Wordpress as a reflective journal, and then moved to using Vox as a mobile enabled eportfolio in semester two of the project. There were three student groups (teams) involved in the 2007 trial. Of these, two groups engaged with the mobile technology aspect of the trial and the move to Vox, while one group chose not to. This led to a stark contrast in feedback on the usefulness of mobile technology in supporting education between the engagers and non-engagers. Discussions with students during the technology sessions and the end of trial student survey indicated that the 'engagers' responded enthusiastically regarding the ability of mobile devices to enhance education

Table 2. Table of trial activities aligned to social constructivist pedagogical outcomes

Activity	Overview	Pedagogical outcomes
Shared Bookmarks	Delicious (http://del.icio.us) is a social bookmarking site – allowing the creation and sharing of Internet bookmark libraries and searching via tags (descriptive keywords). Mobilicious (http://mobilicio.us) a mobile optimised version.	Collaboration
LMS	Moodle is a mobile friendly Learning Management System, hosted on a production level Unitec server. Course notes, discussion forums, and various activities can be hosted on Moodle.	Scaffolding and support
Mobile Google	A gateway into the Google Mobile services (http://mobile.google.com) via the phones web browser. iGoogle (http://www.google.com/ig/i) is a customisable mobile Google Homepage.	Links to tools that support all of the mentioned pedagogies.
Mobile Codes	Mobile Codes (Datamatrix codes in this case) provide sharing of URLs, text and messages via scanning using the smartphones built-in camera. Codes can be created and downloaded from http://mobilecodes.nokia.com and scanned using either a compatible scanning application on the mobile phone.	Scaffolding, support, collaboration.
Web Browsing	The Built-in Web Browser is very good, but in some cases Opera Mini may work better, and Opera Mini has several tools built-in (RSS feeds, synchronisation with Opera on a PC etc…)	Research skills
Document Reading & Editing	Google Docs (http://docs.google.com) is Microsoft Word, Excel and PowerPoint compatible. Documents can be uploaded and shared and edited by a group. They are viewable online in a web browser without MS Office. Docs can be created on mobile devices by emailing the document to a private Google Docs address. To edit uploaded documents you need a full PC web browser, or a full version of 'Quick-Office' on your smartphone – a mobile version of MS Office (~ $60).	Documentation, reflection, critique, description, and collaborative document publishing etc…

Table 3. Typical trial process and timeline

Project Steps	Project Milestones
1. 3 to 6 months pre trial	• Establish a Community Of Practice with potential academic staff members, who are committed to working together and exploring the potential of web 2.0 and mobile web 2.0 technologies in teaching and learning.
2. Pre trial – at end of COP	• Brainstorm mobile web 2.0 project goals and course integration with course Tutors, creating or modifying course outlines and assessment activities.
3. Pre trial	• Purchase appropriate mobile smartphone and accessories (e.g. folding Bluetooth keyboard). • Investigate best option for providing voice and data connectivity • Configure the smartphones with software appropriate for the trial (e.g. Vox client, GMail client, Shozu client, Google Mobile and Moodle shortcuts etc…) • Setup LMS (e.g. Moodle) support course for scaffolding students and forming an focus for the weekly 'technology support' sessions (Effectively a Community Of Practice involving students, staff and the technology steward)
4. Pre including students in trial	• Provide course tutors with smartphone and tutorials on setup.
5. Trial setup with students	• Blog and Web 2.0 setup session with Students and Staff
6. Trial official start with students	• Provide students with smartphone and begin weekly technology support sessions.
7. On going, weekly throughout trial	• Support students and staff during trial via weekly 'technology workshops' • Monitor student progress via their Vox Blogs/eportfolios
8. Mid trial and end of trial	• Student and staff surveys • Focus group • Data analysis and report write up. • Re-evaluation of Trial for second semester
9. During semester break	• Use feedback and evaluation to modify Second semester mobile web 2.0 strategies and assessment activities.
10. On going, weekly throughout second half of trial	• Support students and staff during trial via weekly 'technology workshops' • Monitor student progress via their Vox Blogs/eportfolios
11. End of trial	• Final Data gathering, analysis, and report write up.

Table 4. Outline of Diploma of Landscape Design 2007 mobile web 2.0 trial

Course: Diploma Landscape Design 2007, elective project	
Participants	• 8 students (three teams) –The average age of the students is 28 (19 to 49), and the gender mix was 5 female students and 3 male students. • 1 Course Tutor • Technology Steward (Thom Cochrane – CTLI)
Mobile Technology	Nokia N80 WiFi and 3G smartphone, prepay voice and data SIM
Pedagogical Focus	Design and build a group exhibition garden for the Ellerslie Flower Show
Community of Practice	Focused on beginning and middle of the project, with 4 sessions at the beginning of the trial and 4 sessions mid trial with the introduction of the N80.
Support LMS	Moodle
Deliverables	A reflective blog of the design and build process. (Initially Wordpress, then moved to Vox in July 2007) A portfolio (either electronic using VOX or print-based).
Timeframe	March 2007 to November 2007, with N80 mobile introduced in July 2007.

Table 5. Outline of Bachelor of Product Design 2008, third year class, mobile web 2.0 trial

Course: Bachelor of Product Design, third year class	
Participants	• 9 students – The average age of the students is 24 (19 to 33), and all are male students. • 2 Course Tutors • Technology Steward (Thom Cochrane – CTLI)
Mobile Technology	Nokia N80 WiFi smartphone (upgraded to N95 in Semester2), Bluetooth folding keyboard, 1GB/month 3G data
Pedagogical Focus	Documenting the research and design of three products throughout the year, including working with a client company in small design teams
Community of Practice	Weekly throughout he entire course
Support LMS	Moodle
Deliverables	An online Blog/eportfolio documenting and showcasing your design processes and forming the basis of a collaborative hub with worldwide peers and potential employers/clients.
Timeframe	February 2008 through to November 2008, expanding to the entire course 2009.

Table 6. Outline of Diploma of Contemporary Music 2008 mobile web 2.0 trial

Course: Diploma of Contemporary Music, elective class	
Participants	• 11 students – The average age of the students is 22 (17 to 32), and the gender mix is 6 female students and 5 male students. • 2 Course Tutors • Technology Steward (Thom Cochrane – CTLI)
Mobile Technology	iPod Touch WiFi PDA, upgraded to iPhone with 200MB/month 3G data in Semester2
Pedagogical Focus	A group investigation of the potential of the iPod and iPhone to enhance the Contemporary Music programme
Community of Practice	Weekly throughout the entire course
Support LMS	Blackboard
Deliverables	A regular Blog entry documenting participants experiences A regular PODCast show episode
Timeframe	February 2008 through to November 2008, continuing in 2009.

Table 7. Outline of Diploma of Landscape Design 2008 mobile web 2.0 trial

Course: Diploma Landscape Design 2008, elective overseas field trip	
Participants	• 6 students – The average age of the students is 55 (42 to 69), and the gender mix is 3 female students and 1 male students. • 2 Course Tutors • Technology Steward (Thom Cochrane – CTLI)
Mobile Technology	Sonyericsson P1i WiFi smartphone, Bluetooth folding keyboard, 1GB/month 3G data
Community of Practice	Focused on the beginning of the trial with four introductory sessions, then a further four sessions in August/September before the trip to Japan.
Support LMS	Moodle
Pedagogical Focus	Creation of an eportfolio preparing, researching cultural background, and recording and then exhibiting an investigative trip to Japan
Deliverables	A Vox eportfolio and blog.
Timeframe	April 2008 to October 2008

Table 8. Outline of Bachelor of Product Design second year class 2008 mobile project

Course: Bachelor of Product Design, second year class	
Participants	• 6 students – The average age of the students was 29 (19 to 41), and the gender mix was 3 female students and 3 male students. • 1 Course Lecturer (Did not participate in the project) • Technology Steward (Thom Cochrane – CTLI)
Mobile Technology	Nokia N95 WiFi smartphone, Bluetooth folding keyboard, 1GB/month 3G data
Pedagogical Focus	An informal group investigation of the potential of mobile technologies and moblogging to enhance the Product design second year programme.
Community of Practice	Weekly throughout the second semester, during students lunch hour.
Support LMS	Moodle
Deliverables	No programme or assessable deliverables required, however a reflective personal regular Blog entry documenting participants' mlearning experiences and enhancing their class project was expected of the participants.
Timeframe	July 2008 through to November 2008.

Table 9. Outline of Bachelor of Product Design first year class 2008 mobile project

Course: Bachelor of Product Design, first year class	
Participants	• 10 students – The average age of the students was 25 (19 to 39), and the gender mix was 1 female student and 9 male students. • 1 Course Lecturer • Technology Steward (Thom Cochrane – CTLI)
Mobile Technology	iPhone 3G, 200MB/month 3G data
Pedagogical Focus	Creation of student design teams to research and design a new ergonomic garden trowel. The research was to be documented using a group VOX blog/eportfolio.
Community of Practice	Focused on the Ergonomics paper within the second semester of the course with the first hour of the weekly class devoted to the moblogging project.
Support LMS	Blackboard
Deliverables	An assessed Vox eportfolio and group blog.
Timeframe	August 2008 to November 2008

experiences, while the non-engagers responded strongly in the negative. There was no obvious demographic reason for this contrast. The contrasting response from participants is not unusual, as is illustrated by a similar response from non-engaging students within a mobile learning smartphone trial conducted by Cook et al (2007). This illustrates the need to develop strategies for early identification and scaffolding for such learners.

The non-engaging group were characterised by:

- Reluctant bloggers
- Attended less than 50% of the technology support sessions
- Did not attend the technology sessions introducing the smartphone and mobile blogging
- Either forgot to carry the smartphone with them, or forgot to keep it charged – it did not become part of their social experience.
- Change adverse – they preferred to keep their Wordpress blogs going rather than move to Vox when it was introduced mid way through the project.

- Exhibited little online community building – i.e. they made no comments on each other's blogs, or the other groups blogs.
- A preference for using their own mobile phone and separate digital camera

While initial setup support was required for students moving from Wordpress to Vox the increased level of collaboration exhibited by the increase in comments on each other's Vox blogs compared to Wordpress comments made the move worthwhile. This can be accredited to the way Vox facilitated a group work environment via its 'neighbourhood' feature. Students who used Vox assigned each other as Vox neighbours and were automatically provided with email notifications of comments on their Vox blog and new posts on neighbour Vox blogs. Vox also sends out a weekly email news notification with a summary of Vox neighbourhood activity.

Redesigning the 2008 Trials

Using an action research methodology for the trials provides the flexibility to critique, reflect on, and modify the projects as required. The 2008 trials have built upon the foundation laid by the first mobile trial in 2007 (Cochrane, 2007a, 2008b, 2008c), which found that:

- A context spanning social-constructivist learning environment is facilitated.
- Teachers require a new pedagogical toolkit to capitalise on this environment.
- Students require explicit scaffolding in this environment.
- The capabilities of affordable smartphones are constantly increasing, as is the availability of free mobile web 2.0 services. These can be matched to create highly collaborative and motivating learning environments.
- Good pedagogical design of contextual learning environments is essential.
- Tutor professional development and technology support is critical.
- An ethos of the educational use of mobile web 2.0 technologies needs to be developed within the teaching and learning environment.
- Technology support for students is critical and must be integrated early into the course.
- Student preferences must be considered when choosing appropriate wireless mobile devices.
- Significant time is required to develop skills in the use of the technologies for both students and tutor

The three 2008 mobile learning trials have produced a variety of results that further illustrate the most significant factors highlighted by the 2007 trial. The amount of support required to initiate and nurture the three groups of students and tutors has been more than was envisioned. Nurturing successful intentional Communities of Practice requires significant time and effort (Langelier, 2005; Wenger et al., 2002). However this has been minimised by having a common design to the three trials that has been developed from the experiences of mobile and web 2.0 projects over the past three years. The partnership between the researcher and the three groups of tutors has been built-up over this period as well - initially through communities of practice investigating the use of educational technology, and now this model is being loosely used to create learning communities consisting of the researcher, tutors, and their students. The challenges include modeling the pedagogical use of the technology to the students, and making the learning outcomes explicit for the students while allowing the flexibility for each group to creatively experiment and develop uniquely.

Staff and student feedback has been extremely positive, with significant gains in student output and engagement noted, and a desire for further use of the technology within their courses. The

Figure 2. Survey feedback

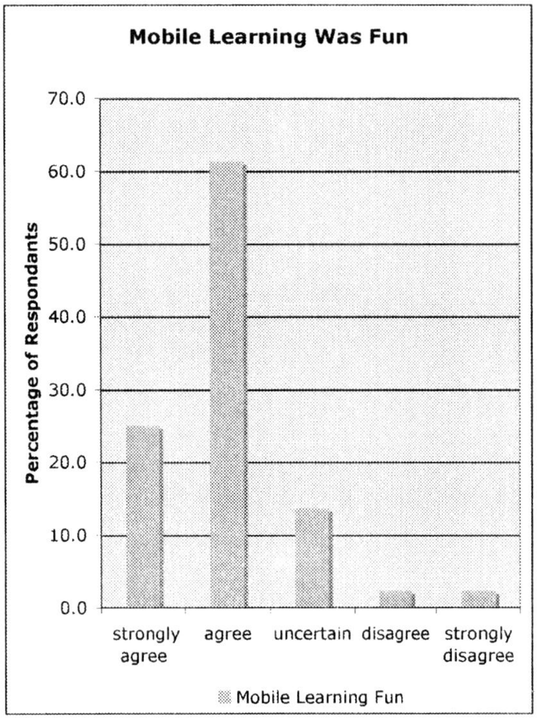

Figure 3. Survey feedback

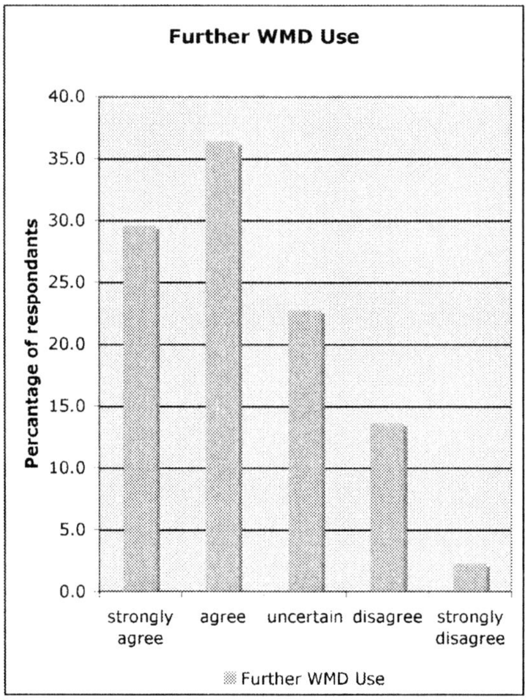

following graphs illustrative student and staff feedback collated and averaged over the six trial groups (Figure 2, Figure 3).

Other schools within the institution are also showing interest – e.g. the School of Screen and Performing Arts, and the School of Architecture. Innovation in programme delivery is a strategic direction for the institution in 2009.

The anticipated learning outcomes from the mlearning trials for students were met.

A graphical representation of the 'tag cloud' (descriptive keywords) generated from Bachelor of Product Design students' VOX blog posts illustrates their use of mobile learning within their course (Figure 4). The relative size of each tag word indicates its frequency of use:

Example Mobile Web 2.0 Scenarios

The following provide illustrative examples of student use of mobile web 2.0 to create context bridging learning environments.

Diploma Landscape Design Student 2007

The camera on the Nokia N80 smartphone was used to capture plant and garden design ideas while off campus. These were then uploaded to the student's blog for sharing with the course tutor and the other students in the design team group. Later on the cameraphone was used to capture the garden design build process on the exhibition site, and then uploaded to the student's blog. Other students and tutors posted feedback comments on the posts from laptops or desktops. Txt messaging was used heavily to coordinate the team members, and email read on the mobile from the course tutor and Vox blog neighbourhood and comment updates. Instant messaging was also used on the smartphone for communication between group members and overseas relatives and friends, showcasing the progress of the garden design.

Figure 4. BDesign student VOX Blogs collated June 2008 tag cloud

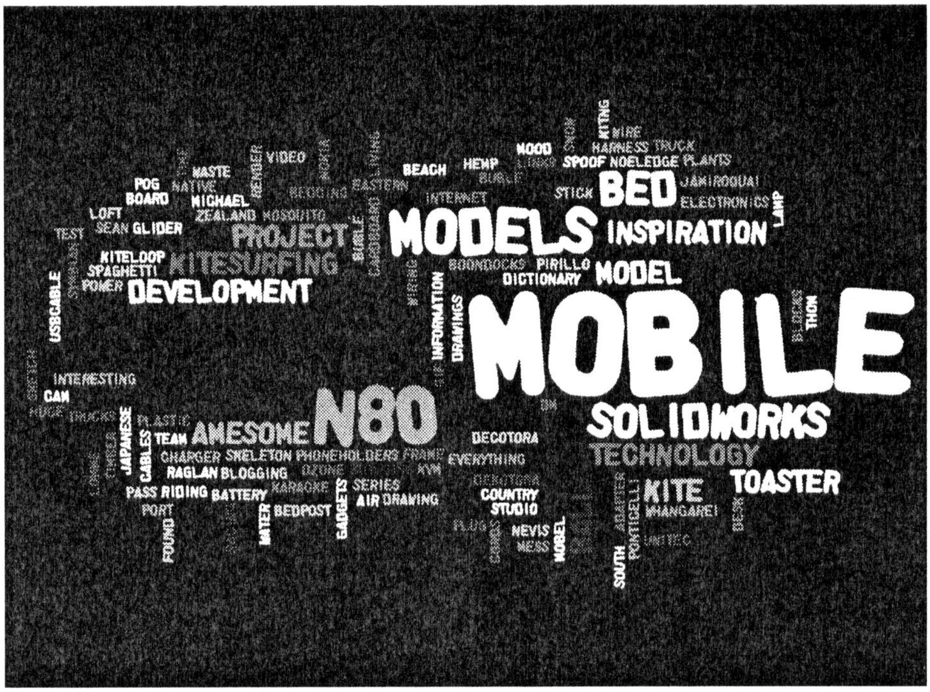

Bachelor of Product Design Student 2008

A student decided to use the smartphone's camera to record still images and video podcasts outlining significant steps in the design process of a snow kite harness. This allowed the student to reflect and critique their design using visual media rather than simply creating a text-based online journal. This took place over the six-month period of the product design. Video clips were recorded from the design studio on campus, from testing in the local park, and from test flights during two ski-field trips. The course tutors followed along with the student's blog posts, offering tips and design guidance while on campus, at home, and while attending overseas conferences. The video clips were then later edited and compiled into a ten-minute video overview of the significant design steps over the six-month design process. The compilation video was then uploaded to YouTube and the student's blog for showcasing and sharing.

Diploma of Contemporary Music Student 2008

Notifications of student performance venues and times were posted to their blog, informing other students' in their Vox neighbourhood via email or RSS to their iPhones of these upcoming events. A second student videoed the student performing live with their band at the venue, and subsequently the video was uploaded and shared via the student's blog. Email and instant messaging were used on the iPhone for communication between students (for social activities and help with assignments), and between the students and the technology steward (asking for help with software issues), and between the students and course tutors (for clarifying assessment requirements).

Diploma of Landscape Architecture Student 2008

The project focused on a research field trip to Japan, gaining landscape design ideas from Japanese garden designs. A student decided to create a story narrative of the trip, using her smartphone to record still photos and videos of the trip mascot (a garden gnome carried on the trip with them) at each of the field trip destinations, uploading and annotating these on her Blog for relatives back in New Zealand to follow along. This also served as the basis of an eportfolio record of the trip from later analysis with the rest of the students and staff when back in New Zealand. Unfortunately the garden gnome suffered a fatal accident before the end of the trip, interrupting the narrative.

Student Feedback

While initially finding learning the smartphone interface daunting, students integrated their use into their everyday lives. Students particularly valued the ability to capture and record ideas and content using the smartphones multimedia capabilities (Cochrane & Bateman, 2008b). They uploaded significantly more media (Mainly still images) to their online eportfolios than actual blog posts. Several students preferred to VODCast (record and upload a video monologue) rather than post text based reflections on their blogs. Students highly valued the potential for mobile web 2.0 technologies to facilitate formative feedback from their course tutors from almost any location and anytime. Least valued by students was the ability to access various types of course content on the

Figure 5. Student perceptions of most useful mobile functions

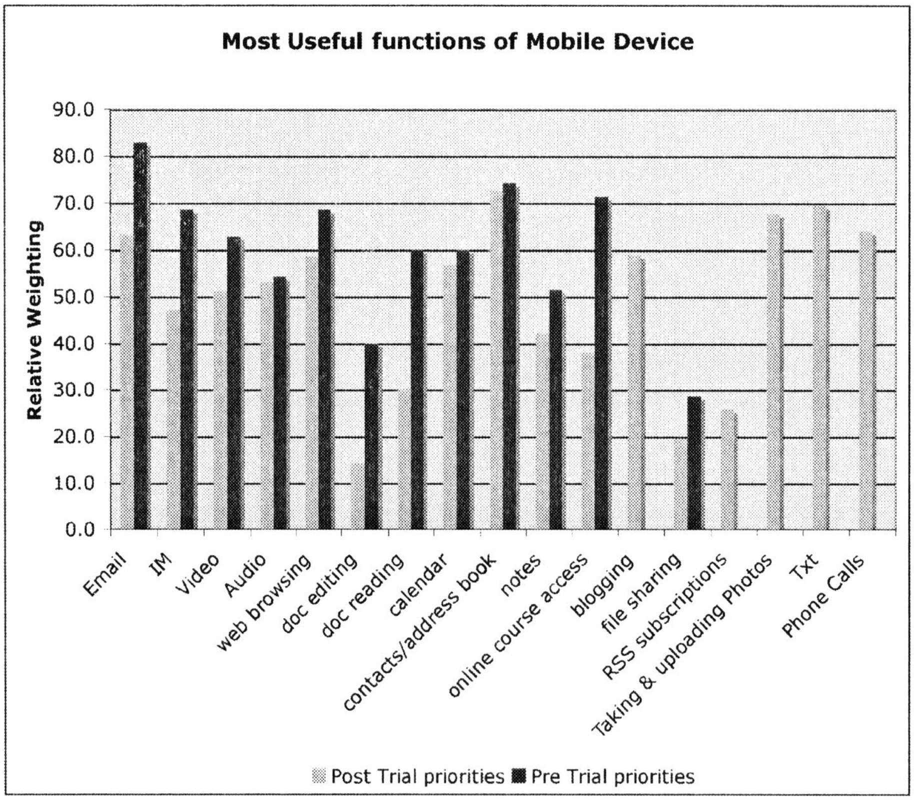

smartphones (see Figure 5.). This is a reflection on the underlying pedagogy chosen for the trials (Social constructivism) where a conscious decision was made to focus on communication, collaboration and user generated content rather than repurpose course content for small screens. However this was also device dependent, with iPhone users rating course content access higher than other mobile device users. In general, students used the smartphones to complement their use of computer laptops.

Students were asked if they would be interested in purchasing their own smartphone as a result of their experiences with the mobile web 2.0 projects. Although a small number of Diploma Landscape Design students rejected the idea of purchasing their own smartphone, BDesign students were unanimous in indicating they would purchase their own smartphone. The most important factors influencing students' own purchase of a smartphone for use in their course were identified as cost, the capability of the built-in camera, the inclusion of wifi connectivity for free internet access on campus, and the ability to integrate the smartphone with their blog for moblogging (see Figure 6). The Nokia N95 smartphones were perceived as a significant leap forward in speed and capability in comparison to the often 'buggy' N80s. The UIQ3 interface of the sonyericsson P1i smartphones was found to be unintuitive for students.

When asked in what situations the WMDs were most effective, students replied:

As a mobile computer – instead of a laptop, and as a communication tool for a team who are in different places all the time, too busy to meet, to transfer information, pictures, documents etc. (Diploma Landscape Design student 2007)

Spur of the moment, spotting something inspirational, documenting an idea when a PC is not around. (Bachelor of Product Design student 2008)

It's the convenience of the small device, nice and handy fits into the pocket. No matter where I was

Figure 6. Most important factors in considering mobile purchase by students

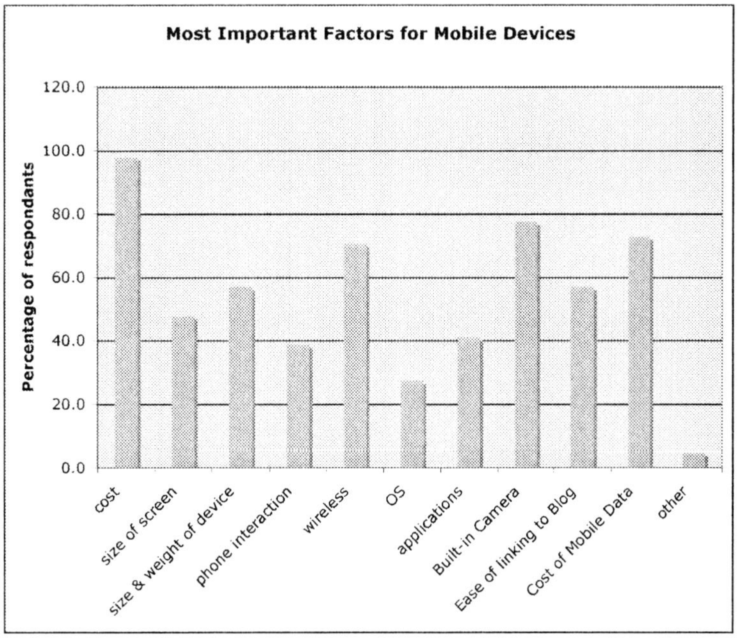

I could use it, spare time having lunch, toilet, even in the classroom while the teacher wanted some information about a particular person. At school looking for information on the net, leisure times, looking at other classmates' webpage's, blog and YouTube videos etc... (Diploma Contemporary Music student 2008).

Staff Feedback

While integration into the courses required significant rethinking of staff pedagogies and assessment procedures, all the staff involved in the trials were very positive at the results (Cochrane & Bateman, 2008a; Cochrane & Cliffin, 2007). However not all teaching staff integrated the use of the mobile web 2.0 tools into their pedagogical toolkits to the same extent.

Once I learnt how to use the technology I then moved on to be able to work with the students. I modified an elective exercise that we didn't formally teach, but was an opportunity for students to put their studies into practice by creating a design for the Ellerslie Flower Show. We decided to make it a course, that doesn't have to have content, but a process, synthesizing all aspects of their Landscape Design course and we can bring in all these learning technologies to support it, including blogs, wikis, and an eportfolio instead of presenting it the traditional way. So in 2006 we trialed it and have built on the idea since then. Thom helped us along the way with this... The Community of Practice that was fostered and the new skills that the students gained in the e-world were fantastic and contributed to them doing so well. It's been a great success and we get savvier every year continuing to experiment with new technologies. Students are feeling more satisfied with the capabilities of the tools they are using and I'm going to keep learning too! (Diploma Landscape Design staff 2007)

It isn't 'easy' working in this way but it is immensely valuable and exciting. I think that it would be very hard go back to traditional teaching only methods now I have begun to use blogging and mobile blogging. (Bachelor of Product Design staff 2008)

Now that I have mastered using WMDs as integrated teaching and learning tools: using up to date technologies to supplement the studio teaching process, I am looking for the next innovation that we can bring to bear on the programme. (Bachelor of Product Design staff 2008)

When asked in what situations the WMDs were most effective, staff replied:

Very useful for blogging, as the WMDs increased interactivity. (Diploma Landscape Design staff 2007)

As an aid to studio based design projects. WMDs allow staff and students to stay in contact outside of the studio as well as allowing staff to point students to on line resources to aid the learning process. (Bachelor of Product Design staff 2008)

WMDs assist when the students are working on live or industry based projects. The clients or companies can easily keep track of the individual students projects thus meaning that when face-to-face meetings do occur, no time is lost getting up to speed. Students seem to take a more professional approach to logging and communicating their projects when they know their client or sponsor company can look at their work at any time. (Bachelor of Product Design staff 2008)

Teaching staff noted that the introduction of the mobile web 2.0 technologies significantly increased student engagement through the creation of a sense of connectivity and the sense of the embedding of current technology into the learning experience. When the mobile web 2.0 technologies were integrated into the course assessment tutors noted the significant facilitation of flexible teaching and learning environments that were no longer bound to on campus facilities.

Embedding assessment is fundamental – because of the time involved in producing these eportfolios and blogs you would not get the uptake or seriousness without it being an assessed deliverable.

Without the mobile devices (as in 2007) blogging was confined to the studio using laptops, so mobile blogging has changed the nature and engagement level! Key therefore is the provision of the mobile devices. Also staff understanding is fundamental, staff have undertaken a learning process as well. Interestingly we assumed that students would know more about web 2.0 technologies than they have!

My teaching approach has changed in that I am now very tolerant of students using technology and not necessarily having to be in the studio as in the past, as they couldn't be interacting with me or other teaching staff. Students are learning on the move and the traditional walls have broken down. My teaching has changed to a balance between being in the studio and reading and marking student blogs. The traditional way of simply being available during the studio sessions has changed to almost being 'on-call' 24/7 because being involved in these blogs becomes quite addictive. Some staff are resistant to this, but using news aggregators is one way to manage this and allows a more flexible working environment. All in all it has been a fantastic experiment. We are looking forward very much to continuing the learning process and seeing how we can reshape the face of studio, art and design education (Bachelor of Product Design staff 2008).

The Future of Mobile Web 2.0

The mobile web 2.0 trials that this chapter has used to illustrate implementation methodologies have so far used a model of providing a common smartphone for the students within a course. The students and staff involved have been encouraged to use the smartphones as if they owned them for the period of the trials. This approach was used to seed the concept and provide proof of concept results. Following the enthusiastic response from the students and lecturers involved in these trials, internal institutional funding was sought, and approved, for extending these small projects to a major large-scale mlearning project in 2009 involving the use of 250 smartphones, and 200 netbooks. This larger scale project is informed by the experiences of the previous trials and will cover a wider range of courses and learning contexts. However, to create a sustainable model, the goal going forward is to move to a student-owned model, where students purchase a smartphone that meets specifications outlined by the course requirements – much as many institutions require students to purchase a specifically specified laptop computer to ease support requirements. As the cost of appropriate smartphones and 3G data costs drop, the purchase cost may be sustainably subsidized by institutions in lieu of other course related costs that the mobile web 2.0 model replaces.

The five mobile web 2.0 trials referenced highlight the following key issues:

- Mobile web 2.0 technologies challenge instructivist pedagogies and provide a rich basis for flexible social constructivist pedagogies.
- A context spanning social-constructivist learning environment is facilitated.
- Mobile web 2.0 technologies facilitate interaction beyond the traditional student-tutor 'conversation'.

- Student engagement is significantly increased and self and peer critical reflection is facilitated.
- Teachers require a new pedagogical toolkit to capitalise on this environment.
- Students require explicit scaffolding in this environment.
- The capabilities of affordable smartphones are constantly increasing, as is the availability of free mobile web 2.0 services. These can be matched to create highly collaborative and motivating learning environments.
- Good pedagogical design of contextual learning environments is essential and should include assessment weighting for students to value the activities.
- Tutor professional development and technology support is critical.
- An ethos of the educational use of mobile web 2.0 technologies needs to be developed within the teaching and learning environment.
- Technology support for students is critical and must be integrated early into the course.
- Student preferences must be considered when choosing appropriate wireless mobile devices.
- Significant time is required to develop skills in the use of the technologies for both students and tutors.

CONCLUSION

This chapter introduces and illustrates the potential for mobile web 2.0 technologies to engage students in a variety of learning contexts, and overviews a transferable model for designing and supporting mobile web 2.0 learning environments. As a limited sample case study the findings and conclusions cannot be used to generalise too broadly, but serve as illustrative principles, strategies used, lessons learned and the results achieved that may help to inform future mobile web 2.0 projects in tertiary education. Student and academic staff feedback is used to illustrate the success of this approach. An intentional Community Of Practice model is presented as a way to support and scaffold mobile web 2.0 projects. The symbiotic relationship developed between the academic advisor (technology steward) and the academic teaching staff involved in each of the mobile learning trials overviewed has proven to be a rich environment for harnessing mobile web 2.0 technologies to design social constructivist learning environments for different groups of tertiary students. The disruptive nature of mobile web 2.0 technologies has been presented as a catalyst to move traditional instructivist pedagogies towards social constructivist pedagogies that bridge both on and off campus learning contexts. It is hoped that the insights gained will be useful for academic teaching staff wanting to implement pedagogical innovation, and for professional development staff seeking insights for facilitating academics to integrate mobile web 2.0 technologies into their pedagogies.

REFERENCES

Alexander, B. (2004, September/October). Going nomadic: Mobile learning in higher education. EDUCAUSE Review, 39, 28–35.

Alexander, B. (2006, March/April). Web 2.0: A new wave of innovation for teaching and learning? EDUCAUSE Review, 41, 33–44.

Alexander, B., Brown, M., Doogan, V., Johnson, L., Levine, A., Sabean, R., et al. (2006). The horizon report 2006 edition. A collaboration between The New Media Consortium and the Educause Learning Initiative.

Anderson, P. (2007). What is Web 2.0? Ideas, technologies, and implications for education. Retrieved in March 2007, from http://www.jisc.ac.uk/whatwedo/services/services_techwatch/techwatch/techwatch_ic_reports2005_published.aspx

Becta. (2006). Emerging technologies for learning. Retrieved on April 6, 2006, from http://www.becta.org.uk/corporate/publications/

Becta. (2007). Emerging technologies for learning: Volume 2. Retrieved in March 2007, from http://partners.becta.org.uk/index.php?section=rh&catcode=_re_rp_ap_03&rid=11380

Bijker, W. (1995). Of bicycles, bakelites, and bulbs. Toward a theory of sociotechnical change. Cambridge: MIT Press.

Boyd, D. M., & Ellison, N. B. (2007). Social network sites: Definition, history, and scholarship. Journal of Computer-Mediated Communication, 13(1), 11.

Bruner, J. (1966). Toward a theory of instruction. Cambridge: Belknap Press of Harvard University.

Bruns, A. (2007, March 21-23). Beyond difference: Reconfiguring education for the user-led age. Paper presented at the ICE3: Ideas in Cyberspace Education: Digital Difference, Ross Priory, Loch Lomond.

Bryant, T. (2006). Social software in academia. EDUCAUSE Quarterly, 2, 61–64.

Cameron, D. (2006, 4-7 December). The rocket in your pocket: How mobile phones became the media by stealth. Paper presented at the 2nd Joint JEANZ/JEA Conference, Rendevous Hotel, Auckland, New Zealand.

Caruso, J. B., & Salaway, G. (2007). Highlights of the 2007 ecar study of students and information technology. ECAR Symposium 2007. Retrieved on January 21, 2008, from http://connect.educause.edu/Library/ECAR/Highlightsofthe2007ECARSt/45912

Cochrane, T. (2007a, October 11). Idf mobile trial1 report: Review and evaluation of first mobile wireless trial. Retrieved from http://docs.google.com/Doc?id=dchr4rgg_215tknwt

Cochrane, T. (2007b, October 16-19). Moving mobile mainstream: Using communities of practice to develop educational technology literacy in tertiary academics. Paper presented at the MLearn 2007-Making the Connections 6th International Conference on Mobile Learning, Melbourne.

Cochrane, T. (2008a, October 8-10). Designing mobile learning environments: Mobile trials at unitec 2008. Paper presented at the MLearn08: The Bridge from Text to Context, University of Wolverhampton, School of Computing and IT.

Cochrane, T. (2008b, July 1-4). Going for gold: A moblogging case study. Paper presented at the HERDSA 2008: Engaging Communities, Millenium Hotel, Rotorua, New Zealand.

Cochrane, T. (2008c). Mobilizing learning: Intentional disruption. Harnessing the potential of social software tools in higher education using wireless mobile devices. International Journal of Mobile Learning and Organisation (Special edition: Developing Themes in Mobile Learning, in pre-press).

Cochrane, T., & Bateman, R. (2008a, June 20). Bachelor of product design blogging reflections video. Retrieved from http://www.youtube.com/watch?v=d44q77cz7H4

Cochrane, T., & Bateman, R. (2008b, June 20). Bachelor of product design moblogging reflections video. Retrieved from http://www.youtube.com/watch?v=V5co1cdzfik

Cochrane, T., & Cliffin, P. (2007). Ctli minisymposium presentation video: Diploma landscape design moblogging. Retrieved from http://www.youtube.com/watch?v=CBWkRrG7-xo

Cochrane, T., & Kligyte, G. (2007, June 11-14). Dummies2delight: Using communities of practice to develop educational technology literacy in tertiary academics. Paper presented at the JISC Online Conference: Innovating eLearning.

Cook, J., Bradley, C., Lance, J., Smith, C., & Haynes, R. (2007). Generating learner contexts with mobile devices. In N. Pachler (Ed.), Mobile learning: Towards a research agenda (Vol. 1, pp. 33-54). London: WLE Centre, Institute of Education.

Elmendorp, R. (2007). Videoreporter.Nl. Retrieved on October 21, 2007, from http://www.videoreporter.nl/videos.htm

Farmer, J. (2004, December 5-8). Communication dynamics: Discussion boards, weblogs, and the development of communities of inquiry in online learning environments. Paper presented at the 21st ASCILITE Conference: Beyond the Comfort Zone, Perth.

Fielder, S. (2004, June 24). Introducing disruptive technologies for learning: Personal webpublishing and weblogs. Retrieved from http://static.cognitivearchitects.com/gems/Seblogging/EdMediaSymposium.pdf

Fulton, N. (2007, October 22). The mobile journalism toolkit contents. Reuters Mobile Journalism. Retrieved on October 24, from http://reutersmojo.com/2007/10/22/the-mobile-journalism-toolkit-contents/

Garrison, D. R., & Anderson, T. (2003). E-learning in the 21st century: A framework for research and practice. London: RoutledgeFalmer.

Glogoff, S. (2005). Instructional blogging: Promoting interactivity, student-centered learning, and peer input. Innovate, 1(5). Retrieved from http://www.innovateonline.info/index.php?view=article&id=126

Herrington, J., Mantei, J., Herrington, A., Olney, I., & Ferry, B. (2008, December 1-4). New technologies, new pedagogies: Mobile technologies and new ways of teaching and learning. Paper presented at the ASCILITE 2008, Deakin University, Melbourne, Australia.

JISC. (2007). In their own words: Exploring the learner's perspective on e-learning (Internet). Bristol: Higher Education Funding Council for England.

Kaplan-Leiserson, E. (2004). RSS: A learning trend. Retrieved on April 4, 2005, from http://www.learningcircuits.org/2004/may2004/0405_Trends.htm

Kennedy, G., Dalgarno, B., Gray, K., Judd, T., Waycott, J., Bennett, S., et al. (2007, December 3-5). The net generation are not big users of Web 2.0 technologies: Preliminary findings. Paper presented at the Ascilite 2007, Singapore.

Kress, G., & Pachler, N. (2007). Thinking about the 'm' in m-learning. In N. Pachler (Ed.), Mobile learning: Towards a research agenda (Vol. 1, pp. 6-32). London: WLE Centre, Institute of Education.

Kukulska-Hulme, A., & Pettit, J. (2007, October 16-19). Self-service education: Smartphones as a catalyst for informal collective and individual learning. Paper presented at the MLearn 2007-Making the Connections 6th International Conference on Mobile Learning, Melbourne.

Lamb, B. (2004). Thewayitwasmeanttobe. Educause Review, 36-48.

Langelier, L. (2005). Work, learning, and networked: Guide to the implementation and leadership of intentional communities of practice. Quebec City: CEFIRO (Recherche et Études de cas collection).

Laurillard, D. (2001). Rethinking university teaching: A framework for the effective use of educational technology (2nd ed.). London: Routledge.

Laurillard, D. (2007). Pedagogcal forms of mobile learning: Framing research questions. In N. Pachler (Ed.), Mobile learning: Towards a research agenda (Vol. 1, pp. 33-54). London: WLE Centre, Institute of Education.

Litchfield, A., Dyson, L. E., Lawrence, E., & Zmijewska, A. (2007, December 3-5). Directions for m-learning research to enhance active learning. Paper presented at the Ascilite 2007, Singapore.

McLoughlin, C., & Lee, M. J. W. (2008). Future learning landscapes: Transforming pedagogy through social software. Innovate: Journal of Online Education, 4(5).

Mishra, P., Koehler, M. J., & Zhao, Y. (Eds.). (2007). Faculty development by design: Integrating technology in higher education. Charlotte: Information Age Publishing.

Moser, F. Z. (2007). Faculty adoption of educational technology. EDUCAUSE Quarterly, 1, 66–69.

New Media Consortium. (2007). The horizon report: 2007 edition. The Horizon Report, 2007. Retrieved from http://www.nmc.org/horizon/2007/report

New Zealand Herald. (2006). The most effective form of emerging media to reach New Zealanders aged 14 to 30. Auckland: New Zealand Herald.

Nokia. (2007). Nokia nseries. Retrieved on April 26, 2007, from http://www.nseries.com/index.html

O'Reilly, T. (2005). What is Web 2.0: Design patterns and business models for the next generation of software. Retrieved in March 2006, from http://www.oreillynet.com/pub/a/oreilly/tim/news/2005/09/30/what-is-web-20.html

Oblinger, D., & Oblinger, J. (2005). Is it age or it? First steps towards understanding the net generation. In D. Oblinger & J. Oblinger (Eds.), Educating the net generation (pp. 10-29). Educause.

Piaget, J. (1973). To understand is to invent. New York: Viking Press.

Prensky, M. (2005a). Engage me or enrage me: What today's learners demand. EDUCAUSE Review, 40(5), 60–65.

Prensky, M. (2005b). What can you learn from a cell phone? Almost anything! Innovate, 1(5). Retrieved from http://www.innovateonline.info/index.php?view=article&id=83

Sharples, M. (2000). Disruptive devices: Personal technologies and education. Retrieved on June 27, 2006, from http://www.eee.bham.ac.uk/handler/ePapers/disruptive.pdf

Sharples, M. (2001). Disruptive devices: Mobile technology for conversational learning. International Journal of Continuing Education and Lifelong Learning, 12(5/6), 504–520. doi:10.1504/IJCEELL.2002.002148doi:10.1504/IJCEELL.2002.002148

Sharples, M. (2005). Learning as conversation: Transforming education in the mobile age. Paper presented at the Conference on Seeing, Understanding, Learning in the Mobile Age, Budapest, Hungary.

Sharples, M., Taylor, J., & Vavoula, G. (2006). A theory of learning for the mobile age (pre-print). Retrieved in February 2007, from http://kn.open.ac.uk/public/document.cfm?docid=8558

Skoeps. (2007). Skoeps-everyone's a reporter. Retrieved on October 24, 2007, from http://www.skoeps.com/landing.html

Stead, G. (2006). Mobile technologies: Transforming the future of learning. Emerging Technologies for Learning. Retrieved on April 6, 2006, from http://www.becta.org.uk/corporate/publications/

Stead, G., & Colley, J. (2008, October 7-10). The power of me: Learning by making your own rich media mobile resources. Paper presented at the MLearn08: The Bridge from Text to Context, Telford, Shropshire, UK.

Uden, L. (2007). Activity theory for designing mobile learning. International Journal of Mobile Learning and Organisation, 1(1), 81–102. doi:10.1504/IJMLO.2007.011190doi:10.1504/IJMLO.2007.011190

Vavoula, G. (2007). Learning bridges: A role for mobile technologies in education. M-Learning Symposium, WLE Centre, Institute of Education, University of London.

Vygotsky, L. (1978). Mind in society. Cambridge, MA: Harvard University Press.

Wadsworth, Y. (1998). What is participatory action research? Retrieved on May 3, 2002, from http://www.scu.edu.au/schools/gcm/ar/ari/p-ywadsworth98.html

Wakabayashi, D., & Auchard, E. (2007, April 23). Mobile phones: Google's next frontier. New Zealand PC World.

Wali, E., Winters, N., & Oliver, M. (2008). Maintaining, changing, and crossing contexts: An activity theoretic reinterpretation of mobile learning. ALT-J. Research in Learning Technologies, 16(1), 41–57.

Wenger, E. (2005, October 14). Communities of practice: A brief introduction. Retrieved on July 17, 2006, from http://www.ewenger.com/theory/index.htm

Wenger, E., McDermott, R., & Snyder, W. (2002). Cultivating communities of practice: A guide to managing knowledge. Boston: Harvard Business School Press.

Wenger, E., White, N., Smith, J., & Spa, K. R. (2005). Technology for communities. Retrieved on July 14, 2006, from http://technologyforcommunities.com/

APPENDIX

Table 10. Wireless mobile study – end of trial questionnaire (DipLSD2007 Students)

QUESTION (This is an anonymous questionnaire)	Your Answer tick or circle most applicable answer/s, or write your answer in the space provided below.					
1. What is your Student ID number?						
2. What is your age?						
3. What is your gender?	Male	Female				
4. What has been your experience of group work facilitated by Blogs and RSS?	Very Good	Good	Not Bad	Neither Good nor Bad	Not Good	Terrible
6. It was easy to use the smartphone (Nokia N80)?	Strongly agree	Agree	Uncertain	Disagree	Strongly disagree	
7. This mobile learning experience was fun.	Strongly agree	Agree	Uncertain	Disagree	Strongly disagree	
8. Based on my experience during this trial, I would use a smartphone in other courses	Strongly agree	Agree	Uncertain	Disagree	Strongly disagree	
9. I would be willing to purchase my own smartphone?	Yes	No				
10. Where did you use the Smartphone? Circle all that apply.	a. At home b. At Unitec in class c. At Unitec not in class d. While Travelling e. On site while investigating or building your project f. Other (specify)					
11. In your opinion, does mobile learning increase the quality of learning?	Strongly agree	Agree	Uncertain	Disagree	Strongly disagree	
12. Mobile blogging helped create a sense of community (group work)?	Strongly agree	Agree	Uncertain	Disagree	Strongly disagree	

Table 10. continued

13. Accessing your course blog was easy using the mobile device?	Strongly agree	Agree	Uncertain	Disagree	Strongly disagree
14. Mobile learning increases access to education?	Strongly agree	Agree	Uncertain	Disagree	Strongly disagree
15. Communication and feedback from the course tutor/lecturer were made easier?	Strongly agree	Agree	Uncertain	Disagree	Strongly disagree
16. Mobile learning is convenient for communication with other students?	Strongly agree	Agree	Uncertain	Disagree	Strongly disagree
17. Rate the usefulness of the following applications using mobile devices? (0 = no use, 10 = extremely useful).	a. Email b. Instant Messaging c. Video d. Audio e. Web Browsing f. Document editing g. Document Reading h. Calendar i. Contacts/Address book j. Notes k. Accessing online course material l. Blogging m. File sharing n. RSS subscriptions o. Taking and uploading photos p. Txt q. Phone calls				
18. What factors would be most important in deciding upon mobile learning?	• Cost of device • Size of the screen • Size & weight of the mobile device • Phone integration • Wireless capability • The operating system: PocketPC, Palm OS, or Symbian • Availability of installable applications • A built-in camera • Ease of linking to your Blog • The cost of mobile data • Other				
19. Do you have any other comments on the mobile project?					

Questions for Discussion

The main purpose of the focus group is to provide critical reflective feedback on the design and implementation of the learning activities and enhanced communication facilitated by the Wireless Mobile Device (WMD) used in the 'trial'. This feedback will provide valuable insights into the design of the following trial, and forms a critical reflective action research cycle of evaluation.

Focus Group Questions

1. How would you rate the effectiveness of the WMD (Smartphone) for accessing your/your students' blogs?
2. How user friendly was the interface of the WMD?
3. How would you rate the effectiveness of the WMD for increasing communication:
    a. Between students
    b. Between Students and Tutors/lecturers?
4. How useful were the WMDs for accessing course content?
5. Describe how the integration into the course of the WMDs may be improved.
6. (For Tutors) How would you rate the usefulness of the WMDs for your own teaching?
7. What level of interactivity did the WMDs provide?
8. What were the benefits of wireless connectivity?
9. What were the support requirements for the WMDs?
10. What other uses did you find for the WMD?
11. In what situations would the WMDs be most effective?
12. What do you think worked well, and what would you do differently another time?

Chapter 8
Mobile Grids:
An Enabling Technology for Next Generation M-Learning Applications

Vassiliki Andronikou
National Technical University of Athens, Greece

Victor Villagra
Universidad Politécnica de Madrid (UPM), Spain

Kleopatra Konstanteli
National Technical University of Athens, Greece

Antonios Litke
National Technical University of Athens, Greece

Athanasia Psychogiou
National Technical University of Athens, Greece

Theodora Varvarigou
National Technical University of Athens, Greece

ABSTRACT

The grid brings a new era to the Internet, by introducing new mechanisms, resources, and concepts which allow it to advance from a passive information medium into an active tool for creating, exploring, and sharing knowledge. In the meanwhile, the realisation of this trend is further spurred by the emergence of next generation grids (NGG) and the far more efficient, cost-effective, and broadly applicable infrastructure they introduce to cover a broader spectrum of business needs. Towards this direction and taking into account that mobility has become a central aspect in business, education, and entertainment, mobile grid has been recently developed as a full inheritor of grid covering the mobility aspects of applications, such as m-learning. In this context, this book chapter focuses on providing a business-technical presentation of mobile grid, as an enabling technology for next generation m-learning applications. We present a general mobile grid architecture able to serve the strict requirements such an m-learning application poses, and analyse the main trends and challenges in the mentioned sector.

DOI: 10.4018/978-1-60566-882-6.ch008

INTRODUCTION

The constantly increasing complexity and volume of interactions among parties, the continuous growth of industrial and business competition and the increased distances between communicating entities, due to globalisation, impose the absolute need for effective and timely communication between all interested parties. In fact, one of the main business-technical challenges is posed by the development of a wide range of continuously evolving services with complex workflows and distributed resources aiming to serve a rapidly increasing number of individuals in varying contexts and with different requirements. In meanwhile, mobility has become a central aspect in the individual's daily life and the business operations through enabling anywhere-anytime connectivity. These challenges combined with the advanced Quality of Service (QoS) requirements narrow the compromise margin for dynamicity, mobility, scalability, performance, security and privacy requirements.

M-learning, as the next generation in e-learning, comprises an exciting new trend in learning techniques allowing for the learner to have an active role in the learning process and enabling continuous education through anytime-anywhere access to and construction of knowledge and expertise as well as collaboration among learners. Following the latest advances in mobile computing and communications and coming to meet the need for advanced knowledge management and undisruptive but still affordable access to learning content, this enhanced learning process brings a new educational era in the academic and business sectors. This revolution in the learning domain, however, is followed by strict accessibility, availability, security, performance non-functional technical requirements that existing infrastructures can address only in small-scale and quite often not sufficiently or resulting in high costs.

These advanced infrastructural needs in combination with the innate business goal for lower cost and higher profit are driving key business sectors such as multimedia, engineering, e-health, gaming, m-learning, among others towards adopting new efficient and scalable solutions into their business. Although initially designed to cover the needs of computationally intensive applications (Foster, Kesselman, & Tuecke, 2001; Leinberger & Kumar, 1999) through facilitating the combination of distributed computational resources, Grid technology of nowadays aims at providing such an infrastructure that can also serve the rising needs of the business and educational domain. As a full inheritor of Grid, Mobile Grid (Litke et al, 2004) with its additional trait being its ability to support mobile resources (serving either as a service provider or a service consumer) in a seamless, transparent, secure and efficient way comes to serve the additional infrastructural needs posed by mobile applications, such as m-learning.

This chapter focuses on presenting and analyzing both from a technical and a business perspective a general Mobile Grid architecture able to serve the strict infrastructural requirements m-learning applications pose based on work performed during the FP6 European project Akogrimo (AKOGRIMO project, 2007). More specifically, work in this chapter presents a Mobile Grid Architecture including the main components and their interconnections as well as the main challenges in such architecture. The driving business needs are presented and a scenario describing the main roles in an advanced m-learning system and their participation in this collaborative environment as well as a set of technical requirements related to this system form the basis for the technical analysis. Finally, the main concerns and challenges are briefly discussed and future research opportunities are suggested, whereas the business future trends are presented.

BACKGROUND

The M-Learning World

The dramatic evolution of Internet and its widespread adoption in combination with recent advances in mobile technologies have incurred tremendous changes in numerous academic, business and governmental sectors. Education and the various related learning activities comprise one of these sectors been strongly influenced by this series of changes. In fact, a new form of learning taking advantage of the minimization of distance effects and the sharing capabilities the Internet offers has been brought at stage; *e-learning*.

M-learning results from the combination of mobile technologies and e-learning. In the learning domain mobility has a threefold meaning; "in terms of space; ... in different areas of life; ... with respect of time" (Vavoula and Sharples, 2002). According to Quinn (2000) m-learning offers "*resources wherever you are, strong search capabilities, rich interaction, powerful support for effective learning, and performance-based assessment*".

When it comes to traditional education, the use of e-learning until recently had been limited to supplementary learning activities. However, gradually e-learning has been adopted in higher education cases more widely with a general tension towards the formulation of virtual educational environments. "Just-in-time" delivery is the main asset e-learning offers; content delivery becomes a non time-consuming process as soon as it has been made available, an extremely important feature in cases in which there is strong need for constant updating of knowledge and change.

The technological advances, the floating market conditions requiring rapid adaptation and the strong competitiveness within the business and industrial world significantly increase the complexity of information as well as the speed of the informational flow. Employers need to absorb knowledge without any delay or geographical barrier, while at the same time new products and services are being brought to market at such a high rate never before having been experienced. In fact, it has been noted that companies offering continuous education and training activities to their employees experience a higher percentage of employees' continual of cooperation with them in a long-term basis whereas their performance rates are higher due to their higher level of knowledge in their line of duties. Thus, in order for an enterprise to be successful there is an imperative need for *"just-in-time"* education of employers as well as *personalization of education* so that the employee being trained is able to adjust the time he requires per learning task in order to absorb the educational content; *two capabilities that currently comprise a great cost for enterprises aiming at becoming more competitive, innovative and productive through the continuous education of their employees and that e-learning environments come to offer in a more affordable, flexible and efficient way.*

Mobile and nomadic eLearning is addressed to allow students and learner in general to have the benefits of "*classical eLearning*" processes beyond a fixed scenario. It is important to note that the learning process takes place in *a social context*, where collaborative group work and sharing with peers (and others) can be a powerful way of confronting one's own conceptions, and the communications can involve teachers, experts, experienced colleagues, workmates, friends and family. The *mobile environment* can make a significant contribution to this process. By facilitating the rapid access to other users anytime/anyplace, sharing contents, knowledge, experiences and gossip, learners can develop '*communities of practice*' as well as informal discussion groups, when needed to optimise their learning processes. As a result, with pervasive and ubiquitous systems it is possible to help students in their student life and enhance their collaboration with other students.

Either serving the academic or the business

world, e- and m-learning improve the collaboration and interaction among the students/trainees through an interactive environment being supported by various means of communication including videos, e-mails, forums, on-line reports, chat rooms, discussion groups. In fact, such a strongly collaborative environment with such numerous types of interaction has proven to be more encouraging and inspiring for students/trainees to learn. Through these interactive means students/trainees are able to absorb knowledge more efficiently, are strongly motivated to participate, have a stronger feeling of responsibility and are able to finalise their classes faster, whereas they feel free to make their mistakes and experiment without feeling exposed. In other words, m-learning brings students/trainees in a more autonomous form of education.

Mobile Grids

Based on the above, apart from the apparent functional requirements, developing an m-learning environment poses great challenges in overcoming their apparent significant non-functional requirements including scalability, availability, performance, interoperability, flexibility, transparency and robustness. Especially in the case of large scale environments, the infrastructural requirements posed are quite strict. In many cases, 24/7 availability of information, complex informational flows, real or 'near' real-time data integration and delivery across heterogeneous data sources as well as real-time analysis of data and fast end-user access and interaction, support of constantly increasing number of users with different privileges, mobility (in case of m-learning) is required. And what is more, issues of data consistency and privacy as well as system flexibility and robustness need to be dealt with in a cost-effective way – with availability, reliability and scalability climbing the higher stairs in the hierarchy. Such advanced infrastructural requirements combined with the innate business goal for lowering costs have driven key educational and business sectors such as e- and m-learning towards the pursuit of new solutions.

The global trend for connectivity independent of the used access mechanism being delivered using (M)IPv6 (Mobile Internet Protocol version 6) in the so called beyond 3G (3rd Generation) or 4G networks sets a robust basis for enabling the delivery of m-learning applications. Within this context, new networking technologies can enable the usage of mobile and nomadic terminals in an m-learning scenario, such as Mobile IPv6 for mobility of terminals, SIP (Session Initiation Protocol) for mobility of users allowing nomadic actors, A4C (Authentication, Authorization, Accounting, Auditing and Charging) for supporting its usage in a commercial environment and Context Management in order to get more information about each actor's environment and to adapt the e-learning services dynamically to it.

In the meanwhile, the Grid can be viewed as a distributed, high performance computing and data handling infrastructure, that incorporates geographically and organizationally dispersed, heterogeneous resources (computing systems, storage systems, instruments and other real-time data sources, human collaborators, communication systems) and provides common interfaces for all these resources, using standard, open, general-purpose protocols and interfaces (Foster, 2002). However, it is also the basis and the enabling technology for pervasive and utility computing due to the ability of being open, highly heterogeneous and scalable.

Thus, in an effort to meet the new challenge of providing new personalised information and advanced communication access capabilities, Grid computing has recently moved beyond traditional high performance distributed computing and incorporated the advanced capabilities of the wireless networks and the lightweight devices, resulting in a new computing paradigm; the *Mobile Grid*. According to Park et al (2003), the idea of Mobile Grid is twofold; not only it enables user mobility offering access to resources of a fixed Grid but also the mobile resources themselves can be part of the Grid. Thus, the devices of the mobile users may have limited capabilities (low processing power, finite battery life and constrained storage space) serving as interfaces to the Grid resource pool through enabling job submission, monitoring and management of the activities allowing for 'anytime, anywhere' operation, or be offered as resources to the Grid.

Despite the short period of time Mobile Grid has entered the infrastructural world which limits the number of adopters, case studies demonstrating the capabilities of such an infrastructure exist. In fact, Mobile Grid has been successfully tested within the e-health and the disaster management domains. In the first case (Loos, 2006) the case study focused on the efficient development, provision and maintenance of complex e-health applications, in an effort to meet the need for mobile ad hoc or pervasive healthcare services (e.g. due to emergencies or chronic diseases) in Heart Monitoring and Emergency Management. In the second case (Bertram, Boniface, Briscombe, Ntuba, & Palmer, 2006) this advanced infrastructure focused on Integrated Emergency Management, and more specifically on enabling the efficient management of crises or disasters related to dangerous and time-critical incidents which are to be jointly handled by medical personnel, security and rescue teams, and other mission-critical mobile personnel.

MOBILE GRIDS: ENABLING M-LEARNING APPLICATIONS

The Business Need

As previously mentioned, m-learning comprises the integration of mobile technologies and e-learning. Thus, it involves a variety of entities, including the communications industry, the e-Learning industry, enterprises in education and business training, trainers, trainees and students. Given the size of the education, training and learning industry and following the technological advances and their great business, educational and financial impact, significant effort is put on information technology and its integration within the learning world. Market figures clearly depict the significant penetration of the mobile technologies in business and personal lives and the proliferation of small, personal devices for voice or data access. According to IDC "By 2008 more than 130 million smartphones will be selling worldwide each year, representing 15% of the overall mobile phone market" (Symbian Limited, 2005).

The interest in this learning vision lies in the capability of exploiting the almost universal availability of mobile devices for educational and training purposes. This next generation of learning allows for a variety of learners and learning environments. The *concept of the learner* now becomes much broader; home users, travelers, children, adults, disabled people, institutional users, employees and employers to be access to and interaction with learning content. In other words, apart from offering an alternative, efficient and less complicated or time-consuming for people to have access to learning content and be involved in knowledge construction, this new m-learning enables the involvement in the learning processes for people may experience a disadvantage due to geographic, economic, social or health status reasons.

After its entrance in the business world, m-learning is gradually supplementing classroom programs and enhancing distance learning in the academic sector as well. Especially in the business world, in an effort to remain competitive and maintain and extend their share in a market that is experiencing an unprecedented growth in the variety of products and services offered, companies are gradually becoming more aware of the need for and the benefit from the continuous education and training of their employees. In fact, depending on their expertise and position in the company, employees need to absorb knowledge without any delay or geographical barrier in a personalised manner with m-learning about to become a competitive necessity.

From the non-functional requirements perspective, on the higher stairs of the priority scale of m-learning environments lie availability, security, performance and mobility. As already mentioned, the infrastructure supporting an m-learning environment must guarantee 24/7 availability of information, complex informational flows, real or 'near' real-time data integration and delivery across heterogeneous data sources, unrestrained, seamless access to learning objects and courseware as well as real-time analysis of data and fast end-user access and interaction. According to Callon (1995), positive contribution – concerning information technology - can come from efficiency measured by productivity, effectiveness (improving the way things are done including what an organisation could never do before) and competitive advantage (doing better and new things for the customer). However, existing infrastructures available to support and offer these functionalities prove to be either inefficient especially for large-scale applications or overly expensive for companies to adopt, whereas mobile devices also usually have much less computing power than static devices. Mobile Grid comes to fill in the missing pieces in current infrastructures and offer an efficient and yet affordable solution within the mobile world.

Mobile Grid-Enabled M-Learning Case Study

Mobile grid technologies can be applied to a variety of scenarios, in which clients and service providers are moving or might be connected from different places at different times. M-learning comprises one of these scenarios: students and teachers are mobile users, but can be also service providers that are moving while connected or can connect from a variety of places and terminals.

Three groups of students are working on their Archaeology class assignments. According to their professor, each group should visit a different archaeological site and apply the techniques they were taught during the semester, whereas they should also combine their findings producing a comparative study. The m-learning environment they are collaborating on provides five distinctive spaces; *the inter-class space*, *the class space*, *the assignment space*, *the group space* and *the private space*.

- The *inter-class space* allows for students to communicate with other students from different departments or universities who are working on the same topic and have been detected at the same site. Through this space the students are able to exchange information, findings and comments.
- The *class space* offers students access to the Archaeological class material (past studies, videos, photos, lectures, etc) and allows for communication, progress reporting, intermediate assessment results and sharing of ideas and findings with the professor as well as with other students at campus. At the same time, the professor can send reminders of important dates, guidance, motivational messages and announce schedule changes.
- The *assignment space* allows for groups to share, compare and discuss their findings, proceed with their comparative study and coordinate their work.
- Through the *group space* mobile members of each group are able to evaluate, prioritize and discuss about their findings, exchange photos and videos, manage their material, share the information they collect through the internet and send notifications to other members of the group.
- Finally, the *private space* allows for each mobile user to keep their personal notes,

Figure 1. Conceptual view of interactions within the spaces

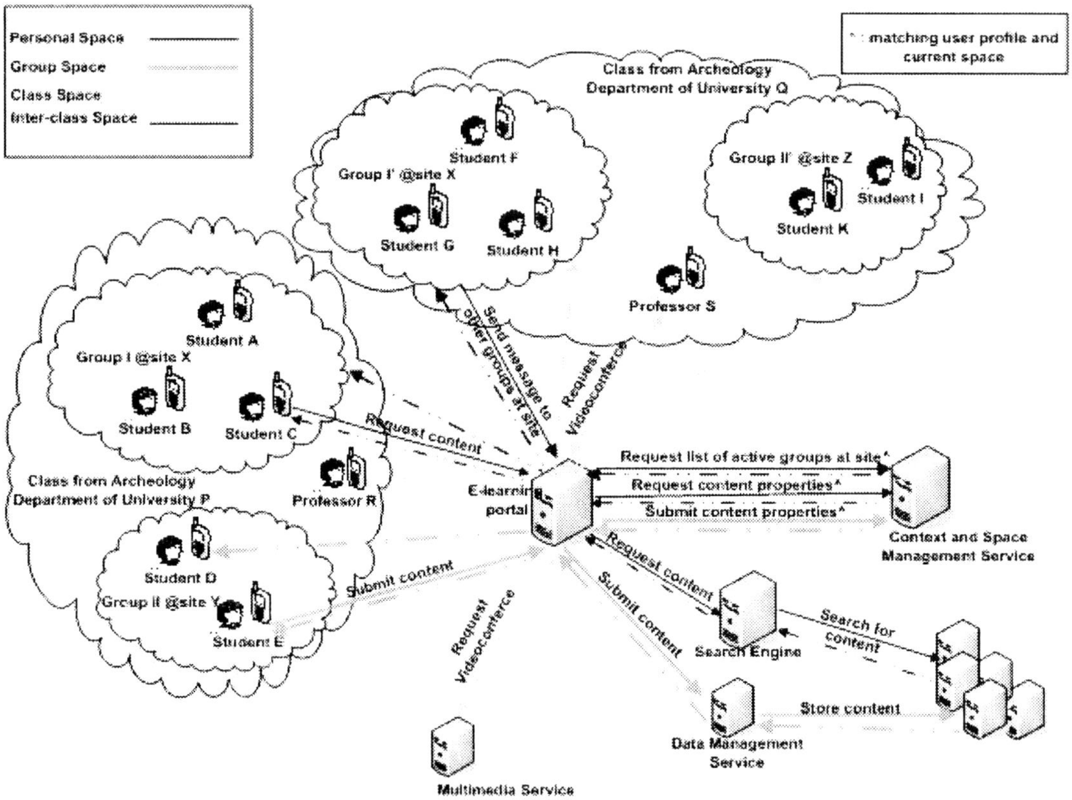

manage their findings (including evaluation, prioritization, editing).

Information sharing and exchange takes place through the appropriate network with the PDA (Personal Digital Assistant) negotiating on the type of network communication based on the bandwidth required, the application type and the agreed-upon QoS (Quality of Service) as well as the price with the Network Service Provider in that zone through the Mobile Grid infrastructure. Taking advantage of location information and combining it with user and group profile information, the PDA automatically indexes the information collected from each individual user based on the group they belong to through appropriate metadata. To secure access to the environment and data transfer, fingerprint-based authentication and encryption are used respectively. Students' findings and professor's guidance and remarks are stored in a Grid repository within the Mobile Grid infrastructure. Each group can share their findings and experiences with other students at university through the class space as well as exchange ideas with students from other universities at the same site through the *inter-class space* (Figure 1).

The Grid m-learning service offered by the Mobile Grid infrastructure orchestrates the video and photo management Grid service X, the speech to text Grid service Y, the next generation semantic text interpretation Grid service W, the advanced assignment management Grid service Z (provided by company A, B, C and D respectively) and elegantly combines them. The professor uploads the assignments' objectives through Grid service Z which translates it into an ontology based knowledge representation. The Grid m-learning service analyses the information students expose to the *class* and *assignment spaces* in order to provide feedback on the progress of the students' work both to the professor and students themselves in group level.

Thus, teachers themselves can have access to a number of different m-learning services: a videoconference service, a service for managing students' contributions (applications for automatic corrections, or applications for managing the m-learning flow). These applications could run in a fixed terminal, but in this case as the service depends on the teacher presence, it will *not be provided continuously*. So, it is more adequate that these services could run in a mobile terminal which is carried by the teacher (i.e. a mobile telephone, advanced PDA, etc.). So Mobile Grid technologies are needed in these cases in order to manage the mobility of the service provider and all the technical requirements presented before. It should be pointed that the teacher is not the only mobile actor in an M-Learning scenario; students can also provide some kind of services in this use case: for example, a service that can be invoked externally (by a teacher or by a learning management system) in order to know the progress of the student, etc.

Within the context of Akogrimo project (AKOGRIMO project, 2007) a Mobile Grid Architecture was developed aiming to serve such applications which involve various both mobile and fixed distributed resources and entities. One of the selected testbeds for this innovative architecture was e-learning (Laria, 2006) serving also mobile users which proved the potential of Mobile Grid to serve mobile users in the e-learning environment.

Technical Requirements

Utilising Mobile Grid concepts to the previously described case study a set of technical requirements arose that are dealt with in the next section:

- Given that m-learning is synonym to "anywhere-anytime" connectivity, mobility comprises one of the most important non-functional requirements. Thus, mobile devices, communication links supporting the Mobile IPv6 protocols and an active Grid middleware serving as mediator between the client side devices and the service operators are essential.
- Provided that the informational load coming from various sources can be rather high and information itself comprises the most valuable resource within such an environment, *fault-tolerant mechanisms* need to be established with the main priority being on *data reliability*.
- Given that the term m-learning is tightly bound with real-time or near real-time information exchange and sharing, *timely communication and integration of information* is required for the successful operation of the established collaborations within this environment.
- As the services are dynamically coupled at runtime, modularity is required.
- Efficient and flexible *SLA* (Service Level Agreement) *monitoring and evaluation mechanisms* are required for monitoring the different SLAs established between the different entities in the m-learning environment and handling unexpected occurrences.
- In order for the different entities to be willing to participate in such a strongly collaborative environment, *security, privacy and flexible identity management* also comprise major challenges that need to be addressed.
- Dynamic workflows that enable the m-learning process as well as the formation and management of the Virtual Organization (VO) that includes all the entities of the m-learning environment.
- There is need for system extensibility, so that new services can be integrated as easier as possible.

Figure 2. Cross-layer cooperation of technologies

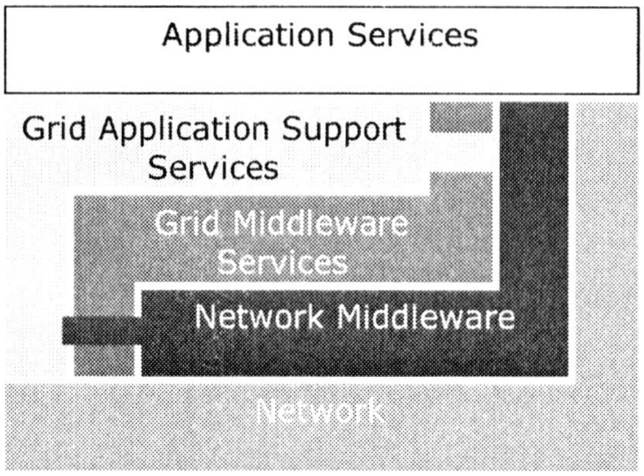

GENERAL MOBILE GRID ARCHITECTURE

Overview

Mobile Grids represent an evolution of the traditional Grid architectures, but supporting mobile and ubiquitous actors in that architecture. Actors can be:

- Mobile or ubiquitous clients, who want to access the services provided by the Virtual Organization from different places, terminals, or while moving with the same terminal.
- Mobile or ubiquitous services, who want to provide services in the Virtual Organization from different places, terminals, or while moving with the same terminal.

For supporting mobile or ubiquitous clients, there is no need to modify the generic Grid architectures, since they are supported with mobile network technologies, like Mobile IPv6 for mobility, and user authentication and authorization technologies for nomadism. The main challenge in a Mobile Grid Architecture is the *support of mobility and nomadicity for services* since it represents an evolution of the classical Virtual Organization composed by a number of fixed services which can cooperate based on the Grid technologies. So, there is a need to combine classical Grid architectures with mobile networks technologies to support the so-called "Mobile Dynamic Virtual Organization" (MDVO), which is the base of the Mobile Grid architecture. In the Case Study presented within this book chapter, mobile groups of students could comprise MD-VOs, so for example if Student A has retrieved from the Grid and stored locally a recent lecture on a study about the monument he and his group have visited at site X, then if Student G from Group I' requests the same lecture, the Grid will direct his retrieval to Student A PDA which is closer to him (see Figure 2). This is accomplished with a cross-layer cooperation of different technologies, as represented in the following figure:

General Architecture

The AKOGRIMO project (AKOGRIMO project, 2007) proposed a Mobile Grid Architecture with different components located in five main domains (Jähnert, J., Wesner, S. & Villagra, V., 2007), as depicted in Figure 3:

- **Base Virtual Organization (BVO):** The Base VO is a Virtual Organisation that is not running a specific business process, but provides the means for creating

Figure 3. Akogrimo Mobile Grid Architecture

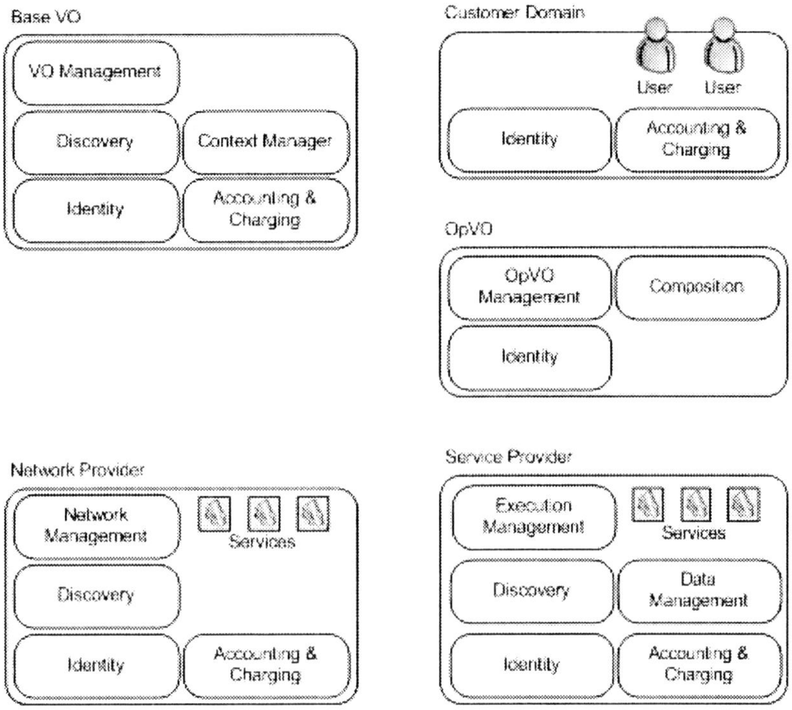

and supporting them. The Base Virtual Organisation allows for registering users, services and other meta-data like SLAs and workflow templates. These repositories are used by the Operative Virtual Organization when a business process is instantiated and executed.

- **Operative Virtual Organization (OpVO)**: The purpose of the Operative VO is to instantiate a business process and to manage the execution. The Base VO has the role of starting the Operative VO creation process. During the creation phase of an Operative VO, all the dedicated management services are instantiated..
- **Customer Domain**: it hosts all the components related to the users' and clients' management, such as identity, accounting and charging management of users (*in our case the students, the professors and the researchers*).
- **Network Domain**: it represents the network infrastructure which is needed for the communication among all the components. In a Mobile Grid scenario, this domain has several added functionalities from the ones of a traditional Grid scenario: it has to include some components to provide support to the Grid Infrastructure service for managing the mobility and nomadism of the users and services. While managing client and user mobility is done transparently through the application of mobile network technology, service mobility and nomadism have to be managed in a cross-layer manner, with components in the network domain providing support to the Grid Infrastructure domain
- **Service Provider (SP)**: This is the key domain for supporting the mobility and nomadism of services, since it is hosting these types of services. The main

component in charge of managing the mobility and nomadism of services is the Execution Management Service, which is cooperating continuously with the network provider components in order *to track the location and context of the service* and react and request the reconfiguration of the virtual organizations if needed.

Main Components

The needed approach for a generic Mobile Grid architecture needs to meet different requirements, which have to be instantiated with the appropriate modules in the architecture. These requirements include:

Base VO (BVO) Management

This functionality is responsible for providing the means for creating and supporting specific business processes which will be instantiated later as an Operative VO. So, it has to provide the means to register users (in our case students, teachers, researchers), services (in our case speech to text service, videoconference service, note service and so on) and other meta-data like SLA (including among others the Quality of Service (QoS) parameters that are important for the efficient operation of the m-learning environment and should be agreed upon and monitored) and workflow (defining the flow of services and users that will be involved for a specific system functionality) templates.

The main components involved in this functionality are:

- A participant registry (in order to store the list of BVO members)
- A BVO manager (in order to manage subscription, authorization and some basilar BVO operation)
- A policy manager to store and distribute policies that apply to VO members.
- A VO Broker (in order to negotiation purchase of services made available from Service Providers)

Apart from the above services that are common to the VOs, the BVO will include a Workflow Repository service as well.

The BVO is a "quite static" environment in the sense that it can be thought as a sort of market place where customers demand for services (*in our case videoconferencing, content management, visualisation of findings etc*) that could be made available in the BVO by Service Providers that are subscribed to the BVO itself. So, summarizing, in a BVO it is possible to:

- Publish available services into the "yellow pages" of the BVO.
- Buy usage of services by searching the latter among the ones available into the "yellow pages".

In order to use the bought services, the BVO will create an OpVO that allows interactions between buyers (in our case teachers, professors, students and so on) and providers (videoconference service provider, speech to text service provider, content management service provider, chat provider, etc). The OpVO bounds a dynamic environment because all the interactions taking action during the run time execution of a workflow will be performed in the frame of an OpVO.

Operative VO (OpVO) Management

The OpVO is responsible of instantiating a specific business process and to manage its execution. In order to perform these operations it needs to encapsulate the following components:

- WorkFlow Manager, which is a management service specific of the OpVO and manages the instantiation of a specific business process as a workflow and its correct execution.

- OpVO Broker to negotiate external services to be involved in the business process execution
- A dedicated participant registry, Policy manager and OpVO manager to manage members of OpVO.
- User Agents, representing external users and responsible of interacting with them
- Service Agents, representing external services and responsible of interacting with them.

Business Process and Workflow

The Mobile Grid architecture is intended to support business process designs that support and take advantage of dynamic, mobile services and users, such as m-learning. Thus, components able to manage (create, instantiate and execute) these business processes are essential, which include:

- Workflow Manager: it provides the functionality to get business process descriptions defined as workflows and store them in a repository related to a specific Virtual Organization. This component is also able to get these descriptions from the repository and trigger their execution by the Workflow Execution Engine.
- Workflow Execution Engine: a module responsible to execute a specific business process representing a workflow.

Mobility and Nomadism Support

The mobility of clients and users is supported by the network infrastructure in a transparent way with mobile network technologies, like Mobile IPv6. So, the network infrastructure needs to include all the components related to Mobile IPv6 management, like Access Routers, Home Agents, and Mobile IPv6 support in terminals.

Mobility and nomadism of services affects directly the management of the Operative Virtual Organizations, since services can appear, disappear, move, etc. So, it is necessary that some Grid infrastructure components keep track of the mobile and nomad services and trigger the reconfiguration of the Virtual Organizations when needed. There are different types of mobility involved with different impacts on the architecture:

- Terminal Mobility: as with clients, this is supported and managed with mobile network technologies like Mobile IPv6 and it is done transparently to the Grid Infrastructure components
- User Mobility: if the service is associated to one user (for example the professor), the user can connect in different places and in different terminals, providing the service in all those connections. So, there is a need to track the presence, location and capabilities of the users in order to react and configure the Virtual Organization for adapt to that situation. This is done with a cross-layer cooperation (Cuevas et al, 2007) between:
    - SIP-based (Session Initiation Protocol) network modules: the SIP protocol is used in the network domain to manage the presence and nomadism of users, so the services need to use the SIP registration functionalities for publishing their presence and current location
    - Execution Management module: the Grid Infrastructure module in charge of providing transparency to the Grid applications in terms of the mobility and ubiquity of the services. Hence this service has to interact with the SIP-based network modules in order to keep track of the presence, location and capabilities of the mobile services (PDAs, laptops etc) and to trigger the

Operative Virtual Organization if required because some service have disappeared (for example Student H has switched off his PDA or has moved to an area with no network coverage), or because now there is a new service which has reappeared and has to be included in the Operative Virtual Organization (for example Professor S has turned on his PDA which has a speech to text service on and is currently at site X).

Identity Management

This functionality is provided by some modules in charge of the correct identification of the users and services, and to provide proofs of this identification to the different modules of the Mobile Grid architecture in order to ensure the security of the transactions. This is done by using the A4C (Authentication, Authorization, Accounting, Auditing and Charging) concept of network technologies: a single point for Authentication, Authorization, Accounting, Auditing and Charging. The provision of Identity Management functionality requires the following components:

- A4C Server, able to act as a *single sign-on* repository which can be queried from different network and service modules.
- A4C clients, running on different modules for querying the server for information related to authentication, authorization, etc.
- SAML (Security Assertion Markup Language) Server, interacting with the A4C Server for providing assertions about the identity, authorization, and so on, of the different users, services and modules of the Mobile Grid architecture.

Context Management

Context comprises any information that can be used to characterise the situation of an entity. Thus, context awareness means that devices, applications and systems have information about the circumstances under which they are operating and can adapt their behaviour to be optimal for the current situation. This increases system usability tremendously by reducing the demands on the end-user and minimizing the need for user attention.

A generic Mobile Grid architecture needs to include support for context-aware mobile Grid services, allowing the user to solve their tasks while devices and technology fade away into the background. The main context involved is the one that describes the state of a mobile user. By knowing this context, the system may easier choose the right service to participate in a workflow, and better adapt service behaviour to the state of those services. Context has many facets:

- Presence: whether the user/service is available or not.
- Physical properties: location, local time, temperature etc.
- Device context: What terminals and other I/O (Input/Output) units are available to the user and service and what are the hardware and software capabilities of those devices?
- Local services: What services are found in their proximity?

The main component delivering Context Management is the Context Manager, a generic context infrastructure that supports context-aware applications (aka context consumers) by gathering, processing and managing basic context information. Context Manager, being a mediator entity, comprises an essential component of a Mobile Grid architecture. This element filters relevant data and converts it to a uniform format prior to delivering it to the interested destination. Additionally it has to solve the possible inconsistencies and infer high level context data from basic context information. Thus, in our Case Study when Professor S turns on his PDA at site X information about his location, available services (speech to text service, chat service) and PDA hardware and software capabilities are gathered. If Student G at site X requests for a speech to text service to take notes about his findings at that site, then the Context Management service will be triggered to send information about any such service within the student's proximity (in this case Professor S PDA) so that the Execution Management module initiates the service at the Professor's PDA.

Discovery

In the dynamic scenario of a Mobile Grid architecture, there can be a number of devices, services, that can be available for being part of the Operative Virtual Organization but are not managed by the mobile network technologies described previously. For example, devices found in the proximity of a user, Grid services available in the domain the user has entered, etc. Hence, there is a need for managing the different types of discovery processes: Network Discovery (NDS), Device Discovery (DDS), Local Service Discovery (LSDS) and Grid Service Discovery (GrSDS).

Accounting and Charging

In a Mobile Grid scenario, multiple administrative domains can be involved, either because they are combining their functionalities/mechanisms or services to provide the services, or due to the mobility and nomadism of the users and services. The multi-domain service provisioning aspect highly impacts the way accounting and charging for composed services is done. These Mobile Dynamic Virtual Organizations group together several Service Providers (SP) and Network Providers (NP) that agree to share their resources for creating more complex value added services that aggregate "sub-services" of more than one organization. In our Case Study for example, the videoconference service offered by Service Provider 1 might be enriched with speech to text capabilities offered by Service Provider 2 in case a user cannot hear well the discussions due to noise in the environment or low quality of the speakers on his PDA. In order for this service provisioning approach to become economically feasible and efficient, appropriate accounting and charging mechanisms are required: *service accounting*, *session records aggregation* and *final bill calculation*, whereas A4C server is the main component.

- *Service accounting* comprises the first step. It takes place inside a single administrative domain and it involves the collection of details about resource consumption of the *basic services*. At the end of this phase, for each service that was instantiated and accounted, a session record containing a summary of consumed resources and associated charges is created. The session records are then sent to the A4C server of the organization who requested these services. By accepting the session record, the requesting organization accepts paying for the respective service session. It is then up to the requesting organization to recover the costs.
- Then, the *session records* received from different organizations are aggregated by the BaseVO's A4C server and the charge for the *composed service* is created. The result of this phase is another session record which is delivered to the home domain of a user. The home domain will be charged by the organization which created the BaseVO for the aggregated service session.
- The home domain will use this *final session record for the bill* that will be issued to the user. Finally, the home domain recovers

Table 1. Mobile grid-enabled m-learning SWOT analysis

Strengths	Weaknesses
• Reduced operating expenses • Innovative product • Operations performance improvement • Cover broader sets of users • Increased efficiency, availability and reliability of the offered services	• Companies are rather unfamiliar with Grid technology • Unwillingness of customers to share their data externally • Difficulty in initially differentiating offered products and services
Opportunities	**Threats**
• Increasing market maturity • International market • First mover advantage • More efficient distribution increases customer satisfaction • Growing and improved networks • Moving into new market segments that offer improved profits.	• Security, profiling and privacy concerns for commercial or user confidential data being exposed through an extended network. • Vague presence of Grid applications (and even more Mobile Grid) in the market

the costs for the BaseVO from the user who actually consumed the service.

CONCERNS, CHALLENGES AND FUTURE TRENDS

This section focuses on analysing the concerns and challenges as well as the expected future trends related to the *Mobile Grid m-learning environment* covering both its academic and business application. Initially a SWOT (Strengths, Weaknesses, Opportunities and Threats) analysis is presented including both strengths and weaknesses (internal factors) and opportunities and threats (external factors), which assists in identifying key concerns and challenges. A summary of the SWOT factors is included in the following table (Table 1).

Based on the above SWOT analysis it can be concluded that the main concerns include the reluctance of companies to adopt new IT solutions and the lack of successful business applications integrated into the Mobile Grid. The first concern stems from the fact that IT departments in enterprises quite often are not eager to proceed with significant infrastructural or generally IT changes, while enterprises need a proven clear financial benefit to be convinced. Although the introduction of Mobile Grid infrastructure promises availability, scalability and reliability leading to more efficient services able to serve a wider range of users, enterprises might find a difficulty in quantifying the business benefits stemming from it. And what is more, as the Mobile Grid m-learning environment brings to front new business models that enterprises adopting it should follow, great transformations are required within the enterprises and their communication with their customers, a process that requires a significant transition period.

Taking into account that one of the most valuable resources in an m-learning environment is information itself, data privacy comprises a major concern. The technological advances, the dynamicity of collaborations, the various forms of knowledge representation and the variety of channels distributing knowledge lead to a new knowledge era that requires great changes in areas such as knowledge ownership. In the case of the *Mobile Grid-enabled m-learning environment* there is a strong need for allowing restricted access to students' findings and professors' notes or books in the academic sector as well as the educational material in the business sector only to members participating in this "collaboration" and with well-specified commitments. In fact, disposal of this information and knowledge to non-privileged parties could hurt interests in both sectors and lead to law infringement. Thus, it can be easily concluded that data security and privacy require a multidisciplinary approach requiring the collaboration of technical, legal, financial and business experts.

At this point it should be noted that Mobile Grid technologies move focus of Grid technologies from serving computational intensive applications to enabling mobile collaborations. Mobile Grid poses new technical requirements; dynamic SLA negotiation and management mechanisms, reliable and efficient data management techniques, user management, data privacy and security, mobility and undisruptive handovers between networks, dynamic workflow management, dynamic Virtual Organisations. All these issues need to be addressed satisfyingly so that Mobile Grid infrastructure reaches its maturity levels and can be then widely adopted by the academic and the business world.

CONCLUSION

M-learning comprises the new generation of learning and training. Applicable both to the educational and business world it pushes forward learning environments into a new knowledge era. The technical and business requirements of such a strongly collaborative data and interaction oriented environment are numerous and their importance and implementation varies according to the target group and their domain. According to our analysis, availability, scalability, reliability, security and efficiency climb to the highest stairs of the non-functional requirements hierarchy. The development of a Mobile Grid infrastructure for enabling m-learning environments comes to meet these requirements opening new horizons to the telecommunication industry, the learning domain and mobile applications in general.

The Mobile Grid infrastructure presented within this book chapter developed in the context of fp6 funded project Akogrimo forms the basis for exploiting and sharing the almost universal availability of mobile devices to the learning and training world. Being a full inheritor of the Grid, Mobile Grid comes to meet the loosely coupled requirements of m-learning with mobile devices offering access to mobile users to the resources of a fixed Grid infrastructure as well as serving themselves as resources to the grid. Such an infrastructure applied in the m-learning environment aims at providing access to educational and training opportunities for disadvantaged populations due to geographical, financial or even social restrictions as well as enabling "anytime anywhere" active and interactive learning and knowledge sharing. However, as it has been mentioned a multidisciplinary approach involving the collaboration of the legal, business and technological world is required for the wide adoption of Mobile Grid within the m-learning environment as well as to other mobile application domains leading to many challenging issues requiring strong collaboration and feverish research.

REFERENCES

AKOGRIMO Project. (2007). Retrieved from http://www.akogrimo.org

Bertram, S., Boniface, M. J., Briscombe, N., Ntuba, M., & Palmer, D. (2006). *Enabling integrated emergency management: Reaping the Akogrimo benefits*. Tech. Rep. UNSPECIFIED, ECS, IT Innovation Centre.

Callon, J. (1995). *Competitive advantage through information technology*. Irwin: McGraw-Hill.

Couros, A. (2000). *Ownership of knowledge and its implications for teacher education*. Retrieved from http://www.usask.ca/education/coursework/802papers/couros/couros.htm

Cuevas, A., Jäehnert, J., Moreno, J. I., Villagrá, V., Olmedo, V., & Wesner, S. (2007). The Akogrimo service provisioning platform. *Proceedings of the 7th International Workshop on Applications and Services in Wireless Networks (ASWN 2007)*, Santander, Spain.

Foster, I. (2002). *What is the grid? A three point checklist, GRID today*.

Foster, I., Kesselman, C., & Tuecke, S. (2001). The anatomy of the grid: Enabling scalable virtual organizations. *The International Journal of Supercomputer Applications, 15*(3).

Jähnert, J., Wesner, S., & Villagra, V. (2007). *The Akogrimo mobile grid reference architecture-overview*. Retrieved from http://www.akogrimo.org/download/White_Papers_and_Publications/Akogrimo_WhitePaper_Architecture_v1-1.pdf

Laria, G. (2006). *Mobile and nomadic user in e-learning: The Akogrimo case*. Akogrimo Whitepaper.

Litke, A., Skoutas, D., & Varvarigou, T. (2004). Mobile grid computing: Changes and challenges of resource management in a mobile grid environment. *Access to Knowledge through Grid in a Mobile World, PAKM 2004 Conference*, Vienna.

Loos, C. (2006). *E-health with mobile grids: The Akogrimo heart monitoring and emergency scenario*. Akogrimo Whitepaper.

Park, S.-M., Ko, Y.-B., & Kim, J.-H. (2003). Disconnected operation service in mobile grid computing. *International Conference on Service Oriented Computing (ICSOC'2003)*, Trento, Italy.

Quinn, C. (2000). M-learning. Mobile, wireless, in-your-pocket learning. *Linezine*. Retrieved from http://www.linezine.com/2.1/features/cqmmwiyp.htm

Symbian Limited. (2005). *Latest version of Symbian OS targets smartphones for mass market*. Retrieved from http://www.symbian.com/news/pr/2005/pr20051892.html

Vavoula, G. N., & Sharples, M. (2002). KleOS: A personal, mobile, knowledge, and learning organisation system. In M. Milrad, H. U. Hoppe & Kinshuk (Eds.), *IEEE International Workshop on Wireless and Mobile Technologies in Education* (pp. 152–156). Los Alimatos: IEEE Computer Society.

Chapter 9
Intelligent M-Learning Frameworks:
Information and Communication Technology Applied in a Laptop Environment

Hazel Owen
Unitec, New Zealand

ABSTRACT

An imperative underpinning the redetermination of education theory and practice is mobility. Mobility encompasses freedom of movement through myriad contexts (physical and cerebral), cultures, and knowledge. Digital natives embrace this mobility, interacting with each other and engaging with new literacies to communicate, access rich contexts, question, and collaborate. There are, however, few studies that investigate the efficacy of blended m-learning as an enhancement to literacy, especially with Gulf learners. Therefore, this chapter describes the background and implementation of ICT enhanced learning and teaching (ICTELT) blended m-learning academic writing intervention piloted at Dubai Men's College (DMC). Findings from the research study are reported and discussed.

INTRODUCTION

Mobility, as in the freedom of movement through myriad contexts (physical and cerebral), cultures and 'knowledge' (Sharples, Taylor, & Vavoula, 2005), is an imperative that underpins the re-determination of education theory and practice. Digital natives (Prensky, 2001a) embrace this mobility, effortlessly interacting with each other, locally and globally (Kloos, 2006), and engaging with new literacies to communicate, access 'rich contexts' (Murchú & Muirhead, 2005), question, and collaborate. In turn, graduates not only need to understand and apply 'content' but must also be able to transfer skills and concepts to real-life contexts (Murchú & Muirhead, 2005) as well as use creative problem solving and critical thinking skills to remain current.

Research supports the theory that learning can be enhanced by the use of information, communication technologies (ICT) (Wenger, 2001). In particular, Web 2.0 tools (also known as 'social software') such as Instant Messaging (IM), wikis, discussion boards, and blogs provide access to 'rich contexts' and limitless sources of skill-support (Brown &

DOI: 10.4018/978-1-60566-882-6.ch009

Duguid, 1991), especially when couched in collaborative activities (Hung & Chen, 2001). Such tools can comprise an efficient heterogeneous system accessible through a wide range of mobile devices. However, such a system may nevertheless prove limited in its effectiveness if it is not compatible with the majority of legacy learning systems, while also remaining flexible, adaptable and scalable. The following chapter seeks to suggest how use of a heterogenous system, informed by a clear pedagogically informed framework, can support learning practices and foster communities of learning.

There are relatively few studies (Kramsch, 'Ness, & Lam, 2000) that identify the needs and effects of using an ICT enhanced learning and teaching (ICTELT) blended mLearning course with specific learners, especially those from the Gulf region (Sharples, 2000). This chapter, as well as considering associated literature, describes the background, design and implementation of the ICTELT blended mLearning writing course that was piloted with Higher Diploma Foundations (HDF) students at Dubai Men's College (DMC). The design was informed by sociocultural theory to stimulate the evolution of an interactive environment, and the tools used included legacy systems as well as freely available Web 2.0 tools. It is hoped that the findings from the associated research study reported in this chapter will be relevant to developers, designers, education organisations, managers and practitioners who are involved with, or interested in, mLearning and creating customised, dynamic learning and teaching frameworks.

THEORETICAL PERSPECTIVES AND RESEARCH

Blended M-Learning and Digital Natives

The term 'digital natives' (Prensky, 2001a) (also known as the 'Net Generation') is often used to refer to people who were born between 1980 and the mid 1990s and have grown up with easy access to ICT (Kennedy, Krause, Judd, Churchward, & Gray, 2006). This notion is somewhat flawed as "online services, or virtual communities as they used to be called, have been around since 1969" (Papworth & Johnson, 2008, p. 2). Oblinger and Oblinger (2005) argue that age is not a central factor, but rather central tenets that define digital natives are the sharing of key characteristics in the use of and attitude toward mobile technology, along with new forms of social practice, expression, and meaning-making. It has been argued that "Digital Natives' brains are ... physically different as a result of the digital input they received growing up" (Prensky, 2001b, p. 1).

For those involved in providing education, the practical implication of this assertion is that digital native students learn differently. For example, they have the ability to multi-task and rapidly process large quantities of hyperlinked, sometimes unrelated, information (including that communicated through multimedia). These students now seek learning that includes inductive discovery where interaction, especially that with peers, is highly valued (Prensky, 2001b). The expectation is that curricula will include some form of online or blended sessions which encourage formal and informal collaboration in discovery-orientated tasks (Rossett, Douglis, & Frazee, 2003). However, "there is often a gap between teachers' hopes and educational outcomes... [resulting in] teacher disappointment and/or student frustration" (Goodyear, 2005, p. 83) which has been identified as, in part, a variation in the quality of practitioners' designs (Goodyear, 2002; Romiszowski & Mason, 2004). Design quality varies partly because design skills and experience for ICT enhanced learning are not yet widespread (Armitage & O'Leary, 2003), and partly because there is still a tendency for technology, and not pedagogy, to be the driving focus (Salmon, 2002).

Mobile Learning (mLearning) as a concept has several interpretations; at a basic level, mLearning involves using handheld or palmtop devices such as mobile phones, iPods and personal digital assistants (PDAs) to facilitate and enhance the learning process (Quinn, 2000; Traxler, 2005). Laptop computers are sometimes excluded from the range of mLearning tools because of size, weight, power requirements, and cost when compared with other mobile devices (Gianna, Scaramuzzi, & Finkelstein, 2004). However, the distinction between laptop computers and mobile phones is blurring as laptops decrease in size and weight, and mobile phones increase in functionality (Attewell & Savill-Smith, 2004).

A more sophisticated view of mLearning refers to the mobility of people, thinking, collaboration, communication and 'knowledge' (Sharples, Taylor, & Vavoula 2006), rather than focussing purely on the tools. Educators and researchers are therefore able to consider the interactions that underlie the process of learning and skills acquisition, rather than looking at the technology or the learner in isolation (Sharples et al., 2006). This chapter, therefore, considers laptops to be mLearning tools, and concentrates on how learners interact with each other through the technology, as opposed to interacting with the technology itself (Warschauer & Kern, 2000).

Blended learning is frequently used interchangeably with hybrid or flexible learning, and usually indicates a blending of face-to-face learning with ICT-enhanced learning. Garrison and Vaughan (2007) suggest that it is "a blending of campus and online educational experiences for the express purpose of enhancing the quality of the learning experience" (p. 5). Heinze and Proctor (2004), on the other hand, define blended learning as "learning that is facilitated by the effective combination of different modes of delivery, models of teaching and styles of learning, and founded on transparent communication amongst all parties involved...." (p. 21). The first definition recognises that blended learning can encourage reassessment of approaches to learning, but limits interaction to on-campus or online. Heinze and Proctor (2004) focus on communication and do not limit the location, the tools or the types of interaction that can be used in blended programmes, and as such, this definition complements the wider notion of mLearning discussed above.

Socio-Cultural Theory as a Framework for Mobile Learning

Three theoretical perspectives have been influential in the design of existing models and frameworks for ICT enhanced learning design, the behaviourist, the cognitive and the sitatuative (Mayes & de Freitas, 2004).

Design from a behaviourist perspective focuses on task-analysis and on writing a set of learning competencies that learners meet by completing structured activities and receiving feedback. Assessment concentrates on the overt demonstration of knowledge or skill components.

Design from a cognitive perspective stresses individual conceptual development within a discipline domain, with learning outcomes couched in meta-cognitive requirements such as self-directed learning. Interactive activities are important for a learner's construction of their own knowledge through experimentation and reflection, and assessment emphasises broad understanding of concepts, often assessed over time.

Design from the situative perspective includes sociocultural theory, which has its foundations in the work of Vygotsky (1986). Underpinning this theory of human development is the central hypothesis that higher order functions develop out of the social interaction of an individual with the external social world (Tharp & Gallimore, 1988), which includes people, objects, and events in various physical settings (Kublin, Wetherby, Crais, & Prizant, 1989). Design informed by sociocultural theory centers around collaborative learning communities that undertake scaffolded activities, and formulate and solve real-world problems. As such, assessment includes elements of participation, peer assessment and authentic practices (Mayes & de Freitas, 2004).

One of the potential advantages of mLearning is the empowerment of learners whereby they have ownership and control over where, when and with whom they participate in learning activities and are also "able to test ideas by performing experiments, to ask questions, collaborate with other people, seek out new knowledge, and plan new actions" (Sharples, 2000, p. 3). The situative perspective seems to allow the most space for this advantage.

Opinions vary as to which perspective in higher and further education is most prevalent in implementing ICT-enhanced learning in general and mLearning in particular. Conole (2005) states that the didactic behaviourist mode, with a focus on the transmission of knowledge, is most influential, whereas Mayes and de Freitas (2004) assert that, although the early 1990s saw a boom of technology initiatives based around traditional instructivist approaches, the majority currently include "blended elements that emphasise all three [perspectives]" (Mayes & de Freitas, 2004, p. 11).

M-Learning and Literacy

The task of writing involves an intricate set of interconnected cognitive skills: "working and long-term memory, procedural and declarative knowledge, motivation, self-regulation, and beliefs and attitudes" (Bruner, Elias, Stein, & Schaefer, 2004, p. 291). Furthermore, researcher and writer Walter Ong (1983) states that writing is a technology which has had a significant influence on verbal expression and thought processes. And David Olsen (1994) – professor at the University of Toronto - places literacy in a context firmly rooted within cultural and social frameworks. Supporting the metalinguistic hypothesis, he indicates that the foregrounding of language by literacy has altered it into an entity that can be reflected upon – enabling, in other words, the 'objectification' of rational thought by writing it down, and therefore making it possible to think about the concept of rationality itself, freeing up the mind for innovative thought because it is not so occupied in the act of remembering. However, writing is not a solitary act (as claimed by Ong, 1982); rather, "it is the result of the interaction among people, contexts and texts" (Murray, 1993, p. 100).

A few studies in the 1960s that focussed on ICT enhanced writing proficiency suggested that 'traditional' instruction tended to be more effective. For instance, findings from a study conducted in 1966 by Izzo (as cited in Al-Jarf, 2004), in Japan, indicated that essays produced on computers were shorter and less well-organised than those that were hand-written. In the last four decades, however, technology has advanced, as have theories, approaches, and pedagogies. Goldberg, Russell, and Cook (2003) advise that " the results of...[their] meta-analyses suggest that on average students who use computers when learning to write produce written work that is about .4 standard deviations better than students who develop writing skills on paper" (p. 20). The reason for the difference was attributed to learner motivation, increased independence, and a greater level of engagement. A further benefit of writing with computers is that students are encouraged to be more creative, write a greater quantity, and are more willing to review and revise their work (Goldberg et al., 2003), especially when writing sessions are a more "socially situated activity, involving issues of epistemology, social identity and social relations and practices" (Cowan, 2004, p. 3). Simic (1994) advises that improvements in writing proficiency can be accelerated when, with sufficient scaffolding, learners are encouraged to experiment concurrently with several aspects of the writing process, thereby overtly comprehending that the separate skills are interconnected and reliant upon each other.

Chun and Plass (1997) also found that multimedia environments stimulate vocabulary acquisition when different medium are used to present new lexical items. Studies which have specifically investigated the effects of using mLearning to enhance literacy (Attewell, 2004) have found that interactions between learners tend to be more collaborative and learner-centered, whereby learners communicate in authentic contexts and there is a dynamic shift away from interacting "with computers to interacting with other humans via the computer" (Warschauer & Kern, 2000, p. 11).

Synchronous communication in general, and instant messaging (IM) in particular, enables context-related learning communities to be formed where common needs and goals are shared, while also remaining "unbounded since the messages can be exchanged anywhere in the world" (Sharples et al., 2005, p. 23). Also, when using IM, learners have an altered connection with the written word compared with oral communication because it is more permanent and yet the interaction is still occurring in a similar timeframe as a spoken conversation (Kramsch et al., 2000). Semones (2001) proposes that the flexibility and spontaneity of chat encourage enthusiastic participation, and as a result "unskilled writers are pushed to achieve higher levels of writing as they learn from others, and skilled writers have the opportunity to exchange ideas and think critically about their writing" (p. 308). In addition, chat history can be saved and referred to as, for example, a record of ideas, or to check back on instructions (Sullivan, 1993).

Research studies around the efficacy of ICTELT mLearning appeared positive and, as such, offered a possible approach to supporting learners facing challenges with writing proficiency, offering an approach that was adaptable and flexible enough to be utilised in a range of contexts.

BACKGROUND

Education Setting

DMC, part of the wider organisation of the Higher Colleges of Technology (HCT) in the UAE, is a tertiary, English language medium institution for Emirati males. All students' language is Arabic, and the majority of Foundations students are between the ages of seventeen and thirty, with approximately 10% of mature students also employed in full-time jobs. In the 2006-2007 academic year, it became mandatory for students to purchase laptops to enroll on the HDF programme. The college campus was also equipped with wireless connectivity to help facilitate 'any time, any place' lifelong learning.

The Problem

Traditionally learning was considered as the transmission of knowledge by a teacher and the absorption of an ultimately knowable 'reality' by a learner. Once the information was assimilated, it was then assumed learners would be able apply it to and in contexts outside of the learning environment (Cobb, 1999). Students who are educated in Arab regions are often still taught within this traditional paradigm of learning, and tend to be reliant on the teacher as a source of instruction and knowledge (Smith, 2001). 'Discussions' are rare and learners are likely to have advanced rote learning and memorisation skills as opposed to critical thinking and self-directed learning skills (Al-Jarf, 2004). Frequent assessments that test the ability to recall and record 'facts' are usual, and results may not be accompanied by feedback. Problems with literacy are common - a phenomenon found in the majority of Arab countries as indicated in the first United Nations publication of *The Arab Human Development Report* (2003) which estimated illiteracy to be approximately 43% in the mid 1990s.

It is, however, a key objective of tertiary education to foster fundamental shifts in learners' understanding of what learning and thinking comprises, and the impact that has on their role (Harrison, 2007). Furthermore, learners who are unable to use higher order thinking and interpersonal skills tend to learn to imitate the disciplines they are studying, memorising unrelated facts, remembering 'right' answers, and focussing on skills that enable them to pass assessments (Ramsden, 1992). As such, they are ill-equipped in authentic situations to apply discipline concepts (Milken, 2007).

Students who enroll on the Higher Diploma Foundations (HDF) programme at DMC often struggle with the expectations of tertiary education, as well as the conventions of academic writing and the requirement to improve their proficiency, especially as they are also processing the challenge of their own changing identities and associated cultural 'double binds' (Perold, 2001). These factors contributed to a high failure rate in the English 070 Key Common Assessments (KCA) administered at the end of the 2004, 2005, and 2006 academic years with 25% of students failing by 20% or more. It was therefore proposed that a pilot research study be conducted in HDF which would document the effectiveness of enhancing the writing proficiency component of Foundations English with mLearning, as well as exploring opportunities to provide scaffolding between traditional learning approaches and more independent, active learning.

THE RESEARCH STUDY

The Questions

Existing research into mLearning and writing proficiency conducted at tertiary level institutions is limited in quantity, sometimes dated, and is not particularly generalisable to the specific circumstances found at DMC. In recognising that the situation was context-bound and shaped by cultural expectations, the pilot study sought to identify key aspects affecting writing proficiency and vocabulary acquisition in an ICTELT blended mLearning setting. Furthermore, because of the recently implemented laptop initiative, stakeholders were keen to find out if the opportunities offered by the mobility of the laptops were having a positive effect on English language acquisition and the uptake and application of appropriate study skills. Research questions included:

1. Do students improve their writing proficiency while they are using mobile, ICT enhanced learning within a blended learning environment?
2. Does mobile, ICT enhanced learning used within a blended learning environment increase vocabulary acquisition (assimilation and meaningful production)?
3. Does blended mLearning facilitate the provision of scaffolding and support during the transition between traditional learning approaches and more independent, active learning?

Participants and Procedures

The participants in this study comprised four HDF sections (seventy-four students in total), and four instructors. The study was conducted in Semester two of the 2006-2007 academic year; students were already members of established communities of learning (Seliger & Shohamy, 1989), so there was no opportunity for random sampling. The sections were selected from the fifteen existing sections to include a representative cross-section of the students in Foundations. Students were all first year, entry level and were 'placed' according to their Common English Proficiency Assessment (CEPA) scores.

Two of the sections were designated as control groups comprising thirty-nine students, and two as quasi-experimental groups ('quasi-' because participants could not be randomly assigned) comprising thirty-five students. This approach was chosen to enable some level of comparison of effect. The two control groups did not participate in the experimental writing interventions. Members of the quasi-experimental groups took part in the pre-test and posttests, questionnaires, interviews, synchronous and asynchronous writing tasks, and reflected on the process in blogs that they completed at regular intervals during the study. The control group did not use synchronous and asynchronous communication tools as part of their writing classes, and teachers used their customary methodology in writing proficiency sessions, which varied in time from week to week – a factor that could not be controlled by the researcher.

Instructors in HDF were randomly approached and assigned either one of the quasi-experimental groups or the control groups. Those instructors participating were asked to allow their writing sessions to be observed, as well as coordinating with the researcher, administering two online questionnaires and one posttest to their students. Furthermore, they made brief reflections, completed two questionnaires, and were interviewed.

Design

Having identified the broad problem with writing, it was necessary to distinguish specific components of the writing curriculum that could be adapted and augmented. In consultation with four instructors who were teaching the quasi-experimental and control groups, sociocultural theory was ascertained to be the underpinning pedagogical philosophy for the design of four interventions based around activities and resources pertaining to advantage/disadvantage and compare/contrast essays.

Research suggests that for ICT to effectively enhance writing proficiency, there needs to be "considerable planning and monitoring on the part of instructors, and training for the students, in order that independent tasks become effective vehicles for socially constructive language development" (Bruton, 2005, p. 17). The ICTELT blended mLearning interventions utilised ICT tools that appeared to offer the greatest potential, as well as being readily available, including the learning management system (LMS) WebCT, MSN instant messenger (IM) and blogs, as well as face-to-face classroom sessions.

The next section briefly outlines of some of the aims, potential learner benefits, and approaches underpinning the design of the interventions and choice of tools. Table 1 also provides a snapshot of the timing and structure of the four interventions.

Face-to-Face Sessions

It was decided that a highly scaffolded course, which blended face-to-face and mLearning approaches, was initially required to assist learners to acquire the skills that would enable them to become more effective self-directed mLearners. Face-to-face sessions were designed to provide participants with a safe forum where they could practise skills that they could then apply in diverse situations and environments (Table 2).

Wireless Laptop Computers

The 2006-2007 wireless laptop computer initiative at DMC illustrated that students embraced the notion of mobility and versatility, using their laptops as an individually tailored resource infrastructure at college, home, and in a variety of other settings (Table 3).

Learning Management System

A course entitled *Improve your Writing and Vocabulary in Foundations* was built for the study in the Learning Management System (LMS), WebCT to provide rich problem and active learning spaces. Furthermore, participants were provided with a shared repertoire of tools, documents, models, explanations, instructions, learning outcomes and rubrics, available in a variety of formats and media (Wenger, 2001)(Table 4).

Multimedia Videos

Students were given access in the LMS to 'how to' videos which they could play, pause, stop and replay as many times as required, and that could be accessed to reinforce face-to-face sessions. For example, the videos were used to take students step-by-step through structuring advantages/disadvantages and compare/contrast essays; these could be downloaded by students onto their laptops or iPods to watch/listen/read, discuss and review, at times and in places of their own choosing. The

Table 1. Timing and outline of interventions

Week (semester 2)	Quasi-experimental Groups	Control Groups
Week 4	**First intervention** (*Topic: Laptops – advantages/disadvantages*) • Conventions of essay genre/reasons for academic writing discussed • Essay rubric discussed/deconstructed • Model/discuss MSN IM • MSN IM 'brainstorm' session • Learners set up blogs & reflect in blog postings (after reviewing model for reflections) • Peers/teachers post comments/replies Learners complete vocabulary pre-test	• Groups' writing sessions observed (*Topic: Laptops – advantages/disadvantages*) Learners complete vocabulary pre-test
Week 5	Vocabulary instruction prior to intervention **Second intervention** • Roles/reasons/instructions for collaborative writing activity introduced/discussed • Learners write/post in pairs • Constructive feedback/evaluation of writing discussed • Model for feedback discussed • Learners undertake review/edit cycle • Peers post feedback • Feedback discussed • Learners post reflections in blogs • Peers/teachers post replies/comments Learners complete vocabulary post-test	• Groups' writing sessions observed Learners complete vocabulary post-test
Week 7	Learners complete vocabulary pre-test **Third intervention** (*Topic: Off-road/on-road driving – compare/contrast*) • Conventions of essay genre discussed • Reasons for academic writing reviewed • Discuss/deconstruct essay rubric • Learners complete vocabulary pre-test • Reasons for using MSN IM reviewed • MSN IM 'brainstorm' session • Learners post reflections in blogs • Peers/teachers post replies/comments	• Groups' writing sessions observed (*Topic: Off-road/on-road driving – compare/contrast*) Learners complete vocabulary pre-test
Week 9	Vocabulary instruction prior to intervention **Fourth intervention** • Roles/reasons/instructions for collaborative writing activities reviewed • Learners write/post in pairs • Constructive feedback/evaluation of writing reviewed • Model for feedback discussed • Learners undertake review/edit cycle • Peers post feedback • Feedback discussed • Learners post reflections in blogs • Peers/teachers post replies/comments Learners complete vocabulary post-test	• Groups' writing sessions observed Learners complete vocabulary post-test
Week 12	Learners complete vocabulary retention-test	Learners complete vocabulary retention-test

Table 2. Aims and potential skills augmentation of the face-to-face sessions

Face to face sessions: Aim(s) (scaffolding / enhancement)	Potential skill augmentation
• Tasks that initially involve structured interaction to help achieve understanding • Provision of opportunities for cumulative, self-regulated & goal-focussed learning • Overt assistance in the use of models as frameworks to enhance creativity & confidence • Raise awareness of the tools & interactions involved in writing activities • Progression toward greater competence & self-direction • Encourage/model collaborative work • Introduction of meaningful tasks, resources & interactions that have transparent, authentic purposes (Wenger, 1998) • Development of students' skills to give, discuss and interpret peer feedback about writing (Semones, 2001) • Encourage reflection/integration of 'new' ideas/construction of 'knowledge' through shared experiences (Oblinger & Oblinger, 2005) • Provide opportunities for learners to 'notice'/discuss conventions of genre (Kramsch et al., 2000)	• Communication • Literacy • Interpersonal • Critical thinking

Table 3. Aims and potential skills augmentation facilitated by the use of wireless laptop computers

Laptop Computer: Aim(s) (scaffolding / enhancement)	Potential skill augmentation
• Facilitation of mobility, choice, and easy access • Choice of time, space, & interactions • Provision of wider audience & associated increase of effort (Semones, 2001) • Increase access to/communication with more advanced peers /teacher & tendency toward peer scaffolding (Semones, 2001) • Foster participation in process-based, experiential activities • Promote extension/completion of meaningful, authentic tasks, resources & interactions (Wenger, 1998) • Collaboration in tasks with authentic purpose that encourage peer support & review • Encourage reflection / integration of 'new' ideas / construction of 'knowledge' through shared experiences (Oblinger & Oblinger, 2005) • Assist learners to take responsibility for own learning • Enable learners to consult & retrieve resources 24/7, from anywhere • Learning cumulative, self-regulated & goal-focussed • Support students who have to travel or be unavoidably absent • Motivate learners by enabling/encouraging multitasking (Oblinger & Oblinger, 2005)	• Communication • Literacy • Data gathering • Organisation • Production & presentation of artifacts • Multi-tasking

Table 4. Aims and potential skills augmentation facilitated by the use of an LMS

Learning Management System: Aim(s) (scaffolding / enhancement)	Potential skill augmentation
• Provision of scaffolding tools & activities that accommodate range of learning preferences (Bowman, 1998) • Provision of scaffolding in form of models, examples, frameworks & step-by-step demonstrations (Passey, 1999) • Searchable, central location for communication tools, calendar, quizzes etc. • Personalise tools/support to meet individual needs of learners • Build a shared repertoire of communal resources (Wenger, 2001) • Access to resources likely to engage learners / encourage 'innovative' participation (Lave & Wenger, 1991) (e.g. models, examples, videos, materials, resources, instructions & rubrics used during interventions) • Enable learners to consult & retrieve resources 24/7, from anywhere • Empower students who do not have to wait for teacher to 'reveal' tasks / requirements / rubrics • More advanced/motivated students can access/complete work ahead of time	• Project management • Self-directed learning • Searching • Critical thinking • Evaluation

Table 5. Aims and potential skills augmentation facilitated by the use of multimedia videos

Multimedia Videos: Aim(s) (scaffolding / enhancement)	Potential skill augmentation
• Complex concepts / processes presented in medium that allows learners to watch/listen/read as many times as need • Break down tasks & represent them step-by-step • Provide for range of learning preferences (Fleming & Bonwell, 1998) • Consistency of approach • Empower learners • 24/7 access • Encourage reinforcement/revision	• Problem solving • Self-directed learning • Critical thinking • Self-direction • Process

potential of these videos was to empower students to solve problems and practise skills independently without reliance on face-to-face sessions and memory (Table 5).

MSN Instant Messaging

Because of the benefits of IM discussed above, it was decided to use MSN Messenger. In the pre-study survey of Foundations students, 14% of respondents indicated that they found it difficult to formulate ideas, and 14% felt that it was complicated to find examples to illustrate opinions. As such, MSN was used to brainstorm ideas as an initial step to writing an essay (Bonk, Cummings, Hara, Fischler, & Lee, 2000) to encourage fluency, and enhance the community of learning. Previous experience had, however, illustrated that unless the reason for and educational benefits of the task were discussed, and very clear model and guidelines given, chat sessions could rapidly disintegrate. As such, a video was made showing a chat session that is initially informal, and then models the type of interchange desired. A whole class discussion (after watching excerpts of the video) encouraged reflection on the authentic purpose for the upcoming chat-sessions, and what the advantages would be. Students also set up MSN so that their chat history could be saved, retrieved, collated, and the ideas made available in WebCT (Table 6).

Vocabulary

Two topics (laptops and driving on-road / off-road) were chosen by students for the intervention sessions. The topics were suitable because of their 1) intrinsic interest, 2) relevance to the syllabus, and 3) suitability for the essay type / genre. A range of topic-related vocabulary was identified by the instructors and researcher, and the quasi-experimental and control groups completed an online vocabulary pre-test to assess prior knowledge of the vocabulary items. The vocabulary was then explicitly taught to the quasi-experimental groups using a range of approaches and tools including smartboards, online bilingual dictionaries, quizzes, interactive activities, & mul-

Table 6. Aims and potential skills augmentation facilitated by the use of instant messaging

Instant Messaging: Aim(s) (scaffolding / enhancement)	Potential skill augmentation
• Increase of language production in 'authentic' context (Nunan, 1999) • Encourage equal participation • Learners' contributions valued & shared (Wenger, McDermott, & Snyder, 2002) • Increase access to peers/teachers • Save chat history to be accessed later to collate learners' ideas • Empowerment of learners • Opportunities to communicate for authentic purposes, & practise range of language functions	• Communication • Interpersonal • Language • Problem solving • Appropriacy / register • Life-long learning

Table 7. Aims and potential vocabulary augmentation facilitated by interventions

Vocabulary support: Aim(s) (scaffolding / enhancement)	Potential skill augmentation
• Encourage participation (learners choose topic) • Stimulate/apply learners' prior knowledge • Foster collaboration	• Literacy • Communication • Vocabulary learning approaches

timedia. Learners collaborated in activities where production, application revision and recycling of the vocabulary were required. Students from the quasi-experimental and control groups were advised that they would repeat the pre-test and have an opportunity to improve their test score. Vocabulary post-tests were administered online. The control group students received no explicit instruction on the lists of words, but did produce and apply the vocabulary as they participated in face-to-face writing sessions. A retention test of all vocabulary items was administered online three weeks after the final intervention session (Table 7).

Blog Postings

One skill that is not used well by digital natives is that of reflection, affecting the ability to generalise and thereby to apply learning experiences (Prensky, 2001a). Blog forums were set up, and example postings were discussed as a group to introduce students to self-reflective practice and the reasons behind it. Introduced by Donald Schon (1996) reflective practice is based around a learner thinking about what they have experienced while utilising a skill or completing an activity – a process that is facilitated by, for example, a teacher. Reflective blog postings were made after each of the four intervention sessions, and learners were asked to describe what they had done, what they felt they had learned from doing this, and how they might do things differently in the future (Table 8).

Discussion Board

The first step of the discussion board task was to collaborate in an activity that would "stimulate real communication in the target language" (Willis, 1996, p. 1) and encourage students to focus on content, accuracy and structure. In pairs (two students per laptop), learners planned and wrote an essay, which was then posted to the discussion board where it was available for further review and editing. Access to scaffolding tools and resources at any point was encouraged. Next, pairs selected another essay, and, using a marking rubric (which was discussed and for which a model was given) (Nunan, 1999), reviewed and gave feedback (Simic, 1994)(Table 9).

Data Collection

This study aimed to generate a rich, examinable body of data, and attempted to "discover how

Table 8. Aims and potential skills augmentation facilitated by the use of blogs

Blog postings: Aim(s) (scaffolding / enhancement)	Potential skill augmentation
• Foster use of high-level skills (Murchú & Muirhead, 2005) • Encourage self-reflection • Provide opportunities for internalisation, reflection, & externalisation of concepts • Enhance learners' confidence to enable them to express own ideas in own style (Boughey, 1997) • Provide opportunities for reflection on writing & learning process (Walther, 2003) • Encourage reflection / integration of 'new' ideas (Oblinger & Oblinger, 2005)	• Self-reflection • Communication • Self-direction • Critical thinking • Evaluation • Analytical

Table 9. Aims and potential skills augmentation facilitated by the use of discussion boards

Discussion board: Aim(s) (scaffolding / enhancement)	Potential skill augmentation
• Construction of knowledge through guided discovery & active engagement with learning activities • Provide greater motivation to write (Semones, 2001) • Encourage increased volume of writing output (essential for improvement in writing proficiency) (Simic, 1994) • Motivate learners by encouraging multitasking (Oblinger & Oblinger, 2005) • Provide opportunities for learners to 'notice'/discuss conventions of genre (Kramsch et al., 2000) • Introduce/model/discuss conventions for writing/giving constructive feedback • Encourage reflection / integration of 'new' ideas / construction of 'knowledge' through shared experiences (Oblinger & Oblinger, 2005) • Raise awareness of writing as recursive process (Semones, 2001) • Provide opportunities for internalisation, reflection, & externalisation of concepts • Encourage focus on/discussion of writing errors & reasons behind them (Kramsch et al., 2000) • All learners' contributions overtly valued & shared (Wenger et al., 2002) • Foster willingness to accept constructive feedback from peers (Walther, 2003) • Use learners' prior knowledge to inform & structure learning • Encourage self-reflection • Raise awareness of appropriacy • Focus on task rather than final grade • Encourage multiple revisions • Foster attention to detail	• Analytical • Language (vocabulary & functions) • Literacy • Appropriacy/register • Communication • Interpersonal • Self-reflection • Problem solving

things work in a particular learning context, using a mixture of qualitative and quantitative sources of data" (Phillips & Gilding, 2000, p. 2). Qualitative was interpreted as "any kind of research that produces findings that are not arrived at by means of statistical procedures or other means of quantification" (Strauss & Corbin, 1990, p. 17) and uses a multi-method approach (Denzin & Lincoln, 1994). The data generated by this pilot research study was mainly qualitative as suggested by Reeves (1993), who proposes that qualitative approaches are more appropriate for the study of tertiary level ICT enhanced learning.

Data was generated using a range of methods and tools including observations, interviews, focus groups, questionnaires, HDF documentation, system-wide exams, pre- and posstests, reflective blog postings, and discussion board postings (Phillips & Gilding, 2000). The volume of data collected was extensive and a thorough discussion of results and findings is not possible within this chapter. Instead, some key findings and associated implications are discussed.

Pre-Research Study

Before beginning the pilot research study, the researcher collected data about HDF instructors' opinions of literacy, and methods that could be used to improve writing proficiency. The pre-study survey was administered to thirteen instructors who had taught or were teaching Foundations level students revealed that 77% of faculty had been teaching ESL/EFL for more that ten years, 15% for five to ten years, and 8% for two to five years. When asked about teaching approach (teacher-centered versus student-centered), 62% felt that initially a teacher-centered approach was necessary with the students entering DMC, but this shifted to a student-centered approach by the end of the academic year. Specific writing instruction was seen as more important than 'learning to learn' by 54% of respondents. Communication was seen by 22% of respondents as the most important factor in academic writing, followed by 20% who felt it was accuracy, 18% academic writing conventions, 16% ideas, 12% fluency, 10% research skills, and 2% other. These findings helped inform the design of the intervention sessions.

Results and Findings

Limitations of the Study

Since this was a pilot study that would inform a future research study, only two quasiexperimental sections and two control group sections were included. Due to time constraints the study was conducted at DMC in one semester of nineteen weeks' duration. Some additional considerations that the researcher had to factor in to the collection, collation, and interpretation of data were the closeness of the researcher to study participants, the reactivity effect, "focusing on the familiar" (Cohen, Manion, & Morrison, 2001, p. 157) and observer bias (Burns, 2000).

Mobility and Spaces

Engeström developed from sociocultural theory an expanded notion of cultural-historical activity theory that is appropriate for analysing tool-mediated learning systems (as cited in Naismith, Lonsdale, Vavoula, & Sharples, 2004). As such, activity theory offers a way of considering an ongoing human sociocultural interaction (activity system) that allows significance to be placed on the space and tools used (including language), along with concepts of 'rules', division of labour, internalisation, externalisation, the hierarchical structure of activity, and continuous development.

Data collected during the research study were analysed, and key factors were represented in a 'system of activity' (adapted from Engeström, 1987, p. 78). The activity settings (learners' social spaces, the environs of Dubai and Academic City, and the LMS, blog, IM and discussion board) were used for collaborative group interactions, whole class interactions, social discussions, and writing exchanges, using the suite of online tools, brainstorming, planning meetings, and finding and evaluating materials. Low-pressure flexible spaces were provided for actors to communicate, negotiate, comment, and question, and this was in part motivated by shared objects, and mediated by rules.

There was sometimes a breakdown in interaction within groups when rules were not known, understood, or were misinterpreted. Overall, students were enthusiastic about collaborating in the interventions, enjoying the freedom of choice, flexibility, and the chance to practise a range of skills and strategies. Student's comments included [errors have been kept as per the original for all student comments]: "Im my openion i have fun... and i learn new ideas", "I really want this course to continue because it helps us a lot when we need it", and "Yesterday i learned how i can improve my writing, and it was very fun and new way to learn". Group dynamics and differing skill sets of participants resulted in exposure to alternative learning strategies and skills, as well as fostering positive interdependence.

Reactions to ICTELT Blended mLearning

Thirty-two learners from the quasi-experimental and control groups responded to a post-study survey. When asked if they felt that technology enhanced their learning, 91% either agreed or strongly agreed that it did, supporting the impression that education technology has a high status with students and that they expect it to be used in their learning experiences. Mobility of learning was important with students explaining that it was good to be able to work where and when they were most comfortable, with some perceiving their laptop to be a constant, helpful companion. On the whole, students from the quasi-experimental group were extremely enthusiastic about the intervention sessions with a lot of requests that "I wish this cousre contenue in the future", and "its a good project and i wish to have more projects like this one". Several students did, however, express concern that technology could be a distraction.

A post-study survey was administered to the four instructors who had participated in the study.

Their responses were followed up with interviews to clarify and expand key points. When asked about whether technology enhances the writing proficiency of students at DMC, three agreed, and one strongly agreed. One quasi-experimental group instructor wrote "they were actually focussing on, not the technology, but the writing itself". For the question whether technology enhances vocabulary acquisition, one agreed, two were undecided, and one strongly disagreed. Open-ended comments were more informative. A quasi-experimental group instructor commented that "I've put 'undecided' because I was rather disappointed by the students' reluctance to make good use of all the vocab which we elicited / provided them with. They tend to revert to 'safe mode' when writing".

Control group instructors felt that technology should be "used in moderation, otherwise it's a distraction", and that "technology based activities should [be] a small percentage of overall activities" because "good books, good activities and good teachers are still the bread and butter of good learning". One instructor commented more specifically on the type of education technology enhancement he uses, indicating that "I use PowerPoint activities rather than presentations and MS word to enhance writing proficiency, and I think it can help if used intelligently. I have no experience with blogs, chat or smartboard". The comments here tend to support the findings above whereby faculty have to be exposed to a fully integrated ICTELT blended mLearning programme before the potential becomes clear. Furthermore, such approaches need to be supported by empirical evidence that the use of technology is enhancing learning, as opposed to distracting students.

In comparison, the quasi-experimental group instructors responded with enthusiasm remarking that the ICTELT blended mLearning intervention approach was "very enjoyable for me and the students", and "useful, very useful". Furthermore, the intervention sessions "fit in with the curriculum and…[are] exactly what they need at the moment". One added that an unforeseen benefit was that "when I followed up the 'technology-base' session with a traditional lesson the following day the students were very productive. They appreciated the variety and also the consistency. The same message in a different way…". Both instructors felt that the students were "comfortable using technology; [and] different learning styles are catered for". In addition, it was observed that the students from both groups "were motivated by the medium…the whole business of getting them to access the stuff from last week and have another look at the…[video] tied it all together". It was also suggested that glitches with technology appeared to be taken in their stride by students.

Roles

The role of the teacher in an ICTELT blended mLearning course is less a transmitter of knowledge, and more of a facilitator and guide. One instructor in this study commented that "you don't have to do very much. You just have to answer the occasional question about…grammar and spelling…the usual questions, but it was nice to be able to deal with them on the spot". Candlin (1993) supports this observation, indicating "one of the most important shifts...in recent years has been from the view of the teacher as the controller...towards a more learner-centered view which stresses the learner's powers of hypothesis formation…." (p. xiii). One instructor did say that they would have to "get used the initial 'messiness' that is quite different to a non-laptop lesson" referring to the fact that students are often multi-tasking, changing location (both virtually and physically), talking to/IM-ing peers, and accessing a variety of resources.

Discussion Board Postings

Students were clearly motivated by the fact that their peers were going to read their work and accessed essays several times to review and edit them. Observations also revealed that more introverted students were encouraged to contribute extensively in the supported environment with access to tools that scaffolded them when compared with interactions observed in the control groups. Quasi-experimental instructor feedback revealed that students' strengths tended to be complementary with 'risk takers', encouraging more cautious writers to be creative, and more accurate writers encouraging their partner to discuss the use of grammar, punctuation and vocabulary. Students felt that working at their own pace, in a place of their own choosing, and collaboratively helped their own understanding, especially when they had to 'externalize' something by explaining it to a peer.

The peer grading and feedback resulted in a wide range of discussion about how to grade an essay, how to give formative feedback, and about the writing process in general. In keeping with existing research findings (e.g. Semones, 2001) there was some initial reservation amongst some students who felt it was not their 'job' to grade essays and give feedback. With use of scaffolding and discussion, though, students were able to take on the role of analytical friend. Students found the feedback model invaluable and gave some thought-provoking, honest feedback that illustrated a high level of understanding of purpose and appropriacy. Reflection on the differences between their own essay and their peers' essays also encouraged dialogue, and raised awareness of their own problem areas. As one instructor commented, "...they do see the point...they overwhelmingly see the point of what we are trying to do".

Writing Proficiency

The quasi-experimental group showed some immediate evidence of improved short-term writing proficiency and vocabulary acquisition, but when students followed up the collaborative activity with an in-class hand-written essay, only 75.4% recycled target vocabulary, showed awareness of the conventions of the essay types, and improved writing accuracy. However, as the intervention session cycles were only completed twice, it could be a result of the brevity of the overall intervention period.

Data collected from the post-research student survey can be categorised into eight key statements, which show that respondents felt that the collaborative essay activity helped them to:

- improve writing proficiency;
- improve knowledge and use of vocabulary;
- share ideas, examples and information;
- improve spelling;
- develop awareness of essay writing conventions;
- increase awareness of essay types;
- prepare for a career in the future; and
- think about writing and the reasons to write

The end of year ENGL 070 KCA exam writing scripts were banded independently of the researcher by the ENGL 070 DMC Foundations team. Scripts were blind double-marked, and third marked where a discrepancy of more that half a band existed. The exams were summative.

Table 10 illustrates that in the exam the quasiexperimental groups improved their mean writing band significantly. During the course of one academic year in Foundations currently the mean band improvement is 1.25, thereby indicating that quasi-experimental group one performed well over one and a half semesters. However, during the period of the intervention sessions, control group one improved by a mean band score of 0.28, group two decreased by 0.14, quasi-experimental group one increased by 0.08, and group two by 0.24. Therefore, based on these statistics alone, it appears that the ICTELT blended mLearning intervention sessions had no direct effect on writing proficiency. This could be for several reasons, the main one being the briefness

Table 10. Comparison of band improvement pre- and post writing proficiency pilot research study

Group	Benchmark writing exam bands (beginning of Sem 1)	End Sem 1 writing exam bands	Sem 2 mid term writing exam bands	Mean increase in writing band
Control group 1	4.01	4.63	4.91	**0.89**
Quasi-experimental group 1	3.02	4.64	4.72	**1.70**
Quasi-experimental group 2	3.97	4.66	4.90	**0.92**
Control group 2	3.22	4.22	4.08	**0.86**

of the intervention period, as it is likely, given the level of engagement, the increased quantity of writing, and the improvement in motivation to write, greater improvement would be seen over a more extended period of time with a larger number of intervention sessions.

Vocabulary

The vocabulary pre-tests, post-tests, and retention test generated comparative statistics for the particular participant population. Tests were self-grading, and students were able to access their grades immediately. The pre- and post-tests were out of fourteen, and the retention test was out of twenty-eight (means were later statistically treated to give a comparative score out of fourteen). The pre- and post-test mean scores for the laptop vocabulary revealed that although control group one's mean was high in the pre-test, comparative gains for the quasi-experimental groups in the post-test exhibited a significant increase while there was a decrease in average mean scores for the control groups. In the second pre-test both control groups scored lower than the quasi-experimental groups and showed a significantly lower mean in the post-test. In contrast, the quasi-experimental groups showed a significant increase in mean scores. The comparison of the two post-test means for each group with the retention test means for each group shows that quasi-experimental group one increased mean gains by 0.15, and group two decreased by 0.13, whereas control group one decreased by 2.65, and group two increased by 1.52.

Several factors need to be taken into account when considering the results outlined above. The control groups did not receive any explicit instruction for the laptop and on-road/off-road driving vocabulary, nor did they have as many opportunities to recycle, review and produce the target vocabulary in meaningful contexts. Students and instructors also regarded the tests as time-consuming, repetitive, and saw little value in completing them. The control groups' relatively high pre-test mean scores for the laptop vocabulary could be attributed to higher frequency of familiarity, as all Foundations students have laptops and many are interested in technology. Whereas, the on-road/off-road driving vocabulary was "more difficult…they had the technical vocabulary in Arabic, but they didn't know the word in English". Combined, these factors help explain the mean scores for the control groups, especially for group one. Interestingly, control group two's gains in the retention test were significant, perhaps suggesting that they made gains through repeated exposure to the target vocabulary.

Analysis of essays written by the quasi-experimental groups indicated that 75.4% of subjects recycled target vocabulary (using more than four of the target words per essay). The end of semester one final exam essays and the mid-semester two exam essays could not be used to measure target vocabulary acquisition directly, as the topics were different. In conclusion, it can be stated that explicit vocabulary instruction, when combined with opportunities for learners to recycle, revise, and produce for a reason, is effective. It is not, however, possible to state that the ICTELT blended mLearning approach had a direct effect on increased vocabulary acquisition. One instructor observed, though, that "some aspects of vocabulary acquisition such as recycling, the need for repeated recall, and systematic organisation and storage are well-suited to technological methods".

WebCT Course

The WebCT course was heavily used by both instructors and students. WebCT usage statistics showed that the most frequently accessed areas of the course were the discussion board (380 hits), the videos (965 hits in total for four videos, and the two most popular pertaining to the writing of the target essay types), and the model for writing feedback for essays (240 hits). All the other tools were used to varying degrees. Comparing the pre-study survey with the post-study survey, of particular interest is the tools the students thought were most useful for assisting improvement in writing proficiency. In pre-study predictions, 42% of respondents indicated a preference for videos as a learning resource (which they use extensively in the Foundations Computer, Research Skills and Projects course). However, after participating in the study intervention sessions, responses in the post-study survey showed a dramatic shift, with 32% of respondents still perceiving videos to be a valuable resource, but with discussion boards increasing from 9% to 43% as a valuable resource. Other tools showed less dramatic alterations of opinion, most noticeably links to grammar Web sites, which decreased from 16% to 3%. Three main conclusions can be drawn from these findings. Firstly, students do not perceive the value of a tool until they have accomplished something meaningful with it and reflected on how it has assisted the learning process. Secondly, once a tool has been established as valuable, it is likely to retain its status until proven otherwise. Thirdly, just making resources available, even if they are directly relevant, has little value unless their use is encouraged as part of specific, authentic tasks.

Instructor feedback suggests that students felt empowered by the easy access to tools and resources, and by an increased sense of communal ownership, especially through participation in collaborative sessions.

MSN IM

The chance to 'chat' with teachers and peers enhanced the learning community with opportunities provided for equal participation, including those learners who did not speak out in face-to-face discussions (Bennett & Pilkington, 2001). Peers and teachers were more accessible, and the informal nature of IM encouraged students who lacked confidence to open dialogues.

Reflective Blogs

Overall student feedback from blog postings showed that students thought the intervention sessions:

- highlighted flexibility and benefits of owning / using a laptop computer
- raised awareness of importance of revision and practice to improve writing skills and strategies;

- enhanced creativity;
- provided opportunities to generate, compare and share ideas;
- helped with strategies to plan an essay;
- improved comfort levels with writing;
- increased ability to work with other people;
- augmented thinking, writing and vocabulary skills;
- gave opportunities to increase vocabulary test scores;
- raised motivation levels;
- fostered ability to use tools and resources that scaffold the learning process;
- encouraged meaningful feedback for other students' essays;
- improved ability to correct common errors;
- helped them learn how to use ICT tools for maximum educational effect;
- provided chance to write about interesting but challenging topic (on-road/off-road driving);
- encouraged increased focus and analysis of essay rubrics; and
- caused frustration because of technical problems.

Feedback in blog postings was positive, even though the medium through which it was collected was challenging because, as one instructor commented, "to get them to reflect like that... you are forcing them to do something that they have never done...to think about the reasons behind why they are doing something...we are trying to forge interconnections". In addition, they had to have confidence that they could give their own opinion as opposed to feeling they had to "give the right answer...say what I say".

CONCLUSION

The need for the enhancement of learning experiences through the inclusion of ICT, and the mobility and freedom of choice it allows, is paramount to enable students to participate in a disparate range of activities using a variety of skills (Warschauer & Kern, 2000). However, the focus should not be the technology itself, but rather the opportunities it affords (Oblinger & Oblinger, 2005). Viewed in light of these notions, the design and implementation of the DMC ICTELT blended learning interventions represent an initial step toward encouraging learners to participate in the active making and ownership of meaning (Sharples et al., 2005), with emphasis placed on the 'process' of collaboration and communication rather than the end product. Participants' cultural and individual needs for learning were largely met, and students were definitely motivated to write a greater volume, with an accompanying attention to quality, although some of the gains proved temporary. The sometimes controversial use of laptops to help enhance literacy skills in this study illustrated that when suitable activities were designed, learners were freed up to select tools and support as required, and the instructor to answer questions and give guidance when it was needed. Furthermore, the systems and tools used provided easily accessible, flexible distribution of learning activities and resources for all participants, irrespective of the time, mobility and location they chose to access them.

Selwyn (2003) states that "the highly significant coupling of...people and mobile technologies has not been well received in educational quarters" (p. 132). Not all educators are keen to integrate mobile, ICT-enhanced activities, nor to improve their understanding of the theory behind its use (Owen & Allardice, 2007). This study, however, indicates that it is the non-digital native educators' mistrust for the tools and related power shifts that creates negativity. Therefore, to ensure the effective integration of ICTELT blended mLearning initiatives, educators need suitable support such as working closely with a technology steward (Wenger, 2004). Furthermore, in a more global setting, formal education needs to participate in the current dialogue exploring how structures such as the curriculum "can be transformed for the mobile age" (Sharples et al., 2005, p. 21).

mLearning couched within a sociocultural interpretive framework therefore appears to be a promising approach that recognises the shifts in digital native learners' skills, needs, and expectations, while also acknowledging the role that institutions and educators play. Studies, such as the one described here, offer a potential basis for the development of larger-scale solutions for emergent e-learning systems. Further research, however, is required, to investigate how digital natives and digital immigrants from different cultures, societies, and educational backgrounds interact within various distributed and mobile e-learning systems and the efficacy of their learning within them.

REFERENCES

Al-Jarf, R. S. (2004). Effect of online learning on struggling ESL college writers. *Foreign Language Annals*, *37*(1), 1–18. doi:10.1111/j.1944-9720.2004.tb02172.x

Armitage, S., & O'Leary, R. (2003). *A guide for learning technologists*. York: Learning and Teaching Support Network (LTSN).

Attewell, J. (2004). *Learning with mobile devices: Research and development*. London, UK: Learning and Skills Development Agency.

Attewell, J., & Savill-Smith, C. (2004). Mobile learning and social inclusion: Focusing on learners and learning. In J. Attewell & C. Savill-Smith (Eds.), *Learning with mobile devices: Research and development* (pp. 3-11). London, UK: Learning and Skills Development Agency.

Bennett, C. L., & Pilkington, R. M. (2001). Using a virtual learning environment in higher education to support independent and collaborative learning. In *Advanced Learning Technologies: Proceedings of the IEEE International Conference* (pp. 285 - 288).

Bonk, C. J., Cummings, J. A., Hara, N., Fischler, R. B., & Lee, S. M. (2000). A ten level Web integration continuum for educational psychology courses: New resources, partners, courses, and markets. Retrieved on January 20, 2007, from http://php.indiana.edu/~cjbonk/paper/10level.html

Boughey, C. (1997). Learning to write by writing to learn: A group-work approach. *ELT Journal*, *51*(2), 126–134. doi:10.1093/elt/51.2.126

Bowman, D. J. (1998). Overcoming reading, writing, spelling deficits: Resource center, learning center and basic skills program, with the application of an Orton-Gillingham Spalding method of instruction [electronic version]. Retrieved on July 2, 2004, from http://www.holmdel.k12.nj.us/pupil/holmdel_reading.htm

Brown, J. S., & Duguid, P. (1991). Organizational learning and communities of practice: Toward a unified view of working, learning, and innovation. *Organization Science*, *2*(1), 40–57. doi:10.1287/orsc.2.1.40

Bruner, C., Elias, V., Stein, D., & Schaefer, S. (2004). *Early learning left out: An examination of public investments in education and development by child age*. Washington, D.C.: Voices for America's Children and the Child and Family Policy Center.

Bruton, A. (2005). Process writing and communicative-task-based instruction: Many common features, but more common limitations? *TESL-EJ*, *9*(3), 1–31.

Burns, R. B. (2000). *Introduction to research methods*. London: Sage Publications.

Candlin, C. N. (1993). Preface. In J. C. Richards (Ed.), *Error analysis: Perspectives on second language acquisition* (12th ed., pp. viiii-xi). Harlow, UK: Longman Group.

Chun, D. M., & Plass, J. L. (1997). Research on text comprehension with multimedia. *Language Learning & Technology, 1*(1), 60–81.

Cobb, T. (1999). Breadth and depth of vocabulary acquisition with hands-on concordancing. *12*, 345-360.

Cohen, L., Manion, L., & Morrison, K. (2001). *Research methods in education* (5th ed.). New York: Routledge.

Conole, G. (2005). Bridging the gap: A review of e-learning research at Southampton [electronic version]. *ELRC Conference*. Retrieved on June 30, 2008, from http://www.elrc.ac.uk/download/presentations/bridgingthegap/four-GrainneConole.ppt

Cowan, J. (2004). *Building students' writing and evaluation skills: Developing reflective self and peer assessment*. Retrieved on February 25, 2007, from http://www.c-sap.bham.ac.uk/resources/project_reports/findings/ShowFinding.asp?id=106

Cummins, J. (2003). *Putting language proficiency in its place: Responding to critiques of the conversational/academic language distinction*. Retrieved on May 15, 2007, from http://www.iteachilearn.com/cummins/converacademlangdisti.html

Denzin, N. K., & Lincoln, Y. S. (1994). Preface. In N. K. Denzin & Y. S. Lincoln (Eds.), *Handbook of qualitative research* (pp. ix-xii). Thousand Oaks, CA: Sage.

Engeström, Y. (1987). *Learning by expanding*. Helsinki: Orienta-Konsultit.

Fleming, N., & Bonwell, C. C. (1998). VARK: A guide to learning styles. Retrieved on January 2, 2005, from http://www.vark-learn.com/english/index.asp

Garrison, R., & Vaughan, N. (2007). Blended learning and course redesign in higher education: Assessing the role of teaching presence from the learner perspective [electronic version]. Retrieved on May 12, 2007 from http://www.ucalgary.ca

Gianna, A., Scaramuzzi, A., & Finkelstein, A. (2004). Evaluating non-functional requirements in mobile learning contents and multimedia educational software. In J. Attewell & C. Savill-Smith (Eds.), *Learning with mobile devices: Research and development* (pp. 13-20). London, UK: Learning and Skills Development Agency.

Goldberg, A., Russell, M., & Cook, A. (2003). The effect of computers on student writing: A metaanalysis of studies from 1992 to 2002. *Journal of Technology, Learning, and Assessment, 2*(1), 1–52.

Goodyear, P. (2002). Psychological foundations for networked learning. In C. Steeples & C. Jones (Eds.), *Networked learning: Perspectives and issues* (pp. 49-75). London: Springer Verlag.

Goodyear, P. (2005). Educational design and networked learning: Patterns, pattern languages, and design practice. *Australasian Journal of Educational Technology, 21*(1), 82–101.

Harrison, R. (2007). Academic skills: What are they and how do we teach them? *Perspectives, 14*(2), 9–11.

Heinze, A., & Proctor, C. (2004). *Reflections on the use of blended learning*. Paper presented at the Education in a Changing Environment, University of Salford, UK. Retrieved on June 10, 2005, from http://www.edu.salford.ac.uk/her/proceedings/papers/ah_04.rtf

Hung, D. W. L., & Chen, D. (2001). Situated cognition, Vygotskian thought and learning from the communities of practice perspective: Implications for the design of Web-based e-learning. *Educational Media International*, *38*(1), 3–12. doi:10.1080/09523980110037525

Kennedy, G., Krause, K., Judd, T., Churchward, A., & Gray, K. (2006). *First year students' experience with technology: Are they really digital natives? Preliminary report findings* [electronic version]. Retrieved on May 16, 2008, from www.bmu.unimelb.edu.au/research/munatives/natives_report2006.pdf

Kloos, M. (2006). *Comm.unities.of.prac.tice 2.0: How blogs, wikis, and social bookmarking offer facilities that support learning in practice in communities of practice*. University of Amsterdam, Amsterdam.

Kramsch, C., 'Ness, F. A., & Lam, W. S. E. (2000). Authenticity and authorship in the computer-mediated acquisition of L2 literacy. *Language Learning & Technology*, *4*(2), 78–104.

Kublin, K. S., Wetherby, A. M., Crais, E. R., & Prizant, B. M. (1989). Prelinguistic dynamic assessment: A transactional perspective. In A. M. Wetherby, S. F. Warren & J. Reichle (Eds.), *Transitions in prelinguistic communication* (pp. 285-312). Baltimore: Paul H. Brookes.

Lave, J., & Wenger, E. (1991). *Situated learning: Legitimate peripheral participation*. Cambridge: Cambridge University Press.

Mayes, T., & de Freitas, S. (2004). *JISC e-learning models desk study: Review of e-learning theories, frameworks, and models* [electronic version]. Retrieved on July 1, 2008 from www.jisc.ac.uk/uploaded_documents/Stage%202%20Learning%20Models%20(Version%201).pdf

Milken, M. *(2007).* What are the characteristics that the globalized workplace increasingly expect and demand of graduates from universities and colleges? Education without borders world forum: Reframing higher education. *Dubai, UAE.*

Murchú, D. Ó., & Muirhead, B. (2005). Insights into promoting critical thinking in online classes. *Instructional Technology and Distance Learning*, *2*(6), 33–48.

Murray, D. E. (1993). Collaborative writing as a literacy event: Implications for ESL instruction. In D. Nunan (Ed.), *Collaborative language learning and teaching* (2nd ed., pp. 100-117). Cambridge: Cambridge University Press.

Naismith, L., Lonsdale, P., Vavoula, G., & Sharples, M. (2004). Literature review in mobile technologies and learning [electronic version]. *Futurelab Series, Report 11*. Retrieved on May 12, 2008, from http://www.nestafuturelab.org/research/reviews/reviews_11_and12/11_01.htm

Nunan, D. (1999). *Second language teaching and learning*. Boston, MA: Heinle & Heinle.

Oblinger, D. G., & Oblinger, J. L. (2005). *Educating the Net generation*. Retrieved on May 16, 2008, from www.educause.edu/educatingthenetgen

Olson, D. R. (1994). *The world on paper: The conceptual and cognitive implications of writing and reading*. Cambridge: Cambridge University Press.

Ong, W. J. (1982). *Orality and literacy: The technologizing of the word*. London: Methuen.

Ong, W. J. (1983). Writing is a humanizing activity. *ADE Bulletin*, *074*(Spring), 13–16.

Owen, H., & Allardice, R. (2007). Managing the implementation of blended e-learning initiatives with the unconverted in a climate of institutionally driven change. *The International Journal of Learning*, *14*(9), 179–192.

Papworth, L., & Johnson, K. (2008). Establishing and managing digital footprints [electronic version]. *Elearning Insights Episode 19*. Retrieved on September 15, 2008 from http://www.edna.edu.au/edna/go/news/podcast/eli/pid/2787

Passey, D. (1999). *Higher order thinking skills: An exploration of aspects of learning and thinking and how ICT can be used to support these processes*. Lancaster, UK: Lancaster University.

Perold, J. J. (2001). Paradox and pedagogy: Double binds and the culture of learning in South African schools. *Culture and Psychology*, *7*(4), 411–431. doi:10.1177/1354067X0174001

Phillips, R., & Gilding, T. (2000). Approaches to evaluating the effect of ICT on student learning. Retrieved on March 9, 2007, from http://www.alt.ac.uk/docs/eln015.pdf

Prensky, M. (2001a). Digital natives, digital immigrants: Part one [electronic version] [from http://www.marcprensky.com/writing/default.asp]. *Horizon*, *9*, Retrieved on May 16, 2008.

Prensky, M. (2001b). Digital natives, digital immigrants: Part two [electronic version]. *On the Horizon, 9*, 1-9. Retrieved on May 16, 2008, from http://www.marcprensky.com/writing/Prensky%20-%20Digital%20Natives,%20Digital%20Immigrants%20-%20Part2.pdf

Quinn, C. (2000). M-learning: Mobile, wireless, in-your-pocket learning. *LiNE Zine, Fall*, 47-50.

Ramsden, P. (1992). *Assessing for understanding*. London: Routledge.

Reeves, T. C. (1993). Pseudoscience in computer-based instruction: The case of learner control research, *20, 2*(39-46).

Romiszowski, A., & Mason, R. (2004). Computer-mediated communication. In D. Jonassen (Ed.), *Handbook of research for educational communications and technology* (2nd ed., pp. 397-431). Mahwah, NJ: Lawrence Erlbaum.

Rossett, A., Douglis, F., & Frazee, R. V. (2003). *Strategies for building blended learning* [electronic version]. Retrieved on June 20, 2008, from http://www.learningcircuits.org/2003/jul2003/rossett.htm

Salmon, G. (2002). *E-tivities. The key to active online learning*. London: Kogan Page.

Schon, D. A. (1996). *Educating the reflective practitioner: Toward a new design for teaching and learning in the professions*. San Francisco: Jossey-Bass.

Seliger, H. W., & Shohamy, E. (1989). What is research? A paradigm for second language research. In *Second Language Research Methods* (pp. 1-41). Oxford, UK: Oxford Unversity Press.

Selwyn, N. (2003). Schooling the mobile generation: The future for schools in the mobile-networked society. *British Journal of Sociology of Education*, *24*(2), 131–144. doi:10.1080/01425690301905

Semones, L. (2001). Collaboration, computer mediation, and the foreign language writer. *Collaboration and Computer Mediation*, *74*(6), 308–312.

Sharples, M. (2000). *Disruptive devices: Personal technologies and education* [electronic version]. Retrieved on May 15, 2008, from http://www.eee.bham.ac.uk/handler/ePapers/disruptive.pdf

Sharples, M., Taylor, J., & Vavoula, G. (2005). *Towards a theory of learning for the mobile age* [electronic version]. Retrieved on April 15, 2008, from www.mlearn.org.za/CD/papers/Sharples-%20Theory%20of%20Mobile.pdf

Sharples, M., Taylor, J., & Vavoula, G. (2006). *A theory of learning for the mobile age* [electronic version]. Retrieved on April 15, 2008, from http://kn.open.ac.uk/public/document.cfm?docid=8558

Simic, M. (1994). *Computer assisted writing instruction*. Retrieved on April 9, 2003, from http://www.indiana.edu/~eric_rec/ieo/digests/d97.html

Smith, B. (2001). Arabic speakers. In B. Smith & M. Swann (Eds.), *Learner English* (2nd ed., pp. 195- 213). Cambridge: Cambridge University Press.

Strauss, A., & Corbin, J. (1990). *Basics of qualitative research: Grounded theory procedures and techniques*. Newbury Park, CA: Sage.

Sullivan, N. (1993). Teaching writing on a computer network. *TESOL Journal,* 34-35.

Tharp, R. G., & Gallimore, R. (1988). *Rousing minds to life: Teaching, learning, and schooling in social context*. Cambridge: Cambridge University Press.

Traxler, J. (2005). *Defining mobile learning*. Paper presented at the Proceedings IADIS International Conference Mobile Learning 2005, Malta.

United Nations Development Programme. (2003). *Arab human development report 2003: Building a knowledge society* (No. 92-1-126157-0). New York: United Nations Publications.

Vygotsky, L. S. (1986). *Thought and language* (rev. ed.). Cambridge, MA: The MIT Press.

Walther, M. (2003). *Integrating English and IT skills via a student newspaper.* Paper presented at the English Language Teaching in the IT Age, 9th Annual TESOL Arabia International Conference, Dubai, UAE.

Warschauer, M., & Kern, R. (2000). Theory and practice of network-based language teaching. In M. Warschauer & R. Kern (Eds.), *Network-based language teaching: Concepts and practice* (pp. 1-19). Cambridge: Cambridge University Press.

Wenger, E. (1998). *Communities of practice: Learning, meaning, and identity*. Cambridge: Cambridge University Press.

Wenger, E. (2001). *Supporting communities of practice a survey of community-oriented technologies*. Retrieved on November 9, 2007, from http://www.ewenger.com/tech

Wenger, E. (2004). Communities of practice: A brief introduction. Retrieved on October 27, 2006, from http://www.ewenger.com/theory/index.htm

Wenger, E., McDermott, R., & Snyder, W. (2002). *Cultivating communities of practice: A guide to managing knowledge*. Cambridge: Harvard Business School Press.

Willis, J. (1996). *A framework for task-based learning*. Harlow, Essex: Addison Wesley Longman.

Chapter 10
Integrating Ontology-Based Content Management into a Mobilized Learning Environment

Gábor Kismihók
Corvinus University of Budapest, Hungary

Barna Kovács
Corvinus University of Budapest, Hungary

Réka Vas
Corvinus University of Budapest, Hungary

ABSTRACT

This chapter describes the architecture of an ontology based content authoring system, developed according to the challenges emerging from Bologna process deployment in Hungary. Considering the needs of Hungarian academic sector, mobility of learners has also been treated as a key requirement. This system has several fundamental components: an educational ontology–which also serves as the domain of curricula development, a content developer, a content repository, and an adaptive knowledge testing engine with a test bank. The services and learning objects are distributed towards the students through a mobilized learning management system.

INTRODUCTION

On 1st February 2008 Carl-Henrich Sandberg, the CEO of Ericsson announced: "*There are now 3.3 billion mobile subscriptions in the world – and every month an additional 50 million people in the world start using their first mobile phone. Broadband is the next step with both mobile and fixed broadband growing rapidly. This figure of 3.3 billion mobile subscriptions far outstrips all previous forecasts.*"

Competition between eLearning solutions is increasing at an alarming rate, while changes of the surrounding environment and the demands of students and the labour market are frequent and substantial. As the announcement of Sandberg indicates, the importance of mobile technology in mainstream education is inevitable. At the same time several questions regarding this impact have not been answered yet. Several factors put pressure

DOI: 10.4018/978-1-60566-882-6.ch010

on higher education institutions to turn towards the development and application of innovative and modern technologies that enable students to easily access, understand and apply complex curricula and other teaching materials.

In this chapter a comprehensive learning environment will be discussed, emphasizing its mobile learning aspects and potentials, stressing its importance in the Bologna System.

We divided this work into two main parts.

In the first part a detailed problem analysis is given about motivating factors behind this project. As it will be visible, the Bologna-process indicated important challenges for the Hungarian higher education, which need to be dealt with. Innovation in education provides competitive advantages for universities therefore, as we argue in this chapter, a combination of an ontology based learning content management with mobile devices enabled content delivery is certainly a solution. Still in this section we show the results of an important empirical research, which examined students' attitudes towards mobile learning. These results are being incorporated into the design and development processes, but also into the deployment strategy of our ontology driven educational environment, namely Corvinno Studio. Further sections discuss the inclusion of mLearning in higher education and other strategic issues of mobile learning deployment.

The second part of the chapter is more technical oriented. It describes steps and important concepts of an ontology based content development system implementation. This system rests on two major pillars. One is a repository layer that has a key role in content development and management. The other one is an ontology layer that supports the creation of reusable learning objects (based on the Educational Ontology) and the promotion of reliable knowledge testing (Adaptive Knowledge Testing System). Mobile learning adds flexibility to this system, since individual learners are not bound to a certain location or time anymore, however the mobilized content is still connected to traditional lectures and seminars. Topics of educational ontology, Studio system architecture, content development and delivery are argued in separate sections. At the end we talk about the first user experiences and our future plans.

SECTION ONE - BACKGROUND

Problems with Bologna System

The Bologna Process is the most important higher educational reform created by European education ministers, inspired by the demand for suiting the requirements of labour markets. On June 19th 1999, 29 European Ministers responsible for higher education signed the Bologna Declaration that contains the aims of this process (European Commission, 2005). With their signature they declared the creation of the European Higher Education Area.

This European Higher Education Area is structured around three cycles where each level has the function of preparing students for the labour market, for further competence building and for active citizenship. This also requires formulation of such descriptors for bachelor and master programs that can be shared within Europe and be used for a variety of purposes, depending on particular national, regional or institutional contexts and requirements. Members of Joint Quality Initiative aimed at developing descriptors for bachelor's and master's that might be shared within Europe and made available for a variety of purposes, depending on particular national, regional or institutional contexts. This was one of the first initiatives, which provided support for facilitating comparison of degrees. The launch of these Dublin descriptors also indicates that competences should have a key role in providing transparent and comparable curricula and qualifications (JQI, 2004). At the same time, methods that enable comparison of curricula and qualifications in everyday practice are still missing.

Figure 1. The Bologna system and the workplace

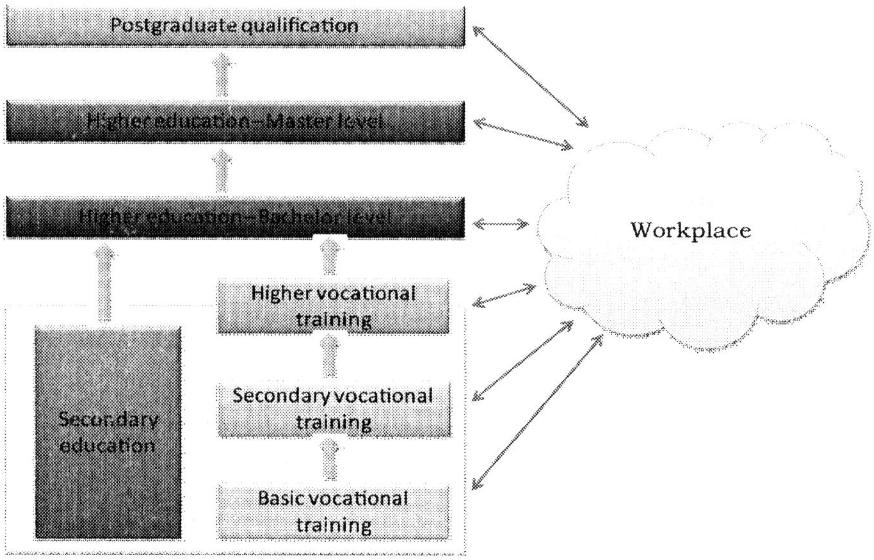

The problem we investigate in this chapter has its roots in the intensification of student's mobilization between the various levels of the European education system, which puts the higher education sector under great pressure. Students, who want to join to a certain cycle (program), have different educational background. They possess diverse combinations of languages, prerequisite courses and learning experience. Due to these reasons, preparation for entrance requirements especially on bachelor and master level is a frequent, barely manageable problem, which may arise in a geographically distributed way – locally, nationwide or on European scale as well.

Ideally, this so called Bologna system (Figure 1) enables an easy enrolment procedure for students, who completed the previous qualification level successfully, at all levels of the unified European qualification system. The BSc (Bachelor)-level cycle consist 180 ECTS points (in minimum 3 years) and provides a degree with a certain profession with clearly defined competencies, as an output. It is possible for students to move horizontally from one educational institution to another within the same academic program, as students can reclaim their obtained ECTS points. A successful BSc degree is the prerequisite of an application to a Master (MSc/MA) program, where students have to collect 120 ECTS points (in maximum 2 years) on a BSc-level knowledge basis. The main difference between the enrolment procedure on master and bachelor cycle is that there is no national, standardized entrance exam on the master level, which may put the students into a ranking order. That's why institutions define and publish, two years in advance, the prerequisites for their master courses.

Students, based on their interest, can decide on an institution freely. The only barrier of this choice is the abovementioned set of prerequisites, defined by the particular institutions. By vertical mobility students move on to a higher level program, if they fulfil its entry requirements (competencies).

Therefore it is visible that students finishing their studies on a certain educational level have to face problems during the Prior Learning Assessment (PLA) of their future educational institution or workplace. The host organization has to convert the students' previous studies, on-campus or off-campus qualifications into valid

Figure 2. Position of the studio interface in the Bologna system

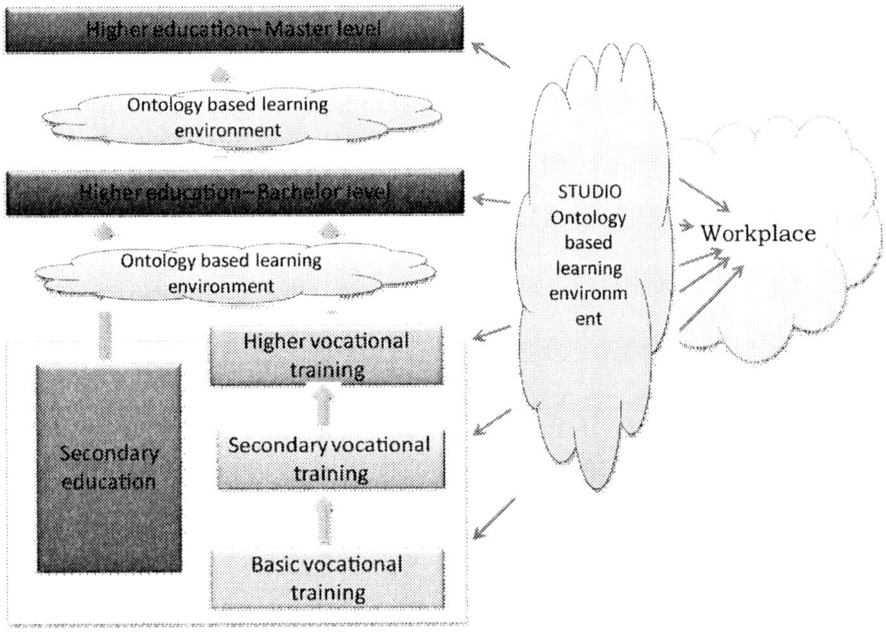

skills and competencies, in order to check whether they fulfil the entrance requirements for a certain academic program or job-role or not. To be more specific, acceptance of students for a certain academic program requires the acknowledgement of their relevant, previously earned ECTS points. Generally 60-120 professional ECTS points are acknowledged from a BSc cycle, when entering to a MA/MSc program on the same educational field. If students can't meet these criteria – for instance points were collected in a different educational field or the receiving organization limits the acceptable ECTS points in the chosen MA cycle –, than they have to collect extra points for entering the desired program.

As it was mentioned above, institutions have the right to define the amount of ECTS points, what they can recognise in their master programs. However, they have to provide opportunities for applicants, who possess bachelor qualifications which are not completely acknowledged, to collect missing ECTS points needed for acceptance.

The domains of the proposed ontology based learning environment were emerging from this conversion problem of the educational sector. As it is visible on Figure 2, our main idea is to introduce an interface between levels of higher education and workplace. This interface, based on the individual's pervious qualifications, completed levels, corporate trainings and practical experiences, should be capable to match students' existing competences with the desired academic programs' entry requirements. Candidates are selected for the particular academic program or job profile, and on the foundation of this assessment learning content will be provided to compensate their missing competences.

We believe that solving this acknowledgement problem of former experiences is to introduce this ontology based learning management system, which can

- successfully map qualifications within the educational sector and also with current and valid job roles,

- test and evaluate students to these valid, labour market driven competencies,
- highlight missing competencies and provide learning content to compensate them,
- be used for correcting failures of certain curricula, as an ad-hoc support of education,
- consider mobility as a key factor of current education.

The system development started in 2003 under the frame of the "Development of Knowledge Balancing, Short Cycle e-Learning Courses and Solutions" project, which aimed to handle the conversion problem between the different levels of Hungarian higher education system (BSc, MSc levels). More specific purpose of this project was to restructure the Business Informatics program's curricula offered by Corvinus University of Budapest (CUB) to facilitate compatibility with other educational programs in this domain, ensuring the above mentioned transparency and assisting student mobility (Gábor, 2007).

Connection to M-Learning

At the same time another Hungarian national project has been launched under the same governmental program aiming to modernize the structure of the Hungarian higher education through redefining its processes (institutional and operational processes, academic processes and supporting innovative processes). The final research output was a major milestone in the reform of the Hungarian higher educational sector (Gábor, 2006).

This project also concentrates on innovative technologies, which scaffold the academic performance of universities. Among these technologies, mLearning was mentioned as a key instrument of educational technology in the near future. The idea of using handheld devices in education provides flexibility, spare time and increase work efficiency. Furthermore with the 3rd generation mobile (UMTS) network and the latest mobile devices it is possible to develop an efficient mobilised distance learning system, which delivers multimedia rich learning objects (Kukulska-Hulme, Traxler, 2005). Therefore the research output also emphasizes the importance of implementing mobile learning technologies in the following main institutional activities (HEFOP FOI, 2006):

- **Administrational processes:** Educational institutions are advised to use mobile communication technologies to contact students regarding administrational issues. This technique should also substitute costly and slow postal services, especially in distance education.
- **Educational processes:** There is visible demand from students for learning anytime, anywhere. To meet this demand, educational institutions should design courses considering possibilities of learning object mobilisation. Therefore they should offer access to educational infrastructure for mobile devices, which enables instructional designers to implement courses (mobilise content) for mobile learners.

On the foundation of educational modernisation projects CUB identified several focal points where the ontology based learning environment and mobile learning can work together successfully:

- Mobile learning has a broad and well developed infrastructure. In 2005 mobile phone penetration was close to 100% (there were 119.1 mobile telecommunication service subscriptions per 100 people in November 2008) (NCA, 2009) providing valid infrastructure for learning content delivery.
- Students, who are stakeholders in the abovementioned problems arising from Bologna process, needed more flexibility in their learning.

- Students are early adopters of technology, especially mobile technology. Universities can reach and involve them better in academic programs, using mobile technology.
- Early adoption of learning technology provides competitive advantage on the educational market of higher education institutions.

In 2005 a strategic decision has been made in order to develop a mobile learning interface to the learning environment in use and provide administrational and educational services through this platform.

Students' Attitudes towards Mobile Learning

Prior to system design a comprehensive empirical study has been carried out, emphasizing mobile learning. As a part of the IMPACT research series (funded by the Socrates-Minerva Programme of the European Commission), this research aimed to compensate current lack of information on the impact of advanced technology in learning and teaching at universities, vocational education institutions and distance education.

In this study it has been investigated empirically how mobile learning managed to break in the world of higher and distance education. A focus and a control group (150 respondents in each group) have been created to measure differences in students' attitudes towards mobile technology in education. The designed questionnaire consisted of three sections:

- Personal information including social indicators like gender, age, profession, or education
- Experiences with technology-enhanced learning
- Questions related to mobile learning

Primary this research aimed to test perceptions, attitudes and opinions about the impact of mobile learning on education. We decided to use intensity questions on five-(Lickert – type) scale, ranging from completely agree to completely disagree. Unfortunately the extent of this chapter doesn't allow us to give detailed description of all aspects of our empirical research. Hence, in case of interest, all research reports are available from the IMPACT project website (www.ericsson.com/impact). The reports there include precise information about the project, the questionnaire, the applied statistical methodologies and the actual results. Here we give only a short summary, related to mobile learning.

One interesting and also significant result of our empirical study was that people, who were engaged in mobile learning before, were more negative in general technology supported educational issues, like the intensity of communication in online education. By the judgement whether the impact of technology on learning is beneficial or not, the control group was again more positive than the focus group, with relatively low uncertainty in both groups.

One possible reason of being positive about mobile learning is that the majority of focus group thinks that mobile devices in general increase access to education and training. 85 out of 150 gave positive answer to this item. This positivism however didn't show up by mobile communication related items. Here the critical tendency of the focus group was robustly represented again. Same amount of people disagreed and was uncertain regarding the communicational benefits of mobile phones in education. This is a surprising result, as the main function of a mobile phone is the communication itself! However from the questionnaire researchers couldn't find out, what sort of mobile services did focus group's respondents use, as there are several mobile learning provisions, where not the communication, but the mobility of the learner is in the centre of attention.

The control group was also more positive regarding how important is the general availability of mobile phones in education. What both groups could agree on is, that a mobile phone only is not sufficient to undertake an academic or professional educational program. Both groups denied this idea (125/149 in the focus group and 110/150 in the control group), but just like before the focus group stressed its negative attitude with high amount of strongly disagree answers (89).

Despite the trend, 74 out of 142 who already used a mobile learning related service said that mobile learning is something what they could recommend to someone else (control group: 55/150). It worth to mention that the number of uncertain answers was high in both groups: 44 in the focus and 55 in the control group.

In general the results of this analysis show that learners approach towards technology may put the system developers under pressure. The scepticism of focus group shows that people, who are engaged in technology based learning, are a bit more careful about articulating their expectations, especially positive expectations towards mobile learning. It was generally accepted that communication has great importance in education and mobile devices might have a positive impact on educational communication between students and educators. There is also no doubt, that mobilised educational services treated positively in both groups. This research also shows, that only robust, reliable systems should be implemented, which serve the general domains of learning. Once this foundation is established should developers concentrate on learners' mobility and deploy mLearning.

Mobilized Content Delivery

Being mobile while studying is not a new idea. It has been incorporated into teaching activities and official curricula a long time ago in the form of field trips and on-spot trainings. Distance learning always carried features of mobility. According to Desmond Keegan (Keegan, 1990), distinguishing characteristics of distance education include the:

- Separation of the teacher from the learner(s)
- Use of technical media supporting communication and collaboration among students
- and their teachers;

The appearance of mobile technology in education in the mid 1990s has extended the scope of teaching and leaded us into a new world of education. Mobility in learning, supported by the latest information and communication technologies (ICT), has become an essential need for both the new generations of students and educational institutions (Naismith, Corlett, 2006.). In order to suit all requirements it is not enough to simply 'mobilize' the ordinary learning environments (Walker, 2006; Keegan, 2005), but conflicts of informal learning and Face-to-Face (F2F) education also have to be eliminated (Sharples, 2006). Integration of mobile devices into education also fosters inclusion of innovative educational practices. (Milard, 2006; Hoppe, 2006).

At the same time the above mentioned transition has its institutional limitations. In traditional educational institutions, just like in the Corvinus University of Budapest, learning technology should be an integral part of knowledge transfer between students and lecturers, but it cannot be the only platform of teaching. However it is essential to follow up students' demand – which forces institutions to involve technology more and more in their everyday teaching activities, enabling students to be flexible in their learning – and construct F2F based learning platforms, which provide elasticity in course content development and delivery. To meet challenges, emerging from combining ICT enhanced learning and traditional classroom education, a blended service framework has been elaborated. This service portfolio designed by the educators of Corvinus (Kismihók, 2007) – see

Figure 3. Mobile learning at the Corvinus University of Budapest

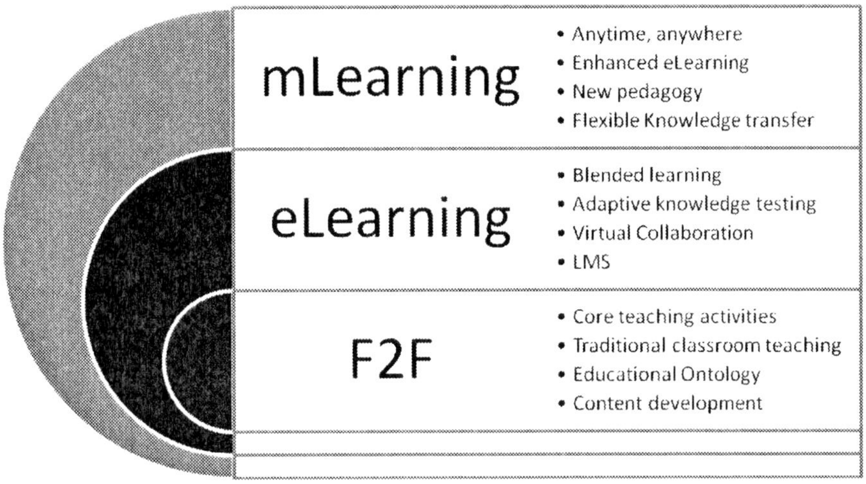

Figure 3 – also put an effort on incorporating theories of navigationism (Brown, 2006) and connectivism (Siemens, 2004).

The core element of the portfolio is the F2F education. The scope of curricula taught in our training programs is represented by the recently developed educational ontology, which is described in the next sections. On the top of traditional classroom teaching a Hungarian, mobilised Learning Management System (mLMS - CooSpace) provides authentication and supports individual learning, enabling the use of rather different, independent learning styles. Supplementary modules, like the ontology driven content authoring environment, see Figure 5, are connected to this platform as well.

SECTION TWO - CONTENT DEVELOPMENT WITH ONTOLOGIES

As it was described in the previous section, one of the most challenging and burning problem of the Bologna system is that outputs of different bachelor programs do not provide homogeneous input for a particular master program. For that very reason such a methodology must be elaborated, which is capable to explore what a student does not know. In other words those knowledge areas must be determined that students must learn before starting a specific master program. In order to promote closing up, curriculum to be learned must be assigned personally to students. After learning, the knowledge of the candidate has to be evaluated again.

The primary objective of our approach is to provide support in exploring missing knowledge areas of students facilitated by an adaptive knowledge testing and evaluating system in order to help them to complement their educational deficiencies. The ontology of curricula, the so called Educational Ontology, provides the fundamentals of this approach. In our solution the exact determination or estimation of the knowledge level is not an objective. The emphasis, which was also taken into consideration when the model of the ontology was formed, is on detailed exploration of missing knowledge areas and on discovering each knowledge area where the candidate lacks acquaintance.

Educational Ontology

Curriculum content may come in many forms and formats, from different departments, with different internal structures and even in different

Figure 4. Educational ontology

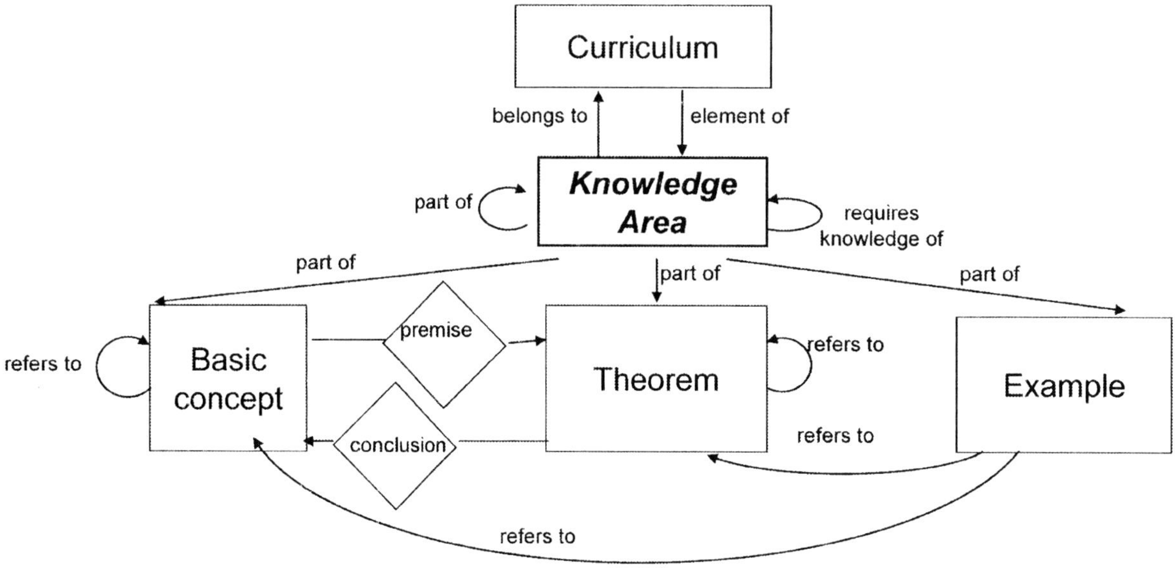

languages. Ontology-based approach provides support for capturing regularities in a single framework, general enough to model the curriculum content management requirements of multiple institutions.

The wide spectrum of ontology applications also proves that both business and scientific world has acknowledged that detailed exploration of semantic relations must stand in the middle of knowledge mapping and processes description – beside the precise definition of concepts (Corcho, Gómez-Pérez, 2000; Gómez-Pérez, Corcho, 2002).

Corcho and his colleagues – by taking into consideration several alternative aspects – constructed a rather precise and practical definition of ontology: „*Ontologies aim to capture consensual knowledge in a generic and formal way, so that they may be reused and shared across applications (software) and by groups of people. Ontologies are usually built cooperatively by a group of people in different locations.*" (Corcho et al., 2003. p. 44.). Characteristics highlighted in this definition also have a key role concerning the Educational Ontology.

The scope of curricula taught in a certain training program can even be rather broad and curricula in general are substantively different in nature, which clearly poses a challenge on the ontology model building process. It should be also taken into consideration that the structure and content of a subject might be at least partly different in diverse institutions. Major classes of the ontology that were developed in the first cycle should meet these challenges (see Figure 4.). Explanation of all the classes follows:

"Knowledge Area" Class: Knowledge areas and competences are connected directly with the "requires" and "ensures" connection. (A competence requires the knowledge of a given knowledge area and the good command of a knowledge area ensures the existence of certain competence(s).)

The internal structure of knowledge areas must be refined to allow effective ontology construction and efficient functioning of the adaptive knowledge testing system. The "Knowledge Area" class represents major parts of a given curriculum. Each "Knowledge Area" may have several Sub-Knowledge-Areas through the "is part of" relation. Not only internal relations, but relations connecting different knowledge areas are also important regarding knowledge testing. Accordingly another relation has to be introduced, namely the "requires knowledge of" relation. This relation has an essential role in supporting adaptive testing. If in the course of testing it is revealed that the student has severe deficiencies on a given knowledge area, then it is possible to evaluate those knowledge areas that must have been learnt before.

For the sake of testing, components belonging to knowledge areas are also listed in the ontology. These objects are called knowledge elements and they have the following major types: "Basic concepts", "Theorems" and "Examples". In order to precisely define the internal structure of knowledge areas, relations that represent the connection between different knowledge elements also must be described. This way both "sides" of "Theorem" class should be analyzed. First of all, a particular theorem should be connected with all its fundamental basic concepts. Hence those basic concepts also have to be defined (and connected to the theorem) which can be inferred from that particular item. Here is an example from a Project management curriculum, where relations of the following basic concepts and theorems should be analyzed:

- Theorem A: Structure of PRINCE project organization
- Theorem B: Accomplishment of Quality Review
- Basic concept 1: project board
- Basic concept 2: project manager
- Basic concept 3: quality management

In the Educational Ontology the relation of Theorem A must be defined with the above-mentioned three concepts. This relation has an essential role, since usually concepts are connected to many theorems not only one. For example, Basic concept 3 is also in relation with Theorem B.

According to the CommonKADS approach, such relations must be defined as coupling objects. These relations are also classes, although they have special properties, like features appearing on both sides of the relation, which must be adequately described. This "relation" class could be applied even in this project management example (expressing that two elements of the ontology are in hierarchical relation with each other). The precise description of this example also requires the thorough analysis of reality that requires defining "relation" class in the ontology. Accordingly the role of "premise" and "conclusion" relations is to determine which basic concepts are used to declare a given theorem and which basic concepts are formed by the declaration of a theorem. The "refers to" relation determines connection between knowledge elements of the ontology. Namely, a basic concept or theorem may refer to another basic concept or theorem and an example may refer to any of the other two knowledge elements. The purpose of introducing this relation is to establish connection between knowledge elements, where it is indispensable ensuring understanding and formation of clear ontology structure.

This way the ontology model that provides the foundation of the application (the content management system with adaptive testing) is completed. The model of Educational Ontology is presented in Figure 4 using the following notation:

- Rectangles sign classes.
- Arrows depict 0-N relations (a competence may have several prerequisites, scope of activities may specify more tasks at the same time and it is also possible that a competence does not have any prerequisites).

Studio Architecture

A learning infrastructure should be developed in order to actively support the entire learning cycle, independently from its form (e.g. workstation- or mobile phone-based learning). This means that the system should contain a Learning Management

Figure 5. The Corvinno studio architecture

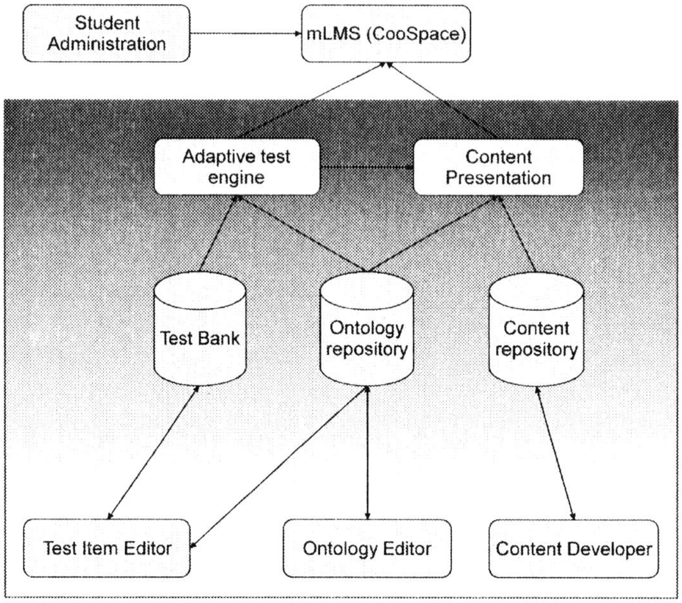

System, which is capable to do transactions with clients using mobile devices as well as clients using desktop computers. This mobilized Learning Management System (mLMS – see next section for a detailed description) is responsible for user administration and authentication tasks. As it is visible on Figure 5, the mLMS is outside of our ontology-based authoring environment, similarly to the system responsible for institutional administration of student accounts.

The mLMS is tied to the ontology-driven content authoring environment. This environment consists of a Content Repository, Ontology Repository and a Test Bank. Ontology Repository has a crucial role as ontologies are the central elements of the content authoring processes. Several ontologies are stored in this repository, all of which are using the structure of the above mentioned Educational Ontology, instantiating it for different domains. These ontologies constitute the central part of other components in this system. Creation and modification of ontologies are carried out by the Ontology Editor module, which guides instructional designers, when they edit ontologies according to the Educational Ontology model. This editor is not applicable as a general ontology editor, it is specifically tailored to support our Educational Ontology model, enabling users to create or edit ontologies, even if they have modest expertise in ontology building.

Students' knowledge is evaluated by using multiple-choice question tests. All questions and possible answers reside in the Test Bank and connected to a specific concept in the ontology. This way, learners' knowledge about a particular concept can be assessed. The Test Item Editor component is responsible for visualizing the ontology structure and allowing users to allocate questions to each node. Numerous questions can be assigned to any concepts in the ontology.

Learning objects are stored in the Content Repository. Additionally, a Content Developer application is also attached, offering content management functions for the authors. The repository has a Content Presentation component, which presents learning objects (LO) for the users. Content uploaded into the system is not format dependent, all extensively used text and multimedia file types are accepted, recognized and supported.

The above mentioned three components (Content Repository, Developer and Presentation) constitute a Content Management System (CMS) specialized for the needs of the ontology-driven environment. These elements enable structuring learning objects according to the ontologies, resulting that every concept in the ontology is connected to a particular piece of LO(s), describing the concept and its relations to other items in the same ontology.

For content management purposes an already existing system has been deployed. The key criterion was to be able to connect the content elements to ontology nodes. For this purpose, Semantic MediaWiki has been selected, as the most appropriate solution. It is an extension to the popular MediaWiki engine, which offers several tools and special wiki-notation in order to use or even construct ontologies to some extent. For instance this engine serves as background of Wikipedia, suggesting that it has the appropriate capabilities for managing large amount of content. One of the advantages of using MediaWiki is that it supports multiple types of contents, including text and various multimedia objects being used broadly in the learning objects of the Studio system.

For students the Adaptive Test Engine is the most essential application, which is also delivered through the mLMS. This component offers an adaptive knowledge evaluation and compiles customized learning materials. The component walks through the ontology structure and asks questions about concepts of the ontology, such as knowledge areas, basic concepts, theorems, examples and their relations. It evaluates the student's answers and decides on the following knowledge elements to be asked. At the end, the user's knowledge is mapped thoroughly and a tailored learning content is offered to be learned. This customized material consists of pieces of learning objects, which are offered by the Content Presentation component.

Content Development Process

Content in the Studio system consists of the following elements:

- the ontology itself
- questions for the concepts in the ontology
- learning objects describing the concepts in the ontology

Content creation begins with the development of the ontology, as it was elucidated in the previous sections. This step provides the basis for all other content authoring activities. The created ontology has to be deployed into the Studio system in order to be able to associate questions and learning objects to its concepts.

The Test Item Editor is used to build up questions for appropriate concepts in a particular ontology. These questions are stored in the Test Bank and queried by the Adaptive Test Engine in order to generate tests. The system supports multiple choice questions with any number of possible replies and one correct answer. The author has to mark the right answer in order to allow the adaptive test system to evaluate the answers. It is advisable to associate several questions to an ontology concept, however the system only verifies the existence of at least one question per node. The Test Item Editor guides the author through the plot of ontology concepts by representing them in a tree-shape. This function also provides support for discovering conceptions without questions attached.

Developing and representing textual and multimedia content is enabled by the Semantic MediaWiki platform. The linkage to an ontology was described in the previous section. Following the ontology import, authors can insert learning objects in the system collaboratively by using MediaWiki features. These elements of content are stored in the repository, in conjunction with appropriate version information that enables authors to follow up and review all changes made in the content. There should be at least one person in the authoring team who has an overview of the status and readiness of the LO(s), since independent authors are responsible only for their own parts. For the Wiki page authors a detailed data formatting and inclusion guideline has been created, with prewritten html codes. Even though the content developer doesn't possess relevant html knowledge, with a simply copy-paste mechanism it is possible to embed rich media content.

Students, who log in the system from a mobile phone, using the mobile interface of our LMS, can access and read the content, which is either in the MediaWiki or in a course related Mobile Learning Space. These learning spaces contain face to face course lecture notes, presentations or other additional learning materials. For some courses location based content is also available. Neither the mLMS nor the MediaWiki are capable to communicate with positioning systems. In order to facilitate location based teaching a flash based application has been developed, which must be downloaded from the Mobile Learning Space and installed locally on the handheld device in order to benefit from location sensitive content delivery.

All materials are accessible via the normal desktop PC interface. PDAs, smartphones with Wireless LAN function are capable to enter the LMS this way as well. In case using a WAP browser of a mobile phone, it is possible that the browser won't be able to access our website. To avoid this problem we recommended students to use the Opera Mini, which is a free internet browser application for wide range of mobile devices. This Java based browser runs on almost all commonly used handhelds. Downloading instructions for the Opera Mini were provided through the mLMS as well.

mLMS

To exploit the advances of mobile technology it is indispensable to transform traditional learning environments into mobilized learning spaces otherwise users can't benefit from mobility. Challenges of limited resources of mobile devices have to be tackled and fitted to the long-established campus-workstation based services. For the Corvinno Studio pilot a Hungarian Learning Management Platform (CooSpace) is being used, which has been deployed at the Department of Information Systems at the Corvinus University of Budapest for several years. CooSpace is a communication-centred solution, which takes place in scenes of this learning environment. A scene is a virtual space of an existing group. Students must join particular scenes through their studies, depending on the task or courses they are currently enrolled. These scenes are supporting co-operation between members of these groups by assuring numerous forms of communication channels and services. These cooperation scenes are treated as social networks, where participants can share their contact and personal information, or they can form study groups. A shared document composition tool supports students to work together on a common project.

Interaction

One of the main driving factors of mobility is collaboration. Fostering interaction between stakeholders of learning processes is a key benefit that has to be supported with reliable services (Keegan, 2005). Collaborative functions like forums, notice boards and messaging services are available within a selected scene. Students can set up conversations, discuss different topics in thematic forums or real-time chat rooms. It is possible to congregate virtual or personal meetings or follow up the learning program related academic or administrative events, with the help of an SMS messaging system.

Students can cooperate and publish their achievements for the closer and the wider circle of stakeholders who are connected to a particular scene. Besides these tasks, the distribution and division of assignments, the evaluation and traceability of distinct subtasks are also possible. It is also feasible to appoint tasks for the whole group or only for individual members of the group, who can submit their documents for evaluation according a predefinable time schedule of the scene.

Content Management

When content is created for the mobile learner, the creator should establish learning scenarios that can be guidelines for content mobilization. On one hand lecturers want their lecture notes available for their students anytime, anywhere. On the other hand there are some applications (quizzes, games or evaluations), which are easy and fun to use on a mobile phone. At the same time being a mobile learner also means that students use content, transferred by the above mentioned means of educational infrastructure, in context. Getting learning content on the right spot at the right time makes formal and also informal learning mobile.

Still, educational documents are accessible in a unified way. A shared document storage provides a common repository of the achievements, templates and draft documents. Users can share documents, media files and with the compilation of bibliographies they can set out curricula, working papers.

User Rights Management

From the technology point of view, CooSpace is a web-based, multi-tier computer application. Regarding the platform, it works with a Microsoft 2003 server, with an MSSQL 2000 database server in .Net framework IIS6/aspx. The user rights management is being handled by a strict set of rules with the help of Microsoft Active Directory Services technology, providing a possibility of Single Sign In. On the web interface of CooSpace every important function (e.g. To Do List, Co-Operation Scenes, Messages, Forum, and Document Storage) is only 'one-click away'. This learning environment can be connected with other systems – including processes of data synchronization and single sign authentication.

User Scenario

In this section, user experience is demonstrated by a description a student case scenario.

The usage of the system begins at the CooSpace authentication screen. Entering the URL of our CooSpace server into a mobile browser takes students to the login page. There they log in with their login name and password (see Figure 6). As it was mentioned before, in CooSpace, educational cooperation takes place on scenes, which is a virtual space for an existing study group.

After signing in, students see all scenes which are associated to their profile. Opening a scene and clicking on the link of the appropriate test initialise an embedded module: the adaptive test engine. Adaptive tests can obviously be assigned to several scenes. This depends on the variety of courses and the policies of course organization in the particular educational institution.

The following step is the face validation. Students receive a short message (top, right picture on Figure 6), informing them about the topic and the nature of the test, the regulation of this assessment and students' options during the test taking. This validation is essential to ensure that students are aware of the test's objectives. The test begins with the acknowledgement of this validation message. Students answer a series of multiple choice questions which are evaluated according the logic described above. At the end students receive their results and the apt explanation (bottom, right picture on Figure 6). This list consists of incorrectly answered questions with links pointing to the corresponding learning materials, organized by the structure of the ontology. As a result, tailored learning units cover the missing elements of the test takers' knowledge. It is students' task and responsibility to visit the provided learning

Figure 6. CooSpace screenshots from a student perspective starting with the login screen (top, left) finishing with the list of missing knowledge areas (right, bottom)

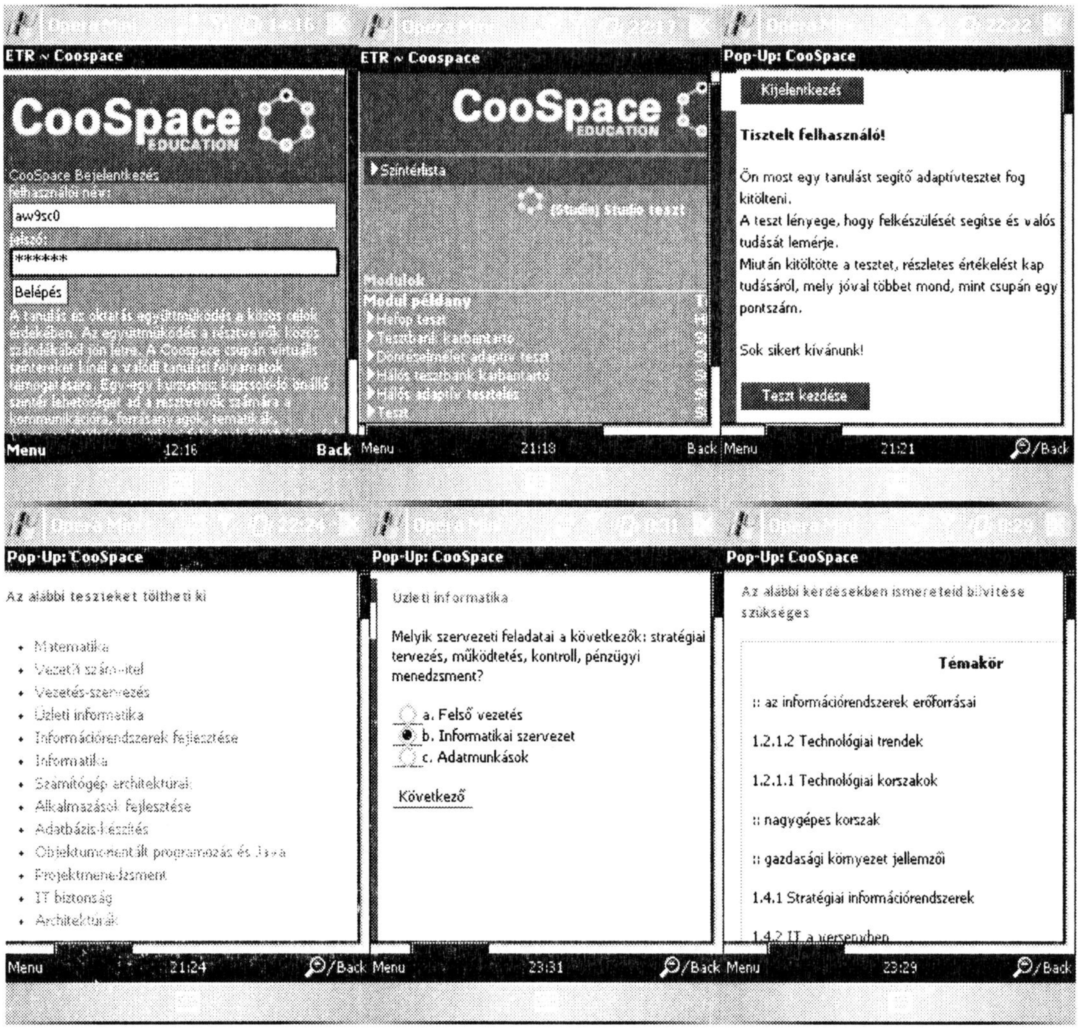

materials. To force continuous self assessment these tests can be repeated anytime. The system logs all attempts and results, which enable users to follow accurately their performance on that particular domain.

The first trial of this ontology based adaptive testing and the mobile learning course content delivery was in the spring semester of 2007. Annually, more than 650 Business BSc students have to take Business Informatics as a compulsory course at the Corvinus University of Budapest. This program is a regular face-to-face program, meaning that knowledge transfer is initiated in classrooms. The technology behind supports blended learning activities through the complete learning cycle:

- Learning content was accessible through traditional eLearning environment with a mobile interface
- Synthesized course summaries were provided for mobile device
- An adaptive test supported self assessment

This trial was part of an EU innovation project "Incorporating mobile learning into the mainstream education". The complete pilot report is available from the project website: www.ericsson.com/mlearning3. The trial mostly validated our efforts. Students were engaged, interested in using their handheld devices in education. The ontology based self assessment trial indicated, that students appreciate a testing system telling them their missing knowledge areas, which need to be practiced before the real exam.

However there were negative feedbacks as well:

- Students demanded simple user interfaces. Content should be available fast and easy.
- Simplicity and clarity is also an issue in case of learning content. Learning objects delivered by mobile learning infrastructure, should be very straightforward, up-to the point. The story should always be more important than technology.
- Services (e.g. access using mobile networks) should be free, students don't want to take any costs

FUTURE PLANS

As our system consists of various components, moreover the majority of these components are already existing software in use, integration is a major issue. For this purpose, Service Oriented Architecture was selected as the state-of-the-art approach to application integration. (He, 2003) Naturally, as SOA is only an approach, interface standards describing integration have to be declared. For this requirement, Web Services has been privileged.

This integration approach enables an enormous degree of freedom in deploying the system or replacing elements with already existing components. During the system development, designers have chosen an existing offline tool (a desktop application) for packaging, which can make use of the resources in the Repository to build content packages. Existing systems can also correspond by appropriate interfaces, which have been used to attach the Adaptive Testing Engine to the Learning Management System.

The SOA approach also enables the deployment of other existing educational environments, which might also be attached to an Enterprise Service Bus by using suitable adaptors. This provides flexibility and opportunities to extend our investigation from academic learning environments towards the needs of corporate training systems.

Another possible way of enriching this environment is introducing IMS capability. IMS stands for IP Multimedia Subsystem, which will be a standard and generic architecture for offering VoIP (Voice over IP) and multimedia services on mobile networks. This internationally recognized standard is expected to be rolled out worldwide from summer 2009. IMS supports all currently used mobile network types (GSM, WCDMA, CDMA2000), but also traditional cable based broadband internet services and WLAN technology. This technology may foster context and location sensitive learning, as it is capable to handle multiple access to services regardless of devices and geographical locations. This technology creates a new layer between content authoring and content delivery. Its main contribution might be to enrich customized learning material with multimedia elements that is presented to the student after completing a test. IMS is also suitable to improve current communication services of our Learning Environment. Audiovisual collaboration and enhanced data transfer between users add value to our system, incorporating several emerging technical platforms (mobile phones, computers, IPTVs, GPS services) into the learning process support. Students might also be able to synchronize their learning activities better.

CONCLUSION

The above discussed pilot research has focused on the application of electronic and mobile learning tools in the academic sector. The introduced approach concerned the deployment of a common framework of transparent and comparable degrees in the Bologna system. As a result a competitive content authoring and knowledge evaluation system has been developed which serves the needs of mobile learners and also promotes the transition between the BSc and MSc levels of higher education. This platform independent learning environment enables the development of customized qualification programs, based on the individual's previous qualifications, completed levels, corporate trainings and practical experiences. Subsequently the potential application areas of this approach are rather wide. Higher education is not the only one, who can enjoy its benefits, public and business sector are also possible targets. This architecture also enables content transfer for individual learning scenarios through traditional Web environment and mobilized learning spaces.

Ontologies, as an abstract and precise way of knowledge description were used to describe the curricula and the needs of the labour market (competencies) in the project. The mobilized learning environment creates flexible learning spaces, which supports individual formal and informal learning either on campus or in individual settings. This approach proved to be fruitful and we are going to extend the scope of this research to the wider academic and business community.

ACKNOWLEDGMENT

The development work has been carried out at the Department of Information Systems, Corvinus University of Budapest (CUB) with the support of learning system engineers of Corvinno Technology Transfer Center (being responsible for the integration between components of the proposed system) and the technical crew of Dexter Ltd (developer of the Corvinus' LMS).

REFERENCES

Brown, T. H. (2006). Beyond constructivsm: Navigationism in the knowledge era. *On the Horizon, 14*(3). Bradford, UK: Emerald Group Publishing Limited.

Corcho, O., Fernández-López, M., & Gómez-Pérez, A. (2003). Methodologies, tools, and languages for building ontologies. Where is their meeting point? *Data & Knowledge Engineering, 46*, 41–64. doi:10.1016/S0169-023X(02)00195-7

Corcho, O., & Gómez-Pérez, A. (2000). Evaluating knowledge representation and reasoning capabilities of ontology specification languages. In *Proceedings of the ECAI 2000 Workshop on Applications of Ontologies and Problem-Solving Methods*, Berlin

European Commission. (2005). *The Bologna declaration on the European space for higher education: An explanation*. Brussels. Retrieved on August 15, 2008, from http://europa.eu.int/comm/education/policies/educ/bologna/bologna_en.html

Gábor, A. (2006, May). *Működéskorszerűsítés a felsőoktatásban*. Paper presented at Felsőoktatás-fejlesztési és felsőfokú szakképzési konferencia, Budapest, Hungary

Gábor, A. (2007, January). *Tudásszintkiegyenlítő, rövidciklusú e-learning kurzusok kifejlesztése*. Paper presented at HEFOP Workshop, Budapest, Hungary

Gómez-Pérez, A., & Corcho, O. (2002). Ontology languages for the Semantic Web. *IEEE Intelligent Systems, 17*(1), 54–60. doi:10.1109/5254.988453

He, H. (2003). *What is service-oriented architecture*. O'Reilly. Retrieved on September 13, 2008, from http://webservices.xml.com/pub/a/ws/2003/09/30/soa.html

HEFOP FOI Project. (2006). *Referencia-modell*. Retrieved on September 24, 2008, from http://informatika.bkae.hu/hefop

Hoppe, U. (2006). How can we integrate mobile devices with broader educational scenarios? In M. Sharples (Ed.), *Big issues in mobile learning: Report of a workshop by the kaleidoscope network of excellence mobile learning initiative*. Nottingham, UK: Learning Sciences Research Institute, University of Nottingham Joint Quality Initiative. (2004). *Shared 'Dublin's descriptors for the bachelor's and master's and doctoral awards*. Retrieved on September 15, 2008, from http://www.tempus.ac.yu/here/tl_files/Dokumenti/Dublinski%20deskriptori.pdf

Keegan, D. (1990). *Foundations of distance education: Frameworks for the future*. First, London, UK: Routledge.

Keegan, D. (Ed.). (2005). *Mobile learning: A practical guide*. Brussels, Belgium: Leonardo da Vinci Programme of the European Commission.

Kismihók, G. (2007, November). *Mobile learning in higher education: The corvinus case*. Paper presented at Online Education Berlin 2007, Berlin, Germany.

Kukulska-Hulme, A., & Traxler, J. (Eds.). (2005). *Mobile learning: A handbook for educators and trainers*. London: Routledge.

Milrad, M. (2006). Media migration and contextual services: Putting content into context to support nomadic learners. In *ICALT 2006* (pp. 1178-1179)

Naismith, L., & Corlett, D. (2006). Reflections on success: A retrospective of the m-learn conference series 2002-2005. In *Proceedings of M-Learn 2006–Across Generations and Cultures Conference*, Banff.

National Communication Authority. (2009). *Digital mobile phone market report, November 2008*. Retrieved on February 2, 2009, from http://nhh.hu/index.php?id=hir&cid=6672

Semantic MediaWiki. (2009). *Semantic media wiki*. Retrieved on January 12, 2009, from http://semantic-mediawiki.org/wiki/Semantic_MediaWiki

Sharples, M. (Ed.). (2006). *Big issues in mobile learning: Report of a workshop by the kaleidoscope network of excellence mobile learning initiative*. Nottingham, UK: Learning Sciences Research Institute, University of Nottingham.

Siemens, G. (2004). *Connectivsm: A learning theory for the digital age*. Retrieved on September 24, 2008, from http://www.elearnspace.org/Articles/connectivsm.htm

Szabó, I. (2006, September 4-5). The implementation of the educational ontology. In P. Fehér (Ed.), *Proceedings of the 7th European Conference on Knowledge Management*, Corvinus University of Budapest, Hungary, ACL, UK (pp. 541-547).

Thissen, D., & Mislevy, R. J. (1990). Testing algorithms. In H. Wainer (Ed.), *Computerized adaptive testing* (pp. 103-135). New Jersey: Lawrence Erlbaum Associates.

Vas, R. (2007). *The role and adaptability of educational ontology in supporting knowledge testing*. Unpublished doctoral dissertation, Corvinus University of Budapest, Budapest

Walker, K. (2006). Mapping the landscape of mobile learning. In M. Sharples (Ed.), *Big issues in mobile learning: Report of a workshop by the kaleidoscope network of excellence mobile learning initiative*. Nottingham, UK: Learning Sciences Research Institute, University of Nottingham

Wikipedia. (2009). *Wikipedia.* Retrieved on February 2, 2009, from http://www.wikipedia.org

Chapter 11
Context-Awareness and Distributed Events in Mobile Learning

Ivica Boticki
University of Zagreb, Croatia

Vedran Mornar
University of Zagreb, Croatia

Natasa Hoic-Bozic
University of Rijeka, Croatia

ABSTRACT

This chapter presents a system called MILE (Mobile and Interactive Learning Environment) which is used to support a blended approach to learning and teaching with mobile devices. The system has a modular and extensible system architecture which aims at supporting different platforms and devices both for students and for teachers. To better adapt to its users the system uses so called contextual widgets-components which gather, process, and store contextual data. To disseminate education–related events, specifically designed distributed events protocol (DEP) is used. Various applicative modules for mobile connected devices can be implemented upon the described architecture. They are, together with the experience gained in the project, described towards the end of the chapter.

INTRODUCTION

Technology enhanced learning has always been of the great interest to educators. The capabilities of modern information and communication technology (ICT) have been perceived as a valuable force in dealing with mundane daily tasks such as exam correction or surveying. Even more intriguing has been the possibility of actually enhancing education so that students learn better (McCormack & Jones, 1997).

Still, computers can enhance educational process only if used correctly - in itself, the technology is neither good nor bad. ICT should be used so that it naturally adapts to its users. They shouldn't be overwhelmed with the capabilities a system offers and they should be able to completely focus on the learning and teaching activities. Therefore, a term

DOI: 10.4018/978-1-60566-882-6.ch011

named context – awareness becomes a buzzword in modern user – oriented systems.

The new technologies need to be complemented with modern teaching practices so today's e-learning forms are more oriented to communication, collaboration, and interactivity (European Commission, 2001) in both face-to-face (f2f) and virtual environments, overcoming the drawbacks of early versions of e-learning which used ICT primarily to improve learning content distribution.

Blended learning is becoming an increasingly popular form of e-learning, particularly suitable in the process of transition from traditional forms of learning and teaching towards e-learning (Alonso, López, Manrique & Viñes, 2005; Thorne, 2003). It combines traditional, or face-to-face teaching with ICT all wrapped in a pedagogically designed courses. Therefore, technology is seen as just one of many elements contributing to the successful teaching and learning.

Miniature mobile devices, ever-rising power and possibilities of communication (e.g. WiFi, 3G etc.) support an area of human activity that has long been technologically neglected: the life on the move. In addition to being used by individuals outside of their living and working environments, mobile technology is used by certain professions in order to acquire contextualized knowledge while on the move (Boticki, Mornar & Andric, 2006; Holzinger & Errath, 2007; Kukulska-Hulme & Traxler 2005).

In addition to desktop computers, mobile technologies begin to influence everyday activities and communication more and more and inevitably enter the world of education. The newest generation of mobile devices combines the power of yesterday's desktop computers with the unique characteristics of being personal, ambient and pervasive. Mobile technologies as a tool can support discursive elements of learning but should be built with the context – awareness in mind (Boticki, Mornar, Hoic-Bozic, 2006). A system designed in such a way can support education and give its social elements a completely new, mobile component.

The research on mobile learning at the Department of Applied Computing, University of Zagreb, Croatia was started in 2004 (Boticki, Mornar & Andric, 2006; Boticki, Mornar & Hoic-Bozic, 2006). After initial implementation dealing with specific, independent applications (e.g. mobile surveying), the need for a systematic approach to mobile learning environment was recognized. A multidisciplinary team had to be gathered in order to provide a pedagogical perspective on one hand and to include deep technological expertise on the other.

In order to support mobile learners in their contexts the system MILE (Mobile and Interactive Learning Environment) has been designed. The main purpose of this system is to support the didactic and the discursive approach to learning (Kukulska-Hulme & Traxler 2005). Students equipped with mobile devices of various kinds (laptops, tablets, PDAs and mobile phones), are connected to the system via faculty or campus wireless networks. They benefit from the central server component which distributes learning – related events to the tools available as a client side MILE application.

MILE's architecture is designed specifically by having mobile learners in mind. Users are not overwhelmed with technological tasks, such as the configuration of the system, filling in server addresses etc., since the system takes care of these in an intelligent way. Furthermore, a core component of the system, context engine, was built to take into account users' context and adapt system's behavior according to it. To achieve that, our context engine utilizes the concepts of subscriptions and contextually triggered actions.

Students using the system benefit from various tools, called modules, whose main aim is to enhance learning by enticing interaction and collaboration in a blended approach to learning. Some of the modules are MCollaboration, MNotebook and MWhiteboard and can be used in everyday classroom to support various educational activities.

The remainder of the chapter is organized as follows: first section of the chapter presents the background of the chapter including pedagogical issues, mobile learning and the use of contextual information in information systems and mobile learning and gives insight into the related work. The second section of the chapter presents the MILE system by describing its architecture. Special emphasis is given on the module for contextual information and the use of distributed events in the system. Towards the end of the chapter applicative modules of the MILE system are presented.

BACKGROUND AND RELATED WORK

Pedagogical Issues

Modern education is being transformed due to the emergence of the new technologies that strongly support constructivism in order to tailor the learning environments that best fit the needs of modern individuals making their learning as effective as possible. The constructivist school sees learning as an active process and emphasizes that „what is learned cannot be separated from how the learning occurs" (Massey, Ramesh & Khatri, 2006). In that sense learning becomes more active, practical and problem based offering students more challenges when constructing their knowledge and extending their competences (Ally, 2004).

Information technology, together with the appropriate pedagogical design, has been found to facilitate the learning process in general. Therefore, learning management systems (LMSs) are gaining more and more popularity and are today used on a daily basis to support the education. However, a LMS tends to be more oriented on online learning with students passively reading contents prepared by their teachers. Therefore, the benefits of the classical, classroom – based, learning environment, often referred to as discursive elements, tend to be missing. Recent years have raised the awareness of that issue through the rise of blended learning (Alonso, López, Manrique & Viñes, 2005; Thorne, 2003) which combines classical methods of teaching with the ICT support.

Blended approach to learning uses various elements to motivate students in their everyday educational tasks. The blend of face – to face lectures, online learning, technology for content delivery and collaboration should help students in successfully completing the course (Bersin, 2004; Thorne, 2003).

The emphasis in blended learning is on the problem identification, blended model definition and careful monitoring of program implementation (Bersin, 2004). Thus a blended learning program should be well structured, with all steps well defined and announced to students in advance. It should use the most adequate technology available, save time both to instructors and students, create a social culture among the students and use experimental learning, peer group collaboration or problem based learning (Bound & Feletti, 2001).

Mobile Learning

Since the beginning of the new millennium mobile devices have become an everyday asset to our lives. Their types range from simpler such as MP4 players to more complex communication enabled personal digital assistants (PDAs). Their technical capabilities are today quite high and open up many possibilities for their use in various everyday activities (Boticki, Mornar & Andric, 2006).

Since younger generations are especially passionate about mobile devices, their use in educational activities in inevitable. Mobile devices are perceived as unwanted by teachers which is not strange since their use in a learning environment is not controlled in an educational sense (Kaleidoscope Network of Excellence, 2006).

Although many debates on the appropriateness of use of mobile devices in education are being led, theorists agree on at least one thing: they strongly support "learning anywhere anytime" paradigm long promoted by the e-learning society. With the traditional technology learning has become independent of the time at which it takes place: one can learn at night or in the morning as long as he or she has access to the technology supported learning resources. Nevertheless, this classical approach heavily lacks the independence of users' location (Kukulsha-Hulme & Traxler, 2005).

The nature of mobile learning rose from the inherent capabilities of mobile devices as well as from the need of removing the location barrier when learning is concerned (Boticki, Mornar & Hoic-Bozic, 2006). Mobile devices have become ubiquitous and their communicational, computational, social and educational powers need to be used to enhance the learning in general. Mobile learning is ambient, that is aware of the surroundings at which the learning occurs, personal since mobile devices are our personal belongings and informal because it occurs whenever and wherever the need exists.

Collaborative activities are especially appropriate for mobility. Collaboration in technology supported learning has been limited by the static nature of desktop computers. Asynchronous collaborative activities such as forums support only certain kinds of collaborative activities, while synchronous communication depends too much on the location at which the hardware is installed. Since many modern mobile devices are communication enabled, they can transform social relationships into the medium for educational and didactical processes (Peters, 1999). Collaboration can be initiated at many levels, some of which are more formal (in-class or teacher – to – student) and the other more informal (on-campus or student – to student). Mobile learning therefore strongly supports the notion of learning as a collaborative activity.

Furthermore, mobility represents a force that inevitably leads to the transformation of education towards a more student-oriented, facilitator-oriented, informal and problem-based (Sharples, Taylor & Vavoula). The shift in the educational process is strongly supported by technology and reflects the competences required by the globalization. Project – based learning is seen as a key competence in today's business society: employees have to be team players, responsible, capable of grasping the bigger picture and be able to make decisions independently. The need for memorization of facts is no longer primary and is being replaced by the need for problem solving and lifelong learning. Individuals are required to manage on their own when dealing with daily tasks. This transformation is sometimes being referred to as to the loss of didactic substance (Peters, 1999).

From the technical point of view there are many projects dealing with mobile learning ranging from simple ones, utilizing mobile devices with preinstalled software to support all sorts of learning activities such as learning foreign languages via SMS (Markett, 2006) or reading e-books (Kukulska Hulme, 2007) to more complex custom made software usually aimed at supporting a specific learning activity such as museum tours (Hsi & Faith, 2005; Proctor and Burton, 2003), fieldwork (Pascoe, Ryan & Morse, 2000) or medicine (Holzinger & Errath, 2007; Kukulska-Hulme & Trayler, 2005). There are some quality reports summarizing projects and activities in the field of m-learning (De Freitas & Levene, 2003; Kukulska-Hulme & Trayler, 2005). Mobile learning community believes that current technological solutions shouldn't be adjusted to fit the needs of mobile learners and that new technological solution (both hardware and software based) should be built from ground up (Kaleidoscope Network, 2006).

In addition to the hardware and software requirements, mobile learning systems can be evaluated by the pedagogical principles they use. They can be purely behavioral, cognitively oriented or designed to support situated approach to learning (Naismith, 2005). Although the relationship between the technical and pedagogical side cannot be firmly established, it seems that the support for the cognitive and situated approaches to mobile learning requires increased technical complexity when software is concerned (Kukulska-Hulme & Trayler, 2005).

Contextual Information in Information Systems

The importance of usage of contextual information rises with the complexity of information systems. They should adapt to their users by anticipating their actions, communicating with other entities which are in some way connected with the user and by taking into account the state of user's surroundings.

This way of adaptation to the state and user's needs is called context-awareness and has been of a special interest to many researchers. This area of science is developing rapidly, a group of researchers has gathered experience through the number of accounts (Dey & Abowd, 2000; Dey, Abowd & Salber, 2001; Hazas, Scott & Krumm) and developed so called "Conceptual framework and a toolkit for supporting the rapid prototyping of context-aware applications" (Dey, Salber and Abowd, 2001). The aim of the conceptual framework is to support the modeling of context-aware applications. It proposes models based on the main principles of software engineering with the most important being the ease of building, the support for reuse and the support for evolution. The authors of the conceptual framework translate these into the entities suitable for implementation into object oriented programming environments. Further in the chapter the framework will be referred to as "the conceptual framework".

The Classification of Contextual Information

Any information that can be used to characterize the situation of entities (whether a person, place or object) that are considered relevant to the interaction between a user and an application, including the user and the application themselves is called contextual information (Dey and Abowd, 2000). Following the definition of contextual information, the contextual framework suggest the classification of contextual information according to entities that can be found in systems and identifies four basic contextual information as entity characteristic: identity, location, status (activity) and time (Dey, Salber and Abowd, 2001). Identity maps unique identifier to an entity (e.g. unique academic person identifier mapped to students in Croatia), location describes spatial relations (e.g. room B1, ground floor, faculty FER, next to room B2), status is about intrinsic entity characteristics that can be inferred from the surroundings (e.g. temperature for room B1) while time is about better characterization of situations.

Basic context categories can be used to define or infer additional contextual information. Basic inferred contextual information are based on one contextual information (e.g. room number is derived from MAC address of a wireless network access point) while complex information get created from multiple contextual information describing the situation (e.g. a prearranged meeting cannot start until all required members are in the room and until a drawing board is turned on).

Context-Aware Services

Knowing, acquiring and deriving contextual information is the base for the so called context-aware services offered by applications:

- presenting information and services (e.g. when a student is positioned next to a room in which a lecture is held, a short lecture

description depending on his or her interests is being displayed to him or her)
- automatically executing a service (e.g. when a student is in a room in which a teacher displays a presentation, the same presentation is forwarded to the student and the currently active slide is presented)
- attaching contextual information for later retrieval (e.g. student makes notes during the presentation which are then enhanced with contextual information to later determine to which course and slide they relate to) (Dey, Salber and Abowd, 2001).

Context-Aware System Characteristics

According to the conceptual framework, context-aware systems should be based on the following principles: separation of concerns, context interpretation, transparent and distributed communications, constant availability of context acquisition, context storage and resource discovery (Dey, Salber and Abowd, 2001). The separation of concerns is about separation of low level details (such as sensors gathering contextual information) from the higher level abstractions called widgets. Widgets hide implementation details, are reusable, support subscriptions and provide a well defined interface for communication with outer world. Context interpretations are about creating mutually connected application layers which deliver contextual information. Distributed and complex systems require transparent and distributed communication in order to hide network communication details and take into account global timeclock mechanisms. Since many software components use contextual information through the widgets and that a request for contextual information can arrive at any time, widgets have to provide constant availability of context acquisition. To reuse contextual information and predict trends contextual information has to be stored. Easy communication of all system entities is, amongst other factors, provided by a well designed mechanism of resource discovery.

Types of Contextual Components

In addition to widgets, the conceptual framework presents four additional categories of contextual components which can be used in designing a context-aware software solution: interpreters, aggregators, services and discoverers (Dey, Salber and Abowd, 2001). Interpreters raise the level of contextual information abstraction by typically using more sources of information (e.g. geo-coordinates can be seen as positions in a city or on a street). Aggregators aggregate related contextual information in a common repository and relate it to a concrete entity (e.g. aggregator for a group meeting can be activated only when all required meeting participants are in the same room). Services are components used to deliver actions depending on the information provided by widgets, interpreters or aggregators according to the application requirements (e.g. a presentation gets delivered to mobile connected devices only if an aggregator for group meeting gets activated). Discoverers take care of all system components (aggregators, interpreters and services) which can be used by applications. They provide a component repository and enable components' dynamic system inclusion.

Contextual Information in Mobile Learning

In his work on context-aware mobile learning (CAML) (Yuan-Kai Wang, 2004), Wang identifies contextual information important for mobile learning. By building the theory of contextual mobile learning, he regards contextual information as contextual space dimensions and identifies the identity dimension, spatio-temporal dimension, facility dimension, activity dimension, student dimension and community dimension. Spatio-temporal and identity dimension map to the basic contextual information of the conceptual framework while the facility dimension could be seen as one of the basic contextual information since it describes the status of various technological components such as mobile devices, sensors, wireless network etc. Activity dimension describes higher order contextual information most often acquired by interpreters and aggregators such as class attendance, discussion participation etc. Student dimension describes intrinsic and psychological student characteristics such as the level of interest which are hard to determine automatically and is therefore, similarly to the activity dimension, based on the information acquired by interpreters and aggregators. The most complex is the community dimension which deals with the process of studying inside the community together with the status and interaction between members of community that make complex social contexts. Social context is about learning activities that evolve through time, place, educational institutions, home and practice making the role of student quite dynamic.

Similarly to the conceptual framework Wang (Yuan-Kai Wang, 2004) identifies four ways in which interaction in mobile contextual learning can be improved. Spatio-temporal dependent interface and contextual event notifications are related to the generic services that context-aware systems have to offer, while navigation and retrieval of learning materials and context-aware communication deals with the usage of contextual information in enhancing existing educational paradigms used in combination with mobile connected devices.

A Generalized Model for Context-Aware Mobile Learning System Architecture

This section of the chapter describes a generalized model of context-aware mobile learning system architecture. Although it is just only one way of looking at the system presented in this section of the chapter, it clearly depicts the use of contextual information to support a learning environment based on mobile devices.

There are some examples of software using context-awareness, collaboration and virtual environments to support learning. Some of them discuss systems that facilitate educational information sources (Sakkopoulos, Lytras & A. Tsakalidis, 2006), others deal with mobile support for problem based learning (Massey, Ramesh & Khatri, 2006), discuss virtual learning environments with location-aware services (Brown, 1996; Morken & Divitini, 2005) or are focused on campus-wide initiatives (Griswold, Shanahan, Brown, Boyer, Ratto, Shapiro & Truong, 2004). They were used as a starting point when the development for the extensible, modular and platform independent architecture presented in this chapter was considered.

Following Wang's definition of CAML (context aware mobile learning) (Yuan-Kai Wang, 2004), the model possesses basic contextual dimensions called identity, spatio-temporal and the facility dimension. The basic contextual dimensions are used to generate the other, higher – order contextual dimensions. Identity is used to identify users; WiFi based location-awareness to provide system and users with location-enhanced services while spatio-temporal dimension and facility dimension are used to fine-tune system's technical characteristics such as devices' display orientation and size (i.e. display size can be adjusted according to the light intensity).

In order to support collaborative activities, the activity and community dimensions of context – aware mobile learning are utilized. Student activity is being aggregated, primarily to support collaborative activities. Community dimension is used to support pedagogical activities in which students form ad hoc learning groups. Community dimension of CAML in the MILE system can be used to support situated approach to learning (e.g. communities of practice).

For defining a model for contextual system architecture we should identify the contextual

Figure 1. Three-tiered contextual system architecture for mobile learning

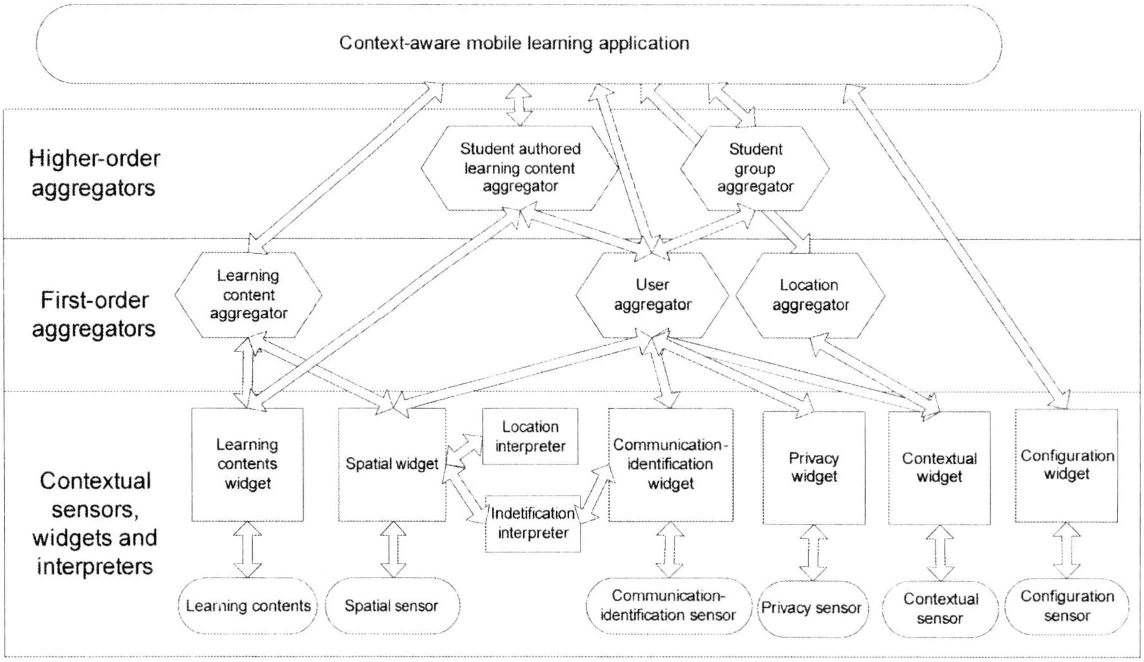

entities and the contextual information used by the entities. The model presented in this section of the chapter is designed to be universally applicable when designing system for teaching and learning with mobile connected devices.

Figure 1 displays three-tiered contextual system architecture for learning with mobile connected devices. The lowest level is made of contextual sensors, widgets and interpreters. Contextual sensors acquire contextual information from physical or logical sensors. Research in the field of contextual information and contextual mobile learning (Dey & Abowd, 2000; Dey, Abowd & Salber, 2001; Dey, Salber and Abowd, 2001; Hazas, Scott & Krumm, 2004) identifies location as the most important contextual information. Communication-identification sensor is used to uniquely identify a user. Contextual sensor is used to acquire contextual information other than location, like the information on noise, light level, temperature etc. That information, according to researchers on context-awareness, can be used to adequately characterize the situation of entities and can be utilized in the realisation of a context-aware mobile learning architecture (Yuan-Kai Wang, 2004). In addition to the physical sensors, a logical learning content sensor is used to generate learning-oriented content to be used in the system (Dey, Salber and Abowd, 2001).

In addition to sensors, the lowest level of the generalized model of context-aware mobile learning architecture is composed of widgets encapsulating sensor functionality and enabling outer entities to create subscriptions to sensor events. The conceptual framework emphasises the importance of a widget object model in which existing sensors can be dynamically replaced to achieve better scalability and the natural use of discoverers. Location widget uses a location interpreter to interpret location sensor information as a specific spatial entity and an identification interpreter to translate user's identification to user entity information.

First order aggregators communicate directly with the widgets. These entities use contextual information to adequately describe the situation of entities they present therefore enabling the number of different services. Students or teachers are the main actors of every learning environment and it is understandable to gather all contextual information related to them. Learning content aggregator contextually positions every learning material used in the system, while the location aggregator defines spatial context in which learning activities occur.

Higher-order aggregators are defined through the first-order aggregators. Examples include student authored materials (e.g. lecture notes) and learning group context determined according to the contexts of individual learners. In the realisation of the generalised model some contextual components can be placed on the server or on the client side, while other reside both on the server and client side uniting the possibilities of client and server modules.

MILE (MOBILE & INTERACTIVE LEARNING ENVIRONMENT)

System Architecture

Main System Characteristics

MILE is a context-aware system that supports learning and teaching facilitated by mobile connected devices and is designed to support everyday classroom activities and different pedagogical models. The system is to be used as a component in a blended approach to learning and teaching. In a typical scenario MILE is used to support just some learning and teaching activities, and as the blended approach to learning and teaching together with modern learning theories advise, is not intended to replace or to support all teaching and learning activities.

MILE is organized as a distributed learning network (Kaleidoscope Network, 2006; Kukulska-Hulme & Traxler, 2005) and supports distributed learning activities. Students use mobile connected devices, communicate and collaborate with teachers in order to fulfil their learning activities. Teachers use the system to deliver teaching activities as easy as possible without the negative interference of technology. System's server side coordinates students and teachers enabling various teaching and learning activities (Figure 2).

The aim of the proposed architecture is to enable the use of mobile connected devices in a learning environment. When dealing with the use of mobile connected devices in the classroom difficulties can be experienced when adjusting current technological solutions to the actual needs of teaching and learning.

Following the advancements in the field of information technology, the architecture is designed to be modular, extensible, and service-oriented. It is based on object oriented principles, and is multi-layered and open.

Main System Libraries

Main parts of the system are libraries called frameworks: the Base Framework, the Device Framework and the Server Framework. The latter two are built upon the Base Framework to provide services to specific parts of the system. The Desktop Framework is used by the applications for desktop computers; the Device Framework by the client application and its applicative modules while the Server Framework provides the base for the Contextual Information Service, Event Service, System and Applicative Services (Figure 2).

Applicative services are used by the applications installed on mobile connected devices to provide different functionality to MILE's users. Applicative services are commonly used as an interface to the central system data repository and to communicate with other server-side components. Applicative services are mutually independent and do not influence the operation of server services in any way which makes easily extendable and replaceable, even during the normal system operation.

Figure 2. Main components and actors in the MILE system

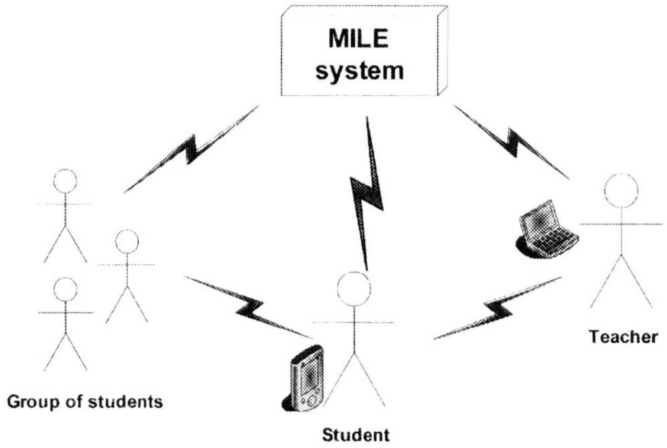

In addition to services as basic building blocks, modular programming structures called libraries need to be created in order to provide common system functionality. The system is therefore divided into layers where higher level layers use the functionality of lower level layers through well defined interfaces (Figure 3).

Base Framework is a system component directly or indirectly used by other components. It is composed of sub-modules and classes designed to provide the means of communication through the Distributed Events Protocol (DEP): sending event messages from the server to the clients, structuring and assembling event messages. This library is composed of specially designed controls called widgets which are used to implement contextual features of the system: privacy, spatial, contextual, configuration and communication-identification widgets. All of them are used to exchange contextual information between mobile connected client devices and server components. Base Framework contains basic building components extended by the Device Framework and Desktop Framework in order to support device specific activity.

Server Framework is a component based on the Base Framework which provides services to higher-lever server components. Server Framework uses common modules for distributed events from the Base Framework and arranges the server side logic of the Distributed Events Protocol. The logic includes assembling event messages, sending event messages to clients, receiving information about the message delivery and retransmission of the message if the need occurs.

Figure 3. MILE system framework stack

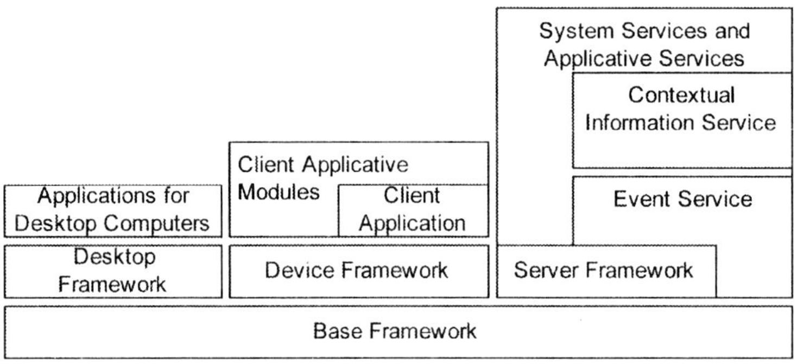

Figure 4. The server framework

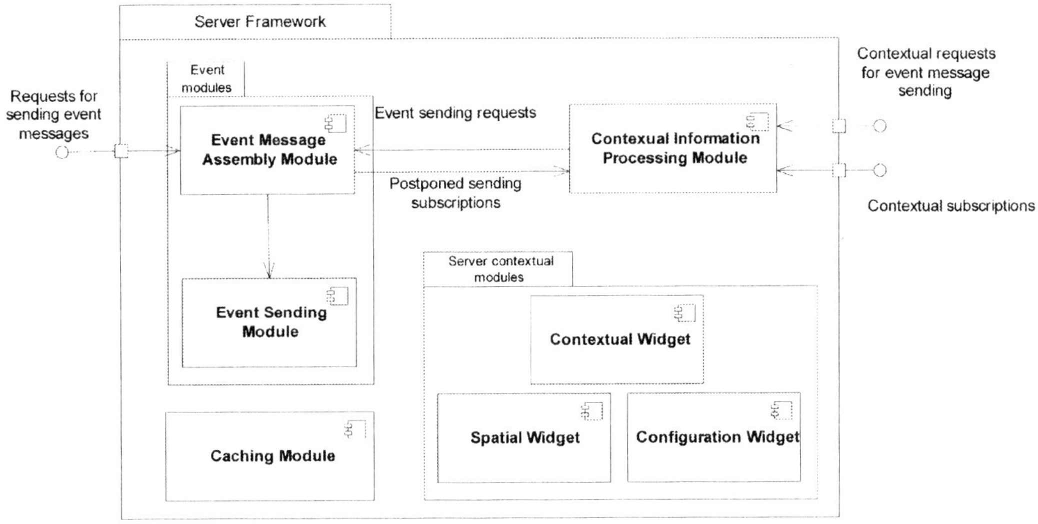

Server Framework uses configuration, location and contextual widgets. These widgets process contextual information on the server side before it is handed over to the module for contextual information to be stored in the database or to be further handed over to the module for event sending. The module for contextual information is used to receive contextual subscription (explained in detail in the chapter "Contextual subscriptions and actions in the MILE system") and contextual requests for event message sending (Figure 4).

In addition to using widgets to deliver contextual system architecture, server framework contains modules for data caching in order to ensure fast data access as well as numerous data and parameters specific to the server side of the system.

Device Framework uses widgets to enable contextual system architecture by extending base widgets' functionality available within the Base Framework. By extending the Base Framework components, new components that enable information exchange between contextual client (mobile connected device) and server components are made possible (Figure 5).

Device Framework contains the elements for the client side of the Distributed Events Protocol (DEP) (explained in detail in chapter "The use of distributed events in the MILE system"), most important of them being the module for message receival and response. To represent an event message with appropriate programming entities, a special module called the Event Factory connected with the mechanism of the Distributed Events Protocol (DEP) is used.

Since all applicative functionality of mobile connected devices in the MILE system is realized as a set of loosely connected modules which can easily be plugged in and out from the system, this library contains additional modules used to drive the communication. To provide secured access to services, a mechanism for acquiring service tickets from the server side and storing them in a special component called Ticket Store is provided. Stored service tickets can be (re)used by all client applicative modules.

Desktop Framework is used to build applications for desktop computers used primarily by teachers in order to track and coordinate events in a learning environment supported by mobile devices. Since desktop computers differ from mobile connected devices by numerous hardware and software characteristics (network connectivity, display size etc.), it was necessary to design

Figure 5. The device framework

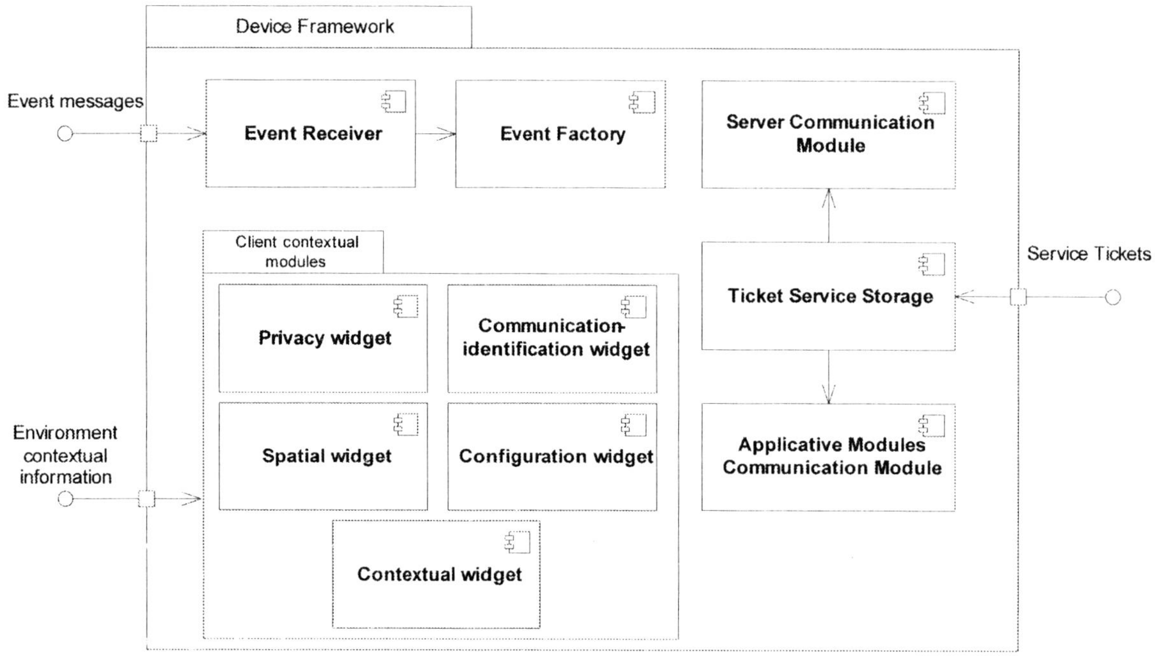

the Desktop Framework as a special component. The most important elements of this component are specific implementation of contextual widgets: privacy, spatial, contextual and configuration-identification widgets with their functionality derived from the Base Framework. Furthermore, proxy modules used to access server side services are contained within the framework taking into account the limitations of the network capabilities of the mobile devices.

Privacy widget is used by the end users to enter or to leave the private mode of use while the configuration widget disseminates the configuration data to the mobile clients. Spatial widget is separated from the contextual widget due to the specific nature of spatial contextual information.

Main System Services

MILE has a complex architecture designed to support different learning and teaching activities. It coordinates teaching activities provided by teachers and learning activities in which students participate. Within its service – orientated architecture several groups of service can be identified: core services, system services and applicative services (Figure 2).

System services are primarily consumed by client applications. Clients receive spatial information by using the Spatial Service, report contextual information by using the Contextual Service, perform automatic configuration using the Configuration Service and use Communication-identification Service to be registered as system users and therefore receive access to other services provided by the system. Authentication Service is used to log into the system, Registration Service to register system users, Security Service to ensure data security, Ticket service to be used by other services as a supplement to the Security Service and Subscription Service to provide access to and manipulation of contextual subscriptions.

Core services are the main components of the system and are used to deliver events to all subscribed system users. Events are generated with the help of all other services or by the Contextual Service. Contextual Service generates events based on contextual subscriptions and current users' context data and hands it over to the Event Service. Event service can be directly used by all server side components. This module encapsulates functionalities for event sending and separates the details of transformation of an event message from a programming entity into a network transferable entity (Figure 3). Event service is used by the Service for contextual information which, depending on the situations in a learning environment or created subscriptions, creates events to be delivered to all interested parties in the system. Contextual Service analyses data stored in the contextual database scheme in order to produce a list of events to be sent to clients. The analysis is preformed depending on the user request, subscription or automatically on a periodical base.

Applicative services are built together with the applicative modules as needed by course designers. Applicative services can utilize core and system services in order to deliver application-specific functionality to mobile devices.

The Client Application and Applicative Modules

Applications for desktop computers use available system architecture through the Desktop Framework (Figure 2) to provide teachers with the possibility for delivery and coordination of educational activities of chosen pedagogical models. Teachers use applications to see all students present in the learning environment, to share educational materials with students, to entice students in their interaction and collaboration or to engage in the interaction and collaboration with students supported by the MILE system.

The Client Application is available on the students' connected mobile devices and is primarily used to support student educational activities. The Client Application receives education related events through the system infrastructure and forwards them to client application modules to be utilized for educational purposes (Figure 4). The Client Application is a host application which can fetch, run or turn off applicative modules through the designated services. The advantage of this approach is that in the case of change in the applicative modules, client application doesn't have to be modified or upgraded. The Client Application provides user with numerous technical details about the system such as contextual information on privacy, locations, network status etc.

Client applicative modules are used to provide specific applicative functionality to clients involved in educational activities of used pedagogical models.

Applicative services are independent components built on top of the Server Framework, Contextual Information Service and Event Service. For the operation they use database as data storage, custom applicative logic and other system services. They use system services as an interface towards the commonly used system level operations and use the Event Service for sending different events to different system users (Figure 3).

The Communication Model

The system communication model is based on a client-server communication model and uses TCP/IP network protocol suite (RFC 675, 1974). There are two basic communication areas: client-server communication area and client-client communication area. Client-server communication area is the base of MILE's system architecture and enables the communication over the HTTP, TCP and UDP protocols as well as over the specifically designed Distributed Events Protocol (DEP) which is discussed in detail in the section "The use of distributed events in the MILE system". Client-client communication area, although controlled by the Device Framework, enables various network activities based on TCP and UDP protocols (Figure 6).

Figure 6. The communication model

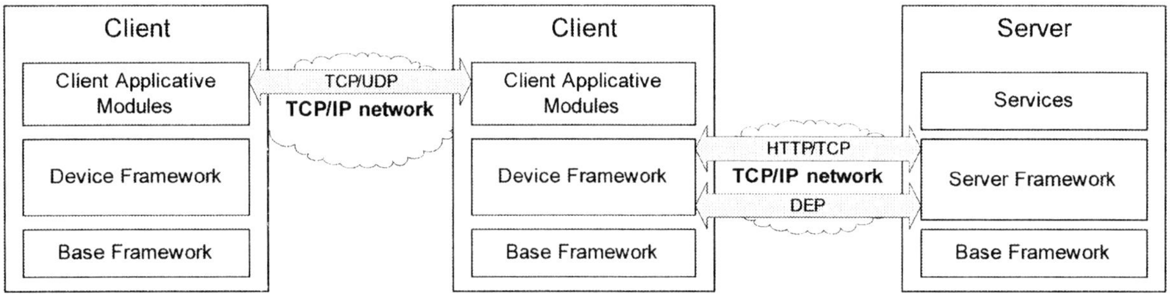

The client-server communication area is used to access system and applicative services and to exchange event messages. System and applicative services are accessed by HTTP or directly by TCP protocol depending on the system configuration. The Device and Server Framework provide communication services to higher level layers: client applicative modules and server applicative and system services. The communication with the services is always initiated by the clients while the event message sending is reserved for the server system side of the client-server communication area. In the latter case the communication is always initiated by the server and is based on the Distributed Events Protocol (DEP).

Client-client communication area is used for communication between clients and is realized at the client application applicative modules level. In contrast to communication with the server, the communication between client modules is not controlled by the server and is designed depending on the applicative requirements (e.g. chat, binary file transfer etc.).

Three-Tiered Data Architecture

Like many business applications, MILE system if composed of three basic layers: presentation layer, business logic layer and data access layer. Data access layer, considered to be the lowest layer, is used to store, fetch and manipulate data. It should have good technical characteristics because it is intensively used by all parts of the system. The system database is considered to be a part of the data access layer as well. The Business logic layer encapsulates system business rules and is used to model business processes that work with business entities. The Presentation layer is applied on top of the business logic layer and delivers the states of business entities to users.

The system is composed of system and applicative services that require data storage. The data architecture in MILE is designed according to the up-to-date paradigms of software engineering and practices (Microsoft patterns & practices Developer Center). It contains a main database component. Furthermore, data access is organized in layers with the main elements of the system represented as business entities and processes. This way of system development enables efficient development, error identification, upgrade and maintenance of the system.

The Module of Contextual Information

Contextual Modules in the MILE System

The implementation of the MILE system is based on the generalized model of context-aware mobile learning architecture. During the realisation several specializations of the model had to be done according to some physical limitations.

Figure 7. MILE's contextual widgets

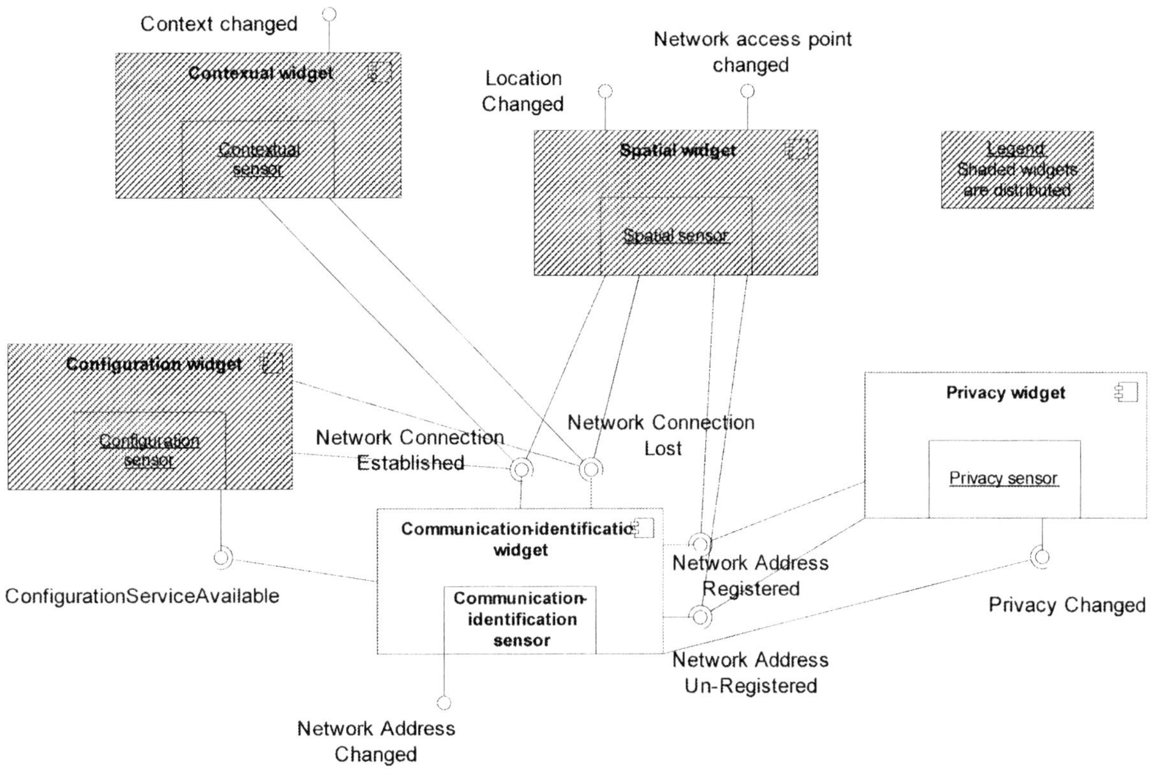

Nevertheless, major conceptual changes to the elements contained in the contextual model have been avoided.

Client side sensors include communication-identification and privacy sensors. Distributed sensors are spatial, contextual and configuration sensor. Learning material sensor is a distributed logical sensor primarily used to fetch learning contents to the user.

Contextual Widgets in the MILE System

Client contextual components of the MILE system collaborate in order to deliver system functionality. Mobile connected devices use contextual information from the learning environment to get connected to a network, fetch the data from the server and communicate with the server (Figure 7).

Communication-identification widget represents a central component of the contextual client in the MILE system and provides some basic communication-identification services to users. The widget is made of two timers used to gather information on network connectivity and network address. Wireless network connectivity is versatile contextual information because of frequent position change and low signal coverage. Therefore it is necessary to test network connectivity periodically and report it to the client application. In addition to changeable network connectivity, mobile connected devices tend to change their network addresses (e.g. IP addresses). Although the situation in which mobile client is assigned a new network address without the loss of connectivity is quite rare, client network identification is often used in the system and it is necessary to ensure it is precise and up-to-date. To achieve that, another timer periodically gathers the information about the network address. Communication-identification widget reacts to the changes of mobile connected device network address and privacy widget's settings. It reports mobile device address change to the server-side components.

Configuration widget is used to provide information about the system server side. Mobile clients have to fetch information about the service access points (addresses) and the ways of communication with services. Configuration widgets look for server on all available network interfaces by broadcasting a specially prepared UDP package. After receiving a client request, configuration server sends to the client detailed information about the way of communication with the server. After receiving the information, communication-identification widget establishes the communication with the server (e.g. registers its IP address).

Privacy widget provides contextual information about the privacy defined by the user. Privacy is considered to be a very important characteristic of context-aware systems since they reveal some information that can, under certain circumstances, be regarded as classified or too personal to be shared (e.g. teacher's location when in a meeting). Therefore, the privacy widget transfers user requests to the communication-identification widget which then performs the registration or the un-registration of users by using communication-identification service. The feedback on the outcome of user registration attempt is submitted back to the privacy widget.

Spatial widget is used to gather contextual information from mobile clients, interpret it by using server side spatial component and to deliver all required information to other client widgets. This widget depends severely on network availability and information provided by the communication-identification widget. Only after the communication network is available, the automatically assigned MAC network address (IEEE Std 802, 2001) can be identified. If the network address is registered, widget communicates with the server side spatial module to interpret the information about the access point and retrieves a learning environment location identifier. It can be used on the client and on the server side to provide numerous context-aware services.

Contextual Subscriptions and Actions in the MILE System

One of the most important elements of context-aware systems is contextual subscriptions. Contextual subscriptions are contextual entities which are triggered by certain contextual prerequisites within the specified time interval. Contextual subscriptions can be defined by the services or by the Event Sending module (Figure 3). Services define subscriptions in order to implement system or application logic while the Event module uses them to store undelivered event messages. Each subscription consists of so called actions which define what should be done when the subscription gets triggered.

There are four possibilities for contextual subscription:

- Contextual user can be subscribed to a context of a user
- Contextual user can be subscribed to a context of a group
- Contextual group can be subscribed to a context of a user
- Contextual group can be subscribed to a context of a group

As an example of the last subscription type, an educational situation in which inter-group collaboration is enticed and in which a message is sent to some groups about a contextual change in another (e.g. members' location change). Action triggered in that case is called "LocationChanged" and is aimed at all subscribed members or groups.

To support the system of contextual subscriptions and actions, active contextual actions and their receivers can be extracted in three ways:

- Periodical data storage analysis for all users and subscriptions

Figure 8. An example of contextual subscription realization

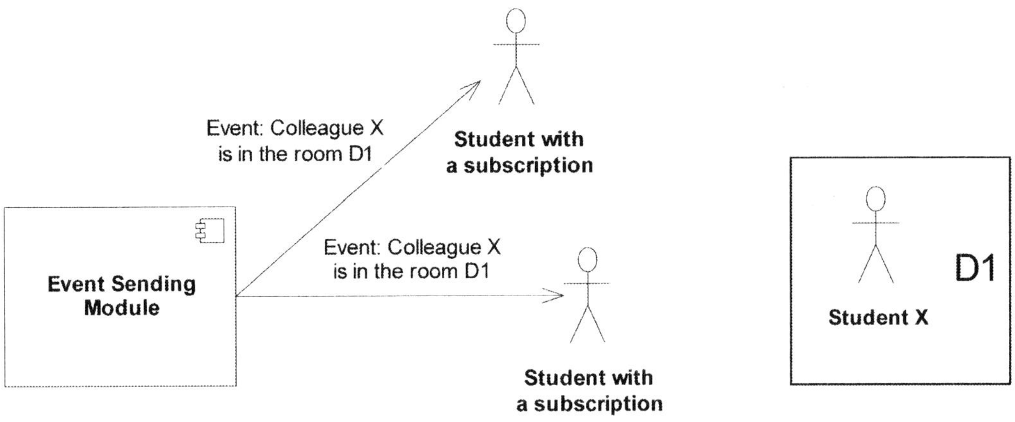

- Data storage analysis for a specific user
- Data storage analysis for a specific subscription

Described components are realized as database stored procedures in the MILE data storage and optimized according to the best practice in order to provide the most efficient results.

The Use of Distributed Events in the MILE System

During the activities of learning and teaching with mobile connected devices a need for transferring information about numerous events between main system actors occurs. Just by being active, clients explicitly spawn many events which are then transferred to all interested system entities. If a teacher opens a presentation on his mobile connected device, students' client applications are notified of the event and react to it appropriately (e.g. fetch presentation opened by the teacher from the central server repository).

Although most events get generated explicitly by students and teachers, some are generated implicitly as a result of server services operations and existing contextual subscription. Events are generated implicitly on the server side when subscriptions get active and are being sent to all subscribed users (e.g. student as a subscription author might have requested to be notified when his colleagues for informal learning enter the room D1). When the context of the subscription is met the server initiates communication and sends event information to all interested users registered as active on the network (Figure 8).

Events need to be transferred in relatively short time to all users they are aimed at. Since there are typically many users in the system and the number of events can get quite high, a special care has to be taken in order to make balance between the use of network resources, response time and reliable event delivery. As an appropriate and tested in practice solution, a TCP/IP protocol family was chosen and its UDP transport layer protocol for package delivery.

In order to ensure the independence of the network transportation mechanism on the one hand, and to satisfy the requests for low network traffic, adequate transfer speed and reliability on the other hand, the Distributed Events Protocol (DEP) was designed. It is used to exchange so called event messages (or DEP messages) which transfer event information and various technical-communicational data as the receiver's and sender's network addresses.

UDP as Base Protocol for the Distributed Events Protocol

Although not as popular as TCP, UDP (eng. User Datagram Protocol) is often applied in specialized systems like real time systems and internet telephony (VoIP – voice over IP) (Jackson, 2007). The UDP protocol is used to exchange short messages called datagrams. It does not guarantee the package delivery or ordered packages. Packages therefore can get lost, be delivered more times or be wrongly ordered. On the other hand, UDP has much shorter diagrams and in practice much faster delivery of packages. It is seen as a protocol for time-sensitive applications and is used in systems with many clients and small amounts of data to be transferred between clients and servers. Furthermore, the advantage of UDP over TCP is in the use of broadcast or multicast mechanisms to deliver a single datagram to more addresses which minimizes network load and utilised physical network infrastructure. UDP is due to its all characteristics appropriate to send events in the MILE system:

- Events are relatively small chunks of data and can be packed as datagrams which in theory can deliver 65,535 bytes (in practice that number is lower and on IPv4 is 65.507 bytes)
- Events need to be transferred as fast as possible. Real time transfer enables high quality service on the client side
- Events can be seen as isolated entities and don't have to be delivered in a specific order other than defined on the application level
- Event transfer should require low system and network resources. UDP enables these since it is not ordered, there are no sessions etc.

Nevertheless, UDP as a candidate for the distributed events protocol has one serious drawback: there are no mechanisms for the received message (UDP datagram) confirmation. Therefore, the Distributed Events Protocol (DEP) should, among other things, ensure event message delivery.

Event Messages

DEP transfers specially designed event messages from senders to receivers. Since every sent event message has to be confirmed with an event response message there are two types of messages: event messages and event response messages.

The logical view on the event message describes it as a system entity, while the physical describes concrete data transferred from the point of sending to the point of receival. On the physical level an event message is composed of message headers and of a message body. Event type (EventType) defines an event in the MILE system, event parameter data type (EventDataType) is a fully qualified data type name describing an event parameter. This header is reserved for simple information about the parameter type being sent, while the data itself can be found in the event body (e.g. for a location change event, event parameters will be the data about the user who changed his or location). Event priority (EventPriority) is information which is transferred to the transport layer in order to determine the priority of the message to be sent. Event destination (EventDestination) contains information on the receiver's type (individual user or group of users), sending time (EventTime) contains the time when the message was sent, unique event identifier (EventId) is temporary attached to an entity to uniquely identify events in the system when sending and responding to event messages. User identifier (UserId) describes a user at the system level to whom the event message is sent. Source IP address and port (SourceIPAddress) contains the information about the sender to whom the event response is to be sent. Reserved element (RFU) is used for future purposes.

An example event message structure used to send information about the user's location change event is depicted in Figure 9.

Figure 9. An example event message for the location change event

Message type: **Event/1.0**		
Event type: **LocationChanged**	Event parameter data type: **BaseFX.DEP.EventData.LocationChangedEventData**	Event priority: **N/A**
Event destination: **User**	Event sending time: **01.01.2009 13:06:39**	Unique event identifier: **1732865868**
User identifier: **8**	Source IP address and port: **192.168.2.10-52606**	Reserved element: **N/A**

```
<?xml version="1.0" encoding="utf-16"?>
<LocationChangedEventData xmlns:xsi="...">
  <LocationInfo>
    <LocationId>55</LocationId>
    <LocationName>Dvorana 1</LocationName>
    <LocationShortName>Dv1</LocationShortName>
    <LocationType>Room</LocationType>
  </LocationInfo>
</LocationChangedEventData>
```

The Distributed Events Protocol

DEP is an applicative TCP/IP layer protocol which uses Internet layer UDP protocol. The need of designing a special protocol together with its event and event response messages came because of the specifics of the MILE system, the most important being fast event transfer and low network traffic. The new protocol is justified by the comparison of the round trip time for message delivery over TCP and DEP. For single message delivery the measured time is of the same order of magnitude (slightly in favor of DEP), while for multiple messages DEP ensures much faster delivery.

In a typical scenario of an event message sending procedure, the server initiates communication by sending message while clients respond to it with the event response message (Figure 10).

For dealing with situations where the server sends more than one event message in parallel, a common port range is used. Before sending event message, the server fetches two available port identifiers from the common range (e.g. [50000, 55000]) and uses one of them to send the event message and the other to receive event responses. All clients, on the other hand, use a reserved port (e.g. 12345) to receive event messages and to send event response messages. If the server does not receive a message response the process of message sending is repeated for a specified number of times (e.g. 3). Should the answer be lost again, the event sending procedure is aborted.

The distributed events protocol is a distributed algorithm realized on the server and clients and uses certain synchronization mechanisms. The complexity of the protocol is in the parallelism that needs to be introduced. On the server side parallel message sending and receiving with the mandatory synchronization points is implemented. Immediately after receiving an event message client responds to it with an event response message. Client tracks unique event identifiers and eliminates duplicate events.

A special care has to be taken of the history of received event messages. The server might resend an event message if a response message is not received in time. This is possible even when a client has already received the event message and its response hasn't reached the server. To solve this problem the server tracks down event message history and discards duplicate event messages.

Figure 10. Event sending and responding to an event in the Distributed Events Protocol

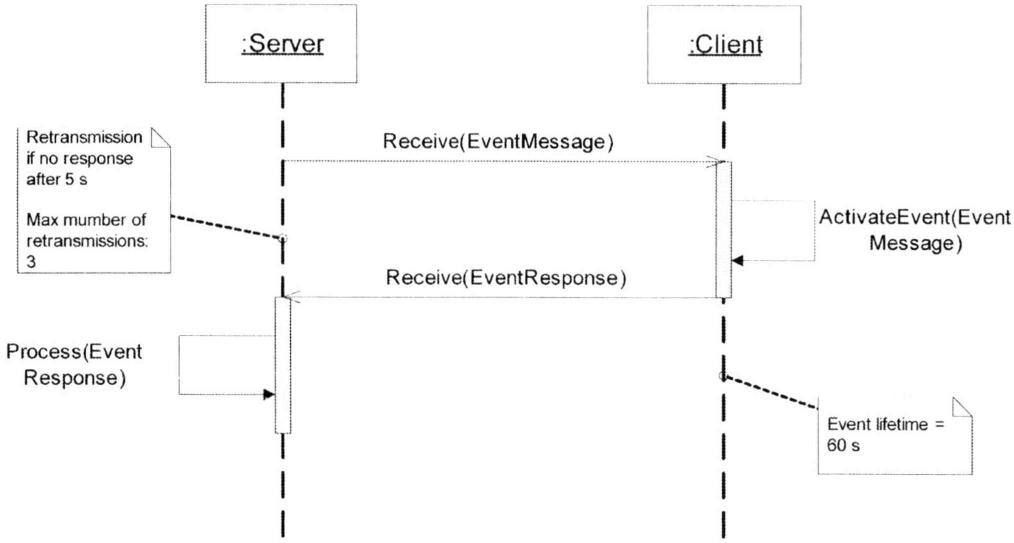

APPLICATION MODULES

MILE offers many different modules that support a learning environment based on mobile devices, some of the most interesting being:

- MCollaboration - used to support collaboration
- MWhiteBoard – an alternative to a classical blackboard available to mobile students and teachers
- MNotebook – used to deliver PowerPoint presentations to mobile devices
- MSchedule – customizable scheduler for mobile devices
- MSurvey – instant in-class mobile assessment and surveying
- MAccessibility – accessibility features for users with special needs
- MVirtualBoard - notice board available anytime anywhere
- MGuide - guide to current education related events

This chapter examines in detail modules that are the most important when collaborative approach to learning and blended teaching model are concerned. According to the constructivism, learning should be interactive to promote higher-level learning and social presence (Kaleidoscope Network, 2006). By using MILE modules students interact online with other students, instructors and the content.

MNoteBook Module

Listening to a lecture, following a displayed presentation, making notes and exchanging them with colleagues all at the same time is challenging even for the most skilful students. MNotebook module is used to automatically display presentations opened by a teacher in a classroom. As the teacher passes on to the next slide, slides are automatically changed on students' mobile devices. In addition to that, students are given the opportunity to tag the bullets with their own notes (Figure 11).

After being created, notes are uploaded to a community web site and become available to other students as a secondary learning resource with the information of significance at a student community level, providing students the possibility to

Figure 11. An MNoteBook slide shown to a mobile user

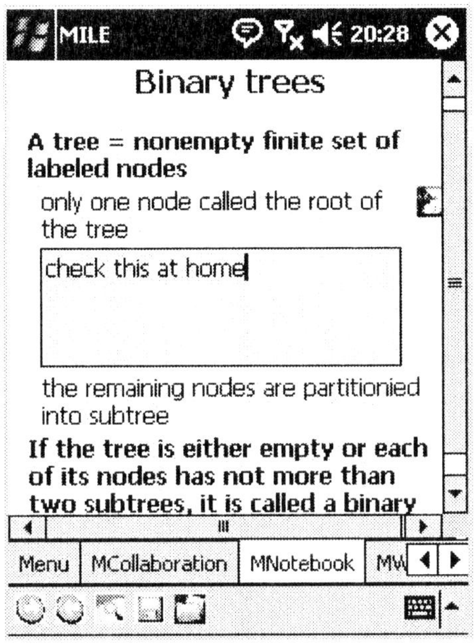

benefit from other students' notes thus facilitating the creation of social networks and clearly demonstrating socializing powers of mobility.

The module presents a process some authors refer to as the digitalization of didactic action since it transforms elements of classical education and inevitably leads to a shift of competences when some standard student activities are concerned (Peters, 1999). In addition to that, such an approach aids recall and reflection similarly to other form of social software such as blogs or discussion groups (Kukulska-Hulme & Trayler, 2005).

MCollaboration Module

The module supports collaborative activities such as chat, file sharing and instant messaging by utilizing wireless network and MILE's central server – side component (left hand side of Figure 12.). Students are notified of the presence of their colleague in the learning environment and are able to, depending on the security and privacy settings, explore colleagues' whereabouts through a digital map of a learning environment (right hand side of Figure 12.).

Socializing powers of mobility are said to facilitate collaborative learning and encourage interaction (Hoic-Bozic, Boticki & Mornar, 2005). Learning is inherently social and mediated through interaction with others, and involves a process of engagement in a community of practice. The MCollaboration module strongly supports the concept of communities of practice, with members sharing common interests, learning together and interacting with each other (Mayes & De Freitas, 2004). By using MILE communities of practice can be formed spontaneously and can be very informal, or they can be formed „artificially" (e.g. by a teacher). Either way the important role

Figure 12. Capabilities of the MCollaboration module

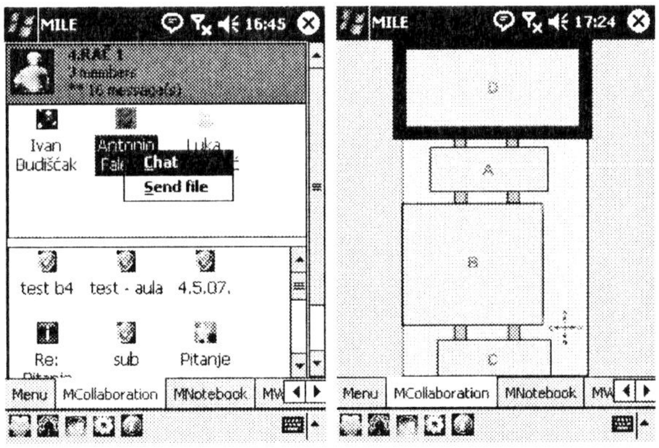

of social interaction and collective learning is strongly emphasized.

MWhiteBoard Module

MWhiteBoard is a module that supports group work in a controlled classroom environment. Students collaborate by sketching ideas on their mobile devices and sharing them on a common canvas (e.g. on a projector) (Figure 13). In this way knowledge can easily be shared, thus offering the possibility for cooperation skills improvement (Mayes & De Freitas, 2004). This is very important since formal learning environments, such as faculties or campuses originally, amongst other reasons, exist to promote chance encounters and awareness of other people's activities (Morken & Divitini, 2005).

CONCLUSION AND FUTURE PLANS

The chapter presented a model for context - aware mobile learning and a system named MILE as an example of its implementation. Context – aware mobile learning utilizes the characteristics of both mobile learning systems and context – aware systems in order to enable learning with mobile devices in contexts.

In addition to being used by individuals outside of their living and working environments, mobile technology is used by certain professions in order to acquire contextualized knowledge while on the move. Mobile learning tries to make learning independent of the location it happens at. In that way learning becomes more personal, less formal and better adapts to learners. Mobile learning is ambient as well. That means it better adapts to students and the environment. The art of developing applications that better adapt to their users is called context – awareness and should be used as a first class concept when designing application for mobile clients.

Following Wang's definition of CAML (context aware mobile learning), MILE possesses basic contextual dimensions called identity, spatio-temporal and the facility dimension. In order to support collaborative activities, the activity and community dimensions of context – aware mobile learning are utilized. The chapter presented a generalized model for context – aware mobile learning designed to be universally applicable when designing system for teaching and learning with mobile connected devices. In addition to sensors, the lowest level of the generalized model of context-aware mobile learning architecture is composed of widgets encapsulating sensor functionality and enabling outer entities

Figure 13. Teacher's view (right hand side) of a student's drawing on MWhiteBoard module (left hand side)

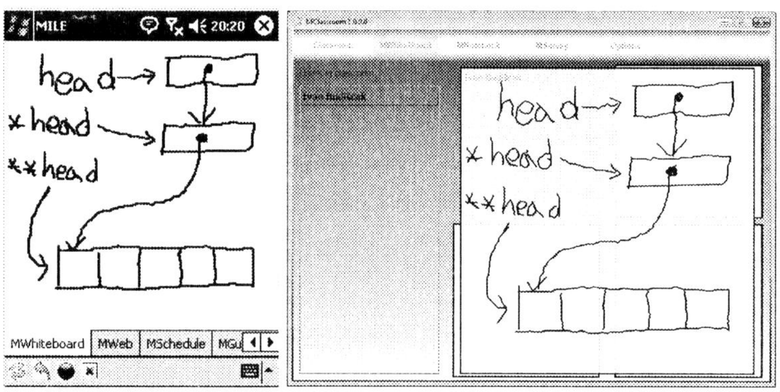

to create subscriptions to sensor events. First order aggregators communicate directly with the widgets and are used as a support to the higher-order aggregators.

Main libraries of the MILE system are the Base Framework, the Device Framework and the Server Framework. The Device Framework and the Server Framework are built upon the Base Framework to provide services to specific parts of the system. The Desktop Framework is used by the applications for desktop computers; the Device Framework for the client application and its applicative modules while the Server Framework provides the base for the Contextual Information Service, Event Service, System and Applicative Services. Since MILE utilizes location-aware data special attention was given to the users' need for privacy. Using the client – side privacy widget, users can switch to the private mode and still use some system resources.

Significant effort was invested into the mechanisms for utilizing network resources in order to achieve adequate communication mechanism in the system. The Distributed Events Protocol was created to disseminate events within a learning environment based on mobile devices. Different synchronization mechanisms had to be implemented since the UDP protocol had to be utilized for communication. Orientation on wireless networks presented a problem since mobile devices tend to change their IP addresses frequently.

Applicative modules for mobile devices were implemented as self-contained and pluggable to enable their easy installation and de-installation. They communicate with the rest of the system through an object oriented programming interface in order to maximize reusability and establish firm module boundaries. Although the code was designed to be reusable, special implementation of the client side applicative modules had to be done for each mobile device platform used.

In order to demonstrate the possibilities of contextual mobile learning, few client applicative modules were implemented. MNoteBook module is designed in order to support the didactical approach to mobile learning, while MCollaboration and MWhiteBoard modules provide support for mobile computer supported collaborative learning.

REFERENCES

Ally, M. (2004). Foundations of educational theory for online learning. In T. Anderson & F. Elloumi (Eds.), *Theory and practice of online learning*. Athabasca University.

Alonso, F., López, G., Manrique, D., & Viñes, J. M. (2005). An instructional model for Web-based e-learning education with a blended learning process approach. *British Journal of Educational Technology*, *36*(2), 217–235. doi:10.1111/j.1467-8535.2005.00454.x

Bersin, J. (2004). *The blended learning handbook*. San Francisco: Wiley.

Boticki, I., Mornar, V., & Andric, K. (2006). *Supporting and enhancing teaching and learning with mobile devices*. CD-ROM edition. ISBN: 3-89958-195-4.

Boticki, I., Mornar, V., & Hoic–Bozic, N. (2006). *Introducing location-awareness into a learning environment supported by mobile devices* (pp. 267-274).

Boud, D., & Feletti, G. (2001). *The challenge of problem based learning*. London: Kogan Page.

Brown, P. J. (1996). *The e-stick document: A framework for creating context-aware applications*. Presented at the Proceedings of the Electronic Publishing (pp. 259-272).

De Freitas, S., & Levene, M. (2003). Evaluating the development of wearable devices, personal data assistants, and the use of other mobile devices in further and higher education institutions (JISC Tech. Rep.). UK: JISC.

Dey, A., & Abowd, D. (2000). Towards a better understanding of context and context–awareness (pp. 304-307).

Dey, A., Abowd, D., & Salber, D. (2001). Conceptual framework and a toolkit for supporting the rapid prototyping of context-aware applications. *Human-Computer Interaction (HCI) Journal*, *16*(2-4), 97–166.

European Commission. (1991). *Communication from the commission to the council and the European parliament: The e-learning action plan*. Retrieved from http://eur-lex.europa.eu/LexUriServ/site/en/com/2001/com2001_0172en01.pdf

Griswold, W. G., Shanahan, P., Brown, S. W., Boyer, R., Ratto, M., Shapiro, R. B., & Truong, T. M. (2004). Activecampus: Experiments in community-oriented ubiquitous computing. *Computer*, *37*(10), 73–81. doi:10.1109/MC.2004.149

Hazas, M., Scott, J., & Krumm, J. (2004). Location-aware computing comes of age. *IEEE Computer Magazine*, *37*(2), 95–97.

Hoic-Bozic, N., Boticki, I., & Mornar, V. (2005). *Interaction and collaborative support in an adaptive Web-based LMS AhyCo* (pp. 123-230).

Holzinger, A., & Errath, M. (2007). Mobile computer Web-application design in medicine: Some research based guidelines. *Universal Access in the Information Society*, *6*, 31–41. doi:10.1007/s10209-007-0074-z

Hsi, S., & Fait, H. (2005). RFID enhances visitors' museum experience at the exploratorium. *Communications of the ACM, 48*(9), 60-65.

IEEE Std. 802®-2001, Media Access Control (MAC). Retrieved from http://standards.ieee.org/getieee802/download/802-2001.pdf

Jackson, B. (2006). *History of VoIP*. University of Texas at Dallas.

Kaleidoscope Network of Excellence. (2006). *Mobile learning initiative big issues in mobile learning* (Report). University of Nottingham. Retrieved from http://mlearning.noe-kaleidoscope.org/public/news/KALEIDOSCOPE%20REPORT_07_Big_Issues_In_Mobile_Learning.pdf

Kukulska-Hulme, A. (2007). Mobile usability in educational contexts: What have we learnt? *International Review of Research in Open and Distance Learning*, *8*(2), 1–16.

Kukulska-Hulme, A., & Traxler, J. (2005). *Mobile learning: A handbook for educators and trainers*. UK: Routledge.

Markett, C., Sanchez, A. I., Weber, S., & Tangney, B. (2006). Using short message service to encourage interactivity in the classroom. *Computers & Education*, *46*(3), 280–293. doi:10.1016/j.compedu.2005.11.014

Massey, A. P., Ramesh, V., & Khatri, V. (2006). Design, development, and assessment of mobile applications: The case for problem-based learning. *IEEE Transactions on Education*, *49*(2), 183–192. doi:10.1109/TE.2006.875700

Mayes, T., & De Freitas, S. (2004). *Review of e-learning theories, frameworks, and models* (JISC e-Learning Models Desk Study). UK. Retrieved from http://www.elearning.ac.uk/resources/modelsdeskreview/

McCormack, C., & Jones, D. (1997). *Building a Web-based education system*. New York: Wiley.

Microsoft Patterns & Practices Developer Center. Microsoft Developer Network. Retrieved from http://msdn.microsoft.com/en-us/practices/default.aspx

Morken, E. M., & Divitini, M. (2005). *Blending mobile and ambient technologies to support mobility in practice based education: The case of teacher education*. Online edition.

Naismith, L. (2005). *Literature review in mobile technologies and learning* (Report 11, Futurelab Series). Bristol, UK: Futurelab. Retrieved from http://www.futurelab.org.uk/resources/documents/lit_reviews/Mobile_Review.pdf

Pascoe, J., Ryan, N., & Morse, D. (2000). Using while moving: Hci issues in fieldwork environments. *ACM Transactions on Computer-Human Interaction*, *7*(3), 417–437. doi:10.1145/355324.355329

Peters, O. (1999). *A pedagogical model for virtual learning spaces. Articles on flexible learning and distance education*. Fernuniversitat Hagen. Retrieved from http://www.tbc.dk/pdf/peters-a_pedagogical_model.pdf

Proctor, N., & Burton, J. (2003). *Tate modern multimedia tour pilots 2002-2003* (pp. 54-55).

RFC 4120. The Kerberos Network Authentication Service (V5). Retrieved from http://www.ietf.org/rfc/rfc4120.txt

RFC 675. Specification of Internet Transmission Control Program. (1974, December). Retrieved from http://tools.ietf.org/html/rfc675

Sakkopoulos, E., Lytras, M., & Tsakalidis, A. (2006). Adaptive mobile Web services facilitate communication and learning Internet technologies. *IEEE Transactions on Education*, *49*(2), 208–215. doi:10.1109/TE.2006.873985

Sharples, M., Taylor, J., & Vavoula, G. (2005). *Towards a theory of mobile learning*. Online edition.

Thorne, K. (2003). *Blended learning*. London: Kogan Page.

Yuan-Kai, W. (2004). Context awareness and adaptation in mobile learning (pp. 154-158).

Chapter 12
'Intelligent Context' for Personalized Mobile Learning

Philip Moore
Birmingham City University, UK

Bin Hu
Birmingham City University, UK

Mike Jackson
Birmingham City University, UK

Jizheng Wan
Birmingham City University, UK

ABSTRACT

There have been significant developments in higher education resulting in interest in personalised educational provision. Concomitant with these changes is the evolving capability and ubiquity of mobile technologies. To facilitate personalisation and leverage the power of mobile technologies in mobile pedagogic systems identification of individuals is a prerequisite; this can be achieved using an individual's profile (termed context). This chapter considers the background to context with related research. Context modelling, the processing of contextual information, context matching and the context matching algorithm, ontology, and the Semantic Web technologies are introduced. Context reasoning and inference in rule-based systems is considered and the context reasoning ontology is presented with scenario-based evaluation. The chapter concludes with a discussion, consideration of future research, and open research questions.

INTRODUCTION

There have been significant developments in higher education (HE) reflecting the evolving socio-economic and demographic make-up of the student population (Cullen *et al*, 2002; Gorrard *et al*, 2002); this has resulted in interest in personalised educational provision – albeit currently at an embryonic stage (generally) in *virtual learning environments* (VLE) such as 'Moodle' (Moodle, 2009). A trial of Moodle was successfully completed at Birmingham City University[1] in 2004 in a third year undergraduate degree module within

DOI: 10.4018/978-1-60566-882-6.ch012

the Department of Computing; subsequently it has been rolled out University wide over a distributed system in a wide area network (WAN) linking multiple campuses delivering a broad range of courses including computing, law, music, and the built environment. For a consideration of VLE see Britain & Liber (1999) and Cullen *et al*, (2002).

Birmingham City University is characterised by a very diverse student base in terms of attainment, demographics, cultural background, and needs from the HE experience, to reflect this a broad range of courses are offered from Batchelor level degrees to Masters and Ph.D. The online presence has demonstrated positive benefits for students by providing learning *'on demand...anytime and anywhere'* as discussed in Goh & Kinshuk (2004), Rushby (1998), and MacKnight (1998). There were, however, additional lessons related to staff involvement in a VLE, as discussed in Weller (2002) teaching staff need to feel comfortable with the increased demands of a VLE [which are manifested in the need to monitor modules delivered in the context of a VLE and provide increased levels if interaction and feedback] for its use to be successful; this is not always the case which can be detrimental to overall process.

Historically, computerised pedagogic systems designed to address the changing HE environment have used networked and Internet-based approaches (generally termed 'e-learning'). Over time developments in mobile technologies have resulted in a blurring of the distinction between the 'e-learning' and mobile learning ('m-learning') concepts, the terms frequently being used interchangeably (Coppola & Della, 2004; Kossen, 2005). In this chapter the term 'm-learning' will be used to refer to both 'e-learning' and 'm-learning' systems.

Concomitant with the interest in personalisation is the evolving capabilities of mobile devices. Mobile devices fall into two broad classifications: (1) laptop and mobile computers (which whilst mobile are not generally useable 'on-the-move'), and (2) *wearable* computing devices (which typically include mobile phones, smart phones, and Personal Digital Assistants (PDA) which can be used in a wider range of environments – albeit characterised by a diverse range of constraints – whilst 'on-the-move'). Additionally, there has been significant convergence in mobile devices and their capabilities resulting in a blurring of the distinction between the two classifications introducing increased complexity in the demands of mobile systems and applications.

The developments in mobile computing will "free users from the desktop" (Abowd *et al*, 1997) however mobile devices have constrained capabilities when compared with desktop alternatives including restricted display, restricted bandwidth and fluctuating availability (Lonsdale *et al*, 2003). Effective 'm-learning' demands that these limitations are addressed, an individuals profile (termed context) offers the potential to mitigate the identified constraints and enable service provision compliant with user need in a format to suit available devices (Moore *et al*, 2008).

There has been significant research targeting m-learning, for example, Goh & Kinshuk (2004) have considered issues in the implementation of learning modules in 'm-learning' using a simple case study and postulate that *"from e-learning to m-learning, mobile learning is going to be the next wave in the evolution of learning environments"*. Goh & Kinshuk (2004) in observing that a number of mobile learning and teaching applications have been deployed and evaluated (see for example Luchini *et al*, 2002; Mifsud, 2002) conclude that while 'm-learning' can compliment e-learning by creating an additional channel of access for mobile users to engage in learning *"anytime and anywhere"* many issues regarding mobile learning have not been exhaustively researched.

Hokyoung & Parsons (2008) discuss recent developments in 'm-learning' techniques and related technologies, emerging innovations are considered with identification of appropriate pedagogies and technology usage methodologies.

Singh & Abu Bakar (2007) describe the educational opportunities of teaching in a wireless classroom using notebooks and PDA's, pedagogic issues are considered with the didactic aspects of mobile learning and the usability issues in accessing information on mobile devices.

There is a large body of research addressing academic and pedagogic issues, a prolific source for such work being the Association for Learning Technology (ALT, 2009). Academic and pedagogic research (generally) investigates socio-economic and demographic issues, course content, and the mode of delivery. A detailed discussion on academic and pedagogic issues is beyond the scope of this chapter however examples of documented research addressing the topic include: Rushby (1998), MacKnight (1998), Cullen *et al* (2002), Gorrard *et al*, (2002), Mungania (2003), Long & Tricker (2004), Bull *et al* (2004), Liaw (2004), Dichev *et al* (2004), Komives (2005), and Scardamalia & Bereiter (2006) etc. Computational research into mobile systems and 'm-learning' typically (again generally) considers implementation issues related to mobility, mobile devices, service infrastructure(s), and service provision. While there are aspects common to research addressing academic / pedagogic and computational issues – as considered in for example Goh & Kinshuk (2004, Hokyoung & Parsons (2008), and Singh & Abu Bakar (2007) – a clear distinction can (generally) be drawn between the two research disciplines.

This chapter focuses on the computational issues as they apply to the use of context to enable personalised service provision in intelligent context-ware pervasive mobile systems. Addressing pedagogic issues is not an aim however where applicable such issues will be introduced as they relate to personalised 'm-learning' in the domain of HE.

Research [undertaken from pedagogical and m-learning perspectives] has demonstrated the potential efficacy of the *anytime and anywhere* approach to address the socio-economic and demographic issues that impact learning. It has, however, failed to address the demands of intelligent context-aware pervasive m-learning systems; 'Intelligent Context' offers the potential to rectify this shortcoming by enabling intelligent context processing and effective personalised mobile learning.

A key concept in 'Intelligent Context' is personalisation; the research discussed in this chapter addresses the twin concepts of 'context' and 'personalisation' [context providing an effective basis for personalisation] and builds on previous work targeted at the development of a generic novel context modelling ontology useable in diverse domains and systems. To this end, an ontology predicated on mobile learning in the domain of HE (see Figure 7) has been developed using domain independent core concepts with domain specific extension concepts that reflect the domain specific nature of context.

In Moore & Hu (2006, 2007b) contextual information (context factors encoded in RDF/S) applicable to a student in the domain of HE for a mobile learning system is identified with consideration of related component (Semantic Web) technologies. It has been shown that an entities' profile (context) in combination with ontology is an effective approach to personalisation (Moore & Hu, 2006, 2007b). The work documented in Moore & Hu (2006, 2007b) is extended in Moore *et al* (2008). *'Intelligent Context'* revises and extends the previous work introducing a novel system architecture with a revised generic context reasoning ontology and *Context Processing Rules* (CPR). These elements are designed to provide an effective basis for *'context-matching'* in a rule-based system capable of efficient *'context management'*.

The chapter is structured in two sections. Section 1 (Background) addresses the background with an introduction to the component technologies. Context and context-awareness with related research is addressed along with context modelling and design considerations. Ontology, semantics and the Semantic Web are introduced. Section 2 (Intelligent Context) addresses the specifics of *'Intelligent Context'*. Context reasoning and inference are addressed with context processing in a rule-based system using CPR. The context reasoning ontology is presented with a context reasoning example and a scenario-based evaluation using an online context-aware mobile learning and collaboration simulation. The final section presents a discussion with conclusions, open research questions, and potentially profitable directions for future research activity.

SECTION ONE: BACKGROUND

Context and Context-Awareness

The first use of context in computer systems runs concurrently with the development of pervasive computing as envisioned by Mark Weiser in his seminal papers (Weiser, 1991, 1993) and the emergence of mobile computing components in the early 1990's. These developments have led to the desire to support computer usage in a diverse range of environments and domains. Context forms an important element in pervasive computing; for example, in location-based services (such as context-aware tour guides) context is a pivotal function. This analogy clearly extends to personalised education in m-learning systems.

Context-Awareness

Context-awareness describes a concept in which the profile of an entity is defined by its 'context', an entity being defined in Dey *et al* (1999a) as: *"a person, place or a physical or computational object"*. Context-awareness employs context to identify individuals to enable targeted service provision based on location, preferences and current needs with minimal user effort (Lonsdale *et al*, 2003; Moore *et al*, 2006, 2008). Context is also pivotal in the matching of users in Computer Supported Collaboration (CSC) in interactive systems (Lonsdale *et al*, 2003).

There are two principal approaches to the building context-aware artefacts, *Technology* and *Application* driven approaches (Lonsdale *et al*, 2003).

- **Technology** driven approaches focus on hardware and software capabilities, the concept being one where system-derived data and processing capabilities determine resource targeting and formatting based on the available device capabilities.
- **Application** driven approaches concentrate on specific applications and the use of context to define user needs and preferences.

From a design perspective the two approaches can be treated as independent. However, effective implementation of context-awareness to enable 'm-learning' in mobile systems clearly requires the implementation of both approaches working in concert, each being dependent on the other for an intelligent context-aware system to function effectively.

Context-Awareness and Mobile Learning

To effectively personalise learning and leverage the power of mobile technologies context performs a pivotal role (Goh & Kinshuk, 2004), Sharples *et al* (2002) observing that there is a *"natural alliance between learning as a contextual activity and personal mobile technologies: mobile learning being strongly mediated by its context"*. Personalised m-learning involves the targeting of resources and the matching of users in CSC (Lin-Hsiao, 2005; Hu *et al*, 2007a; Hu *et al*, 2007b; Moore *et al*, 2007b, 2008), this has a corollary in the provision of personalised services in related research which addresses issues related to the identification of entities based on their needs and preferences (Abowd *et al*, 1997; Pascoe *et al*, 1999; Poslad *et al*, 2001; Chen & Kotz, 2002; Lonsdale *et al*, 2003; Kaasinen, 2003).

Context

The effective definition of context is an important element in context-aware computing, a context consisting of contextual information (context properties) that describe a users profile to enable personalised service provision based on a users current situation (termed *situated role*). The notion of context has a dual origin, *technical* and *social science* based (Dourish, 2004). The technical notion refers to the role of context in human computer interaction, the social science notion relating to social settings. There is considerable confusion surrounding the notion of context, it's meaning, and the role it plays in interactive systems (Dourish, 2004). The literature contains many definitions of the term context including:

1. *"Any information that can be used to characterise an entity"* (Dey *et al*, 1999a)
2. *"A broad concept... incorporating information relating to the inner state of the person describing it"* (Laerhoven & Aidoo, 2001)
3. *"Context refers to the physical and social situation in which computational devices are embedded"* (Dourish, 2004)
4. *"The current situation the user of a mobile device experiences while using it"* (Coppola et al, 2004)
5. *"The location and the identity of nearby people and objects"* (Schilit et al, 1994, Schilit, 1995)
6. *"The location, identity, environment, and time"* (Ryan et al, 1997)

In a comprehensive investigation into context-based computing Dey *et al* (1999a) define context as:

7. *"Any information that can be used to characterise the situation of entities"* and extend this definition to include *"typically the location, identity and state of people, groups, and computational and physical objects"*

One of the earliest, broadest, and most comprehensive definitions of context has been proposed by Schilit *et al* (1994):

8. *"Context encompasses more than just the users location, because other things of interest are also mobile and changing. Context includes lighting, noise level, network connectivity, communication costs, communication bandwidth and even the social situation, e.g., whether you are with your manager or with a co-worker"*

While the definitions (1-7) point to a broadly common view on the concept of context they also identify the failure to agree on a common definition. Definition (8) (Schilit *et al*, 1994) clearly extends the range and scope of contextual information encompassing many factors that effect mobile computing. The failure to agree on a common definition is arguably due to the inherent complexity of context and the differing perspectives from which it is viewed, this points to the domain specific nature of context.

Context is purpose and application specific requiring the identification of the function(s) and properties specific to individual domains. This is exemplified in 'm-learning' where the starting point in the definition of a context is *the "identification of the function and purpose in which we are interested"* (Lonsdale *et al*, 2003). Given the domain-specific nature of context, definitions 1-8 fail to properly define context for a Personalised Mobile Learning (PML) domain, a derived context definition for PML (9) is proposed (Moore *et al*, 2008):

9. *Information consisting of properties that combine to describe and characterise an*

entity and its situated role in computer readable form

Location is central to context in mobile systems, context however includes more than just location (Dey *et al*, 1999a; Kaasinen, 2003; Schilit *et al*. 1994; Schilit, 1995). As identified in Schilit *et al* (1994) a broad and diverse range of context factors combine to form a context definition, in fact, almost any information available at the time of an interaction can be viewed as contextual information including:

a) The variable tasks demanded by users
b) The diverse range of mobile devices and the associated service infrastructure
c) Resource availability (connectivity, battery condition, display, network, and bandwidth etc)
d) Nearby resources (accessible devices and hosts including I/O devices (MIT, 2004)
e) The physical situation (temperature, air quality, light, and noise level etc)
f) The social situation (who you are with, people nearby etc – proximate information)
g) Spatial information (location, orientation, speed and acceleration etc)
h) Temporal information (time of the day, date, and season of the year)
i) Physiological measurements (blood pressure, heart rate, respiration and muscle activity etc)

The range of contextual information [identified in points a to i], whilst not comprehensive, effectively demonstrates the inherent complexity of context, its domain specific nature, and the difficulty in defining and measuring it. This difficulty is exemplified in the need to accommodate two general types of context: ***static*** context and ***dynamic*** context (Moore *et al*, 2007b):

- ***Static*** context (termed *customisation*) relates to a use-case in which a users profile (context) is created manually, the user being actively involved in the process and having an element of control.
- ***Dynamic*** context (termed *personalisation*) relates to a condition in which the user is seen as being passive, or at least somewhat less in control. In such a use-case the system monitors, analyses, and reacts dynamically to a users behaviour and situated-role.

The two types of context are reflected in the two principal ways context is used, these are: (1) as a retrieval indicator (a *static* context) and (2) to tailor system behaviour to match users system usage patterns (a *dynamic* context).

RELATED RESEARCH

Context-aware solutions have been applied in many diverse domains where the provision of personalised services mapped to an entities context is a system requirement, set out below are representative examples of documented research utilising context (Table 1). The research projects are considered under three general headings: (1) the application of context-awareness, (2) personalisation and adaptation in mobile systems, and (3) ad-hoc networks. Each project is classified under three parameters: (1) the domain the project is designed to address, (2) the (general) nature of the contextual information the project employs, and (3) the mode of operation.

The Application of Context-Awareness

Personalisation and Adaptation in Mobile Systems

The research considered above, whilst addressing aspects of personalisation, fails to fully address the systemic demands of constrained mobile devices in context-aware mobile systems. Given

Table 1. Examples of research utilizing context

Research Project	Domain	Contextual Data	Mode of Operation
Active Badge (Want *et al*, 1992, 1995) (Ward *et al*, 1997)	Office Environment	Spatio-Temporal Identity	IR badge
ParcTab (Want *et al*, 1995) (Brown *et al*, 1997)	Office Environment	Spatio-Temporal Identity Proximate	IR mobile device
In/Out board (Salber *et al*, 1999)	Office Environment	Spatio-Temporal Identity	RF tag
DUMMBO (Salber *et al*, 1999)	Office Environment	Spatio-Temporal Identity	IR or RF tag
Chameleon (Fitzmaurice, 1993)	Tour Guide	Location	Mobile device
Cyberguide (Abowd *et al*, 1997)	Tour Guide	Location	Mobile device IR Beacons GPS
FLUMP (Flexible Ubiquitous Monitor Project) (Finney et *al*, 1996)	Tour Guide	Spatio-Temporal Identity	IR badge
Guide (Davies *et al*, 1998)	Tour Guide	Location Preferences	Portable PC
Virtual Information Towers (VIT) (Leonardi *et al*, 1999)	Tour Guide	Location	Mobile *wearable* device with GPS over GSM or Wireless LAN
Smart Sight (Jie Yang *et al*, 1999)	Tour Guide	Location Language Environmental	Mobile PC Audio Visual GPS
PALIO (Andreadis *et al*, 2001)	Personalised pervasive Tour Guide	Location Identity Preferences	Wireless or wired Mobile device
CRUMPET (Poslad *et al*, 2001)	Tour Guide	Location Identity	Wireless mobile device
MOBIlearn (Lonsdale *et al*, 2003)	Mobile Learning	Spatio-Temporal	Wireless mobile device
Archaeological Assistant (Ryan *et al*, 1997)	Research Field Tools	Spatio-Temporal	*PalmPilot* with GPS
Animal Observation (Pascoe, 1998, 1999)	Research Field Tools	Spatio-Temporal	*PalmPilot* GPS
Forget-Me-Not (Lamming & Flynn, 1994)	Memory Aids	Location Proximate Autobiographical	PDA (*ParcTab* terminals)
Remembrance Agent (Rhodes, 1997)	Memory Aids	Spatio-Temporal Proximate Subject / Note body	*Wearable* device
Stick-e-Notes (Pascoe *et al*, 1999)	Memory Aids	Note body	*PalmTop* computer
Startle-Cam (Healey & Picard, 1998)	Sensing / Monitoring and outdoor or ambulatory	Events (conscious and preconscious)	*Wearable* computer, Video camera Sensing system
Group Interaction Support (Ferscha *et al*, 2004)	Mobile distributed computing environments	Spatio-Temporal	Mobile distributed computing environments

continued on following page

Table 1. continued

Research Project	Domain	Contextual Data	Mode of Operation
Portolano (University of Washington, 2008).	Pervasive computing environments	Identity BDI	Internet-based computing
Cooltown & Ubicomp (Kindberg, 2008)	Pervasive computing environments	Spatio-Temporal Identity	Wireless networks with portable devices
Oxygen (MIT, 2004)	Ad-Hoc Network	Spatio-Temporal Identity	Mobile and stationary devices
Wireless ECG (Liu *et al*, 2005)	Sensing/Monitoring and outdoor ambulatory	Physical status	Wireless physical sensors
Wireless Communication in Hospital environments (Senses, 2003)	Sensing/Monitoring and outdoor ambulatory	*Medical Device & Diagnostic Industry*	Wireless mobile devices and systems
Motion Capture for every day health exercise (Majoe *et al*, 2008)	Sensing / Monitoring	Posture Ambulatory Work activity	Wearable computing devices Wireless sensors
Intelligent Mobile Computing to Assist in the Treatment of Depression (Wan, *et al*, 2008)	Sensing / Monitoring	Mental states	Mobile device
Conference Assistant (Dey *et al*, 1999b)	Information Provision	Spatio-Temporal Activity Preferences	RF tags with wireless LAN
Context-Aware Modelling of Concept Sketch (Cuixia *et al*, 2008)	Graphic Design Application	User Properties Machine Properties	Workstations and PCs

the broad range of computing devices available [that may be used in mobile systems] and their evolving convergence, the mode of delivery is a pivotal consideration. This points to the need to adapt the mode of delivery to suit the diverse range of mobile devices; the following documented research considers personalisation and adaptation in mobile systems (Table 2).

Ad-Hoc Networks

Ad-Hoc networks are (generally) established and maintained dynamically by mobile and wearable devices acting as network nodes, the nodes coming online and going off-line dynamically (Johnson & Maltz, 1996; Royer & Chai-Keong, 1999). This results in dynamic change in network topology and membership, as such ad-hoc networks are generally autonomous and self-configuring. Ad-hoc networks can be viewed as inherently context-aware, contextual information being applied on a number of levels including: (1) establishing an ad-hoc network, (2) establishing and managing routing mechanisms, and (3) on an application level.

Ad-hoc networks employ (in the main) spatio-temporal and identity based contextual information to establish dynamic connections between devices situated at specific logical or physical locations. A relatively common type of application is locating nearby resources including I/O devices such as printers and displays etc. Oxygen (MIT, 2004) [a project to create an infrastructure of mobile and stationary devices connected to a self-configuring network] is an example of an ad-hoc network research.

Table 2. Examples of research considering personalization and adaptation in mobile systems

Research Project	Domain	Contextual Data	Mode of Operation
Pocket PiCoMap (Luchini *et al*,2002)	Mapping Activities to Handheld Devices	Concept mapping	Wearable devices
Mobile Adaptation with Multiple Representation Approach as Educational Pedagogy (Kinshuk & Goh, 2003)	Adaptation in Mobile Learning Systems	Context related to interface adaptivity	Adaptation to a diverse range of mobile and stationary devices
Adaptivity in web and mobile learning services (Kinshuk *et al*, 2004)	Adaptivity in computing related to mobile learning	Adaptivity in mobile learning services	Mobile devices
Cognitive Trait Model for Persistent Student Modelling (Lin *et al*, 2003)	Student Modelling	Context Modelling	Context modelling

Approaches to Rule-Based Systems

'Intelligent Context' (discussed in section two) is predicated on the use of *Context-Processing Rules* (CPR) in an event driven system. There is a large body of documented research into rule-based systems addressing a broad and diverse range of approaches (Hayes-Roth, 1985; Gonzales & Dankel, 1993; Mitchell, 1997) including database systems (Elmasari & Navathe, 1994; Berndtsson & Hansson, 1995), data mining and warehousing (Roiger *et al*, 1997), fuzzy logic (Berndtsson & Lings, 1995; Alvarado & Vázquez, 2004; Berkan & Truebatch, 1997), decision trees (DT's) (Cerkvenik, 1997; Basak & Krishnapuram, 2005; Berger *et al*, 2006), and logical reasoning and inference (Jena, 2009; Horrocks *et* al, 2004). The literature demonstrates the adaptability of rules and points to a number of conclusions:

1. The use of rules with fuzzy logic with the associated *defuzzification* (Berkan & Truebatch, 1997) based on a predetermined threshold provides the basis for partial matching and enables effective context matching.
2. IF – THEN rules have been shown to be an effective solution to arrive at binary decisions in decision-centric systems using: (1) approaches implementing Event:Condition:Action (ECA) rules (Berndtsson & Ling, 1995;), and (2) approaches applying fuzzy extensions (Berkan & Truebatch, 1997).
3. The use of rule-based approaches in the construction of decision trees (DT) has been shown to be effective in decision support systems. Context processing and the matching of *input* and *output* contexts results in a binary decision relative to the suitability of an individual represented by the *output* context, thus DT's represent a potentially usable solution where such decision support is required.
4. The research into logical reasoning and inference (generally) addresses the defining of complex relationships (frequently based on family or work-based P2P relationships).
5. Context matching (a fundamental concept in *'Intelligent Context'*) represents a novel concept that is not addressed in the research.

DESIGN CONSIDERATIONS

Context has been shown to be an effective means to realize *personalisation*, what has not been considered is how a context can be described and defined in a suitable formalism. Realising this goal points to a number of important design considerations which must be addressed:

1. Develop a suitable formalism in an appropriate data structure to describe and define a context in both human and computer readable form.
2. The use of context in mobile information systems (a mobile learning system can be viewed in terms of a mobile information system) is (generally) restricted to location and spatio-temporal context factors; the inherent complexity of context has not been effectively addressed – thus we must develop a suitable means to accommodate the inherent complexity of context.
3. Context must be viewed from two perspectives (see Section Two): (1) the *input* context (the problem), and (2) the *output* context (the potential solution). The process of comparing the input and output contexts is termed 'context-matching' within the 'context-space' (Moore *et al*, 2008). Given the remote likelihood of a perfect match, partial validation with decidability is vital; addressing this identified the need to develop a suitable approach to effectively match the input and output contexts to enable effective context matching.

Addressing issues 1 to 3 requires the accessing and implementation of a stored context (context property values). Data storage can be in a diverse range of data structures and database systems (including legacy systems), thus a generic and adaptable approach to enable access and updating of data must be realised. Thus further design issue is:

4. Develop a suitable approach [using a recognised technology] to enable the realisation of a generic system of data storage and access usable in a diverse range of data storage and database systems.

Design issues 1 to 4 fails to address the implementation issue; this demands the effective management of context processing, this points to a further design issue:

5. Develop a suitable approach to enable effective context management to manage and integrate the solutions adopted to address the design issues (1 to 4) in a technology generalisable to a diverse range of domains, systems and technologies.

The design issues (1 to 5) address the principal design issues, however a further issue is security, thus an additional design issue is:

6. Develop a suitable system to describe and define policy constraints to effectively implement rights and permissions and data security.

The design issues (1 to 6) represent the principal design issues, *'Intelligent Context'* is the posited approach to address the issues identified. There are a number of design sub-issues that must be considered in any generic system, such issues will be considered under the sections to which they apply.

CONTEXT MODELLING

Context modelling is arguably a research topic in itself and there is no consensus on the best approach to the modelling of context or how context influences context modeling of a decision-centric context-aware information system, the representation of context being dependent on the utilisation of context resulting from the domain specific nature of context. Context modelling approaches fall under 6 general headings (Moore *et al*, 2007a): (1) Key-Value Models (KVM), (2) Markup Scheme Models (MSM), (3) Graphical Models (GM), (4) Object-Oriented Models (OOM), (5) Logic-Based

Models (LBM), and (6) Ontology-Based Models (OBM). In addition to these approaches there are machine learning (ML) approaches using both supervised and unsupervised learning (Flanagan, 2005; Brdiczka, 2005).

The [context modelling] approaches are not independent; there is a significant degree of interdependence. For example, in developing systems using ontologies, OBM may be used to model the relationships and constraints that exist between entities. OBM however inherits elements from LBM, OOM, GM and MSM. Space restricts a detailed analysis of the context modelling approaches listed however in summary the review set out in Moore *et al* (2007a) concludes that:

1. When viewed from a data structures perspective, classifying the context modelling approaches points to the need to accommodate the processing of contextual information (generally) expressed in a textual format. Such a format when used with the Semantic Web technologies accommodates the varying levels of granularity with relatively simple specification of constraints and relationships.
2. Context is generally *entity-based* resulting in ontologies with inference and reasoning being the dominant approach to the issue of context recognition in mobile environments.
3. OBM is the optimal approach to context modeling providing a cross-platform basis upon which intelligent context using inference and reasoning can be realised.

Flanagan (2005) [in a paper entitled 'Context Awareness in a Mobile Device: Ontologies Versus Unsupervised/Supervised Learning'] considers context-awareness as an approach to enable interaction between a user and a mobile device, the interaction requiring: *"personalisation of the context-awareness"*. Recall that OBM is proposed as the optimal approach to context modelling; in addressing the personalisation issue Flanagan (2005) proposes an alternative to ontology using a machine learning approach using unsupervised learning. In arguing for unsupervised learning Flanagan (2005) notes that one principal difference between machine learning and ontology is the immediate availability [of an ontology once defined] as opposed to the need for each [machine] learned context to be experienced at least once before being recognised.

The approach posited in Flanagan (2005) presents significant issues for the realisation of *static* and *dynamic* context definitions using pre-defined and updateable context definitions based on heterogeneous back-end resources (a basic system pre-requisite). Ontology therefore remains the optimal approach (Moore *et al*, 2006; Moore *et* al, 2007a; Moore *et al*, 2008); the issue is one of effective implementation in an intelligent context-aware system.

ONTOLOGY AND THE SEMANTIC WEB

The Greek term 'metaphysica' [literally: *"after the physical"*] was used to refer to what Aristotle described as *"the science of being qua being"* (Corrazzon, 2009); this was subsequently termed ontology. Ontology has traditionally been considered to be a branch of philosophy known as metaphysics (Corrazzon, 2009) where an ontology is a systematic account of existence (Gruber, 1993a, 1993b). The use of ontology in computer science can be traced to Artificial Intelligence (AI) research in the 1960's (Russell & Norvig, 1995). A formal dictionary definition of the term ontology[2] when used in AI is (Middleton *et al*, 2004):

1. *An explicit formal specification of how to represent objects, concepts and other entities that are assumed to exist in some area of interest and the relationships that hold among them ... for AI systems, what "exists" is that which can be represented*

... and... *"A conceptualisation of a domain into a human-understandable but machine-readable format consisting of entities, attributes, relationships and axioms".*

Ontology defines a set of representational terms that associate the names of entities (e.g., classes, relations, functions or other objects) in an area of interest (universe of discourse) with human-readable text describing meaning and formal axioms that constrain the interpretation and 'well-formed' use of these terms. In computer science and information systems an ontology is a representation of a knowledge model with semantic detail and structure; the "most prominent definition is" (Weisenberg *et al.* 2004):

2. *An explicit formal specification of a shared conceptualisation...the objects, concepts, and other entities that are assumed to exist in some area of interest and the relationships that hold among them* (Gruber, 1993a, 1993b; Borst, 1997).

There are a number of alternative definitions proposed define an ontology including:

3. *A conceptualisation of a domain into a human-understandable, but machine-readable format consisting of entities, attributes, relationships, and axioms* (Guarino & Giaretta, 1995).
4. *A formal explicit description of concepts (or classes) in a domain of discourse, properties of each class describing various features and attributes of the class, and restrictions on properties* (Noy & McGuinness, 2001).
5. *A well founded and broadly agreed upon system of concepts and relationships between them ... can be used as common vocabularies for domain knowledge representation in specific domains that allow sharing, reuse, and exchange of knowledge bases and courseware functional components among* [different] *courses and instructors* [authors] (Dichev *et al*, 2004)

The definitions (1-5) address the general case whereas definition (6) extends the general case to consider pedagogic systems. The definitions (1-5) are representative definitions of the term ontology, there being general agreement on the fundamental characteristics with a number of common features characterising the concept of ontology. Given the range of definitions and the domain specificity of 'm-learning', a derived definition for ontology when used in the domain of 'm-learning' is (Moore *et al*, 2008):'

6. *An explicit formal specification conceptualising a specific domain of interest [m-learning] with semantic detail and structure to represent concepts, entities, attributes, relationships, constraints, axioms and their properties in human and computer readable form*

Formally, ontology is a statement of logical theory to represent objects (e.g., entities) and enable inference and reasoning thereby providing the basis upon which a degree of computational intelligence can be realised. An important concept that underpins the concept of ontology is semantics and semantic relationships between objects and entities, a semantic context reasoning ontology implemented using the W3C Semantic Web Technologies forms an important element [in *'Intelligent Context'*] to enable effective reasoning and inference and realise intelligent context.

The ability of ontologies to represent entities has recognised benefits; these are (1) the capacity to communicate information, and (2) the ability to name concepts in machine-readable form (Middleton, *et al*, 2004). There are however disadvantages including:

a) The potential size and scale of an ontology capable of handling context can be an issue when new concepts can be added. Each time a new concept is added to an ontology a consistency check should be made, as well as updating all interpretations of concepts and semantic links in the ontology to take into consideration the new concept (Flanagan, 2005).

b) Ontologies are based on *"well-defined concepts and logic making concept definition potentially difficult"* (Flanagan, 2005).

In considering (a), the consistency checking and updating of relationships is relatively easily mitigated using ontology creation and editing software (such as Protégé3) which (generally) has inbuilt ontology consistency checking and classification functions predicated in the use of inferred models and relationships. Adding concepts and facts can however result in ontologies growing very large very quickly resulting in possible tractability issues.

In considering (b), humans (generally) understand what is meant by different concepts such as ***at_home*** or ***at_work***. Computationally it is necessary to define such concepts using inference rules on an ontology which can present difficulties which must be addressed to realise intelligent context.

Ontology languages allow users to write explicit formal conceptualisations of domain models. The main requirements of such models are (Antoniou *et al*, 2003): (a) *well-designed syntax* (b) *well-designed semantics* (c) *efficient reasoning support* (d) ***Sufficient*** *expressive power* (e) *convenience of expression*. A number of ontology languages have been developed, the most widely known being the Web Ontology Language OWL (a component in the W3c Semantic Web). OWL is an extension of RDF/S (this is a generalisation as there are 3 OWL sub-languages) and is (partially) mapped onto a description logic (Antoniou *et al*, 2003), description logic being a subset of predicate logic for which efficient reasoning support is possible (Baader *et al*, 2003).

A Semantic Ontology: A Simple Example

Ontology "establishes a common conceptual description and a joint terminology between members of communities of interest (human and autonomous software agents)" (Geroimenko & Chen, 2002). For example, a semantic ontology may be constructed to represent the animal kingdom built using assertions such as: #1: *a tiger is a type of cat*, #2: *all cats are carnivores, and* #3: *carnivores eat meat*. Additional geographical assertions can be made to the effect that: #4: *Bengal is a province of India*, and #5: *a Bengal tiger is a type of tiger from Bengal*. Using assertions #1 to #5 it is possible to achieve two objectives: (1) to draw inferences based on the assertions (axioms) and (2) to query the data as the following simple example shows:

```
   IF #1 ∩ #2 ∩ #3 THEN tigers eat meat
   IF #4 ∩ #5 THEN all Bengal tigers
originate from Bengal
   IF A1 ∩ A2 THEN all Bengal tigers eat
meat
   Inference query? - Find meat-eating
animals in India? = 'BengalTiger'.
```

The example demonstrates: (1) the potential power of reasoning and inference using semantic ontologies (2) the use of rules in computation and inference based on a *closed world* assumption [briefly discussed under context reasoning and inference in section two] and (3) the ability to formulate queries based on reasoning and inference. In the example, inference relies on the use of axioms (atomic concepts), the *Context Processing Rules* (CPR) (see Section Two) are predicated on the use of atomic context properties in Horn-style rules to realise reasoning and inference.

The Semantic Web

Ontology is an important concept in theW3C *Semantic Web*, the Semantic Web technologies being important elements in *'Intelligent Context'*. Space restrictions preclude a full exposition of the Semantic Web – a comprehensive introduction can be found in W3C Semantic Web (2009) – however the following brief introduction points to the principal aspect as they apply to *'Intelligent Context'*.

The Semantic Web is a concept predicated on the goal of transforming the WWW into a set of connected applications forming a consistent logical web of data realised by adding 'semantic annotations' to the XML/RDF tagging schema to impart meaning to web content. In the Semantic Web information has explicit meaning enabling automated processing (as opposed to merely presenting content to users). The Semantic Web functions using Semantic Metadata and is predicated on the idea that data can be arranged in the form of [an] ontology and can be viewed in terms of 'a set of logical assertions about specific things and their relationships'.

Ontologies establish a common conceptual description and a joint terminology between members of communities of interest – human and autonomous software agents. The Semantic Web consists of four W3C recommendations: (1) the *Extensible Markup Language* (XML), (2) *XML Schema*, (3) the *Resource Description Framework* (RDF/S), and (4) the *Web Ontology Language* (OWL). XML, XML Schema and RDF/S are well-understood concepts, the principal concepts that characterise OWL are considered below.

The Web Ontology Language (OWL)

The expressivity of RDF and RDF Schema (RDF/S) is (deliberately) very limited (Antoniou *et al*, 2003; W3C Semantic Web, 2009). RDF is (generally) limited to binary ground predicates, RDF/S being (generally) limited to subclass and property hierarchies with domain and range definitions of these properties (Antoniou *et al*, 2003). OWL extends the expressive power of RDF and RDF Schema (RDF/S) adding additional vocabulary enabling constraints including: (1) *relationships*, (2) *equality*, (3) *richer typing of properties*, (4) *characteristics of properties*, and (5) *enumerated classes*. OWL provides three sub-languages (Antoniou *et al*, 2003; W3C Semantic Web, 2009):

- **OWL Full**: uses all OWL language primitives enabling their use with RDF and RDF Schema. The disadvantage is that OWL Full is undecidable, making effective reasoning support at best impractical and at worst impossible.
- **#OWL DL** (Description Logic): to enable effective reasoning OWL DL restricts the use of OWL and RDF constructors, thus ensuring that the language corresponds to a description logic. The disadvantage is that full compatibility with RDF is lost, RDF documents requiring extending or restricting before they are legal OWL DL documents. Conversely, every OWL DL document is a legal RDF document.
- **OWL Lite**: represents a further restriction in limiting OWL to a subset of the language constructors. OWL Lite exclusions include: (1) *enumerated classes*, (2) *disjoint statements* and (3) *cardinality*. The disadvantage of OWL Lite is its restricted expressivity and limited reasoning capability.

Ontological context modelling requires *sufficient* expressive power to enable effective reasoning support; *OWL Full* and *OWL Lite* fail in this regard. *OWL DL* is predicated on description logics providing effective support for context reasoning. For a comprehensive exposition on Description Logics see Nardi & Brachman (2002) and Baader *et al* (2003).

The Jena 2 Semantic Web Framework

A significant benefit derived from using RDF/S and OWL is the existence of the Java based Jena RDF API (Powers, 2003; Wilkinson *et* al, 2003; Jena, 2009,). Jena 2 is the second generation of the Jena toolkit conforming to a revised RDF specification with *"new capabilities and internal architecture"* (Wilkinson *et* al, 2003). A design focus of Jena 2 was performance and scaling to reflect the *"renewed interest in applying semantic web technology to real world applications"* (Berners-Lee, 2003). Recall that context is domain specific, an example of a 'real-world' application is context-aware personalised mobile learning; the Semantic Web technologies provides an effective basis upon which this can be realised in a broad range of domains. Among the lessons learnt from Jena 1 was the value of database portability to the open source community and this was retained in Jena 2. (Wilkinson *et al*, 2003). A detailed discussion is beyond the scope of this chapter however in summary Jena 2 provides a broad range of functionalities including:

- A programming environment for RDF/S and OWL enabling complex context definitions to be defined using application specific schema vocabularies.
- Rule-based inference using both built-in inference engines and external inference engines implementing OWL DL; for example *Pellet* (Clarke& Parsia LLC, 2008) and *Sesame* (OpenRDF.org, 2008) can be implemented within the Jena environment.
- The capability to work with 'in-memory' and persistent storage data formats including the capacity to use a broad range of relational databases. There is support within each database system for multiple data storage layouts including: *Generic*, *GenericProc*, *MMGeneric*, *Hash* and *MMHash* (Powers, 2003).

These capabilities provide the capability to implement context-aware applications in diverse domains, systems and technologies using heterogeneous backend systems. Jena and its built-in functionalities provide an effective basis upon which intelligent context [as discussed in section two] can be implemented.

SECTION TWO: 'INTELLIGENT CONTEXT' - INTRODUCTION

Section 1 has addressed the background and introduced the component technologies; this section addresses *'Intelligent Context'*, a system designed to enable intelligent context reasoning in a decision-centric context-aware mobile environments. The processing of contextual information (context properties) is pivotal to the realisation of *'Intelligent Context'*. Context processing requires that a number of issues are addressed, these are: (1) the system architecture (2) context processing (3) context-processing rules (CPR) and (4) the context-reasoning ontology, these elements are addressed below.

SYSTEM ARCHITECTURE

The system architecture (see Figure 1) models the principal component technologies and processes that combine to realise the 'Intelligent Context' system.

The RDF Model, RDF Schema (RDF/S vocabularies) and OWL provide the basis for the data structure and context reasoning ontology, Jena providing the interface between the data structure and the RDMS which provides the storage capability for the contextual information (context properties and their values). Recall that Jena incorporates the capability to implement 'in-memory' and 'persistent storage', in practice Intelligent Context' employs both approaches to data storage in the context matching process.

Figure 1. The system architecture

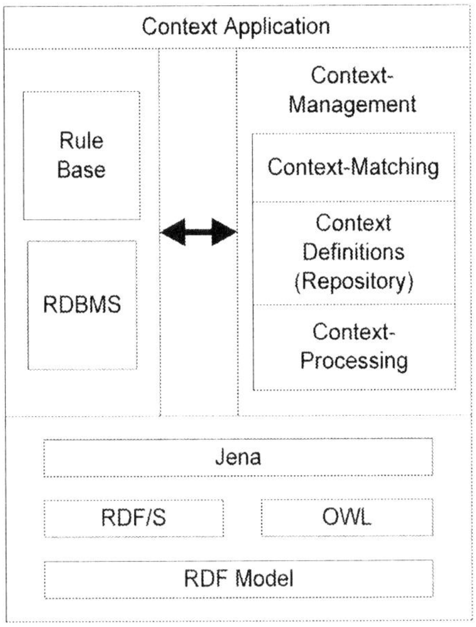

The Rule-Base is the repository for the CPR used in the context matching and processing (see the sections addressing these topics), these functions forming components in the Context Management module. The Context Application addresses the data capture (the system inputs) requirement.

The modules identified are relatively simple to comprehend, however, a brief explanatory note regarding the *Context Definitions Repository* will be useful. The *Context Definitions Repository* models the *'context-space'* (Moore & Hu, 2007b, 2008) which is a conceptual space in which the *input* context and the *output* context (s) are held for use in context matching process.

CONTEXT MATCHING

The *Context Matching* function is designed to access the *input* and *output* context definitions and using a context matching process determine if the *output* context forms an acceptable match with the *input* context. Essentially, the context-matching process is one of reaching a decision as to the suitability of a specific individual based on his or her situated role as a suitably qualified recipient for service provision in the form of a resource or in an interactive collaboration.

The context-matching process involves the matching of contextual information (context properties) that describes the *input* context and the *output* context. Given that a perfect match is highly unlikely the context matching process must accommodate partial matching with a high degree of predictability at a pre-determined level. Figure 2 graphically models the partial matching issue, Figure 3 graphically modelling the context-matching (input/output context) evaluation.

The 'context-matching' algorithm is set out in the following section however in summary the process involves *fuzzy (logic) extensions* (to the ECA concept as discussed in the section addressing CPR) with *defuzzification* (Berkan & Trubatch, 1997) based on a predefined threshold using a normalized value in the range {0...1}. Figure 3 graphically models the context-matching process representing the *input* and *output* context(s), each context is made up of a number of context properties $[x_1 \ldots x_n]$, in Figure 3 the properties are $[a_1, b_1, b_2, c_1, c_2]$. The 'context-matching' algorithm is as follows where:

a = the numerical evaluation of an individual property match

n = the summation of the individual property evaluation matches

x = the value for a perfect match (for example in Fig 3 all matches evaluate to a normalised value of [1] resulting in a value for **x** of [5].

m = the normalised value (**n** / **x**)

t = the preset threshold value {0...1}

The Context-Matching Algorithm

Evaluate the context match for each individual context property:

Figure 2. Context matching schematic

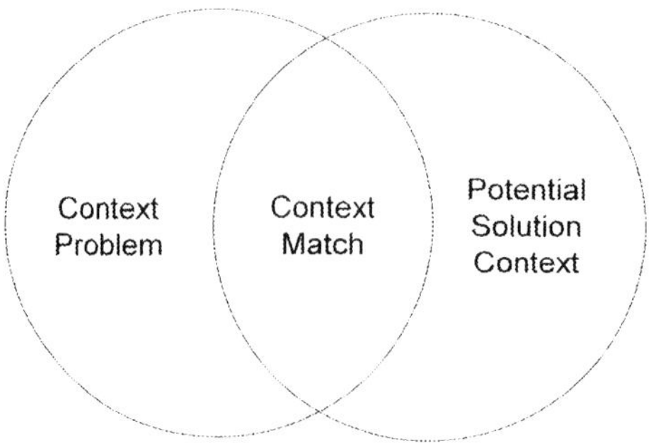

IF (a_1(input) **equalTo** (a_1(output)
THEN (a = [1])

IF (a_1(input) **notEqualTo** (a_1(output)
THEN (a = [0])

Sum the values derived from the matching process
($n = \sum(a_1, b_1, b_2, c_1, c_2)$)

Using the value for a perfect match (x = [5] (based on a_1, b_1, b_2, c_1, c_2 all = [1])) calculate the normalised value {0...1}
($m = n / x$)

Using the preset threshold value {0...1} determine if the output (potential solution) context definition is a suitably qualified match with the input (problem) context:

IF(m >= t) **THEN** (context-match = *true*)

IF(m < t) **THEN** (context-match = *false*)

Implement the context-matching decision. Using fig 5 as an example applying the algorithm using the following values for [a]: a_1 = [1], b_1 = [0], b_2 = [1], c_1 = [1], c_2 = [0] and a threshold value of [0.75] the context-matching formula is:

($n = \sum (a_1$ = [1], b_1 = [0], b_2 = [1], c_1 = [1], c_2 = [0]))
(n = [3], x = [5])
($m = (n / x)$) ∴ (m = (3 / 5)) ∴ (m = 0.60)

The result of the context matching is a normalised value of (0.60). As this is less than the preset threshold value (0.75) the context match is *false* and the individual us therefore not a suitably qualified individual.

Figure 3. Context matching (condition) model

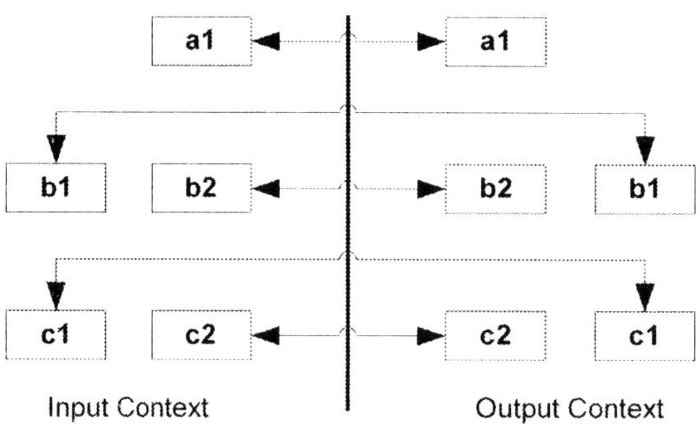

CONTEXT PROCESSING

The context-processing function addresses the creation, accessing and updating of a stored context definition(s) in a rule-based event driven system. A context can be viewed as a ***state*** with ***transitionalstates***, Figure 4 graphically models the overall system function and the context process model which commences with a stored context (Current Context [A]) and terminates with the replacement of the initial stored context (Current Context [A]) with the (Implemented (updated) Context [D]). The process is cyclic with a back-up context always retained to address issues such as a systems failure.

The context-process model presented in Figure 4 details the context processing function; the notes (1 to 6) shown in Figure 4 are expanded below:

- **Note 1**: the initial stored Current Context [A] is created (in the first instance default values will be used to create an initial current context [A]).
- **Note 2**: upon an event triggering the system the sensory input data is processed and the Updated Context [B] created to reflect the new situated role.
- **Note 3**: based on context processing rules if no further context processing is required the Updated Context [B] will replace the initial stored Current Context [A]. The initial Current Context [A] is stored in a back-up system.
- **Note 4**: in situations where context-processing rules dictate the Updated Context [B] will be replaced by the Updated Context [C] (following context processing) to reflect the changing situated role.
- **Note 5**: The Updated Context [C] is implemented and the Updated Context [C] becomes the Implemented Context [D].
- **Note 6**: Finally the Implemented Context [D] replaces the Current Context [A]. The initial Current Context [A] is stored in a back-up system.

Figure 4. The context process model

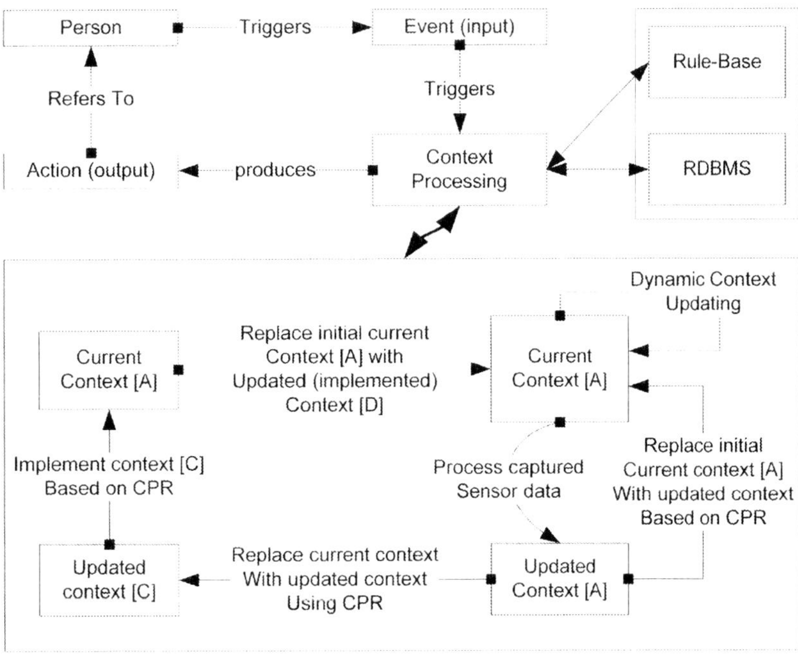

CONTEXT PROCESSING RULES (CPR)

The context-process model is predicated on the use of CPR's [in a rule-based system] to enable both the context processing and context management. CPR's are predicated on 3 elements (1) ***Event*** (2) ***Condition*** (3) ***Action***. The basic structure of the rules is:

On <Event> ***IF*** <Condition> ***THEN*** <Action>

- An ***Event*** relates to an input which can be either: (1) the < *event_Type* > plus the contextual data capture or (2) the output resulting from the firing of a rule [which triggers a subsequent rule].
- A ***condition*** (a rule antecedent / body) relates to the evaluation of the context properties (contextual information) in which comparisons are drawn between the input property(s) (contextual data capture) and the output context property(s) [a potential solution(s) properties and related property values derived from the database] as discussed in the context matching algorithm.
- An ***action*** (a rule consequent / head) is the result derived from the processing of the rule condition(s) (the rule antecedent / body) and results in either: (1) the triggering of a related simple or block (a complex or composite) rule or (2) a Boolean decision based on context matching arrived at using context processing. In (1) there is a pre-defined sequence incorporating built in stopping criteria setting out termination and/or satisfaction criteria based on pre-defined threshold functions.

Figure 5. Event-rule / rule Set association with specific rule / rule set subscription related to a specific <Event_Type>

Figure 6. Prototypical rule structure based on the association / subscription paradigm – shown is the association between an event and the associated subscription rule (or rule set) with examples of contextual information (context properties) on data capture

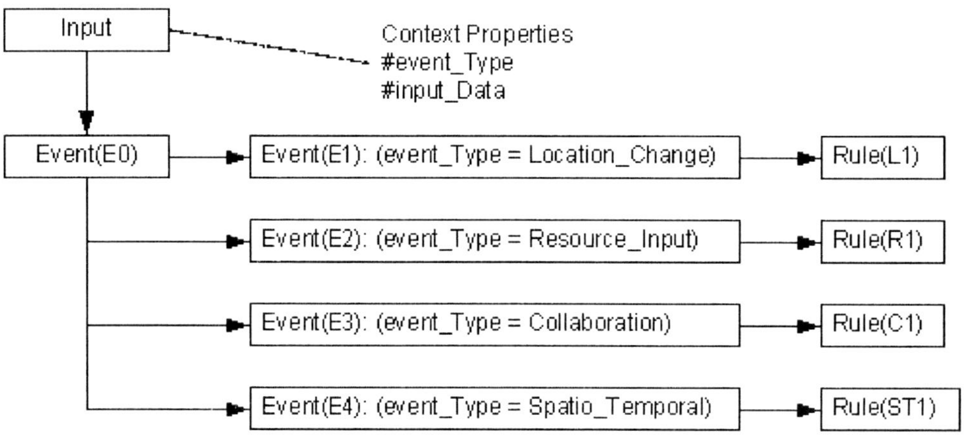

Relating a specific Event to a specific rule or rule set is achieved using the association / subscription approach (Berndtsson, 1995), the process is modelled in Figures 5 and 6.

The advantage gained [using this approach] is a reduction in the computational overhead due to the reduction / elimination in the searching of inappropriate rules or rule sets not applicable to a specific < *event_Type* >. Figure 6 models the association / subscription approach from a class diagram perspective, the < *event_Type* > context property is the principal trigger in context processing function.

CPR's function on the basis of logic function(s) which implement a *Condition* → *Action* process in a binary structure similar to a *Horn* style rule in a complex rule structure using complex rule structure using multiple conditions to address cases where multiple (complex) conditions must be parsed to derive actions (Note: the Semantic Web Rule Language (SWRL) framework adds "a simple form of Horn-style rules" to the OWL DL (part of the Ontology Web Language predicated on Description Logics (DL) – OWL and the SWRL are important desiderata in the proposed system). This rule structure provides the potential to assign numerical values to each context property [as discussed under context-matching] to enable *defuzzification*, an essential element in the application of fuzzy logic in a decision-centric system.

The rules structure is predicated on each < *condition* > being an atomic property reflecting the concepts and properties defined on the context reasoning ontology [discussed in a later section], complex rules being constructed using a combination of logic operators to enable conjunctive (*AND*), disjunctive (*OR*), and compliment (*NOT*) logical relationships to be realised.

Context Processing Logic Functions

Implementation of the CPR structure requires the use of logic functions. The (initial) essential primary logic functions required to implement context reasoning and inference are: (1) *conjunction* (AND) (2) *disjunction* (NOT) and (3) *action* (THEN). Functions (1 and 2) are conditional, function (3) is Boolean. In addition to the primary logic functions there is a requirement for secondary logic functions to implement additional conditional functions including: (a) *equality*, (b) *unary, (c) enumeration,* and (d) *transitivity*. In actuality CPR's will incorporate the logic functions as applicable to address specific issues raised by semantic relationships [as defined in the context reasoning ontology], constraint implementation, and the realisation of *inference* and *reasoning* and *fuzzy logic* in a modular system using *Description Logics*.

The design aim [of the system] is to enable cross platform implementation in a diverse range of technologies and systems. Given that the logical operators are present in most Turing complete high-level programming languages [including Java and C++ etc] the logic functions identified satisfy the design criteria. Additionally precedence, associativity, overriding and strict datatyping are fundamental concepts in Java; this provides the basis upon which variable sequential use of the logic function can be realised thus satisfying the design demands of the CPR's.

CONTEXT REASONING AND INFERENCE

The key to realising intelligent context lies in implementing effective reasoning and inference. Section One introduced the *Semantic Web* and *OWL* with related technologies (such as inference engines – including Jena built-in inference engines and external inference engines such as *Pellet*). These technologies provide a basis upon which context reasoning and inference can be achieved however prior to considering context reasoning and inference as it relates to mobile systems it is necessary to consider the two approaches to reasoning and inference: (1) *monotonic* and (2) *non-monotonic* reasoning.

There is an on-going debate around the approach to reasoning and inference based on the twin concepts of: (1) the *Open-World-Assumption* (monotonic reasoning), and (2) the *Closed-World-Assumption* (non-monotonic reasoning) which is predicated on *negation-as-failure* (if it is not provably true, conclude that it's false); when viewed from the perspective of knowledge representation systems, SQL databases make the same assumption. A further example of the *Closed-World-Assumption* is the *Unique-Names-Assumption* (entities with differing names are different – there are no aliases or synonyms). The *Semantic Web* is predicated on the *Open-World-Assumption*; however, ensuring that all *Closed-World-Assumptions* are explicit is a key aspect of the *Semantic Web* architecture. Space restricts a full exposition on the *Open-World* and *Closed-World* assumptions however a discussion on the topics considered above with references can be found in Sheth & Ramakrishnan (2003), Russell (2003), Horrocks *et al* (2003), and W3C OWL (2009). *'Intelligent Context'* is predicated on the *closed-world-assumption* to enable reliable and effective *decidability* in the context reasoning and inference process.

The Context Reasoning Ontology

The [context reasoning] ontology (see Figure 7) defines the entity concepts (Classes) and the semantic relationship between them. The ontology is constructed using a combination of Core Concepts (Classes) with Domain Specific Concepts (Classes). The core concepts are designed to be generic, incorporating the ability to address a diverse range of contextual information applicable across a broad range of domains and applications. The domain specific concepts are designed to address the prototypical mobile learning application used to evaluate the context matching process.

It is important to note that the ontology is predicated on Object-Orientation (OO). OO is a fundamental concept in RDF, RDF being predicated on class and sub-class with property and sub-property structures. The principle of OO is similarly applicable to Java thus providing a common development platform upon which to implement the ontology. This relates directly to the use of Java and the Java Jena API, the use of the Semantic Web technologies, and the proposed use of Description Logics (DL) using OWL DL.

The context-reasoning ontology (Figure 7) sets out the concepts [in the ontology the concepts are in actuality OWL:Class(s)] with the associated semantic relationships. The semantic relationships relate to the OWL *object Properties* and *inverse properties*. The syntax for the *object Properties* and *inverse properties* is shown in the following code snippet (1) which sets out the semantic relationship between the #Person *core concept* and the #Course *domain concept*. Shown is the <owl:Objectproperty> and <rdf:ID=#teaches"> with the inverse property <rdf:resource="#isTaughtBy">:

```
<owl:ObjectProperty rdf:ID="teaches">
<rdfs:range rdf:resource="#course"/>
<rdfs:domain rdf:resource="#academicStaff
Member"/>      (1)
<owl:inverseOf
rdf:resource="#isTaughtBy"/>
<owl:Objectproperty/>
```

In actuality, a *domain* and *range* can be inherited from the *inverse property* (interchange *domain* with *range*). The semantic relationships are fundamental in the process of reasoning and inheritance.

Syntactically, <owl:inverseOf> is a built-in OWL property with <owl:ObjectProperty> as its domain and range. Note the domain identifies an '#academicStaffMember', this identifies the ability to differentiate between, for example, *academic staff*, *technical staff*, and *students* thus

Figure 7. The Context Reasoning Ontology

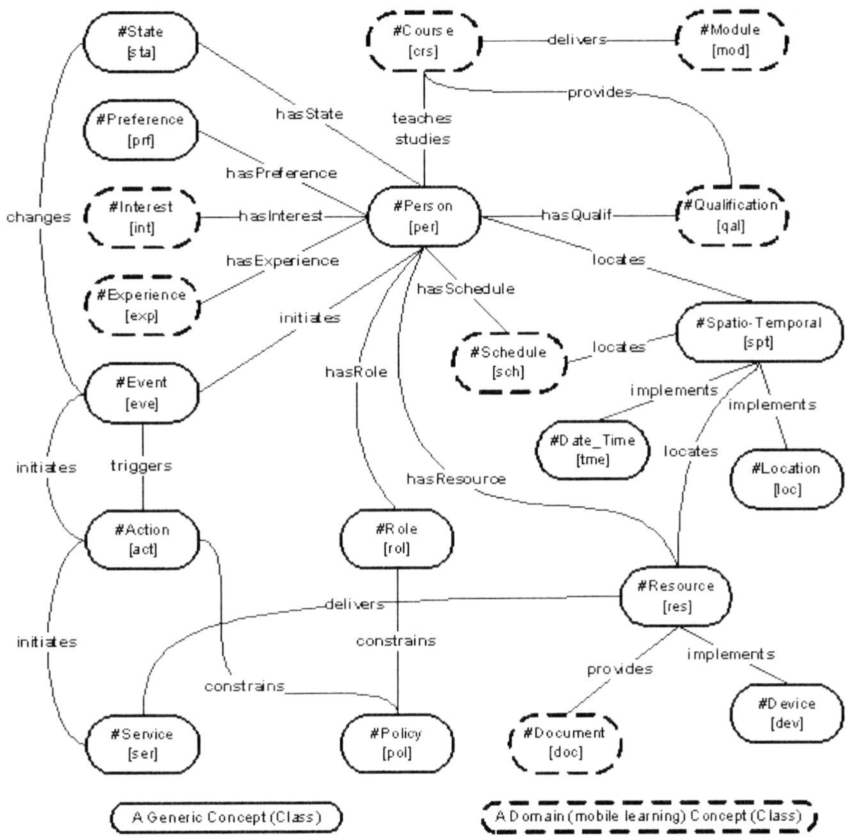

providing an effective basis for the implementation of *policy* rules.

Recall that the rule structure is predicated on the concept of atomic conditions – an axiom of the form [P1: owl:inverseOf -> P2] asserts that for every pair (x, y) in the property extension of P1, there is a pair (y, x) in the property extension of P2 (and vice-versa). Thus, owl:inverseOf can be seen to be a symmetric property. The use of owl:ObjectProperty and owl:inverseOf with the related <rdfs:range> and <rdfs:domain> can be seen in the code snippet (1). For a full exposition of the OWL Semantic Web Language vocabulary and language constructs see (Antoniou *et al* 2003; W3C OWL (2008).

EVALUATION AND SIMULATION

'Intelligent Context', a system to enable the effective implementation of context in a context-aware decision-centric system has been introduced; this section presents an evaluation of the approach set out in this chapter. Set out below is a context reasoning example and a simulation demonstrating the results obtained from the processing of context.

Context-Reasoning Example

A Bluetooth enabled PDA enables user identification and initiates event [in the scenario a collaboration query – see the CPR section and **B3** in the following example] driven context updating and input (task/problem) < *event_Type*

> tagging. The scenario sets out a typical online cooperative learning interaction with an example of context reasoning including conjunctions (∩) and disjunctions (∪). Context reasoning enables context processing facilitating context matching of the questioner (the input/problem) to the advisor(s) (the output/solution).

In the scenario the concepts relate to the context reasoning ontology and relate to the following OWL concepts: (1) #Spatio-Temporal (2) #Person (3) #State (4) #Event (5) #Preference (6) #Course (7) #Module and (8)#Qualification. Context reasoning with inference using the property values enables the availability of "Lisa" and her suitability as an advisor to the questioner "Bob" to be decided with their respective roles, ("Bob"="student") and ("Lisa"= "tutor") inferred. The ontology identifies the semantic relationships for the scenario context components and the schedule, resource and device context components.

A Location Based On-Line Cooperative Computing Scenario

```
A1: #Spatio-Temporal<date="2006:18:12">
[Monday]
A2: #Spatio-Temporal<time="10:50:48">
[am]
B1: #Person<name="Bob">
isLocatedAt#Spatio-
Temporal<location="library">
B2: #Person<name="Bob">
hasState#State<state="on-line">
B3: #Status<status="on-line">  initiates#
Event<question<subject="Java">
B4: "Bob" is on line, is located in the
library and has a role of student
C1: #Person<name="Lisa">
isLocatedAt#Spatio-Temporal<location="on-
campus">
C2: #Person<name="Lisa">  hasPreferen
ce#Preference<availability<location=
"on campus"><day = "Monday-friday"><
time="am">
C3: #Person<name="Lisa">  hasStatus#Perso
n<available="yes">
C4: #Person<name="Lisa">  studies#Course<
course="computing">
C5: #Course< course="computing">
delivers#Module<module="Java">
C6: #Person<name="Lisa">  hasQualif#Quali
fication<qualification="Java ">
C7: "Lisa" is available, is an appropri-
ate advisor to "Bob" and has a role of
tutor
((B1  ∩  B2  ∩  B3)  ⇒  B4)
((A1  ∩  A2)  ∩  (C1  ∩  C2 )  ⇒  C3)
(C3  ∩  ((C4  ∩  C5)  ∪  C6)  ⇒  C6)
```

Identification of individuals based on their context clearly reduces to a decision problem. The ontology in defining relationships based on the semantic links defined by context properties and their associated values (e.g. <location="library">) enables reasoned decisions including disambiguation to be realised.

Scenario-Based Evaluation

The simple scenario set out below describes a typical application of context to enable personalisation in a mobile environment. The scenario addresses a number of functions a context-aware system is designed to provide and is based on a fictional Birmingham City University student 'Toby' Philip' using a context-aware mobile learning system. The functions demonstrated are: (1) logging on to the system (2) information provision (3) a library search function (4) a collaborative interaction and (6) a system advice (schedule) function.

The system design is predicated on the use of both PC monitor(s) and mobile devices. The argument has been made that in a mobile learning system all devices are mobile devices, the differences are their capabilities and whether or not they are 'wearable', this is however an esoteric argument which will not be addressed here. Accommodating such a diverse range of devices and

Figure 8. Logon screen

Figure 9. Welcome screen

their widely differing interfaces clearly requires a high level of adaptation [to accommodate service provision and to suit the HCI considerations]. To accommodate this design requirement a number of interface designs are required to address screen size and connectivity constraints, however, given the importance of mobility in the system the scenario set out below demonstrates how the system is applied to a wireless mobile device.

On-Line Mobile Learning and Collaboration Scenario

1. Toby Philip is a computing student requiring information relating to an assignment.
2. Using a wireless hand-held mobile device he logs on to the system using his personal identification (in the scenario this is his student number). Figure 8 shows a screenshot of the logon screen with Figure 9 showing a screen shot of the welcome screen.
3. The welcome screen shows the basic information about Toby Philip including his: (1) name, (2) e-mail inbox, (3) schedule details (an upcoming lecture and its time), and (4) library record (number of books currently on loan).
4. Using the function selection menu, Toby Philip selects the "Library" function from the menu; Figure 10 is a screen shot illustrating this function selection.
5. Based on the context, the system identifies suitable books relevant to the assignment Toby must complete; Figure 11 is a screenshot showing the books identified.
6. Toby has some queries relating to the identified book "Java How to Program". He enters a collaboration query with the aim

Figure 10. Menu function

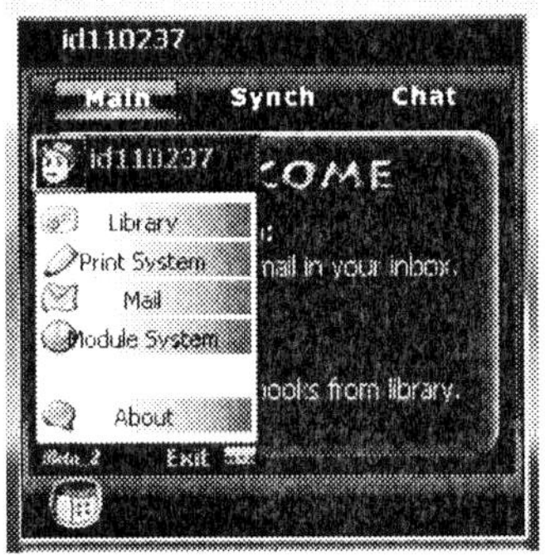

Figure 11. Library selection

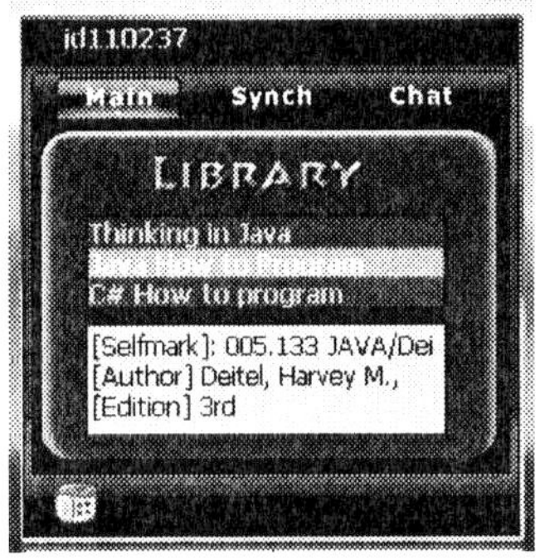

Figure 12. Collaboration screen

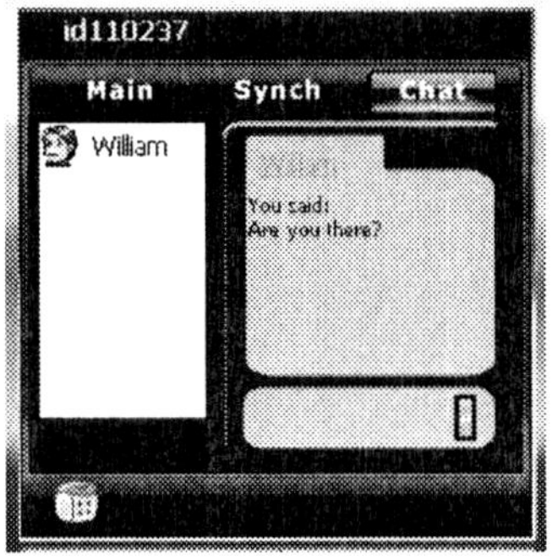

Figure 13. Lecture screen

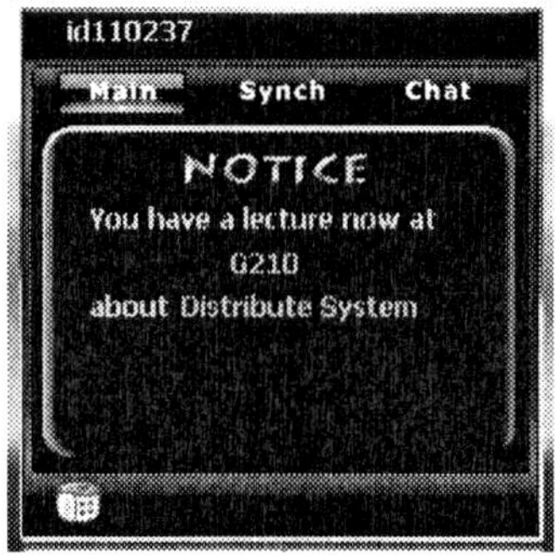

of location a suitably qualified person with the knowledge and experience to assist with and discuss his queries. Following the context matching process the system identifies 'William' as a suitably qualified person.

7. Contact is made with 'William' and an online collaboration is commenced. Figure 12 is a screen shot showing the online contact.
8. During their discussion, Toby gets a system generated notification that his lecture will start shortly in room G210, this points to the need to terminate the online conversation to attend the lecture. Figure 13 is a screen shot showing the notification and notice details.

The scenario and the related Figures 8 to 13 illustrate the context matching process. Shown is a typical constrained mobile device [interface] with the output derived from the processing of contextual information.

The scenario demonstrates the output for a *wearable* recipient device (such devices typically include mobile phones, smart phones and PDA's which can be used in a wider range of environments – albeit characterised by a diverse range of constraints – whilst 'on-the-move'). Personalisation in intelligent context-aware mobile learning systems must however consider potential alternative recipient devices such as: (1) *laptop* and *mobile computers* (which whilst mobile are not generally useable 'on-the-move'), and (2) PCs' or workstations.

In all the cases identified, the information presented must be consistent, however adaptation must be used to tailor the presentation using alternative formats (graphical user interface designs) to suit device, HCI, and usability engineering constraints whilst addressing constraint satisfaction and preference compliance issues.

DISCUSSION, CONCLUSION AND FUTURE WORK

This chapter has addressed the background to context as it relates to personalised service provision and CSC in mobile systems. Research related to contextual computing has been considered, the *Semantic Web* and its related component technologies introduced, and *'Intelligent Context'* presented with a scenario based evaluation.

The related research has identified a broad and diverse range of domains (including ad-hoc networks and adaptation) to which context has been applied, this is exemplified in the diverse nature and range of contextual information identified in the discussion addressing context. The general aim of the related research is the personalization of service provision. Additionally, context has been shown to be purpose and application specific requiring the identification of the function(s) and properties specific to individual domains; the domain specificity applying to 'm-learning' which is a specific type of mobile information system.

An important conclusion drawn from the related research is the predominance of spatio-temporal and identity contextual information in mobile systems, this is (arguably) the result of the inherent complexity of context (as demonstrated in the broad range of potential context properties identified) and the difficulty in defining dynamically a users context (h/her situated role). Addressing these limitations demands the use of computational intelligence; *'Intelligent Context'*, in applying computational intelligence to the processing of contextual information (context properties) has been shown to provide an effective basis upon which computational intelligence can be implemented and the inherent complexity of context leveraged.

'Intelligent Context', whilst targeting a prototypical 'm-learning' application in the domain of HE, has the potential to be applied across a broad range of domains and systems. To this end the aim of the research is the development of a generic approach and *'Intelligent Context'* has been developed to realise this aim. Recall that 'Intelligent Context' is event-driven and rule-based and while it [the prototypical application] is implemented in Java [in conjunction with the W3C Semantic Web Technologies and Jena 2 with the context properties encoded in RDF/S] the rules are conceived as a generic structure portable to other high-level Turing complete programming languages.

The evaluation and simulation has shown the potential of *'Intelligent Context'* to achieve intelligent context processing and demonstrated proof-of-concept. However, providing a coherent basis for intelligent context processing fails to address the inherent issues and challenges that must be addressed if a generic (and equally important, useful and usable) intelligent context-aware system is to be developed. Realising this aim is the goal of our continuing research activities and this along with the open research questions is addressed in the following section.

Future Work and Open Research Questions

The research conducted to date has focused on developing a generic novel semantic context modelling ontology with a rule-based context processing and matching system incorporating effective decision support. While the research has focused on the development of a Java based system predicated on the W3C Semantic Web Technologies including Jena; a primary goal [of the research] has been the development of a simple and portable rule structure usable in a divers range of domains, systems, and technologies.

While the work completed to date has net the initial research goals it has identified a number of issues and challenges which must be addressed in future work. The identified issues and challenges can be summarised under five headings: (1) data capture, (2) data description, (3) data storage, (4) statistical context processing, and (5) the development of modular context middleware.

Data Capture

Input contextual information is a trigger function in the initiation of context processing. There are essentially three data sources, (a) sensor derived data, (b) user input data: and (c) system derived data:

1. *Sensor derived data*: is dynamically created and includes the event (e.g., location change) with location and identity contextual information. The sensor location is continuously polled and monitored, the user triggering an input using for example RFID or Bluetooth enabled devices.
2. *User derived data*: is directly entered by a user and includes a broad range of contextual information including contextual information that: (1) identifies a resource input to be distributed, (2) identifies suitable recipients

for a resource input, (3) identifies suitable collaborators, and (4) personal data including registration, and preferences etc.

3. *System derived data*: generated in response to sensor and user input events including spatio-temporal data (using OS functions).

It is envisaged that there are two direct input modes: (1) sensor input, and (2) user input using a GUI. The work to date has used contextual data directly entered to simulate these input modes. All the component technologies currently exist however developing the input and data capture systems remains an open research question.

Data Description

Data description relates to the context factors entered by users. The issue is one of how to represent user input to enable effective context matching. Approaches under consideration include: (a) *Keywords*, and (b) *Natural Language Processing* (NLP).

a) Initially, the selected option is *Keywords*, there are however issues relating to the keyword corpus usable across a broad range of domains. Investigations have failed to locate such a corpus, the available corpora being highly domain and topic specific. The development of a suitable corpus [for an 'm-learning' application but potentially for other domains] is an open research question.
b) To enable users to enter data and queries with a greater degree of granularity and specificity NLP would provide enhanced ability to express resource properties or the nature of a collaboration query. The use of NLP is challenging and additionally creates greatly increased system complexity and overhead, thus it is not currently a research goal. It however remains an open research question that presents a desirable research direction.

Data Storage

The RDF data model is typically found in online applications such as e-commerce systems which are predicated on datasets which are highly dynamic, constantly evolving, sparsely populated, and may contain numerous null values (Agrawal *et al*, 2001). *'Intelligent Context'* is however characterised by a dataset where data is dense, evolves relatively slowly (as compared to e-commerce sites where product inventories are subject to dynamic change), and does not have null values (as is the case with e-commerce applications.

Additionally, ontology mapping to the data store to enable efficient database operations is required. Wilkinson et al (2003) in addressing 'efficient RDF Storage and Retrieval in Jena 2' has observed that: "*...the mixing of property tables and statement tables in a graph database complicates query processing and optimization... more work is needed on efficient algorithms for this case*". For 'Intelligent Context', the initial intuition is that a relational database model represents the optimal approach to the storage of contextual data (RDF metadata being defined in the RDF vocabularies) however identifying the optimal approach remains an open research question.

Statistical Context Processing

An issue identified in the research relates to use-cases where (for example) users web surfing activity is captured and rated to enable effective resource delivery and collaborative matching. An additional issue identified is the need to disambiguate and resolve conflicts in sensor derived location data.

Investigations have identified a number of potentially interesting research directions to address this issue including Bayesian methods (Mitchell, 1997), unsupervised learning (Flanagan, 2005), and decision trees (Moore *et al*, 2008). Developing the optimal approach(s) remains a challenging open research question.

The Development of a Modular Context Middleware

The effective implementation of *'Intelligent Context'* demands the realisation of a number of important functions: (1) context management, (2) context processing, and (3) context matching in a decision-centric context-aware system. Effective implementation requires the development of a context middleware capable of achieving these functions, the system architecture forming the model upon which the development of the middleware is predicated.

There are essentially two types of system function: (1) 'real-time' operations where time is of the essence (such as collaborative activities), and (2) background' functions where time constraints are less of an issue (such as resource delivery activities. The building of an intelligent context middleware capable of implementing a decision-centric system to realise these demands in a generic, robust and tractable approach capable of addressing the inherent complexity of context is the subject of ongoing current research.

CONCLUSION

This chapter has introduced 'Intelligent Context', considered the design issues and addressed the component technologies. The design of the posited approach has been addressed, the context reasoning ontology with the context processing rules have been presented and 'Intelligent Context' has been evaluated using a prototypical mobile learning application to demonstrate proof-of-concept. The nature and scope of outstanding research issues and challenges have been identified and considered with potentially promising future research directions.

'Intelligent Context' is posited as an effective, portable, and realistic 'real-world' solution to begin to achieve effective use of context in pervasive systems; the difficulty of achieving this is not underestimated, however, while it is recognised as a difficult challenge it is considered to be a realistic ultimate goal.

REFERENCES

W3C OWL. (2009). OWL Web ontology language reference W3C recommendation [online]. Retrieved from http://www.w3.org/TR/owl-ref/

W3C Semantic Web. (2009). *W3C Semantic Web activity* [online]. Retrieved from http://www.w3.org/2001/sw/

Abowd, G. D., Atkeson, C. G., Hong, J., Long, S., Kooper, R., & Pinkerton, M. (1997). Cyberguide: A mobile context-aware tour guide. *Wireless Networks*, *3*, 421–433. doi:10.1023/A:1019194325861

Agrawal, R., Somani, A., & Xu, Y. (2001). Storage and querying of e-commerce data. In *Proc. of VLDB 2001* [online]. Retrieved from http://wotan.liu.edu/docis/lib/sisl/rclis/dbl/vldbvl/(2001)%253C149%253ASAQOED%253E/www.dia.uniroma3.it%252F~vldbproc%252F019_149.pdf

ALT. (2009). *ALT-the Association for Learning Technology* [online]. Retrieved on January 12, 2009, from http://www.alt.ac.uk/index.html

Alvarado, M., & Vázquez, M. (2004). *Decision making automation based on fuzzy event-condition-action rules* [online]. Retrieved from http://delta.cs.cinvestav.mx/~matias/PDF/

Andreadis, A., Benelli, G., Bianchi, A., Fedele, P., & Giambene, G. (2001, July). *Universal access to personalised information services*. (Tech. Rep.). Siena, Italy: Dipartimento di Ingegneria dell'Informazione, Universita di Siena. IST-PALIO project.

Antoniou, G., & Van Harmelen, F. (2003). Web ontology language: OWL. In S. Staab & R. Struder (Eds.), *Handbook on ontologies*. Germany: Springer.

Baader, F., Calvanese, T. D., McGuinness, D. L., Nardi, D., & Patel-Schneider, P. F. (Eds.). (2003) *The description logic handbook: Theory, implementation, applications*. Cambridge, UK: Cambridge University Press.

Basak, J., & Krishnapuram, R. (2005). Interpretable hierarchical clustering by constructing an unsupervised decision tree. *IEEE Transactions on Knowledge and Data Engineering*, *17*(1), 121–132. doi:10.1109/TKDE.2005.11

Berger, H., Merkl, D., & Dittenbach, M. (2006). Exploiting partial decision trees for feature subset selection in e-mail categorisation. *Proceedings of the 2006 ACM Symposium on Applied Computing*, Dijon, France. *SESSION: Information Access and Retrieval (IAR)* (pp. 1105–1109).

Berkan, R. C., & Trubatch, S. L. (1997). *Fuzzy systems design principles: Building fuzzy IF-THEN rule bases*. Piscataway, NJ: IEEE Press.

Berndtsson, M., & Hansson, J. (1995, June). Issues in active real-time databases. In *Proceedings of the 1st International Workshop on Active and Real-Time Database Systems (ARTDB-95)*, Skovde, Sweden, Workshops in Computing (pp. 142-157). London: Springer Verlag.

Berndtsson, M., & Lings, B. (1995). *Logical events and ECA rules*. (Tech. Rep. HS-IDA-TR-95-004). University of Skovde [online]. Retrieved from http://citeseerx.ist.psu.edu/legacymapper?did=77063

Berners-Lee, T. (2003). Web services and Semantic Web. *Keynote speech, World Wide Web Conference 2003* [online]. Retrieved from http://www.w3.org/2003/Talks/0521-www-keynote-tbl/

Borst, P. (1997). *Construction of engineering ontologies for knowledge sharing and reuse*. Unpublished doctoral dissertation, Twente University [online]. Retrieved from http://www.ub.utwente.nl/webdocs/inf/1/t0000004.pdf

Brdiczka, O., Reignier, P., & Crowley, J. L. (2005). Supervised learning of an abstract context model for an intelligent environment. In *Proceedings of the 2005 Joint Conference on Smart Objects and Ambient Intelligence: Innovative Context-aware Services: Usages and Technologies*. Grenoble, France, SESSION: Context-aware Systems (pp. 259-264).

Britain, S., & Liber, O. (1999, October). Pedagogical evaluation of virtual learning environments. (Rep. 41). JISC Technology Applications Programme.

Brown, P. J., Bovey, J. D., & Chen, X. (1997). Context-aware applications: From the laboratory to the marketplace. *IEEE Personal Communications*, *4*(5), 58–64. doi:10.1109/98.626984

Bull, S., Yanchun, C., McEnvoy, A. T., Reid, E., & Wei Yang. (2004, March). Roles for learner models. In *Proceedings of the 2nd IEEE International Workshop on Wireless and Mobile Technologies in Education (WMTE 2004)*. Taoyuan, Taiwan (pp. 124-128).

Cerkveinik, G. (2007). Decision trees and automatic learning in medical decision making. In *Proceedings of the 1997 IASTED International Conference on Intelligent Information Systems (Iis'97)*. Grand Bahamia Island, Bahamas (pp. 8-10 & 37-45).

Chen, G., & Kotz, D. (2002). *Solar: An open platform for context-aware mobile applications*. (Tech. Rep.). Hanover, NH & Italy: Department of Computer Science, Dartmouth College & Dipartimento di Scienze dell'Informazione, Universit`a of Bologna.

Clarke & Parsia LLC. (2008). *Pellet* [online]. Retrieved from http://pellet.owldl.com/

Coppola, P., & Della, M. A. (2004). The concept of relevance in mobile and ubiquitous access. *Mobile and Ubiquitous Info 2003.* (. *LNCS, 2954*, 1–10.

Corrazzon, R. (2009). *Ontology. A resource guide for philosophers* [online]. Retrieved from http://www.formalontology.it/

Cuixia, M., Hongan, W., Teng, D., & Dai, G. (2008, October 6-8). Context-aware modeling of concept sketch. In *Proceedings of the Third International Conference on Pervasive Computing and Applications* (pp. 520-525). Alexandria, Egypt.

Cullen, J., Hadjivassiliou, K., Hamilton, E., Sommerlad, E., & Stern, E. (2002). *Report submitted to the Economic and Social Research Institute, London. Review of current pedagogic research and practice in the fields of post-compulsory education and lifelong learning.* The Tavistock Institute.

Davies, N., Mitchell, K., Cheverest, K., & Blair, G. (1998). Developing a context sensitive tourist guide. (GIST Tech. Rep. G98-1). *First Workshop on Human Computer Interaction with Mobile Devices.*

Dey, A. K., & Abowd, G. D. (1999a). Towards a better understanding of context and context-awareness. (GVU Tech. Rep. GIT-GVU-99-22). Georgia: College of Computing, Georgia Institute of Technology.

Dey, A. K., Salber, D., Abowd, G. D., & Futakawa, M. (1999b). The conference assistant: Combining context-awareness with wearable computing. In *Proceedings of the 3rd International Symposium on Wearable Computers* (pp. 21-28), San Francisco, CA, October 18-19.

Dichev, C., Dicheva, D., & Arroyo, L. (2004). Using topic maps for Web-based education. *Advanced Technology for Learning, 1*(1), 1–7. doi:10.2316/Journal.208.2004.1.202-1450

Dourish, P. (2004). What we talk about when we talk about context. *Personal and Ubiquitous Computing, 8*, 19–30. doi:10.1007/s00779-003-0253-8

Elmasari, R., & Navathi, S. B. (1994). *Fundamentals of database design*, 2nd ed. Redwood City, CA: Benjamin/Cummins.

Ferscha, A., Clemens, H., & Oppl, S. (2004, October 1). Context awareness for group interaction support. In [Philadelphia, PA.]. *Proceedings of MobiWac, 04*, 88–97. doi:10.1145/1023783.1023801

Finney, J., Wade, S., Davies, N., & Fridal, A. (1996). *FLUMP: The flexible ubiquitous monitor project.* (Tech. Rep.). Distributed Multimedia Research Group, Department of Computing, Lancaster University, Lancaster, UK [online]. Retrieved from http://citeseerx.ist.psu.edu/viewdoc/summary?doi=10.1.1.53.2268

Fitzmaurice, G. W. (1993, July). Situated information spaces and spatially aware palmtop computers. In *Proceedings of CACM, 36*(7), 39-48.

Flanagan, J. A. (2005). *Context awareness in a mobile device: Ontologies vs. unsupervised/supervised learning* [online]. Retrieved from http://www.cis.hut.fi/AKRR05/papers/akrr05flanagan.pdf

Geroimenko, V., & Chen, C. (2002). (Eds). *Visualising the Semantic Web.* Berlin: Springer Verlag.

Goh T., & Kinshuk. (2004, June 21-26). Getting ready for mobile learning. In L. Cantoni & C. McLoughlin (Eds.), *Proceedings of ED-MEDIA 2004-World Conference on Educational Multimedia, Hypermedia & Telecommunications* (pp. 56-63), Lugano, Switzerland: AACE.

Gonzales, A. J., & Dankel, D. D. (1993). *The engineering of knowledge-based systems theory and practice*. NJ: Prentice-Hall.

Gorrard, S., Selwyn, N., Madden, L., & Furlong, J. (2002). Technology and lifelong learning: Are we cutting IT? *All-Wales Education Research Conference*, Gregynog, July 3-5, 1993.

Gruber, T. R. (1993a). A translation approach to portable ontology specification. *Knowledge Acquisition, 5*(2), 199–220. doi:10.1006/knac.1993.1008

Gruber, T. R. (1993b). Toward principles for the design of ontologies used for knowledge sharing. *International Journal of Human-Computer Studies, 43*(5-6), 907–928. doi:10.1006/ijhc.1995.1081

Guarino, N., & Giaretta, P. (1995). Ontologies and knowledge bases: Towards a terminological clarification. In N. Mars (Ed.), *Towards very large knowledge bases: Knowledge building and knowledge sharing* (pp. 25-32). Amsterdam, Holland: IOS Press.

Hayes-Roth, F. (1985). Rule-based systems. *Communications of the ACM, 28*(9), 921–932. doi:10.1145/4284.4286

Healey, J., & Picard, R. W. (1998, October 1-20). Startlecam: A cybernetic wearable camera. In *Proceedings of the 2nd International Symposium on Wearable Computers* (pp. 42-49), Pittsburgh, PA.

Hokyoung, R., & Parsons, D. (2008). *Innovative mobile learning: Techniques and technologies*. Hershey, PA: IGI Global.

Horrocks, I., Patel-Schneider, P. F., Boley, H., Tabet, S., Grosof, B., & Dean, M. (2004). *SWRL: A Semantic Web rule language combining OWL and RuleML* [online]. Retrieved from http://www.w3.org/Submission/SWRL/

Horrocks, I., Patel-Schneider, P. F., & van-Harmelen, F. (2003). From SHIQ and RDF to OWL: The making of the ontology Web language. *Journal of Web Semantics, 1*(1), 7–26. doi:10.1016/j.websem.2003.07.001

Hu, B., & Moore, P. (2007b). Smart context: An ontology based context model for cooperative mobile learning. *Computer Supported Cooperative Work in Design, 10th International Conference (CSCWD 2006)* (LNCS 4402, pp. 717-726), Nanjing, China, May 2006.

Hu, B., Moore, P., & Chen, H.-H. (2007a). A semantic model for location based cooperative learning. In *Proceedings of the International Conference on Communications (ICC-2007)* (pp. 326-331), Glasgow, Scotland, June 24-28.

Jena. (2009). *Jena–a Semantic Web framework for java* [online]. Retrieved from http://jena.sourceforge.net/index.html

Jie, Y., Weiyi, Y., Denecke, M., & Waibel, A. (1999, October 18-19). Smart sight: A tourist assistant system. In *Proceedings of the 3rd International Symposium on Wearable Computers* (pp. 73-78), San Francisco, CA.

Johnson, D. B., & Maltz, D. A. (1996). Dynamic source routing in ad hoc wireless networks. In *The International Series in Engineering and Computer Science* (Vol. 353, pp. 151-181). USA: Springer.

Kaasinen, E. (2003). User needs for location-aware mobile services. *Personal and Ubiquitous Computing, 7*, 70–79. doi:10.1007/s00779-002-0214-7

Kindberg, T. (2008). *Cooltown & ubicomp* [online]. Retrieved from http://www.hpl.hp.com/archive/cooltown/

Kinshuk, & Goh, T. T. (2003). Mobile adaptation with multiple representation as educational pedagogy. In W. Uhr, W. Esswein & E. Schoop (Eds.), *Wirtschaftsinformatik 2003-Medien-Markte-Mobilitat* (pp. 747-763).

Kinshuk., Kommers, P., & Sampson, D. G. (2004). Adaptivity in Web and mobile learning services. In *Proceedings of the Int. J. Cont. Engineering Education and Lifelong Learning 2004, 14*(4/5), 313-317.

Komives, S. R. (2005). *The changing nature of work in higher education* [online]. Retrieved from http://www.acpa.nche.edu/seniorscholars/trends/trends6.htm

Kossen, J. S. (2005). Mobile e-learning when e-learning becomes m-learning [online]. Retrieved from http://www.palmpowerenterprise.com/issuesprint/issue200106/elearning.html

Laerhoven, K. V., & Aidoo, K. (2001). Teaching context to applications. *Personal and Ubiquitous Computing, 5*, 46–49. doi:10.1007/s007790170029

Lamming, M., & Flynn, M. (1994, February 2-4). Forget-me-not: Intimate computing in support of human memory. In *Proceedings of FRIEND21 _94, the International Symposium on Next Generation Human Interface*, Magufo Jagoen, Japan.

Leonhardi, A., Kubach, U., Rothermel, K., & Fritz, A. (1999, October 18-19). Virtual information towers–a metaphor for intuitive, location-aware information access in a mobile. In *Proceedings of the 3rd International Symposium on Wearable Computers* (pp. 15-20), San Francisco, CA.

Liaw, S.-S. (2004). Considerations for developing constructivist Web-based learning. *International Journal of Instructional Media, 31*(3), 309.

Lin, T. Kinshuk, & Patel, A. (2003). Cognitive trait model for persistent student modelling. In D. Lasser & C. McNaught (Eds.), *EdMedia 2003* (pp 2114-2147). Norfolk, USA: AACE.

Lin Hsiao, J. D. (2005). *CSCL theories* [online]. Retrieved from http://www.edb.utexas.edu/cscl-student/Dhsiao/theories.html

Liu, J. A. Kardashian, Goo, J., Smith, C., Yap, F., & Kapur, A. (2005). *Wireless ECG*. (Tech. Rep.). Duke University Smart House Pratt School of Engineering [online]. Retrieved from http://www.smarthouse.duke.edu/projects/wirelessecg.php

Long, P., & Tricker, T. (2004, September 16-18). Do first year graduates find what they expect? *British Educational Research Association Conference 2004*, University of Manchester.

Lonsdale, P., Barber, C., Sharples, M., & Arvanitis, T. N. (2003). A context awareness architecture for facilitating mobile learning. In *Proceedings of MLEARN 2003*, London, UK.

Luchini, K., Curtis, M., Quintana, C., & Soloway, E. (2002). Supporting learning in context: Extending learner-centered design to the development of handheld educational software. In M. Milrad, H.U. Hoppe & Kinshuk (Eds.), *IEEE International Workshop on Wireless and Mobile Technologies in Education 2002* (pp. 107-111).

MacKnight, C. B. (1998). Electronic learning materials: The crisis continues. *ACM SIGCUE Outlook, 26*(2), 8–16. doi:10.1145/281083.281088

Majoe, D., Estermann, M., Ranieri, N., & Gutknecht, J. (2008, October 6-8). Ergonomic low cost motion capture for every day health exercise. In *Proceedings of the Third International Conference on Pervasive Computing and Applications (ICPCA08)* (pp. 627-632). Alexandria, Egypt.

Middleton, S. E., Shadbolt, N. R., & De-Rour, D. C. (2004). Ontological user profiling in recommender systems. *ACM Transactions on Information Systems, 22*(1), 54–88. doi:10.1145/963770.963773

Mifsud, L. (2002, August 29-30). Alternative learning arenas-pedagogical challenges to mobile learning technology in education. In *Proceedings of the IEEE International Workshop on Wireless and Mobile Technologies in Education (WMTE 2002)* (pp. 112-116), Växjö, Sweden. Washington, D.C.: IEEE Computer Society.

MIT. (2004). *MIT project oxygen: Pervasive human-centered computing* [online]. Retrieved in January 2009, from, http://oxygen.lcs.mit.edu/

Mitchell, T. M. (1997). *Machine learning*. Singapore: McGraw-Hill.

Moodle. (2009). *Moodle*. Retrieved from http://moodle.org/about/

Moore, P., & Hu, B. (2006, August 3-5). Entity profiling: Context with ontology. *Proceedings of the 1st International Symposium on Pervasive Computing and Applications (SPCA06)* (pp. 172-177), Urumqi, P.R. China. USA: IEEE Press.

Moore, P., & Hu, B. (2007b). A context framework with ontology for personalised and cooperative mobile learning. *Computer Supported Cooperative Work in Design, 10th International Conference (CSCWD 2006)*, Nanjing, China, May 2006 (LNCS 4402, pp. 727-738). Berlin, Germany: Springer-Verlag.

Moore, P., Hu, B., & Wan, J. (2008). Smart-context: A context ontology for pervasive co-operative applications. *The Computer Journal*, doi:10.1093/comjnl/bxm104. Retrieved from http://comjnl.oxfordjournals.org/cgi/content/abstract/bxm104v1?

Moore, P., Hu, B., Zhu, X., Campbell, W., & Ratcliffe, M. (2007a). A survey of context modeling for pervasive cooperative learning. In *IEEE Proceedings of the First International Symposium on Information Technologies and Applications in Education (ISITAE '07)*, Kunming, Yuan, P.R. China, November 23-25, 2007. K5-1-K5-6. USA: IEEE.

Mungania, P. (2003). *The seven e-learning barriers facing employees*. USA: University of Louisville.

Nardi, D., & Brachman, R. J. (2002). *An introduction to description logics*. Cambridge, UK: Cambridge University Press.

Noy, N. F., & McGuinness, D. L. (2001). *Ontology development 101: A guide to creating your 1st ontology* [online]. Retrieved from http://protege.stanford.edu/publications/ontologydevelopment/ontology101.shtml

OpenRDF.org. (2008). *The Sesame API* [online]. Retrieved from http://www.openrdf.org/doc/sesame/users/ch07.html

Pascoe, J., Ryan, N. S., & Morse, D. R. (1998). Human computer giraffe interaction-HCI in the field. *Workshop on Human Computer Interaction with Mobile Devices* [online]. Retrieved from http://www.dcs.gla.ac.uk/~johnson/papers/mobile/HCIMD1.html

Pascoe, J., Ryan, N. S., & Morse, D. R. (1999, September). Issues in developing context-aware computing. In *Proceedings of the International Symposium on Handheld and Ubiquitous Computing* (pp. 208-221), Karlsruhe, Germany.

Poslad, S., Laamanen, H., Malaka, R., Nick, A., Buckle, P., & Zipf (2001, March). A crumpet: Creation of user friendly mobile services personalised for tourism. 3G 2001. In *Proceedings of the Second International Conference on 3G Mobile Communication Technologies*, London.

Powers, S. (2003). *Practical RDF*. Cambridge, MA: O'Reilly.

Rhodes, B. J. (1997, October 13-14). The wearable remembrance agent: A system for augmented memory. In *Proceedings of the 1st International Symposium on Wearable Computers* (pp. 123-128), Cambridge, MA.

Roiger, R. J., Azarbod, C., & Sant, R. R. (1997, December 8-10). A majority rules approach to data mining. In *Proceedings of the 1997 IASTED International Conference on Intelligent Information Systems(Iis'97)* (pp. 100-107), Grand Bahamia Island, Bahamas.

Royer, E. M., & Chai-Keong, T. (1999). A review of current routing protocols for ad-hoc mobile wireless networks. *Personal Communications, IEEE, 6*(2), 46–55. doi:10.1109/98.760423

Rushby, N. (1998). Where are the desks for the virtual class. *ACM SIGCUE Outlook, 26*(2), 33–36. doi:10.1145/281083.281093

Russell, S. (2003). *Readings about the question: It is said that reasoning on the Semantic Web must be monotonic. Why is this so, when human reasoning, which seems to have served us well, is nonmonotonic?* [online]. Retrieved from http://robustai.net/papers/Monotonic_Reasoning_on_the_Semantic_Web.html

Russell, S., & Norvig, P. (1995). *Artificial intelligence: A modern approach*. NJ: Prentice Hall.

Ryan, N., Pascoe, J., & Morse, D. (1997). Enhanced reality fieldwork: The context-aware archaeological assistant. In Gaffney, Leusen & Exxon (Eds.), *Computer applications in archaeology*. Oxford, UK: British Archaeological Reports.

Salber, D., Dey, A. K., & Abowd, G. D. (1999, May 15-20). The context toolkit: Aiding the development of context-enabled applications. In *Proceedings of the ACM CHI 99 Human Factors in Computing Systems Conference (CHI 99)* (pp. 434-441), Pittsburgh, PA.

Scardamalia, M., & Bereiter, C. (2006). Knowledge building: Theory, pedagogy, and technology. In K. Sawyer (Ed.), *Cambridge handbook of the learning sciences* (pp. 97-118). New York: Cambridge University Press.

Schilit, B. N., Adams, N. I., & Want, R. (1994). Context-aware computing applications. In *Proceedings of the Workshop on Mobile Computing Systems and Applications*, IEEE Computer Society (pp. 85-90), Santa Cruz, CA.

Schilit, W. N. (1995). System architecture for context-aware mobile computing. Unpublished doctoral dissertation, Columbia University, Columbia.

Senses, B. (2003, July). Implementing wireless communication in hospital environments with Bluetooth, 802.11b, and Other Technologies. (Tech. Rep.). *Medical Device & Diagnostic Industry*.

Sharples, M., Corlett, D., & Wesmancott, O. (2002). The design and implementation of a mobile learning resource. *Personal and Ubiquitous Computing*, (3): 220–234. doi:10.1007/s007790200021

Sheth, A., & Ramakrishnan, C. (2003, December). Semantic (Web) technology in action: Ontology driven information systems for search, integration, and analysis. In U. Dayal, H. Kuno & K. Wilkinson (Eds.), *IEEE data engineering bulletin, special issue on making the Semantic Web.*

Singh, D., & Abu Bakar, Z. (2007). Wireless implementation of a mobile learning environment based on students' expectations. *International Journal of Mobile Learning and Organisation, 1*(2), 198–215. doi:10.1504/IJMLO.2007.012678

University of Washington. (2008). *Portolano: An expedition into invisible computing* [online]. Retrieved from http://portolano.cs.washington.edu/

Wan, J., Hu, B., Moore, P., & Ashford, R. (2008, October 6-8). Intelligent mobile computing to assist in the treatment of depression. In *Proceedings of the Third International Conference on Pervasive Computing and Applications (ICPCA 08)* (pp. 650-655), Alexandria, Egypt.

Want, R. (1995, December). An overview of the PARCTAB ubiquitous computing environment. *IEEE Personal Communications, 2*(6), 28–43. doi:10.1109/98.475986

Want, R., Hopper, A., Falcao, V., & Gibbons, J. (1992). The active badge location system. *ACM Transactions on Information Systems, 10*(1), 91–102. doi:10.1145/128756.128759

Ward, A., Jones, A., & Hopper, A. (1997). A new location technique for the active office. *Personal Communications, IEEE, 4*(5), 42–47. doi:10.1109/98.626982

Weisenberg, N. N., Voisard, A., & Gartmann, R. (2004, November 12-13). Using ontologies in personalised mobile applications. In *Proceedings of the 12th Annual ACM International Workshop on Geographic Information Systems (GIS '04)* (pp. 2-11), Washington, D.C.

Weiser, M. (1991). The computer for the 21st century. *Scientific American,* 94-104. Reprinted in *IEEE Pervasive Computing*, Jan.-Mar. 2002, 19-25.

Weiser, M. (1993). Some computer science issues in ubiquitous computing. *Communications of the ACM, 36*(7), 75–84. doi:10.1145/159544.159617

Weller, M. (2002). *Delivering learning on the net–the why, what, and how of online education.* London: Kogan Page.

Wilkinson, K., Sayers, C., Kuno, H., & Reynolds, D. (2003). *Efficient RDF storage and retrieval in Jena2.* (HP Laboratories Tech. Rep. HPL-2003-266).

ENDNOTES

1 Birmingham City University (http://www.bcu.ac.uk/) – formerly The University of Central England (UCE)

2 Dictionary.com: (www.dictionary.com)
3 Protégé – a free open source ontology editor (http://protege.stanford.edu/)

4 A target range in the order 60% - 80% (normalised to 0.6 – 0.8) can be viewed as realistic based on previous results obtained in studies addressing information retrieval. Given that there is no identified documented research into context matching there is no recorded benchmarks to asses the context matching performance therefore initial thresholds in the range o.6 – 0.8 will be used in the context matching process.

Section 3

Architecture Applications and Case Studies on Mobile Learning Practices

Chapter 13

Schools in Action: Pedagogical Evaluation of COLLAGE, a Case Study on Mobile and Location Game-Based Learning

Mario Barajas
University of Barcelona, Spain

Sofoklis Sotiriou
Ellinogermaniki Agogi, Greece

Martin Owen
Medrus Learning, UK

Manfred Lohr
BG/BRG Schwechat, Austria

ABSTRACT

This chapter looks at the implementation and evaluation of mobile learning scenarios with location-based features, done under the project COLLAGE (Collaborative Learning Platform Using Game-like Enhancements). Five scenarios are examined. Evaluating different implementations within the same project gives an appraisal of the technical and pedagogical value of the mobile learning scenarios, but also informs the research community of appropriate evaluation models and evaluation parameters, which are lacking in the game-based mobile learning with location-based components. The project responds to questions about designing mobile learning scenarios that are pedagogically sound and attractive to secondary school students, and presents the pedagogical evaluation of the effectiveness of mobile game-based learning scenarios in the COLLAGE platform. The project makes a case for a close collaboration with teachers and students in elaborating and validating complex mobile learning scenarios.

INTRODUCTION

This chapter looks at the implementation and evaluation of five mobile learning scenarios with location-based features. We had the following research and development questions:

- What are the approaches to design learning scenarios to be implemented in a mobile

DOI: 10.4018/978-1-60566-882-6.ch013

learning platform that are pedagogically sound and attractive to secondary school students?
- What should be the procedures for designing games for mobile-learning location-based scenarios? What evaluation procedures and parameters are best for evaluating mobile learning?

We approached these issues through a series of cases developed in the frame of the project COLLAGE (Collaborative Learning Platform Using Game-like Enhancements). COLLAGE was an 2-year project funded by the European Commission, eLearning Programme, focused on secondary education as the students are more familiar with the use of the mobile technology and game-like applications. This Chapter can be considered the continuation of *"Developing tools that support effective Mobile and Game Based Learning: The COLLAGE Platform"*, a chapter of this book.

There are only a few examples of mobile learning applications devoted to secondary education which have been extensively evaluated in real learning settings. There is still not enough accumulated experience on using mobile learning, and most of the examples refer to informal education and to higher education projects. Evaluating different implementations within the same project, not only gave us an appraisal of the technical and pedagogical value of these mobile learning scenarios, but also informed the research community of appropriate evaluation models and evaluation parameters, which are lacking in the game-based mobile learning and location-based learning area.

In addition, sound pedagogical principles for designing mobile learning scenarios were explored for the enabling technologies and learning platforms. The complexity of the design increases because the learning strategies include games as an added motivating aspect, and outdoors location-based scenarios are part of the learning context. Furthermore, best practice principles have been consulted to inform the design and specially, the operationalisation of the implementation of the scenarios, the novelty of the approach in secondary education, and the complexity of the technologies all added an extra difficulty to put into practice these rich scenarios in real learning situations. The complex panorama was completed by the fact that the users, teachers and students were included in the process from the very beginning.

Usage scenarios in COLLAGE have been developed combining several pedagogical approaches within the constructivism pedagogical theory where the individual learner constructs knowledge based on his/her pre-existing and current experiences. The learning environment build throughout the project resembles computer games for children, facilitating pupils' interaction and acquisition of new knowledge. On the other hand, the situated learning approach suggests the acquisition of knowledge through social participation and collaboration. In COLLAGE scenarios students and teachers confront problems together in authentic learning situations.

The aim of this chapter is twofold: first, to present the COLLAGE learning scenarios and learning games; second, to discuss the pedagogical evaluation results of these learning scenarios implemented in the COLLAGE platform.

Five scenarios are presented with descriptions of the learning activities and the technologies used, which illustrates the unique nature of COLLAGE in the field of mobile learning. Each scenario has unique features, showing variety and richness. The five scenarios presented are:

- **Carnuntum:** archaeological site in the outskirts of Vienna, Austria. COLLAGE created a role-play game with different learning "paths", in which students follow a character representing an inhabitant of the city. They have to answer questions at certain places and fulfil tasks (e.g. take a picture of this location) on a PDA.

- **Mozart:** role-play mobile game designed and uploaded by the students in the COLLAGE platform, in which the historical character "Mozart" is a member of the team of students visiting today's city of Salzburg.
- **Knossos:** Archaeological site in Crete, Greece. During the site visit, with the help of PDA students identify specific places, respond to questions, take pictures and gather data on the site while playing a game uploaded in the COLLAGE platform.
- **Tholos/Agora:** a combination of augmented reality and mobile learning game. The students toured virtually the ancient Agora, at the modern 3D theatre of Tholos (Foundation of the Hellenic World in Athens), then visited the Agora, and played the game designed by the teachers using PDAs and mobile phones.
- **Fodele:** A group activity firmly based on the existing curriculum, which consist on a visit to an ecosystem, where they study the quality of the environment, taking samples of the river, compiling the data on the PDA, and responding questions in a game uploaded in the COLLAGE platform.

For the purpose of the evaluation, COLLAGE is considered a case study as a whole, implemented in five different scenarios, which will be described in detail. The scenarios use pedagogical strategies using game-based learning, such as participatory simulations, narrative learning and enquiry-based learning. Role-playing and collaborative learning are also part of the scenarios. However, for the purpose of evaluation, all scenarios were analysed according to a set of parameters defined in collaboration with the teachers that matched the pedagogical framework. The pedagogical evaluation analysed teachers and students' attitudes and views about mobile learning after participating in the project.

Although the chapter does not address a technical evaluation of the platform used, the evaluation took into account the technological opportunities and constraints identifies by both teachers and students. The project had, by circumstance, a mix of opportunities which varied according to the availability of technology the students had, the affordances of the technology (GPS, video capture, etc.), the networks available to the students via the mobile devices (WAP was minimum) and realistic expectations of connection bandwidth.

EVALUATING MOBILE AND LOCATION-BASED SCENARIOS

In a recent workshop about mobile learning undertaken by the Kaleidoscope Network of Excellence (http://www.noe-kaleidoscope.org/pub/) on technology-enhanced learning, there was recognition of the difficulty of formative evaluations of specific applications for mobile learning, since few teachers and learners have experienced mobile learning scenarios, with the added problem of rapidly changing technologies (Taylor, 2007) and mobile learning platforms. If we add that we are dealing with experiments in formal learning settings, but within informal learning scenarios, the difficulties increase substantially. Therefore, the evaluation design and the evaluation parameters have to be necessarily tentative. We take the view of learning being mediated by mobile devices in mobile settings, so that evaluation cannot be based just on laboratory experiments.

There are few studies on evaluating mobile learning applications. In the review of evaluation methods for mobile learning by Traxler and Kukulska (2005), responding to the growing number of mobile learning pilots and trials taking place, the efficacy of traditional evaluation techniques is questioned and the need for innovative and varied evaluation approaches suggested.

Two of the key trends in evaluation mobile learning applications are usability testing and pedagogical evaluation, which are done sometimes separately, and sometimes complementarily. The first method calls for looking at the component software and platform interface, whereas the second looks mainly at the pedagogical value of the mobile learning applications.

Usability tests often use heuristic evaluation (Nielsen, 1993) done by experts, along with other methods that give a quick assessment of the technical aspects and reactions of the users towards the devices and interfaces, such as SUS methodology (Brooke, 1996).

In terms of mobile learning there are few evaluative frameworks, and usually, general evaluation models are used, for instance the one mentioned by Jones el al. (1999), which outlines three dimensions for evaluating educational software: context of use, interactions, and attitudes and outcomes. Motiwalla (2007) suggests a) observing the usage of the mobile learning application, and b) determining student opinions on the role and value of m-learning application. Taylor (2003) proposes testing the usability of the system and later the pedagogical value. The same author uses the socio-cognitive method (based on activity theory), which allows analysing learners in their contexts in order to understand the nature of their learning tasks and how they go about them (Taylor, 2007). Another model proposed by Syvänen and Nokelainen (2004) suggests four dimensions for evaluation of mobile learning projects: level of collaboration, level of control, effectiveness of the multimodal learning experience and transferability of learning structures.

If we introduce the mobile game dimension, there are few examples on stage. Freitas and Oliver (2006) introduce a model for evaluating educational games, following the increasing use of games and simulations for teaching and the need to assess the effectiveness of these varied learning scenarios. Rather than a prescriptive approach, these authors promote a model that allows practitioners to be more critical about how they embed games and simulations into their lesson plans. Four key dimensions are suggested: a) the particular context where play/learning takes place; b) the attributes of the particular learner or learner group, c) the internal representational world of the game or simulation (the mode of presentation, the interactivity, the levels of immersion and fidelity used in the game or simulation), and d) the processes of learning both during the course of formal curricula based learning time and during informal learning. In another example Schwabe & Göth (2005a) in evaluating learning games look at the following dimensions: a) user satisfaction, b) motivational aspects of the game, and c) usability of the functions, apart from data about the users.

In terms of location-based learning, innovative projects in this area are scarce. But one good example is the project Frequency 1550, a mobile location-based learning game that was developed by the Dutch Waag Society in Amsterdam in 2005, in which students aged 12 to 14, acquire historical knowledge about the city of Amsterdam (Raessens, 2007; Huizenga et al., 2007). The project has been evaluated in two stages, using participatory methods and narrative methods of enquiry, evaluating motivation, attitudes towards collaborative learning, engagement, and learning effects. Another project, Savannah http://www.futurelab.org.uk/projects/savannah, is a location-based role playing game where the school soccer pitch is turned into an African Savannah and the students become a pride of lions is another good example. The aim of the Savannah experience was to encourage understanding of particular content (in Savannah this was animal behaviour). The evaluations sought evidence from contextual mobile games of conceptual understanding of the context of the game and of relationships to the context (empathy, further engagement, etc.). Further, generic skills were expected to be developed and therefore the researchers needed to provide a framework for recognizing and evaluating these activities (e.g. strategies for working with problems as a team). Additionally game-like learning requires identification, imagination, and reutilization of learned knowledge. There is a strong narrative of place, role and time, and an evaluation framework was required for this (Facer et al., 2004; Owen, 2008).

COLLAGE, A MOBILE GAME-BASED AND LOCATION-BASED APPROACH

During the two years of the project COLLAGE, four institutions from four different countries have designed and implemented different location-based and mobile learning scenarios. For the purpose of this chapter, we analyse the implementation and validation of the COLLAGE scenarios developed in two countries, Austria and Greece, since the ones done in the other two countries, Estonia and Denmark, were done at the test level and were discontinued.

Mobile learning takes place when learning activities are mediated by mobile devices (McManus, 2002), and also when the learner is mobile, meaning outside the classroom (Vavoula and McAndrew, 2005). COLLAGE capitalises on four components: game-based learning, mobile learning activities, the "mobile learner", and a new one, location-based learning. The COLLAGE project studied mobile game-based learning on the assumption that, when engaged in the learning process, students learn and retain more. Engagement may come through emotion, and especially through fun. At the same time, the games are taking place on location, so that the students visit sites where the learning game takes place. Within this perspective, it is obvious that games on location are a strong motivating and engaging factor (Anand, 2008).

Within the COLLAGE project's framework, students participated in a series of entertaining and fun activities, playing different learning games uploaded in the COLLAGE platform and accessed through PDA, 3G mobile phones when visiting different places, such as archaeological sites, natural parks, and museums. By placing a game at the core of the learning strategy, the learning platform provided students with the opportunity to participate in an active learning process in competition with other peers, enabling them to gain knowledge and skills beyond 'traditional' classroom results.

The pedagogical concepts and consequently, the methodological approaches underlying COLLAGE, followed learning theories based upon:

- **Constructivism:** A learning theory according to which the individual learners' construction of knowledge is based on pre-existing and developing schemata. The learning environment built around a game is familiar and resembles computer games children are accustomed and attracted to. In this way the learning process is facilitated.
- **Situated Learning:** An instructional strategy where knowledge is acquired through a process of social participation. Teachers working alongside the students confront problems in authentic learning situations. Location-based learning with the help of mobile technologies can facilitate the construction of these type of learning scenarios and teaching strategies. Context-aware computing is one of the approaches within this paradigm, "which means gathering information from the environment to provide a measure of what is currently going on around the user and the device" (Johanson, 2007, Wang, 2004Naismith et al., 2004, p. 14). Collaborative data gathering (Roschelle, 2003. p. 264) is also part of this approach.
- **Game-based learning:** An instructional approach that facilitates and support meaningful learning of pupils, merging informal and school learning (Colella, 2000; Prensky, 2003; Shaffer, 2006). Gee (2005) lists a number of principles of learning or practices to be built into digital pedagogy

characterizing game-based learning. These principles of learning deal with the empowerment of the learner, the learning task as a problem-solving task, and the learning process as a process of understanding.

- **Exploratory learning**: A learning process in which the learners take control of their own learning. By placing a game at the core of an interactive learning environment, the mobile activities provide an active learning process enabling the students to gain knowledge and skills beyond 'traditional' classroom results.

COLLAGE takes a pragmatic approach and is informed by all these approaches. The pedagogical strategy for designing the mobile learning scenarios follows a set of practical pedagogical principles set by Anderson and McCormick (2005) in agreement with the above mentioned learning theories: 1) Match to the curriculum; 2) Inclusion; 3) Student engagement; 4) Innovativeness of the approach; 5) Effective learning; 6) Formative assessment; 7) Summative assessment; 8) Coherence, consistency and transparency; 9) Ease of use, and 10) Cost-effectiveness.

These principles represent the underpinning values that can apply to a range of expressions of digital learning, and are meaningful for the different stakeholders involved in technology-based innovations: designers, teachers and learners. These principles, reinterpreted for mobile learning, helped COLLAGE to build the learning scenarios with pedagogically sound underpinnings.

THE COLLAGE SCENARIOS AND IMPLEMENTATION

A variety of scenarios have been developed and tested throughout the project. These are documented in the Internet-based project library (http://neseredete.forthnet.gr/collage/library.asp). Examples of the COLLAGE scenarios are presented in this section of the chapter. Each of them have specific characteristics, and were evolving in the lifetime of COLLAGE, from an initial design undertaken by the project team, which included teachers, to a latter phase in which the students were also participating, redesigning or authoring new scenarios. Here we describe the most evolved scenarios.

The COLLAGE scenarios were designed from a multidisciplinary team of academic experts, teacher trainers and teachers from many European countries. As mentioned before, we will look at the scenarios implemented in Greece, and Austria. Below we describe the scenarios selected, which were designed, developed and improved along the lifetime of the project COLLAGE.

The Carnuntum Scenario

The Carnuntum scenario was implemented in the archaeological excavation areas of Carnuntum, situated on the border of the Roman Empire in the outskirts of Vienna, Austria. The excavation sites of the civil settlements and the military *castra* are the largest archaeological areas in Austria and are visited by almost all schools in the eastern part of Austria, mostly in a very traditional way with guides or questionnaires for a self-guiding tour. The main attractions are houses, gardens and part of the limes road, reconstructed under scientific supervision only with tools and methods that were used in the 4th century A.D.

There are, among other ruins the "house of Lucious". Archaeologists studied the excavated basements and attempted to reveal as exactly as possible how the house was built, and reconstructed the house using original tools. The interior of the house, including a *hypocauston* heating system, furniture, vessels and food is authentic. Visitors who are no experts in ancient history and archaeology can imagine what a Roman city looked like and how people lived and worked there (Figure 1).

Figure 1. Archaeological site of Carnuntum with the House of Lucius at the back

The aim in this scenario was to give the students a chance to get a vivid impression of the daily life in the Roman Empire - exemplified by the ancient Roman city of Carnuntum - supported by new mobile technologies. COLLAGE created a role-play game with three "paths". Along each path a character representing an inhabitant of Carnuntum walks around the city, meets friends, enters the shops and public buildings, and so on. The students are told the story of this person on the PDA; they "follow" him/her and learn about the former functions of the ruins and the reconstructed buildings. They have to answer questions (multiple choices) at certain places or fulfil tasks (e.g. take a picture of this location). On the fourth path, located at the military amphitheatre, students have to change their roles and find questions and tasks themselves and upload them on the PDA.

The characters could have lived there. The name Maximianus, the soldier, is taken from an original inscription at a tomb at Carnuntum, the others are typical names of slaves and gladiators. The details of the story are designed as closely as possible to the original historical background. The characters of the game were: 1) Fusca, a 14 year old slave; 2) Gigas, a gladiator, and 3) Maximianus, a soldier.

The participants in the evaluation of this implementation were 17 students of the 3rd grade (13-year old) and 17 students of the 7th grade (age 17) of the BGS school, Vienna, Austria. The students were divided into 10 groups consisting of 3 students each and in 2 groups consisting of 2 children each. Two teachers observed the students as coordinators and assistants at technical problems. The tasks carried out in this activity were related to the subjects Latin, History and Physics.

Each group of students was equipped with one PDA with GPRS connection. During the game the students alternated in using the device (Figure 2). The teacher was able to monitor the log-books and the position of the teams by using a tablet PC with wireless internet connection.

Students had to answer multiple choice questions. After the selection of the chosen answer a window of their logbook opened, and they had to explain the reasons for their choice. The logbook is a record of how the team dealt with the questions of each Game Path. The players had to add a comment in order to support their answers, regardless they are right or wrong. On entering the logbook the player can infer from the points collected whether they have chosen the correct answer or not. The pedagogical objective of the

Figure 2. 13-year old girls playing the game

logbook is to allow the players and the teams to review their game plan. By providing support for every answer the players are encouraged to think critically. The students had previously visited the Museum Carnuntum. In the museum the results of the excavations at Carnuntum are displayed. Some of the questions of the learning scenario were based on the experiences they had gained during this visit.

The students were trained in the classroom how to work with the COLLAGE platform and how to use the mobile device, the MDA vario II. Also, during the bus ride to the outside experiment, the students watched a DVD about the ancient city of Carnuntum made by the ORF, the Austrian Television Company.

Once in the excavation site of Carnuntum the students should get an idea how common people lived 1600 years ago. The game gives scientifically correct information, based on the curriculum in Latin, History and Physics; and the use of mobile technologies adds a "third dimension", which is to move around through the ancient city while playing the interactive game.

Learning Objectives and Implementation

The game started when each group logged in with their PDA in the COLLAGE platform and chose the path to take. Every team had to solve 10 questions and critical thinking tasks in the main excavation. The tasks of the Carnuntum Scenario consisted of instructions where the pupils had to move to a new location, or instructions to take pictures with their PDAs and upload them to a logbook in the COLLAGE platform (Figure 3).

An important activity was the creation of a new learning path and the uploading of the questions by the students (Figure 4). This task, when students had to create their own questions and tasks and to upload them in their logbooks, open the possibility for the next level of students' engagement in the game: students as creators of the game. This took place in the next scenario described, named Mozart.

To exemplify the activity evolved within the different teams, we look at the soldier' character: the teams playing this role were directed to the House of Lucius (number 2 on Figure 5), where the soldier met his old friend Lucius: students had to explore the functions of the heating system of the house, and outside in the garden they had to

Figure 3. Carnuntum scenario. Beginning of the game as seen in the COLLAGE interface

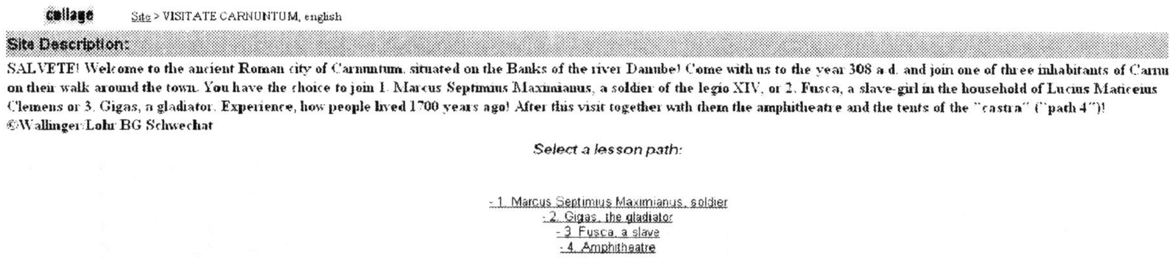

deal with flowers, vegetables, fruits and herbs. After they had left the house, while walking over an old Roman street, they got questions about the surface of the street and the nearby public baths and toilets. Then they were directed to a building with columns and had to answer questions about this Roman temple.

After the students had played the part of the game which took place in the main excavation site, they had to go out of this area. Because of the fact that only 1% of the ancient city of Carnuntum has been excavated, one of the intentions of the game was to give to the students an impression of the size of the ancient city. The students had to use the GPS coordinates to find the next point of interest. They had to find and translate Roman inscriptions in the walls of an old farmer's house (site nr. 2 on the map). Following their story, they had to walk in their roles of the soldier, the gladiator and the slave to the ancient Roman public baths, another big excavation site (site nr. 3 on the map).

The game ended when the soldier, the gladiator and the slave arrived in the Amphitheatre of Carnuntum. There the students had to solve the final task: they had to create two new questions and tasks related to their roles in the game and to upload their questions to the COLLAGE platform.

As for the technical aspects, during the outdoor activities 12 PDAs, namely MDA vario II, were used. These devices are working with the Windows Mobile 5.0 operating system, equipped with

Figure 4. Carnuntum scenario, once a learning path has been selected. Question as seen in the COLLAGE interface

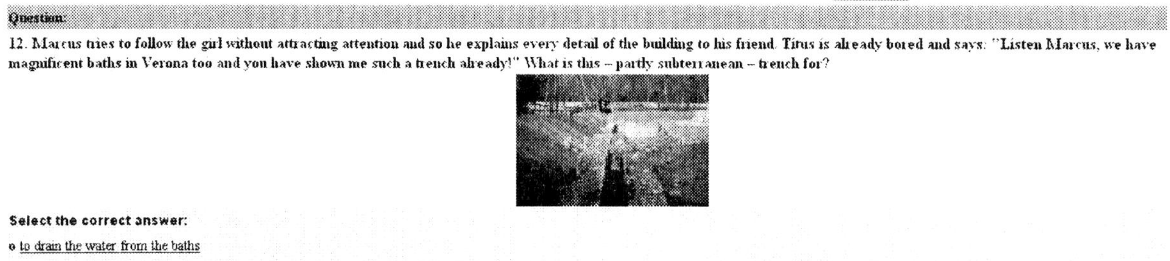

Figure 5. Map of the location of the game in Carnuntum

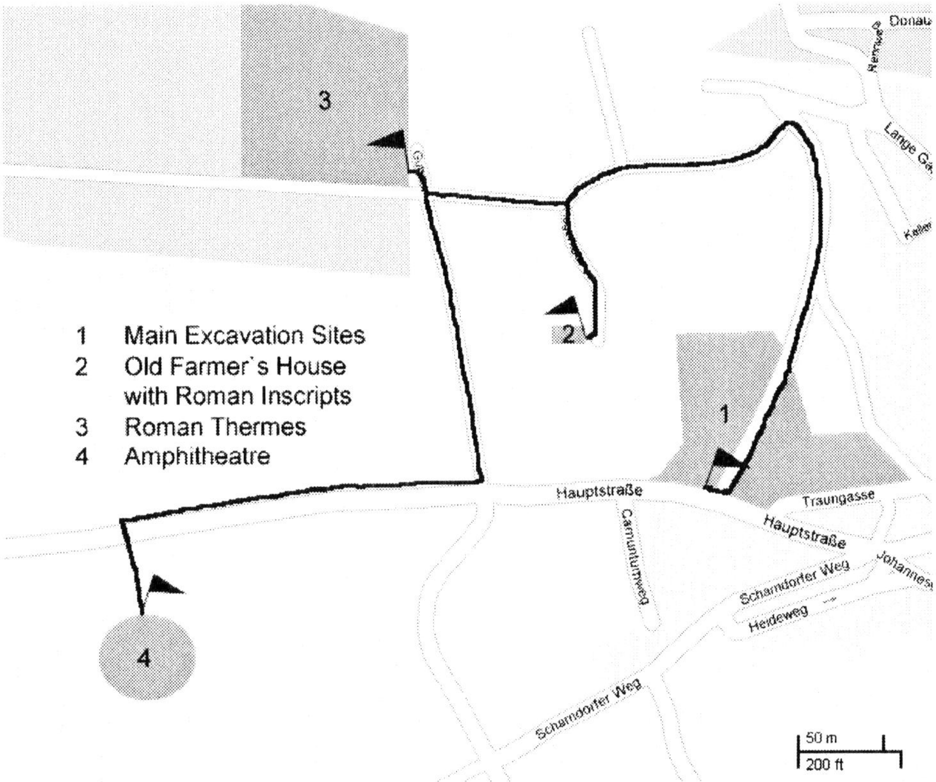

a QWERTZ keyboard and a 2 mega pixel photo camera. The MDA devices were connected by Bluetooth to a GPS mouse, the GPS coordinates were read by the BeeLineGPS software installed on the MDAs. The devices were connected to the COLLAGE platform by GPRS connection; a broadband connection like UMTS was not available in Carnuntum.

The teacher used a Siemens tablet notebook, which was connected to the internet by GPRS. The COLLAGE platform enables the teacher to have a look at the logbooks of all teams playing the game. It is also possible for the teacher to see in Google Earth the tracks of the teams based on their GPS coordinates. These tools allow the teacher to have an overview of the students' work progress. If the teacher recognizes that a particular group needs help, he/she can use the COLLAGE platform to send an SMS to this group.

The Mozart Scenario

This scenario was designed by the students of the same school in the framework of the "Interpaedagogica", the greatest fair of education in Austria. The students designed and implemented a new learning path named "Mozart is back!". They took pictures and uploaded their questions and tasks to the platform.

The number of participants was 10 secondary school students and 2 teachers who were using 3 PDA devices.

The game took place in only one day. The high schools students at BGS school (Schwechat, Austria) were introduced to the ideas and aims of COLLAGE and then started without the teacher to explore the old city of Salzburg in order to create a learning game called "Mozart is back" in which Mozart comes to live and visit the city of Salzburg.

The game was to find things Mozart would be interested in now in the city. On the very same day, students started uploading their game items to the platform: they designed twelve questions/tasks, translated them into English and finished the German as well as the English path. The students liked very much working with the platform and asked to learn about other COLLAGE paths from other participants.

The Knossos Scenario

This scenario takes place in the Palace of Knossos, Crete (Greece), one of the most important archaeological site of ancient Greece. In this scenario, students are divided into teams. Each team has a specific mission and the target of all teams is to arrive to the Central Court of the Palace and from there to the King's room. Again the teacher has prepared a series of tasks for the students. Using their PDAs (with embedded GPS in order to be aware of the specific positioning all the time) students have to identify specific areas in the palace, explain the possible usage of the rooms they are crossing, discuss the way of living of the citizens of the palace, explain symbols and paintings, and finally, after answering a series of questions correctly, find their way to the Central Court. Each wrong answer is taking them away from the target while correct answers are bringing them closer to their final destination.

In order to liven up the experience of the game the teachers came up with a back story: A group of time travellers returned from the Knossos Place of Bronze Age back to modern time. It is a group of friends and colleagues with various interests, characters and backgrounds: a painter, a civil engineer, a sociologist, a journalist and a fashion designer. Thanks to their time travel in the past they lived an extraordinary day in Knossos Palace and they left with the best memories and a painting of the Palace created by their painter friend (Figure 6). With a great desire to re-live their fantastic experience the five friends decide to go for a holiday to modern Crete. They are eager to go again to Knossos, to visit the ruins of Knossos Palace.

Figure 6. The interface of the Knossos mobile game, as seen in the PDA

Learning Objectives and Implementation

The learning objectives of this scenario are concerned with specific History school curriculum: a) the Minoans' worship of nature through female representations; b) the role of the palace as place of religious worship; c) the sacred symbols of Minoan religion.

The history teachers compiled a set of questions that animates the back story (narrative). The questions were associated with specific rooms and spots of the palace to form a sequence or path that could be drawn on the Knossos map. The curator of the archaeological site was asked to read the questions they prepared and provide comments. Here is an example of a question that could be addressed to the civil engineer of the story:

What do you think is the reason why there are no fortification works?

A. The Minoans did not know how to construct such structures.

B. There had been some fortification but they have all been destroyed.

C. Fortification was not necessary as the Minoan control of the sea safeguarded them against intruders

(C: correct answer according to teachers' suggestions).

The teachers, students and consortium partners who visited the Knossos site were given maps of the site on which the paths were drawn.

Fodele (Crete)

Each year, the 11th Gymnasium of Heraklion has a well organised and established activity related to environmental education. This group activity is included in the curriculum although not compulsory. Also on an annual basis, a visit to an ecosystem is proposed as part of the third class Biology lesson. Fodele is a preserved area near Heraklion (Crete, Greece). By using biological indicators, a creek is investigated by the students in order to find out more about the quality of the environment in this area. The Fodele scenario can easily be used by all the high schools of Heraklion through the activities of environmental education.

Learning Objectives and Implementation

Two secondary school biology teachers, two biologists from the Natural Science Museum in Crete, together with the director of Fodele, joined the site visit. Twenty one students divided into 4 teams, using a PDA, investigated different aspect of the river. The learning scenario concentrated on a site visit to Fodele, with the aim of finding responses to the key question "is the creek in Fodele in environmental health conditions?" An ecosystem by its nature can easily reveal the presence of life and its variability and the dependence of the living creatures on their environment, as well as the human factor interference.

Students gathered data about the number of species in the water creek, as well as other biotic factors such as speed of the water, PH, temperature, etc. They use a meter, speedometer, etc. and then they fill up the data in the PDA. They respond to the questions posed in the COLLAGE game, so the team who get more responses right, wins the game.

All groups were designated to play the paths "Safety rules" at the site "Fodele the biotope". Two groups were designed to play the path "Human community" while the other two were engaged in the path "Biotic and abiotic factors" of the same site. In the first case the "Human community" path was dealing with the history of the area and the economical activities (recreation and agriculture) which are related to the river.

The path "Biotic and abiotic factors" guided the participating pupils to take pictures of the vegetation, record the sound of the water, determine the flow of the river by measuring the time for which a floating object, such as a piece of wood, travels to cover a specific distance and the acidity of the water using a portable pH meter. Then all students gathered at the river banks to search for any of the twenty four (24) small animals mainly insects and molluscs described in their instructions. Each animal was represented as a path at the site "Fodele small animals of the water identities". Successful identification of one of these animals helped the group to answer simple questions and perform the tasks required in the corresponding path (Figure 7).

The intended learning outcomes have been: a) Presence of life and its variability; b) Dependence of the living creatures on their environment; c) Role of abiotic factors; d) Human factor interference.

The teacher designed the visit using an activity book available to all biology teachers in Greece, and adapted its dynamics to the COLLAGE environment.

The Ancient Agora / Tholos Scenario

This scenario was designed and implemented by the teachers of history who have already been involved in the development of the Knossos scenario. They applied the experience they gained in the implementation of a new game: this game evolves across a number of paths that navigate the players in the archaeological site of Ancient Agora in the centre of Athens, below the hill where the Acropolis stands. The teachers authored the lesson plan, which was introduced in the COLLAGE platform.

There is not a particular story or narration to accompany the game in Ancient Agora. However, the experience of visiting the archaeological site is complemented by navigating the same place through a 3D interactive movie, in a modern theatre a few kilometres away. Before visiting the ruins of ancient agora, the secondary school students toured virtually the ancient Agora, at the modern 3D theatre of Tholos, at the foundation of the Hellenic World in Athens. They had the opportunity to get a glimpse into the Agora during the Classical, Hellenistic, and Roman periods, and thus get an understanding of how important the place was across periods. The Ancient Agora had been the heart of ancient Athens, the focus of political, commercial, administrative and social activity, the religious and cultural centre, and the seat of justice.

After the end of the movie the students went to the archaeological site in order to play the game using PDAs and mobile phones. On site, the students followed pre-defined paths that represented a specific navigation through historic periods and by category of interest: economy, politics

Figure 7. Students taking biological samples in the Fodele scenario and discussing the data with the teacher

and religion. Driven by the game questions, the students were guided to observe different places, ruins and labels, making relations between their observation and their knowledge on the role and the history of the Ancient Agora of Athens. Drawing on the experience of the virtual navigation and the actual tour of the ruins the students answered questions and provided evidence in support of answers by taking pictures and entering notes collaboratively.

Following paths on site, answering questions and providing evidence was done in groups so that each member could contribute in a different way. After the visit the students could review online the comments and evidence they provided during the game and reflect on the way they worked together in order to provide answers.

Learning Objectives and Implementation

The students had most of the responsibility for planning and organising their learning (autonomous learning). Although they could draw on their existing knowledge and the experience of Tholos, many of the questions required the students to answer based on the experience they had on site (learning through discovery). Specific learning goals, which are closely related to the curriculum and the current schooling conditions, were set. The teachers aspired that the students would be able to place historical events in time and space and identify the political, commercial, religious, social aspects of the Ancient Agora through the buildings, and understand that the place was important across historical periods.

The students worked collaboratively and they were engaged in a series of preparatory activities. Educational material had been developed aiming to inform the students on the Ancient Agora of Athens. Furthermore, activities and exercises were designed aiming at the consolidation of the learning results. Also, the students were familiarized with the computer and PDA applications of the COLLAGE project.

Before going to the Ancient Agora, students visited the cultural center "Hellenic World", where they took part in a 3D interactive virtual tour. The virtual tour allowed students to gain an understanding of how the place evolved from the classic, to the roman and Byzantine period. At the site of ancient agora the students formed three groups and each group was given a PDA to use. The main aim of the educational activities was to study an important aspect of Ancient Agora: economic, religious and commercial. The students had to follow separate learning paths that corresponded to each of the three aspects. At the end of the tour the three different groups gathered together and presented the results of the games to each other (Figure 8).

A few days after the visit the students were engaged in activities that motivated them to reflect on the visit and the experience they gained. They visited the logbooks they had created on the COLLAGE platform as points of reference of how they played the game. They were also encouraged to visit relevant web sites in order to clarify the mistakes and misconceptions identified through the logbooks.

In a second phase the students participated in designing the learning game. Apart from the previous steps mentioned in the initial phase of this scenario, the students were introduced to the concept of designing a learning game, including new questions and challenges around the theme of Ancient Agora. They were asked, first, to collect material (in digital format, text, photos, etc.) and to upload it into a content management platform.

Students were organized in groups to work collaboratively. They started to produce new questions, which were assigned to different groups to answer at a later stage. The best questions for the game were evaluated by the teacher and short-listed to enter the final game. A content management system was used to support the exchange process and upload the contents to produce new

Figure 8. Tour visit of the "green team" to the Ancient Agora

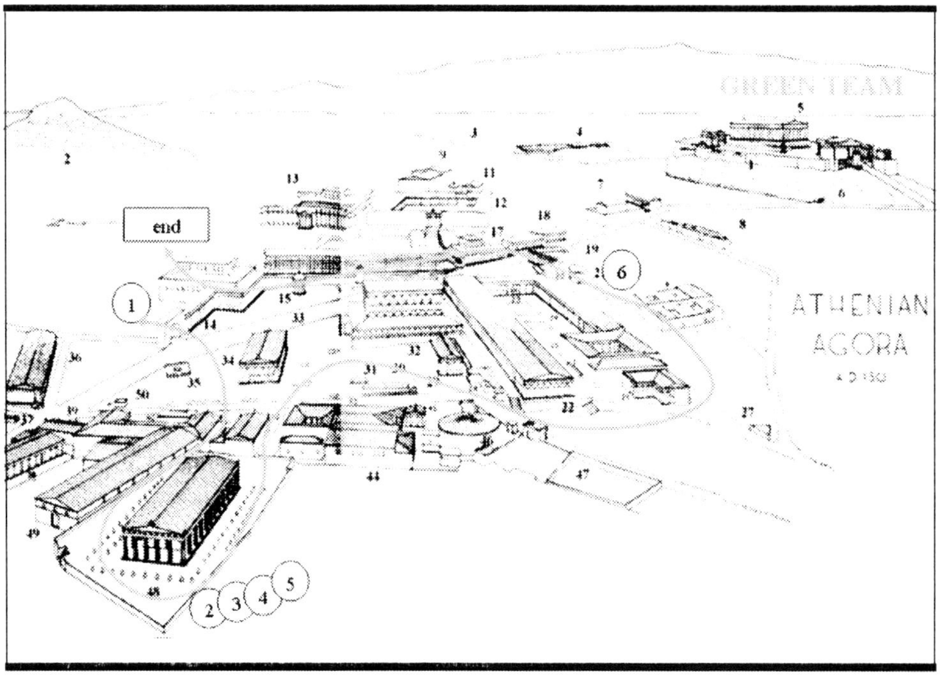

questions. Finally the students uploaded the questions and went back to the ancient Agora to play the game.

COLLAGE PEDAGOGICAL EVALUATION

Evaluating technology-based learning innovations asks primarily for the pedagogical value of these approaches. Evaluation in the COLLAGE project referred to the learning opportunities presented by the new mobile learning scenarios, the way students and teachers performed the learning tasks in it, the impact on pupils' and teachers' social processes and interactions and how they are modified by the technology. In the context of the project, the evaluation examined and validated the pedagogical added-value of the mobile learning scenarios developed, and determined how the COLLAGE platform supported the didactical approaches. This resulted in a review of the potential of the developed tools considering their effectiveness in school education improvements and learning.

The evaluation approach of COLLAGE was seen in a constructivist context, which means that the project outcomes are a common construction of the partners involved, which integrates the different views of the stakeholders in continuous feedback-loops. The project development is considered as an open adaptable process which uses the initial project work plan as a guiding framework but not as a limiting constraint (Cullen and Kelleher, 1995). Evaluation is an iterative process attempting to achieve a balance between formative and summative practices. The success of an innovation at the implementation phase depends on how this process evolves and adapts to the changes, and not only on strictly following the project calendar and achieving the project milestones.

An important aspect from the very beginning has been the need to involve the users in the evaluation process. This implies in practice to negotiate what is relevant to evaluate, how, where and when. There are important reasons for that. First of all, the innovative nature of the technologies and scenarios call for team work, exchange of ideas of what is important for success in pedagogical terms. Second, school teachers know the school reality, the constraints and opportunities. From this point of view, evaluation needs to be embedded within the design process from the very beginning. The evaluation experts have played a role of making the evaluation process sound and consistent with the project goals.

In the analysis we concentrated on the pedagogical evaluation of the scenarios and the way they are linked (enhanced or limited) to the platform features. Five case studies were analysed. Each case has its own pedagogical approach using game-based learning: participatory simulations, narrative learning and enquiry-based learning. Learning strategies as role-playing and collaborative learning are also part of the usage scenarios.

Evaluation Design

From the evaluation point of view, COLLAGE project as a whole was considered as a case study. Following Yin (1993), the approach explored a range of 'exemplars' of application of the COLLAGE platform (the scenarios) by triangulating data from different sources and from the perspective of different stakeholders. The evaluation approach was based on qualitative data analysis, while data was drawn from primary sources, using instruments such as questionnaires, focus groups discussions, observation and interviews. Direct observations implied engagement with participants, for example following up the trials with the students and teachers, or getting learners to 'think aloud' during the trials. The evaluation procedures revolved around the follow-up of the game-based learning scenarios throughout the project's implementation in real learning situations.

The evaluation took place in three cycles, (Table 1). Different phases and evaluation activities during the lifetime of the project were planned. A pilot test took place on a small scale at the beginning of the project, whereas trials started during the first and continued through the second year.

In this process, key stakeholders participating in the evaluation included the people whose support and cooperation was necessary for the project to succeed, as well as the people who were expected to use or to act on the evaluation findings. Involving the end users, from teachers and researchers to students and educational managers, as participants in the development process increases the likelihood that the final products will meet their needs and achieve project goals. At the beginning of an innovation, user needs and expectations generally cannot be well specified since they evolve as opportunities arise for trying out early versions of the system. Furthermore, users' understanding of what the technology can do and how it relates to changes in user work practices increases.

In the case of COLLAGE, key stakeholders were active participants in the evaluation. Students and teachers offered clear insights on how to improve the game strategies and the platform

Table 1. COLLAGE scenarios and evaluation cycles

	1st cycle: testing (initial test)	2nd cycle: pilot phase (co-design with teachers)	3rd cycle: validation (co-design with students)
Greece	Knossos	- Ancient Agora / Tholos 1 - Fodele	Ancient Agora / Tholos 2
Austria	Carnuntum	Carnuntum 2	Mozart scenario

features, and provided ideas for new game scenarios.

Evaluation Parameters and Instruments

The teachers participated in setting the evaluation goals from the very beginning. They started participating in a survey on the pedagogical framework in order to set out the evaluation parameters. These parameters included issues such as interactions (nature of feedback), communication processes, roles of learning actors, motivation, team work, learning outcomes, and assessment. In a second stage, in a participatory exercise with the teachers, the parameters were refined. Here we have the most relevant ones related to not only curriculum oriented learning aspects, but implicit learning aspects (Table 2).

Data on demographics, experience with mobile devices, ownership of mobile devices, among other factors, were also gathered. Then, the evaluation took into consideration key aspects as: a) Technological background and usability; b) Attitudes and motivation; c) Learning outcomes; d) game-based scenarios; e) team work; f) organisational aspects.

With these target groups in mind, the evaluation instruments were developed. The instruments used with teachers and students were questionnaires (disseminated in printed and/or electronic version), interviews, focus groups with teachers (as scenario developers), and a key one, field observations of each implementation.

SUMMARY OF EVALUATION RESULTS

The data shows the potential of the mobile learning platform and of the selected learning scenarios and strategies. There were a few concerns and recommendations to be given at different levels and various aspects. Here we present, from a qualitative approach, some of the most interesting data according to the users, secondary school students and teachers.

Student Feedback

Data was gathered from a sample of thirty-five students from two different countries that were directly involved in the learning scenarios. Before doing the site visits and play the game, they were trained in using the PDAs and the COLLAGE platform by the teachers, something that was evaluated as very clear and positive.

Those student who participated during the three project' phases demonstrated an evolution in their understanding of the COLLAGE platform

Table 2. Evaluation parameters to take into account during the project

Evaluation parameters
- Match between the curriculum and the learning objectives - Learning outcomes, expected and unexpected - Assessment of learning - Teachers and students´ attitudes - Links between the outdoors and the classroom activities - Game storytelling transparency - Level of interactions, students-students and students-teachers - Team work and team size - New roles of teachers and students - Attitudes towards mobile technologies - Motivational aspects - Organizational requirements - Usability aspects - Socio-cultural differences and accessibility gaps

and, more interestingly, in their ability to design new learning paths and game strategies. They were willing to improve the experiment suggesting changes or creating their own scenarios and questions. Students used correctly the previous information given to them in the classroom and understood well the game dynamics from the beginning.

According to almost all the students, learning in the mobile learning context was motivating or very motivating; all found the "on location" aspect of learning a very productive experience that helped the students to learn in a different way. Having access to other resources, both online and on paper, other than school text books, was also considered very positive. They felt that doing the COLLAGE activities helped them to better understand the subject contents. However, they asked for a better integration of the mobile learning activities into their regular classroom activities before and after the site visits.

As for the specific mobile games design and mechanisms, one third of the students reported that too many questions requested the same type of actions (answering, uploading photo, adding comment). Some other concerns were also mentioned, for instance the lack of feedback from the COLLAGE platform immediately after they responded to a question or did an activity.

For more than two third of the students, the difficulty level of the game was average and generally they didn't have major problems in answering the questions and doing the activities in their teams. However, they mentioned that some game questions were much easier than others.

The level of collaboration among the students in the teams was high in order to complete the assignment. The teams in a pragmatic approach divided up the responsibilities among them, since the aim was to complete the game by getting the highest score: the most knowledgeable in using the PDAs was in charge of exchanging with the COLLAGE platform. However, students claimed to find ways to all team members been able to interact with the platform, and not only one per team.

To complete the overview, here we have some comments of the students about their perceptions after participating in the projects:

I liked it very much because it was much more fun than the normal lesson. It is a nice alternative.

It was really interesting to learn in a different way. I really enjoyed interactive learning, taking photos and writing comments. It would be better if there were more learning paths. But anyway, I liked it and I think it is a good change for the students.

Generally it was an interesting experience. We need more time to find the responses to some of the questions posed in the PDA. It was fun to design the questions with our fellow students.

I liked the experience. It shows that we can do things with computers and not depend only on the schoolbook. When we were asked to write new questions we had a lot of material that we could use. However, we needed more time to elaborate on this material.

It was a perfect way to study and get to know your own hometown in a different way. And of course in fresh-air! It was fun to be outside the classroom and play a game that is related to school work.

I loved it! It was superb! Great to see and learn how to use a PDA. But the platform could be made for simpler mobile devices as well.

I liked the fact that we could make our own questions, but it was difficult to think of an interesting scenario that could be related to the questions.

Teacher Feedback

Ten teachers participated in the evaluation from three secondary schools. For them, the whole experiment helped them to organize their learning contents in a better way than the traditional classroom methods. Moreover, the students' learning outcomes from the experiment were more complete in the experiment than in the typical classroom lesson.

Comparing the COLLAGE experiment and the traditional teaching methods, for all the teachers the project made a positive difference in the level of interest and motivation shown by the students.

The assessment of learning was mostly formative. As the students were authoring the questions, suggestions were given to them for making the questions better. In the end, all the questions were assessed by the student peers of the other participating groups. If the questions and activities were fairly easily answered and done, it was because all students were more knowledgeable about the subject.

One interesting result that occurred as the games proceeded was that the teachers reported soon ways to improve the games. As the games were initially designed, there was no immediate feedback on the questions provided by the COLLAGE platform. Since this is an important condition for learning, an effective feedback mechanism needs to be considered in the design of the games. Also, there should be continuous access to scores by the teams, not only when the game ends. In respect to the contents, teachers reported avoiding very easy questions/answers, or easy quizzes, because they would make the game less interesting.

Teachers found little collaboration in the games and suggested embedding, formal collaboration mechanisms within them. They also suggested more interaction among the teachers' and the students' teams; for example, sending teacher-student SMS if they got lost in the field, or needed to get more instructions. The size of the teams, four to five students, hindered communication and use of the mobile devices, since each team had only one PDA for doing the learning paths..

After their experience in COLLAGE, the schools were, overall, very positive towards adopting this kind of activities in the mainstream school curriculum. However, the they foresaw certain difficulties concerning such integration: a) teachers' hesitation to try it, since most teachers are conservative; b) time constraints, since the scenarios need a time schedule which is not allowed by the regular curriculum (some teachers had to borrow time from other courses); c) nowadays the equipment necessary is rather expensive for schools, although it will be eventually more accessible.

To complete the overview, here we have some comments made by the teachers in the final evaluation interview:

I am very happy to participate in this project and from the first minute until now I have enjoyed it. The project could be applied in other subjects. It is very important to mention that the students of our school that weren't selected to participate were angry and they were asking us why we chose only the students from the humanities and not the students from sciences.

Having access to other resources, both on line and on paper, other than school text book, was very positive for me. At the same time, though, it needs a lot of time in order to integrate extracurricular material. For authoring games, students need more time. In the last year of secondary education, projects like this cannot be done, because students have to dedicate all of their time to studying for university entrance exams.

Definitely the school can afford some PDA devices for the students. But for sure it is very difficult to afford 25-30 PDAs for a whole class. It is very expensive. Five devices for every 25 students could be possible to buy and maintain.

It was nice to get outside the classroom! The students seemed to enjoy it and I had a chance to encourage them to learn and use mobile phones for it!

I think the experiment was very successful, as both students and teachers learned a lot about this new technology and improved their skills in using mobile communication devices. Students perhaps got an idea about everyday life in an ancient Roman town when they imagined the historical characters in the learning paths and the functions the ruins once had.

Platform

In general, the COLLAGE platform worked well, with very few failures. The affordances of the technology, which developed over the duration of the project, were a variable. The project started by developing multiple-choice questions to be asked at the location and gradually developed more two-way communication and GPS enabled activity. Similarly, as teachers became more confident in the use of the technology there was a gradual shift from the simple structures about direct recall questions based in location to greater amounts of problem solving and student generated games.

Some obstacles appeared during the implementation in the sites. Teachers reported that some of the mobiles phones used didn't have the necessary WAP-platform. Also, poor Internet connection in the sites interrupted the game dynamics several times.

Not all the features of the platform were used, or were barely used, such as the SMS capabilities, for the following reasons: a) they were difficult to implement within the game; b) they were not useful within the context of the given scenario; c) they were not fully available when needed. A more effective use could be achieved if more training were provided on the handling of the technologies concerned. This would enable the users to get a better idea about all the functionalities and make navigation easier.

Listed below are the most significant constraints identified during the experiments:

- Problem with the COLLAGE Platform: after a collapse of the server, the teams lost the points they had gained in the game, and had to start again from the beginning.
- There were some problems concerning the PDAs; for instance, making and uploading photos, changing the size of the data, and limited visibility of the PDA screen in the field.
- Not everybody had the opportunity to use the PDA (there was only one PDA per team).
- Students with no expertise in using a PDA were afraid to use it (or even to damage it).

Finally, some suggestions were made with respect the improvement of the COLLAGE interface, such as a simpler user interface with the possibility to use different fonts or colours.

FUTURE RESEARCH DIRECTIONS

In COLLAGE, as a research and implementation project, the evolution of the platform system was complex, especially at the point of implementing new features. From the experience gained, some lines of research are envisioned for the future. Here are some remarks for further developments:

- Although the game approach showed capacity for motivation and engagement (creating of different learning paths, allowing role playing, etc.), it needs more sophistication at the time of creating the learning paths, breaking the linearity of question-answer-activity approach. A future challenge is to adapt the platform features for designing non-linear games according to identified COLLAGE models. Then, the platform would need to include easy ways to deal with the different types of games, such as templates for designing other more complex game-based designs defined in COLLAGE.

- Web 2.0 open source applications are becoming part of the school culture. It would be advisable to integrate these applications within the COLLAGE platform, for example, instant messaging embedded in the interface. The same can be said about the increasingly popular location-based applications (interactive maps, excursion paths, etc.). The integration of these applications within the COLLAGE platform would make it more attractive to students and teachers.
- In order to improve transferability and validation of in the field mobile learning games, more experiments are needed, especially in knowledge areas other than history and archaeology. The challenge is to design new game strategies building new narratives, with storylines and back-up stories for a wide variety of school subject areas.
- The COLLAGE technological environment is still complex to programme, difficult to manage, and lacks standardisation. In order to appeal to mainstream education, an approach would be to develop software systems to build learning scenarios that are both content and context independent. These systems should be easy for teachers to use in building their own scenarios. A good step has been the first preliminary studies for integrating the COLLAGE platform into a leaning management system (Moodle).

CONCLUSION

COLLAGE has been one of the ground-breaking school projects using sophisticated technologies for innovative learning tasks, adding to the successes that have been reported in other mobile game and location-based learning school projects (Swan et al., 2005; Schwabe et al., 2005b; Raessens, 2007). The activities required a degree of relatively unsupervised movement of students in public spaces, which prove to be easily achieved with secondary schools students. This cannot be accomplished with primary age students. The game approach, however, could be easily adapted to higher education settings.

Following, we would like to reflect on some aspects of the project as a whole and to look to the future of game-based mobile learning.

First of all, it is clear that the mobile technology affects the pedagogy and vice versa. The system platforms, the mobile devices, while allowing new ways for motivating and engaging students and teachers, proved to be complex and sometimes problematic in some aspects. In this endeavour, stronger collaboration between technological and pedagogical developers as well as final users could contribute to more coherent approaches.

Engagement

The project achieved most of its goals, opening the door to new learning strategies using mobile technologies, mainly PDAs and cellular phones. The level of engagement of all actors was very high, especially in those scenarios that were evolving in time to the point of including students in both the design of new ones and the improvement of the ones tested in early stages. Teachers were enthusiastic about using the system in situations in which learning takes place outside the classroom. The same can be said about students who were always very keen on "learning mobile", outside the school, and using mobile technologies in the different scenarios. Team size, especially when using only one device per team, should be reconsidered, making smaller teams, in the line suggested by Schwabe et al. (2005b), so it will be easier for all to use the COLLAGE platform.

Games

A positive aspect of COLLAGE has been the evolution of the project scenarios in each of the participating sites, especially in Agora/Tholos and Carnuntum. For instance, the Carnuntum scenario first designed a path, and in the end three more were implemented, the last one with the help of the students. Furthermore, students became authors in designing a totally new game (Mozart), demonstrating the possibilities of the COLLAGE platform and interface. The new scenarios included new storylines and back-stories, fundamental element for making the games more attractive (Juul, 2005; Hug, 2005).

The game structure implemented was successful, as demonstrated during the third phase, in helping the teachers to create engaging learning activities adapted to the site. Teachers had the opportunity to improve the game strategies according to mostly two different leaning approaches: enquiry-based learning (Fodele) and narrative-based learning (the others). Strategies such as role-playing (Carnuntum, Mozart, Agora/Tholos) and collaborative learning (in all of them), were successfully embedded within the scenarios.

The level of difficulty of the questions and activities is an important design factor since it very much influences motivation, both positively and negatively; for instance, if simple questions or activities dominate the game, the students lose interest, and the same happens if they are all difficult. The game challenges need to be both real and complex, as pointed out in other mobile game projects (Facer et al., 2004, p. 408; Schwabe et al., 2005b, p. 204).

Scenario Co-Design

Teachers in this project, who co-created the scenarios, discovered the need to look at content from new perspectives. Students found that the scenarios done or designed by them were a creative and effective way to learn. This is an example of constructivist learning that worked well in technology-enhanced learning scenarios.

For re-designing a learning path or creating new scenarios, students and teachers need also to fully understand both the game strategy used and all the platform features. A dialog between the software developers and the users could resolve these kinds of problems.

Although a pedagogical and technical handbook for using the system was published as the COLLAGE implementation handbook it was recognised that, for taking full advantage of the possibilities of the platform, specific training is needed, particularly for users as designers.

Despite these challenges, the project clearly demonstrated its pedagogical value and potential for school innovation. In each of the sites the mobile learning scenarios gave the students the opportunity to see the history lesson or the biology lesson from a different perspective.

Finally, we can conclude that the mobile learning technologies have significant potential, as demonstrated by the project COLLAGE. It is clear that, as mobile technologies, which are already a part of the student culture, continue to evolve throughout society, there will be other successful mobile learning projects devoted to school education, breaking the conservative environment of the educational structures. We have seen that new learning approaches can be implemented in location-based scenarios, and there has been enough success in this project to warrant future experimentation and, eventually, mobile learning innovation take-up in mainstream schools.

ACKNOWLEDGMENT

The COLLAGE research work was partially financed from the European Commission in the framework of the Life Long Learning programme (Contract Number: 2005-3873 eLearning).

REFERENCES

Anand, P. (2008, June 18-21). Constructivist-based location aware mobile learning activity. *Proceedings of the Emerging Technologies Conference*, University of Wollongong.

Anderson, J., & McCormick, R. (2005). *Ten pedagogic principles for e-learning. INSIGHT–Observatory for new technologies in education.* Retrieved on September 2, 2008, from http://insight.eun.org/ww/en/pub/insight/thematic_dossiers/articles/quality_criteria/equality2.htm

Brooke, J. (1996). SUS-a quick and dirty usability scale. In P. W. Jordan, B. Thomas, B. A. Weerdmeester & I. McLelland (Eds.), *Usability evaluation in industry* (pp. 189-194). London: Taylor and Francis.

Colella, V. (2000). Participatory simulations: Building collaborative understanding through immersive dynamic modeling. *Journal of the Learning Sciences*, *9*(4), 471–500. doi:10.1207/S15327809JLS0904_4

Cullen, J., & Kelleher, J. (Eds.). (1995). *Evaluation guidelines handbook for learning technology innovation*. London: The Tavistock Institute.

de Freitas, S., & Oliver, M. (2006). How can exploratory learning with games and simulations within the curriculum be most effectively evaluated? *Computers & Education*, *46*, 249–264. doi:10.1016/j.compedu.2005.11.007

Facer, K., Joiner, R., Stanton, D., Reid, J., Hull, R., & Kirk, D. (2004). Savannah: Mobile Gaming and Learning? *Journal of Computer Assisted Learning*, *20*, 399–409. doi:10.1111/j.1365-2729.2004.00105.x

Facer, K., Joiner, R., Stanton, D., Reid, J., Hull, R., & Kirk, D. S. (2004). Savannah: Mobile learning and gaming? *Journal of Computer Assisted Learning*, *20*, 399–409. doi:10.1111/j.1365-2729.2004.00105.x

Gee, J. P. (2005). Learning by design: Good video games as learning machines. *E-Learning*, *2*(1), 5–16. doi:10.2304/elea.2005.2.1.5

Hug, T. (2005, May 6-8). *Microlearning and narration.* Paper presented at the Fourth Media in Transition Conference, MIT, Cambridge, MA. Retrieved on September 10, 2008, from http://web.mit.edu/comm-forum/mit4/papers/hug.pdf

Huizenga, J., Admiraal, W., Akkerman, S., & Dam, G. (2007, October). Learning history by playing a mobile city game. In D. Remenyi (Ed.), *Proceedings of the 1st European Conference on Game-Based Learning (ECGBL)* (pp. 127–134), University of Paisley, Paisley, Scotland. Reading, UK: Academic Conferences Limited.

Johnson, S. (2007). A framework for mobile context-aware applications. *BT Technology Journal*, *25*(2), 106–111. doi:10.1007/s10550-007-0033-5

Jones, A., Scanlon, E., Tosunoglu, C., Morris, E., Ross, S., Butcher, P., & Greenberg, J. (1999). Contexts for evaluating educational software. *Interacting with Computers*, *11*(5), 499–516. doi:10.1016/S0953-5438(98)00064-2

Juul, J. (2005). Games telling stories? In J. Raessens & J. Goldstein (Eds), *Handbook of computer game studies* (pp. 219–226). Cambridge, MA: The MIT Press.

McManus, T. (2002). *Mobile what? The educational potential of mobile technologies.* World Conference on E-Learning in Corporate, Government, Healthcare, and Higher Education 2002, Montreal, Canada, AACE.

Motiwalla, L. (2007). Mobile learning: A framework and evaluation. *Computers & Education, 49*(3), 581–596. doi:10.1016/j.compedu.2005.10.011

Naismith, L., Lonsdale, P., Vavoula, G., & Sharples, M. (2004). *Literature review in mobile technologies and learning.* NESTA Futurelab. Retrieved on September 10, 2008, from http://www.futurelab.org.uk/resources/documents/lit_reviews/Mobile_Review.pdf

Nielsen, J. (1994). Heuristic evaluation. In J. Nielsen & R. L. Mack (Eds.), *Usability inspection methods.* New York: John Wiley & Sons.

Owen, M. (2008). From individual learning to collaborative learning-location, fun, and games: Place, context, and identity in mobile learning. In H. Riu & D. Parsons (Eds.), *Innovative mobile learning: Technique and technologies.* Hershey, PA: Information Science Reference.

Prensky, M. (2003). Digital game-based learning. *ACM Computers in Entertainment, 1*(1), 1–4. doi:10.1145/950566.950567

Raessens, J. (2007). Playing history: Reflections on mobile and location-based learning. In T. Hug (Ed.), *Didactics of microlearning. Concepts, discourses, and examples* (pp. 200-217). Münster: Waxmann.

Roschelle, J. (2003). Unlocking the learning value of wireless mobile devices. *Journal of Computer Assisted Learning, 19*(3), 260–272. doi:10.1046/j.0266-4909.2003.00028.x

Schwabe, G., & Göth, C. (2005a). Mobile learning with a mobile game: Design and motivational effects. *Journal of Computer Assisted Learning, 21,* 2004–2016. doi:10.1111/j.1365-2729.2005.00128.x

Schwabe, G., Göth, C., & Frohberg, D. (2005b). Does team size matter in mobile learning? *Proceedings of the International Conference on Mobile Business (ICMB'05),* July 11-13, 2005, Sydney Australia.

Shaffer, D. W. (2006). Epistemic frames for epistemic games. *Computers & Education, 46,* 223–234. doi:10.1016/j.compedu.2005.11.003

Swan, K., Hooft, M., Kratkoski, A., & Hunger, D. (2005). Uses and effects of mobile computing devices in K-8 classrooms. *Journal of Research on Technology in Education, 38*(1), 99.

Syvänen, A., & Nokelainen, P. (2004). Evaluation of the technical and pedagogical mobile usability. In Murelli, et al. (Eds.), *Proceedings of the 3rd International Conference on Mobile Learning (MLEARN 2004)* (pp. 191-195). Rome, Italy: LSDA.

Taylor, J. (2003, May 19-20). A task-centred approach to evaluating a mobile learning environment for pedagogical soundness. *Proceedings of the 2nd International Conference on Mobile Learning (MLEARN2003),* London.

Taylor, J. (2007). Evaluating mobile learning. What are appropriate methods for evaluating learning in mobile environments? In M. Sharples (Ed.), *Big issues in mobile learning: Report of a workshop by the kaleidoscope network of excellence mobile learning initiative.* LSRI, University of Nottingham. Retrieved on September 10, 2008, from http://www.lsri.nottingham.ac.uk/msh/Papers/BIG_ISSUES_REPORT_PUBLISHED.pdf

Traxler, J., & Kukulska-Hulme, A. (2005, October 25-28). Evaluating mobile learning: Reflections on current practice. *Proceedings of MLEARN 2005*, Cape Town, South Africa.

Vavoula, G., & McAndrew, P. (2005). *Pedagogical methodologies and paradigms. A study of mobile learning practices. Mobilearn Project.* Retrieved on September 10, 2008, from http://www.mobilearn.org/download/results/public_deliverables/MOBIlearn_D4.4_Final.pdf

Wang, Y. K. (2004). Context awareness and adaptation in mobile learning. *Proceedings of the 2nd IEEE International Workshop on Wireless and Mobile Technologies (WMTE'04)* (pp. 154-158).

Yin, R. K. (1993). Advancing rigorous methodologies: A review of towards rigor in reviews of multivocal literatures. *Review of Educational Research, 61*(3).

Chapter 14
Technical Evaluation of Wireless Communications in a Mobile Learning Architecture

Javier Carmona-Murillo
University of Extremadura, Spain

Jaime Galán-Jiménez
University of Extremadura, Spain

José-Luis González-Sánchez
University of Extremadura, Spain

ABSTRACT

Due to the high growth of mobile networks and portable devices, learning process is evolving from desktop computer to mobile devices. In this sense, technologies and services that support this change are also evolving. The appearance of portable devices has made users to take part in this process from anywhere. On the other hand, architectures used in a mobile learning environment are designed to offer users the ability of participate in learning activities from its embedded devices. Campus Ubicuo is a mobile architecture over which learning services can be developed. The successful of any mobile learning platform fundamentally depends on the quality in learning services and also in the good operation of wireless technologies. In this chapter, we focus on this second aspect. We have evaluated the behaviour of wireless technologies in a mobile learning architecture when different services are offered through diverse networks.

INTRODUCTION

Mobile learning is defined as the type of learning characterized by the usage of mobile communications technologies. M-learning also takes advantage of portable devices such as mobile phones, laptops or PDAs. The development of mobile learning is not intended to replace the traditional classroom learning, but to enhance the value of wireless communications networks (Yu-Liang, 2005). Mobile learning scope is not only focused on learning centers. In fact, over the last years, mobile learning popularity has grown significantly and many projects about this subject have been developed in

DOI: 10.4018/978-1-60566-882-6.ch014

schools, workplaces, hospitals, museums, cities and rural areas.

We have designed an architecture called Campus Ubicuo (Carmona-Murillo, 2007) and several telematic applications to provide mobility in a university campus environment which is being adapted to other organizations with mobility needs. In fact, starting from Campus Ubicuo architecture, we are working in two projects focused on offer mobility services in a hospital and in a city for tourist industry. These projects are called MESEAS (Meseas, 2008) and Libre Movicuidad (Gitaca, 2008) respectively.

In Campus Ubicuo, several technologies are involved, such as GSM (Global System for Mobile communications), GPRS (General Packet Radio Service), UMTS (Universal Mobile Telecommunications System), Bluetooth, Wi-Fi; portable devices such as laptops, mobile phones and PDAs; and some applications developed to offer mobility and learning services to the users.

Usually, when mobile learning architectures are evaluated, the model is analyzed from a learning process point of view. Obviously, this is a main aspect, however there is another point of view based on mobile technologies. We are talking about a mobility platform over which offer m-learning services, and the most important feature in the mobile environment is mobility itself. That is why in this chapter we show a performance evaluation of wireless communication in Campus Ubicuo. We have done this evaluation from two points of view: Local wireless networks such as Bluetooth or Wi-Fi, and global mobility communications such as GSM, GPRS or UMTS.

If mobile learning platforms are used by lots of users in a localized area, technologies that use the ISM (Industrial, Scientific and Medical) bands of the electromagnetic spectrum are exposed to interferences that can diminish the quality of the communication up to suspend the connection (Farpoint Group, 2006; Fairpoint Group, 2003). For that reason, it is important for a m-learning administrator to have some information about the state of the wireless connections. With the analytical study presented in this chapter, an administrator has all the information needed to avoid, or at least, to know the problems caused by this situation.

On the other hand, global mobile communications are used a lot in multimedia communications like virtual classes or other similar advanced services. We have done an evaluation of collaborative communications in next generation mobile networks. This will show a real scene useful to those developers who need to know the capacity of the network over which the services will be deployed.

The rest of the chapter is organized as follows. First, a brief explanation of theoretical content related to this chapter is given in the background section. Then, the main section is focused on the analytical study and performance evaluation of the proposed mobile learning architecture. Finally the main conclusions of this work are exposed.

BACKGROUND

In this section, we present important topics necessaries to understand the rest of the chapter. First of all, we introduce multimedia communications applied to mobile learning platforms and the environment in which they work. After this, it is shown a brief description about the physical knowledge necessary to understand the analytical study carried out to evaluate the technical performance of the mobile learning architecture. In this way, if the technical performance has a high level, the educational performance of the platform would be analyzed.

Multimedia Communications

In multimedia communications we must look for different quality parameters. With these parameters we can make an evaluation of the multimedia communication. These parameters are:

- **Throughput:** The average rate of successful message delivery.
- **Delay:** This is the round trip time of a packet in the Internet usually introduced by the routers of the backbone.
- **Jitter:** The variation in delay between packets is known as jitter and can seriously affect the quality of streaming audio and/or video.
- **Reliability:** This is the amount of packet loss in a network.

Moreover, multimedia traffic has special features that must be considered. Next, these ones are briefly explained.

Firstly, the throughput in a multimedia communication can be variable or constant. Furthermore, there is a hard dependence with respect to the timestamp of multimedia content and to the network. For example, if a videoconference has any delay, both video and audio flow can be unsynchronized and make the communication unfeasible. Finally, the multimedia flow is symmetric, so it usually needs the same throughput in server and receiver hosts.

The Electromagnetic Spectrum

The electromagnetic spectrum classifies the existing waves according to their frequencies and wavelength magnitude. It is composed of different ranges: radio waves, with the highest wavelength, microwaves, infrared rays, visible light, ultraviolet rays, and the lowest wavelength electromagnetic waves: the X and gamma rays. Furthermore, it is defined as the amount of electromagnetic radiation that a particular substance can emit or absorb. This radiation can be used to identify a substance in a similar way to a digital track. The wavelength magnitude of a particular substance is the inverse of the frequency value. So, when the wavelength is greater, the frequency will be minor and vice versa. The relation between both of them is expressed with the following mathematical formula:

Frequency (KHz) = 300,000 (km/s) / wave length (m)

Once the electromagnetic spectrum has been defined, Figure 1 represents the information about the frequency radio bands of the wireless technologies. For each wireless technology, we can see clearly the frequency bands where it operates and how the spectrum is shared by all the different wireless technologies. This helps the mobile learning system administrator to know where the possible interferences from each other are.

The main problem is located in the called ISM Bands, one of them is the 2.4 GHz band. Up to five wireless technologies can be operating at the same time using the same band. Moreover, other devices like microwave ovens, baby monitors, wireless video game controllers and medical devices can also use them.

ISM Bands

ISM bands are those internationally reserved and not intended for commercial use. These bands correspond with the 902-928 MHZ, 2,400-2,483.5 and 5,725-5,850 frequency ranges; they were defined in the article number five of the Regulations Radio by the ITU, specifically in points 5.138 and 5.150. The use of these ranges is opened to everyone who wants to use them. According to the regulations that limit the transmitted power levels, no governmental license is required in order to freely use them. Wi-Fi technology (Wi-Fi Alliance, 2008), Bluetooth (The Official Bluetooth Technology Info Site, 2008), WiBree, ZigBee and HomeRF are examples of technologies that use these unlicensed bands.

Other devices are located in the same bands like the aforementioned medical devices, microwave ovens, garage door openers, baby monitors or cordless telephones in the U.S.A. and South America.

Figure 1. Frequency overlap scheme

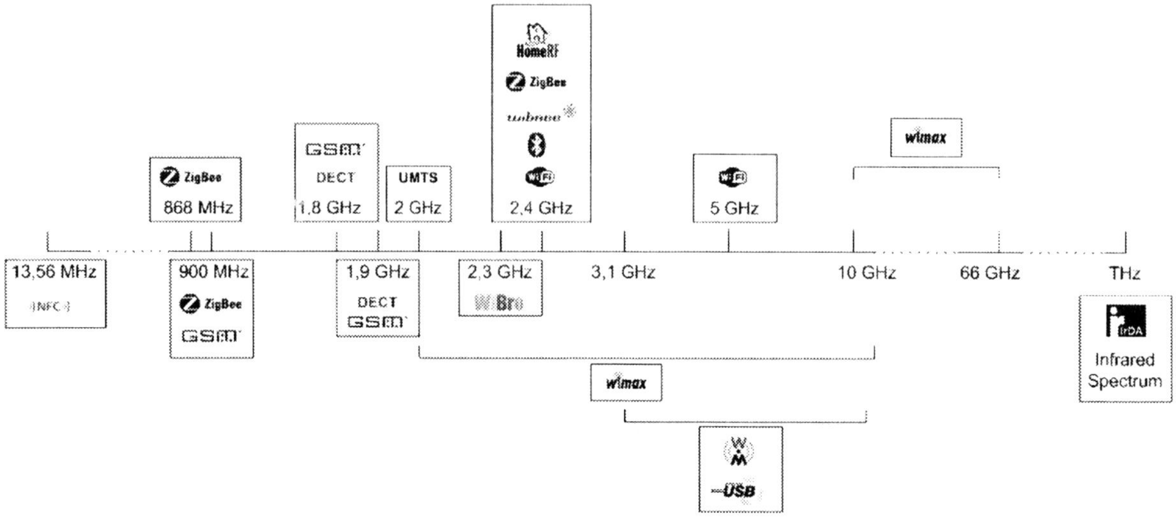

Spread Spectrum

The spread spectrum is a data transmission method where the main information is distributed over a larger bandwidth than the conventional one. It can use less power level and a high interference protection. This implies that throughput can be improved. Thus, the information is not transmitted using only a frequency or channel; it uses the entire frequency band available to do it, in such a way that the possibilities of using the same operation frequency among different devices that can be active at the same time are minimized. There are two variants of this method: *Frequency Hopping Spread Spectrum (FHSS)* and *Direct Sequence Spread Spectrum (DSSS)*.

Interferences

The term interference has different meanings, depending on the context where it is used:

- In communications and similar areas, interference is any process that alters, modifies or destroys a signal in the channel established between the emitter and the receiver.
- In ondulatory mechanics, it is the result of the superposition of two or more waves, thus, a new wave pattern is created.
- In electromagnetism, it is the disturbance caused by an electromagnetic radiation from an external source over any electrical circuit. A signal mixture among different systems can be generated and interrupt, degrade or limit the performance of a transmission. It is also known as *EMI (ElectroMagnetic Interference)* or *RFI (Radio Frequency Interference)*.

Waves Superposition Principle establishes that the ondulatory displacement magnitude in any midpoint is equal to the sum of every present wave displacement in that point. In this way, if two waves are not in phase, they will interfere with each other in a destructive way, resulting in a new wave with lower amplitude. In wireless technologies context, the interferences can happen if they use the same frequencies or the same area of the electromagnetic spectrum (channels). Furthermore, the existing materials in the environment in which wireless technologies are operating can also produce a high interference degree over the communication.

ANALYTICAL STUDY AND PERFORMANCE EVALUATION OF THE PROPOSED MOBILE LEARNING ARCHITECTURE

Proof Planning

Multimedia Technologies in Mobile Learning Environments

In this section we present a study about the performance of the designed mobile learning platform using multimedia communications.

In the platform that we propose in Campus Ubicuo project, we use a new multimedia application called VLinex. It can transmit video and audio to multiple clients using multicast (Graham & Zhang, 2005). This application has been developed in Java using an API called Java Media Framework (JMF) to handle multimedia content. It can communicate two multicast islands using a tunnel between them.

In that sense, the platform designed in addition to VLinex can provide collaborative communications for virtual classes or tele-working in heterogeneous networks, and it allows to the users to be connected to the platform all around the world.

Internet cannot transmit multicast flows because of the fact that the routers in the backbone are not prepared for this communications. Furthermore, the first router that processes the packets in the path of the communication will discard every multicast flow. This is called multicast island because the multicast flow cannot be sent to Internet.

In this scene, tunneling mechanism allows sending and receiving multicast flows between islands. In our proposal we have developed an end-to-end TCP (Transmission Control Protocol) tunnel. We have decided to implement these tunnels with TCP protocol because LANs (Local Area Network) usually are protected with firewalls that block UDP (User Datagram Protocol) traffic and they use several routing protocols like NAT (Network Address Translation), which uses private addresses. For this reason, the tunneling with UDP is very difficult without modifying the network structure or the rules implemented in the routers.

VLinEx needs an auxiliary application to connect with a UMTS network. For this reason, we have developed another application called Gnome-GPRS to the architecture. This application uses the mobile phone as a modem and it allows users to connect to the Internet using the mobile network infrastructure.

Gnome-GPRS simplifies the process, offering GNU/Linux users a mechanism to connect to the Internet using portable devices and mobile technologies. Furthermore, it can negotiate different parameters of Quality of Service (QoS) and offers information about the real status of the connection.

This is the architecture proposed to evaluate the performance of the mobile learning platform using multimedia content. The scenario of the study is shown in Figure 2. In all tests we have used a PC with GNU/Linux as a server of the session (multicast session and tunnel). The client (laptop) is connected to a mobile network or to a wired network using Gnome-GPRS or a fixed line respectively. This laptop is connected to the tunnel created by the server of the session and it generates a new multicast island.

With this method, all the problems mentioned are avoided because of the fact that the system developed returns the information needed to configure the tunnel. Once the transmission is finished, the tunnel is closed.

Deployment Scenario

The proposed architecture can be deployed in scenes like universities, hospitals or city councils, with a high amount of users sharing the same environment all at the same time, the same physical area, and, therefore, the same resources: the electromagnetic waves.

Figure 2. Diagram of the communication

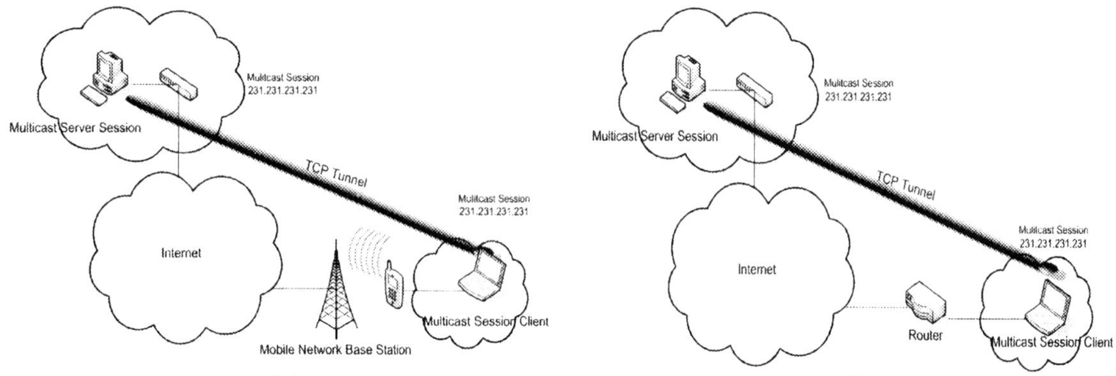

(a) *(b)*

The most used devices in this architecture are PDA terminals and mobile phones. Both of them have Bluetooth and Wi-Fi capabilities. We have carried out a study to know which kinds of effects are obtained by using so many devices in a closer environment full of electromagnetic signals. This way, the main goal of this section is to measure how the existing interferences are produced, under which circumstances, and what repercussions they have over the rest of the coexisting wireless devices and wireless technologies (Iwireless, 2008). This is a very important key point to the mobile learning platform network administrator.

Referring to hospitals, most of the devices which are used for medical treatment utilize the unlicensed ISM bands, created for this purpose. These bands are also used by wireless technologies like Bluetooth o Wi-Fi, needed to provide ubiquity to users of the mobile learning platform. Thus, several tests have been done with the aim to analyze the performance of these devices when they are all operating at the same time and in the same environment.

Due to we can't use these medical devices, we have done the performance analysis using several non-medical devices with similar features like the same frequency to emit and similar signal strength.

Test Bed

Technologies and devices used in tests are: Wi-Fi (802.11g), Bluetooth, microwave oven, mobile phone, Pocket PC, Bluetooth headsets, baby monitor, wireless video game controller and radio frequency jamming devices. Tests have been carried out using two different types of traffic: TCP traffic such as FTP (File Transfer Protocol) or HTTP (Hyper Text Transfer Protocol) downloads and UDP traffic.

The place where tests have been carried out is the Telematic Engineering lab at the Polytechnic School of Cáceres, at the University of Extremadura. We have measured the radio frequency environment in that location, detecting active devices, signal power, power level of the interfering signals, channel utilization, etc. This situation is the so-called *test environment* and it is used in all the tests carried out.

Apart from the access point we have in the laboratory, there are other active access points that belong to other nearby wireless networks. Furthermore, they will have to be considered when we propose the appropriate conclusions.

Tools and Wireshark Extensions Used in the Measurement Process

In order to analyze interferences among wireless technologies, the WildPackets OmniSpectrum Analyzer (WildPackets, 2008) has been used. It consists of hardware-based spectrum sensors and a GUI-based spectrum console application; together, these tools provide complete visibility of the radio frequency environment in which wireless networks technologies operate. The sensor card incorporates a transceiver, a Spectrum Analysis Engine (SAgE) and a CPU. It captures data from the external antenna and shows them after applying several algorithms aimed to summarize them. It analyzes data from the sensor card and provides a GUI-based view of network and radio frequency activity. Thus, network administrators can analyze different electromagnetic spectrum charts, active devices both at the current moment and historically, a summary of the used channels both in the 2.4 GHz and 5 GHz bands and, finally, options that allow locating the desired devices. This tool supports various bands for spectrum monitoring, as well as some other information.

Devices that can be classified by OmniSpectrum are the following ones:

- Wi-Fi Access Points and Wi-Fi Stations.
- A wide variety of Bluetooth devices.
- Cordless phones that operate in 2.4 and 5 GHz bands.
- Microwave Ovens.
- Generic TDD.
- Continuous transmitters (e.g., FM Phones, NTSC, etc.).
- Radio frequency jamming devices.
- 802.11 FH devices.

With the purpose to obtain real data about the performance variation in wireless networks when other devices interfere due to they are all operating in the same frequencies or channels, we have developed an extension to the Wireshark network protocol analyzer (Wireshark Network Protocol Analyzer, 2008).

Its possible uses are:

- Visualizing both, TCP and UDP throughput, and the possible retransmissions, in the same graph.
- Obtaining statistics of the captured data.
- Analyzing graphs by dividing them into intervals to compare different situations to know when and why a throughput decrease is produced.
- Storing data in a text file (from .pcap to .txt) in order to create charts using third-part applications.

The Wireshark software extension has two different ways of execution: one in real time and another after loading a previously saved trace file. In the latter, a new window has been developed to analyze the network performance decrease of both, TCP and UDP traffic (performance analysis window).

Next we explain those new windows developed to analyze the performance decrease in wireless networks.

Performance Window

It is a window divided into two areas as we can see in Figure 3 (a). The upper one has a three-in-one graph depending on the analyzed traffic: throughput TCP, throughput UDP and TCP retransmissions; the lower area contains a button panel (left), there is another area where chart axis can be modified (center), and lastly, numeric information (right).

In the button panel, one can press the "performance analysis window" button for both, TCP and UDP traffic, which will open a new window that is explained in the next paragraphs.

Performance Analysis Window

In this window, the chart can be divided at the most into five intervals by setting the end time

Figure 3. Performance windows developed for the Wireshark Network Protocol Analyzer

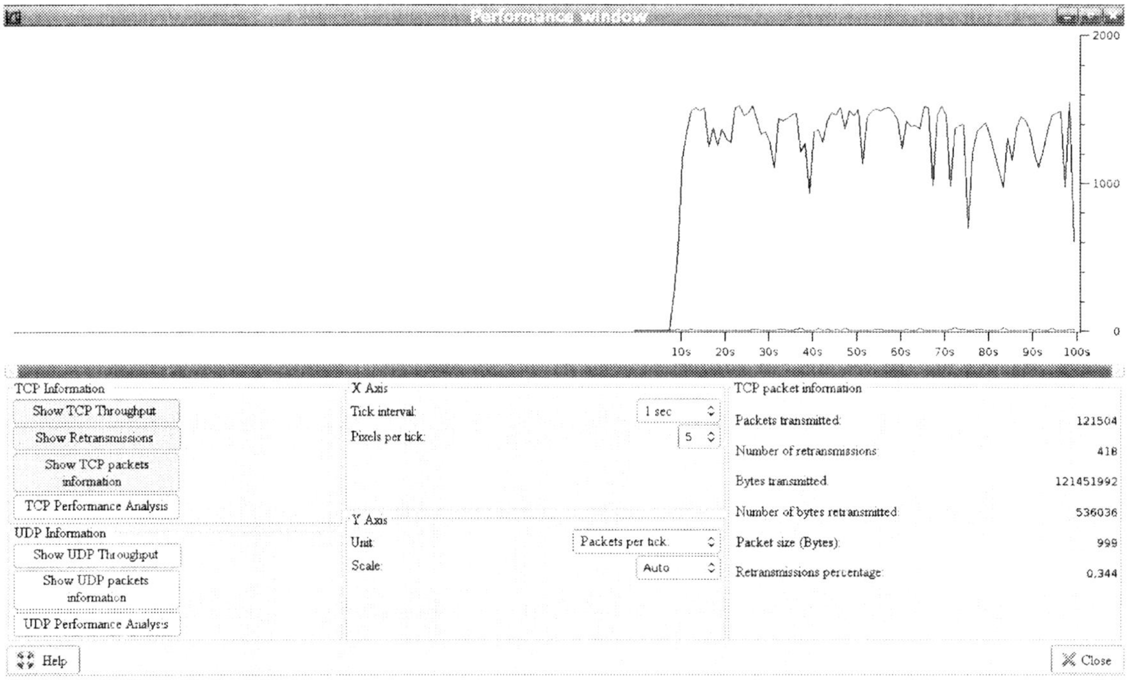

(a) Performance Window

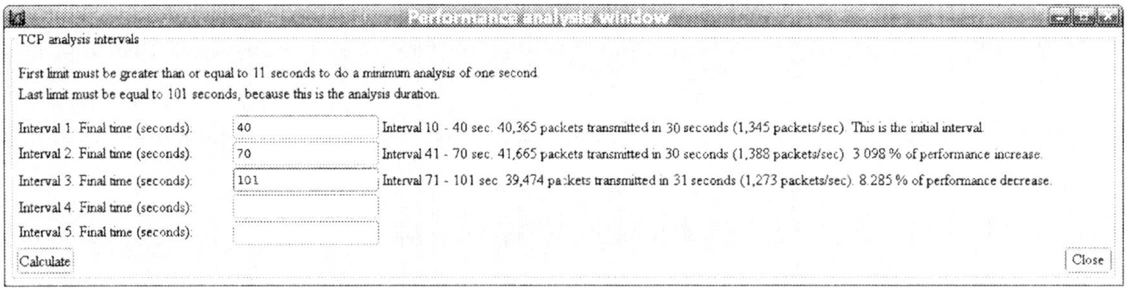

(b) Performance Analysis Window

for each one of them. This is shown in Figure 3 (b). The aim is to check if there has been a performance increase or decrease, by comparing each interval to the previous one. Thus, network administrators can know the reason about the performance increase or decrease, by analyzing the wireless devices that were active at every moment.

This way, we can see information about the interval time in seconds, the number of transmitted packets in that time and the percentage of performance increase or decrease respecting to the previous interval for each one of the ranges in which the chart has been divided.

Evaluation Results of the M-Learning Architecture Proposed

Evaluation of Campus Ubicuo in Multimedia Transmissions

In this section we present the results obtained from different test carried out conforming to the scenarios presented in the previous section.

Figure 4. Multicast stream in the multicast island (receiver side)

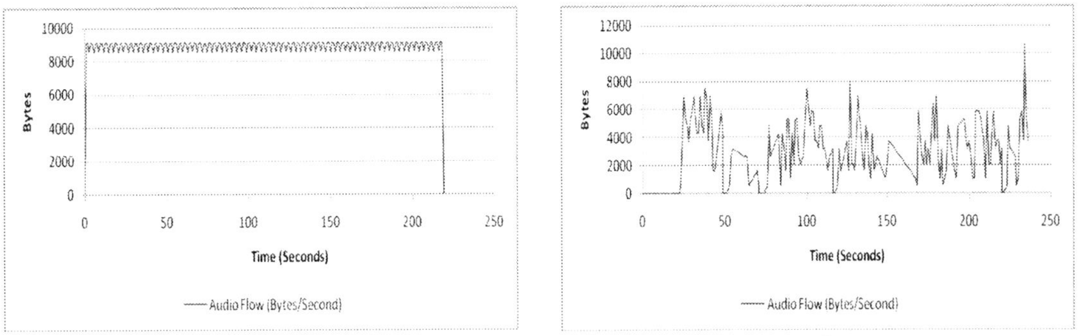

(a) *(b)*

The first test consists in an audio transmission. The data are obtained from a MP3 file and encoded in μLaw format to transmit the information.

The second test is a video transmission. The data are obtained from a WebCam and the latest test is a multimedia file transmission. The data are encoded in DIVX5 and MP3 and recoded in H.263 and μLaw (video and audio) when it is transmitted. These codec have been used due to they are included in the RTP (Real-Time Transport Protocol) with minimal control standard (Schulzrinne, Casner, Frederick & Jacobson, 2003; Schulzrinne, 1996).

The results obtained are compared with a transmission over a wired network as we can see in Figure 2 (b). There are two different Ethernet subnets. This implies that there are two multicast islands and a tunnel is necessary between them.

Audio Transmission

This is the first test; we compare the results in the audio transmission test using a mobile network (UMTS) versus the proof using a wired network. The multimedia content is an audio file coded in MP3 and it is transmitted in the scenario presented in Figure 2 (a and b).

The file is opened and recoded in μLaw by the server of the session. When the tunnel is established, the server of the session sends the information through the tunnel to the multicast island (receiver side).

Figure 4 (a) graphically shows the communication in the multicast island (receiver side). In this test, the server of the session transmits a constant bit rate stream. The information is packaged in RTP and sent to the network. We can also observe that the throughput is constant; the variation depends on the amount (a variation of one package) of packages received per second. This effect is caused by the delay introduced by the network.

So, the transmission is fluent in the multicast islands and the reproduction of the sound is clear without interruptions due to the delay in the reception of the packets. This is the ideal scenario. The test in the mobile network (Figure 2 (a)) will be compared with these results.

Figure 4 (b) shows the same transmission in the mobile network. We can observe that the packets are not received with a constant throughput and the network drops some packets of the stream. This situation can be observed in the figure because some maximums and minimums are produced in it. One example of this can be observed around the second 50, the throughput downs nearly to zero. A high packet loss ratio in the nodes of the network produces this effect.

In this case, we use the same modification to the Wireshark application explained in the pre-

Figure 5. Video results

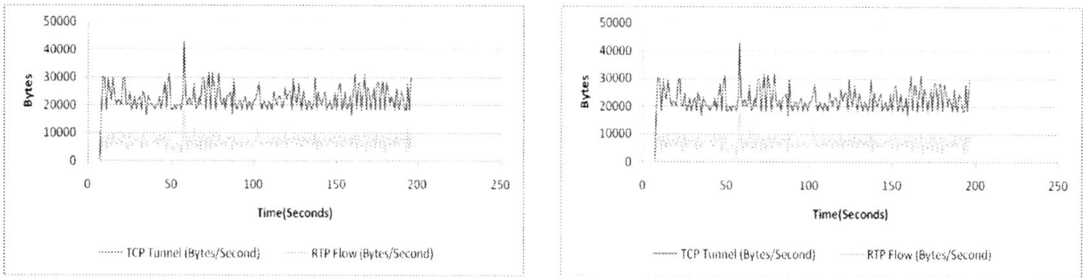

(a) *(b)*

vious section. We have obtained the packet loss percent in the network. This value is around the 5.2% of the overall packets transmitted through the tunnel. These packets are not received or they are received with a significant delay. This situation produces a discontinuous reproduction due to the packet loss.

Video Transmission in Real Time

This test transmits a video captured from a WebCam and encoded in the H.263 format. Figure 5 (a) shows the transmission through the TCP tunnel in the wired network.

We can observe that the throughput is not constant like the last test. The encoder codifies the video frames depending on the previous and subsequent frames of the video captured.

Furthermore, the information codified is related to the data that contains the frame itself (Ghanbari, 2003). If the frame is dark the amount of information to compress is lower than if the frame is rich in color.

The server of the session transmits 10,318 packets in 200 seconds. The average packet size is around 418 Bytes and the information transmitted is around 4.5MB.

There is no packet loss and the reproduction has not any failure. Furthermore, the temporal sequence is reconstructed in time. No frame is lost and the information can be reproduced without gaps.

The second function is represented in Figure 5 (a). It corresponds to the RTP stream in the multicast island (receiver side). All the devices connected to this island receive this stream. The information received is the same information that was transmitted through the tunnel. The throughput needed to transmit the information in the tunnel is greater due to the TCP headers. When the packet is translated into a UDP segment, the information to retransmit is lower.

In this test, the transmission showed in Figure 5 (a) is the reference model and we will compare it with the results obtained in the test using the UMTS network as we could see in Figure 2 (a).

Figure 5 (b) shows the results obtained in the test using the mobile network. The graphics obtained are similar to Figure 5 (a) but not identical. This test is a real time video transmission, and the content is not recorded previously. This implies that the codified images are different in the two tests (wired and mobile networks). Even so, the two graphics contained in Figure 5 (b) are similar each other.

In this test we are using a UMTS network (Figure 2 (a)), and the throughput of the channel is not the same as the throughput in the wired network. The UMTS network provides connection about 320 Kbps (40 KBps) and the stream generated by the application of videoconference does not exceed this throughput. This implies that

Figure 6. Resilience test

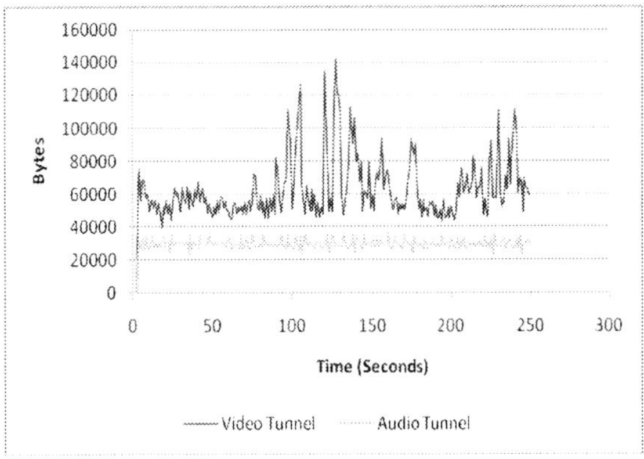

(a)

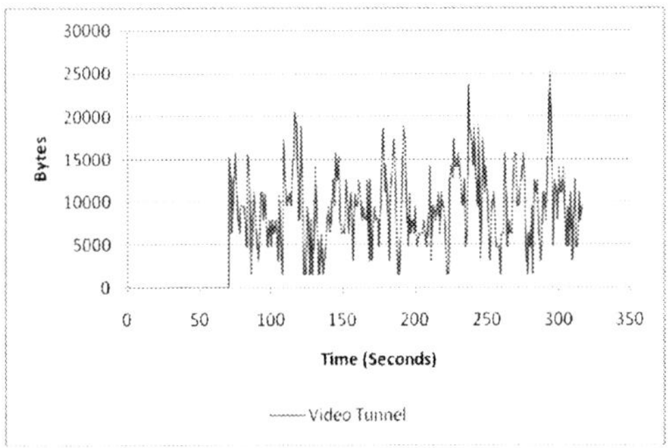

(b)

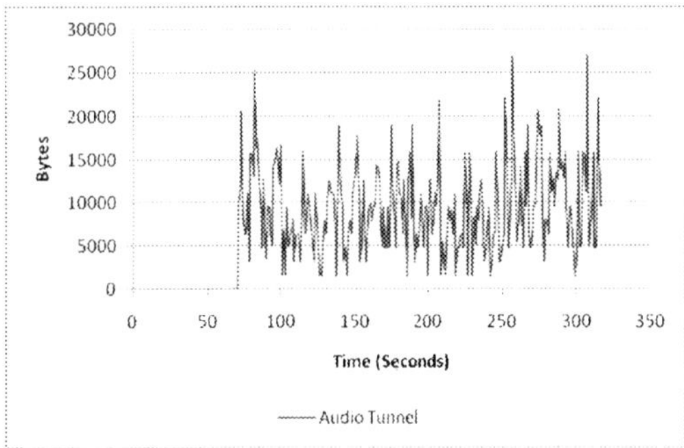

(c)

we can transmit video in real time using UMTS networks.

In the test, we transmit 4,380 packets in 165 seconds. The average packet size is around 843 Bytes and the information transmitted is around 3.7MB. In all tests, we are using the same protocols stack and the same codec. The expected results should be the same as the last test, but the obtained results are different. In the mobile network test, the average packet size is double than the wired network test.

The mobile network produces this effect to increase its performance. The packet decrease improves the performance of the network and the number of packets that have to be routed and processed in it. However, the mobile network loses around the 0.78% of the packets. The reproduction in the multicast island (receiver side) is discontinuous and the packet loss produces pixelation in the frames.

Resilience Test to the UMTS Network

With the results obtained in this test, we can know how the UMTS network reacts when the stream transmitted is three times greater than the throughput of the network.

In this test, we transmit a multimedia file encoded in DIVX5 and MP3; it is recoded in H.263 and μLaw when the stream is transmitted to the network.

Figure 6 (a) shows the results of the multimedia transmission through the tunnel in the wired network. In this test the video stream needs a bigger throughput than the audio stream. This is produced because of the multimedia file to encode and transmit is bigger and more complex.

The throughput used by the video stream is not constant as the previous test and many variations are produced by the information encoded. The audio stream is constant because of the payload of the RTP packet specifies this property. The bit rate of the flow is constant and the reproduction has not any failure. This will be our model and we are going to compare it with the results obtained in the test with the mobile network.

Figure 6 (b and c) shows the TCP tunnel in the mobile network. We can observe that the video (Figure 6 (b)) and the audio transmission are different from the results showed in Figure 6 (a).

Analyzing the video tunnel, we can observe that the throughput is near to 0 Bytes many times. This effect is produced by the packet loss in the tunnel. If we study analytically the stream, we obtain that the packet loss rate is around 6.6% of the packet transmitted.

We can observe in the audio tunnel that the problem is similar to the video tunnel. In this case, the function of the graphic should be constant, but there are many maximums and minimums that imply the packet loss. The loss rate is about 6.2% of the transmitted packets. This has a negative influence on the stream reconstructed at the multicast island (receiver side). These results were expected because we are transmitting a multimedia content that needs three times the throughput that the UMTS network can provide.

The average packet loss ratio is about 6.6% of the packets transmitted. The throughput necessary to transmit the multimedia file is about 90 KBps and the throughput provided by the mobile network is 40MBps. Thus, the packet loss is comprehensible and expected in this test.

Moreover, as we could see in the previous test, the mobile network merges the packets. The average packet size is about 444 Bytes in the wired test and in the mobile test is about 773 Bytes.

Summarizing all tests, due to this merging, the average packet size in the UMTS network is bigger than the same value in the wired network and the amount of packets in the mobile network is lower. This implies that the routing and processing packet cost is lower than the wired network.

The merging can benefit to some type of traffic like web or mail traffic (best-effort streams) that do not generate a big amount of packets. However, the multimedia streams are penalized by this technique because if a packet has been lost in the UMTS network, the server of the session has to retransmit two packets.

As a result, the communication performance decrease and the delay increase in the communication. When the stream is going to be reproduced, if the packets are received with delay, the frames or the audio cannot be reconstructed and this information cannot be reproduced. Thus these packets are going to be discarded in upper layers of the protocol stack.

When the RTP layer tries to rebuild the information received but some packets are missed or delayed, the multimedia content has to be discarded.

Finally, the packet delay produces gaps and pixelations in the images due to the error correction algorithms applied in the upper layers (RTP, multimedia codecs etc.).

Evaluation of the Effects among the Wireless Technologies Used in the Mobile Learning Architecture

Once we have explained the test environment in "Deployment scenario" section, we are going to describe the steps followed to carry out the test and analyze the impact of the wireless devices over the mobile learning platform.

Four types of tests have been done in this study from the laboratory where the proofs have been done. The path between source and destination is explained next:

- File download from Rediris server using the FTP protocol (Figure 7 (a)). Rediris is

Figure 7. Path between source and destination

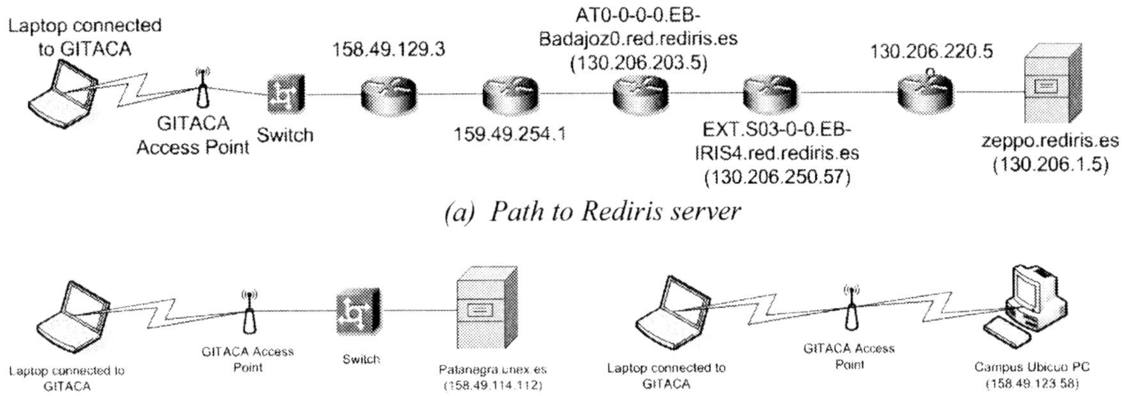

(a) Path to Rediris server

(b) Path to patanegra server

(c) Path to Campus Ubicuo PC

the Spanish National Academic Network.

- Download of the same file using HTTP protocol from patanegra server, located in the laboratory where we have carried out the tests (Figure 7 (b)).
- Download of the same file using FTP protocol from Campus Ubicuo PC, also located in the same laboratory and connected to the wireless network.
- A video file transmission using RTP protocol between two workstations located in the laboratory, both connected to the network via a wireless link. Figure 7 (c) shows the paths followed in the last two tests. Both of them fit in.

The four aforementioned tests have been done for each of the following devices, all of them with similar features to the devices used in the proposed architecture:

- Microwave oven.
- File transfer via Bluetooth.
- Bluetooth headsets connected to PC.
- Baby monitor.
- Wireless video game controller.

In other words, we have introduced a new source of interference to measure the variation of the wireless network performance caused by that specific device.

To obtain reliable and consistent results, several tests have been made following the same methodology:

1. With the spectrum analyzer we have obtained the interference values that the specific device was producing in an environment where it was the only signal emitter.
2. Once we knew these values, it was necessary to set the same channel in both the laboratory access point and the device.
3. Next, we started the data capture using the Wireshark software extension.
4. After some seconds, the file download or the video transmission starts, depending on the particular test.
5. Soon after (30 sec.) we switched on the interferences source (e.g. microwave oven, baby monitor, etc.), getting the effect that it causes to the wireless network performance. Meanwhile the file download or the video transfer continued.
6. After the device kept working for a short period of time, we switched it off while the test continued.
7. Finally, the test finished and the data collected could be analyzed.

Figure 8. Results of a test with an interference source active

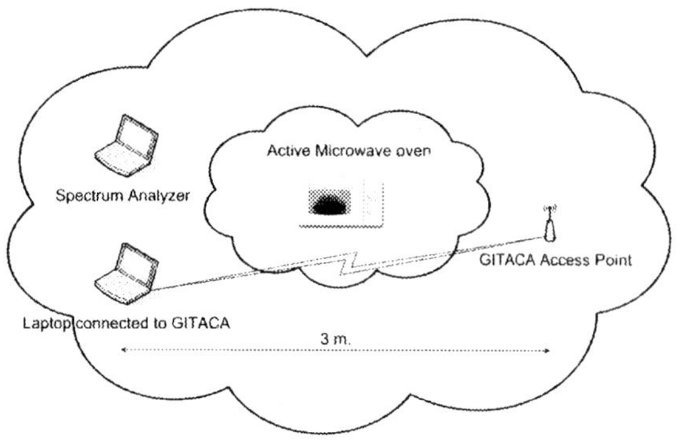

(a) Test environment with an interference source

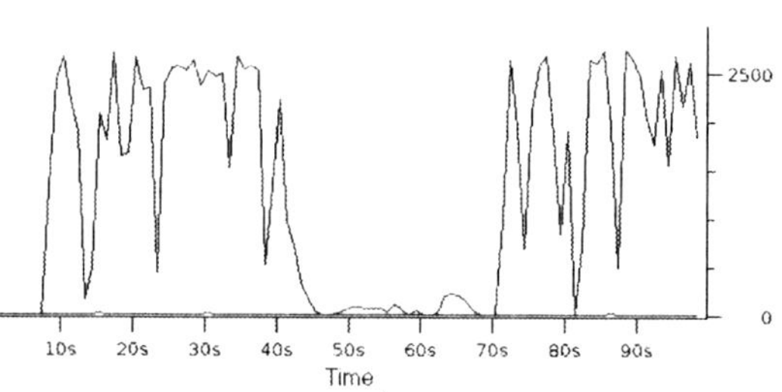

(b) Performance graph of a download with the interference source active

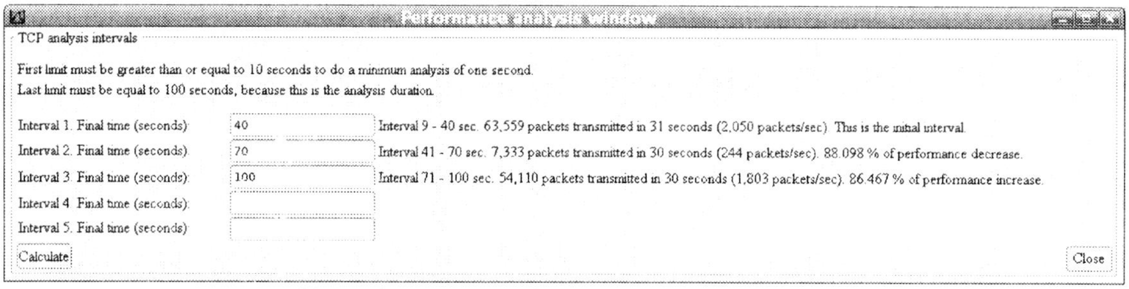

(c) Performance analysis window of the download

An Example of an Interference Source

Next, a test using a microwave oven as an interference source is explained in detail. Figure 8 (a) shows the laboratory layout for this test.

Figure 8 (b) shows the chart provided by Wireshark corresponding to a file downloaded from the laboratory server.

In the chart, tree parts are clearly differentiated: the first interval includes from the beginning to the second 40. In this time, 2,500 packets are transmitted. However, when the microwave oven is switched on, the throughput goes down considerably, transmitting just some packets by second or even not arriving any of them. This second interval lasts 30 seconds, finishing when the microwave oven is disconnected (second 70). After this instant the throughput goes up again and reaches similar values to the obtained before the device was switched on.

The performance analysis window shows the download details for each one of the abovementioned intervals, when a new source of interferences like a microwave oven is introduced. As we can see in Figure 8 (c), time period during which the microwave oven is switched on (second interval) 7,333 packets are transmitted in 30 seconds in a data rate of 244 packets per second. Comparing this data with the 2,050 packets per second of the first interval while the device was disconnected, the performance decrease is over 88%. Moreover, comparing the second interval with the third interval, the growth performance is over 86.5%, so the network recovers its previous state. With these data we can summarize that, in this test, a microwave oven affects to the wireless network performance, approximately in an 88%.

Figure 9 (a) shows this situation from another point of view. In this new chart, the line means the cumulative data sent in the transfer. During the first interval the amount of information increases following a linear function. The second interval starts when the microwave oven is switched on. In

Figure 9. Overall results

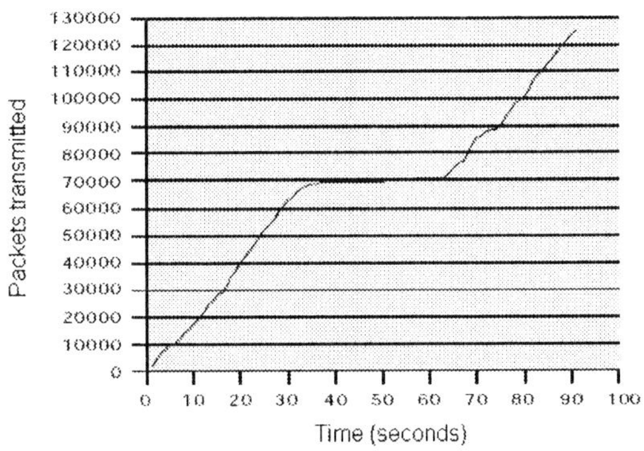

(a) Cumulative chart of the download when the microwave oven is active

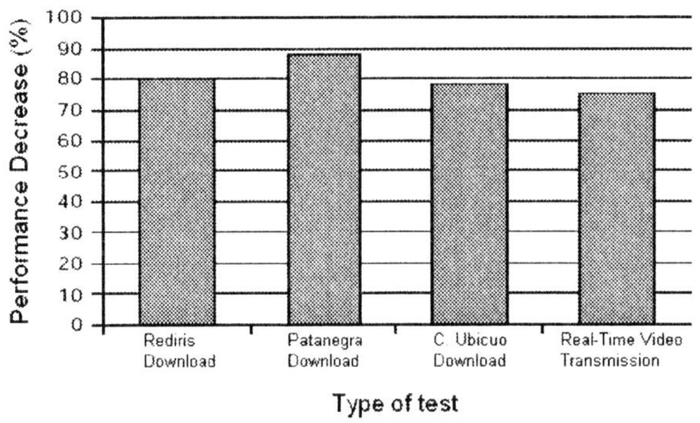

(b) Performance decrease caused by a microwave oven

Device \ Test	Rediris download	Patanegra download	Campus Ubicuo Download	Real-time video transmission
Microwave oven	80 %	88 %	78 %	75 %
Bluetooth transfer	50 %	50 %	30 %	0 %
Bluetooth Wireless headset	0 %	0 %	0 %	0 %
Baby monitor	100 %	100 %	100 %	100 %
Wireless video game controller	33 %	50 %	50 %	0 %

(c) Percentage of performance decrease caused by test

this period, the amount of data transmitted keeps without a significant increase. Once the device is disconnected, there are not interferences, so the data transferred describes again a linear function, similar to the first interval.

The influence of the microwave oven in a wireless network, when both of them use the same channel, produces a decrease by 80% of the wireless network. Figure 9 (b) shows the performance decrease in the test using the microwave oven as an interference source in a wireless network.

Figure 9 (c) shows the result of the test obtained from Figure 9 (b) repeated for other devices, showing the performance decrease of the wireless network in each case.

We can observe that the biggest performance decrease is produced by the baby monitor (100%), followed by the microwave oven in which case is around 80%. Otherwise, the test done with the Bluetooth headsets does not affect to the performance of the wireless network. The test done with the wireless controller affects to the test that involves TCP traffic (around 50% of performance decrease) and it does not affect to the multimedia transmission with RTP. By means of the last table, we can assure that wireless technologies interacts each other. The performance of the devices depends on the type of traffic and on the other devices that are operating in the same environment.

Radio Frequency Jamming Devices

The last test tries to prove whether wireless networks near an official organism building with radio frequency jamming devices operating in the same environment have an optimal performance or not.

Normally, a city council has several security video cameras to record what is happening outside and hospitals or universities can be placed near an official organism building. In this test, we used the spectrum analyzer near an official organism and we detected some Wi-Fi access points, two analog video cameras and one radar (CW modulation). The two cameras use the full range of wireless channels. This produces a dreadful effect in the access points that are near those devices. Whereas, the radio frequency jamming device does not affect to the wireless network because it does not use the 2.4 GHz band and the spectrum analyzer does not detect it as a source of interferences. Therefore, medical and other devices which use the ISM bands to operate, should work with a high performance by forgetting the presence of this kind of jamming devices.

CONCLUSION

In this chapter we show a method to evaluate a mobile learning platform using different technologies like UMTS, multicast, RTP, TCP, UDP, etc. The performance of the communications has been measured with TCP tunnels in wired and UMTS networks.

We can obtain several conclusions about this chapter. The first one is that the throughput provided by UMTS (more expanded than HDSPA networks) is insufficient to handle services that transmit a huge amount of information.

As we can observe in the third test of the "Evaluation of Campus Ubicuo in multimedia transmissions" section, when the throughput needed exceed the throughput provided by the UMTS network, the packet loss increase produce different effects like gaps or pixelation.

Even so, UMTS networks can be useful to deploy new services to the mobile learning platforms and increase the added value of these innovative platforms that use the mobile technologies as the basis of the knowledge.

Additionally, other main conclusion derived from this work is the great problem that involves the simultaneous use of different wireless technologies and the way that they transmit to the medium in a mobile learning platform. This is a consequence of the ISM bands and the technologies that operate using them.

Furthermore, manufacturers choose their own portion of the radio frequency spectrum for their devices implementation. Sometimes it is possible that two devices of the same manufacturer operate in different frequencies, so, it is more difficult to try to avoid the existence of interference between them. It is also necessary to say that the tests carried out in this study have been made in a reduced environment, not excessively polluted by different wireless devices.

We can extrapolate it to a bigger city or bigger environments where there is much pollution on the frequency bands due to the amount of the devices working near other. With respect to future research lines, other types of traffic and wireless technologies that have not been analyzed could also be studied to complete this analytical study.

ACKNOWLEDGMENT

This work is sponsored in part by the regional Economy, Commerce and Innovation Ministry belonging to the Extremadura (Spain) Regional Government, through the following projects: Campus Ubicuo (numbered as PDT05A041) and LibreMovicuidad (numbered as PRI08A079).

REFERENCES

Carmona-Murillo, J., González-Sánchez, J. L., & Castro-Ruiz, M. (2007). Technological innovation in mobile communications developed with free software: Campus ubicuo. *UPGRADE. The European Journal for the Informatics Professional*, *8*(6), 27–33.

Farpoint Group Technical Note 2003-201.1. (2003, September). *Beyond the site survey: RF spectrum management for wireless LANs.*

Farpoint Group Technical Note 2006-321.1. (2006, October). *The invisible threat: Interference and wireless LANs.*

Ganjam, A., & Zhang, H. (2005). Internet multicast video delivery. *Proceedings of the IEEE, 93*(1), 159–170. doi:10.1109/JPROC.2004.839602

Ghanbari, M. (2003). *Standard codecs: Image compression to advanced video coding.* Great Britain: Institution of Electrical Engineers. GITACA Research Group. (n.d.). Retrieved on October 15, 2008, from http://www.gitaca.com

MESEAS Project. (n.d.). Retrieved on October 15, 2008, from http://www.meseas.com

Page, I. W. (n.d.). Retrieved on October 15, 2008, from http://www.gitaca.com/iwireless

Page, W.-F. A.-H. (n.d.). Retrieved on October 15, 2008, from http://www.wi-fi.org

Schulzrinne, H. (1996). *RTP profile for audio and videoconferences with minimal control.* Internet Engineering Task Force.

Schulzrinne, H., Casner, S., Frederick, R., & Jacobson, V. (2003). *RTP: A transport protocol for real-time applications.* Internet Engineering Task Force. The Official Bluetooth Technology Info Site. (n.d.). Retrieved on October 15, 2008, from http://www.bluetooth.com/bluetooth

WildPackets Web Page. (n.d.). Retrieved on October 15, 2008, from http://www.wildpackets.com

Wireshark Network Protocol Analyzer. Retrieved October 15, 2008. http://www.wireshark.org.

Yu-Liang Ting, R. (2005). *Mobile learning: Current trend and future challenges.* Paper presented at Fifth IEEE International Conference on Advanced Learning Technologies (ICALT'05), Kaohsiung, Taiwan.

KEY TERMS AND DEFINITIONS

Bluetooth: A short-range radio technology aimed at simplifying communications of 10 meters or fewer.

FHSS (Frequency Hop Spread Spectrum): a modulations technique which spreads data across the entire transmission spectrum by transmitting successive data on different channels ("hopping").

FTP (File Transfer Protocol): Protocol that allows users to copy files between their local system and any system they can reach on the network

GSM (Global System for Mobile Communications): A European standard for digital mobile cellular networks. One of the world's main second generation (2G) digital wireless standards

GPRS (General Packet Radio Service): A mobile data service available to users of GSM mobile phones. It is often described as 2.5G, that is, a technology between the second generation (2G) and third generation (3G) of mobile telephony.

HSDPA (High-Speed Downlink Packet Access): New mobile telephony protocol that represents an upgrade of the UMTS network and is sometimes referred to as a 3.5G technology.

HTTP (HyperText Transfer Protocol): A protocol to transfer hypertext requests and information between servers and browsers.

ISM Bands: Industrial, Scientific, Medical Band. A global, public, high frequency, license free radio band. 433MHz, 868MHz, 915MHz, 2.4GHz.

ITU (International Telecommunication Union): The leading United Nations agency for information and communication technology issues.

NAT (Network Address Translation): Is the process of modifying network address information in datagram packet headers while in transit across a traffic routing device for the purpose of remapping a given address space into another.

RTP (Real-Time Transport Protocol): The Internet-standard protocol for the transport of real-time data, including audio and video.

TCP (Transmission Control Protocol): Transport layer protocol that establishes a reliable, full duplex, data delivery service used by many TCP/IP application programs

UDP (User Datagram Protocol): A protocol within the TCP/IP protocol suite that is used in place of TCP when a reliable delivery is not required

UMTS (Universal Mobile Telecommunications System): Third-generation international mobile communications standard that unites mobile multimedia and telematics services in the frequency spectrum of 2 GHz.

WI-FI (Wireless Fidelity): A radio frequency standard that is used to connect devices, such as computers, together using a wireless connection.

Chapter 15
Supporting Mobile Access to VLE Resources through MobiGlam

Fatma Meawad
German University in Cairo, Egypt

Geneen Stubbs
University of Glamorgan, UK

ABSTRACT

MobiGlam is a generic framework of interoperability with existing virtual learning environments (VLEs) that provides a compact and easy to use implementation of learning activity on Java enabled mobile devices. A case study was conducted at the University of Glamorgan, UK where MobiGlam was seamlessly integrated with the university's VLE to support the delivery of computer courses at the foundation level. Such integration showed an added value to the participants and in many cases, it improved their use of the VLE. This chapter reports on the deployment, the evaluation, and the results of this case study. The results are analysed from two views: the impact on the participants' use of the VLE and the framework's overall usability.

INTRODUCTION

The computer literacy courses for foundation year students at the University of Glamorgan are delivered through the Virtual Learning Environment (VLE) Moodle (Moodle, 2008). Even though Moodle is configured to enable students to undertake all course work remotely, face to face tutor assistance is available during regular sessions throughout the week. Regardless of the numerous ways available for communication among students and tutors through the VLE, tutors find it difficult to keep the students updated or engaged with the activities being offered through the VLE. Furthermore, many students can be unreachable even through their emails. Providing mobile access to the VLE resources has the potential to address these issues and enhance the use of the VLE. However, there are several challenges associated with introducing such technology, for example, achieving wide acceptance and support from involved staff while considering cost issues and extra staff time. In addition, the threat of poor usability of mobile devices can influence the users' whole experience.

DOI: 10.4018/978-1-60566-882-6.ch015

MobiGlam is a framework that is designed in a way that achieves flexibility of use in various learning contexts and for a wide range of mobile devices (Meawad & Stubbs, 2008). MobiGlam can provide seamless mobile support to students and tutors who use the VLE. Their regular use of the VLE will not be affected and supporting mobile access will not require extra effort or preparation for the tutors. For example, when tutors assess course work on the VLE, notifications are automatically generated to the assessed students with their personal information without the tutors being involved in the process. Additionally, students will able to instantly access this information without further work from the tutor. Such instant access and SMS notifications can be achieved for various resources of the VLE, including, exercises, assignments, messages, grades, quizzes, events, workshops, forums, news and users' information.

A case study was conducted at the University to evaluate the feasibility and the impact of using MobiGlam with foundation year students. This chapter discusses the details, observations and results of the case study. The chapter starts with a background about similar work in higher education; then we give a description of the evaluation context and the deployment process. This is followed by an analysis of the participants' background and pre-use expectations. Then, the results and post-use feedback are reported. The results are analysed in detail from two views: the framework's overall usability and the value of the mobile support for the participants.

MOBILE ACCESS TO LEARNING SERVICES IN HIGHER EDUCATION

In the University context, there are several attempts to support students in managing, organising and enhancing their learning experience through mobile access to a variety of activities. The University of Birmingham introduced a mobile learning organiser that provided a set of integrated tools to students: a Time Manager, a Course Manager, a Communication Manager and a Concept Mapper (Corlett et al., 2004). As indicated by the names of these tools, they provided various activities to help learners organise their schedules, communicate and take notes on their mobile devices. Additionally, desktop based applications were provided to help tutors in creating content for some of these tools, for example, time schedules, events and deadlines. Such content can be downloaded as demanded by students on their devices through the mobile organiser. An evaluation of the mobile learning organiser took place with seventeen students from the University of Birmingham where students were loaned PDAs with the dedicated software (Corlett et al., 2004). Additionally, they were allowed to download any additional applications for their personal use. The results showed that students used the organiser mainly for communication and time management purposes.

The mobile learning organiser was one of the first initiatives to support mobile access in a University context. However, it was only introduced for a specific series of devices which forced the evaluators to introduce these specific devices to the participants. Consequently, they were unwilling to invest time or money in using the device. Students reported the usual usability issues that could result from the limitations of mobile devices, for example, memory size, battery life and portability issues. The lack of the sense of ownership of the mobile device among the participants caused lack of interest in investing time or money in using the device. Additionally, this evaluation has raised institutional issues because the content was not updated frequently which added a source of uncertainty to the students.

SMILE, Sussex Mobile Interactive Learning Environment, is another mobile learning initiative that gave flexibility to learners in creating their own learning experiences (Luckin et al., 2003). Students were loaned XDA devices which have

PDA capabilities, mobile office tools and always-on Internet connection. Students were asked to explore opportunities for using mobile devices for collaboration and communication. In this project, there was little work done towards automating or enhancing the process of accessing content as much as it was directed towards assessing the potential of the devices in enhancing the learning experience. Even though such evaluation is indeed important, we argue that without improving the use of the technology, the result of the evaluation will be affected. They will not reflect an accurate description of what the technology can offer. This was seen in students' feedback that often indicated that the idea was good but the technology was not there yet.

The technical and institutional problems faced by existing m-learning initiatives has led many researchers to suggest that an integration with existing content management systems or VLEs used by institutions can be beneficial. Throughout this chapter, several examples of integrating mobile access with existing content management systems were introduced, for example, the Mobile Learning Engine (MLE) (Meisenberger, 2004), the e-learning lab in Shanghai (Wang et al., 2005) or the Finesse client (Millard et al., 2005). Claroline is another VLE that was adapted for mobile access as a collaboration project between a mobile media company and the national college of Ireland (Hayes et al., 2004). This work resulted in stressing several technical issues that relates to designing engaging content for mobile learners and investigating approaches for adapting content for several mobile platforms. The researchers in this project came to the conclusion that the success of mobile learning will be always related to its ease of use, cost effectiveness and how seamlessly it is integrated in learners' lives.

Current and on-going initiatives to enable flexible access to VLEs in a University context hold promise for the future of mainstreaming mobile learning in higher education. For instance, *exact Mobile* (Giunti, 2008), offers interoperation with learning management systems or VLEs to deliver context-aware SCORM compliant content seamlessly and flexibly to wireless devices, palmtops or even wearable PCs. *Exact Mobile* is a commercial product developed by Giunti labs (Giunti, 2008a), and targets work based learners or blended academic learning programmes. *Engage* is another interesting project that aims to enable access of personalised learning material on mobile devices from several VLEs such as Domino, Moodle and uPortal (Race, 2006). *Engage* is being developed by Lancaster University in collaboration with several of its partners. The main motivation of the project *Engage* is the recognized need for better communication and access to learning material for learners and teachers. Both *exact Mobile* and *Engage* share the same objectives as the work proposed by this thesis in attempting to achieve flexibility of access by interoperating with various VLEs. However, as will be discussed throughout this thesis, this work proposes scalable and generic techniques to achieve interoperability with VLEs based on conceptual models of mobile activities. In the meantime, the proposed framework maintains automation and seamless use to enhance usability for users and scalability for institutions.

THE EVALUATION CONTEXT

As mentioned earlier, Moodle is used at the University of Glamorgan to teach the information technology courses to foundation year students. Students from various disciplines register to this instance of Moodle with several tutors per course and one module leader for the whole instance of Moodle. Foundation year students vary in their ages, their background and their level of computer literacy. It is worth mentioning that the offered courses do not require the students to be computer literate. Therefore, some students might not have any prior knowledge about using computers, the Internet or e-mails; however, relying on a VLE in their courses throughout the

Figure 1. The main course layout on Moodle showing a classification of activities by topics

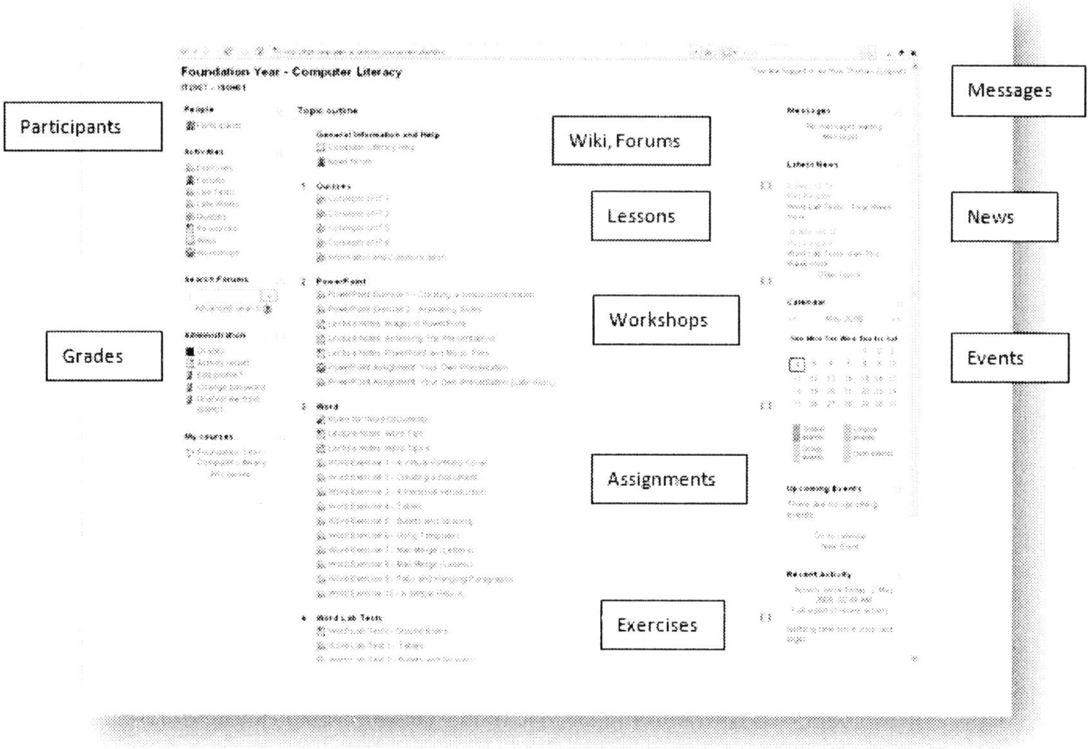

year makes them more comfortable with the use of IT and the Internet.

It was important to introduce MobiGlam without interrupting the regular delivery of the course in order to make it a seamless process for the course participants. Consequently, the scenarios available for this case study were dependent on what the module leader had configured for this instance of the VLE. As shown in Figure 1, there was a wide variety of activities set up for Moodle at that time including: messages, news, events, assignments, forums, workshops, exercises, lessons, wikis, contacts and grades. Additionally, MobiGlam provides some standard features by default such as preferences and profile.

One Step Deployment

The actual link between MobiGlam and a Moodle instance, already running in an institution, requires only one step: the VLE registration. This process simply requires an administrator to fill a form that permits MobiGlam to access the VLE database. Afterwards, MobiGlam processes the database and automatically identifies the content and the modules that can be supported according to the built-in SQL specifications for Moodle. Additionally, a web administration module is provided to help administrators in configuring how MobiGlam extends the activities and how it operates in general. In line with this description and in this case study, the database of the VLE shown in figure 1 was dynamically processed by the framework to be configured by an administrator as shown in figure 2 after filling the registration form. This is what we refer to as a one-step deployment process. This process shows the simplicity of integrating the framework in the institutional infrastructure which is envisaged to promote large scale use. In practice, such simplicity allowed the VLE admin-

Figure 2. MobiGlam's administration home page showing the dynamically recognised courses and listing several configuration options

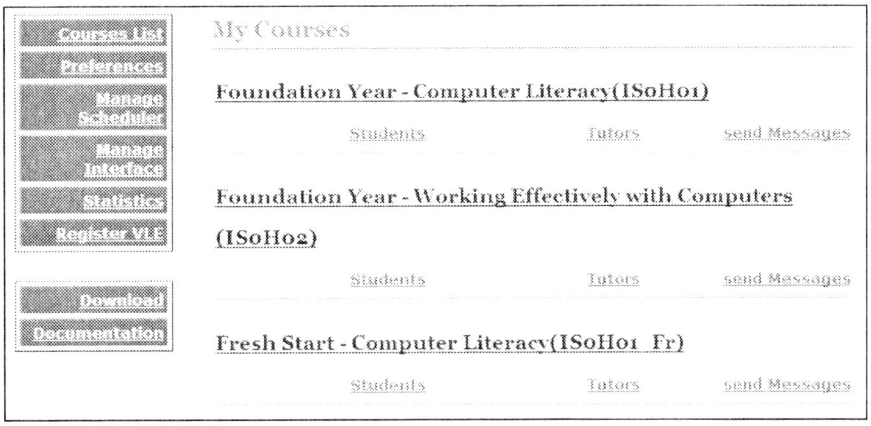

istrator at the University to integrate MobiGlam into the live instance of Moodle as the courses are being delivered.

As shown in figure 2, there are several administration options to configure MobiGlam's extension of Moodle or monitor users' mobile activity. MobiGlam runs independently as a dynamic web application over a Tomcat web server (Apache, 2007) which is an open source tool. The framework runs on a different server from the VLE server and communicates remotely with the VLE database. After the completion of this step, users can register their mobile numbers and download a light java-based browser that allows a pleasant mobile interface to the VLE resources. Users who do not wish to download the browser can still benefit from the automated notifications about any related events that are created through the VLE.

Methodology

The system was introduced to tutors and students in their regular tutorial sessions with a request for volunteers in its evaluation. Thirty volunteering users participated in the evaluation with 28 students and 2 tutors. In order to provide opportunities for authentic use, it was important to observe the participants' use over a complete course delivery period. Such a period can be the start and the end of a course, an academic term, or a project. This case study was carried out in the autumn term of 2007 over the duration of 12 weeks. It is worth noting that the availability of MobiGlam for the participants does not end by the end of the course delivery. As will be reported later in this chapter, users accessed MobiGlam even after the end of their course to check grades or to communicate with peers.

In addition to pre and post questionnaires, informal feedback and comments were continuously exchanged during the evaluations through interviews, emails, messages or arranged chats online. Due to the nature of the technology and its intended merge in users' daily lives, some important feedback and comments were reported individually, as experienced by user to the author. Collectively, the analysis reported in this chapter is based on three sources of information: (a) data collected by MobiGlam's monitoring module, (b) data logs of the VLE itself and (c) user's feedback.

Figure 3. Percentages of users in different age groups

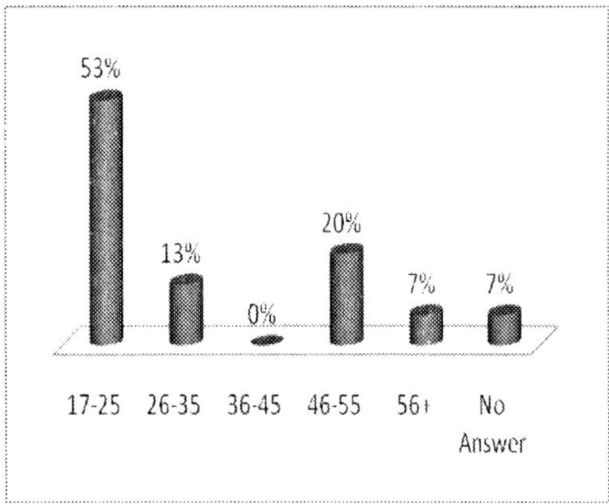

BACKGROUND AND PRE-USE FEEDBACK

Prior to installing the MobiGlam browser on their mobile devices, the participants were asked to fill in a pre-use questionnaire. This questionnaire was intended to collect some background information about the participants particularly in using the Moodle VLE. The participants belonged to various age groups (see figure 3). Even though the dominant age group (53%) was between the age of 17 and the age of 25, a considerable percentage of mature participants starting from the age of 46 were involved. Out of these participants, only 30% were males while 66.7% were females. Moreover, most of the participants were at the intermediate level or above in their computer proficiency skills (see figure 4). Only 10% of the participants were novices in using computers. The participants were given a description of the skills for various skill levels before answering this question.

VLE Use

The participants' experiences with using Moodle as a VLE differed as well. Figure 5 shows that the majority of the participants (66.7%) were familiar with Moodle as they had taken 3 or more courses through it. On the other hand, 30% of the participants were using Moodle for the first time. It is worth mentioning this percentage as these participants will be experiencing two new technologies at the same time. The participants normally spend a considerable number of hours on accessing Moodle weekly as exhibited in figure 6. The regular number of hours seems to lie between 1 to 10 hours per week. Yet, some participants have indicated that their access time can reach up to 20 hours per week.

The participants rated the usefulness of the specific activities of the VLE pre-using MobiGlam on a 1 to 5 point scale. Figure 7 shows the participants' ratings of the activities grouped into

Figure 4. Percentages of users with various levels of computer proficiency

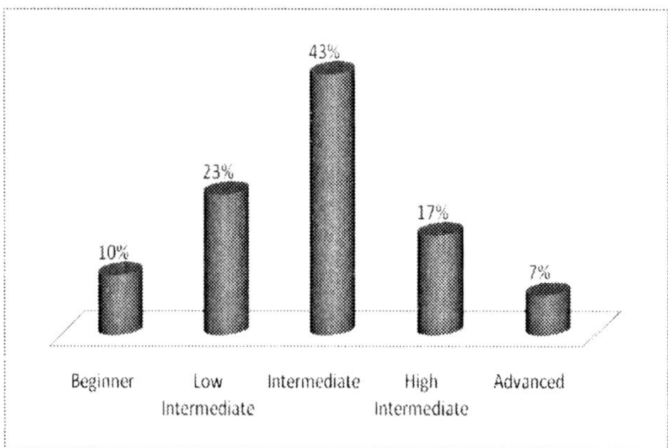

Figure 5. The percentages of the participants according to the number of courses taken through Moodle

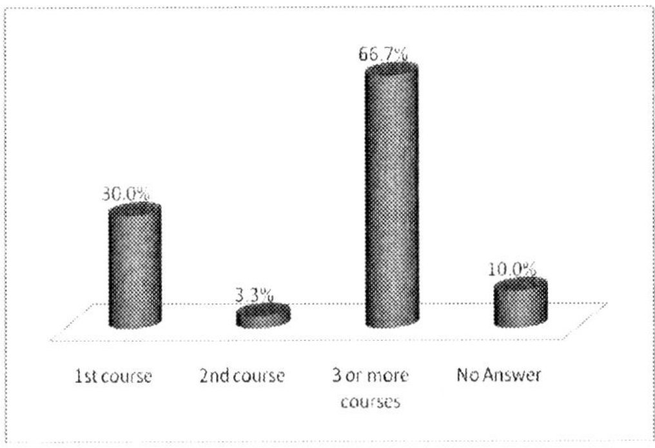

Figure 6. The approximate number of hours spent by participants on accessing Moodle weekly

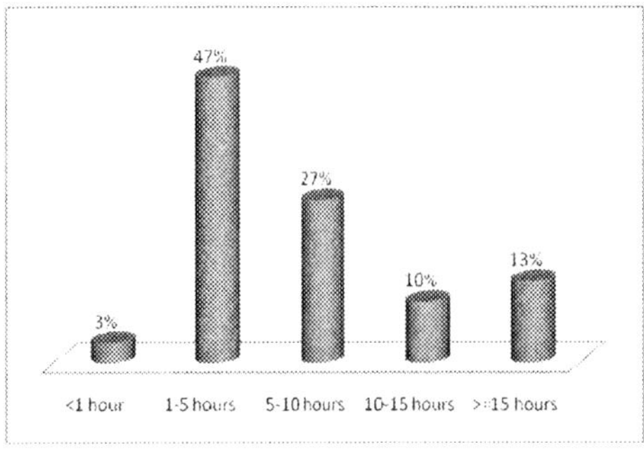

useful, not useful and never used. Their feedback shows many activities that were never used for example, wikis, chat, forums and contacts. The participants shared the opinion on the usefulness of the assignments, exercises, messages and the grades. On the other hand, forums, chat and wiki activities were rated as not useful compared to other activities. Some participants explained that their rating of some activities as not useful is because they are not regularly updated or used by tutors, for example chats and wikis. Our analysis of the participants' interest in specific activities or features of a VLE prior to using MobiGlam helps us form an opinion of the expected value of providing mobile access to these activities. The resulting behaviour can be quite different from any expectations which will also be an interesting pattern to observe.

Mobile Use

Fifty percent of the participants use their mobile devices extensively in their daily lives, while 27% of them rely on messaging and 20% use

Figure 7. A value table showing the ratings (in percentages) of different activities on Moodle as useful, not useful or never used

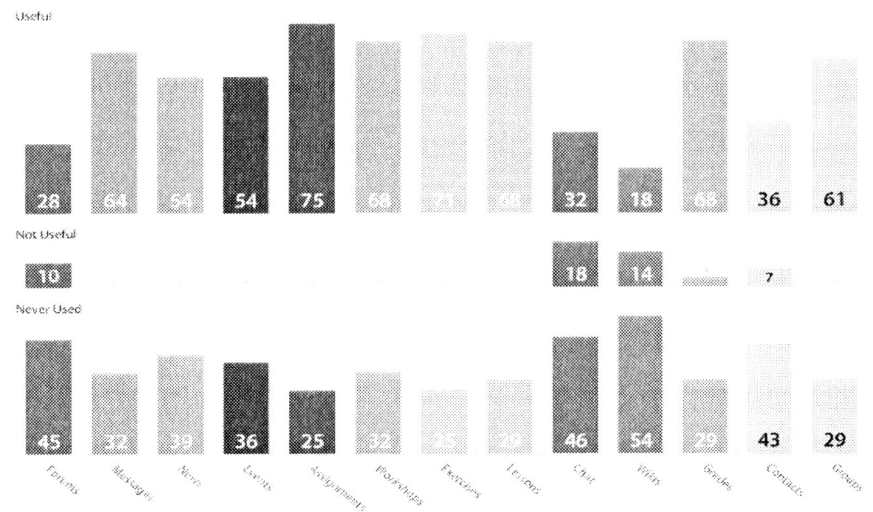

their mobile devices as phones only (see figure 8). When asked about their specific interest in the mobile Internet, 70% of the participants indicated that they use it for social networking through Facebook, Bebo, Myspace, MSN or for seeking general information such as cinema time, train times. Additionally, 27% of these participants indicated that they had had experience of downloading or syncing games, movies, music, photos, themes and Nokia life.

Impressions of Mobile Learning

All the participants expressed interest in having anytime and anywhere access to Moodle. In the previous sections, the participants' ratings of different services provided by a VLE were reported. Based on this, they were asked if providing mobile access to such services could achieve the following benefits:

- **Mobile services can enhance their communication with tutors and other learners:** 80% of the participants agreed with this statement and none of them disagreed. The rest of the participants were either neutral or provided no answer. Some participants commented mentioning existing issues in communication where students or tutors are unreachable even for important matters.
- **Instant access to information can be useful during idle time waiting in a queue or in a train:** The majority of the participants (83%) agreed with this statement and none of them disagreed.
- **Instant notification can keep them up to date with the online learning system:** Again the majority of the participants (87%) agreed with this statement and none of them disagreed.
- **Mobile services can help them in time management:** Only 63% of the participants agreed while 3% disagreed. This statement had a lower appreciation among the participants compared to the other benefits. Later in this chapter, a comparison with the participants' feedback about this value is provided to show the impact of using MobiGlam on the participants' impressions.

REGISTRATION AND DOWNLOAD

The participants were required to register with MobiGlam and download the Java-ME browser on their devices. This step is done through an online registration form that only takes the user's mobile

Figure 8. The participants' different patterns of use of mobile devices

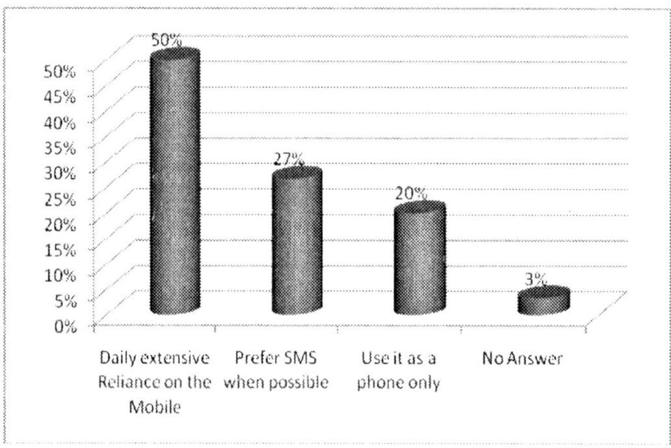

number, username and password already used with the existing VLE (see figure 9). At this point, the user is not required to enter any information about the accessing device. Upon registration, a WAP push message and an SMS message are sent to the device to guide the user in the installation process. As shown in figure 10, there is a link in the sent message from which the installation starts automatically. Afterwards, the user is only required to approve the steps that proceed with the installation.

The participants were expected to be able to register and download on their own. Additionally they had the opportunity for face-to-face help in their regular tutorial sessions. The participants should use their personally owned devices. This was an important factor in the evaluation so that realistic behaviours can be observed. In the meantime, to avoid the cost issue, a system was developed that estimated data connectivity costs. That system was based on the fact that mobile operators use the amount of kilobytes being transferred to charge users for GPRS data connectivity. An estimation of the amount of data used by each user is feasible through the data logged by the system. The question was how to decide on the cost for each kilobyte knowing that it differs according to each operator's plan and according to the user's pricing plan. The only solution was to apply a maximum estimate that will guarantee that the cost for each user is less than the calculated maximum estimate. The estimate was set through several experiments using SIM cards from Orange, T-Mobile, Vodafone and

Figure 9. User registration form to MobiGlam. The form only requires existing username and password in addition to the phone number. No information about the device used is required.

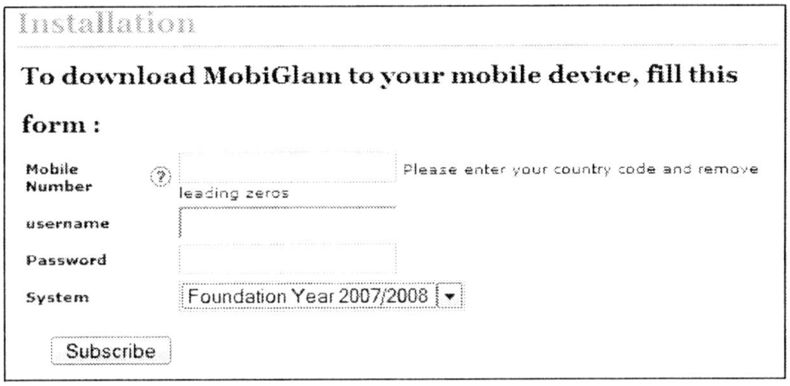

Figure 10. Snapshots from a Nokia N70 device showing the process of installing MobiGlam after receiving the WAP Push message

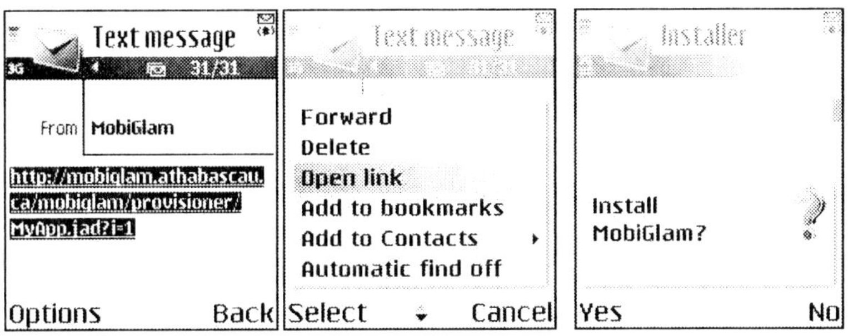

O2 to be a maximum of one pence per kilobyte. Thus, if a user accessed 40 kilobytes per session, he is entitled to a 40 pence refund. Based on this, the participants were encouraged to use any data connectivity at anytime they needed it.

Installation and Download

The installation process of the Java-ME browser returns a notification string to the server upon the following events: success, cancellation or error. The case of no notifications is usually due to connection problems or device-related constraints. By analysing the participants' installation activity, it was observed that many of them have requested installation more than once even if they have installed the browser successfully the first time. In fact, some of the participants repeated their request to install the application for the same device for up to 17 times. Further observations from the collected data show that a few of these participants would realise that re-requesting installation was not necessary and cancelled; while most of them would proceed with the installation steps again till the end. Such repeated pattern of behaviour is most likely related to users' confusion about how to open the application from a mobile device once it is successfully installed. Opening an installed application could be very unclear on some devices. Similar evaluations of mobile applications have reported the same difficulties in finding the application after the download (Kaikkonen et al., 2005) which supports the proposed cause of such behaviour. As shown in figure 11, only 42.8% of the participants installed the MobiGlam browser from the first attempt. There were exactly 2 failures during installations. Failed installation instances were identified by checking two conditions in the database: (a) the number of successful installations is zero and (b) the number of sessions accessed from this particular device is also zero.

Three of the participants had very old phones that were not data enabled. These phones can only send messages and make phone calls. The first reaction of these participants, when knowing that they do not have a suitable device, was offering to purchase new ones. However, it is important to acknowledge the fact that some users are only interested in using a mobile device with minimal phone capabilities that fulfil their needs. Therefore, participants with such devices were asked to register without downloading the browser. Even though they will not be able to browse information and interact from their devices, they will receive notifications and updates from their VLE. Meanwhile, the participants were encouraged to try out the emulator environment before giving post-use feedback.

Figure 11. The percentages of participants according to the number of attempts towards successful installation or failure

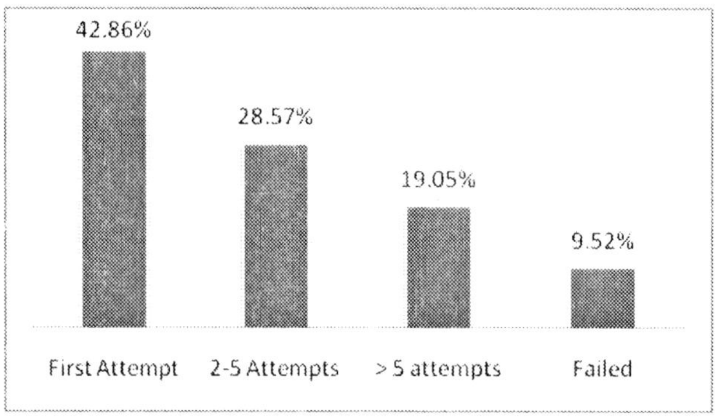

User Feedback on Installation

The previous section provided an analysis of the installation behaviour through the information logged by MobiGlam. Additionally, the participants were asked to rate their experiences with the registration, download and installation. Seventy seven percent of the participants agreed that the registration was an easy process while only 3% disagreed. Seventy percent of the participants agreed that it was easy to understand the download process from the received message, while 6% disagreed. There was a relatively lower percentage (50%) of participants who agreed on their ability to go through the whole process without help. Table 1 shows the mean of the participants' ratings of several aspects of the installation process on a scale from 1 (strongly disagree) to 5 (strongly agree). The table shows that the participants' satisfaction with the process was above average but they still believed that they needed help with the installation process.

POST-USE FEEDBACK

Even though a total of 30 users registered to MobiGlam, there were only 21 active users overall. Active users are the ones who initiated access through MobiGlam based on their specific need and in their own time. In this section, an analysis is provided of (a) the participants' activity throughout their terms of use, (b) the value of the notifications, (c) the feedback on usability and (d) the general impressions on the added benefits of using MobiGlam.

User Activity Analysis

Context and Time of Access

Using the logged data of user access times, the percentages of users' sessions were grouped according to 4 different periods of the day: midnight till 6 AM, 6 AM till noon, noon till 6 PM and 6 PM till midnight. Even though the highest level of access took place in the afternoon period (35.6%), the participants were accessing the system throughout the day (see figure 12). Twenty four percent of the participants accessed during the period from midnight till 6 AM. Additionally, there was no specific place for accessing MobiGlam as indicated by the participants' feedback when asked about context of use. Many participants frequently mentioned that they accessed MobiGlam whenever they had a few minutes to spare in different places at home, at work, in a train or in a bus. For example, one participant, who travels for 1 hour to get to the University, has reported that it was "very useful" to be able to access course information and send/reply to messages to peers about where to meet and what to do upon arrival. Another participant found the best use was to check grades when away over Christmas. Such feedback implies that MobiGlam was only accessed whenever users had some time to do something useful. However, this access can be interrupted by other unexpected factors. For example, one tutor, who relies ex-

Table 1. A table comparing the means of the participants' ratings of the corresponding statements about installation and download

The online registration process was easy and straight forward.	3.8
It was easy to understand how to download the application from the SMS	3.6
The installation of the application on the device was smooth	3.7
Overall, I didn't need much help to install and open the application.	3.3
Overall Average	3.6

Figure 12. This table shows the access level during different times of the day. The participants were accessing MobiGlam throughout the day.

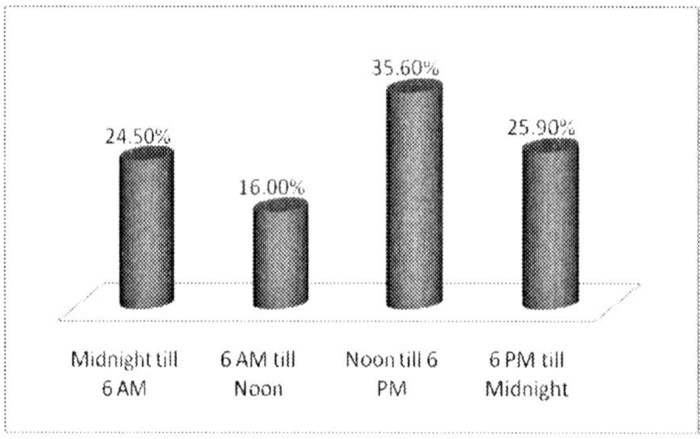

Figure 13. This table the number of hours per week in which the participants accessed MobiGlam

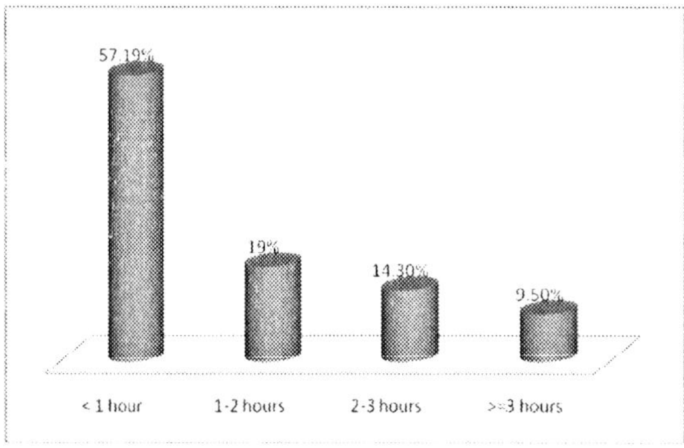

tensively on messages in communicating with students, expressed frustration in attempting to make use of time while waiting in a hospital and found that there was no network signal to allow connection. Such factors are uncontrollable but they do affect the user's experience especially if there was an intended plan to make use of a long period of waiting time.

Activity Level and Activity Type

In order to view the time spent weekly by each user in accessing MobiGlam, the average of the total time taken for all the sessions of a user in a week was calculated. The majority of the participants accessed MobiGlam for less than an hour per week (see figure 13). It is not necessary to relate these observations to the participants' access times of the web version of Moodle (see figure 6) because the mobile access is supposed to help in capturing short unused periods of times. It was surprising to see some participants reaching to 2 or 3 hours per week. There were also participants who had an average as low as 6 minutes per week.

A participant's activity level is defined as the number of transactions made. Each transaction also indicates the activity type which gives us a chance to see what users were actually looking for. Figure 14 shows the activity level of the participants over time. It is clear that the participants were particularly active in the middle period of the evaluation from week 4 to week 9. The significant increase in activity coincides with the assessment period in the course delivery which

Figure 14. The activity level of the participants over 12 weeks time. The activity increased with the SMS notifications for grades and messages.

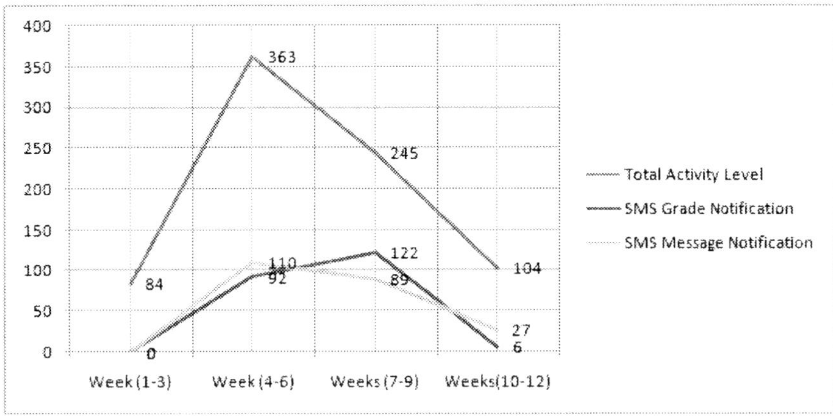

justifies the increase in the SMS notifications for grades. Figure 15 compares the access level for all the activity and it is so sorted from bottom up. From that figure, it is clear that checking grades was most popular among the participants during the middle period. The figure shows other popular activities among the participants such as exercises, messages, profile, etc. The proportional increase of the activity level with the SMS notifications implies that the notifications kept the participants up to date with events in the VLE which motivated them to interact. The same observation is supported by the participants' own feedback about being interested in grades and deadline notifications and being able to access when there is not a computer connection:

You can access things more often, for example if you are somewhere where there are no computers, you can still access your grades and assessment details.

Knowing when your deadlines are and when you are out of reach of computer you can check and make it a benefit.

Messages about deadlines changing for assignments is the main thing.

Another observation on the activity type is that contacts, events and news, which were rated useful pre-using MobiGlam (see figure 7), were not used much during the evaluation. Additionally, messages which were on top of the list in their interest came after grades and exercises in actual use. Based on these observations, it is clear that the main interest for campus based learners was in course assessed information while their use of communication activities was mainly with the tutors and not as much with each other. Even after the end of the course, 2 learners used the mobile access to re-check their grades.

Profiled Notifications

The participants were receiving notifications throughout the evaluation time. These notifications were triggered by various events from the VLE. The level of notifications sent over the weeks was already shown in the previous section (see figure 14). Each notification message is supposed to only notify users of the specific event then invite them to login to MobiGlam for further action. The communication does not involve showing the actual mobile numbers of the participants to maintain the anonymity of personal mobile numbers. Additionally, to prevent any intrusion

Figure 15. The level of the participants' use of each activity over time sorted bottom up

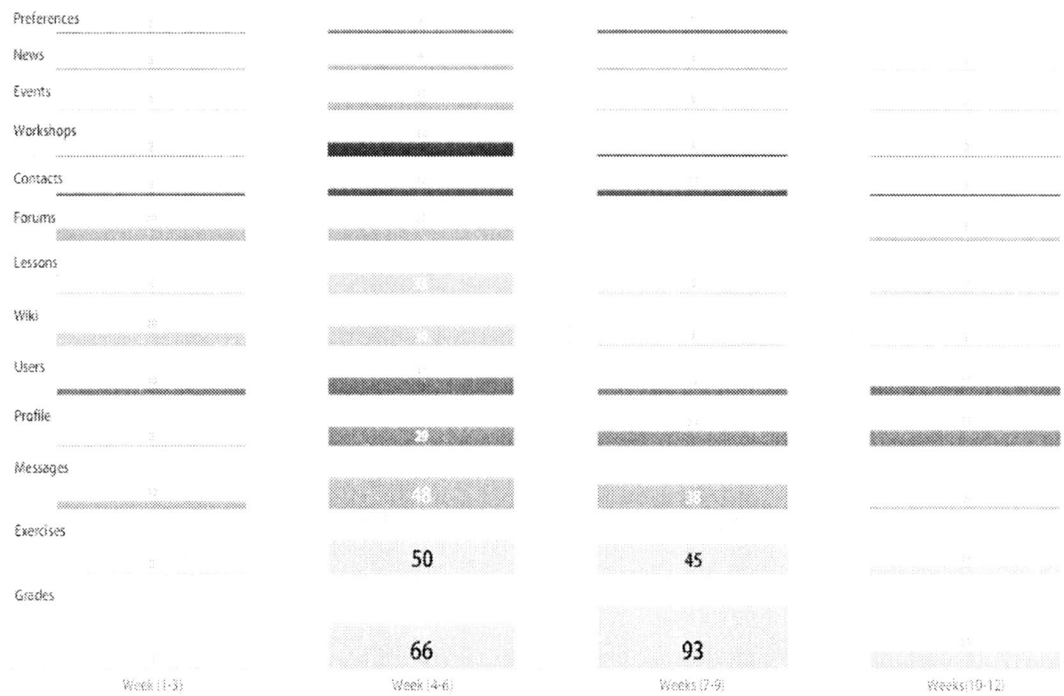

on users' personal space, the preferences feature of MobiGlam allows a user to control the type of notifications received.

Notifications are triggered by new items added as news, events, assessments, messages, posts in subscribed forums and replies to one's posts. On a scale from 1 (not useful) to 5 (very useful), the participants were asked to rate the usefulness of these notifications. Table 2 shows the mean of the participants' rating of usefulness for each type of notification. Grades and messages had the highest ratings which are related to their most used activities as shown in the previous section.

Tutors with active roles were developing their own time saver behaviour through the notifications. For example, tutors, who are heavily involved in communicating with students through messages, reported that the notifications helped them "preview" what is going on the VLE and think over what kind of reply or what sort of action should be taken. Then, once they sit down in-front of a computer, they reply back in much less time. Additionally, all the participants indicated that they find the notifications useful and not obtrusive:

...the messages never annoying and it is better to get them [on] your phone than checking the email reminder.

it is not necessary to keep checking the VLE for updates.

Besides describing the notifications as fun, one mature student mentioned that when she received notifications in the company of other people, she bragged about getting notifications from the University. Finally, a request that was often repeated by the students was that they wanted this feature for all their courses not just foundation ones.

Table 2. This table compares the mean of the participants' ratings of different types of notifications

News	4.04
Events	4.26
Forum posts	3.65
Assessments	4.74
Messages	4.64
Replies to Forums	4.22

Table 3. The means of the participants' ratings of their satisfaction with the usability aspects of the system

Efficiency	4.2
Learn-ability	3.9
Content Layout	3.9615
Overall Performance	3.09

Usability

After analysing the participants' activity and patterns of use, their feedback was collected on the following usability points: efficiency, learn-ability, content layout and overall performance. Table 3 summarises the mean of the participants' ratings of their satisfaction of the mentioned aspects of usability on a scale of 1 (not satisfied) to 5 (very satisfied). The participants were more satisfied with the system's efficiency than with other aspects.

Under the efficiency aspect, the focus was on discovering if MobiGlam allowed the participants complete their intended tasks without errors. Eighty percent of the participants agreed that MobiGlam was efficient and none of them disagreed. Additionally, the participants were asked about their satisfaction with the different elements of content layout such as readable text, clear images and finding menu items. Over 95% of the participants indicated their satisfaction with the content layout and none of them disagreed. Similarly, 70% of the participants indicated that it was easy to learn how to use the mini-browser from the mobile device and none of them disagreed. However, when it comes to the overall performance, 27% of the participants indicated that they were dissatisfied with this aspect.

Added Values

Earlier in this chapter, the participants' general impressions about mobile learning were reported. Even though the majority were interested in mobile access to Moodle, there was some doubt about the possible benefits when it comes to saving time or improving their access. In this section, the overall impressions post-using MobiGlam is reported from three views: time management, communication and providing anytime and anywhere access. It should be interesting to see if the participants' opinions have changed from their impressions pre-using MobiGlam

Time Management

Making use of idle time that we spend in travelling, queuing or waiting is probably the first benefit that comes to mind when thinking of mobile learning.

The participants were asked if using MobiGlam helped them to make use of such idle time. Figure 16 shows a comparison in the pre and post use impressions about the value of time management. Eighty two percent of the participants agreed that MobiGlam helped them in managing their time. There is a 19% increase in the number of participants who agreed to such benefit. There is also a 3% decrease in the number of participants who disagree leaving it to no disagreement from the participants.

Communication

Another expected benefit of enabling mobile access is to improve the communication among the participants especially the remote ones who rely on the VLE for communicating with one another or with tutors. Over 90% of the Glamorgan participants agreed that using MobiGlam has improved their communication with students or tutors using Moodle. There is a 12% increase in the number of participants who agreed compared to the pre-use feedback (Figure 17).

Anywhere, Anytime Access

Was the application successful in providing anytime and anywhere access or were the notifications its only attraction? To answer this question, the activities that involve interactions such as sending a message, replying to a message, searching or creating discussions were analysed. Using the mobile device to send, reply to or search messages represented only 14% of the participants' access to the messages activity. The level of use of features that involves interaction is very low. Even with such evidence of low interaction, one participant reported the following:

The ease by which you can reply is amazing and sending messages but with predictive text, I can actually reply more.

Another important measure of "anywhere and anytime" access is the level of practicality and affordability of the technology. Estimating costs per user was an attempt to overcome the costs issue associated with using GPRS. The interesting part was that the costs were not an issue with most users because the system sends and receives small amounts of data per transaction. Seventy five percent of the users totally disagreed that the cost was an issue. Two of the participants mentioned that it costs them less to check a message through MobiGlam than the normal cost of an SMS message.

Figure 16. A chart showing pre and post use impressions about achieving the benefit of time management by using MobiGlam

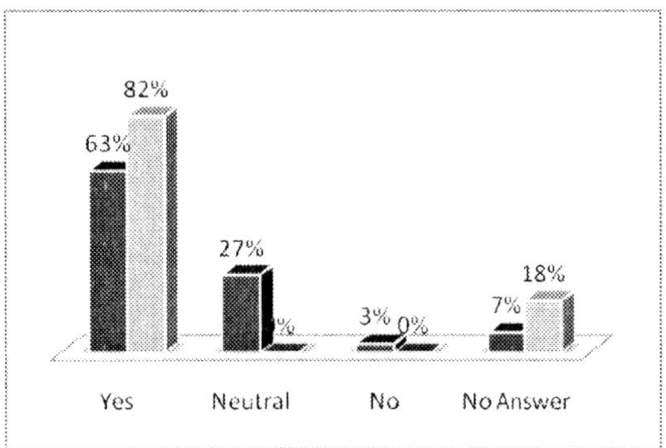

CONCLUSION

MobiGlam was integrated with the VLE used by foundation year tutors and students in order to address their communication issues and enhance their use of the VLE resources. Throughout the chapter, an analysis based on the system's logged data and users' feedback from a 12 weeks evaluation period is provided. This analysis started by showing the diverse background of the participants and their interest in mobile access to their VLE and continued to their feedback about the usability and the added benefits of using such technology in their lives. It is important to note that MobiGlam was not meant to replace the VLE but enhance it and provide more flexibility to its use.

MobiGlam's flexibility in deployment and in targeting a wide variety of devices provided an in-hand solution that addresses the institutional challenges in introducing the technology. Such flexibility allowed integrating MobiGlam for a truly ubiquitous experience without any supervision on how, when or where it can be used. Many of the participants' comments and patterns of use support the fact that MobiGlam was successful in achieving this. For example, some students indicated that they accessed MobiGlam in a train or when away during Christmas. Furthermore, tutors have changed the way they use the messages activity through Moodle and relied on having a prior knowledge of what to expect when they access the web VLE. Additionally, knowing that important notifications will go through to the participants' personal devices increases the trust in reaching delivering information and the reliance on the VLE to do that. Additionally, comparing the participants' ratings of the added benefits of mobile use showed an increase from before and after their experience with MobiGlam. This is again an indicator to the success of the technology in enhancing the experience for the participants. The following subsections highlight the lessons learned from this case study.

Real Use, Real Need

The use of mobile technologies has many challenges that come along with the benefits of portability and presumed pervasive access. Thus, when introducing such technologies, there should be a real need and expected value in the lives of potential users. The participants had a relatively low activity level and they could be inactive for a week or more. However, their feedback shows that they had had a very positive experience with MobiGlam that they recommended the application to other potential users and institutions. Additionally, the request to add this technology to all courses was frequently encountered. Therefore, the main value of the system came on demand whenever and wherever needed by the participants. This is again explained by the increase of their activity level in relation to the notifications about their grades.

Therefore their access was meaningful and based on a real demand. An interesting observation was that the participants still accessed the system even after the end of their courses to check their already known grades or to communicate with peers.

Simplicity and Interoperability

One big challenge for any mobile learning application is how to introduce the technology and

Figure 17. A chart showing pre and post use impressions about improving the communication by using MobiGlam

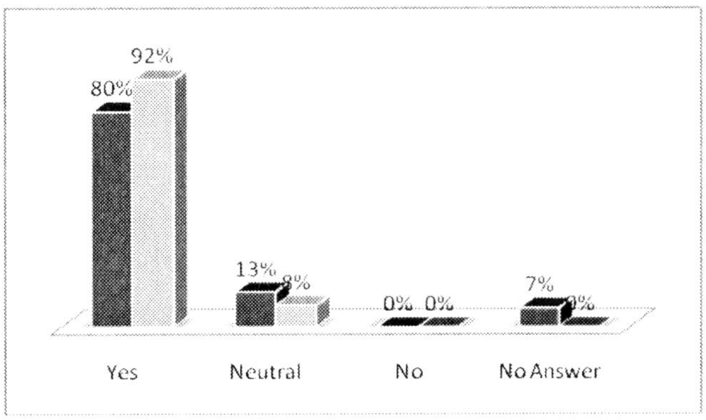

bypass the institutional obstacles. Many of the design and development principles adopted for MobiGlam made the integration of the technology for this case study possible, for example, ease of deployment, flexibility of extending content, alignment with institutional policies, cost control, user and administrator control. Without these principles, setting up and taking part in the discussed evaluation would not have been possible in practice. Interoperability was one huge advantage for the application. Another important aspect that contributed to the success of this case study was the flexibility given to tutors to create content from a VLE that they are familiar with or to extend what they already have without extra effort. Such feature of the system resulted in a rich application that is consistent with the existing VLE which created many opportunities for authentic and valuable use.

Feature Discovery

Several participants were overwhelmed with the number of functionalities introduced and as a result they felt confused. This was shown by the fact that they were mostly unaware of what the application could do. Many remarks were made about the need to add a certain feature that already existed in the application. It is even more alarming when a user's main frustration comes from believing that such a feature is not there to help. This was more obvious with the preferences that allow the participants to control the notifications or when users browse through long lists of content while they can use "Search" to decrease their effort. Improving feature discovery was a big challenge in this pilot implementation. By the end of the evaluations, there were still several functionalities that were not well explored, such as, scheduling alerts, group messages, searching in different activities, contextual feedback messages and saved items.

REFERENCES

Apache. (2007). *Apache tomcat*. The Apache Software Foundation. Retrieved on July 3, 2008, from http://tomcat.apache.org/

Corlett, D., Sharples, M., Chan, T., & Bull, S. (2004). A mobile learning organiser for university students. In *Wireless and Mobile Technologies in Education, 2004, Proceedings of the 2nd IEEE International Workshop* (pp. 35-42).

Giunti. (2008a). *Exactmobile, giunti labs*. Retrieved on November 23, 2008, from http://www.giuntilabs.com/info.php?vvu=34

Kaikkonen, A., Kallio, T., Keklinen, A., Kankainen, A., & Cankar, M. (2005). Usability testing of mobile applications: A comparison between laboratory and field testing. *Journal of Usability Studies*, *1*, 4–16.

Luckin, R., Brewster, D., Pearce, D., Siddons-Corby, R., & du Boulay, B. (2003). Smile: The creation of space for interaction through blended digital technology. In J. Attewell & C. Savill-Smith (Eds.), *MLearn* (pp. 87-94). Learning and Skills Development Agency.

Meawad, F., & Stubbs, G. (2008). A framework for enabling on-demand personalized mobile learning. [Inderscience Publishers.]. *Int. J. Mobile Learning and Organisation*, *2*(2), 133–148. doi:10.1504/IJMLO.2008.019765

Meisenberger, M. (2004). *Mobile learning engine*. Retrieved on April 6, 2008, from http://drei.fh-joanneum.at/mle/start.php

Millard, D., Woukeu, A., Tao, F. B., & Davis, H. (2005). Experiences with writing grid clients for mobile devices. In *1st International ELeGI Conference on Advanced Technology for Enhanced Learning*, BCS Electronic Workshops in Computing (eWiC).

Moodle. (2008). *Moodle: A free open source course management for online learning*. Retrieved on April 3, 2008, from http://moodle.org

Race, N. J. P. (2006). Engage: Enabling personalised learning across vle platforms using mobile devices. (Tech. Rep.). Lancaster University.

Wang, M., Shen, R., Tong, R., Yang, F., & Han, P. (2005). Mobile learning with cellphones and pocketpcs. (. *LNCS*, *3583*, 332–339.

Chapter 16
Using Technology to Support Quality Learning for School Activities Involving Field Studies

K.M. Stewart
Macquarie University, Australia

K. Thompson
University of Sydney, Australia

J.G. Hedberg
Macquarie University, Australia

W.Y. Wong
University of Sydney, Australia

ABSTRACT

The term mobile learning provides an image of active learning, of moving out into the world beyond the confines of the desk, beyond the classroom, beyond the school. The affordances of mobile, networked digital computers can provide learners with seamless access to and between information systems including data capture facilities and global positioning systems in real world settings. Mobile learning has come to represent a fruitful partnership between innovation in pedagogy and innovation in information and communication technologies. This chapter explores this nexus as it appears in emerging practices of a range of classroom teachers who are working to combine their aspirations for high quality student learning with the affordances of mobile technologies.

INTRODUCTION

The increasing use of mobile technologies to support global communities has impacted on all sectors of education and has resulted in changes in the conceptualisation of mobile learning in schools and the discipline of science in particular. Earlier definitions of mobile learning focussed upon the devices themselves and on strong links to e-learning (Traxler, 2007). However recent considerations of the scope of work identified as mobile learning have suggested that a single definition of mobile learning is not adequate (Sharples, 2007; Kukulska-Hulme

DOI: 10.4018/978-1-60566-882-6.ch016

& Traxler, 2007; Naismith, Lonsdale, Vavoula, & Sharples, 2004). Indeed the wide range of applications of mobile technologies evident in the literature indicates that mobile learning may be more appropriately conceptualised by a cluster of dimensions or common factors including the learning environment, curriculum, tools and community links (Winters, 2007; Laouris & Eteokleous, 2005). Rather than defining mobile learning these dimensions or factors represent areas to be considered when developing learning activities that require the use of mobile technologies.

Mobile learning implies the concept of the mobility of the learner so that there is no constraint to the data or the real world contexts in which it is collected. Reflections by educators and researchers working in this area emphasise the "broader concept of learning taking place in the mobile age, rather than the use of the narrower term 'mobile learning'" (Taylor, 2007, p. 26). "What needs to move with the learner is not the device, but his/her whole learning environment." (Laouris & Eteokleous, 2005, p. 7). Hence the pedagogical options that are supported by mobile technology become a critical focus for consideration (Beetham & Sharpe, 2007; Luckin, Brewster, Pearce, du Boulay, & Siddons-Corby, 2005). These options can be combined into a framework that comprises firstly a theoretical stance on the nature of knowledge and on how people learn then secondly a pedagogical approach informed by this stance.

This chapter contains an account of a project that focused on supporting school teachers in their use of mobile technologies to enhance learning in the field. This two-year project was funded by an Australian government initiative concerned with innovation in science, technology and mathematics education in schools. The project team included specialists in curriculum design, ICT education, outdoor education, software design and system analysis. Five publically funded schools from Sydney's southern and south-western suburbs responded to an invitation from the University of Sydney to join the project. These schools comprised two high schools and three primary schools with student populations reflecting the culturally diverse, urban population of Sydney. The project team focused on providing a group of 12-15 teachers from these project schools with the resources and support they required to design, conduct and evaluate a high quality learning experience for their classes of students incorporating the use of tablet PCs and digital cameras.

The first of four sections in this chapter discusses the pedagogical framework constructed by the participants in the project and provides an insight into the theoretical background of the project's educational approach. The second section considers requirements of mobile technologies viewed from the perspectives of school students, their teachers and researchers. The third section provides closer detail of the work of two of the project schools – a high school and a primary school. The final section discusses issues arising from the implementation of the project and considers future directions in this work.

CREATING A PEDAGOGICAL FRAMEWORK FOR MOBILE LEARNING

Over several years, there has been an increasing focus upon the nature of high quality learning and the theoretical ideas emerging from this activity formed the basis of a common approach to pedagogy constructed and adopted by the participants of this project focusing on the design of school field work activities. These activities were to be supported and enhanced by the use of mobile personal computers (in particular tablet PCs) and associated technologies that support learning in contexts that are no longer bounded by wires and walls.

The theoretical orientation of the project is grounded in social constructivist perspectives (von Glasersfeld, 1995; Vygotsky, 1978) which support group processes of collaboration and consultation as learners seek to construct shared understandings around areas of significant content. The pedagogical approach arising from this theoretical view of learning is informed by research associated with the concept of 'authentic pedagogy' (Newmann & Associates, 1996). Newmann's research describes learning of high intellectual quality occurring in situations where students are actively involved in constructing knowledge rather than replicating or reproducing someone else's expression of knowledge. Furthermore, authentic learning involves deeper understanding of areas perceived as highly valuable by students and the communities within which they live.

Other researchers have continued Newmann's work, focussing on being able to describe the nature of practices in schools that really make a difference to student learning (Hayes, 2003; Lingard, Hayes, & Mills, 2003). Their findings confirm what many already know – it is good teachers and their pedagogies that make the difference to student learning within the school environment. Concrete realization of aspirations for high quality learning can be located in the activities created for students by these successful classroom teachers. As Herrington, Reeves, Oliver, & Woo, (2004) state:

A complex and sustained activity can motivate students to learn. It can provide meaning and relevance to complex content, enable collaborative problem solving, justify the creation of polished products, and provide integrated assessment of achievement. (p. 5)

The approach employed in the projects described in this chapter was to provide innovative classroom teachers with the opportunity and support to embed the use of mobile technologies into specific learning activities. These activities were not limited to traditional classwork but included less traditional curriculum approaches such as across class mentoring by students within a school and across school mentoring between schools. The project activities required teachers to include in their planning a component of local biodiversity monitoring using tablet PCs and digital cameras.

A major outcome from early stages of the project was the clear agreement between participating teachers' perceptions of high quality learning. The resulting insights formed the basis of a common pedagogical approach for the development of curriculum and the selection of learning activities.

- The project incorporated the use of teaching and learning strategies that focussed on sustained *student engagement* and *self-direction*. There would be a focusing question or idea around which students would work *individually* and/or *collaboratively* to construct a response based on *collected real-world data* and *shared representations*.
- The content of the project was focused on knowledge and understandings that could be *integrated across topics* and/or subject areas.
- The content focus of the project was *meaningfully significant* to both the students and the wider community.
- The project provided *in the field opportunities for communication and collaboration* between students; between students and teachers; between students and other adults including community members and subject experts.
- The project viewed students as *knowledge communicators*. Students had access to knowledge and understandings held in the community about the local environment with the tacit understanding that they were able *contribute to this knowledge base* by re-working and re-presenting their understandings in a form *accessible to and shared with the local community*.

Once articulated, these shared statements guided the curriculum development work of project teachers as they interpreted these principles in the light of their particular school and the needs of the students involved in the project. Unlike many mobile learning projects the focus for learning remained with the classroom teacher rather than with the project team itself. There was no formula or pre-designed program imposed on project teachers who were given time and support to develop their own approaches to authentic learning activity design incorporating the use of mobile technologies.

STAKEHOLDERS' EXPECTATIONS OF TECHNOLOGY

Both students and teachers have reported that students benefit from the use of mobile learning (Swan, van 't Hooft, Kratcoski, & Unger, 2005; Vahey & Crawford, 2002; van 't Hooft, Diaz, & Swan, 2004). Thus studies are no longer addressing *whether* mobile learning is successful, but how and why it can be successful. The three stakeholder groups discussed in this section are students, teachers and researchers. At some point in the process of planning for mobile learning, a decision has to be made about the technologies that will support the learning activities. This section of the chapter discusses the attributes of mobile technologies that support mobile learning for these three stakeholder groups.

Students

Mobile technologies support student-centred learning so the needs of students should be taken into account when deciding on the technologies required. The attributes identified from these studies and from a review of the literature focus on the usability of the technologies and on the provision of learning scaffolds.

Usability

In the context of this discussion, usability focuses on the interface, the incorporation of digital products into class work, and the task itself. It appears that if usability of any of these areas is inadequate, students would find another way to do the task in some cases avoiding the use of the mobile technology.

Mobile learning technologies often involve tools with small screen sizes such as the screen on a mobile phone or personal digital assistant (PDA). In these cases, screen size can be a frustration for students if the interface is not appropriately designed (Swan et al., 2005). Tasks should be designed around the tools, or tools with an appropriate screen size for the task should be selected. Other devices such as Nova 5000 computers and tablet PCs, despite larger screens, have interfaces that still need a degree of customisation for the learning tasks. Customisation of the interface allows students to concentrate on the learning activity rather than the operation of the technology.

Students in any class will have a range of abilities which can be addressed by the attributes of the technology or by the pedagogical approach of the classroom teacher. For example employing a jigsaw structure in group work involves students each becoming specialists with one particular piece of technology then sharing their expertise with other members of the group (Thompson & Stewart, 2007). One of the areas in which students may have a range of abilities is in the use of technology itself. For students already interested in the technology there should be some challenge involved in its use. In our experience, if the use is too simple or provides little opportunity to expand their skills, students can become dis-engaged. For students who are not interested in technology, the mobile technologies should be straightforward to ensure the students have some degree of success in operating the technology. Usually, the opportunity to use mobile technologies in or out of the classroom is generally met with some excitement.

File types should be compatible across the mobile system and the local school computer system. Students need to be able to easily save their work in a format they can open when they don't have access to the mobile technology. This ensures that students will be able to access their field records and incorporate their data into class work on another date.

Scaffolding Technology Use

Professional development for teachers is discussed in the literature as a requirement for any mobile learning project (see for example van 't Hooft et al., 2004). However students also need appropriate support in how to use the technology as part of the learning task. While it is true that many students will determine how to use the tools themselves and teach each other, they will achieve more and be able to focus on the learning outcome if they have some formal training in the use of the technologies.

Where pen input is used, instruction is necessary for effective use of the computer. Pen input has a number of advantages such as organising and searching handwritten notes, taking notes in subjects where students need to draw, converting handwriting to text and sharing notes for collaborative work (Center for Digital Education & Gateway, 2005). It also allows the computer to simply lie flat and so encourages collaboration between students. Critics of this style suggest that text entry accuracy is affected and that audio-based input would better support the mobility aspect of the devices used (Lumsden & Gammell, 2004).

In considering which mobile technology, or combination of technologies, to include in a task, the scaffolding of the students' skills should be included in the discussion. In order to do this, teachers themselves must determine how the technology will be incorporated into their learning activities. The following section discusses teachers' requirements of the technology utilised in this project.

Teachers

The main attribute for the teacher stakeholder group is that they need to be able to manage the learning experience for their students. This presents itself in terms of coordinating student activities, synchronisation between work in the classroom and the field, lesson planning and pedagogy, and appropriate professional development.

Coordinating Student Activities

Teachers need to be able to coordinate students' activities. This is perhaps one of the biggest challenges for using technology in the classroom. As discussed above, students have a range of abilities and being able to coordinate and help any one of those students at any point in the task is essential for their classroom teacher. The solution to this challenge may require a routine to be developed (for example, rotation of students through specific tasks) or it may mean that extra support staff are required.

Extra staff can be made available to support the requirements of classroom teachers involved in designing learning activities utilising mobile technologies. Support staff may include experts in the use of the mobile technology who are familiar with the project. The use of support staff can add costs and may not be sustainable through the life of the project, however there are advantages in terms of teacher and student mastery of new devices in the early stages of the project.

Synchronisation of Work

Synchronisation of work across different learning contexts was discussed to some extent in the previous section on usability. It is worth considering from a teacher's perspective. Mobile learning most often happens away from the classroom, however teachers still need to be able to continue the work with students in the classroom. A system that allows the learning activities completed in the field to be synchronized with those occurring in the classroom will ensure that records are captured and then built upon. Teachers need to have a good understanding of their technology options and choose those that they think will best suit the task.

Teachers can take a number of approaches. Some decide that part of the advantage of using mobile technology can be that students do not have to re-enter data collected in the field. Hence synchronisation with classwork requires special consideration of the way in which field data is captured. In other cases, the purpose of the activity can be to produce a digital photograph or piece of art that can be incorporated into other work, and so the way in which this is recorded in the field is of less importance. The USB drive can be an invaluable tool in transferring student work between computer systems. However in the future wifi connections may be a more streamlined solution.

Lesson Planning and Pedagogy

Teachers need to be given opportunities to plan the incorporation of new technology, and new pedagogy into their lessons. This may involve support from the school in terms of time and also flexibility and ongoing changes to work practices (Cobcroft, 2006).

Mobile technologies can support student-centred and inquiry-based learning environments (Tan, Chen, Looi, Zhang, Seow, & Chan, 2007) and also both personalized and collaborative learning (Swan et al., 2005). Our experience has focused on student-centred, inquiry-based, collaborative learning activities (Stewart, 2007; Thompson & Stewart, 2007). Project teachers are interested to have the opportunity to trial these more innovative pedagogies along with innovative technologies. "Technology in itself won't make the difference; it's what students do with it that does." (Swan et al., 2005, p. 110) The way in which the mobile technology is used has to be appropriate to the learning outcomes, and therefore there needs to be some way to assess these learning outcomes. Technology may be able to support these two needs of educators by adapting the outputs such that they can easily be assessed or by having a core set of skills that can be mapped to learning outcomes.

The classroom culture has been indicated as a factor that may influence the success of these technologies (Swan et al., 2005). One way in which teachers can support a student-centred learning environment is to allow students to choose which technology they want to use – it is certainly an area that warrants further research (Swan et al., 2005). From the literature and experience with mobile learning projects, successful projects involve teachers and schools making use of the mobile technologies to build on existing programs of work and involve a variety of activities that build on students' experiences with the technologies (Swan et al., 2005; Warschauer, Grant, Del Real, & Rousseau, 2004). The technology should be flexible, sustainable and educators should be able to reuse the technology for another project at another time, with a different group of students.

Ongoing Professional Development

Ongoing professional development is required for educators (Attewell, 2005; van 't Hooft et al., 2004). Similar to the students, many teachers will be able to adapt their practice to the new technology, however they will be better able to do this if they have been trained in use of the technology.

Any professional development should incorporate the above points of learning outcomes and assessment – helping teachers to map learning outcomes to the use of the technology. Teachers will benefit from adopting an iterative approach towards developing their innovative activities. These areas are new and cycles of design and development of materials informed by learner feedback will be useful for further work (Attewell, 2005). This process is related to the sustainability of the technology and the learning activities where teachers need to be able to use the same processes in following years or for other projects, otherwise the time invested in the original project could be wasted.

Researchers

Researchers can play an important role in school-based mobile learning projects. They often choose and supply the technology, provide professional development and classroom support for teachers, and train students in the use of the technology. However, researchers are not often discussed as a stakeholder group. Yet the needs of this group are important because they often plan mobile learning projects and their reports can inform further work.

Data Capturing

From the point of view of research, ways in which all the above experiences can be captured for further analysis are to be considered. The use of mobile technology for education is still relatively new and research-based practice is encouraged. If the design of the technology or the activities around it incorporates some way of capturing the experiences then this will only further help practice. This may involve the setup of a server to store the information, and a database, so that it can be found again.

User Support

Researchers are in an appropriate position to provide training both in use of mobile technology and in classroom logistics incorporating student access to and use of the new technologies. Attewell (2005) comments that a fast response to mentor and learner problems is crucial to avoid disillusionment of project participants which can lead to stalling of momentum. Furthermore, proactive support for those just starting to support mobile learning plus ongoing access to advice is helpful.

Many students have indicated that failures with the equipment can constrain how mobile technology is used (for example Swan et al., 2005). While there can be issues with the tools themselves, such as battery life and screen visibility, other issues occur when, for example, the tools are integrated with a school's wireless network. Wireless infrastructure can add substantially to the power of a mobile learning environment offering ubiquity, portability and flexibility for collaborative learning projects (Sotillo, 2003). However a wireless network usually requires a set up, an IT person who can train users and maintain the system, and ongoing costs of some kind. Researchers often provide advice on synchronisation of files and are often in the best position to develop system and procedures that can be used in a range of project schools.

CASE STUDIES

Participating teachers from the five project schools were highly experienced classroom teachers interested in using the novel technology to provide their students with a different kind of learning experience. Some of the group were uncertain about their competence in using the new technology and were willing to learn along with their students. Teachers demonstrated that they were able to operate effectively and comfortably with a situation where control of their students' learning was often shared with the students themselves as well as with a range of project participants.

The early stages of the project involved collective planning and preparation with the project team and participating teachers. The group discussed pedagogical approaches and tentative ideas about the focus of the activities incorporating the use of the resources available to the project. A starting point for exploration of the use of mobile technologies to support student learning in the field was provided by records of innovative projects such as Ambient Wood (Rogers, Price, Harris, Phelps, Underwood, Wilde, Smith, Muller, Randell, Stanton, Neale, Thompson, Weal, & Michaelides, 2002) and Warriewood Wetlands (Bennett, 1998). The Ambient Wood project utilized a range of ubiquitous technologies to engage students in their study of their local woodland. The scope of this inspirational project with its purpose built hardware and software, while beyond the resources of our situation, provided an insight into some of the issues involved in using technology in the field.

The Warriewood Wetland project involved 10-12 year old students creating a website containing information about the biodiversity of their local natural environment. This website is linked to a community environmental education centre and represents an engaging record of local plant and animal species. This useful product served as a tool to focus project participants on possible concrete outcomes of student fieldwork.

Initial meetings also involved exploration and training in the use of the technology. Participants grappled with learning how to use the technology to achieve a desired outcome or simply to master the basic features of the technology itself eg creating, using and saving work; transferring files between the mobile technology system and the school computer systems etc. The focus of the project then turned to individual schools as they continued with their site-based curriculum development process. The following case descriptions present the mobile learning projects designed in two schools (refer to the project website for details of all schools, http://coco.edfac.usyd.edu.au/mobilelearning).

Case One: Student Biodiversity Project

Project teachers from the first school – a public co-educational high school from Sydney's southern suburbs, elected to involve both Year 11 biology students and Year 7 students as part of a syllabus-based peer mentoring program. The two project teachers conceptualized the focus of the learning and its associated activities as well as facilitated links with local naturalists, biologists and environmental educators from the student alumni, the local municipal council, and an environmental education centre.

The project team supported this initiative by providing tablet PCs and digital cameras for student use and training for students in their use. Expertise from across the tertiary sector was also sought to assist the school with its work. Two undergraduate computer engineering students were engaged to construct a web site containing a touch sensitive map of the school grounds and a database shell for the biodiversity records. An entomologist volunteered to be available on line to respond to student inquiries about identification and other information they required for their work.

Curriculum Context

Project teachers viewed the project as 'co-curricula' as it spanned both the formal and informal curriculum of the school. The project was linked to formal assessment and evaluation processes for the senior biology students requiring them to submit a report which included their area of study. The inquiry focus of the work was also particularly relevant to the junior science syllabus. Processes such as the generation of hypotheses, data collection and record keeping, field work, species identification, use of scientific language etc are all critical components of investigating and communicating scientifically.

Located in the informal or 'hidden' curriculum of this project school is its aspiration to support the personal and social needs of its students. This goal is served by programs such as peer mentoring where older students in the junior secondary school meet and work with beginning Year 7 students. The subsequent relationships formed are seen to assist younger students adjust to the secondary school environment and to develop counselling and communication skills in the older group of students. Project teachers perceived the advantage of combining the peer mentoring project with the learning potential of students using mobile technology to construct a collaborative product. Hence the curriculum focus of this project was both within and beyond the mainstream subject structure of the normal high school.

The content focus of the project was located in studying the biodiversity of the school grounds which contain a small but significant remnant of Sydney's turpentine-ironbark woodland. Teachers perceived the activity as a 'rich task' where students would work collaboratively to construct an interactive on-line database showcasing the flora and fauna of the local area. Senior students acted as project managers and worked with their younger students to locate, identify and describe trees and associated fauna in the group's specifically allocated area of the school grounds.

The project teachers held the following learning objectives:

1. to provide students with experience identifying plants in the school playground using scientific criteria.
2. to provide students with an opportunity to appreciate the diversity of species found in their grounds.
3. to provide students with an opportunity to use the latest digital technology in recording and reporting their discoveries.
4. to develop a database of the species of flora and fauna found at the school.

The school project team designated four 'incursion' days through the school year for students to have access to the group of specialists from the local community and to the entomologist on line. Typically the ten groups of up to six students alternated between collecting data in the field using tablet PCs and digital cameras and returning to the school computer room to download and organize their information. Students used the internet, reference books, project staff and internet access to the scientist-on-line to augment and confirm their field data. Over the four days students continued to refine their inventory and data collection techniques as they compiled and wrote up their biodiversity study.

Expectations of Mobile Technology

Project teachers and students anticipated access to a mobile learning platform that provided Wiki software, local wireless LAN, and positioning technology (GPS). Both teachers and students required instruction in the use of these technologies by ICT specialists in order to best achieve the desired learning outcomes. The final mobile learning platform that was designed for this project was the IRIS Mobile Learning Platform developed within the Faculty of Education and Social Work, University of Sydney.

The IRIS mobile learning platform integrated local wireless network technology, GPS, and Wiki software to facilitate collaborative learning for students and teachers in the field. Specifically, the IRIS ICT infrastructure consisted of a mobile laptop server with a portable wireless access point and a collection of wireless client laptops. Each wireless client laptop was fitted with a dongle to access GPS information. Via the local wireless network, the mobile laptop server provided Wiki services for social information construction activities and collaborative construction of multimedia information. The mobile laptop server also provided a GPS linked knowledge base for various points of interest in the outdoor school environment.

Outcomes and Reflections

The project teachers reported successful achievement of: student identification of plants in the playground; student appreciation of the diversity of species' found in the school grounds; effective student use of tablet PCs to record and report their discoveries. Teachers noted the enthusiastic response of the students to the learning task. Students realized the effectiveness of digital field records over paper-based records and began to develop methods incorporating the use of the tablet PC and their school computing facilities. Coordination of information across digital systems was considered as students themselves developed methods to link their field notes about a particular found species with their digital photographs. Students also addressed the issue of storing and retrieving the work of the group over the four field trip events.

Interest in the project was not confined to the school itself. Experts from the local municipal council worked with students and in doing so, provided the task with an authenticity and rigour that took it beyond a normal class activity. Student interaction with the scientist-on-line generally involved a single round of communication between the student inquirer and the scientist's response – even if the latter response required students to find more information to assist with the identification of the animal. Students would have benefited from focused input on ways of communicating and interacting with external experts.

Sustainability of the project with its requirement for mobile computing capabilities and wireless internet access was ensured by the school's acquisition of a bank of lap top computers stored on a movable trolley with a router linked to the school's network. While the laptops are more cumbersome than the tablet PCs, they support a wider range of purposes within the school. The work of the project continued beyond its initial trial with members of the original project team continuing to work on the wireless platform for GPS location and access to the on-line database whilst in the field.

Case Two: Salt Pan Creek Biodiversity Study

The two project teachers from a public primary school in Sydney's south-west, involved their classes of high ability students. One class consisted of students from Year 1 to Year 3, the second class had students from Year 4 to Year 6. Both teachers decided to incorporate the use of mobile technology into units of classwork, with the older class of students being involved earlier in the year and then acting as mentors for the younger class. Teachers made contact with the environment officer at the local municipal council who provided the school with maps of the local area and its storm water drainage system as well as species lists of local plants.

The local amateur naturalist society was approached to work with students to assist them to identify plants and animals in the field. The volunteer group was able to provide up to four members to accompany students on their field trips and to visit the school to speak with classes about the plants and animals of the local area.

The project team was involved in a wide range of activities within the school. Initial work involved assisting project teachers to design their units of classwork. The students were trained to develop a range of skills focusing on their use of the tablet PC and digital camera. Two undergraduate computer engineering students were engaged to design the project website where the primary students could locate their plants on a map of the local area. The website would also contain a database where students could upload information about their plants.

Curriculum Context

Project teachers were interested in designing curriculum to support sustained student inquiry focusing on their local creek. The period of inquiry would result in a polished product which reflected student knowledge and understanding of detailed content and competence in using technology to communicate scientifically. The curriculum design process commenced with setting learning outcomes for the unit of work. Consideration was then given to assessment procedures that would determine if students had achieved these outcomes.

Knowing what was to be achieved and how it would be measured, attention turned to the design of a teaching and learning sequence. The resulting units of classwork can be viewed at http://coco.edfac.usyd.edu.au/mobilelearning/

The older class commenced their unit with training in the use of the tablet PC and digital camera. Students were divided into small groups of four with two students working with a particular piece of equipment (eg two students using a tablet PC and two students using a digital camera). Initial investigations of the local flora and fauna included a visit from members of the local naturalist society. Students had designed questions to seek direct information from these local experts around a set of 30 local plants found at the study site. A field day to the local creek was organised for the students to work with a range of adult experts to research specific characteristics of their plant and of the environment in general. Information was gathered using the tablet PC, digital camera and binocular microscopes.

Digital information collected in the field was then used to create student presentations on the biodiversity of their local creek. The older class had also created a field herbarium of their plants. This pressed plant collection was then passed onto the younger class and a second field day was organised so that older students could familiarise their younger friends with their particular plant.

The task of the younger class was to create an information page about a specific plant that could be used by their families and other members of the local community. An assessment rubric was compiled for this task and discussed with students in the initial stages of their project. Students were trained in the use of the tablet PC and digital camera and used these on a further field trip to the creek. Explicit teaching was conducted around developing effective research skills and communicating scientifically. Students were able to use reference books and other sources of scientific information to add to the information about their plant. Specific instruction also focussed on using digital photographs to communicate scientific information and resulted in high quality products. Students' information sheets can be viewed on the project web site and are exemplary samples of work from the youngest of our primary students.

Expectations of Technology

Project teachers required access to mobile technologies not normally available to schools and to develop their personal skills in using tablet PCs, digital cameras, USB drives and the internet. They also expected to be supported by a team of specialists in using these technologies with their class of students to achieve set learning outcomes.

A class of approximately 30 students was divided into eight groups of three to four students. Each group required a tablet PC, digital camera and USB drive. The project team provided the required numbers of fully charged, ready to use equipment for each visit to the school. Progress in a particular activity slowed and in some cases stalled when equipment failed. This critical requirement necessitated procedures such as a specific member of the project team nominated to book, prepare and pack the equipment ready for the visit. This seemingly elementary consideration remains a fundamental factor in the successful delivery of learning outcomes relating to use of this technology.

The project team trained specific students in each group to use the tablet PC and the digital camera. Students also learned a range of computing skills including: creating and saving documents and folders; downloading pictures from the digital camera; saving fieldwork data held on tablet PCs to a USB drive. Students appeared to have little difficulty mastering these skills and were fully engaged with the technology and the tasks required of them during these training sessions.

A further expectation of the project technology was for seamless transfer of student work between computer systems. Both the classroom teachers and project team discussed the use of the USB drive to transfer digital information between the tablet PC and the school computer system. Some initial difficulties were encountered where documents had been created using software that was specific to the tablet PC. These documents were unable to be opened on the school system.

The group of undergraduate students working on the website for this project encountered insurmountable problems when they endeavoured to install their website onto the school system. The resourcefulness of the project teachers resulted in adjustment of their unit of work to accommodate this failure. Software compatibility between computer systems remains a critical factor in the success of these types of projects.

Outcomes and Reflections

The project team was overwhelmed by the high quality of work produced by the students involved in the project. A delegation of students from the school presented their work to a special meeting of the local naturalist society who had supported the project. The community group responded by making further offers of collaboration to assist students with their studies of the local environment. Student work samples stand as a testament to the potency of a learning environment where meeting the learning needs of the student is the priority of a well resourced team in collaboration with the classroom teacher.

ISSUES AND FUTURE DIRECTIONS

Many issues have arisen from this project and further experience trialling technologies to support mobile learning. The main issues can be grouped into three categories: issues concerned with technology; issues relating to school and classroom culture; the broader issue of researching in a school context.

Issues Concerning the Technology

The way in which the mobile technology (tablet PCs, digital cameras, USB drives) assists students to capture data in the field may not allow this data to be transferred easily to the school's computer system. Ideally students should be able to create, access and manipulate their field data across a range of computer systems. A system can be devised allowing students and teachers to transfer files from one device to another. This requires an understanding of the two devices and some training of teachers and students. Another solution is the development of a system to synchronise work done in the field with a server once students return to the classroom.

The amount of time required for the project team to develop specialised programs or websites and the process involved in this development is often underestimated. The need for specialised software to support learning in the field can be met by a range of experts including undergraduate honours students as well as paid professionals. University students who are able to create such programs as part of their study produce a high standard of work, however they are limited by a semester time frame of three to four months. Migration of the newly constructed software to the school's system can also be a lengthy process over which the schools themselves may have little control.

School access to mobile technology is often restricted to those times when they are involved with a project providing equipment such as tablet PCs, digital cameras and USB drives etc. While this means that schools are able to participate with low costs, it also means that teachers and students have restricted access to the equipment. Furthermore the project itself may have limited access to expensive devices such as tablet PCs. In this case teachers have less control over lesson planning as pedagogical concerns give way to factors such as group size and equitable access to equipment. Ideally the classes involved with the project should have unlimited access to mobile devices for at least the duration of their involvement with the activities. Schools may consider purchasing mobile devices such as tablet PCs, however a major concern is that the technology will advance, leaving the school with outdated equipment.

Issues Concerning School and Classroom Culture

Support for change within the classroom and possibly within the school is required from both the school principal and the project teachers. Teachers and school administrators are required to recognise the need for appropriate time to be made available for teachers and students to be involved in the authentic tasks envisaged by the rhetoric of quality learning. Flexibility in school routines can facilitate pedagogically desirable activities such as student mentoring, field work and visits to museums and local community groups etc. Rigid timetables – especially in the secondary school, can work against the conditions required to develop the more student-centred approaches relevant to authentic learning.

Inquiry-based approaches also require re-thinking both the role of the teacher and the role of the student. In an environment of teacher-directed learning approaches teachers are accustomed to leading and controlling the direction and scope of day-to-day student learning. Students are accustomed to following the directions of their teacher and mastering the content and skills placed before them. To change this paradigm, teachers can be required to attend professional development activities and be allocated time to plan the new learning context and to scaffold its implementation for their students. Students are required to play a more active role in their learning. Assessment strategies and reporting processes need to reflect the depth and quality of the authentic tasks which involve sustained student activity over longer periods of time.

A further hindrance to the development and implementation of more student-directed pedagogies is the increasing domination of testing regimes implemented at the state, federal and international levels of education administration. A perception held by school administrators and classroom teachers of the need to prepare students specifically to be able to respond to these regimes appear to take precedence over responding to the learning needs of the students themselves.

Researching in a School Environment

Researching mobile learning projects in schools involves consideration of a special range of issues beyond defining the research questions, devising a methodological approach and seeking ethics approval. Continued re-focussing on the research aspects of the project is required to prevent them being made subject to the needs and demands of the school situation.

A large number of project staff is needed to manage and support a mobile learning project. The professional development of project teachers is required in both the pedagogical approach of the work and the use of mobile technologies. Students also need training in the use of the equipment (and perhaps other basic computer skills). Project staff attend field days where they interact with students and attend to difficulties with equipment and with systems. All staff associated with school students are required to obtain formal clearance to work with children – a necessary but time-consuming process.

Adequate support of a mobile learning project involves an assurance of reliability and durability of the mobile technology used by project schools. Mobile equipment needs to be ready to work in a remote location in sufficient numbers for the required period of time. Clearly researchers need to be familiar with the field work site and the requirements of the classroom teacher in preparation for project field days.

Researchers may experience difficulty in being able to locate and communicate with classroom teachers. The project itself is just one of the many tasks facing the teacher in their daily work and its priority may not match that of the researcher. Recognition of and respect for the dedication of the project classroom teacher is an essential feature of this type of research projects being conducted in school context.

Future Directions

In many ways future directions in the technology will depend on developments in the devices themselves, and determining ways of linking with or enhancing current devices to accommodate these advances. The use of wikis and GPS involves enhancing wireless capabilities in conjunction with development of methods to synchronise the learning activities in the field with those in the classroom.

Future directions in scaffolding learning in the field will concentrate on many of those areas already outlined as essential to successful mobile learning projects. These include the provision of teacher professional development in student-centred approaches, construction of collaborative learning environments and authentic assessment. Large investment in time and resources across a range of project participants would require evidence of high quality learning outcomes and an indication of ways in which the work of the project would be sustained beyond its life. A highly desirable outcome of classroom teachers' involvement with mobile learning projects is change in practice to more student-led inquiry-based pedagogies. The shared resources produced by project teachers are an essential building block in the process of developing informed communities of practice around innovative pedagogies supported by innovative technologies.

ACKNOWLEDGMENT

Project mentor, Professor Peter Reimann; school principals, Christine Geelan and Terry Wylie; dedicated classroom teachers: Jenny Hoskings, Elisabeth Lloyd, Alan Ewings and Peter Turbet; enthusiastic students of these teachers; colleagues who made comments on earlier drafts of this work.

REFERENCES

Attewell, J. (2005, October 25-28). *From research and development to mobile learning: Tools for education and training providers and their learners*. Proceedings of mLearn 2005, Cape Town, South Africa.

Beetham, H., & Sharpe, R. (Eds.). (2007). *Rethinking pedagogy for a digital age*. Oxon: Routledge.

Bennett, J. (1998). *Warriewood wetlands*. Retrieved on April 24, 2007, from http://www.schools.ash.org.au/elanorah/wwetland.htm

Center for Digital Education, & Gateway. (2005). *Higher education mobile learning handbook: A resource on one-to-one computing environments for administrators, faculty, and the higher education community*. Retrieved on October 7, 2008, from http://media.centerdigitalgov.com/reg2view/CDE05_HigherED_Gateway.pdf

Cobcroft, R. (2006). *Literature review into mobile learning in the university context*. Queensland University: Queensland University of Technology, Creative Industries Faculty.

Hayes, D. (2003). Making learning an effect of schooling: Aligning curriculum, assessment, and pedagogy. *Discourse: Studies in the Cultural Politics of Education, 24*(2), 223–243. doi:10.1080/01596300303039

Herrington, J., Reeves, T. C., Oliver, R., & Woo, Y. (2004). Designing authentic activities in Web-based courses. *Journal of Computing in Higher Education, 16*(1), 3–29. doi:10.1007/BF02960280

Kukulska-Hulme, A., & Traxler, J. (2007). Designing for mobile and wireless learning. In H. Beetham & R. Sharpe (Eds.), *Rethinking pedagogy for a digital age* (pp. 180-192). Oxon: Routledge.

Laouris, Y., & Eteokleous, N. (2005, October 25-28). *We need an educationally relevant definition of mobile learning*. Proceedings of mLearn 2005, Cape Town, South Africa. Retrieved on April 11, 2007, from http://www.mlearn.org.za/CD/papers/Laouris%20&%20Eteokleous.pdf

Lingard, B., Hayes, D., & Mills, M. (2003). Teachers and productive pedagogies: Contextualising, conceptualizing, utilizing. *Pedagogy, Culture & Society, 11*(3), 397–422. doi:10.1080/14681360300200181

Luckin, R., Brewster, D., Pearce, D., du Boulay, B., & Siddons-Corby, R. (2005). Whether it's m-learning or e-learning, it must be ME learning. In A. Kukulska & J. Traxler (Eds.), *Mobile learning* (pp. 116-124). Oxon: Routledge.

Lumsden, J., & Gammell, A. (2004, September 13-16). *Mobile note taking: Investigating the efficacy of mobile text entry*. Paper presented at the 6th International Conference on Human Computer Interaction with Mobile Devices and Services, Glasgow, Scotland, United Kingdom.

Naismith, L., Lonsdale, P., Vavoula, G., & Sharples, M. (2004). *Literature review in mobile technologies and learning*. Bristol: NESTA Futurelab. Retrieved on April 24, 2007 from http://www.futurelab.org.uk/download/pdfs/research/lit_reviews/futurelab_review_11.pdf

Newmann, F., & Associates. (1996). *Authentic achievement: Restructuring schools for intellectual quality*. San Francisco: Jossey-Bass.

Rogers, Y., Price, S., Harris, E., Phelps, T., Underwood, M., Wilde, D., et al. (2002). *Learning through digitally augmented physical experiences: Reflections on the ambient wood project*. Retrieved on April 26, 2007, from http://www.cogs.susx.ac.uk/interact/previousSite/papers/Rogers_Ambient_Wood2.pdf

Sharples, M. (Ed.). (2007). *Big issues in mobile learning*. Nottingham: Learning Sciences Research Institute.

Sotillo, S. M. (2003). *Pedagogical advantages of ubiquitous computing in a wireless environment*. The Technology Source. Retrieved on January 16, 2006, from http://education.korea.ac.kr/innwoo/edu603/Wireless/Pedagogical%20Advantages%20of%20Ubiquitous%20Computing%20in%20a%20Wireless%20Environment.htm

Stewart, K. (2007, October 16-19). *Mobile learning: Designing the learning context*. Proceedings of mLearn 2007, Melbourne, Australia.

Swan, K., van 't Hooft, M., Kratcoski, A., & Unger, D. (2005). Uses and effects of mobile computing devices in K-8 classrooms. *Journal of Research on Technology in Education, 38*(1), 99–113.

Tan, N., Chen, W., Looi, C.-K., Zhang, B., Seow, P., & Chan, A. (2007). Handheld computers as cognitive tools: An environmental learning project in Singapore. In T. Hirashima, U. Hoppe & S. Shwu-Ching Young (Eds.), *Supporting learning flow through integrative technologies* (pp. 377-384). Amsterdam: IOS Press.

Taylor, J. (2007). Evaluating mobile learning. In M. Sharples (Ed.), *Big issues in mobile learning* (pp. 26-28). Nottingham: Learning Sciences Research Institute.

Thompson, K., & Stewart, K. (2007, October 16-19). *The mobile jigsaw: A collaborative strategy for mlearning about the environment*. Proceedings of mLearn 2007, Melbourne, Australia.

Traxler, J. (2007). Defining, discussing, and evaluating mobile learning: The moving finger writes and having writ.... *International Review of Research in Open and Distance Learning*, *8*(2).

Vahey, P., & Crawford, V. (2002). *Palm(TM) education pioneers program final evaluation report*. CA: SRI International.

van 't Hooft, M., Diaz, S., & Swan, K. (2004). Examining the potential of handheld computers: Findings from the Ohio PEP project. *Journal of Educational Computing Research*, *30*(4), 295–311. doi:10.2190/M1W6-A94D-3NKM-KBUU

von Glasersfeld, E. (1995). *Radical constructivism: A way of knowing and learning*. London: Falmer Press.

Vygotsky, L. S. (1978). *Mind in society: Development of higher psychological processes*. Cambridge: Harvard University Press.

Warschauer, M., Grant, D., Del Real, G., & Rousseau, M. (2004). Promoting academic literacy with technology: Successful laptop programs in K-12 schools. *System*, *32*, 525–537. doi:10.1016/j.system.2004.09.010

Winters, N. (2007). What is mobile learning? In M. Sharples (Ed.), *Big issues in mobile learning* (pp. 7-11). Nottingham: Learning Sciences Research Institute.

Chapter 17
Exploring Learner Identities through M-Learning:
Learning across Regional and Knowledge Boundaries

Ruth Wallace
Charles Darwin University, Australia

ABSTRACT

Learning is about making connections: connections from the known to the unknown through interactions and dialogue; connections between people's ideas and identities. Participation in learning is informed by an understanding of participants' connections to understanding of themselves and their membership of different groups. The engagement of disenfranchised learners is supported by the opportunities for learners to participate in learning experiences where their knowledge is valued and they are partners in co-producing knowledge and materials. Mobile technologies have considerable potential to support disenfranchised learners to participate in creating and defining a space where they belong in formal education settings. M-learning provides opportunities for learners and educators to be active agents in learning, share their own worlds and perspectives, and together create and recreate their understandings of the world and their own place within it. This chapter analyses a range of learning programmes that have utilised m-learning to engage disenfranchised learners in regional areas across Northern Australia. The author argues that m-learning is more than a tool to engage learners, it provides an insight into understanding how people learn and develop strong identities as learners. The discussion demonstrates the potential of m-learning to engage with ways of knowing and representing knowledge in ways that build strong connections to broad and diverse learning and knowledge societies.

INTRODUCTION

The development of m-learning pedagogy is informed by understanding its potential to engage learner identities, explore different forms of knowledge, engage learners in the co-production of knowledge and resources. The development of m-learning pedagogy has resulted in practices that also inform the construction of learning theoretical frameworks. Learning is about making connections:

DOI: 10.4018/978-1-60566-882-6.ch017

connections from the known to the unknown through interactions and dialogue; connections between people's ideas and identities; embodied though practice, collaboration, sharing, experiences, trial and error and relationships with fellow learners, experts, peers and others. Learners' engagement is informed by their learner identity, an empowered learner identity supports learner engagement as it contributes to learners' sense that they can negotiate their own learning participation, their knowledge is valued and they are partners in co-producing knowledge and materials. Powerful pedagogies implementation supports the development of social partnerships in learning that engage learning stakeholders and empower learners. The integration of mobile technologies, for example mobile phones and MP3 players, into a broad range of learning communities has been rapid and extensive, many of these communities have historically, had limited access to digital technologies for learning. The availability and flexibility of m-learning has been utilised to actively engage disenfranchised learners in meaningful learning experiences.

Mobile technologies have considerable potential to support disenfranchised learners to participate in creating and defining a space where they belong in formal education settings. Learners can access, capture, interpret, remix and present information about theirs and others worlds in multimedia formats. They can use their own devices to participate in the production and sharing of resources about their own lives without being restricted by extensive and expensive infrastructure. In short, mobile technologies have the potential to support learners to make connections about and through learning. This impact on infrastructure-poor or disengaged learners' experiences of and participation in learning should not be underestimated.

This chapter examines some of the ways partners in learning (including learners, teachers, para-professional support staff) use m-learning to deepen learning experiences and engage disenfranchised learners. The vignettes provide examples of various m-learning uses in Northern Australian regional areas and provide a basis to discuss some of the key concepts in relation to active engagement in learning, learner identities and m-learning. In particular, the learning from the vignettes examine the ways m-learning can engage disenfranchised learners in regional areas and the identities represented and given voice through m-learning. The discussion includes the kinds of media that have been used effectively for learning and the ways educators can use m-learning to build bridges across knowledge and learning systems. Where the literature or the projects broadly focused on e-learning is made explicit. The analysis of the literature, projects and implication focuses on the contribution of m-learning to students' learning.

M-LEARNING

M-learning uses a range of emerging technologies, consequently m-learning is continually being transformed as technology and its uses change. The uses of technology have developed with the technological advances and, as Kress and Pachler (2007) note, the incorporation of a range of devices into many peoples' social and cultural practices. Consider the impact of changes in battery size, voice recognition, touch screens, digital photographs and being able to beam files on your use of use of mobile technologies. M-learning has been described in terms of the mobile devices and software used in learning, tools that are available for immediate interaction in educational settings without physical restrictions; tools that are personal and pervasive (Kukulska-Hulme 2005). That is not to say there are no physical restraints, consider impact of battery life or being out of range of telecommunication services. As mobile technology is further integrated into daily life, people's expectations of their capacity to be available and fully functioning increases (or tolerance of being non-functional deceases). Mobile technologies' use is being integrated into social and cultural practices of a range of societies. Mobile technologies include digital media in common use such as digital cameras, audio recorders, mobile telephones, personal media devices (such as iPods), laptop computers, smartphones, personal digital assistants (PDAs), SMS (Short Message Service) text messaging (Kukulske-Hulme 2005) wireless modems, and through sharing audio, visual and text files.

Haythornthwaite (2007) notes that the digital divide (related to the access to and competence in use of a range of technologies like computers and high speed internet) impacts on communities' access and therefore their engagement in e-learning (including m-learning). The digital divide can be described in terms of income, education, access to infrastructure, occupation, ethnicity, regionality and life stage. Mobile technologies and their use may provide a tool to address the boundaries that educational and social results of the digital divide. The use of mobile technologies has extended rapidly across a wide range of communities across the globe; including communities that have limited access computer technologies.

Contrary to trends in the developed world, where the PC and Internet-connectivity is almost ubiquitous, mobile phones are currently the most important networked knowledge exchange technology used in the developing world. From a developing country perspective, features such as limited or no dependence on permanent electricity supply, easy maintenance, easy to use audio and text interfaces and the affordability of these devices are critical of mobile technology in education. (van den Berg, Botha, Krause, Tolmay and van Zyl (2008:290-1).

Africa is a case in point, where mobile technologies have been adopted in areas where the general lack of infrastructure, regular electricity supply, access to networks and technical support has previously restricted access to many communication technologies whereas the affordability and easy to use interface of mobile technologies, particularly mobile phones has provided opportunities for access (Traxler and Leach, 2006, Botha and Ford 2008). This rapid adoption would seem to indicate that people in infrastructure–poor and disenfranchised communities have found mobile technologies to be valuable in their lives.

Defining m-learning in terms of hardware and software helps to recognise m-learning tools in daily life but is limited by the technology advances at the time of any publication. It is may be more useful to describe m-learning in terms of its use and purpose. Mobile technologies are frequently connected to people's lives, are used for people's own purposes for recording and communication information. These uses of mobile technologies focus on making meaning and connection beyond the educational to the social. Mobile devices are characterised by potential for making connection through spontaneous collaboration and communication, location focused information, being readily available i.e. within sight, beaming information between devices and providing portable means of collecting and sharing audio and visual information (Kukulska-Hulme and Traxler 2005). Mobile devices provide opportunities for a wider group of people to create and share new forms of information using multimedia forms for their own purposes. Some examples are collecting videos on a mobile phone, creating a digital story, responding to an automated bill by text message or a wedding invitation by MMS (Multimedia Messaging Service).

The use of mobile technologies in learning environments has been integrated into formal educational contexts to enhance the communication of knowledge and development of ideas between learners, experts and their peers. 'The mobile learning community has demonstrated that it can (t)ake learning to individuals, communities and countries that were previously too remote, socially or geographically, for other educational initiatives'(Traxler 2008:9). Access to mobile technologies and m-learning pedagogies can provide learners (including teachers) meaningful, context driven ways to introduce and share their knowledge and worlds.

As mobile technologies and their use are a product of, a part of social and cultural practices, the issues related to social purpose, are worth considering in developing their use for educational purposes i.e. for m-learning. Field (2005:115-6) discusses the impact of emerging technologies on social capital, the trust and reciprocal relationships between people in society and the development of communities and places in cyberspace 'where people actively construct their identities as parts of wider sets of shared relationships.' The use of m-learning approaches presents opportunities to engage with a range of knowledge sets, constructs and contexts beyond those found in many formal or desk based educational settings. This might include multimedia based representations of diverse home life and beliefs systems, representations of knowledge as constructed by different social and cultural constructs. Though educational experiences, learners can use m-learning to make connections between learners' worlds, make unfamiliar contexts more accessible and create ways of interpreting knowledge that reflect different ways of knowing.

The focus on developing m-learning to meet disenfranchised learners' needs is based on more than the provision of technology. Sawyer (2004) found, in a study of issues around the digital divide in a remote desert Australian Indigenous community although technology and infrastructure issues were addressed, key issues of pedagogy, teacher skills and institutional barriers remained (Boyle and Wallace 2008). The related pedagogical issues of m-learning are key in optimising the use of mobile technologies in learning. M-learning tools and material have been used in conjunction with a range of software and content management systems. These include system wide mandated systems such as Blackboard or with freely available software and open source programs that provide access to instant messaging, emails, SMS text messages, Web 2.0, digital stories, voicethreads, scrapbooking, social networking, audio recording, and m-portfolios. The challenge, then, is utilising mobile phones (and other technologies) pragmatically rather than trying to replicate desktop computer functionalities (Botha, Traxler and Ford 2008:44).

M-learning is 'personal learning, which could be remote and individual, or social and collaborative' (Kukulska–Hulme and Traxler 2005:30-1). M-learning pedagogy integrates into learning experiences, the personal devices that many people own, access or use as individuals without being restricted to a particular space. The degree to which learners and teachers can negotiate their own identities, the contexts that inform them and are able to work in and across a range of local, regional and knowledge systems impacts on learning engagement. This involves moving away from one size fits all systems approaches as a single answer but looking at ways to utilise a range of m-learning tools together to support learners to express and connect to their diverse identities and knowledge. M-learning offers opportunities to explore a range of identities and connect to different ways of knowing and sharing.

LEARNING ACROSS DIVERSE KNOWLEDGE SYSTEMS

Lifelong, or lifewide, learning relates to the 'many different areas of life in which people continue to acquire and create new skills and knowledge throughout their lifespan' (Field 2005:1). Learning is socially constructed (Scott 2001:32), people learn through interaction with others in socially and culturally based contexts and knowledge (Gee 2004). These interactions are informed by people's identity as a learner and connected to the social cultural, historical and economic forces that surround and determine their lives. The decisions people make about their engagement in learning is related to the learner identities that they draw on, and the opportunities that are available to connect to a range of empowered community, family and workplace identities (Gee 2003, Wallace 2008). These are informed by learners' diverse cultures, contexts, knowledge systems and experiences. For disenfranchised learners, opportunities to explore their identity as learners and connect with different knowledge systems can make the difference in participating in formal education and undertake qualifications.

Learners and their learning contexts, practices and identities are socially situated, they are informed and created by people's lives, knowledge systems and relationships. Lave and Wenger (1991:35) proposed that learning is more than *situated in practice; it is* an identifiable process that is located in a particular place, *learning is an integral part of the generative social practice in the lived-in world.* As such, learning activities and contexts, their engagement and interpretation, are essentially connected in the broader relevant social based structures and their discourses (Scott 2001). Social constructions of learning are informed by and integrated into the knowledge and power relationships that function in societal structures; which are based on cultural, historic, social and economic influences. Learning sites are not value-free, as Billett (2001:7) noted workplaces as learning sites *are contested terrain,* evident in employees and management relationships and bonds based on age, gender, ethnicity, affiliation and bases for employment.

Understanding the social aspects of learning includes developing an understanding of the students' learning community, community membership (as described by Wenger 1998:149), multiple ways of knowing (e.g. multiliteracies as described by New London Group 2000), and community priorities. These may challenge an educational institution's curriculum and accepted knowledge base, providing a point of conflict for learners attempting to balance their membership in the formal education institutions curriculum and that of a workplace or community. The New London Group (2000:10-8) have explored pedagogical approaches that recognise issues related to language, culture and gender to minimise their negative impact on educational success. By developing pedagogies that make space for and value diversity, educational experiences invites learners to make connections between the known and the unknown and to make sense of learning experiences. This is particularly valuable as Gee (2004:39) notes learning is a cultural process, enacted through experiences and action, 'no one just reads: rather they read *something*... learning to read is about learning to read different types of text with real understanding.' M-learning, then, is a part of situated learning, as Gee (2003:15) states, 'knowing about a social practice always involves recognizing various distinctive ways of acting, interacting, valuing, feeling, knowing, and using various objects and technologies that constitute the social practice.'

Gee (2004) asserts that people learn better through embodied processes, where content is related to activities, discussion and sharing ideas. Embodied knowledge is embedded in educational systems' element and interactions (Sharples, Taylor and Vavoula 2007). Through these interactions and experiences related to specific contexts, people learn and become partners in creating ways of understanding those elements in that context. The interactions related to learning create connections that are mediated through communities of common interest, that may be connected through m-learning processes across regional, social and workplace boundaries, just to name a few. Gee (2003) describes the communities of learners as affinity groups that form around a common endeavour first and secondarily about sociocultural connections, their knowledge is holistic rather than separated into a specific narrow disciplines and intensive, deep knowledge about matters of importance to the community.

There are multiple routes to learning: learners make choices based on their experiences; their strengths preferred ways of learning and exploring other ways of learning. The ways people learn is based on reflecting on their own cultural models of the world that do not denigrate their identities, social connections, strengths and contrast them to new models (Gee 2003). M-learning tools extend the ways information can be collected, formatted, mixed and shared, particularly as learners can use readily available technologies in socially approved and recognised ways. For example, young people taking photographs with mobile phones, creating digital stories about their lives or recording elders' oral histories.

Digital tools create new possibilities for getting access to information, for producing sharing and reusing... The main point is more and more people in our culture can take part on these remixing activities; not only elite or specific groups. Everyone engages in remix in this general sense of the idea...what id ne is, of course, the impact of digital technologies. The possibilities of remixing all kinds of textual expressions and artefacts have thereby changed (Erstad 2008:185).

Learners, more than passive consumers of knowledge, are producers and teachers of knowledge and ideas as they relate to specific contexts (Gee 2003) as they relate to specific contexts. Learners are active interpreters of all learning, including m-learning, its use and potential. These interpretations relate to a sound understanding of the relevant context and relationship to people, places and knowledge systems. In an analysis of the ways Australian Aboriginal people produced resources in their own digital environments, Christie (2007:2-3) noted;

(Aboriginal) People use the digital resources in a social context as props or artefacts, in the same way that they would use nondigital resources like paintings, photos, diagrams, ceremonial objects, and of course the land itself and natural phenomena in talking about and representing themselves and their histories, and making agreements... the use of Aboriginal digital resources is serious business, making claims about ownership, about rights and responsibilities, and appropriate behaviour. In these cases the ways that the resources are identified and validated, the way they are accessed and displayed and the ways assemblages are put together and used in context, is a crucial part of the knowledge production process, and negotiations over resources (Christie 2007:2-3)

M-learning has provided access to envisage and share different forms of knowledge, strengths and skills. This is key in involving diverse ways of knowing, being and acting in the world. M-learning has the potential to support and reflect on effective approaches to learning. The potential of m-learning is about extending and deepening the ways learners explore, analyse and create in meaningful ways. To understand what is meaningful to learners and the power of connection between people's lives and diverse forms of knowing and being.

LEARNING IDENTITIES

Learning involves taking on and playing with identities in such a way that the learner has real choices ... and ample opportunity to mediate on the relationship between the new identities and the old ones. (Gee 2003:67)

Understanding the contexts in which learners operate, the role and implications of learning practices, means understanding the role of identity in learning. Falk and Balatti (2003) have found that a link exists between education and identity, that learners are affected by the ways they understand themselves and understand their identity as a learner in relation to education; both formal and informal education. Crenshaw (2003) contends identities are socially constructed, with particular reference to socially constructed notions of gender and race and their impact on identities. A person's identity, their knowledge and view of themselves or the way they are identified by others, impacts on the way they interact with learning domains, including m-learning domains. In terms of its relationship to learning, Gee (1999) notes the concept of 'socially situated identity' describes the multiple identities that people take on in different practices and contexts while the term core identity is used to describe the continuous and relatively fixed identities that underlie the social constructions of multi-faceted identities. Socially situated identities are developed through peoples' relationship to a range of family, local, peer, workplace and global communities. They are 'concerned with situated means, social languages, cultural models and Discourses. Discourses cover what has been described as communities of practice, cultural communities, distributed knowledge or distributed systems' (Gee 1999:38). Consider the impact of SMS on the way people communicate or the way participating in a m-learning community relates to one's reflection on the ways they see themselves as a learner or teacher.

For Wenger (1998), identity in practice as a *negotiated experience,* where people are identified by their participation, or lack thereof, in a group, as *community membership*, where people understand what is familiar, or not, as a *learning trajectory*, defined in terms of historical influences. Wenger describes identity in terms of a *nexus of membership* and is defined by the reconciliation of different types of membership of communities that people have. These communities can be at a local and a global level. Identity is being continuously renegotiating through participants' interpretation of themselves in terms of learning events and contexts and their membership with relevant communities. This practice involves negotiating diverse ways of engaging in practice that reflect the participants' individuality, accountability to significant communities, and performance elements that are recognised or not as valid by the relevant communities(p155). Negotiating a learner identity through a nexus of membership in different communities is complex; m-learning can provide access to means to explore a range of identities and to make connections to learners own worlds.

The impact of learning approaches that ignore or denigrate learners' identities as an empowered learner, either actively or by omission has been found by Smyth and Hattam (2004), Gee (2004) and Wallace (2008) to have significant impacts on learners' engagement in formal education processes. This can occur through misinterpretation or assumptions made about learners' lives and misrepresentations of their knowledge, or privileging certain content and contexts. They found that identities related to learning are constructed through interactions with their worlds; that of the media, peers, families and school. Their studies point to examples of disenfranchisement that had lead to lack of connection to learning experiences; where the experiences created a struggle over identity; to be negotiating or suppressing their own identities to survive or withdrawing from learning experiences. People with empowered identities see themselves as learners in ways that do not denigrate their own abilities, identities and connections to work, local and global communities and contrast them to other models (Gee 2003, Wallace 2008).

The integration of m-learning has the potential for learners, particularly disenfranchised learners, to accurately represent and share their own worlds while also exploring others in safe environments. A range of people, knowledge and contexts that are meaningful for empowering learners identity can be shared and explored to support individual's learning. Learners are able to organise and create information in ways that are mediated by a range of digital tools. Mobile technologies are accessible to a wide range of people who do not have ready access to mother forms of e-learning such as desktop computers and high speed internet.

The enacted learner identity framework I have developed to understand learners' identities draws on learning identity (Gee 2003, Falk and Balatti 2003Wenger 1998 Falk and Kilpatrick 2001) and social capital (Woolcock 2001, Grootaert, Narayan, Nyhan Jones and Woolcock 2004, Gitell and Vidal 1998, Putnam 2000, Fukyama 1995) theoretical frameworks assists in describing learning elements that impact on learner identity. The analysis identifies learner identity as it pertains to;

- types of training undertaken
- purpose for learner engagement
- networks accessed and supported through engagement
- types of learner identity evident through engagement
- resources used and demonstrated through engagement
- degree of student centred negotiability and learner empowerment
- alignment of learners' identities with informing identities i.e. professional, institutional, global and community.

This provides a framework for discussing the ways m-learning supports the engagement of disenfranchised learners in empowering learning experiences and to build connections between learners; their worlds and other identities. This is explored through a range of case studies.

FOUR M-LEARNING VIGNETTES

An analysis of broad range of examples of m-learning implemented in regional areas of Northern Australia explored the concept of identities and m-learning. These learner-centred projects, while not focussed on m-learning, have utilised m-learning in the implementation. The projects operated across compulsory and vocational education programs, school and work based programs, teaching and assessment pedagogy. The learning communities that developed and enhanced educational uptake of these approaches are particularly considered in each vignette. The following key learnings are drawn from the four vignettes and focus on the aspects of the projects that have utilised and explored m-learning. The case studies range across Indigenous and non-Indigenous teacher and student groups, adult, vocational and school based learning contexts. The projects' groups ranged from 12 to 120 participants. The projects involved Indigenous learners and educators in exploring ways to maximise learning and workforce outcomes with people who have often had negative experiences of formal education. Each project is discussed in terms of the key learnings about the role of m-learning in making connections for learners' identities.

Vignette 1: The Top End Groove – Indigenous Tourism E-Learning

A national Indigenous Engagement project, funded by Australian National Training Authority, was conducted in 2006 with Indigenous Tourism Operators from the Top End of Australia through which Indigenous enterprise operators trialled and developed e-learning and e-business tools and information for the establishment phase of an enterprise. Through the workshops, key issues in using digital technologies were identified by successful enterprises and training partners. Key in this process was an exploration and negotiation of ways e-tools can be used to support enterprise development training. The outcomes were analysed and presented as an Indigenous tourism enterprise community on a website. This website continues as a work in progress, Indigenous tourism operators were trained as administrators of the website so they can manage their own material and web content, create blogs and gain online feedback from visitors to their business.

M-learning was maximised as a useful art of the overall toolkit for building a business, learning about digital literacies by focusing on the purpose for participation and exploring the range of m-learning tools potential to support that goal. People explored the resources, support for building competence focussed on making connections using the tools. Participants were encouraged to explore the areas they needed and decide how they will use the technologies or their own purpose. People were not necessarily comfortable with, or regular users, of many technologies. M-learning tools were less daunting and more familiar. People were prepared to take, for example, a digital camera and explore how to use it in pairs or set up networks through online communication tools and talk online. People were not formally trained in how to use the technology; rather the focus was on exploring the tools for learners' purpose. They are experts in their own areas and are making informed decisions about how they can integrate the m-learning tools into their practice. Once learners had made those connections, people were interested in testing a range of e-learning and m-learning approaches and resources for their enterprise teams.

Enterprise teams worked in transgenerational teams to use the tools to make digital stories about their contexts; their enterprises' products, the history of their place or documenting the work they are doing. This enabled people who were reticent about being involved were encouraged by focusing sharing their strengths and knowledge through image and audio. By working in teams, one could work the technology while another was narrating etc in this way people could experiment with their workplace and learning identities in relation to significant people from their communities, the knowledge owned by that group and participation in a new community, an m-learning community. This approach meant together people had the opportunity to experiment and extend/deepen their learner identity in terms of education and the use of mobile technologies. M-learning in teams, for their purpose, engaged through just in time learning supported people effectively. Through experimentation and continued ownership, people involved became the experts in the relationships between the m-learning, content and contexts. The materials were published to their part of the website for wider local, international and web-based audiences. This could be used for assessment but first had a genuine purpose. As the processes were not mandated for assessment, people learnt from each other and through bringing their knowledge of place, context and content to the learning experience.

Vignette 2: Working from Our Strengths – Recognising and building literacy through the Training and Assessment Competencies

This was a project built on the work of Indigenous enterprise operators across Northern Australia to develop effective strategies to ensure relevant, quality training and qualifications are implemented that support economic independence and knowledge management at a local and national level. Funded by the Department of Education, Science and Training, the project used e-learning tools and technologies to support Indigenous enterprise operators' needed to map the development of training plan with their current and potential staff. The processes recognised the knowledge that is developed and owned by that enterprise and establishes opportunities for leading e-learning training for Indigenous people involved in enterprise training. Established Indigenous tourism enterprise operators and staff from a range of Indigenous businesses participated. Participants undertook recognition of prior learning (RPL) and current competence (RCC) processes that reflect the work undertaken in locally based enterprises and Aboriginal businesses using digital photographs, videos and stories, m-portfolios and web-based conferencing. The final product outlined the process for developing a training plan with an Indigenous enterprise team, ways to use m-learning tools to collect evidence and examples of successful e-applications of RPL and training plans.

While the project started by considering a range of e-learning approaches, m-learning strategies and resources were found to be most useful. The projects were based in remote Indigenous communities and were best managed by collecting and organising information with people, while they were involved in relevant work based and learning activities. In low information and communication technologies (ICT) infrastructure and support environments, it was beneficial not to rely on complicated technology and use approaches that can work anywhere, anytime. M-learning approaches, such as using laptops and cameras were less intrusive and already, integrated into people's daily lives, even if they were not used regularly by participants. M-learning based evidence collection strategies ranged across making digital stories, audio files to collating images and texts from various sources. Once these were accepted by students as viable, people identified a broad range of ways to collect evidence. Of particular benefit were peer teams who collected evidence for each other in their own workplace contexts and then reflecting on the images and recordings before remixing the information to be presented to the assessor. As the learning and evidence collection strategies were a part of people's lives and accepted made different ways to think about what is involved in learning and what counts for assessment. This encouraged people to focus on what they can do and how to document and communicate it so others could recognise those skills and competences. Learners also noted the empowerment they experienced by being involved in a learning process that included their worlds, worked from their own strengths in managing information and included more than text based ways of making connections. Assessors found alternative ways of recognising students' knowledge, strengths and potential points for connection around assessment.

Vignette 3: The Safe Houses Training Framework

This was developed to guide the professional development and qualification of Indigenous community members to work in and manage the Safe Places programme; designed to support family harmony based on Indigenous perspectives of life, family and health issues in Northern Territory (NT) Indigenous communities. The framework was designed to ensure training and assessment met the learning needs of Indigenous people, prepared and built people's capacity to work as community workers in the Safe Places programme. The innovative approach to professional development and training works to develop a professional community of practice of Indigenous and non-Indigenous Safe Places staff, field officers and management who are developing, implementing and documenting a community partnerships to addressing domestic violence. The framework was mapped to nationally accredited qualifications, employability skills, position descriptions and a sustainable employment path (for more detail see Wallace and Chick 2008). The principles of the training framework are that the locations of the Safe Places are remote and contextually unique; training and professional development would take place on-site and integrated into the community and workplace. The training is based on the relevant position's skills sets, context and their relationship to endorsed competencies' description. Resources developed that respect and incorporate Indigenous literacies and contexts, knowledge of and understandings about family, relationships and community services. As such content was developed with community approval and includes the mandatory data collection. The program has developed digital visually based data collection methods with Indigenous people working in the area

The learning materials and approach focus on portability, visual and accurate representations of the relevant concepts as they operate in

Indigenous communities. This framework development and design also recognises the value of positive relationships in developing positive and self sustaining learning experiences, networks and environments. The approach recognises the significant knowledge all the participants have about working in complex remote environments and socially based programmes. All resources are inclusive, include visual and digital resources for teaching and the programme does not rely on strong written Standard Australian English literacy skills mastery to enter the program.

M-portfolios were identified as an effective strategy for collecting evidence for assessment and RPL as well as exemplars of work based projects. For example digital stories and videos developed in the Safe Houses. By analysing the work tasks and resources with NTDHCS team we designed a range of projects using existing ICT and tasks required in the job role as well as the requirements of the funding body, the NTDHCS team designed the case studies that would be used for training to ensure there was high congruence with the environment that the Safe Places programme would operate within. The learning approach needed to move away from traditional text based learning using work books to using the literacies that are required in the job roles and the emerging digital age, i.e. visual and digital literacies.

Vignette 4: Integrating ICT as a Teaching and Learning Tool

To support classroom teachers, was a project that explored the use of ICT as a Teaching and Learning Tool, specifically in the engagement of reluctant and disengaged learners in regional contexts. A partnership between Charles Darwin University and the NT Catholic Education Office in 2008 established a professional learning community of teachers across a range of non-government schools in NT. Through this community, teachers shared and were introduced to and shared a variety of ICT tools (photo story, moviemaker and PowerPoint, interactive whiteboards, free photo manipulation programs) and the ways these can be used as effective teaching and learning tools to engage children in learning. The project's aim was to ensure teachers can identify good practice, what is needed to develop that practice and develop strong e-learning leaders.

The study identified the ICTs technologies and pedagogies that could be used effectively as a teaching and learning tool, and the professional development practice required for developing the use of ICT to engage students in more effective ways. Many of the tools and approaches related to m-learning and they are discussed here. The participants had greatly varied levels of confidence and experience in using m-learning technologies, integrating ICT effectively into their teaching and learning sequences which can be implemented by teachers in various locations and contexts and acting as mentors and critical colleagues in schools.

Teachers used a range of strategies including using iPods, digital cameras, laptops, multimedia animation and audacity to teach about story telling, developing posters for a public campaign. Students preferred working towards an external publishable purpose, and noted publishing was more important than playing games on ICT equipment as the games became boring. It was important to be involved in the use of m-learning as a co-producer and having an authentic purpose. Different input systems were attractive to students who were not confident with their handwriting. Students were keen to spend a lot of time on the content of their stories, felt ownership was important and were protective of their work. The use of m-learning in well designed learning experiences had a significant impact on student's engagement and participation. An identified advantage of m-learning was encouraging self critique and discussing how to can work differently, this was particularly noticeable with reluctant learners. These learners worked well in peer groups to share their expertise and experience. Effective approaches recognised the social aspects of using computers as important and were the focus of activities along with some basic computer skills. Teachers identified the importance of being available to help students on demand and accessing mentor peer groups. It was also valuable to recognise the different skills of teachers and encourage them to be confident in their skills and to develop networks that support their practice rather then feeling they had to have mastery of everything before working with students.

M-LEARNING THAT ENGAGES LEARNER IDENTITIES

These vignettes provide keys for thinking about the role of m-learning in formal education. M-learning provides powerful tools and approaches to make connections to learners' purpose for engagement. M-learning provides alternative and evolving ways of collecting, representing and sharing knowledge that may not be well understood or represented by formal education systems. These ways of sharing knowledge need to be controlled and owned by learners themselves for their own purposes and help to build bridges across knowledge systems. M-learning can be used to connect people across regions, generations and common interests to co-produce materials that utilise what they have learnt in relation to their own and others contexts. Learners can explore m-learning resources and their potential, given the tools to access and freedom to experiment, the focus is how the tool can help meet the purpose. The emergent and interactive nature of mobile technology encourages this flexibility in educational settings.

Incorporating different forms of knowledge are part of a rich tapestry where knowledge is valued within its context and for a purpose. Learners and teachers are involved in co-production of knowledge that references their experience and makes links to other forms of knowledge. M-learning, then, has a role in developing strong learner identity and re-engaging regional learners in formal education that meets their purposes. Any learning, including m-learning is mediated by the learners' informing networks and communities; this is true for teachers and students who will connect to local, work related and global communities through m-learning. Peers and knowledge brokers are important in working out the connections between knowledge and learning in ways that are supportive of learners' identities. Learners are active partners in the production of m-learning objects for their own purposes; m-learning can provide the environment and tools for innovation and creative problem solving. The m-learning outcomes are owned by learners and continue to be used for their purposes, for example sharing items from an m-portfolio for assessment and applying for a job.

M-learning pedagogy provides ways to collect information that accords with the knowledge and its social construct and informants i.e. community, learner and learning centred education. By seeing learners as competent in their own environments and gaining an insight into the complexity and depth of their knowledge systems, teachers understand learners in affirming ways. Effective approaches to m-learning focused on the pedagogy and purpose drawing on a fusion of available hardware and software. It was more important for the learners to be able to access, manage, solve problems and make critical decisions about the use of m-learning resources.

The value of m-learning that is well integrated into rich learning environments, then, is the opportunity for learners to engage in learning experiences where they are co-producers of knowledge, can actively engage in negotiating ideas, connecting to different people around common areas of interest. The particular value of m-learning is the potential for people to represent and introduce ideas in relation to their own worlds in diverse ways. 'Digital technologies create new possibilities for how people relate to each other, how knowledge is defined in negotiation between actors and changes our conception of learning environments in which actors make meaning' (Erstad 2008:181). Portable, accessible mobile learning devices and software provide the powerful tools for people to share and interpret their knowledge in ways that are meaningful to them rather than only in relation to curriculum based contexts. They incorporate ways of presenting ideas in visual, audio and written forms, and for people at basic entry level of skill and technology to remix those forms as they understand it.

In this approach, learners, particularly disenfranchised learners, have a chance to explore ideas, practice articulating their ideas and have the space to change their position completely and regularly. By developing a sense of self as a competent learner who has agency and has an impact on the learning context and content, learners have the chance to become the centre of their learning experience and able to negotiate a range of learning institutions. Learning is based in generation of the performative before competence, it starts from learners and encourages formal customisation of the curriculum – as a way to include and represent diversity, multiple identities, continually negotiated nexus of membership and multiliteracies. Activities have strong elements that reflect students' strengths such as oracy, spatial relations, visual representations, regional contexts and communities.

CONNECTIONS TO M-LEARNING BY FORMAL EDUCATION SYSTEMS

What could the integration of m-learning approaches mean for educational systems, particularly for those providing services to disenfranchised learners? Learning concepts, contexts and pedagogies utilized are effective when linked to the students' perceptual frameworks, there is a space in which to explore ideas and their connections to learners' identities and lifeworlds, the learners previous experience is not only valued it informs the learning process formally. It may be more appropriate to start learning from experience and link to a range of other experiences before considering the theoretical frameworks that help in articulating and discussing this experience. A range of learner identities are recognised as valid, individuals may adopt, explore and reject these at any time and repeatedly. This is part of the learning process and classes may have to change direction, stop for a time or provide a range of options which are more different from each other than just to topic or context. The inter-agency, institutional, personal, community relationships are overtly recognised and discussed as part of growing understanding about the world. These are complex and difficult and rather than seeking resolution, provide a rich source of understanding what is happening, why and how it may evolve.

Teachers engage as active participants in integrating m-learning to support learners to make connections and practise articulating their own ideas in relation to others. Teachers facilitate and support disenfranchised learners to develop an empowered identity as a learner. Co-trainers and assessors could be based in the communities in which learners identify. Their expert knowledge of context and content can assist in deepening knowledge a particular practice and support rigorous assessment of outcomes in situ. Empowerment is related to the active use of different tools, as long as learners have the competence and critical perspectives to use them for learning (Erstad 2008:181).

Educational institutions who decide to access the potential of emerging technologies and m-learning need to consider the implications for investment in systems. Investment needs to focus on supporting systems that support individuals to access and combine different information forms in unexpected ways, ways that reflect their ideas and worlds. Investment then will concentrate on systems that support individuals and communities to connect to a range of hard and software and combine information for learners purposes' rather than investing in single platform systems. The systems will adapt to emerging technologies, for example, a new multimedia programme to present information. Professional development supports teachers learn how to make strong networks and invest in being part of learning communities that share ideas and emerging technologies. Its important teachers feel confident to support innovation and concentrate on the product. Samples of learning and assessment products need to be available to teachers and learners to inspire innovation and experimentation.

Systems planners are challenged by rapid technological change and the integration of mobile technologies into teaching practice and educational support systems. The maintenance and development of systems wide solutions take time and infrastructure support. The introduction of m-learning tools adds another level if complexity. The focus of system planning needs to be on facilitating the interfaces between technology and providing platforms whereby learners can access the array of co-production tools and can experiment, create and remix files and images. Interoperability issues are the focus of integrating m-learning tools into educational systems, just as they have been in people's lives.

CONCLUSION

M-learning has engaged disenfranchised learners from regional areas in active and engaged learning that recognises and values their knowledge. The flexibility of m-learning means it is context and place driven and uses a range of visual, audio and multimedia files to represent knowledge in accordance with the relevant knowledge structures. Learners' identities are represented in terms of their local and global communities, peers, and given voice through m-learning. A hybrid of useful and readily available mobile devices and media worked together to support learners to engage and build strong identities. The integration of m-learning doesn't provide the only or one size fits all solution for engaging students and their learning identities. M-learning isn't a cure-all, a kits of gadgets to distract students, its efficacy is predicated on its integration into an engaging learning program. It is a key component of an engaging program and challenges education systems to appreciate m-learning as more than being engaging as they are fun but has an important impact on rethinking the ways learner's knowledge, skills and identities are recognised, valued and extended. M-learning is more than a tool to engage learners, it also provides an insight into understanding how people think. It provides new ways to think about the nature of learning from different perspectives and to better understand difference and the strength different ways of knowing and representing knowledge provides to learning and knowledge societies.

M-learning tools can be used to focus learning on exploring and engaging learner identities, local and global knowledge. By recognising the diverse knowledge systems and contexts of a range of disenfranchised learners, such as youth, regional communities and small enterprise owners, there are opportunities to build bridges between their worlds and that of formal education curriculum. The bridges provide points of connection and sharing, not for one to dominate or denigrate the other, rather to make connections to share ideas, build mutual understanding and extend possibilities for learning. M-learning pedagogy can be implemented to involve disenfranchised learners in positive learning experiences and active construction of knowledge and learner identities. Learners are able to work with and be assessed using material from their worlds as they relate to the worlds of work, community life and lifelong learning, to explore new possibilities and develop strong empowered learner identities.

REFERENCES

Billett. (2003). *Learning at work: Strategies for effective practice.* Sydney: Allen and Unwin.

Botha, A., & Ford, M. (2008). Digital life skills for the young and mobile digital citizens. *Proceedings of the mLearn 2008 Conference: The Bridge from Text to Context,* UK.

Botha, A., Traxler, J., & Ford, M. (2008). MobilED: A tool by any other name. *Proceedings of the mLearn 2008 Conference: The Bridge from Text to Context*, UK.

Boyle, A., & Wallace, R. (2008). The role of e-learning in 'holistic' approaches to VET in remote Australian Indigenous contexts. *Proceedings of the 2008 AVETRA Conference*, Adelaide.

Christie, M. (2007) Fracturing the skeleton of principle: Australian law, Aboriginal law, and digital technology. *Learning Communities: International Journal of Learning in Social Contexts.* Darwin: Charles Darwin University.

Crenshaw, K. (2003). Mapping the margins: Intersectionality, identity politics, and violence against women of color. In L. M. Alcoff & E. Mendieta (Eds.), *Identities: Race, class, gender, and nationality* (pp.175-200). Malden, MA: Blackwell Publishing.

Erstad, O. (2008). Trajectories of remixing: Digital literacies, media production, and schooling. In C. Lankshear & M. Knobel (Eds.), *Digital literacies* (pp.177-202). New York: Peter Lang Publishing.

Falk, I., & Balatti, J. (2003). *Role of identity in VET learning.* Paper presented at the 11th Annual International Conference on Post-compulsory Education and Training, Gold Coast, Centre for Learning Research, Griffith University.

Falk, I., & Kilpatrick, S. (2000). What is social capital? A study of interaction in a rural community. *Journal of the European Society for Rural Sociology . Sociologia Ruralis, 40*(1), 87–110. doi:10.1111/1467-9523.00133

Field, J. (2005). *Social capital and lifelong learning.* Bristol: The Policy Press.

Fukuyama, F. (1995). *Trust: The social virtues and the creation of prosperity*. New York: Free Press.

Gee, J. P. (2003). *What video games have to teach us about learning and literacy.* New York: Palgrave Macmillan.

Gee, J. P. (2004). *Situated language and learning: A critique of traditional schooling.* New York: Routledge.

Gittell, R., & Vidal, A. (1998). *Community organizing: Building social capital as a development strategy.* Thousand Oaks, CA: Sage Publications.

Grootaert, C., Narayan, D., Nyhan Jones, V., & Woolcock, M. (2004). *Measuring social capital: An integrated questionnaire.* World Bank Working Paper No. 18. Washington, D.C.: The World Bank.

Haythornthwaite, C. (2007). Digital divide and e-learning. In R. Andrews & C. Haythornthwaite (Eds.), *The Sage handbook of e-learning research* (pp. 97-118). London: Sage Publications.

Kress & Pachler. (2007). Thinking about the 'm' in m-learning. In N. Pachler (Ed.), *Mobile learning: Towards a research agenda.* London: WLE Centre, IoE.

Kukulska-Hulme, A. (2005). Introduction. In A. Kukulska-Hulme & J. Traxler (Eds.), *Mobile learning: A handbook for educators and trainers* (pp. 1-6). Oxon: Routledge.

Kukulska-Hulme, A., & Traxler, J. (2005). Mobile teaching and learning. In A. Kukulska-Hulme & J. Traxler (Eds.), *Mobile learning: A handbook for educators and trainers* (pp. 25-44). Oxon: Routledge.

Lave, J., & Wenger, E. (1991). *Situated learning: Legitimate peripheral participation.* Cambridge: Cambridge University Press.

Mendieta, E. (2003). Afterword. In L. M. Alcoff & E. Mendieta (Eds.), *Identities: Postcolonial and global in identities race, class, gender, and nationality* (pp. 407-416). Oxford, UK: Blackwell.

Putnam, R. (2000). *Bowling alone: The collapse and revival of American community.* New York: Simon and Schuster.

Sawyer, G. (2004). *Closing the digital divide: Increasing education and training opportunities for Indigenous students in remote areas.* Brisbane: New Practices in Flexible Learning. Australian Flexible Learning Framework.

Scott, D. (2001). Situated views of learning. In R. E. C. Paechter, R. Harrison & P. Twining (Eds.), *Learning, space, and identity.* London: Paul Chapman Publishing.

Seddon, T., &. Billett, S. (2004). *Social partnerships in vocational education: Building community capacity.* Adelaide: National Centre of Vocational Research.

Sharples, M., Taylor, J., & Vavoula, G. (2007). A theory of learning for the mobile age. In R. Andrews & C. Haythornthwaite (Eds.), *The Sage handbook of e-learning research* (pp. 221-247). London: Sage Publications.

Smyth, J., &. H. R. (2004). *Dropping out, drifting off, being excluded: Becoming someone without school.* New York: Peter Lang.

The New London Group. (2000). A pedagogy of multiliteracies: Designing social futures. In B. Cope & M. Kalantzis (Eds.), *Multiliteracies: Literacy learning and the design of social futures* (pp. 9-37). London: Routledge.

Traxler, J. (2008). From text to context. *Proceedings of the mLearn 2008 Conference: The Bridge from Text to Context*, UK.

Traxler, J., & Leach, J. (2006). *Innovative and sustainable mobile learning in Africa.* Paper presented at the Fourth IEEE International Workshop on Wireless, Mobile, and Ubiquitous Technology in Education (ICHIT'06).

van den Berg, M., Botha, A., Krause, C., Tolmay, C. J. P., & van Zyl, P. (2008). MobilED: A step backwards to look ahead. *Proceedings of the mLearn 2008 Conference: The Bridge from Text to Context,* UK.

Wallace, R. (2008). *Reluctant learners: Their identities and educational experiences.* Adelaide: NCVER.

Wallace, R., & Chick, L. (2008). *Safe places training framework: Building Indigenous capacity through work based VET in remote communities.* Paper presented at the 2008 AVETRA Conference, Adelaide

Wenger, E. (1998). *Communities of practice learning, meaning, and identity.* Cambridge: Cambridge University Press.

Woolcock, M. (2001). The place of social capital in understanding social and economic outcomes. *ISUMA: Canadian Journal of Policy Research, 2*, 11–17.

Compilation of References

3Home Page, G. P. P. Retrieved on October 15, 2008, from http://www.3gpp.org/

Abowd, G. D., Atkeson, C. G., Hong, J., Long, S., Kooper, R., & Pinkerton, M. (1997). Cyberguide: A mobile context-aware tour guide. *Wireless Networks, 3*, 421–433. doi:10.1023/A:1019194325861

AccessGrid. (2008). *Access grid*. Retrieved from www.accessgrid.org

Agrawal, R., Somani, A., & Xu, Y. (2001). Storage and querying of e-commerce data. In *Proc. of VLDB 2001* [online]. Retrieved from http://wotan.liu.edu/docis/lib/sisl/rclis/dbl/vldbvl/(2001)%253C149%253ASAQOED%253E/www.dia.uniroma3.it%252F~vldbproc%252F019_149.pdf

AKOGRIMO Project. (2007). Retrieved from http://www.akogrimo.org

Alexander, B. (2004, September/October). Going nomadic: Mobile learning in higher education. EDUCAUSE Review, 39, 28–35.

Alexander, B. (2006, March/April). Web 2.0: A new wave of innovation for teaching and learning? EDUCAUSE Review, 41, 33–44.

Alexander, B., Brown, M., Doogan, V., Johnson, L., Levine, A., Sabean, R., et al. (2006). The horizon report 2006 edition. A collaboration between The New Media Consortium and the Educause Learning Initiative.

Al-Jarf, R. S. (2004). Effect of online learning on struggling ESL college writers. *Foreign Language Annals, 37*(1), 1–18. doi:10.1111/j.1944-9720.2004.tb02172.x

Ally, M. (2004). Foundations of educational theory for online learning. In T. Anderson & F. Elloumi (Eds.), *Theory and practice of online learning*. Athabasca University.

Ally, M., Lin, F., McGreal, R., & Woo, B. (2005). *An intelligent agent for adapting and delivering electronic course materials to mobile learners*. Retrieved from http://www.mlearn.org.za/CD/papers/Ally-an intelligent.pdf

Alonso, F., López, G., Manrique, D., & Viñes, J. M. (2005). An instructional model for Web-based e-learning education with a blended learning process approach. *British Journal of Educational Technology, 36*(2), 217–235. doi:10.1111/j.1467-8535.2005.00454.x

ALT. (2009). *ALT-the Association for Learning Technology* [online]. Retrieved on January 12, 2009, from http://www.alt.ac.uk/index.html

Alvarado, M., & Vázquez, M. (2004). *Decision making automation based on fuzzy event-condition-action rules* [online]. Retrieved from http://delta.cs.cinvestav.mx/~matias/PDF/

Amory, A. (2007). Game object model version II: A theoretical framework for educational game development. *Educational Technology Research and Development, 55*(1), 51–77. doi:10.1007/s11423-006-9001-x

Anand, P. (2008, June 18-21). Constructivist-based location aware mobile learning activity. *Proceedings of the Emerging Technologies Conference*, University of Wollongong.

Anderson, J., & McCormick, R. (2005). *Ten pedagogic principles for e-learning. INSIGHT–Observatory for new technologies in education.* Retrieved on September 2, 2008, from http://insight.eun.org/ww/en/pub/insight/thematic_dossiers/articles/quality_criteria/equality2.htm

Anderson, P. (2007). What is Web 2.0? Ideas, technologies, and implications for education. Retrieved in March 2007, from http://www.jisc.ac.uk/whatwedo/services/services_techwatch/techwatch/techwatch_ic_reports2005_published.aspx

Andreadis, A., Benelli, G., Bianchi, A., Fedele, P., & Giambene, G. (2001, July). *Universal access to personalised information services.* (Tech. Rep.). Siena, Italy: Dipartimento di Ingegneria dell'Informazione, Universita di Siena. IST-PALIO project.

Andronico, A., Carmonaro, A., Colazzo, L., Molinari, A., Ronchetti, M., & Trifonova, A. (2003). *Designing models and services for learning management systems in mobile settings.* Udine, Italy: Mobile and Ubiquitous Information Access.

Antoniou, G., & Van Harmelen, F. (2003). Web ontology language: OWL. In S. Staab & R. Struder (Eds.), *Handbook on ontologies.* Germany: Springer.

Apache. (2007). *Apache tomcat.* The Apache Software Foundation. Retrieved on July 3, 2008, from http://tomcat.apache.org/

Armitage, S., & O'Leary, R. (2003). *A guide for learning technologists.* York: Learning and Teaching Support Network (LTSN).

Attawell, J. (2005). Mobile technologies and learning: A technology update and m-learning project summary. London: Learning and Skills Development Agency.

Attewell, J. (2004). *Learning with mobile devices: Research and development.* London, UK: Learning and Skills Development Agency.

Attewell, J. (2005, October 25-28). *From research and development to mobile learning: Tools for education and training providers and their learners.* Proceedings of mLearn 2005, Cape Town, South Africa.

Attewell, J., & Savill-Smith, C. (2004). Mobile learning and social inclusion: Focusing on learners and learning. In J. Attewell & C. Savill-Smith (Eds.), *Learning with mobile devices: Research and development* (pp. 3-11). London, UK: Learning and Skills Development Agency.

Australian Bureau of Statistics. (2007). Retrieved on April 27, 2007, from http://www.abs.gov.au/ausstats/abs%40.nsf/

Australian Mobile Data. (2006a). Retrieved on December 1, 2006, from http://www.budde.com.au/e-Newsletters/Contents/Australia-Mobile-Communications-Data-1180.html

Australian Mobile Data. (2006b). Retrieved on December 1, 2006, from http://www.budde.com.au/publications/annual/australia/australia-mobile-data-and-content-markets-summary.html

Baader, F., Calvanese, T. D., McGuinness, D. L., Nardi, D., & Patel-Schneider, P. F. (Eds.). (2003) *The description logic handbook: Theory, implementation, applications.* Cambridge, UK: Cambridge University Press.

Bachmair, B. (2007). M-learning and media use in everyday life: Towards a theoretical framework. In N. Pachler (Ed.), Mobile learning: Towards a research agenda. WLE Centre Occasional Papers in Work-based Learning 1. London: The WLE Centre, Institute of Education.

Barnes, K., Marateo, R., & Ferris, P. (2007). Teaching and learning with the Net generation, Innovate Journal of Online Education, 3(4). Retrieved on April 1, 2007, from http://www.innovateonline.info/index.php?view=article&id=382

Basak, J., & Krishnapuram, R. (2005). Interpretable hierarchical clustering by constructing an unsupervised decision tree. *IEEE Transactions on Knowledge and Data Engineering, 17*(1), 121–132. doi:10.1109/TKDE.2005.11

Beckett, D., & Hager, P. (2000). Making judgements as the basis of workplace learning: Towards an epistemology of practice. *International Journal of Lifelong Education, 19*(8), 300–311.

Becta. (2006). Emerging technologies for learning. Retrieved on April 6, 2006, from http://www.becta.org.uk/corporate/publications/

Becta. (2007). Emerging technologies for learning: Volume 2. Retrieved in March 2007, from http://partners.becta.org.uk/index.php?section=rh&catcode=_re_rp_ap_03&rid=11380

Beetham, H., & Sharpe, R. (Eds.). (2007). *Rethinking pedagogy for a digital age*. Oxon: Routledge.

Benford, S., Rowlanda, D., Flintham, M., Hull, R., Reid, J., Morrison, J., et al. (2004). Savannah: Designing a location-based game simulating lion behaviour. *International Conference on Advances in Computer Entertainment Technology*.

Bennett, C. L., & Pilkington, R. M. (2001). Using a virtual learning environment in higher education to support independent and collaborative learning. In *Advanced Learning Technologies: Proceedings of the IEEE International Conference* (pp. 285 - 288).

Bennett, J. (1998). *Warriewood wetlands*. Retrieved on April 24, 2007, from http://www.schools.ash.org.au/elanorah/wwetland.htm

Berger, H., Merkl, D., & Dittenbach, M. (2006). Exploiting partial decision trees for feature subset selection in e-mail categorisation. *Proceedings of the 2006 ACM Symposium on Applied Computing*, Dijon, France. *SESSION: Information Access and Retrieval (IAR)* (pp. 1105–1109).

Berkan, R. C., & Trubatch, S. L. (1997). *Fuzzy systems design principles: Building fuzzy IF-THEN rule bases*. Piscataway, NJ: IEEE Press.

Berndtsson, M., & Hansson, J. (1995, June). Issues in active real-time databases. In *Proceedings of the 1st International Workshop on Active and Real-Time Database Systems (ARTDB-95)*, Skovde, Sweden, Workshops in Computing (pp. 142-157). London: Springer Verlag.

Berndtsson, M., & Lings, B. (1995). *Logical events and ECA rules*. (Tech. Rep. HS-IDA-TR-95-004). University of Skovde [online]. Retrieved from http://citeseerx.ist.psu.edu/legacymapper?did=77063

Berners-Lee, T. (2003). Web services and Semantic Web. *Keynote speech, World Wide Web Conference 2003* [online]. Retrieved from http://www.w3.org/2003/Talks/0521-www-keynote-tbl/

Bersin, J. (2004). *The blended learning handbook*. San Francisco: Wiley.

Bertram, S., Boniface, M. J., Briscombe, N., Ntuba, M., & Palmer, D. (2006). *Enabling integrated emergency management: Reaping the Akogrimo benefits*. Tech. Rep. UNSPECIFIED, ECS, IT Innovation Centre.

Bijker, W. (1995). Of bicycles, bakelites, and bulbs. Toward a theory of sociotechnical change. Cambridge: MIT Press.

Billett, S. (2004). Workplace participatory practices, conceptualising workplaces as learning environments. *Journal of Workplace Learning, 16*(6), 312–324. doi:10.1108/13665620410550295

Billett. (2003). *Learning at work: Strategies for effective practice*. Sydney: Allen and Unwin.

Bonk, C. J., Cummings, J. A., Hara, N., Fischler, R. B., & Lee, S. M. (2000). A ten level Web integration continuum for educational psychology courses: New resources, partners, courses, and markets. Retrieved on January 20, 2007, from http://php.indiana.edu/~cjbonk/paper/10level.html

Borst, P. (1997). *Construction of engineering ontologies for knowledge sharing and reuse*. Unpublished doctoral dissertation, Twente University [online]. Retrieved from http://www.ub.utwente.nl/webdocs/inf/1/t0000004.pdf

Botha, A., & Ford, M. (2008). Digital life skills for the young and mobile digital citizens. *Proceedings of the mLearn 2008 Conference: The Bridge from Text to Context*, UK.

Botha, A., Traxler, J., & Ford, M. (2008). MobilED: A tool by any other name. *Proceedings of the mLearn 2008 Conference: The Bridge from Text to Context*, UK.

Boticki, I., Mornar, V., & Andric, K. (2006). *Supporting and enhancing teaching and learning with mobile devices*. CD-ROM edition. ISBN: 3-89958-195-4.

Boticki, I., Mornar, V., & Hoic–Bozic, N. (2006). *Introducing location-awareness into a learning environment supported by mobile devices* (pp. 267-274).

Boud, D., & Feletti, G. (2001). *The challenge of problem based learning.* London: Kogan Page.

Boughey, C. (1997). Learning to write by writing to learn: A group-work approach. *ELT Journal, 51*(2), 126–134. doi:10.1093/elt/51.2.126

Bourne, J. R. (1998). Net-learning: Strategies for on-campus and off-campus network-enabled learning. [JALN]. *Journal of Asynchronous Learning Networks, 2*(2).

Bowman, D. J. (1998). Overcoming reading, writing, spelling deficits: Resource center, learning center and basic skills program, with the application of an Orton-Gillingham Spalding method of instruction [electronic version]. Retrieved on July 2, 2004, from http://www.holmdel.k12.nj.us/pupil/holmdel_reading.htm

Boyd, D. M., & Ellison, N. B. (2007). Social network sites: Definition, history, and scholarship. Journal of Computer-Mediated Communication, 13(1), 11.

Boyle, A., & Wallace, R. (2008). The role of e-learning in 'holistic' approaches to VET in remote Australian Indigenous contexts. *Proceedings of the 2008 AVETRA Conference*, Adelaide.

Brdiczka, O., Reignier, P., & Crowley, J. L. (2005). Supervised learning of an abstract context model for an intelligent environment. In *Proceedings of the 2005 Joint Conference on Smart Objects and Ambient Intelligence: Innovative Context-aware Services: Usages and Technologies.* Grenoble, France, SESSION: Context-aware Systems (pp. 259-264).

Britain, S., & Liber, O. (1999, October). Pedagogical evaluation of virtual learning environments. (Rep. 41). JISC Technology Applications Programme.

Brooke, J. (1996). SUS-a quick and dirty usability scale. In P. W. Jordan, B. Thomas, B. A. Weerdmeester & I. McLelland (Eds.), *Usability evaluation in industry* (pp. 189-194). London: Taylor and Francis.

Brown, J. S., & Duguid, P. (1991). Organizational learning and communities of practice: Toward a unified view of working, learning, and innovation. *Organization Science, 2*(1), 40–57. doi:10.1287/orsc.2.1.40

Brown, P. J. (1996). *The e-stick document: A framework for creating context-aware applications.* Presented at the Proceedings of the Electronic Publishing (pp. 259-272).

Brown, P. J., Bovey, J. D., & Chen, X. (1997). Context-aware applications: From the laboratory to the market-place. *IEEE Personal Communications, 4*(5), 58–64. doi:10.1109/98.626984

Brown, T. H. (2006). Beyond constructivsm: Navigationism in the knowledge era. *On the Horizon, 14*(3). Bradford, UK: Emerald Group Publishing Limited.

Bruce, B., & Hogan, M. (1998). The disappearance of technology: Toward an ecological model of literacy. In D. Reinking, M. McKenna, L. Labbo & R. Kieffer (Eds.), Handbook of literacy and technology: Transformations in a post-typographic world. Mahwah, NJ: Lawrence Erlbaum Associates.

Bruner, C., Elias, V., Stein, D., & Schaefer, S. (2004). *Early learning left out: An examination of public investments in education and development by child age.* Washington, D.C.: Voices for America's Children and the Child and Family Policy Center.

Bruner, J. (1966). Toward a theory of instruction. Cambridge: Belknap Press of Harvard University.

Bruns, A. (2007, March 21-23). Beyond difference: Reconfiguring education for the user-led age. Paper presented at the ICE3: Ideas in Cyberspace Education: Digital Difference, Ross Priory, Loch Lomond.

Bruton, A. (2005). Process writing and communicative-task-based instruction: Many common features, but more common limitations? *TESL-EJ, 9*(3), 1–31.

Bryant, T. (2006). Social software in academia. *EDUCAUSE Quarterly, 2*, 61–64.

Bull, S., Yanchun, C., McEnvoy, A. T., Reid, E., & Wei Yang. (2004, March). Roles for learner models. In

Proceedings of the 2nd IEEE International Workshop on Wireless and Mobile Technologies in Education (WMTE 2004). Taoyuan, Taiwan (pp. 124-128).

Burleigh S., et. al. (2003). Delay-tolerant networking: An approach to interplanetary Internet. *IEEE Communications Magazine*, June.

Burns, R. B. (2000). *Introduction to research methods*. London: Sage Publications.

Callon, J. (1995). *Competitive advantage through information technology*. Irwin: McGraw-Hill.

Cameron, D. (2006, 4-7 December). The rocket in your pocket: How mobile phones became the media by stealth. Paper presented at the 2nd Joint JEANZ/JEA Conference, Rendevous Hotel, Auckland, New Zealand.

Candlin, C. N. (1993). Preface. In J. C. Richards (Ed.), *Error analysis: Perspectives on second language acquisition* (12th ed., pp. viiii-xi). Harlow, UK: Longman Group.

Carmona-Murillo, J., González-Sánchez, J. L., & Castro-Ruiz, M. (2007). Technological innovation in mobile communications developed with free software: Campus ubicuo. *UPGRADE. The European Journal for the Informatics Professional*, *8*(6), 27–33.

Caruso, J. B., & Salaway, G. (2007). Highlights of the 2007 ecar study of students and information technology. ECAR Symposium 2007. Retrieved on January 21, 2008, from http://connect.educause.edu/Library/ECAR/Highlightsofthe2007ECARSt/45912

Center for Digital Education, & Gateway. (2005). *Higher education mobile learning handbook: A resource on one-to-one computing environments for administrators, faculty, and the higher education community.* Retrieved on October 7, 2008, from http://media.centerdigitalgov.com/reg2view/CDE05_HigherED_Gateway.pdf

Cerkveinik, G. (2007). Decision trees and automatic learning in medical decision making. In *Proceedings of the 1997 IASTED International Conference on Intelligent Information Systems (Iis'97)*. Grand Bahamia Island, Bahamas (pp. 8-10 & 37-45).

Chaintreau, P., et al. (2006). Impact of human mobility on the design of opportunistic forwarding algorithms. In *Proceedings of IEEE INFOCOM*, 2006.

Chen, G., & Kotz, D. (2002). *Solar: An open platform for context-aware mobile applications*. (Tech. Rep.). Hanover, NH & Italy: Department of Computer Science, Dartmouth College & Dipartimento di Scienze dell'Informazione, Universit'a of Bologna.

Chen, N. S. (2005). Synchronous learning model over the Internet. *Innovations in Education and Teaching International*, *42*(2). doi:10.1080/14703290500062599

Chen, Y. S., Kao, T. C., & Sheu, J. P. (2005). Realizing outdoor independent learning with a buttery-watching mobile learning system. *Journal of Educational Computing Research*, *33*, 395–417. doi:10.2190/0PAB-HRN9-PJ9K-DY0C

Cheng, S., Tsai, W., & Chen, Y. (2008). Rescue knowledge m-learning system by 3G mobile phones. *Fifth IEEE International Conference on Wireless, Mobile, and Ubiquitous Technology in Education (WMUTE08)*, Beijing, China. Cityware Project Home Page. Retrieved on January 26, 2009, from http://www.cityware.org.uk/

ChinaGrid. (2008). Retrieved from http://www.chinagrid.edu.cn/chinagrid/index.jsp

Christie, M. (2007) Fracturing the skeleton of principle: Australian law, Aboriginal law, and digital technology. *Learning Communities: International Journal of Learning in Social Contexts*. Darwin: Charles Darwin University.

Chun, D. M., & Plass, J. L. (1997). Research on text comprehension with multimedia. *Language Learning & Technology*, *1*(1), 60–81.

Clarke & Parsia LLC. (2008). *Pellet* [online]. Retrieved from http://pellet.owldl.com/

Cobb, T. (1999). Breadth and depth of vocabulary acquisition with hands-on concordancing. *12*, 345-360.

Cobcroft, R. (2006). *Literature review into mobile learning in the university context*. Queensland University of Technology Creative Industries Faculty.

Cochrane, T. (2007, October 11). Idf mobile trial1 report: Review and evaluation of first mobile wireless trial. Retrieved from http://docs.google.com/Doc?id=dchr4rgg_215tknwt

Cochrane, T. (2007, October 16-19). Moving mobile mainstream: Using communities of practice to develop educational technology literacy in tertiary academics. Paper presented at the MLearn 2007-Making the Connections 6th International Conference on Mobile Learning, Melbourne.

Cochrane, T. (2008). Mobilizing learning: Intentional disruption. Harnessing the potential of social software tools in higher education using wireless mobile devices. International Journal of Mobile Learning and Organisation (Special edition: Developing Themes in Mobile Learning, in pre-press).

Cochrane, T. (2008, July 1-4). Going for gold: A moblogging case study. Paper presented at the HERDSA 2008: Engaging Communities, Millenium Hotel, Rotorua, New Zealand.

Cochrane, T. (2008, October 8-10). Designing mobile learning environments: Mobile trials at unitec 2008. Paper presented at the MLearn08: The Bridge from Text to Context, University of Wolverhampton, School of Computing and IT.

Cochrane, T., & Bateman, R. (2008, June 20). Bachelor of product design blogging reflections video. Retrieved from http://www.youtube.com/watch?v=d44q77cz7H4

Cochrane, T., & Cliffin, P. (2007). Ctli minisymposium presentation video: Diploma landscape design moblogging. Retrieved from http://www.youtube.com/watch?v=CBWkRrG7-xo

Cochrane, T., & Kligyte, G. (2007, June 11-14). Dummies2delight: Using communities of practice to develop educational technology literacy in tertiary academics. Paper presented at the JISC Online Conference: Innovating eLearning.

Cohen, L., Manion, L., & Morrison, K. (2001). *Research methods in education* (5th ed.). New York: Routledge.

Colella, V. (2000). Participatory simulations: Building collaborative understanding through immersive dynamic modeling. *Journal of the Learning Sciences*, *9*(4), 471–500. doi:10.1207/S15327809JLS0904_4

Collage Project Home Page. Retrieved on January 26, 2009, from http://www.ea.gr/ep/collage/main.asp

Compact HTML for Small Information Appliances. Retrieved on February 9, 1998, from http://www.w3.org/TR/1998/NOTE-compactHTML-19980209/

Composite Capabilities/Preference Profiles Retrieved on October 25, 2007, from http://www.w3.org/Mobile/CCPP/

Comvu. (2007). Press release 04/24/07 Comvu Media Inc. Retrieved on April 26, 2007, from http://www.comvu.com/comvu/presscenter/News042407.htm

Conole, G. (2005). Bridging the gap: A review of e-learning research at Southampton [electronic version]. *ELRC Conference*. Retrieved on June 30, 2008, from http://www.elrc.ac.uk/download/presentations/bridgingthegap/four-GrainneConole.ppt

CONTSENS (Using Wireless Technologies for Context Sensitive Education and Training) Project Home Page. Retrieved on January 26, 2009, from http://www.ericsson.com/ericsson/corpinfo/programs/using_wireless_technologies_for_context_sensitive_education_and_training/

Cook, J., Bradley, C., Lance, J., Smith, C., & Haynes, R. (2007). Generating learner contexts with mobile devices. In N. Pachler (Ed.), Mobile learning: Towards a research agenda (Vol. 1, pp. 33-54). London: WLE Centre, Institute of Education.

Cook, J., Pachler, N., & Bradley, C. (2008). Bridging the gap? Mobile phones at the interface between informal and formal learning. *Journal of the Research Center for Educational Technology*, *4*(1), 3–18.

Coppola, P., & Della, M. A. (2004). The concept of relevance in mobile and ubiquitous access. *Mobile and Ubiquitous Info 2003, LNCS*, *2954*, 1–10.

Corcho, O., & Gómez-Pérez, A. (2000). Evaluating knowledge representation and reasoning capabilities of ontology specification languages. In *Proceedings of the ECAI 2000 Workshop on Applications of Ontologies and Problem-Solving Methods*, Berlin

Corcho, O., Fernández-López, M., & Gómez-Pérez, A. (2003). Methodologies, tools, and languages for building ontologies. Where is their meeting point? *Data & Knowledge Engineering*, *46*, 41–64. doi:10.1016/S0169-023X(02)00195-7

Corlett, D., Sharples, M., Chan, T., & Bull, S. (2004). A mobile learning organiser for university students. In *Wireless and Mobile Technologies in Education, 2004, Proceedings of the 2nd IEEE International Workshop* (pp. 35-42).

Corrazzon, R. (2009). *Ontology. A resource guide for philosophers* [online]. Retrieved from http://www.formalontology.it/

Couros, A. (2000). *Ownership of knowledge and its implications for teacher education*. Retrieved from http://www.usask.ca/education/coursework/802papers/couros/couros.htm

Coursaris, C. K., & Kim, D. J. (2006). A qualitative review of empirical mobile usability studies. *In Proceedings of the Twelfth Americas Conference on Information Systems*, Acapulco, Mexico.

Cowan, J. (2004). *Building students' writing and evaluation skills: Developing reflective self and peer assessment*. Retrieved on February 25, 2007, from http://www.c-sap.bham.ac.uk/resources/project_reports/findings/ShowFinding.asp?id=106

Crenshaw, K. (2003). Mapping the margins: Intersectionality, identity politics, and violence against women of color. In L. M. Alcoff & E. Mendieta (Eds.), *Identities: Race, class, gender, and nationality* (pp.175-200). Malden, MA: Blackwell Publishing.

CSF. (2008). *Community scheduler framework, CSF.* Retrieved from www.globus.org

Cuevas, A., Jäehnert, J., Moreno, J. I., Villagrá, V., Olmedo, V., & Wesner, S. (2007). The Akogrimo service provisioning platform. *Proceedings of the 7th International Workshop on Applications and Services in Wireless Networks (ASWN 2007)*, Santander, Spain.

Cuixia, M., Hongan, W., Teng, D., & Dai, G. (2008, October 6-8). Context-aware modeling of concept sketch. In *Proceedings of the Third International Conference on Pervasive Computing and Applications* (pp. 520-525). Alexandria, Egypt.

Cullen, J., & Kelleher, J. (Eds.). (1995). *Evaluation guidelines handbook for learning technology innovation.* London: The Tavistock Institute.

Cullen, J., Hadjivassiliou, K., Hamilton, E., Sommerlad, E., & Stern, E. (2002). *Report submitted to the Economic and Social Research Institute, London. Review of current pedagogic research and practice in the fields of post-compulsory education and lifelong learning.* The Tavistock Institute.

Cummins, J. (2003). *Putting language proficiency in its place: Responding to critiques of the conversational/academic language distinction.* Retrieved on May 15, 2007, from http://www.iteachilearn.com/cummins/converacademlangdisti.html

Davies, N., Mitchell, K., Cheverest, K., & Blair, G. (1998). Developing a context sensitive tourist guide. (GIST Tech. Rep. G98-1). *First Workshop on Human Computer Interaction with Mobile Devices.*

de Freitas, S. (2006). Learning in immersive worlds: A review of game based learning. Joint Information Systems Committee (JISC). Retrieved on October 10, 2008, from http://www.jisc.ac.uk/media/documents/programmes/elearninginnovation/gamingreport_v3.pdf

de Freitas, S., & Levene, M. (2003). Evaluating the development of wearable devices, personal data assistants, and the use of other mobile devices in further and higher education institutions (JISC Tech. Rep.). UK: JISC.

de Freitas, S., & Oliver, M. (2006). How can exploratory learning with games and simulations within the curriculum be most effectively evaluated? *Computers & Education*, *46*, 249–264. doi:10.1016/j.compedu.2005.11.007

Dennis, T., & El-Gayar, O. (2005). Effectiveness of hybrid learning environments. *Issues in Information Systems*, *6*(1).

Denzin, N. K., & Lincoln, Y. S. (1994). Preface. In N. K. Denzin & Y. S. Lincoln (Eds.), *Handbook of qualitative research* (pp. ix-xii). Thousand Oaks, CA: Sage.

Device Independent Authoring Language (DIAL). (2007). Retrieved from http://www.w3.org/TR/dial/

Dey, A. K., & Abowd, G. D. (1999a). Towards a better understanding of context and context-awareness. (GVU Tech. Rep. GIT-GVU-99-22). Georgia: College of Computing, Georgia Institute of Technology.

Dey, A. K., Salber, D., Abowd, G. D., & Futakawa, M. (1999b). The conference assistant: Combining context-awareness with wearable computing. In *Proceedings of the 3rd International Symposium on Wearable Computers* (pp. 21-28), San Francisco, CA, October 18-19.

Dey, A., & Abowd, D. (2000). Towards a better understanding of context and context–awareness (pp. 304-307).

Dey, A., Abowd, D., & Salber, D. (2001). Conceptual framework and a toolkit for supporting the rapid prototyping of context-aware applications. *Human-Computer Interaction (HCI) . Journal*, *16*(2-4), 97–166.

Dichev, C., Dicheva, D., & Arroyo, L. (2004). Using topic maps for Web-based education. *Advanced Technology for Learning*, *1*(1), 1–7. doi:10.2316/Journal.208.2004.1.202-1450

Dix, A., Finlay, J., Abowd, G., & Beale, R. (2004). *Human computer interaction* (3rd ed.). Harlow, UK: Prentice Hall.

Document Management-Part 1: PDF 1.7: ISO 32000-1:2008. Retrieved from http://www.iso.org/iso/iso_catalogue/catalogue_tc/catalogue_detail.htm?csnumber=51502

Doering, N. M. (2007). The mainstreaming of mobile learning at a German university. In *Pervasive Computing and Communications Workshops (2007). PerCom Work Fifth Annual IEEE International Conference* (pp. 159-164).

Dourish, P. (2004). What we talk about when we talk about context. *Personal and Ubiquitous Computing*, *8*, 19–30. doi:10.1007/s00779-003-0253-8

Economides, A. A. (2007). Requirements of mobile learning applications. *International Journal of Innovation and Learning*.

E-Grid. (2008). *EU-US learning grid*. Retrieved from http://us-eu.ncsa.uiuc.edu/domains/elearning.htm

Elmasari, R., & Navathi, S. B. (1994). *Fundamentals of database design*, 2nd ed. Redwood City, CA: Benjamin/Cummins.

Elmendorp, R. (2007). Videoreporter.Nl. Retrieved on October 21, 2007, from http://www.videoreporter.nl/videos.htm

Embedded Debian Home Page. *The universal embedded operative system*. Retrieved on October 15, 2008, from http://www.emdebian.org

Engeström, Y. (1987). *Learning by expanding*. Helsinki: Orienta-Konsultit.

EPC. (2008). Retrieved on January 27, 2008, from http://www.epcglobalinc.org

Eraut, M. (2004). Informal learning in the workplace. *Studies in Continuing Education*, *26*(2), 247–273. doi:10.1080/158037042000225245

Erstad, O. (2008). Trajectories of remixing: Digital literacies, media production, and schooling. In C. Lankshear & M. Knobel (Eds.), *Digital literacies* (pp.177-202). New York: Peter Lang Publishing.

ETSI TS 07.07. (2003). *Digital cellular telecommunications system (phase 2+); AT command set for GSM mobile equipment (ME)*. Familiar Project Home Page. Retrieved on October 15, 2008, from http://familiar.handhelds.org/

European Commission. (1991). *Communication from the commission to the council and the European parliament: The e-learning action plan*. Retrieved from http://eur-lex.europa.eu/LexUriServ/site/en/com/2001/com2001_0172en01.pdf

European Commission. (2005). *The Bologna declaration on the European space for higher education: An explanation.* Brussels. Retrieved on August 15, 2008, from http://europa.eu.int/comm/education/policies/educ/bologna/bologna_en.html

EXPLOAR Project. (2008). About the EXPLOAR project. Retrieved on February 16, 2009, from http://www.ea.gr/ep/exploar/

Facer, K., Joiner, R., Stanton, D., Reid, J., Hull, R., & Kirk, D. (2004). Savannah: Mobile gaming and learning? *Journal of Computer Assisted Learning, 20*(6), 399–409. doi:10.1111/j.1365-2729.2004.00105.x

Falk, I., & Balatti, J. (2003). *Role of identity in VET learning.* Paper presented at the 11th Annual International Conference on Post-compulsory Education and Training, Gold Coast, Centre for Learning Research, Griffith University.

Falk, I., & Kilpatrick, S. (2000). What is social capital? A study of interaction in a rural community. *Journal of the European Society for Rural Sociology . Sociologia Ruralis, 40*(1), 87–110. doi:10.1111/1467-9523.00133

Falk, J. H., & Dierking, L. D. (2000). Learning from museums. Walnut Creek, CA: AltaMira Press.

Fall, F. (2003, August 25-29). A delay-tolerant network architecture for challenged Internets. *SIGCOMM 2003*, Karlsruhe, Germany.

Farmer, J. (2004, December 5-8). Communication dynamics: Discussion boards, weblogs, and the development of communities of inquiry in online learning environments. Paper presented at the 21st ASCILITE Conference: Beyond the Comfort Zone, Perth.

Farpoint Group Technical Note 2003-201.1. (2003, September). *Beyond the site survey: RF spectrum management for wireless LANs.*

Farpoint Group Technical Note 2006-321.1. (2006, October). *The invisible threat: Interference and wireless LANs.*

Feisst, M., Santos, D., Mitic, J., & Christ, A. (2005). *Adaptive heterogeneous learning system, mLearn2005.* Retrieved from http://www.mlearn.org.za/CD/papers/Feist.pdf

Ferscha, A., Clemens, H., & Oppl, S. (2004, October 1). Context awareness for group interaction support. In [Philadelphia, PA.]. *Proceedings of MobiWac, 04*, 88–97. doi:10.1145/1023783.1023801

Field, J. (2005). *Social capital and lifelong learning.* Bristol: The Policy Press.

Fielder, S. (2004, June 24). Introducing disruptive technologies for learning: Personal webpublishing and weblogs. Retrieved from http://static.cognitivearchitects.com/gems/Seblogging/EdMediaSymposium.pdf

Finney, J., Wade, S., Davies, N., & Fridal, A. (1996). *FLUMP: The flexible ubiquitous monitor project.* (Tech. Rep.). Distributed Multimedia Research Group, Department of Computing, Lancaster University, Lancaster, UK [online]. Retrieved from http://citeseerx.ist.psu.edu/viewdoc/summary?doi=10.1.1.53.2268

Fitzmaurice, G. W. (1993, July). Situated information spaces and spatially aware palmtop computers. In *Proceedings of CACM, 36*(7), 39-48.

Flanagan, J. A. (2005). *Context awareness in a mobile device: Ontologies vs. unsupervised/supervised learning* [online]. Retrieved from http://www.cis.hut.fi/AKRR05/papers/akrr05flanagan.pdf

Fleming, N., & Bonwell, C. C. (1998). VARK: A guide to learning styles. Retrieved on January 2, 2005, from http://www.vark-learn.com/english/index.asp

Foster, I. (2002). *What is the grid? A three point checklist, GRID today.*

Foster, I., Kesselman, C., & Tuecke, S. (2001). The anatomy of the grid: Enabling scalable virtual organizations. *The International Journal of Supercomputer Applications, 15*(3).

Fukuyama, F. (1995). *Trust: The social virtues and the creation of prosperity.* New York: Free Press.

Fulton, N. (2007, October 22). The mobile journalism toolkit contents. Reuters Mobile Journalism. Retrieved on October 24, from http://reutersmojo.com/2007/10/22/the-mobile-journalism-toolkit-contents/

Gábor, A. (2006, May). *Működéskorszerűsítés a felsőoktatásban.* Paper presented at Felsőoktatás-fejlesztési és felsőfokú szakképzési konferencia, Budapest, Hungary

Gábor, A. (2007, January). *Tudásszintkiegyenlítő, rövidciklusú e-learning kurzusok kifejlesztése.* Paper presented at HEFOP Workshop, Budapest, Hungary

Gaedke, M., Beigl, M., Gellersen, H.-W., & Segor, C. (1998). *Web content delivery to heterogeneous mobile platforms.* University of Karlsruhe. Retrieved from http://www.teco.edu/~gaedke/paper/1998-lncs1552.pdf

Ganjam, A., & Zhang, H. (2005). Internet multicast video delivery. *Proceedings of the IEEE, 93*(1), 159–170. doi:10.1109/JPROC.2004.839602

Garrison, D. R., & Anderson, T. (2003). E-learning in the 21st century: A framework for research and practice. London: RoutledgeFalmer.

Garrison, R., & Vaughan, N. (2007). Blended learning and course redesign in higher education: Assessing the role of teaching presence from the learner perspective [electronic version]. Retrieved on May 12, 2007 from http://www.ucalgary.ca

Gee, J. P. (2003). *What video games have to teach us about learning and literacy.* New York: Palgrave Macmillan.

Gee, J. P. (2004). *Situated language and learning: A critique of traditional schooling.* New York: Routledge.

Gee, J. P. (2005). Learning by design: Good video games as learning machines. *E-Learning, 2*(1), 5–16. doi:10.2304/elea.2005.2.1.5

Georgiev, T., Georgieva, E., & Trajkovski, G. (2006). Transitioning from e-learning to m-learning: Present issues and future challenges. *Proceedings of the Seventh ACIS International Conference on Software Engineering, Artificial Intelligence, Networking, and Parallel/Distributed Computing (SNPD '06)*, Las Vegas, NV. GITACA Research Group Home Page. Retrieved on October 15, 2008, from http://www.gitaca.com

Geroimenko, V., & Chen, C. (2002). (Eds). *Visualising the Semantic Web.* Berlin: Springer Verlag.

Ghanbari, M. (2003). *Standard codecs: Image compression to advanced video coding.* Great Britain: Institution of Electrical Engineers. GITACA Research Group. (n.d.). Retrieved on October 15, 2008, from http://www.gitaca.com

Ghim, S. J., Yoon, Y. I., & Ra, I. (2004). *A context-adaptive model for mobile learning applications.* (LNCS 3307/2004, pp.102-113). Springer Berlin / Heidelberg.

Gianna, A., Scaramuzzi, A., & Finkelstein, A. (2004). Evaluating non-functional requirements in mobile learning contents and multimedia educational software. In J. Attewell & C. Savill-Smith (Eds.), *Learning with mobile devices: Research and development* (pp. 13-20). London, UK: Learning and Skills Development Agency.

Gittell, R., & Vidal, A. (1998). *Community organizing: Building social capital as a development strategy.* Thousand Oaks, CA: Sage Publications.

Giunti. (2008). *Exactmobile, giunti labs.* Retrieved on November 23, 2008, from http://www.giuntilabs.com/info.php?vvu=34

Glogoff, S. (2005). Instructional blogging: Promoting interactivity, student-centered learning, and peer input. Innovate, 1(5). Retrieved from http://www.innovateonline.info/index.php?view=article&id=126

GNU/LinEx Operative System Home Page. Retrieved on October 15, 2008, from http://www.linex.org

Goh T., & Kinshuk. (2004, June 21-26). Getting ready for mobile learning. In L. Cantoni & C. McLoughlin (Eds.), *Proceedings of ED-MEDIA 2004-World Conference on Educational Multimedia, Hypermedia & Telecommunications* (pp. 56-63), Lugano, Switzerland: AACE.

Goh, T. T., & Hooper, V. (2007). To txt or not to txt: That's the puzzle. *Journal of Information Technology Education, 6*, 441–453. doi:10.3923/itj.2007.441.447

Goldberg, A., Russell, M., & Cook, A. (2003). The effect of computers on student writing: A metaanalysis of studies from 1992 to 2002. *Journal of Technology, Learning, and Assessment*, *2*(1), 1–52.

Gómez-Pérez, A., & Corcho, O. (2002). Ontology languages for the Semantic Web. *IEEE Intelligent Systems*, *17*(1), 54–60. doi:10.1109/5254.988453

Gonzales, A. J., & Dankel, D. D. (1993). *The engineering of knowledge-based systems theory and practice*. NJ: Prentice-Hall.

Goodlad, J. (1984). A place called school: Prospects for the future. New York: McGraw-Hill.

Goodyear, P. (2002). Psychological foundations for networked learning. In C. Steeples & C. Jones (Eds.), *Networked learning: Perspectives and issues* (pp. 49-75). London: Springer Verlag.

Goodyear, P. (2005). Educational design and networked learning: Patterns, pattern languages, and design practice. *Australasian Journal of Educational Technology*, *21*(1), 82–101.

Gorrard, S., Selwyn, N., Madden, L., & Furlong, J. (2002). Technology and lifelong learning: Are we cutting IT? *All-Wales Education Research Conference*, Gregynog, July 3-5, 1993.

Griswold, W. G., Shanahan, P., Brown, S. W., Boyer, R., Ratto, M., Shapiro, R. B., & Truong, T. M. (2004). Activecampus: Experiments in community-oriented ubiquitous computing. *Computer*, *37*(10), 73–81. doi:10.1109/MC.2004.149

Grootaert, C., Narayan, D., Nyhan Jones, V., & Woolcock, M. (2004). *Measuring social capital: An integrated questionnaire*. World Bank Working Paper No. 18. Washington, D.C.: The World Bank.

Grossglauser, M., & Tse, D. (2002). Mobility increases the capacity of ad hoc wireless networks. *IEEE/ACM Transactions on Networking, 2002*.

Gruber, T. R. (1993). A translation approach to portable ontology specification. *Knowledge Acquisition*, *5*(2), 199–220. doi:10.1006/knac.1993.1008

Gruber, T. R. (1993). Toward principles for the design of ontologies used for knowledge sharing. *International Journal of Human-Computer Studies*, *43*(5-6), 907–928. doi:10.1006/ijhc.1995.1081

Guarino, N., & Giaretta, P. (1995). Ontologies and knowledge bases: Towards a terminological clarification. In N. Mars (Ed.), *Towards very large knowledge bases: Knowledge building and knowledge sharing* (pp. 25-32). Amsterdam, Holland: IOS Press.

Gulliver, R., Randall, B., & Pok, Y. (1999). The orbicular model-cognitive learning in cyberspace. *Association for the Advancement of Computing in Education*, *1*(12), 18–22.

Hadzilacos, T., & Tryfona, N. (2005). *Mobile learning: Current trend and future challenges*. Paper presented at Fifth International Conference on Advanced Learning Technologies (ICALT '05), Kaohsiung, Taiwan.

Harrison, R. (2007). Academic skills: What are they and how do we teach them? *Perspectives*, *14*(2), 9–11.

Hartnell-Young, E. (2004). Mapping the e-portfolio territory. Personal hand out, International Society for Performance Improvement, Melbourne chapter, Presentation, November 2004.

Hawkey, R. (2004). Learning with digital technologies in museums, science centres, and galleries. Report No. 9, NESTA FutureLab. Retrieved on February 16, 2009, from http://www.futurelab.org.uk/resources/documents/lit_reviews/Museums_Galleries_Review.pdf

Hayes, D. (2003). Making learning an effect of schooling: Aligning curriculum, assessment, and pedagogy. *Discourse: Studies in the Cultural Politics of Education*, *24*(2), 223–243. doi:10.1080/01596300303039

Hayes-Roth, F. (1985). Rule-based systems. *Communications of the ACM*, *28*(9), 921–932. doi:10.1145/4284.4286

Haythornthwaite, C. (2007). Digital divide and e-learning. In R. Andrews & C. Haythornthwaite (Eds.), *The Sage handbook of e-learning research* (pp. 97-118). London: Sage Publications.

Hazas, M., Scott, J., & Krumm, J. (2004). Location-aware computing comes of age. *IEEE Computer Magazine*, *37*(2), 95–97.

He, H. (2003). *What is service-oriented architecture*. O'Reilly. Retrieved on September 13, 2008, from http://webservices.xml.com/pub/a/ws/2003/09/30/soa.html

Healey, J., & Picard, R. W. (1998, October 1-20). Startlecam: A cybernetic wearable camera. In *Proceedings of the 2nd International Symposium on Wearable Computers* (pp. 42-49), Pittsburgh, PA.

HEFOP FOI Project. (2006). *Referencia-modell*. Retrieved on September 24, 2008, from http://informatika.bkae.hu/hefop

Heinze, A., & Proctor, C. (2004). *Reflections on the use of blended learning*. Paper presented at the Education in a Changing Environment, University of Salford, UK. Retrieved on June 10, 2005, from http://www.edu.salford.ac.uk/her/proceedings/papers/ah_04.rtf

Herrington, J., Mantei, J., Herrington, A., Olney, I., & Ferry, B. (2008, December 1-4). New technologies, new pedagogies: Mobile technologies and new ways of teaching and learning. Paper presented at the ASCILITE 2008, Deakin University, Melbourne, Australia.

Herrington, J., Reeves, T. C., Oliver, R., & Woo, Y. (2004). Designing authentic activities in Web-based courses. *Journal of Computing in Higher Education*, *16*(1), 3–29. doi:10.1007/BF02960280

Hoic-Bozic, N., Boticki, I., & Mornar, V. (2005). *Interaction and collaborative support in an adaptive Web-based LMS AhyCo* (pp. 123-230).

Hokyoung, R., & Parsons, D. (2008). *Innovative mobile learning: Techniques and technologies*. Hershey, PA: IGI Global.

Holzinger, A., & Errath, M. (2007). Mobile computer Web-application design in medicine: Some research based guidelines. *Universal Access in the Information Society*, *6*, 31–41. doi:10.1007/s10209-007-0074-z

Holzinger, A., Nischelwitzer, A. K., & Kickmeier-Rust, M. D. (2006). Pervasive e-education supports lifelong learning: Some examples of x-media learning objects (xlos). In *10th IACEE World Conference on Continuing Engineering Education (WCCEE)*, Vienna University of Technology, Vienna.

Hoppe, U. (2006). How can we integrate mobile devices with broader educational scenarios? In M. Sharples (Ed.), *Big issues in mobile learning: Report of a workshop by the kaleidoscope network of excellence mobile learning initiative*. Nottingham, UK: Learning Sciences Research Institute, University of Nottingham Joint Quality Initiative. (2004). *Shared 'Dublin's descriptors for the bachelor's and master's and doctoral awards*. Retrieved on September 15, 2008, from http://www.tempus.ac.yu/here/tl_files/Dokumenti/Dublinski%20deskriptori.pdf

Horrocks, I., Patel-Schneider, P. F., & van-Harmelen, F. (2003). From SHIQ and RDF to OWL: The making of the ontology Web language. *Journal of Web Semantics*, *1*(1), 7–26. doi:10.1016/j.websem.2003.07.001

Horrocks, I., Patel-Schneider, P. F., Boley, H., Tabet, S., Grosof, B., & Dean, M. (2004). *SWRL: A Semantic Web rule language combining OWL and RuleML* [online]. Retrieved from http://www.w3.org/Submission/SWRL/

Hsi, S., & Fait, H. (2005). RFID enhances visitors' museum experience at the exploratorium. *Communications of the ACM*, *48*(9), 60-65.

HTML 4.01 Specification. Retrieved on December 24, 1999, from http://www.w3.org/TR/html401/

Hu, B., & Moore, P. (2007). Smart context: An ontology based context model for cooperative mobile learning. *Computer Supported Cooperative Work in Design, 10th International Conference (CSCWD 2006)* (LNCS 4402, pp. 717-726), Nanjing, China, May 2006.

Hu, B., Moore, P., & Chen, H.-H. (2007). A semantic model for location based cooperative learning. In *Proceedings of the International Conference on Communications (ICC-2007)* (pp. 326-331), Glasgow, Scotland, June 24-28.

Hug, T. (2005, May 6-8). *Microlearning and narration*. Paper presented at the Fourth Media in Transition Conference, MIT, Cambridge, MA. Retrieved on September

10, 2008, from http://web.mit.edu/comm-forum/mit4/papers/hug.pdf

Huizenga, J., Admiraal, W., Akkerman, S., & Dam, G. (2007, October). Learning history by playing a mobile city game. In D. Remenyi (Ed.), *Proceedings of the 1st European Conference on Game-Based Learning (ECGBL)* (pp. 127–134), University of Paisley, Paisley, Scotland. Reading, UK: Academic Conferences Limited.

Hung, D. W. L., & Chen, D. (2001). Situated cognition, Vygotskian thought and learning from the communities of practice perspective: Implications for the design of Web-based e-learning. *Educational Media International, 38*(1), 3–12. doi:10.1080/09523980110037525

IEEE Std. 802®-2001, Media Access Control (MAC). Retrieved from http://standards.ieee.org/getieee802/download/802-2001.pdf

Jackson, B. (2006). *History of VoIP*. University of Texas at Dallas.

Jähnert, J., Wesner, S., & Villagra, V. (2007). *The Akogrimo mobile grid reference architecture-overview*. Retrieved from http://www.akogrimo.org/download/White_Papers_and_Publications/Akogrimo_WhitePaper_Architecture_v1-1.pdf

Jawad, B., Rachid, B., & Yacine, A. (2006). Ontology-based framework for context-aware mobile learning. In *IWCMC 2006, Proceedings of the 2006 International Wireless Communications and Mobile Computing Conference* (Vol. 2006, pp. 1307-1310).

Jena. (2009). *Jena– a Semantic Web framework for java* [online]. Retrieved from http://jena.sourceforge.net/index.html

Jie, Y., Weiyi, Y., Denecke, M., & Waibel, A. (1999, October 18-19). Smart sight: A tourist assistant system. In *Proceedings of the 3rd International Symposium on Wearable Computers* (pp. 73-78), San Francisco, CA.

JISC. (2007). In their own words: Exploring the learner's perspective on e-learning (Internet). Bristol: Higher Education Funding Council for England.

Johnson, D. B., & Maltz, D. A. (1996). Dynamic source routing in ad hoc wireless networks. In *The International Series in Engineering and Computer Science* (Vol. 353, pp. 151-181). USA: Springer.

Johnson, S. (2007). A framework for mobile context-aware applications. *BT Technology Journal, 25*(2), 106–111. doi:10.1007/s10550-007-0033-5

Jones, A., Scanlon, E., Tosunoglu, C., Morris, E., Ross, S., Butcher, P., & Greenberg, J. (1999). Contexts for evaluating educational software. *Interacting with Computers, 11*(5), 499–516. doi:10.1016/S0953-5438(98)00064-2

Jorgensen, C. (2004). Connecting work and education: Should learning be useful, correct, or meaningful? *Journal of Workplace Learning, 16*(8), 455–465. doi:10.1108/13665620410566423

Jukes, I. (2005). Understanding digital kids. The Infosavvy Group. Retrieved on February 23, 2007, from http://ianjukes.com/infosavvy/education/handouts/ndl.pdf>

Juul, J. (2005). Games telling stories? In J. Raessens & J. Goldstein (Eds), *Handbook of computer game studies* (pp. 219–226). Cambridge, MA: The MIT Press.

Kaasinen, E. (2003). User needs for location-aware mobile services. *Personal and Ubiquitous Computing, 7*, 70–79. doi:10.1007/s00779-002-0214-7

Kaikkonen, A., Kallio, T., Keklinen, A., Kankainen, A., & Cankar, M. (2005). Usability testing of mobile applications: A comparison between laboratory and field testing. *Journal of Usability Studies, 1*, 4–16.

Kaleidoscope Network of Excellence. (2006). *Mobile learning initiative big issues in mobile learning* (Report). University of Nottingham. Retrieved from http://mlearning.noe-kaleidoscope.org/public/news/KALEIDOSCOPE%20REPORT_07_Big_Issues_In_Mobile_Learning.pdf

Kaplan-Leiserson, E. (2004). RSS: A learning trend. Retrieved on April 4, 2005, from http://www.learningcircuits.org/2004/may2004/0405_Trends.htm

Keegan, D. (1990). *Foundations of distance education: Frameworks for the future*. First, London, UK: Routledge.

Keegan, D. (2005). Mobile learning: The next generation of learning. *Distance Education International.*

Keegan, D. (Ed.). (2005). *Mobile learning: A practical guide.* Brussels, Belgium: Leonardo da Vinci Programme of the European Commission.

Kember, L. (2001). *Introducing mobile learning.* IT Solutions, SYS-CON Media.

Kennedy, G., Dalgarno, B., Gray, K., Judd, T., Waycott, J., Bennett, S., et al. (2007, December 3-5). The net generation are not big users of Web 2.0 technologies: Preliminary findings. Paper presented at the Ascilite 2007, Singapore.

Kennedy, G., Krause, K., Judd, T., Churchward, A., & Gray, K. (2006). *First year students' experience with technology: Are they really digital natives? Preliminary report findings* [electronic version]. Retrieved on May 16, 2008, from www.bmu.unimelb.edu.au/research/munatives/natives_report2006.pdf

Kiili, K. (2005). Digital game-based learning: Towards an experiential gaming model. *The Internet and Higher Education, 8*, 13–24. doi:10.1016/j.iheduc.2004.12.001

Kindberg, T. (2008). *Cooltown & ubicomp* [online]. Retrieved from http://www.hpl.hp.com/archive/cooltown/

Kinshuk, & Goh, T. T. (2003). Mobile adaptation with multiple representation as educational pedagogy. In W. Uhr, W. Esswein & E. Schoop (Eds.), *Wirtschaftsinformatik 2003-Medien-Markte-Mobilitat* (pp. 747-763).

Kinshuk., Kommers, P., & Sampson, D. G. (2004). Adaptivity in Web and mobile learning services. In *Proceedings of the Int. J. Cont. Engineering Education and Lifelong Learning 2004, 14*(4/5), 313-317.

Kismihók, G. (2007, November). *Mobile learning in higher education: The corvinus case.* Paper presented at Online Education Berlin 2007, Berlin, Germany.

Kloos, M. (2006). *Comm.unities.of.prac.tice 2.0: How blogs, wikis, and social bookmarking offer facilities that support learning in practice in communities of practice.* University of Amsterdam, Amsterdam.

Klopfer, E., Squire, K., & Jenkins, H. (2002). Environmental detectives: PDAs as a window into a virtual simulated world. IEEE International Workshop, Wireless, and Mobile Technologies in Education, 95-98.

Kneebone, R., & Brenton, H. (2005). Using PDAs to support a new professional healthcare role: A case study. In A. Kukulska-Hulme & J. Traxler (Eds.), *Mobile learning: A handbook for educators and trainers.* London: RoutledgeFalmer.

Komives, S. R. (2005). *The changing nature of work in higher education* [online]. Retrieved from http://www.acpa.nche.edu/seniorscholars/trends/trends6.htm

Koodli, R. S., & Perkins, C. (2007). *Mobile internetworking with IPv6: Concepts, principles, and practices.* Hoboken, NJ: John Wiley & Sons, Inc.

Kossen, J. S. (2005). Mobile e-learning when e-learning becomes m-learning [online]. Retrieved from http://www.palmpowerenterprise.com/issuesprint/issue200106/elearning.html

Kramer, B. J. (2005). *Mobile learning: The next generation of learning, fernuniversitts contributions to the 2nd year of the leonardo project mlearn2.* (Tech. Rep.) ISSN 0945-0130, 5/2005, FernUniversitt in Hagen, 58084 Hagen, Germany.

Kramsch, C., 'Ness, F. A., & Lam, W. S. E. (2000). Authenticity and authorship in the computer-mediated acquisition of L2 literacy. *Language Learning & Technology, 4*(2), 78–104.

Kress & Pachler. (2007). Thinking about the 'm' in m-learning. In N. Pachler (Ed.), *Mobile learning: Towards a research agenda.* London: WLE Centre, IoE.

Kress, G., & Pachler, N. (2007). Thinking about the 'm' in m-learning. In N. Pachler (Ed.), Mobile learning: Towards a research agenda (Vol. 1, pp. 6-32). London: WLE Centre, Institute of Education.

Ktoridou, D., & Eteokleous, N. (2005). Adaptive m-learning: Technological and pedagogical aspects to be considered in Cyprus tertiary education. In *Recent research developments in learning technologies* (pp. 676-683). Spain: Badajoz.

Kublin, K. S., Wetherby, A. M., Crais, E. R., & Prizant, B. M. (1989). Prelinguistic dynamic assessment: A transactional perspective. In A. M. Wetherby, S. F. Warren & J. Reichle (Eds.), *Transitions in prelinguistic communication* (pp. 285-312). Baltimore: Paul H. Brookes.

Kukulska-Hulme, A. (2007). Mobile usability in educational contexts: What have we learnt? *International Review of Research in Open and Distance Learning*, *8*(2), 1–16.

Kukulska-Hulme, A., & Pettit, J. (2007, October 16-19). *Self-service education: Smartphones as a catalyst for informal collective and individual learning*. Paper presented at the MLearn 2007-Making the Connections 6th International Conference on Mobile Learning, Melbourne.

Kukulska-Hulme, A., & Traxler, J. (2005). *Mobile learning: A handbook for educators and trainers*. UK: Routledge.

Kukulska-Hulme, A., & Traxler, J. (2007). Designing for mobile and wireless learning. In H. Beetham & R. Sharpe (Eds.), *Rethinking pedagogy for a digital age* (pp. 180-192). Oxon: Routledge.

Kukulska-Hulme, A., Traxler, J., & Pettit, J. (2007). Designed and user-generated activity in the mobile age. *Journal of Learning Design*, *2*(1), 52–65.

Laerhoven, K. V., & Aidoo, K. (2001). Teaching context to applications. *Personal and Ubiquitous Computing*, *5*, 46–49. doi:10.1007/s007790170029

Lamb, B. (2004). Thewayitwasmeanttobe. Educause Review, 36-48.

Lamming, M., & Flynn, M. (1994, February 2-4). Forget-me-not: Intimate computing in support of human memory. In *Proceedings of FRIEND21 _94, the International Symposium on Next Generation Human Interface*, Magufo Jagoen, Japan.

Langelier, L. (2005). Work, learning, and networked: Guide to the implementation and leadership of intentional communities of practice. Quebec City: CEFIRO (Recherche et Études de cas collection).

Language, E. M. (XML) 1.0, 16. Retrieved in August 2006, from http://www.w3.org/TR/xml/

Language, E. S. (XSL) Version 1.1.5. Retrieved in December 2006, from http://www.w3.org/TR/xsl11/

Laouris, Y., & Eteokleous, N. (2005, October 25-28). *We need an educationally relevant definition of mobile learning*. Proceedings of mLearn 2005, Cape Town, South Africa. Retrieved on April 11, 2007, from http://www.mlearn.org.za/CD/papers/Laouris%20&%20Eteokleous.pdf

Laria, G. (2006). *Mobile and nomadic user in e-learning: The Akogrimo case*. AkogrimoWhitepaper.

Laurillard, D. (2001). Rethinking university teaching: A framework for the effective use of educational technology (2nd ed.). London: Routledge.

Laurillard, D. (2007). Pedagogcal forms of mobile learning: Framing research questions. In N. Pachler (Ed.), Mobile learning: Towards a research agenda (Vol. 1, pp. 33-54). London: WLE Centre, Institute of Education.

Lave, J., & Wenger, E. (1991). *Situated learning: Legitimate peripheral participation*. Cambridge: Cambridge University Press.

Leonhardi, A., Kubach, U., Rothermel, K., & Fritz, A. (1999, October 18-19). Virtual information towers–a metaphor for intuitive, location-aware information access in a mobile. In *Proceedings of the 3rd International Symposium on Wearable Computers* (pp. 15-20), San Francisco, CA.

Levy, M., & Kennedy, C. (2005). Learning Italian via mobile SMS. In A. Kukulska-Hulme & J. Traxler (Eds.), *Mobile learning: A handbook for educators and trainers*. London: RoutledgeFalmer.

Liaw, S.-S. (2004). Considerations for developing constructivist Web-based learning. *International Journal of Instructional Media*, *31*(3), 309.

Lin Hsiao, J. D. (2005). *CSCL theories* [online]. Retrieved from http://www.edb.utexas.edu/csclstudent/Dhsiao/theories.html

Lin, C., & Liu, D. (2006). An intelligent virtual piano tutor. ACM International Conference Proceedings: Virtual Reality Continuum and Its Applications, Hong Kong, China (pp. 353–356).

Lin, T. Kinshuk, & Patel, A. (2003). Cognitive trait model for persistent student modelling. In D. Lasser & C. McNaught (Eds.), *EdMedia 2003* (pp 2114-2147). Norfolk, USA: AACE.

Lingard, B., Hayes, D., & Mills, M. (2003). Teachers and productive pedagogies: Contextualising, conceptualizing, utilizing. *Pedagogy, Culture & Society, 11*(3), 397–422. doi:10.1080/14681360300200181

LISTEN. (2005). Project LISTEN–a reading tutor that listens. Retrieved on February 16, 2009, from http://www.cs.cmu.edu/~listen/

Litchfield, A., Dyson, L. E., Lawrence, E., & Zmijewska, A. (2007, December 3-5). Directions for m-learning research to enhance active learning. Paper presented at the Ascilite 2007, Singapore.

Litke, A., Skoutas, D., & Varvarigou, T. (2004). Mobile grid computing: Changes and challenges of resource management in a mobile grid environment. *Access to Knowledge through Grid in a Mobile World, PAKM 2004 Conference*, Vienna.

Liu, J. A. Kardashian, Goo, J., Smith, C., Yap, F., & Kapur, A. (2005). *Wireless ECG.* (Tech. Rep.). Duke University Smart House Pratt School of Engineering [online]. Retrieved from http://www.smarthouse.duke.edu/projects/wirelessecg.php

Long, P., & Tricker, T. (2004, September 16-18). Do first year graduates find what they expect? *British Educational Research Association Conference 2004*, University of Manchester.

Lonsdale, P., Barber, C., Sharples, M., & Arvanitis, T. N. (2003). A context awareness architecture for facilitating mobile learning. In *Proceedings of MLEARN 2003*, London, UK.

Loos, C. (2006). *E-health with mobile grids: The Akogrimo heart monitoring and emergency scenario.* Akogrimo Whitepaper.

Luchini, K., Curtis, M., Quintana, C., & Soloway, E. (2002). Supporting learning in context: Extending learner-centered design to the development of handheld educational software. In M. Milrad, H.U. Hoppe & Kinshuk (Eds.), *IEEE International Workshop on Wireless and Mobile Technologies in Education 2002* (pp. 107-111).

Luckin, R., Brewster, D., Pearce, D., du Boulay, B., & Siddons-Corby, R. (2005). Whether it's m-learning or e-learning, it must be ME learning. In A. Kukulska & J. Traxler (Eds.), *Mobile learning* (pp. 116-124). Oxon: Routledge.

Luckin, R., Brewster, D., Pearce, D., Siddons-Corby, R., & du Boulay, B. (2003). Smile: The creation of space for interaction through blended digital technology. In J. Attewell & C. Savill-Smith (Eds.), *MLearn* (pp. 87-94). Learning and Skills Development Agency.

Luckin, R., Brewster, D., Pearce, D., Siddons-Corby, R., & du Boulay, B. (2005). *Mobile learning: A handbook for educators and trainers* (pp. 116-124). London: Routledge.

Lumsden, J., & Gammell, A. (2004, September 13-16). *Mobile note taking: Investigating the efficacy of mobile text entry.* Paper presented at the 6th International Conference on Human Computer Interaction with Mobile Devices and Services, Glasgow, Scotland, United Kingdom.

Luo, Z., Chan, T., & Li, J. (2005). A lightweight mutual authentication protocol for RFID networks. *ICEBE, 2005*, 620–625.

Luo, Z., Fei, Y., & Liang, J. (2006). On demand e-learning with service grid technologies. *Edutainment, 2006*, 60–69.

Luo, Z., Zhang, J., & Badia, R. (2005). *Service grid for business computing. Grid technologies: Emerging from distributed architectures to virtual organizations.* WIT Press.

Luyten, K., Van Loon, H., Gabriels, K., Teunkens, D., Robert, K., Conix, K., & Manshoven, E. (2006). Designing for interaction: Socially-aware museum handheld guides.

Document Server@UHasselt, Research Groups, Dept. Mathematics, Physics, Informatics (WNI), Expertise Centre for Digital Media (EDM). Retrieved on October 25, 2008, from http://hdl.handle.net/1942/1740

MacKnight, C. B. (1998). Electronic learning materials: The crisis continues. *ACM SIGCUE Outlook*, *26*(2), 8–16. doi:10.1145/281083.281088

Maginnis, F., White, R., & Mckenna, C. (2000). Customers on the move: M-commerce demands a business object broker approach to EAI. *eAI Journal*, 58-62.

Majoe, D., Estermann, M., Ranieri, N., & Gutknecht, J. (2008, October 6-8). Ergonomic low cost motion capture for every day health exercise. In *Proceedings of the Third International Conference on Pervasive Computing and Applications (ICPCA08)* (pp. 627-632). Alexandria, Egypt.

Markett, C., Arnedillo Sánchez, I., Weber, S., & Tangney, B. (2006). Using short message service (SMS) to encourage interactivity. *Computers & Education*, *46*(3), 280–293. doi:10.1016/j.compedu.2005.11.014

Markett, C., Sanchez, A. I., Weber, S., & Tangney, B. (2006). Using short message service to encourage interactivity in the classroom. *Computers & Education*, *46*(3), 280–293. doi:10.1016/j.compedu.2005.11.014

Massey, A. P., Ramesh, V., & Khatri, V. (2006). Design, development, and assessment of mobile applications: The case for problem-based learning. *IEEE Transactions on Education*, *49*(2), 183–192. doi:10.1109/TE.2006.875700

Mayes, T., & de Freitas, S. (2004). *JISC e-learning models desk study: Review of e-learning theories, frameworks, and models* [electronic version]. Retrieved on July 1, 2008 from www.jisc.ac.uk/uploaded_documents/Stage%202%20Learning%20Models%20(Version%201).pdf

Mayes, T., & De Freitas, S. (2004). *Review of e-learning theories, frameworks, and models* (JISC e-Learning Models Desk Study). UK. Retrieved from http://www.elearning.ac.uk/resources/modelsdeskreview/

McCormack, C., & Jones, D. (1997). *Building a Web-based education system*. New York: Wiley.

McGreen, N., & Arnedillo Sánchez, I. (2005). Mapping challenge: A case study in the use of mobile phones in collaborative, contextual learning. *International Association for Development of the Information Society Press*, 213-217. MILE (Mobile and Interactive Learning Environment) Project Home Page. Retrieved on January 26, 2009, from http://www.mile-project.net/

McKenzie, M., & Kernig, W. (1975). The challenge of informal education: Extending young children's learning in the open classroom. London: Darton, Longman, and Todd.

McLoughlin, C., & Lee, M. J. W. (2008). Future learning landscapes: Transforming pedagogy through social software. Innovate: Journal of Online Education, 4(5).

McManus, T. (2002). *Mobile what? The educational potential of mobile technologies*. World Conference on E-Learning in Corporate, Government, Healthcare, and Higher Education 2002, Montreal, Canada, AACE.

Meawad, F., & Stubbs, G. (2008). A framework for enabling on-demand personalized mobile learning. [Inderscience Publishers.]. *Int. J. Mobile Learning and Organisation*, *2*(2), 133–148. doi:10.1504/IJMLO.2008.019765

Meisenberger, M. (2004). *Mobile learning engine*. Retrieved on April 6, 2008, from http://drei.fh-joanneum.at/mle/start.php

Mendieta, E. (2003). Afterword. In L. M. Alcoff & E. Mendieta (Eds.), *Identities: Postcolonial and global in identities race, class, gender, and nationality* (pp. 407-416). Oxford, UK: Blackwell.

MESEAS Project. (n.d.). Retrieved on October 15, 2008, from http://www.meseas.com

Microsoft Patterns & Practices Developer Center. Microsoft Developer Network. Retrieved from http://msdn.microsoft.com/en-us/practices/default.aspx

Middleton, S. E., Shadbolt, N. R., & De-Rour, D. C. (2004). Ontological user profiling in recommender systems. *ACM Transactions on Information Systems*, *22*(1), 54–88. doi:10.1145/963770.963773

Mifsud, L. (2002, August 29-30). Alternative learning arenas-pedagogical challenges to mobile learning technology in education. In *Proceedings of the IEEE International Workshop on Wireless and Mobile Technologies in Education (WMTE 2002)* (pp. 112-116), Växjö, Sweden. Washington, D.C.: IEEE Computer Society.

Milken, M. *(2007).* What are the characteristics that the globalized workplace increasingly expect and demand of graduates from universities and colleges? Education without borders world forum: Reframing higher education. *Dubai, UAE.*

Millard, D., Woukeu, A., Tao, F. B., & Davis, H. (2005). Experiences with writing grid clients for mobile devices. In *1st International ELeGI Conference on Advanced Technology for Enhanced Learning*, BCS Electronic Workshops in Computing (eWiC).

Milrad, M. (2006). Media migration and contextual services: Putting content into context to support nomadic learners. In *ICALT 2006* (pp. 1178-1179)

Mishra, P., Koehler, M. J., & Zhao, Y. (Eds.). (2007). Faculty development by design: Integrating technology in higher education. Charlotte: Information Age Publishing.

MIT. (2004). *MIT project oxygen: Pervasive human-centered computing* [online]. Retrieved in January 2009, from, http://oxygen.lcs.mit.edu/

Mitchell, J., & Young, S. (2005). Innovation and the national training system: Core ideas. Elizabeth, South Australia: Reframing the Future.

Mitchell, T. M. (1997). *Machine learning.* Singapore: McGraw-Hill.

Mobile Web Application Best Practices. Retrieved on July 29, 2008, from http://www.w3.org/TR/mwabp/#bp-devcap-classify

Moodle. (2008). *Moodle: A free open source course management for online learning.* Retrieved on April 3, 2008, from http://moodle.org

Moore, P., & Hu, B. (2006, August 3-5). Entity profiling: Context with ontology. *Proceedings of the 1st International Symposium on Pervasive Computing and Applications (SPCA06)* (pp. 172-177), Urumqi, P.R. China. USA: IEEE Press.

Moore, P., & Hu, B. (2007). A context framework with ontology for personalised and cooperative mobile learning. *Computer Supported Cooperative Work in Design, 10th International Conference (CSCWD 2006)*, Nanjing, China, May 2006 (LNCS 4402, pp. 727-738). Berlin, Germany: Springer-Verlag.

Moore, P., Hu, B., & Wan, J. (2008). Smart-context: A context ontology for pervasive cooperative applications. *The Computer Journal*, doi:10.1093/comjnl/bxm104. Retrieved from http://comjnl.oxfordjournals.org/cgi/content/abstract/bxm104v1?

Moore, P., Hu, B., Zhu, X., Campbell, W., & Ratcliffe, M. (2007). A survey of context modeling for pervasive cooperative learning. In *IEEE Proceedings of the First International Symposium on Information Technologies and Applications in Education (ISITAE '07)*, Kunming, Yuan, P.R. China, November 23-25, 2007. K5-1-K5-6. USA: IEEE.

Morken, E. M., & Divitini, M. (2005). *Blending mobile and ambient technologies to support mobility in practice based education: The case of teacher education.* Online edition.

Moser, F. Z. (2007). Faculty adoption of educational technology. EDUCAUSE Quarterly, 1, 66–69.

Motiwalla, L. (2007). Mobile learning: A framework and evaluation. *Computers & Education, 49*(3), 581–596. doi:10.1016/j.compedu.2005.10.011

Mungania, P. (2003). *The seven e-learning barriers facing employees.* USA: University of Louisville.

Murchú, D. Ó., & Muirhead, B. (2005). Insights into promoting critical thinking in online classes. *Instructional Technology and Distance Learning, 2*(6), 33–48.

Murray, D. E. (1993). Collaborative writing as a literacy event: Implications for ESL instruction. In D. Nunan (Ed.), *Collaborative language learning and teaching* (2nd ed., pp. 100-117). Cambridge: Cambridge University Press.

Naismith, L. (2005). *Literature review in mobile technologies and learning* (Report 11, Futurelab Series). Bristol, UK: Futurelab. Retrieved from http://www.futurelab.org.uk/resources/documents/lit_reviews/Mobile_Review.pdf

Naismith, L., & Corlett, D. (2006). Reflections on success: A retrospective of the m-learn conference series 2002-2005. In *Proceedings of M-Learn 2006–Across Generations and Cultures Conference*, Banff.

Naismith, L., Lonsdale, P., Vavoula, G., & Sharples, M. (2004). *Literature review in mobile technologies and learning*. NESTA Futurelab. Retrieved on September 10, 2008, from http://www.futurelab.org.uk/resources/documents/lit_reviews/Mobile_Review.pdf

Naismith, L., Sharples, M., & Ting, J. (2005). *Evaluation of caerus: A context aware mobile guide.*

Naismith, N., Lonsdale, P., Vavoula, G., & Sharples, M. (2004). Literature review in mobile technologies and learning. Futurelab. Retrieved on April 18, 2007, from http://www.futurelab.org.uk/research/lit_reviews.htm

Nardi, D., & Brachman, R. J. (2002). *An introduction to description logics*. Cambridge, UK: Cambridge University Press.

National Communication Authority. (2009). *Digital mobile phone market report, November 2008*. Retrieved on February 2, 2009, from http://nhh.hu/index.php?id=hir&cid=6672

New Media Consortium. (2007). The horizon report: 2007 edition. The Horizon Report, 2007. Retrieved from http://www.nmc.org/horizon/2007/report

New Zealand Herald. (2006). The most effective form of emerging media to reach New Zealanders aged 14 to 30. Auckland: New Zealand Herald.

Newmann, F., & Associates. (1996). *Authentic achievement: Restructuring schools for intellectual quality*. San Francisco: Jossey-Bass.

Nielsen, J. (1994). Heuristic evaluation. In J. Nielsen & R. L. Mack (Eds.), *Usability inspection methods*. New York: John Wiley & Sons.

Nokia. (2007). Nokia nseries. Retrieved on April 26, 2007, from http://www.nseries.com/index.html

Norman, D. A. (2001). The future of education: Lessons learned from video games and museum exhibits. Commencement address, Northwestern University, School of Education and Social Policy.

Noy, N. F., & McGuinness, D. L. (2001). *Ontology development 101: A guide to creating your 1st ontology* [online]. Retrieved from http://protege.stanford.edu/publications/ontologydevelopment/ontology101.shtml

Nunan, D. (1999). *Second language teaching and learning*. Boston, MA: Heinle & Heinle.

Nyiri, K. (2002). Towards a philosophy of m-learning. In *Wireless and Mobile Technologies in Education 2002. Proceedings. IEEE International Workshop* (pp. 121-124).

O'Reilly, T. (2005). What is Web 2.0: Design patterns and business models for the next generation of software. Retrieved in March 2006, from http://www.oreillynet.com/pub/a/oreilly/tim/news/2005/09/30/what-is-web-20.html

OASIS UDDI Specifications TC–Committee Specifications. Retrieved from http://www.oasis-open.org/committees/uddi-spec/doc/tcspecs.htm

Oblinger, D. G., & Oblinger, J. L. (2005). *Educating the Net generation*. Retrieved on May 16, 2008, from www.educause.edu/educatingthenetgen

Oblinger, D., & Oblinger, J. (2005). Is it age or it? First steps towards understanding the net generation. In D. Oblinger & J. Oblinger (Eds.), Educating the net generation (pp. 10-29). Educause.

Ocakoglu, O., & Ercetin, O. (2006). Energy efficient random sleep-awake schedule design. *IEEE Communications Letters*, *10*(7), 528–530.

ODSG. (2008). *On demand service grid, ODSG*. Retrieved from www.ibm.com

OGSA-DAI. (2008). Retrieved from www.globus.org

Oloruntoba, R. (2006). Mobile learning environments: A conceptual overview. Retrieved on October 1, 2008, from https://olt.qut.edu.au/udf/OLT2006/gen/static/papers/Oloruntoba_OLT2006_paper.pdf

Olson, D. R. (1994). *The world on paper: The conceptual and cognitive implications of writing and reading.* Cambridge: Cambridge University Press.

Omari, R. (2006). *A SW module for mobile device content delivery.* Master thesis, University of Applied Sciences Offenburg. Web Services Description Language (WSDL) Version 2.0 Part 0: Primer. Retrieved on June 26, 2007, from http://www.w3.org/TR/wsdl20-primer/

Ong, W. J. (1982). *Orality and literacy: The technologizing of the word.* London: Methuen.

Ong, W. J. (1983). Writing is a humanizing activity. *ADE Bulletin, 074*(Spring), 13–16.

Openembedded Home Page. *The cross-compile environment.* Retrieved on October 15, 2008, from http://www.openembedded.org/

OpenRDF.org. (2008). *The Sesame API* [online]. Retrieved from http://www.openrdf.org/doc/sesame/users/ch07.html

Openwave. (2007). 5 things you need to know about personalization. Openwave Systems Inc. Retrieved on April 18, 2007, from http://www.openwave.com/docs/openwave_5things_about_personalization.pdf

Owen, H., & Allardice, R. (2007). Managing the implementation of blended e-learning initiatives with the unconverted in a climate of institutionally driven change. *The International Journal of Learning, 14*(9), 179–192.

Owen, M. (2006). Social software and learning. Bristol: Futurelab.

Owen, M. (2008). From individual learning to collaborative learning-location, fun, and games: Place, context, and identity in mobile learning. In H. Riu & D. Parsons (Eds.), *Innovative mobile learning: Technique and technologies.* Hershey, PA: Information Science Reference.

Pachler, N. (2007). Mobile learning: Towards a research agenda. WLE Centre Occasional Papers in Work-based Learning 1. London: The WLE Centre, Institute of Education. Retrieved on February 16, 2009, from http://www.wlecentre.ac.uk/cms/files/occasionalpapers/mobilelearning_pachler2007.pdf

Page, I. W. (n.d.). Retrieved on October 15, 2008, from http://www.gitaca.com/iwireless

Page, W.-F. A.-H. (n.d.). Retrieved on October 15, 2008, from http://www.wi-fi.org

Papworth, L., & Johnson, K. (2008). Establishing and managing digital footprints [electronic version]. *El-earning Insights Episode 19.* Retrieved on September 15, 2008 from http://www.edna.edu.au/edna/go/news/podcast/eli/pid/2787

Park, S.-M., Ko, Y.-B., & Kim, J.-H. (2003). Disconnected operation service in mobile grid computing. *International Conference on Service Oriented Computing (ICSOC'2003)*, Trento, Italy.

Parsons, D., Ryu, H., & Cranshaw, M. (2006). A study of design requirements for mobile learning environments. In *Advanced Learning Technologies 2006. Sixth International Conference* (pp. 96-100).

Pascoe, J., Ryan, N. S., & Morse, D. R. (1998). Human computer giraffe interaction-HCI in the field. *Workshop on Human Computer Interaction with Mobile Devices* [online]. Retrieved from http://www.dcs.gla.ac.uk/~johnson/papers/mobile/HCIMD1.html

Pascoe, J., Ryan, N. S., & Morse, D. R. (1999, September). Issues in developing context-aware computing. In *Proceedings of the International Symposium on Handheld and Ubiquitous Computing* (pp. 208-221), Karlsruhe, Germany.

Pascoe, J., Ryan, N., & Morse, D. (2000). Using while moving: HCI issues in fieldwork environments. *ACM Transactions on Computer-Human Interaction, 7*(3), 417–437. doi:10.1145/355324.355329

Passani, L. (2006). *DDR Workshop WURFL, WALL and the Community of Mobile Developers.* Retrieved from http://www.w3.org/2005/MWI/DDWG/workshop2006/presentations/WURFL/WURFLandWALL.pdf

Passey, D. (1999). *Higher order thinking skills: An exploration of aspects of learning and thinking and how ICT can be used to support these processes*. Lancaster, UK: Lancaster University.

Pastore, S. (2005). Experiences of mobile learning in science: Technological solutions for wireless network and content delivery. *7th Internet Users Conference*, Dubrovnik, Croatia.

Patten, B., Arnedillo-Sánchez, I., & Tangney, B. (2006). Designing collaborative, constructionist, and contextual applications for handheld devices: Virtual learning? *Computers & Education*, *46*(3), 294–308. doi:10.1016/j.compedu.2005.11.011

Peng, P. (2008). A P2P based collaborative RFID data cleaning model. *The 2008 International Symposium on Advances in Grid and Pervasive Systems (AGPS 2008)* in conjunction with the *3rd International Conference on Grid and Pervasive Computing (GPC 2008)*, Kunming, China.

Perez-Romero, J., Sallent, O., Agustí, R., & Díaz-Guerra, M. A. (2005). *Radio resource management strategies in UMTS*. West Sussex, England: John Wiley & Sons.

Perold, J. J. (2001). Paradox and pedagogy: Double binds and the culture of learning in South African schools. *Culture and Psychology*, *7*(4), 411–431. doi:10.1177/1354067X0174001

Peters, O. (1999). *A pedagogical model for virtual learning spaces. Articles on flexible learning and distance education*. Fernuniversitat Hagen. Retrieved from http://www.tbc.dk/pdf/peters-a_pedagogical_model.pdf

Phillips, R., & Gilding, T. (2000). Approaches to evaluating the effect of ICT on student learning. Retrieved on March 9, 2007, from http://www.alt.ac.uk/docs/eln015.pdf

Piaget, J. (1973). To understand is to invent. New York: Viking Press.

Poslad, S., Laamanen, H., Malaka, R., Nick, A., Buckle, P., & Zipf (2001, March). A crumpet: Creation of user friendly mobile services personalised for tourism. 3G 2001. In *Proceedings of the Second International Conference on 3G Mobile Communication Technologies*, London.

Powers, S. (2003). *Practical RDF*. Cambridge, MA: O'Reilly.

Preece, J., Rogers, Y., & Sharp, H. (2002). *Interaction design: Beyond human-computer interaction*. New York: John Wiley

Prensky, M. (2001). Digital natives, digital immigrants: Part one [electronic version] [from http://www.marcprensky.com/writing/default.asp]. *Horizon*, *9*, Retrieved on May 16, 2008.

Prensky, M. (2001). Digital natives, digital immigrants: Part two [electronic version]. *On the Horizon, 9*, 1-9. Retrieved on May 16, 2008, from http://www.marcprensky.com/writing/Prensky%20-%20Digital%20Natives,%20Digital%20Immigrants%20-%20Part2.pdf

Prensky, M. (2003). Digital game-based learning. *ACM Computers in Entertainment*, *1*(1), 1–4. doi:10.1145/950566.950567

Prensky, M. (2005). What can you learn from a mobile phone?–almost anything! Innovate Journal of Online Education, 1(5). Retrieved on October 30, 2006, from http://innovateonline.info/index.php?view=article&id=83

Prensky, M. (2005). Engage me or enrage me: What today's learners demand. EDUCAUSE Review, 40(5), 60–65.

Prensky, M. (2005). What can you learn from a cell phone? Almost anything! Innovate, 1(5). Retrieved from http://www.innovateonline.info/index.php?view=article&id=83

Prensky, M. (2006). Don't bother me, Mom, I'm learning!: How computer and video games are preparing your kids for 21st century success and how you can help! St. Paul, MN: Paragon House.

Price, S. (2007). Ubiquitous computing: Digital augmentation and learning. In N. Pachler (Ed.), Mobile learning:

Towards a research agenda. WLE Centre Occasional Papers in Work-based Learning 1. London: The WLE Centre, Institute of Education.

Price, S., Rogers, Y., Stanton, D., & Smith, H. (2003). A new conceptual framework for CSCL: Supporting diverse forms of reflection through multiple interactions. In B. Wasson, S. Ludvigsen & U. Hoppe (Eds.), Designing for change in networked learning environments. Proceedings of the International Conference on Computer Supported Collaborative Learning 2003.

Proctor, N., & Burton, J. (2003). *Tate modern multimedia tour pilots 2002-2003* (pp. 54-55).

Putnam, R. (2000). *Bowling alone: The collapse and revival of American community*. New York: Simon and Schuster.

Quinn, C. (2000). M-learning: Mobile, wireless, in-your-pocket learning. *LiNE Zine, Fall*, 47-50.

Quinn, C. N. (2005). Engaging learning: Designing e-learning simulation games. San Francisco: Pfeiffer.

Race, N. J. P. (2006). Engage: Enabling personalised learning across vle platforms using mobile devices. (Tech. Rep.). Lancaster University.

Raessens, J. (2007). Playing history: Reflections on mobile and location-based learning. In T. Hug (Ed.), *Didactics of microlearning. Concepts, discourses, and examples* (pp. 200-217). Münster: Waxmann.

Ramsden, P. (1992). *Assessing for understanding*. London: Routledge.

Reeves, T. C. (1993). Pseudoscience in computer-based instruction: The case of learner control research, *20, 2*(39-46).

RFC 4120. The Kerberos Network Authentication Service (V5). Retrieved from http://www.ietf.org/rfc/rfc4120.txt

RFC 675. Specification of Internet Transmission Control Program. (1974, December). Retrieved from http://tools.ietf.org/html/rfc675

Rhodes, B. J. (1997, October 13-14). The wearable remembrance agent: A system for augmented memory. In *Proceedings of the 1st International Symposium on Wearable Computers* (pp. 123-128), Cambridge, MA.

Rogers, Y., Price, S., Fitzpatrick, G., Fleck, R., Harris, E., Smith, H., et al. (2004). *Ambient wood: Designing new forms of digital augmentation for learning outdoors* (pp. 3-10).

Rogers, Y., Price, S., Harris, E., Phelps, T., Underwood, M., Wilde, D., et al. (2002). *Learning through digitally augmented physical experiences: Reflections on the ambient wood project*. Retrieved on April 26, 2007, from http://www.cogs.susx.ac.uk/interact/previousSite/papers/Rogers_Ambient_Wood2.pdf

Roiger, R. J., Azarbod, C., & Sant, R. R. (1997, December 8-10). A majority rules approach to data mining. In *Proceedings of the 1997 IASTED International Conference on Intelligent Information Systems (Iis'97)* (pp. 100-107), Grand Bahamia Island, Bahamas.

Romiszowski, A., & Mason, R. (2004). Computer-mediated communication. In D. Jonassen (Ed.), *Handbook of research for educational communications and technology* (2nd ed., pp. 397-431). Mahwah, NJ: Lawrence Erlbaum.

Roschelle, J. (2003). Unlocking the learning value of wireless mobile devices. *Journal of Computer Assisted Learning, 19*(3), 260–272. doi:10.1046/j.0266-4909.2003.00028.x

Rossett, A., Douglis, F., & Frazee, R. V. (2003). *Strategies for building blended learning* [electronic version]. Retrieved on June 20, 2008, from http://www.learningcircuits.org/2003/jul2003/rossett.htm

Royer, E. M., & Chai-Keong, T. (1999). A review of current routing protocols for ad-hoc mobile wireless networks. *Personal Communications, IEEE, 6*(2), 46–55. doi:10.1109/98.760423

Rushby, N. (1998). Where are the desks for the virtual class. *ACM SIGCUE Outlook, 26*(2), 33–36. doi:10.1145/281083.281093

Russell, S. (2003). *Readings about the question: It is said that reasoning on the Semantic Web must be monotonic. Why is this so, when human reasoning, which seems to have served us well, is nonmonotonic?* [online]. Retrieved from http://robustai.net/papers/Monotonic_Reasoning_on_the_Semantic_Web.html

Russell, S., & Norvig, P. (1995). *Artificial intelligence: A modern approach*. NJ: Prentice Hall.

Ryan, N., Pascoe, J., & Morse, D. (1997). Enhanced reality fieldwork: The context-aware archaeological assistant. In Gaffney, Leusen & Exxon (Eds.), *Computer applications in archaeology*. Oxford, UK: British Archaeological Reports.

Sakkopoulos, E., Lytras, M., & Tsakalidis, A. (2006). Adaptive mobile Web services facilitate communication and learning Internet technologies. *IEEE Transactions on Education*, *49*(2), 208–215. doi:10.1109/TE.2006.873985

Salber, D., Dey, A. K., & Abowd, G. D. (1999, May 15-20). The context toolkit: Aiding the development of context-enabled applications. In *Proceedings of the ACM CHI 99 Human Factors in Computing Systems Conference (CHI 99)* (pp. 434-441), Pittsburgh, PA.

Salmon, G. (2002). *E-tivities. The key to active online learning*. London: Kogan Page.

Salt, B. (2007, May 7). Will learning communities cope with our future. Presentation, Frankston Arts Centre.

Sandford, R., & Williamson, B. (2005). Games and learning. NESTA Futurelab. Retrieved on October 1, 2008, from http://www.nestafuturelab.org/download/pdfs/research/handbooks/games_and_learning.pdf on 02/03/2006

Sandford, R., Ulicsak, M., Facer, K., & Rudd, T. (2006). Teaching with games: Using commercial off-the-shelf computer games in formal education. Bristol: Futurelab.

Sawyer, G. (2004). *Closing the digital divide: Increasing education and training opportunities for Indigenous students in remote areas*. Brisbane: New Practices in Flexible Learning. Australian Flexible Learning Framework.

Scardamalia, M., & Bereiter, C. (2006). Knowledge building: Theory, pedagogy, and technology. In K. Sawyer (Ed.), *Cambridge handbook of the learning sciences* (pp. 97-118). New York: Cambridge University Press.

Schema Part, X. M. L. 0. Retrieved on October 28, 2004, from http://www.w3.org/TR/xmlschema-0/

Schilit, B. N., Adams, N. I., & Want, R. (1994). Context-aware computing applications. In *Proceedings of the Workshop on Mobile Computing Systems and Applications*, IEEE Computer Society (pp. 85-90), Santa Cruz, CA.

Schilit, W. N. (1995). System architecture for context-aware mobile computing. Unpublished doctoral dissertation, Columbia University, Columbia.

Schon, D. A. (1996). *Educating the reflective practitioner: Toward a new design for teaching and learning in the professions*. San Francisco: Jossey-Bass.

Schulzrinne, H. (1996). *RTP profile for audio and video-conferences with minimal control*. Internet Engineering Task Force.

Schulzrinne, H., Casner, S., Frederick, R., & Jacobson, V. (2003). *RTP: A transport protocol for real-time applications*. Internet Engineering Task Force. The Official Bluetooth Technology Info Site. (n.d.). Retrieved on October 15, 2008, from http://www.bluetooth.com/bluetooth

Schwabe, G., & Göth, C. (2005). Mobile learning with a mobile game: Design and motivational effects. *Journal of Computer Assisted Learning*, *21*, 2004–2016. doi:10.1111/j.1365-2729.2005.00128.x

Schwabe, G., Göth, C., & Frohberg, D. (2005). Does team size matter in mobile learning? *Proceedings of the International Conference on Mobile Business (ICMB'05)*, July 11-13, 2005, Sydney Australia.

Scott, D. (2001). Situated views of learning. In R. E. C. Paechter, R. Harrison & P. Twining (Eds.), *Learning, space, and identity*. London: Paul Chapman Publishing.

Scratchbox Home Page. *The cross-compilation toolkit project*. Retrieved on October 15, 2008, from http://www.scratchbox.org/

Seddon, T., &. Billett, S. (2004). *Social partnerships in vocational education: Building community capacity.* Adelaide: National Centre of Vocational Research.

Seliger, H. W., & Shohamy, E. (1989). What is research? A paradigm for second language research. In *Second Language Research Methods* (pp. 1-41). Oxford, UK: Oxford Unversity Press.

Selwyn, N. (2003). Schooling the mobile generation: The future for schools in the mobile-networked society. *British Journal of Sociology of Education, 24*(2), 131–144. doi:10.1080/01425690301905

Semantic MediaWiki. (2009). *Semantic media wiki.* Retrieved on January 12, 2009, from http://semantic-mediawiki.org/wiki/Semantic_MediaWiki

Semones, L. (2001). Collaboration, computer mediation, and the foreign language writer. *Collaboration and Computer Mediation, 74*(6), 308–312.

Senses, B. (2003, July). Implementing wireless communication in hospital environments with Bluetooth, 802.11b, and Other Technologies. (Tech. Rep.). *Medical Device & Diagnostic Industry.*

Seong, D. S. K. (2006). Usability guidelines for designing mobile learning portals. In *Mobility '06: Proceedings of the 3rd International Conference on Mobile Technology, Applications, & Systems*, 25. New York: ACM.

Shaffer, D. W. (2006). Epistemic frames for epistemic games. *Computers & Education, 46*, 223–234. doi:10.1016/j.compedu.2005.11.003

Sharples, M. (2000). Disruptive devices: Personal technologies and education. Retrieved on June 27, 2006, from http://www.eee.bham.ac.uk/handler/ePapers/disruptive.pdf

Sharples, M. (2002). Disruptive devices: Mobile technology for conversational learning. *International Journal of Continuing Engineering Education and Lifelong Learning, 12*(5/6), 504–520. doi:10.1504/IJCEELL.2002.002148

Sharples, M. (2005). Learning as conversation: Transforming education in the mobile age. Paper presented at the Conference on Seeing, Understanding, Learning in the Mobile Age, Budapest, Hungary.

Sharples, M. (Ed.). (2006). *Big issues in mobile learning: Report of a workshop by the kaleidoscope network of excellence mobile learning initiative*. Nottingham, UK: Learning Sciences Research Institute, University of Nottingham.

Sharples, M., Corlett, D., & Wesmancott, O. (2002). The design and implementation of a mobile learning resource. *Personal and Ubiquitous Computing*, (3): 220–234. doi:10.1007/s007790200021

Sharples, M., Taylor, J., & Vavoula, G. (2005). *Towards a theory of mobile learning.* Online edition.

Sharples, M., Taylor, J., & Vavoula, G. (2005). *Towards a theory of learning for the mobile age* [electronic version]. Retrieved on April 15, 2008, from www.mlearn.org.za/CD/papers/Sharples-%20Theory%20of%20Mobile.pdf

Sharples, M., Taylor, J., & Vavoula, G. (2006). *A theory of learning for the mobile age* [electronic version]. Retrieved on April 15, 2008, from http://kn.open.ac.uk/public/document.cfm?docid=8558

Sheth, A., & Ramakrishnan, C. (2003, December). Semantic (Web) technology in action: Ontology driven information systems for search, integration, and analysis. In U. Dayal, H. Kuno & K. Wilkinson (Eds.), *IEEE data engineering bulletin, special issue on making the Semantic Web.*

Siemens, G. (2004). *Connectivsm: A learning theory for the digital age.* Retrieved on September 24, 2008, from http://www.elearnspace.org/Articles/connectivsm.htm

Simic, M. (1994). *Computer assisted writing instruction.* Retrieved on April 9, 2003, from http://www.indiana.edu/~eric_rec/ieo/digests/d97.html

Singh, D., & Abu Bakar, Z. (2007). Wireless implementation of a mobile learning environment based on students' expectations. *International Journal of Mobile Learning and Organisation, 1*(2), 198–215. doi:10.1504/IJMLO.2007.012678

Skoeps. (2007). Skoeps-everyone's a reporter. Retrieved on October 24, 2007, from http://www.skoeps.com/landing.html

Smith, B. (2001). Arabic speakers. In B. Smith & M. Swann (Eds.), *Learner English* (2nd ed., pp. 195- 213). Cambridge: Cambridge University Press.

Smyth, J., &. H. R. (2004). *Dropping out, drifting off, being excluded: Becoming someone without school.* New York: Peter Lang.

Song, Y., & Fox, R. (2008). Affordances of PDAs: Undergraduate student perceptions. *Journal of the Research Center for Educational Technology, 4*(1), 19–38.

Sotillo, S. M. (2003). *Pedagogical advantages of ubiquitous computing in a wireless environment.* The Technology Source. Retrieved on January 16, 2006, from http://education.korea.ac.kr/innwoo/edu603/Wireless/Pedagogical%20Advantages%20of%20Ubiquitous%20Computing%20in%20a%20Wireless%20Environment.htm

Sotiriou, S., Chryssafidou, E., Owen, M., Barajas Frutos, M., Zistler, E., Lohr, M., et al. (2008). The COLLAGE project: Guide of good practice on mobile and game based learning. Athens, Greece: EPINOIA Ed.

Spikol, D., & Milrad, M. (2008). Combining physical activities and mobile games to promote novel learning practices. Fifth IEEE International Conference on Wireless, Mobile, and Ubiquitous Technology in Education (pp. 31-38).

Squeak. (2007). About squeak. Retrieved on October 10, 2008, from http://www.squeak.org

Stead, G. (2005). Moving mobile into the mainstream. In *4th World conference on m-Learning.*

Stead, G. (2006). Mobile technologies: Transforming the future of learning. Emerging Technologies for Learning. Retrieved on April 6, 2006, from http://www.becta.org.uk/corporate/publications/

Stead, G., & Colley, J. (2008, October 7-10). The power of me: Learning by making your own rich media mobile resources. Paper presented at the MLearn08: The Bridge from Text to Context, Telford, Shropshire, UK.

Stenton, S. P. (2007). Mediascapes: Context-aware multimedia experiences. *IEEE MultiMedia, 14*(3), 98–105. doi:10.1109/MMUL.2007.52

Stewart, K. (2007, October 16-19). *Mobile learning: Designing the learning context.* Proceedings of mLearn 2007, Melbourne, Australia.

Strauss, A., & Corbin, J. (1990). *Basics of qualitative research: Grounded theory procedures and techniques.* Newbury Park, CA: Sage.

Su, J., et al. (2004). User mobility for opportunistic ad-hoc networking. In *Proceedings of IEEE WMCSA.*

Sullivan, N. (1993). Teaching writing on a computer network. *TESOL Journal,* 34-35.

Swan, K., Hooft, M., Kratkoski, A., & Hunger, D. (2005). Uses and effects of mobile computing devices in K-8 classrooms. *Journal of Research on Technology in Education, 38*(1), 99.

Swan, K., van 't Hooft, M., Kratcoski, A., & Unger, D. (2005). Uses and effects of mobile computing devices in K-8 classrooms. *Journal of Research on Technology in Education, 38*(1), 99–113.

Symbian Limited. (2005). *Latest version of Symbian OS targets smartphones for mass market.* Retrieved from http://www.symbian.com/news/pr/2005/pr20051892.html

Syvänen, A., & Nokelainen, P. (2004). Evaluation of the technical and pedagogical mobile usability. In Murelli, et al. (Eds.), *Proceedings of the 3rd International Conference on Mobile Learning (MLEARN 2004)* (pp. 191-195). Rome, Italy: LSDA.

Szabó, I. (2006, September 4-5). The implementation of the educational ontology. In P. Fehér (Ed.), *Proceedings of the 7th European Conference on Knowledge Management*, Corvinus University of Budapest, Hungary, ACL, UK (pp. 541-547).

Tan, N., Chen, W., Looi, C.-K., Zhang, B., Seow, P., & Chan, A. (2007). Handheld computers as cognitive tools: An environmental learning project in Singapore. In T. Hirashima, U. Hoppe & S. Shwu-Ching Young (Eds.), *Supporting learning flow through integrative technologies* (pp. 377-384). Amsterdam: IOS Press.

Tatar, D., Harrison, S., Crandell, A., & Schaefer, M. (2008). Using place as provocation: In Situ collaborative narrative construction. *Journal of the Research Center for Educational Technology, 4*(1), 49–60.

Taylor, J. (2003, May 19-20). A task-centred approach to evaluating a mobile learning environment for pedagogical soundness. *Proceedings of the 2nd International Conference on Mobile Learning (MLEARN2003)*, London.

Taylor, J. (2007). Evaluating mobile learning. In M. Sharples (Ed.), *Big issues in mobile learning* (pp. 26-28). Nottingham: Learning Sciences Research Institute.

Taylor, J. (2007). Evaluating mobile learning. What are appropriate methods for evaluating learning in mobile environments? In M. Sharples (Ed.), *Big issues in mobile learning: Report of a workshop by the kaleidoscope network of excellence mobile learning initiative*. LSRI, University of Nottingham. Retrieved on September 10, 2008, from http://www.lsri.nottingham.ac.uk/msh/Papers/BIG_ISSUES_REPORT_PUBLISHED.pdf

Text.it. (2007). Media Centre. Retrieved on April, 19, from http://www.text.it/mediacentre/press_release_list.cfm?thePublicationID=351A37F2-C5A0-881E-03C5B18AAC2AE745

Tharp, R. G., & Gallimore, R. (1988). *Rousing minds to life: Teaching, learning, and schooling in social context*. Cambridge: Cambridge University Press.

The Australian Psychological Society. (2004, November). Psychological aspects of mobile phone use among adolescents. The Australian Psychological Society, 3. Retrieved on March 2, 2007, from http://www.pshychology.org.au/news/psychology_week/10.10_2.asp

The New London Group. (2000). A pedagogy of multiliteracies: Designing social futures. In B. Cope & M. Kalantzis (Eds.), *Multiliteracies: Literacy learning and the design of social futures* (pp. 9-37). London: Routledge.

Thissen, D., & Mislevy, R. J. (1990). Testing algorithms. In H. Wainer (Ed.), *Computerized adaptive testing* (pp. 103-135). New Jersey: Lawrence Erlbaum Associates.

Thomas, S. (2005). Pervasive, persuasive e-learning: Modeling the pervasive learning space. In *Pervasive Computing and Communications Workshops, 2005. PerCom 2005 Workshops. Third IEEE International Conference* (pp. 332-336).

Thompson, K., & Stewart, K. (2007, October 16-19). *The mobile jigsaw: A collaborative strategy for mlearning about the environment*. Proceedings of mLearn 2007, Melbourne, Australia.

Thorne, K. (2003). *Blended learning*. London: Kogan Page.

Tracey, I. (2004). Social protocol: Mobile phone and Internet. M/cyclopedia of New Media, Creative Industries Faculty, QUT. Retrieved on March 20, 2007, from http://wiki.media-culture.org.au/index.php/Youth_Culture_and_New_Technologies_-_Social_Protocol>

Traxler, J. (2005). *Defining mobile learning*. Paper presented at the Proceedings IADIS International Conference Mobile Learning 2005, Malta.

Traxler, J. (2007). Defining, discussing, and evaluating mobile learning: The moving finger writes and having writ.... *International Review of Research in Open and Distance Learning, 8*(2).

Traxler, J. (2008). From text to context. *Proceedings of the mLearn 2008 Conference: The Bridge from Text to Context*, UK.

Traxler, J., & Kukulska-Hulme, A. (2005, October 25-28). Evaluating mobile learning: Reflections on current practice. *Proceedings of MLEARN 2005*, Cape Town, South Africa.

Traxler, J., & Leach, J. (2006). *Innovative and sustainable mobile learning in Africa.* Paper presented at the Fourth IEEE International Workshop on Wireless, Mobile, and Ubiquitous Technology in Education (ICHIT'06).

Trifonova, A. (2006). *Towards hoarding content. In m-learning context.* Unpublished doctoral dissertation, DIT-University of Trento.

Uden, L. (2007). Activity theory for designing mobile learning. *International Journal of Mobile Learning and Organisation, 1*(1), 81–102. doi:10.1504/IJMLO.2007.011190

United Nations Development Programme. (2003). *Arab human development report 2003: Building a knowledge society* (No. 92-1-126157-0). New York: United Nations Publications.

University of Washington. (2008). *Portolano: An expedition into invisible computing* [online]. Retrieved from http://portolano.cs.washington.edu/

Uther, M. (2002). Mobile Internet usability: What can 'mobile learning' learn from the past? In *Wireless and Mobile Technologies in Education 2002. Proceedings. IEEE International Workshop* (pp. 174-176).

Vahey, P., & Crawford, V. (2002). *Palm(TM) education pioneers program final evaluation report.* CA: SRI International.

van 't Hooft, M., Diaz, S., & Swan, K. (2004). Examining the potential of handheld computers: Findings from the Ohio PEP project. *Journal of Educational Computing Research, 30*(4), 295–311. doi:10.2190/M1W6-A94D-3NKM-KBUU

van den Berg, M., Botha, A., Krause, C., Tolmay, C. J. P., & van Zyl, P. (2008). MobilED: A step backwards to look ahead. *Proceedings of the mLearn 2008 Conference: The Bridge from Text to Context,* UK.

Vas, R. (2007). *The role and adaptability of educational ontology in supporting knowledge testing.* Unpublished doctoral dissertation, Corvinus University of Budapest, Budapest

Vavoula, G. (2007). Learning bridges: A role for mobile technologies in education. M-Learning Symposium, WLE Centre, Institute of Education, University of London.

Vavoula, G. N., & Sharples, M. (2002). KleOS: A personal, mobile, knowledge, and learning organisation system. In M. Milrad, H. U. Hoppe & Kinshuk (Eds.), *IEEE International Workshop on Wireless and Mobile Technologies in Education* (pp. 152–156). Los Alimatos: IEEE Computer Society.

Vavoula, G., & McAndrew, P. (2005). *Pedagogical methodologies and paradigms. A study of mobile learning practices. Mobilearn Project.* Retrieved on September 10, 2008, from http://www.mobilearn.org/download/results/public_deliverables/MOBIlearn_D4.4_Final.pdf

von Glasersfeld, E. (1995). *Radical constructivism: A way of knowing and learning.* London: Falmer Press.

Vygotsky, L. S. (1978). *Mind in society: Development of higher psychological processes.* Cambridge: Harvard University Press.

Vygotsky, L. S. (1986). *Thought and language* (rev. ed.). Cambridge, MA: The MIT Press.

W3C OWL. (2009). OWL Web ontology language reference W3C recommendation [online]. Retrieved from http://www.w3.org/TR/owl-ref/

W3C Semantic Web Activity/Resource Description Framework (RDF). (2004). Retrieved from http://www.w3.org/RDF/

W3C Semantic Web. (2009). *W3C Semantic Web activity* [online]. Retrieved from http://www.w3.org/2001/sw/

Wadsworth, Y. (1998). What is participatory action research? Retrieved on May 3, 2002, from http://www.scu.edu.au/schools/gcm/ar/ari/p-ywadsworth98.html

Wagner, E. D. (2005). Enabling mobile learning. *EDUCAUSE Review, 40,* 4053.

Wakabayashi, D., & Auchard, E. (2007, April 23). Mobile phones: Google's next frontier. New Zealand PC World.

Wali, E., Winters, N., & Oliver, M. (2008). Maintaining, changing, and crossing contexts: An activity theoretic reinterpretation of mobile learning. ALT-J. Research in Learning Technologies, 16(1), 41–57.

Walker, K. (2006). Mapping the landscape of mobile learning. In M. Sharples (Ed.), *Big issues in mobile learning: Report of a workshop by the kaleidoscope network of excellence mobile learning initiative*. Nottingham, UK: Learning Sciences Research Institute, University of Nottingham

Wallace, R. (2008). *Reluctant learners: Their identities and educational experiences.* Adelaide: NCVER.

Wallace, R., & Chick, L. (2008). *Safe places training framework: Building Indigenous capacity through work based VET in remote communities.* Paper presented at the 2008 AVETRA Conference, Adelaide

Walther, M. (2003). *Integrating English and IT skills via a student newspaper.* Paper presented at the English Language Teaching in the IT Age, 9th Annual TESOL Arabia International Conference, Dubai, UAE.

Wan, J., Hu, B., Moore, P., & Ashford, R. (2008, October 6-8). Intelligent mobile computing to assist in the treatment of depression. In *Proceedings of the Third International Conference on Pervasive Computing and Applications (ICPCA 08)* (pp. 650-655), Alexandria, Egypt.

Wang, J., et al. (2007). RFID based object tracking for automating manufacturing assembly lines. *ICEBE 2007*, Hong Kong.

Wang, M., Shen, R., Tong, R., Yang, F., & Han, P. (2005). Mobile learning with cellphones and pocketpcs. *LNCS, 3583*, 332–339.

Wang, Y. K. (2004). Context awareness and adaptation in mobile learning. *Proceedings of the 2nd IEEE International Workshop on Wireless and Mobile Technologies (WMTE'04)* (pp. 154-158).

Want, R. (1995, December). An overview of the PARCTAB ubiquitous computing environment. *IEEE Personal Communications, 2*(6), 28–43. doi:10.1109/98.475986

Want, R., Hopper, A., Falcao, V., & Gibbons, J. (1992). The active badge location system. *ACM Transactions on Information Systems, 10*(1), 91–102. doi:10.1145/128756.128759

Ward, A., Jones, A., & Hopper, A. (1997). A new location technique for the active office. *Personal Communications, IEEE, 4*(5), 42–47. doi:10.1109/98.626982

Warschauer, M., & Kern, R. (2000). Theory and practice of network-based language teaching. In M. Warschauer & R. Kern (Eds.), *Network-based language teaching: Concepts and practice* (pp. 1-19). Cambridge: Cambridge University Press.

Warschauer, M., Grant, D., Del Real, G., & Rousseau, M. (2004). Promoting academic literacy with technology: Successful laptop programs in K-12 schools. *System, 32*, 525–537. doi:10.1016/j.system.2004.09.010

Waycott, J., & Kukulska-Hulme, A. (2003). Student experiences with PDAs for reading course materials. *Personal and Ubiquitous Computing, 7*(1), 30–43. doi:10.1007/s00779-002-0211-x

Weisenberg, N. N., Voisard, A., & Gartmann, R. (2004, November 12-13). Using ontologies in personalised mobile applications. In *Proceedings of the 12th Annual ACM International Workshop on Geographic Information Systems (GIS'04)* (pp. 2-11), Washington, D.C.

Weiser, M. (1991). The computer for the 21st century. *Scientific American*, 94-104. Reprinted in *IEEE Pervasive Computing*, Jan.-Mar. 2002, 19-25.

Weiser, M. (1993). Some computer science issues in ubiquitous computing. *Communications of the ACM, 36*(7), 75–84. doi:10.1145/159544.159617

Weiss, S. (2002). *Handheld usability.* Chichester: John Wiley & Sons.

Weller, M. (2002). *Delivering learning on the net–the why, what, and how of online education.* London: Kogan Page.

Wenger, E. (1998). *Communities of practice: Learning, meaning, and identity.* Cambridge: Cambridge University Press.

Wenger, E. (2001). *Supporting communities of practice a survey of community-oriented technologies*. Retrieved on November 9, 2007, from http://www.ewenger.com/tech

Wenger, E. (2005, October 14). Communities of practice: A brief introduction. Retrieved on July 17, 2006, from http://www.ewenger.com/theory/index.htm

Wenger, E., McDermott, R., & Snyder, W. (2002). *Cultivating communities of practice: A guide to managing knowledge*. Cambridge: Harvard Business School Press.

Wenger, E., White, N., Smith, J., & Spa, K. R. (2005). Technology for communities. Retrieved on July 14, 2006, from http://technologyforcommunities.com/

Wentzel, P., Lammeren, R. v., & Molendijk, S. M. Bruin, & Wagtendonk, A. (2005). Using mobile technology to enhance students' educational experiences. *Educause, (ECAR Case Study 2)*, 18. Boulder.

Wikipedia. (2009). *Wikipedia*. Retrieved on February 2, 2009, from http://www.wikipedia.org

WildPackets Web Page. (n.d.). Retrieved on October 15, 2008, from http://www.wildpackets.com

Wilkinson, K., Sayers, C., Kuno, H., & Reynolds, D. (2003). *Efficient RDF storage and retrieval in Jena2*. (HP Laboratories Tech. Rep. HPL-2003-266).

Williams, K., & Paparozzi, E. (2002). Model to develop a synchronous interinstitutional course using distance technologies. *NACTA Journal*.

Willis, J. (1996). *A framework for task-based learning*. Harlow, Essex: Addison Wesley Longman.

Winters, N. (2007). What is mobile learning? In M. Sharples (Ed.), *Big issues in mobile learning* (pp. 7-11). Nottingham: Learning Sciences Research Institute.

Wireshark Network Protocol Analyzer. Retrieved October 15, 2008. http://www.wireshark.org.

Woolcock, M. (2001). The place of social capital in understanding social and economic outcomes. *ISUMA: Canadian Journal of Policy Research*, *2*, 11–17.

World, G. S. M. (2008). *Subscriber connections-Q2 2008*. Retrieved from http://www.gsmworld.com/news/statistics/pdf/gsma_stats_q2_08.pdf

XHTML 1.0 Recommendation. Retrieved on January 26, 2000, from http://www.w3.org/TR/xhtml1/

XHTML Mobile Profile. Retrieved on October 29, 2001, from http://www.openmobilealliance.org/tech/affiliates/wap/wap-277-xhtmlmp-20011029-a.pdf

Yin, R. K. (1993). Advancing rigorous methodologies: A review of towards rigor in reviews of multivocal literatures. *Review of Educational Research*, *61*(3).

Yuan-Kai, W. (2004). Context awareness and adaptation in mobile learning (pp. 154-158).

Yu-Liang Ting, R. (2005). *Mobile learning: Current trend and future challenges*. Paper presented at Fifth IEEE International Conference on Advanced Learning Technologies (ICALT'05), Kaohsiung, Taiwan.

Yu-Liang, R. (2005). *Mobile learning: Current trend and future challenges*. Paper presented at Fifth IEEE International Conference on Advanced Learning Technologies (ICALT'05), Kaohsiung, Taiwan.

Zanev, V., & Clark, R. (2005). Wireless course management system. *In ACM SE 43: Proceedings of the 43rd Annual Southeast Regional Conference* (pp. 118-123). New York: ACM Press.

Zemke, R., & Zemke, S. (1995). Adult learning: What do we know for sure? *Training (New York, N.Y.)*, *32*(6), 31–40.

Zhang, T., & Luo, Z. (2008). Developing a trusted system for tracking asset on the move. *ICYCS*, *2008*, 2008–2013.

Zhang, T., et al. (2008, June 11-13). Mobile intelligence for delay tolerant logistics and supply chain management. *SUTC 2008*, Taichung, Taiwan.

Zhang, T., Li, Z., & Liu, M. (2006). Routing in partially connected wireless network. *Journal of System Simulation*, *18*(10), 2972–2975.

Zhang, Y., Li, W., & Fu, Y. (2007). A mobile learning system based on bluetooth. *Third International Conference on Natural Computation, 2007 (ICNC 2007)* (Vol. 5, pp.768-771).

Zhang, Y., Zhang, S., Vuong, S., & Malik, K. (2006). Mobile learning with bluetooth-based e-learning system. *Wireless Ad Hoc and Sensor Networks Symposium*, Vancouver, Canada.

Zoakou, A., Tzanavari, A., Papadopoulos, G. A., & Sotiriou, S. (2007). A methodology for e-learning scenario development: The UNITE approach. In D. Remenyi (Ed.), The 6th European Conference on e-Learning, Copenhagen Business School, Trinity College Dublin, Ireland (pp. 683-692).

About the Contributors

Santi Caballé has a PhD, Masters and Bachelors in Computer Science from the Open University of Catalonia. Since 2003, he has been an Assistant Professor at the Open University of Catalonia teaching a variety of curses in Computer Science in the areas of Information Systems, Software Engineering and Collaborative Learning. Since 2006 he has been working as an Associate Professor of the department of Computer Science, Multimedia and Telecommunication at the Open University of Catalonia where he coordinates several online courses in the area of Software Engineering. He is a member of the Distributed, Parallel and Collaborative Systems Research Group at the Open University of Catalonia. His research focuses on e-learning, m-learning, computer-supported collaborative learning, distributed learning, software engineering, network technologies, grid technologies. His email address is scaballe@uoc.edu

Fatos Xhafa received his PhD in Computer Science from the Polytechnic University of Catalonia (Barcelona, Spain) in 1998. He joined the Department of Languages and Informatics Systems of the Polytechnic University of Catalonia as an Assistant Professor in 1996 and is currently Associate Professor of this department. He is member of the ALBCOM Research Group of this department and also is external member of the Distributed, Parallel and Collaborative Research Group of the Open University of Catalonia. His research is supported by several research projects from Spain, European Union and NSF/USA. He has published in leading international journals and conferences. He serves in the editorial board of the International Journal of Computer Supported Collaborative Learning and has served as Co-chair / PC member for many conferences and workshops. His email address is fatos@lsi.upc.edu

Thanasis Daradoumis has a PhD in Information Sciences from the Polytechnic University of Catalonia-Spain, a Masters in Computer Science from the University of Illinois, and a Bachelors in Mathematics from the University of Thessaloniki-Greece. Since 1984, he has been an Assistant Professor at several universities in the USA, Greece and Spain, teaching a variety of courses in Mathematics and Computer Science. Since 1998, he has been working as a Professor in the department of Computer Science, Multimedia and Telecommunication at the Open University of Catalonia where he coordinates several online courses as well as the development of teaching materials appropriate for virtual learning. His research focuses on e-learning and learning technologies, ontologies and semantic web, distributed learning, CSCL, CSCW, interaction analysis, grid technologies. His email address is adaradoumis@uoc.edu

Angel Juan holds a Ph.D. in Applied Computational Mathematics (UNED), an M.S. in Information Technology (Open University of Catalonia), and an M.S. in Applied Mathematics (University of Valencia). His research interests include computer simulation, educational data analysis and mathematical e-learning. He has published several papers in international journals, books and proceedings regarding these fields. As a researcher, he has been involved in several international research projects. He is an editorial board member of the Int. J. of Data Analysis Techniques and Strategies, and a member of the INFORMS society. His email address is ajuanp@uoc.edu

* * *

Vassiliki Andronikou obtained her diploma from the Electrical and Computer Engineering Department of the National Technical University of Athens in 2004. She has worked in the National Bank of Greece and the Organization of Telecommunications of Greece, while since 2004 she has been a research associate and PhD candidate in the Telecommunications Laboratory of the NTUA. In 2005 she was given the Ericsson award for her Thesis on Mobile IPv6 with Fast Handovers. Her research has involved her participation in many European projects, with her interests focusing on the fields of the security and privacy aspects of biometrics and data management in Grid.

Mario Barajas, PhD in Education, teaches at the University of Barcelona, Department of Didactics and Educational Organisation. His background encompasses a degree in Philosophy and Education, in engineering and a Master's Degree in Educational Technology by the San Francisco State University (USA). He is head of the research group Future Learning (http://www.ub.es/euelearning), an interdisciplinary team aiming at developing theoretical and applied research into e-Learning. He has done an extensive work on the evaluation of ongoing research tackling educational, institutional, organisational and symbolic aspects of learning mediated by ICT. During the last years he has coordinated and participated in numerous European Union funded projects in the area of technology-enhanced learning. He is author of numerous publications on the use and evaluation of ICT in learning.

Ivica Boticki received the B.Sc. and Ph.D. degree in computing from the Faculty of Electrical Engineering and Computing (FER), University of Zagreb, Croatia, in 2004 and 2009, respectively. He has been a research assistant and has been teaching programming, algorithms and data structure and programming paradigms and languages at the Faculty of Electrical Engineering and Computing, University of Zagreb since 2004. His main areas of research are information systems, programming languages, e-learning, blended learning and mobile learning.

Javier Carmona-Murillo is a PhD student in the Computing Systems and Telematics Engineering Department at the University of Extremadura, Spain, where he received his BEng (2003) and MEng (2005) in Computer Science Engineering. During 2006 and 2007 he worked as the main developer for the Campus Ubicuo project. Since November 2007 he held a pre-doctoral research scholarship from the regional government of Extremadura. He has published many articles in journals and conferences related to computing and networking. His main research topics are broadband networks, QoS provision in mobile networks and IP mobility. He is also doing research support work at Advanced and Applied Communications Engineering Research Group (GITACA).

Rodger Carroll has been heavily involved in the building industry for 34 years as a Registered Building Practitioner in residential and commercial construction. In 1998 he commenced teaching building courses with Chisholm Institute. His current position is Department Manager, Building and Furniture, Chisholm Institute, Australia. He regularly undertakes further training and study, actively participating in professional networks to keep his skills and knowledge up to date. He recently completed a Master of Education at Victoria University and he is Programs Director and a past President of the International Society for Performance Improvement (ISPI) Melbourne chapter.

Andreas H. Christ received the doctoral degree in electrical engineering from Technische Universität Darmstadt, Germany, in 1988. He joined the Central Research and Development Laboratories and later on the Public Communication Department of Siemens AG, Munich, Germany, where he was engaged in microwaves, mobile communications and fiber-to-the-home projects. In 1993, he became a Professor at the Hochschule Offenburg, University of Applied Sciences, Germany. In 1997, he became Head of the Department 'Media and Information' and since 2007 he is Vice-President of the Hochschule Offenburg, University of Applied Sciences. Also, as Head of the Informationszentrum he is responsible for the deployment of and support for e-learning and electronic media for education and research purpose. His professional interests include technologies for mobile learning, mobile internet and 3D visualisation. His main focus lies on concepts, software architectures and exemplary implementations.

Evi Chryssafidou graduated from the Department of Mass Media and Communication, University of Athens, in 1994 and received her M.Sc degree in Human-Centred Computer Systems from the School of Cognitive and Computing Sciences, University of Sussex, in 1997. She has submitted her PhD thesis at the School of Electronic and Electrical Engineering (Educational technology group), University of Birmingham. Her PhD research focuses on the design, implementation and evaluation of an interactive software programme that helps students to write well-structured essays. From 2003 she completed two research projects at the University of Birmingham, first, at the School of Electronic and Electrical Engineering and, then, at the Medical School, supporting the design and evaluation of e-learning modules for the teaching of Evidence-based Medicine. Since October 2005 she works as researcher of the R&D of Ellinogermaniki Agogi and she is mainly involved in mobile learning (e.g. COLLAGE) and in music education and ICT (e.g. VEMUS) projects.

Thomas Cochrane is an Academic Advisor (elearning and Learning Technologies) with Unitec (March 2004 to present). His role at Unitec includes providing support for elearning and learning technologies for Unitec teaching staff, and pushing the boundaries of educational technology for enhancing teaching and learning at Unitec. His research interests include mobile learning, web 2.0, and communities of practice. He is currently implementing mobile learning trials for his PHD thesis: "Mobilizing Learning: The potential impact of wireless mobile computing on teaching and learning in higher education in New Zealand". Harnessing the potential of social software tools (such as: Mobile Blogging, RSS, Instant Messaging, Moodle and Elgg...) using wireless mobile devices, such as: PDAs, laptops, and the new generation of mobile phones.

David Cortés-Polo is a PhD student in the Computing Systems and Telematics Engineering Department at the University of Extremadura (Spain), where he received his engineering degree in Computer Science (2006). He is currently working in IPfonos proyect financed by the regional government of

Extremadura (http://gitaca.unex.es/ipfonos). He is involved in the Advanced and Applied Communications Engineering Research Group (GITACA). His main research topics are multimedia communcations, broadband networks and IP mobility. He has published several articles in different national and international conferences.

Markus Feißt received his Diploma in "Electrical Engineering and Automation" in 1998 and his M.Sc. Degree in "Communication and Media Engineering from "Hochschule Offenburg", University of Applied Sciences (Germany), in 2000. In 2001 he started with his doctoral thesis researching the possibility of displaying interactive 3D content on mobile phones in monoscopic and stereoscopic view. He obtained is doctoral degree from the University Louis Pasteur Strasbourg (France) in 2006. Since 2006 he has worked at the "Informationszentrum" (information centre) of the University of Applied Science Offenburg. His main focus lies on research and implementation of student services mainly concerning mobile devices and mobile learning.

Jaime Galán-Jiménez received his Engineering degree in Computer Science Engineering at the University of Extremadura (Spain) in 2007, where he is currently working as professor in the Computing Systems and Telematics Engineering Department. He has worked in several projects at private enterprises and public organizations, such as the University of Extremadura. His main research topics are wireless technologies and the performance evaluation in wireless and mobile networks. He is also doing research support work in the Advanced and Applied Communications Engineering Research Group (GITACA) of the University of Extremadura.

José-Luis González-Sánchez is a full time associate professor of the Computing Systems and Telematics Engineering department at the University of Extremadura, Spain. He received his Engineering degree in Computer Science and his Ph.D degree in Computer Science (2001) at the Polytechnic University of Cataluña, Barcelona, Spain. He has worked, for years, at several private enterprises and public organizations, accomplishing functions of System and Network Manager. He is the main researcher of the Advanced and Applied Communications Engineering Research Group (GÍTACA) of the University of Extremadura. He has published many articles, books and research projects related to computing and networking.

John Hedberg holds the Millennium Innovations Chair in ICT and Education and is Head of the Department of Education at Macquarie University, Sydney, Australia. He is well known for his research into learning environments that engage students and employ problem-based learning. He has worked in several countries exploring how interactive and digital media can be employed as part of innovative pedagogies. His current work is on the role of digital technologies in new approaches to discipline knowledge and how the technologies can be employed to represent ideas that cannot be represented in any other ways.

Natasa Hoic-Bozic received the B.S. degree in mathematics and information science from the University of Rijeka, Croatia, in 1990, the M.S. degrees in computer and information science from the University of Ljubljana, Slovenia, in 1997, and the Ph.D. degree in computing from the Faculty of Electrical Engineering and Computing (FER), University of Zagreb, Croatia, in 2002. Currently, she is an assistant professor at the Department of Information Science, Faculty of Arts and Sciences, University of

Rijeka. Her main research interests include adaptive hypermedia, multimedia systems, and educational technologies, focusing on blended learning approaches.

Bin Hu, Ph,D in Computer Science, Reader in the department of computing, TID, Birmingham City University, UK. He is the leader of context aware Computing group in the pervasive computing centre; a Chair/PC Chair/member of quite a few international conferences, e.g. ICPCA07, CSCWD, IEEE ICC 2007, UIC'08, IEEE DSSC'08, BCS HCI 2008, etc.; an editor/a guest editor of some pervasive computing journals, e.g. The Computer Journal, Wireless Communications and Mobile Computing; Keynote Speaker in IEEE & BCS International Conference on Pervasive Computing and Applications 2006 and IEEE International Conference on ICT in Education (2007), IEEE International Conference on ICT in Education and Health Care (2008), etc.

Mike Jackson obtained a degree in Computer Science at Sheffield City Polytechnic (now Sheffield Hallam University). He went on to do research at Manchester University. After a year working for Manchester Polytechnic as a systems programmer, he joined Wolverhampton Polytechnic (now University of Wolverhampton) as a lecturer. He worked at Wolverhampton for over 20 years as Principal Lecturer, Reader in Software Engineering and Professor of Data Engineering. He moved to Birmingham City University in 2004. Mike has been very active in the UK Database community and is closely associated with the British National Conference of Databases. He was Programme Chair for the conference in 2005.

Gábor Kismihók is graduated from Budapest University of Economic Sciences and Public Administration (BUESPA) in 2004 as a Master of International Business. Currently he is a PhD candidate at the Department of Information Systems at the Corvinus University of Budapest. He is busy with various EU Research projects in eLearning and in mLearning, dealing with mLMS development, content development, Ontology engineering. Recently he is interested in the relationship between advanced learning environments and Human Resource Management.

Barna Kovács is graduated from Budapest University of Economic Sciences and Public Administration (BUESPA) as economist. Since 2003 he is a researcher at the Department of Information Systems of the Corvinus University of Budapest while being a Ph.D. student at the Faculty of Business Administration. His main field of research is the application of semantic technologies in content management, but his research interests include the field of open-source software, software development methodologies in system integration and developing knowledge-based systems. He took part in various research projects like ADVISOR (Development of an expert system for non-cash compensation system in the field of HR), COBIR (Developing an Intelligent System supporting IT audit and control activities), ECRIME (Creating knowledge management tools and procedures to support the modernization and development of justice systems), LEFIS (Legal Framework for the Information Society) and he is actively participating in SAKE project developing an agile knowledge management system using semantic technologies supporting the e-Government.

Pavlos Koulouris is a graduate of Literature and Linguistics (University of Athens, Greece), with postgraduate studies and research (Institute of Education-University of London, UK) in the field of ICT in education, life-long learning, applied linguistics, multimodal discourse and social semiotics. His work experience is diverse, ranging from teaching (language, literature and humanities) to educational and social research (university research officer on a number of research projects), and, since 2001, EU-funded applied research and development projects in the fields of school education, professional development, and life-long learning.

Antonios Litke received the diploma from the Dept. of Computer Engineering and Informatics of the University of Patras, Greece in 1999, and the PhD from Electrical and Computer Engineering Department of National Technical University of Athens in 2006. Currently, he is working in the Telecommunication Laboratory of Electrical and Computer Engineering Department of National Technical University of Athens as researcher participating in numerous EU and National funded projects. His research interests include Grid computing, resource management in heterogeneous systems, Web services and information engineering.

Manfred Lohr holds a Master's degree in Mathematics and Physics at the University of Vienna. In 1981 he began to work as teacher of Mathematics and Physics and since 1988 of Computer Science and recently IT coordinator at the BG/BRG Schwechat. Since 2005 he is the e-learning coordinator responsible for the pedagogical concept of usage of the learning management system Moodle at BG/BRG Schwechat as well as for teacher training in the field of e-learning. Since 1997 he has been participating as teacher and project coordinator in many European projects. Since 2003 he has been cooperating with the Austrian Ministry of Education in order to present his experiences with European projects to other Austrian schools.

Zongwei Luo has been a senior researcher of the E-Business Technology Institute at the University of Hong Kong since 2003. Before he came to Hong Kong, he worked at the IBM TJ Watson Research Center in Yorktown Height (NY, USA). He also served as the Affiliate Senior Consultant to ETI Consulting Limited. His research has been supported by various funding sources including HKU seed funding, HK RGC, and HK ITF. Dr. Luo is the founding Editor-in-Chief of the International Journal of Applied Logistics. An expert in service oriented architecture and RFID, his current interests include developing enabling technologies and applications in e-logistics and supply chain management.

Fatma Meawad is a currently an assistant professor at the German University in Cairo. Fatma holds a PhD in Mobile Learning from the University of Glamorgan, UK, a masters in advanced computer science from Birmingham University and Bachelor of Science in computer science from the American University in Cairo. Currently, Fatma teaches a variety of topics in computer science and educational technology. Fatma's research interests include mobile application development, Human Computer interaction and innovative uses of technology in education.

Antonis Miliarakis, was born in Crete, Greece on 27 June 1978. He holds an MPhil degree by the Systems Engineering Department, at BRUNEL University, UK. He graduated with honors from the Electrical Engineering Department of the Technological Educational Institute of Crete, Greece, in 2002. Since October 2000 he has worked at Forthnet S.A. where his main responsibility is the technical management of ICT research projects and the design of mobile service platforms and wireless networks. During his activities at the research and development department he has participated in the implementation of many European and national IT projects. Since September 2004 he has been lecturing

Computer Systems Architecture, Medical Informatics and Microprocessors at the Applied Informatics and Multimedia department of Technological Education Institute of Crete.

Marcelo Milrad is a professor in Media Technology at the department of computer science, school of mathematics and systems engineering, at Växjö University in Sweden. His current research interest focuses on the design and development of mobile and wireless applications to support collaborative learning. He has published more than 100 articles in international journals, refereed conferences, books and technical reports. Professor Milrad has also presented and given lectures about his work in more than 35 countries worldwide. In recent years he has been serving as a program committee and editorial board member for a number of international scientific conferences and journals. He was one of the initiators of the IEEE international conference on Wireless and Mobile Technologies in Education (WMTE).

Philip Moore obtained a first class honours degree in computing with artificial intelligence at University of Central England in the UK (now Birmingham City University). Following a Masters degree in computing (Internet Applications) he is currently working to a Ph.D in computer science researching ontological intelligent context-aware pervasive applications, the focus being on personalised mobile learning in rule-based systems. His work has been published conference proceedings and journals. He has acted as a reviewer of conference papers as program committee member for a number of international conferences and journal articles for a number of international computing journals. He is currently a member of the Context Aware Computing Research Group.

Vedran Mornar received the B.S., M.S. and Ph.D. degree in computing from the Faculty of Electrical Engineering and Computing (FER), University of Zagreb, Croatia, in 1981, 1985, and 1990, respectively. Currently, he is a Full Professor of computer science and Dean at FER. His professional interest is in application of operational research in real world information systems, database design, development and implementation. He is an editor of international journal "Computing and Information Technology".

Hazel Owen is an Academic Advisor (Education Technology Consultant) at Unitec, NZ. She has been involved with implementing ICT enhanced learning for ten years to date and is involved with training for faculty around the design and adaptation of blended and distance courses, as well as developing them herself. Her research interests include developing learning spaces (physical and virtual) for effective learning, Web 2.0, mLearning ePortfolios, eAssessment, literacy and numeracy embedding/support, communities of learning, theories and practice around effective PD, and ICT enhanced learning and teaching (ICTELT) underpinned by Sociocultural principles.

Martin Owen is at present developing unique playful, tangible devices for early learning with his own company Smalti. He is also working as an independent researcher in European Union projects in technology enhanced learning with particular emphasis on games, mobility and augmented reality. He was until recently the Director of Learning and Head of Concept Development at Futurelab (http://www.futurelab.org.uk/). At Futurelab he was responsible for the key concepts in the mobile game Savannah and the physics game Racing Academy. Previously he was an academic researcher and teacher trainer at University of Wales, Bangor. He has also been a school teacher.

Athanasia Psychogiou obtained her diploma from the Electrical and Computer Engineering Department of the National Technical University of Athens in 2007. Since then she has worked at the Telecommunication Laboratory of the National Technical University of Athens as a Research Associate as well as in the private sector as computer engineer in the telecommunication sector. Her main research interests involve next generation e-learning applications.

Sofoklis Sotiriou has worked at CERN, at the National Center for Scientific Research "DEMOKRITOS" in Athens and in the Physics Laboratory of Athens University. He holds two PhD titles, one in High Energy Neutrino Astrophysics and one in Science Education. He is the Head of R&D Department of Ellinogermaniki Agogi, one of the biggest educational institutions in Greece, where has coordinated research projects focusing on advanced technologies (e.g. mobile applications, wearable computers, VR and AR applications, robotics) in science education. His main research field is the design, application, and evaluation of virtual and digital media environments that could bridge the gap between formal and informal science learning. He has been involved in a long series of EU joint research and technology funded projects. He is a member of the European Academy of Sciences, and author of numerous articles and publications on the use of ICT in science education.

Daniel Spikol is a Ph.D. student in Computer Science at the school of Mathematics and Systems Engineering, at Växjö University (VXU) in Sweden. He works for the Center for Learning and Knowledge Technologies (CeLeKT). His current research interests include the design of mobile learning environments that explore modes of collaboration that foster discovery. He is presently involved in a number of European and National projects exploring how mobile and wireless technologies can be used to support new ways of learning and how these technologies can support groups of learners when they, collectively, share their understanding in these learning environments. Previously he has worked for the Interactive Institute that is part of the Swedish Institute of Computer Science (SICS) and the LEGO group.

Kathy Stewart lectures in science and environmental education at Macquarie University, Sydney, Australia and researches in the area of mobile learning. Her PhD was based on botanic gardens as locations for learning. Her academic interest is now focussed on curriculum and pedagogies that support student-led inquiry in environments beyond the classroom. She has held elected positions on boards of community environmental education centres and organisations developing resources to support environmental education.

Manolis Stratakis was born in Heraklio, Crete, Greece. He holds an MSc by research in Computer Networks and Digital Communications and a BSc in Electronic Computer Systems, both from the University of Salford, UK. He is currently the Head of Research Projects in the R&D department of FORTHnet S.A., where he is managing European and National research projects, primarily related to Internet and web applications and the development of Value Added Services in the areas of Mobile Internet, Advanced Messaging Systems, mobile Learning, Electronic Commerce, Teleworking, eHealth, Telemedicine and 3G Technologies. He has worked from 1992 to 1997 at the Institute of Computer Science, FORTH-Greece. He has also worked as a visiting professor in the Technological Education Institute of Heraklio, School of Technological Applications, from 1993 to 2000.

Geneen Stubbs is a senior Lecturer in the Division of Computer Science. Having gained a First Class Honours degree in Computer Studies at the University of Glamorgan, she was employed as a Research Assistant on the TLTP project W.I.S.D.E.N. Subsequently, she began lecturing in CBL and Instructional Design. She gained a PhD in June 2001 in the area of CBL design and development modelling. Current research interests include the design and development of CBL/eLearning resources; the use of Virtual Learning Environments (VLEs) to support learning; Learning Styles of undergraduate students; Reusable Information and Learning Objects and Web 2.0. She is currently Director of Studies for three research students and a supervisor for a fourth. She takes an active part in research and is a member of the University Research Group.

Kate Thompson is a research fellow at the Centre for Research in Computer-supported learning and Cognition (CoCo), University of Sydney, Australia. Her research in the use of technology in environmental education has focused on the use of models to understand a complex socio-environmental system and also the use of mobile learning for environmental education. She graduated with an honours degree in Environmental Science from the University of New South Wales in 2001, and has worked as a research assistant in the field of innovation in industry at the University of Western Sydney before beginning her PhD with CoCo in 2004. She is a member of the National Advisory Committee for the Australian Association of Environmental Education.

Theodora A. Varvarigou received the B. Tech degree from the National Technical University of Athens, Athens, Greece in 1988, the MS degrees in Electrical Engineering (1989) and in Computer Science (1991) from Stanford University, Stanford, California in 1989 and the Ph.D. degree from Stanford University as well in 1991. She worked at AT&T Bell Labs, Holmdel, New Jersey between 1991 and 1995. Between 1995 and 1997 she worked as an Assistant Professor at the Technical University of Crete, Chania, Greece. Since 1997 she was elected as an Assistant Professor while since 2007 she is a Professor at the National Technical University of Athens, and Director of the Postgraduate Course "Engineering Economics Systems". Prof. Varvarigou has great experience in the area of semantic web technologies, scheduling over distributed platforms, embedded systems and grid computing. In this area, she has published more than 150 papers in leading journals and conferences. She has participated and coordinated several EU funded projects.

Réka Vas was born in Szeged, Hungary and educated at the University of Szeged, where she studied economics and received her MSc. Since 2002 she is a researcher and lecturer at the Department of Information Systems of Corvinus University of Budapest, where she also took part in a doctoral program and received her Ph.D. degree. Her research fields include knowledge representation, ontology engineering and knowledge management. She took part in several R&D projects including GUIDE (Creating an European standard for interoperable and secure Identity Management Architecture for eGovernment).

Victor A. Villagra is an Associate Professor of Telematics Engineering at the Technical University of Madrid, Spain (DIT-UPM). He received his M.Sc. degree in 1989 and his Ph.D. in Telematics Engineering in 1994, both from the Technical University of Madrid. He has participated in National and International Research Projects focused on service and network management and its application to the management of new distributed e-services. His current research interests include integrated management of distributed networks and services, network security, application of formal knowledge representation mechanisms to network management and security and cross-layer interactions between networks and services technologies.

Ruth Wallace is the Director of the Social Partnerships in Learning Research Consortium at Charles Darwin University, Darwin, NT. Ruth's particular interests are related to engaging in research that improves outcomes for workforce stakeholders in regional and remote Australia. Ruth's research focus is in vocational education and training practice and workforce development in regional and remote contexts. Ruth has undertaken research into flexible learning, engaged learning and developing effective pedagogy, materials and assessment for marginalized students. In particular, this work explores approaches that focus on recognising marginalised learners' strengths and developing systems that connect to and value learners' diverse knowledge systems. Her research examines the links between identity and adult's involvement in post-compulsory schooling and development of effective pathways through flexible learning and recognition of diverse knowledge systems.

Jizheng Wan received his Bachelor degree from Guilin University of Technology in 2006. One year later he obtained his Master degree at Birmingham City University (formerly the University of Central England) majoring in Pervasive Computing. Subsequently, he became a Research and Development assistant in the Corporate ICT (Information and Communication Technology) at Birmingham City University. He currently works as Research and Development Change Manager at the same institution and is preparing for his part time Ph.D. His research areas include pervasive computing in Mental Health Treatment, Context Ontology and Ontology Versioning and Evolution.

Wai Yat Wong is currently a researcher at the Centre for Research in Computer-supported learning and Cognition (CoCo) at the Faculty of Education and Social Work, University of Sydney. He is also the information systems manager at the Faculty of Education of Social Work, University of Sydney. He is the principal investigator on an ICT project titled 'Educational Video with Annotation (EVA) collaboratory and teaching and learning management framework' funded the University of Sydney. He was also the principal investigator on two previous ICT projects in mobile learning and web based collaborative video teaching and learning. He has lectured in information technology at the University of Newcastle and has worked as a computer scientist with CSIRO on the areas of knowledge base, computational intelligence, and multimedia delivery. He has been the author or co-author on 4 journal papers, 21 international conference papers and 24 technical reports on various ICT related and application areas.

Index

D

E

F

G

H

I

J

K

L

M